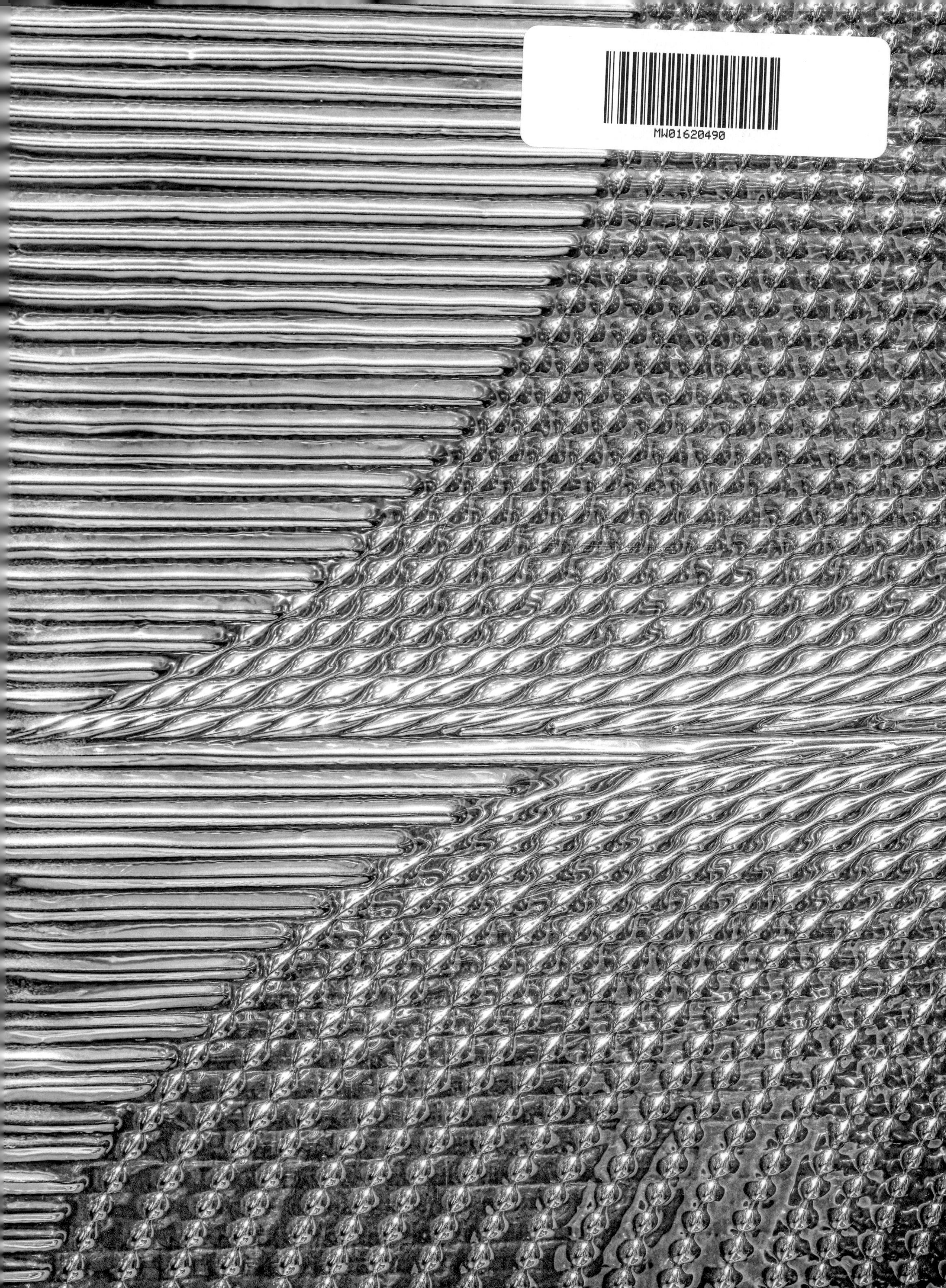

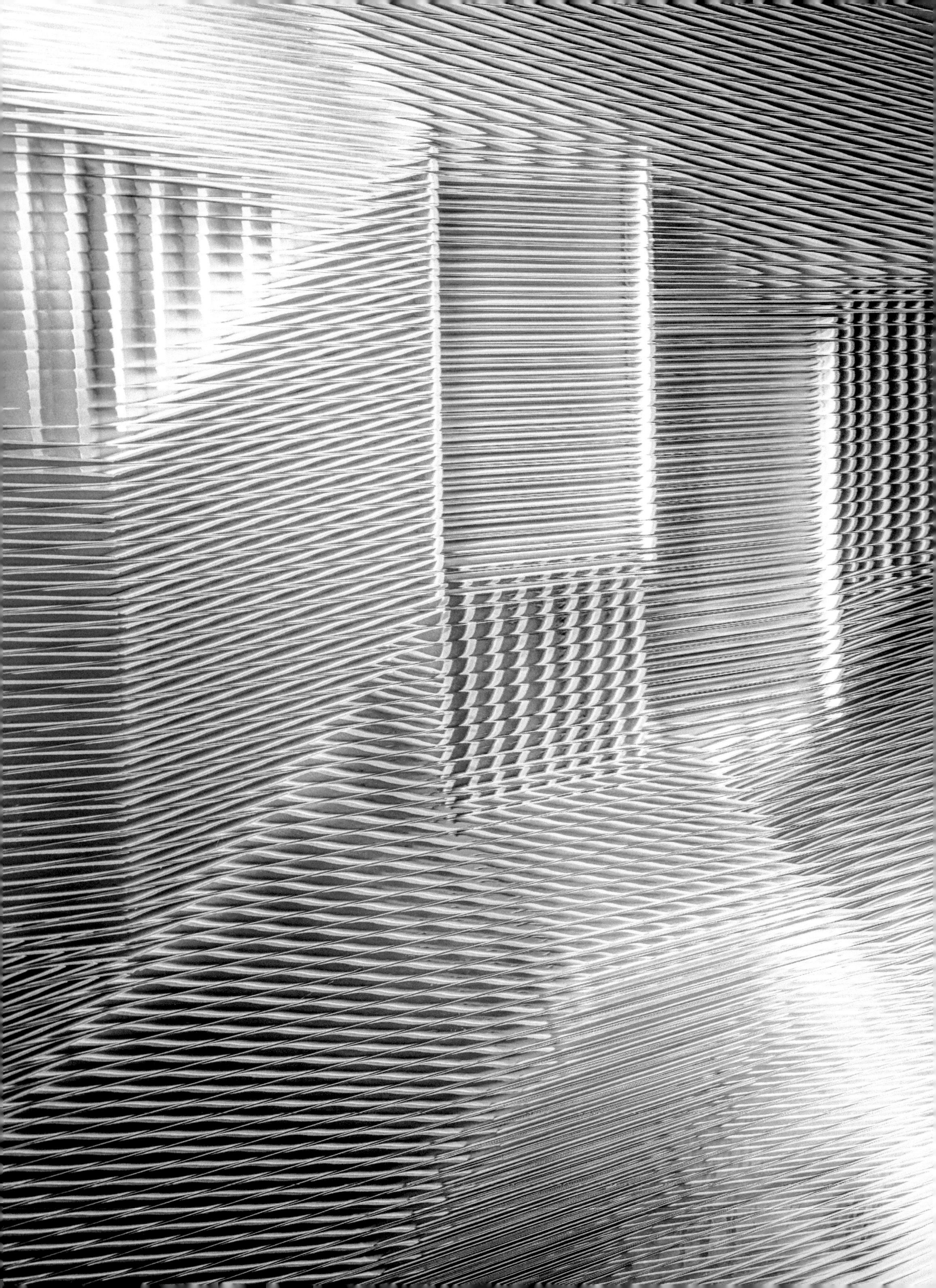

MACK REFLECTED
expanding the ZERO code

Edited by Alistair Hudson

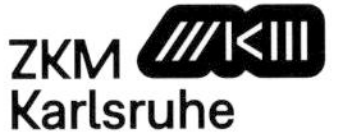

HIRMER

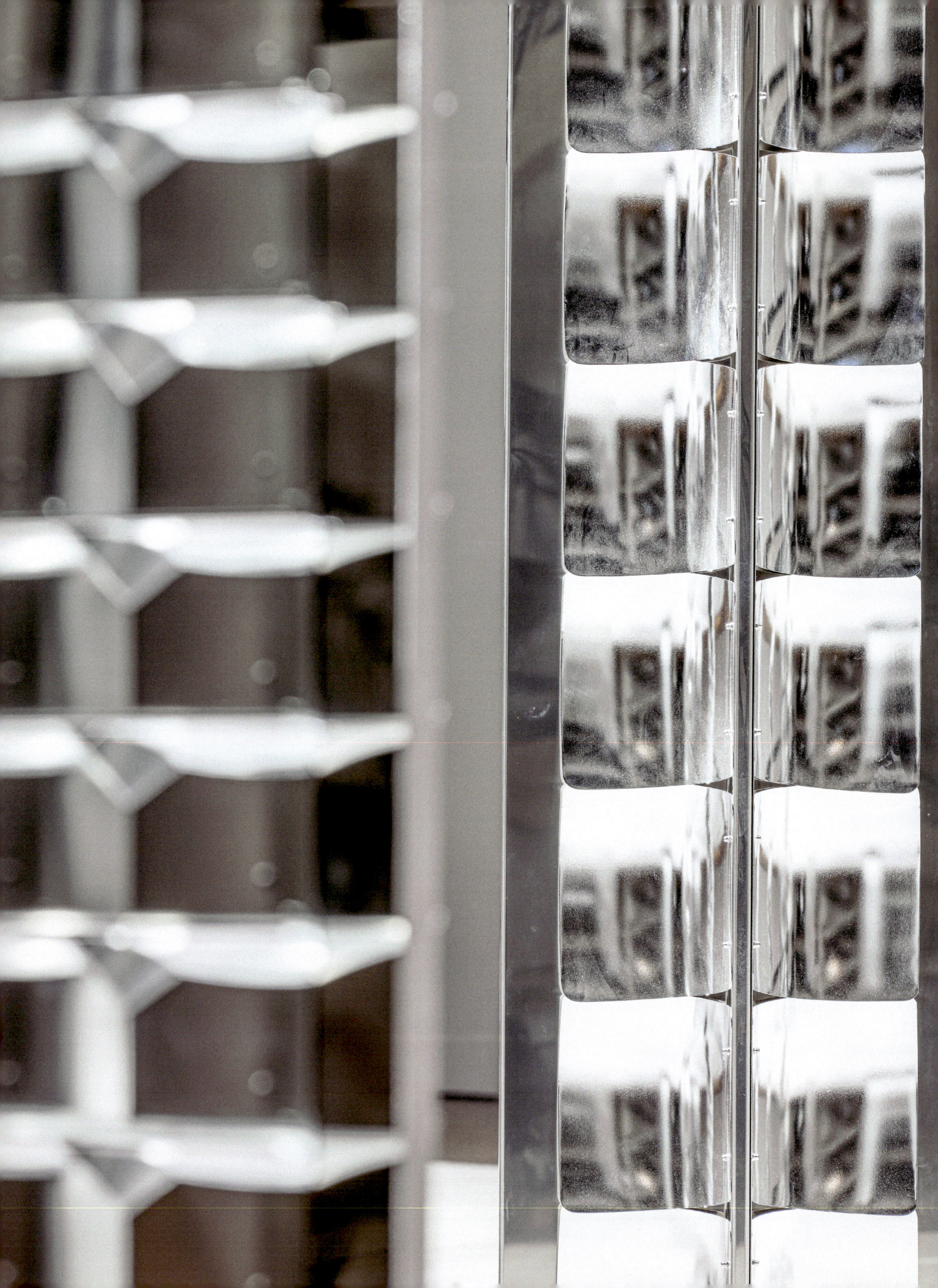

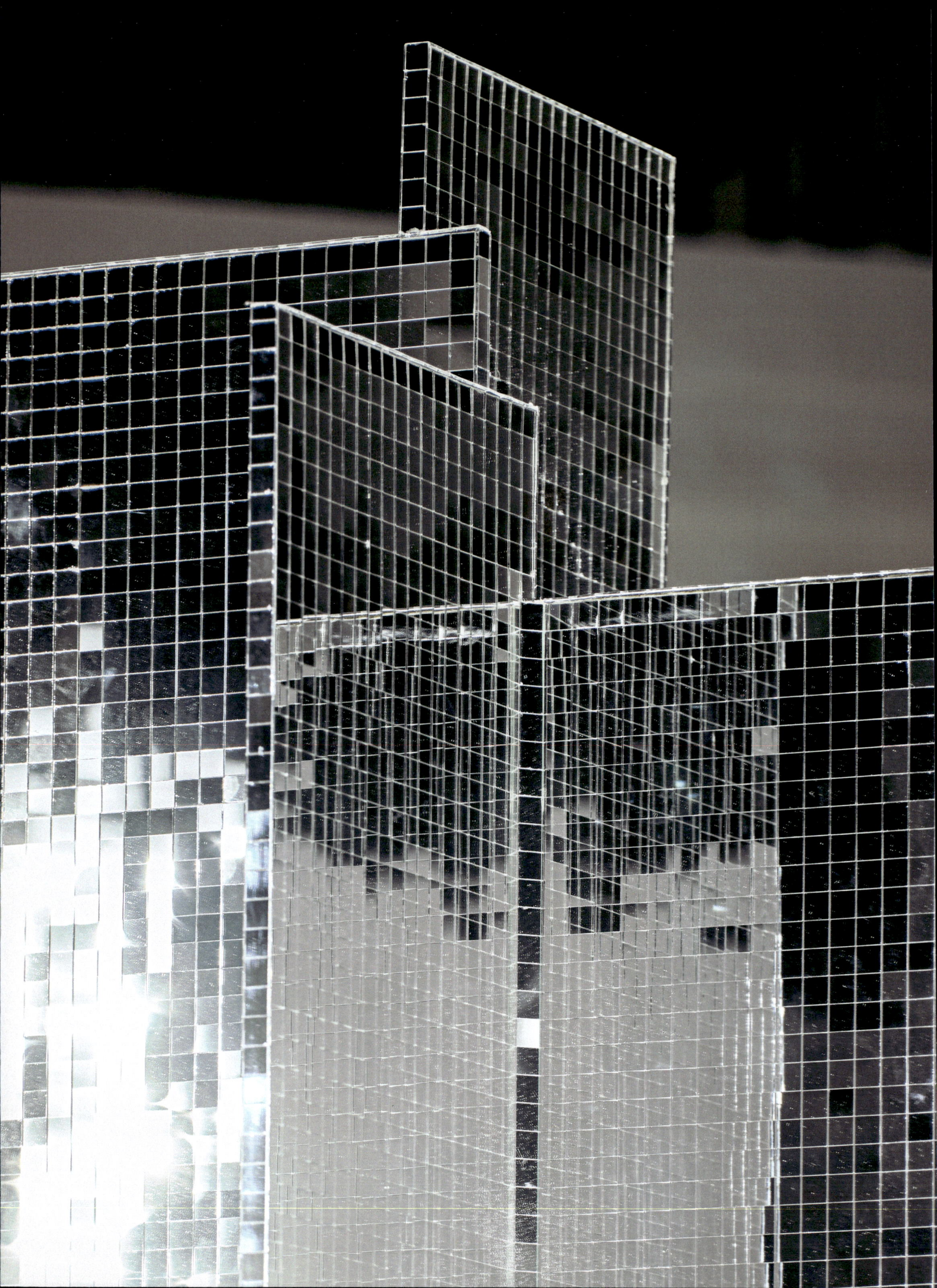

Mack Reflected

This publication offers a timely re-evaluation of Heinz Mack in the context of numerous shifting paradigms. We are now a quarter of the way through the twenty-first century; our globalized society is leaving the modern era behind and embracing the complexities of a multi-polar and pluralistic world. The centers of power and influence that were once so certain, so solid, are redistributing, reforming in other geographies – both physical and virtual. Demands to redress the environmental and social impacts of industrial modernity are now urgent, and this calls for an ecological mode of thinking, not the autonomous mindset of old.

From this viewpoint, it is possible to understand the cosmos of Heinz Mack in a different way, spanning an era of transition, from the catastrophe of World War II, the collapse of Empires and working towards a new vision of how we might see and understand our planet anew. In the aftermath of 1945, the ZERO movement sought to reset and recalibrate everything in a future facing, future embracing mission of hope and energetics. This utopia, naturally, has never been fully realized, but the aesthetic impetus of Mack's work has certainly shaped our vision of what the future could be like.

It is clear from the texts in this volume that the artist has had huge influence on the formal development of art in the second half of the twentieth century; his thirst for the new allowing him to test forms, materials, and languages that were to become widely established in land art, minimalism, kinetic art, installation art, and more. But the authors in this book also point to a wider appreciation of Mack in the context of today's planetary and societal issues.

For a long time, the story of the post-war progression of art in the natural environment was dominated by a certain kind of purist, male persona. With a closer and more nuanced analysis, and multiple perspectives, we are now able to unpick the history more delicately and reveal other stories that have been missed, ignored, or suppressed. Mack's embrace of technology and natural phenomena link him also with female artists such as Steina Vasulka, Nancy Holt, or Margaret Benyon. His work, like theirs, was operating outside of the logic of the art market for many years, and he had to self-support or find new spaces for his work that were not acknowledged by the avant-gardist establishment. His ventures into wildernesses and commissions for trade fairs are perhaps the most pertinent projects in this sense, and ones we wished to highlight in our recent exhibitions at both ZKM | Center for Art and Media Karlsruhe and EnBW Energie Baden-Württemberg AG. This is a methodology which is very much about working in the world, embracing complexity and far from the seemingly autonomous zones of museums and galleries.

Furthermore, approaching these works from today's perspective, where our relationship with the natural world and a plurality of cultures is shifting, reveals a subtlety and poignancy that runs through Mack's entire œuvre, and it is one which comes from the concentration, manipulation, and consideration of the nature of light as a fundamental force. This is the essence of Mack, and it overrides the hardware and mechanics that are there to supply its effects.

For me, this intention overwrites a reading in terms of modernist histories and speaks of something more universal and cosmic. It echoes the fascination with the sun and stars that has been at the center of human cultures from the very beginning. It brings to mind the earliest writings on aesthetics, as a field of perception and transformation, and in particular the thirteenth-century treatise by Saint Bonaventure, *On the Reduction of the Arts to Theology* (*De reductione artium ad theologiam*). Bonaventure maintains that all knowledge is ultimately derived from various forms of light, which emanate from a single source – in his case, God, but we might also say in these times the Big Bang. St. Bonaventure enumerates four categories of light in order of increasing importance: mechanical arts (which illuminate the forms produced by man), sensitive knowledge (natural forms), philosophical knowledge (intelligible truths), and the Sacred Scripture (the salvific truths). Closer readings reveal six categories, which further differentiate rational philosophy, natural philosophy, and moral philosophy.

Even though every illumination of knowledge is ultimately internal, he says we can reasonably distinguish what may be called an *exterior* light, or the light of mechanical arts; and an *interior* light, the light of philosophical knowledge. Bonaventure describes how the first light illumines with respect to the forms of *artifacts*; the second, with respect to *natural forms*; the third, with respect to *intellectual truth*; the fourth and last, with respect to *saving truth*. In Heinz Mack's work, all these facets come together.

Whilst this is firmly embedded in the traditions of western theology, it also opens a door that could connect Mack with other world views, spiritualisms, philosophies, cosmologies that are now emerging and considered relevant; views that are intent on crafting a world with technology that is in tune with nature, not against it. Even more so, Mack, with his post-war space adventure, directs us beyond a planetary ecology to the galactic ecology that we must surely consider in the coming century.

Today, therefore, we see contradictions and complications with this work that make it all the more engaging. On the one hand, a resetting of our relationship with nature and the modern era is currently underway, and this can make Mack's adventures into the wide and deserted expanses of the Sahara and Arctic seem to be avoiding the geopolitical, cultural, and economic realities of these regions. Yet his works can also be read as an invitation by an artist, a fellow human, to look to what unifies us under one star, a prefiguring of a global ecological sensibility. His work is firmly entangled with the late modernity of post-war rebuilding, but it is also imbued with a universal hope and connectivity between people and ideas; between art, science, technology, and realpolitik.

That he was able to manifest his grandest projects outside of the white walls of the gallery, with the support of great expos and industry fairs as well as countless public commissions, and communicate on prime-time television, situates him in a different category of artist, one who is willing to engage and operate in the world as it really is, in dialogue with all its complexity, and subsequently influence it on a bigger scale.

In this sense, it was important that this publication and our exhibitions were realized in partnership with EnBW, reflecting this interplay between technological advancement in industry and culture.

The exhibition *MACK at ZKM* proved to be a great public success, and for this I wish to express sincere thanks to the late Peter Weibel, who had the very first idea for an exhibition that would situate Heinz Mack as a key figure in the development of media arts and also present his large-scale projects in natural and industrial contexts.

I also would like to praise the whole team of ZKM who, as always, form a collective of passion, insight, and professionalism around every project, one that allows artists to achieve their fullest expression. Thanks are due in particular to the dedicated curatorial team of Daria Mille, Clara Runge, and Katharina Kern, as well as the technical and collection teams at ZKM for their ability rise to any technical challenge to present works of such great complexity: Andrea Hartinger, Matthias Gommel, Marlies Peller, Leonie Rök, Regina Linder, Martin Mangold, Volker Becker, Claudius Böhm, Götz Dipper, Mirco Fraß, Rainer Gabler, Gregor Gaissmaier, Jan Gerigk, Martin Häberle, Ronny Haas, Daniel Heiss, Christof Hierholzer, Werner Hutzenlaub, Gisbert Laaber, Bernd Lintermann, Nolan Ashvin Miranda, Christian Nainggolan, Marco Preitschopf, Martin Schläfke, Marc Schütze, Niklas Wallbaum, Manuel Weber, Andreas Brehmer, Christina Zartmann, Max Clausen, and Andy Koch. We are also grateful to the external companies who support the exhibition production: Artinate, COMYK, Essential-Art-Solutions, Pollux Edelstahlverarbeitung GmbH, and Richfelder Kunstprojekte.

Studio Mack have been exceptional in their general support for the exhibition and book, especially in providing image material. The studio team of Ute Mack and Sophia Sotke have been wonderfully generous in their time and dedication to a truly collaborative project. I wish to pay a special tribute to the Friends of ZERO foundation and EnBW for their continuous support throughout.

This publication has been realized by the relentlessly dedicated ZKM publications team and managed with great acuity by Ulrike Havemann. Thanks also go to all the authors, Demian Bern for the accomplished graphic design, Felix Grünschloß and Tobias Wootton for the atmospheric photography, the editors at Hirmer for their confidence and support when it comes to the production of the book, and our translators Anna Galt, Gérard Goodrow, and Dan Lawler for their impeccable work.

Alistair Hudson

Chairman and CEO of ZKM | Center for Art and Media Karlsruhe

Opening Remarks

For almost two decades now, EnBW Energy Baden-Württemberg has been involved with the ZKM | Center for Art and Media Karlsruhe. As a provider of energy and infrastructural services, our company supports this cultural institution and its activities surrounding innovative developments in technology and digital media. The ZKM enjoys an excellent world-wide reputation.

From time to time, the ZKM and EnBW work together on special exhibition projects. During these collaborations, the foyer at our headquarters in Karlsruhe turns into a satellite branch of the ZKM for additional exhibits that augment the current exhibition at the ZKM itself. This is also the case for *Mack at ZKM*. Alongside this exhibition, a key element of one of the most ground-breaking projects created by the internationally renowned ZERO artist Heinz Mack is on display at EnBW: *Jardin Artificiel*.

As early as the 1950s, the artist worked towards a new beginning in art and turned his attention to the relationship between humanity, nature, and technology. To this end, he sought out new spaces to perfect his art, which he found in the sand deserts of Tunisia and Algeria as well as the Arctic desert of Greenland. In the Sahara, he "planted" his unusual objects to create the original *Jardin Artificiel*, an artificial garden in which he experimented with new materials and their textures to investigate their interactions with movement, color, space, and light.

Mack was especially fascinated with light and its inherent energy. In his artistic experiments, he explored these phenomena and their creative potential. He erected monumental *Light Plantations* to capture light and transform it. This approach seems like an artistic anticipation of solar power plants, which have since taken on a crucial role in the transition to renewable energy and become a widespread technology – although there is still work to be done here.

In this respect, Heinz Mack was a pioneer whose ideas were ahead of his time. From today's perspective, his art is not only visually fascinating, but also proof of the artist's creativity, foresight, and courage. These are characteristics which we urgently need today in order to overcome the challenges of our time. The transition to renewable energy requires the same visionary willpower and targeted creativity to stave off climate change.

That is why it was an easy decision to support this ZKM publication documenting the extensive work of Heinz Mack. We hope that many readers will benefit from its insights into the work and mind of this extraordinary artist.

Colette Rückert-Hennen

Member of the Board of Management
EnBW Energie Baden-Württemberg AG

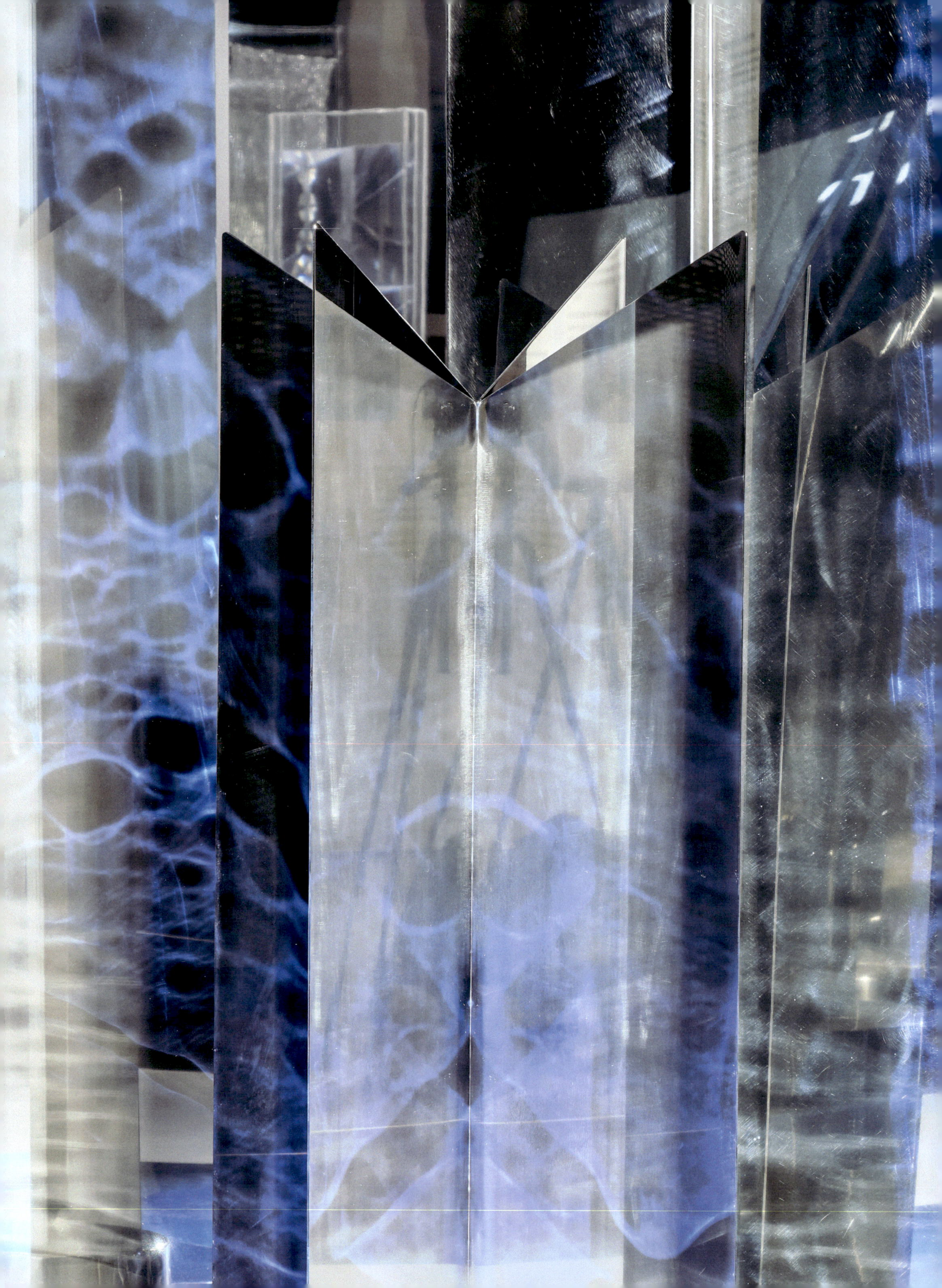

Light Choreography

In the center of the atrium is the *Light Choreography*, a combination of several works by Heinz Mack, shown here for the first time in this form. *The Mechanical Ballet* (1966/2015) is an ensemble of seven stainless steel steles of various sizes set in rotation by motors, standing on and in front of mirrored surfaces. The idea for this group of moving light steles dates back to 1966, but the first public presentation only took place in 2018. The title of the work refers to the Dadaist silent film *Ballet méchanique*. This early experimental film was made in 1924 by Fernand Léger together with Dudley Murphy. Mack's kinetic ensemble can be read as a tribute to the French artist. The kinetic steles made of polished stainless steel originally moved to the 1961 orchestral piece *Atmosphères* (1961) by the renowned composer of New Music György Ligeti; at the ZKM, the music is not included in the exhibition.

In addition, an arrangement of steles of different heights – some of them motor-driven – made of various metals, optical lenses, acrylic glass, and mirrors is on show. As "instruments of light," they reflect the incidence of light in multiple directions, which seems to dissolve their own physical materiality. Such steles have been part of the artist's wide range of sculptural forms since the 1950s. In his earlier years, the artist made them out of wood and stone and, from 1958, versions made of new industrial materials followed. Mack finds inspiration in tall trees as a natural connection between heaven and earth, but also in the skyscrapers of the urban environment. With regard to the art scene, he is particularly fascinated by the work of Constantin Brâncuși and his concept of the *Endless Column*.

Two large mirror sculptures frame this environment. They reflect, refract, and multiply what is happening at the center and accentuate the effects of the light steles. Mack sets light and space in vibration and literally makes them dance, thereby creating a multisensory, immersive experience.

← *fig. 8* Heinz Mack, *The Mechanical Ballet*, 2015 (idea: 1966), detail

*Although it may seem as though I have dedicated my work to light exclusively, I must clarify that it has always been my sole intention to make objects whose appearance is immaterial; to this end, I rely – more than anything else – on light and movement.**

Works in the exhibition:
All works courtesy of the artist
unless otherwise noted

The Mechanical Ballet
2015 (idea: 1966)
Kinetic ensemble: stainless steel, motors, mirrors, light
Environment, dimensions variable, 7 steles à 120, 140, 160, 180, 200, 200 and 250 cm
→ *figs. 8, 9, 10, 44*

Stele With 9 Wings
1960 (replica from 2018)
Light stele: acrylic glass, aluminum
400 × 53.5 × 15.5 cm, plinth 4 × 60 × 80 cm
→ *figs. 11, 12, 117*

Nemesis
2014
Light stele: aluminum, stainless steel
374.5 × 46 × 15 cm, plinth 4.5 × 46 × 110.5 cm
→ *figs. 5, 11, 12, 13, 117*

Themis
2020
Light stele: aluminum, stainless steel, wood
360.5 × 33.5 × 10 cm, plinth 4.5 × 33.5 × 90 cm
→ *figs. 11, 12, 13, 117*

Helios
1973 (replica from 2019)
Light stele: mirror mosaic, acrylic glass
304 × 55 × 55 cm, plinth 2 × Ø 69 cm
→ *figs. 6, 11, 12, 13, 117*

Grid Stele
2020
Light stele: aluminum, stainless steel, wood
297.5 × 40.5 × 12 cm, plinth 4.5 × 40.5 × 90 cm
→ *figs. 11, 12, 13, 117*

Paravent for Light
1964
Light stele: aluminum, acrylic glass
295 × 55.4 × 2.2 cm, plinth 2.5 × 55.4 × 69.5 cm
→ *figs. 11, 12, 117*

Untitled
2007
Kinetic light stele: acrylic glass, stainless steel, aluminum, electric motor
244.5 × 31.5 × 31.5 cm
→ *fig. 11*

Untitled (II. Version)
2007
Kinetic light stele: acrylic glass, stainless steel, electric motor
259.5 × 26 × 26.5 cm
→ *fig. 11*

Semitransparent Stele
2020
Light stele: acrylic glass, aluminum, stainless steel, wood
228 × 46 × 11.5 cm, plinth 4 × 46 × 76 cm
→ *figs. 12, 13, 117*

The Time of Stars
1963
Light stele: Fresnel lenses, acrylic glass
227.5 × 42.5 × 10 cm, plinth 1,7 × 42.5 × 70 cm
ZERO foundation, Düsseldorf / donation Heinz Mack
→ *figs. 12, 117*

Mirror-Object
2022
Mirror sculpture: EasyMirror special mirror glass
Hight 396 cm, Ø 240 cm
→ *fig. 11*

Untitled
2016
Mirror sculpture: stainless steel
298 × 148 × 148 cm
→ *fig. 11*

* Heinz Mack, "Licht ist nicht Licht," 1966, (typoscript, Archive Heinz Mack), first published in: *Mackazin* (Frankfurt/Main: Typos, 1967). Translated from the German.

→ *figs. 9, 10* Heinz Mack, *The Mechanical Ballet*, 2015 (idea: 1966)

→→ *figs. 11, 12, 13* *Mack at ZKM*, exhibition view, ZKM | Karlsruhe 2023

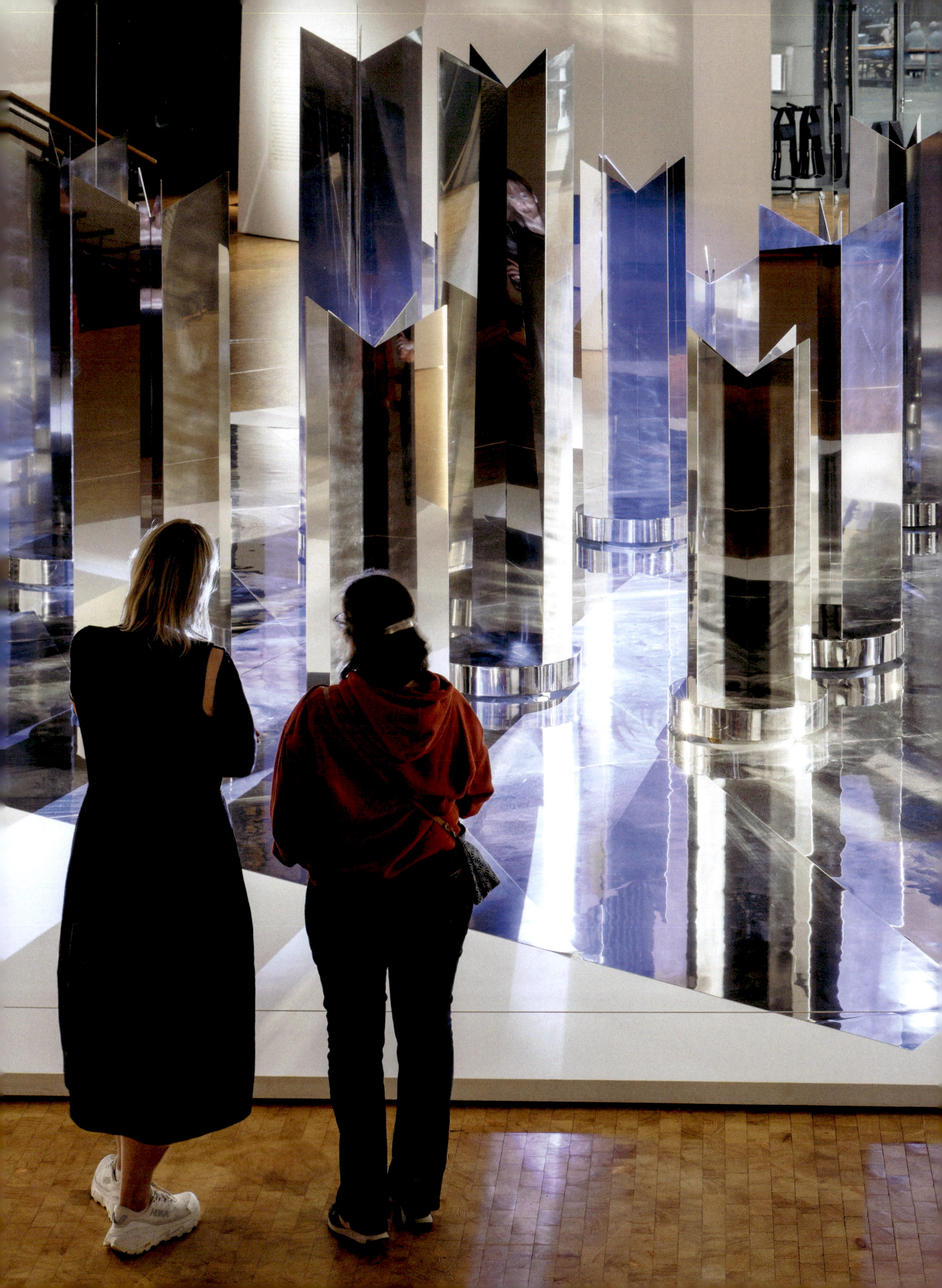
HOKA

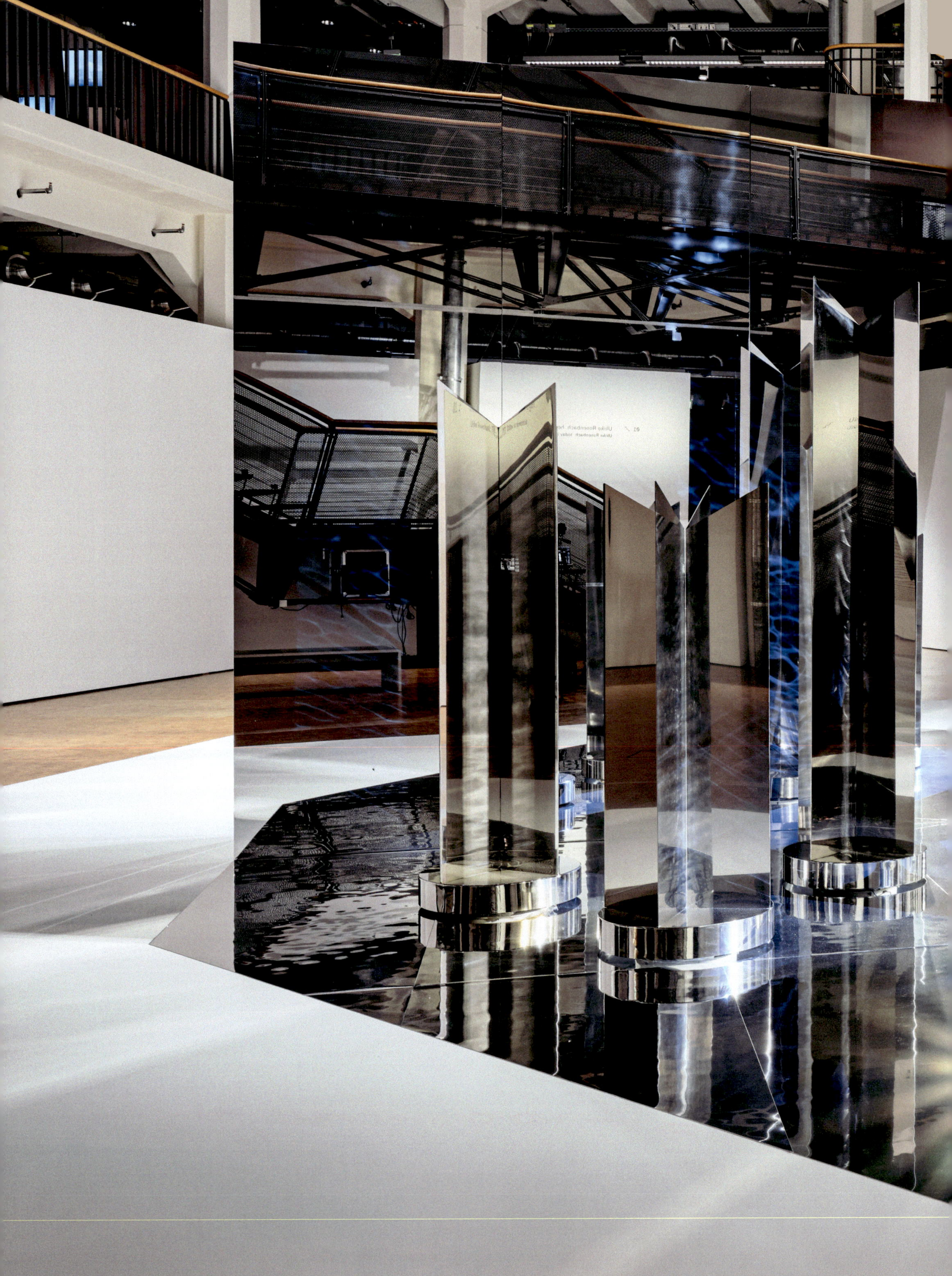

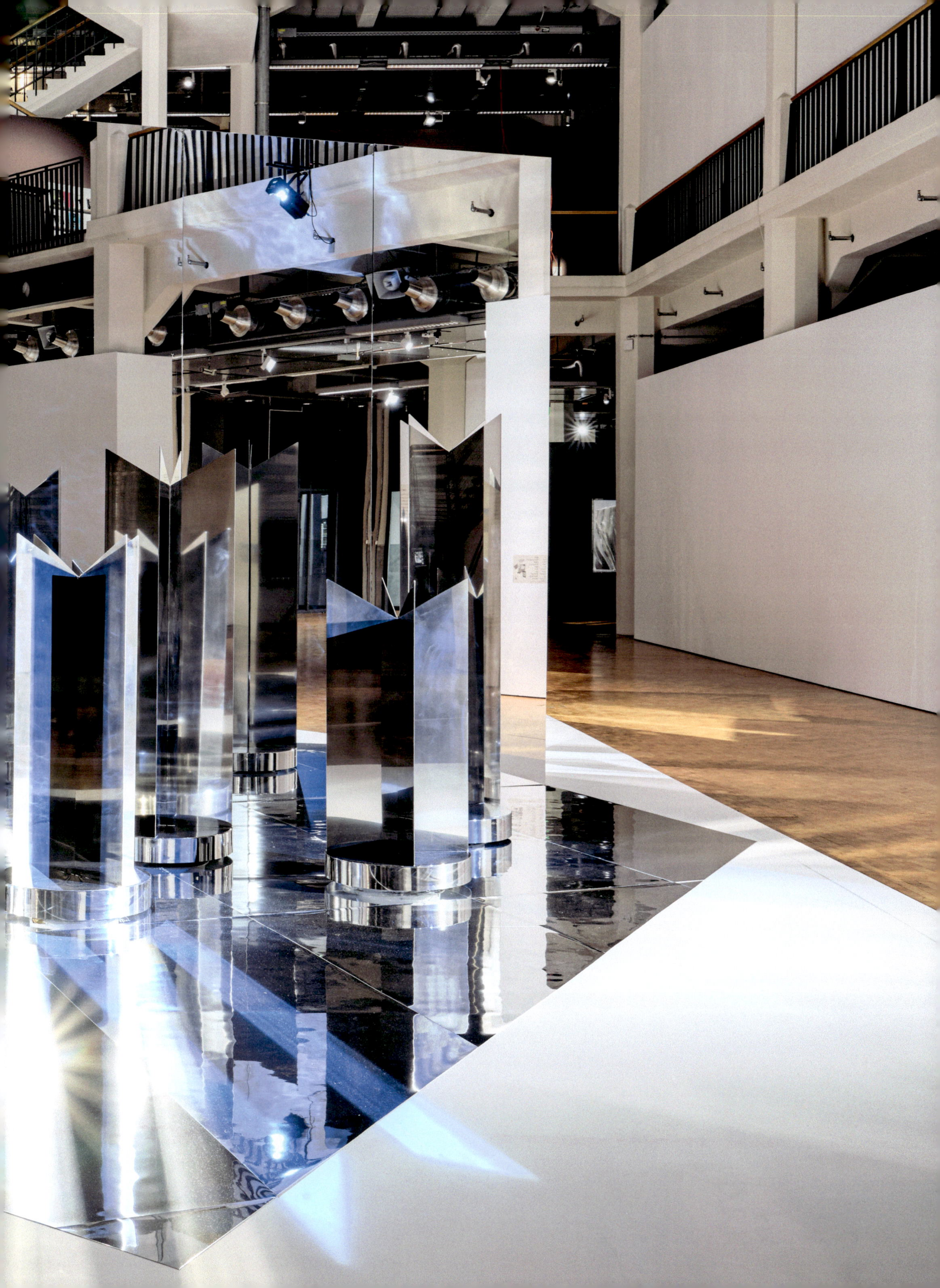

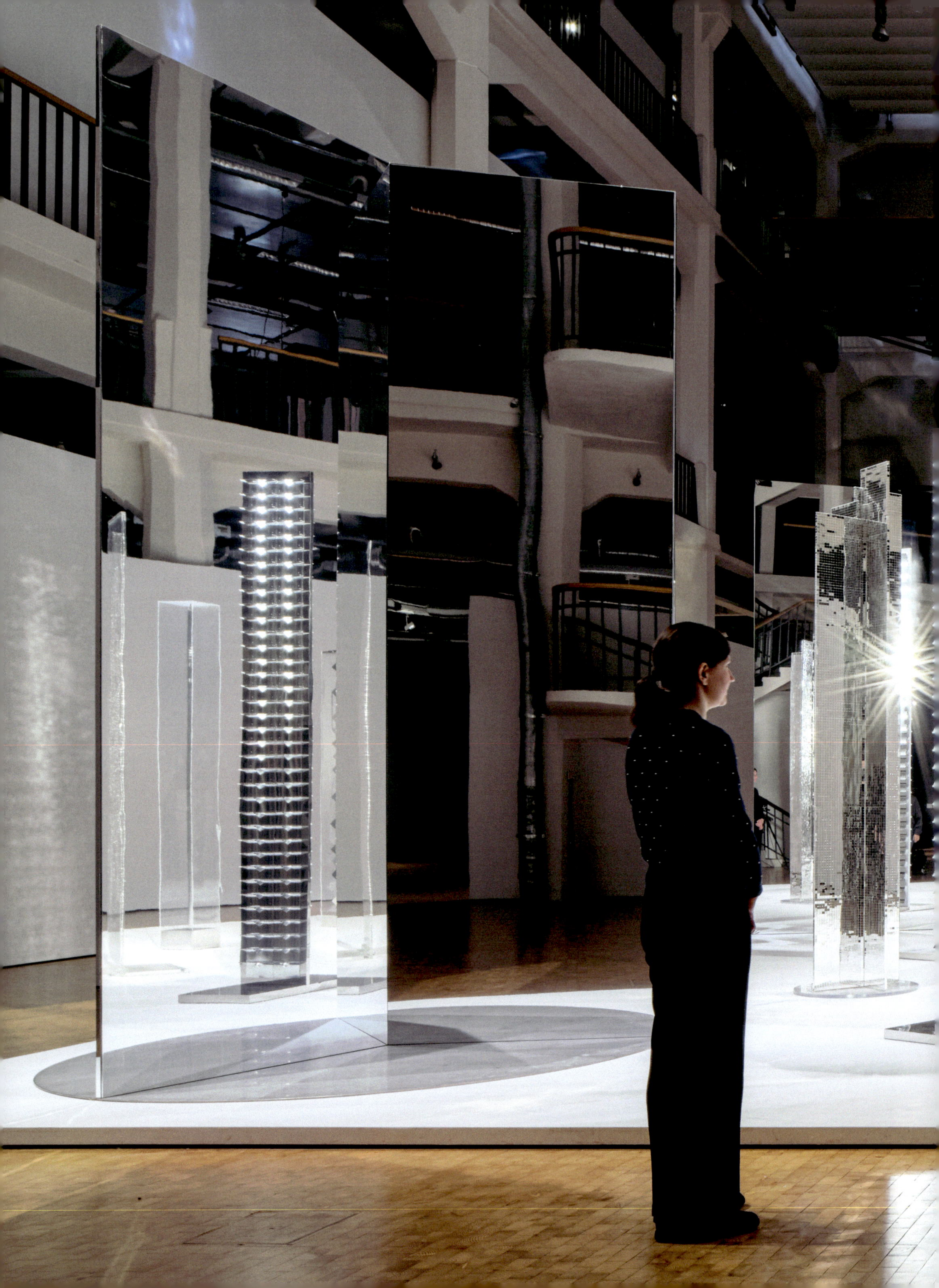

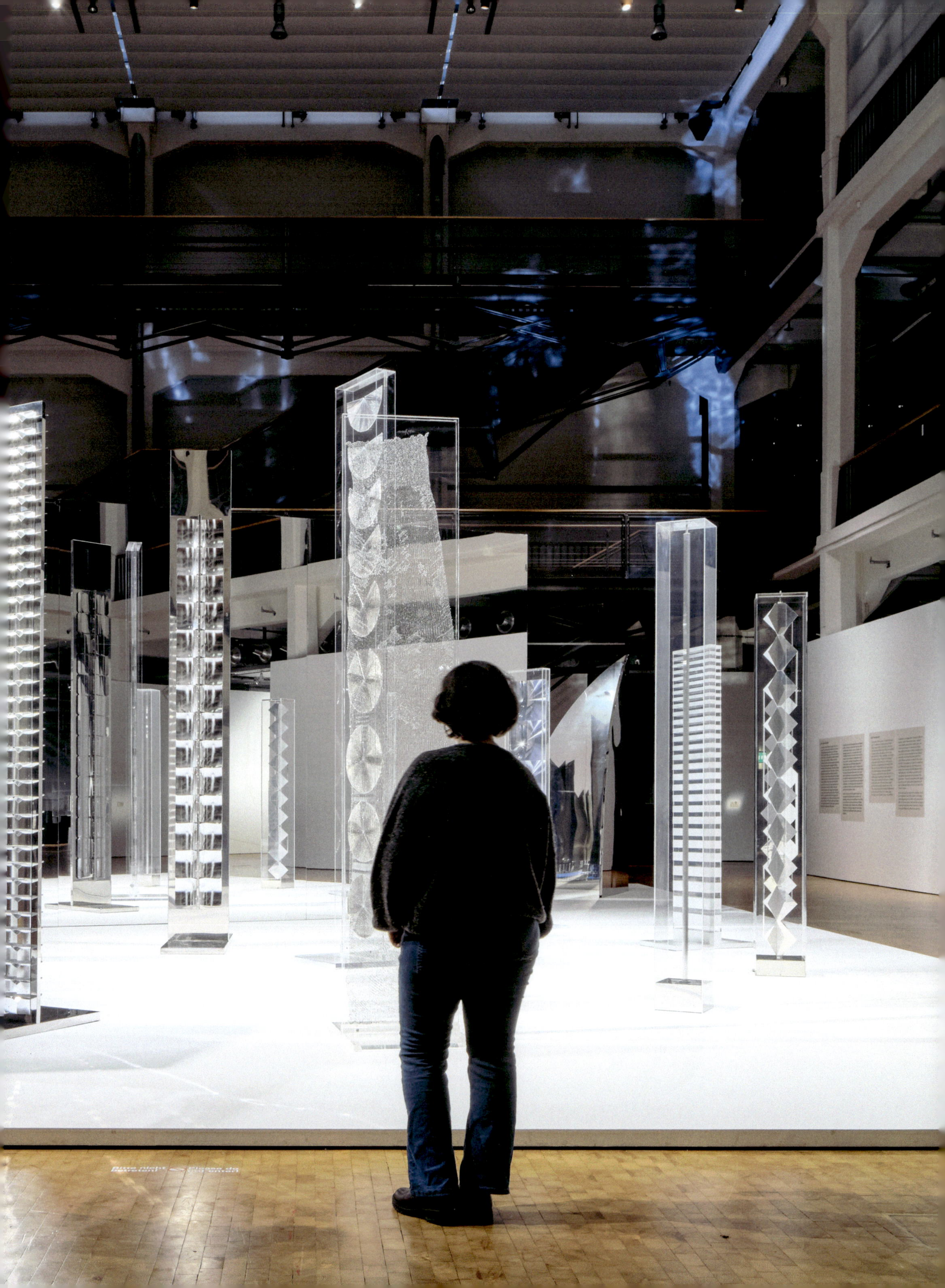

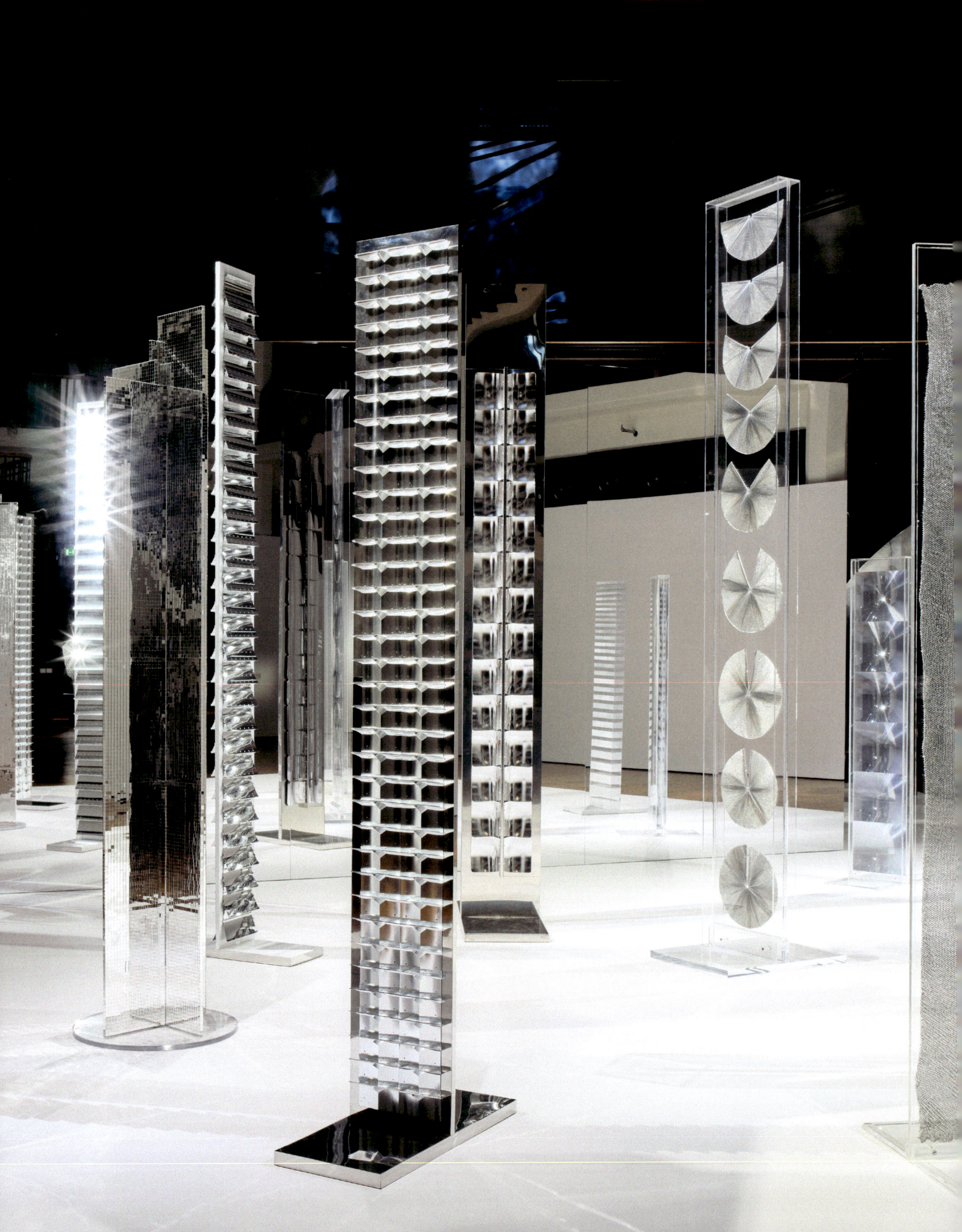

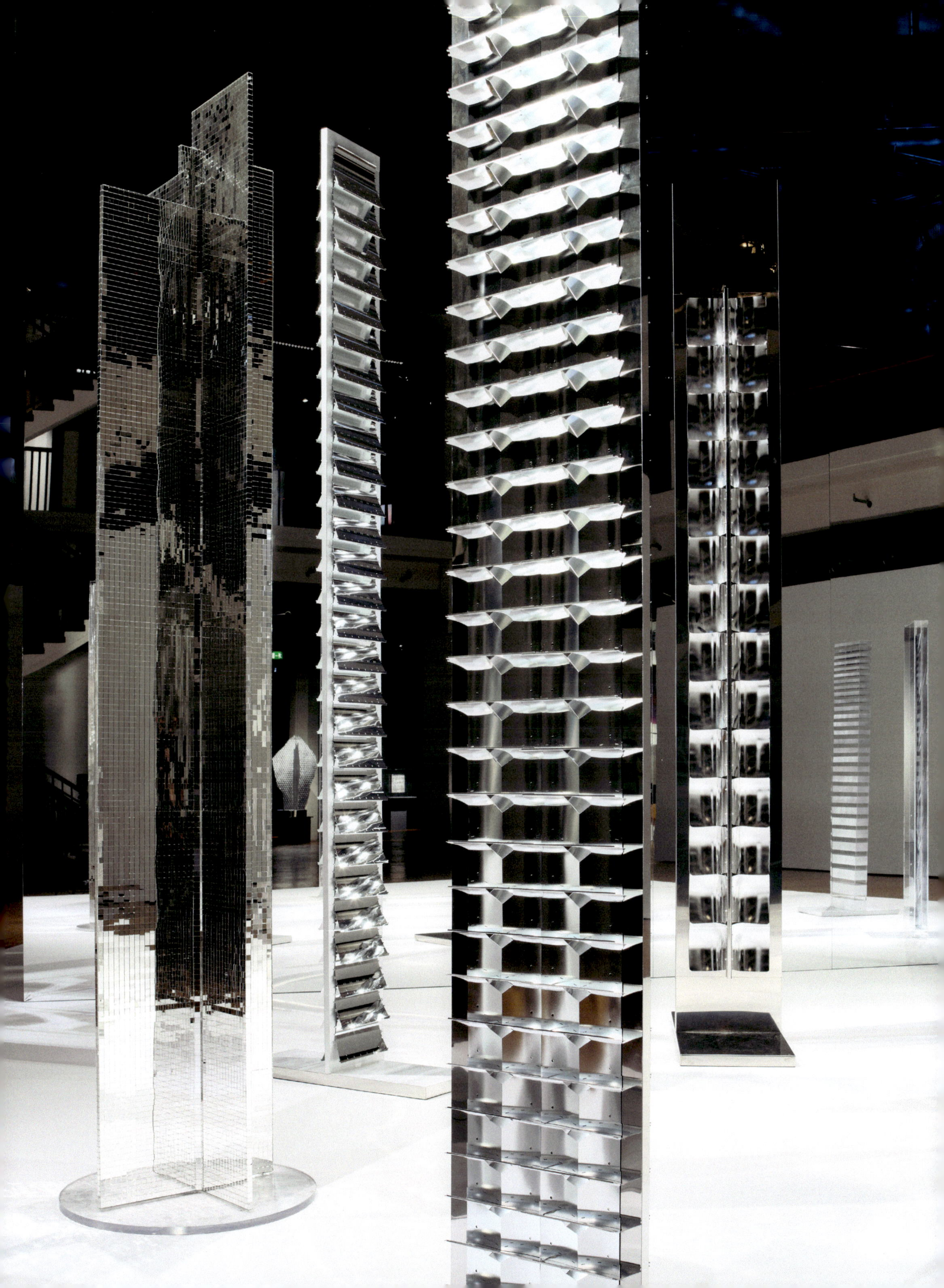

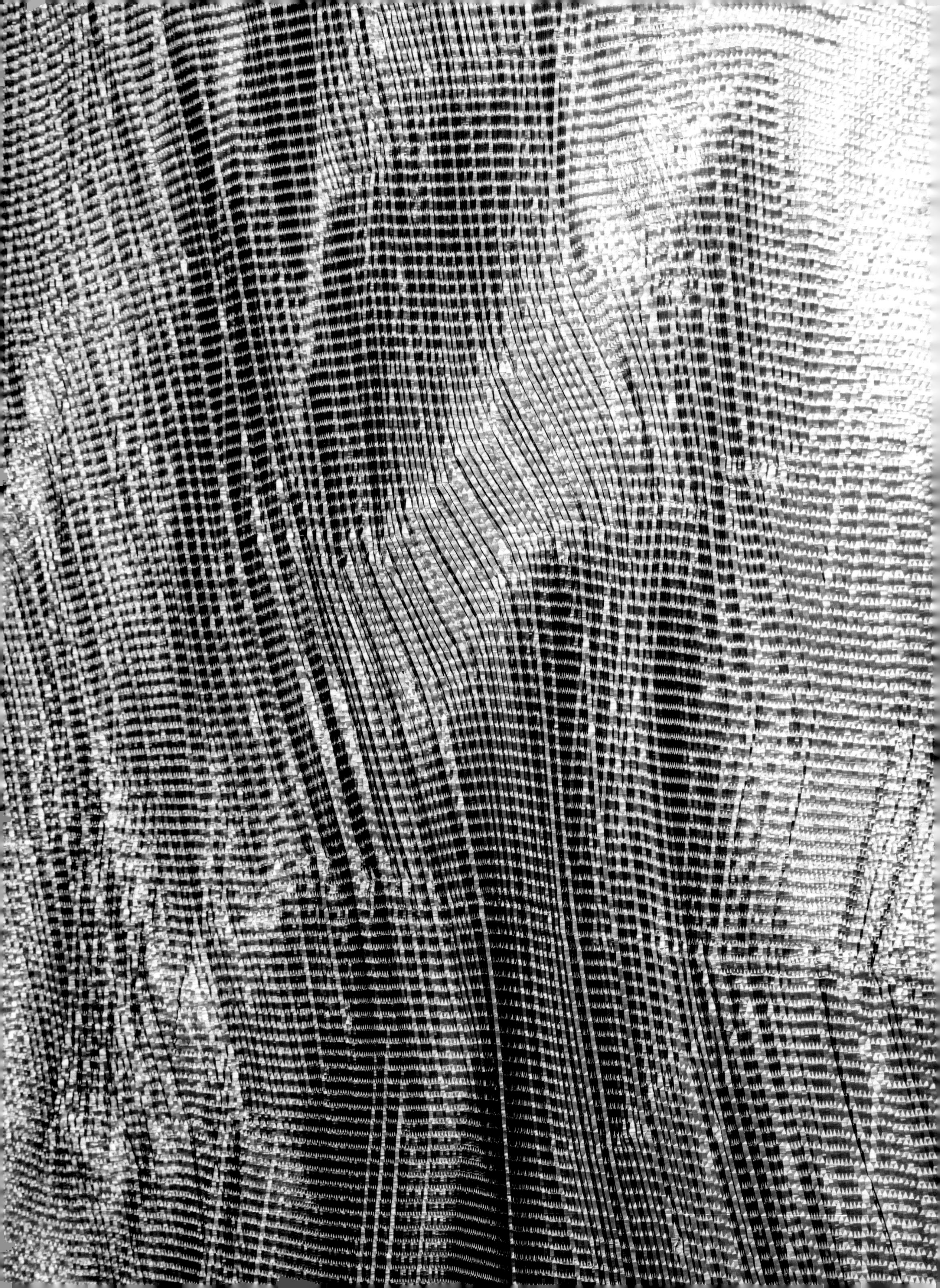

Instruments of Light

In post-war Germany, the ZERO artists looked to the future with optimism and a spirit of renewal. Mack speaks of the artists' fight against a prevailing mood of conservatism and anti-science in the art scene after the trauma of Nazism.

The ZERO group, reflecting this spirit of optimism, created a new repertoire of artistic media. At the end of the 1950s, Heinz Mack began to use new industrial materials for his works: stainless steel, aluminum, acrylic glass, the honeycomb aluminum mesh used in the aerospace industry, and Fresnel lenses developed for use in lighthouses and aerospace applications. His enthusiasm for new, forward-looking technologies and his desire to try out new means of expression also led him to experiment with chemical substances such as mercury.

For Mack, art, nature, and technology are not irreconcilable opposites, but rather categories that are mutually intensifying. Combining them opens up new spaces of possibilities for experimenting with technological innovations and expanding sensory perception. All of these shimmering silvery surfaces interact with the wavelengths of natural light, whether polished to a mirror finish or deformed by hand to create new shapes and structures in the material.

These light objects are not self-contained, but open to the changing perspective of the viewer and surrounding conditions. Depending on the incidence of light, surfaces become dynamic and materiality is suspended, dematerialized. The use of transparent materials like glass or acrylic increases the effect, the boundaries between things dissolve. The light replaces paint or patina.

Little-known architectural models, also shown in this exhibition area, underline the close connection between utopia and reality in Mack's work. Mack has repeatedly put forward concrete proposals for utopian projects that rethink museum or urban spaces, for example. Many and varied crystalline mirror facets produce a kaleidoscopic fragmentation that leads to abstract forms. For Mack, the driving force is and always has been beauty, which emerges from the use of light, space, color, and time.

← *fig. 14* Heinz Mack, *Paravent for Light*, 1970, detail

*The works which I have created in the last 30 years only come to life if they have 'their' light, the 'right' light. These works are objects of light, instruments of light, and an expression of its energy.**

Works in the exhibition:
All works courtesy of the artist
unless otherwise noted

Wind Chime for Light
1958
Light sculpture: aluminum, chrome-plated steel
198 × 60 × 60 cm, plinth 0.5 × 44 × 44 cm
→ *fig. 33*

Cube with Glass Chunks
2015 (idea: 1964)
Cube: acrylic glass, stainless steel, breakage of glass
31 × 30 × 30 cm, base 100 × 30 × 30 cm
→ *figs. 21, 255*

The Silence of the Material III
2019
Cube: aluminum, acrylic glass, stainless steel, wood
40 × 40 × 40 cm, cover 70 × 70 × 70 cm, plate 2 × 90 × 90 cm, base 80 × 50 × 50 cm
→ *fig. 23*

Untitled
2020
Cube: acrylic glass
65 × 65 × 65 cm, plate 1 × 110 × 110 cm, base 60 × 60 × 60 cm
→ *fig. 110*

Light Relief (with Rotation)
1963
Light relief: aluminum, wood, acrylic glass
216 × 116 × 10 cm
→ *figs. 27, 29*

The Dance (Light-Relief)
1963
Light relief: aluminum, wood, stainless steel, acrylic glass
217 × 117 × 10 cm
→ *figs. 3, 30, 115*

Law and Freedom
1973
Light relief: aluminum
137 × 102 × 4.5 cm
→ *fig. 31*

Paravent for Light
1970
Light sculpture: aluminum, stainless steel, acrylic glass
235 × 158.4 × 3.5 cm, plinth 15 × 158.4 × 81.5 cm
→ *figs. 14, 15*

Optical Light
1964
Light-kinetic sculpture: mercury vapor-coated acrylic glass, metal grid, electric equipment
184 × 37 × 37 cm
→ *fig. 20*

The Shrine of the Void (Green and Yellow Version)
1968
Cube: acrylic glass, crystal glass, marble
65 × 60 × 60 cm, plate 4 × 80 × 80 cm, base 50 × 40 × 40 cm
→ *fig. 22, 23*

Untitled
1964 (replica from 2017)
Light relief: aluminum, stainless steel, wood, acrylic glass
139.5 × 104.5 × 7.5 cm
→ *fig. 27*

Untitled
1970 (replica from 2023)
Interactive sculpture: acrylic glass, mercury, mirror, wood
Mercury object 3 × 100 × 100 cm, glass case 30 × 100.5 × 95 cm, wooden base 36 × 100.5 × 95 cm, interactive base plate 1 × 190 × 185 cm
→ *figs. 25, 26*

Emanation of Light
1960
Rotor: aluminum, wood, acrylic glass, motor
30 × 29.3 × 8 cm
→ *fig. 18*

Light-Ball
1965
Light-kinetic sculpture: aluminum, stainless steel, electric equipment
25 × 17 × 25 cm
→ *fig. 19*

Light Pavillion I
2006
Cube: mineral vapor-coated glass, mirror glass
30.5 × 30.5 × 30.5 cm, plate 1 × 40 × 40 cm
→ *figs. 23, 113*

Light Pavillion II
2006
Cube: mineral vapor-coated glass
50 × 50 × 50 cm
→ *figs. 23, 163*

Untitled
2006
Cube: mineral vapor-coated glass, mirror glass
30 × 30 × 30 cm, plate 1 × 40 × 40 cm
→ *figs. 23, 406*

The Sculptural City – The City of the Future (model)
1970–1997
Photo print
→ *figs. 16, 17*

Night-Light-Sculpture (Light Wing)
1970
Kinetic light sculpture: aluminum, motor
158 × 105 × 100 cm
→ *figs. 17, 18, 407*

Light Harp
1971
Light sculpture: acrylic glass, glass, stainless steel
158 × 44 × 40.5 cm, plate 1 × 43.5 × 39.5 cm
→ *figs. 17, 32, 118*

Very Little Cube in Silver
2020 (idea: 1974)
Cube: aluminum, wood, acrylic glass
23 × 23 × 23 cm, cover 33.5 × 34 × 34 cm
→ *figs. 17, 24*

Mirror Pavillon (Model for a Mirror-Hall as a Silver-Light-Space-Architecture)
2013 (idea: 1995)
Model: mirror, aluminum, cardboard, wooden silver panel
13 × 31 × 22 cm

Wing Pyramid (Model for a Sacred Architecture)
1978 (idea: 1964)
Model: stainless steel
33.5 × 48 × 48 cm
→ *fig. 28*

Creamcheese (Model for a Bar Wall)
1966/1967
Model: mirror glass, stainless steel
12 × 66 × 33 cm

* Dieter Honisch, "Interview mit Heinz Mack," in: Dieter Honisch, *Mack. Skulpturen 1953–1986* (Düsseldorf: Econ, 1986), 462. Translated from the German.

→ *fig. 15* Heinz Mack, *Paravent for Light*, 1970

→→ *fig. 16* Heinz Mack, *The Sculptural City – The City of the Future (model)*, 1970–1997

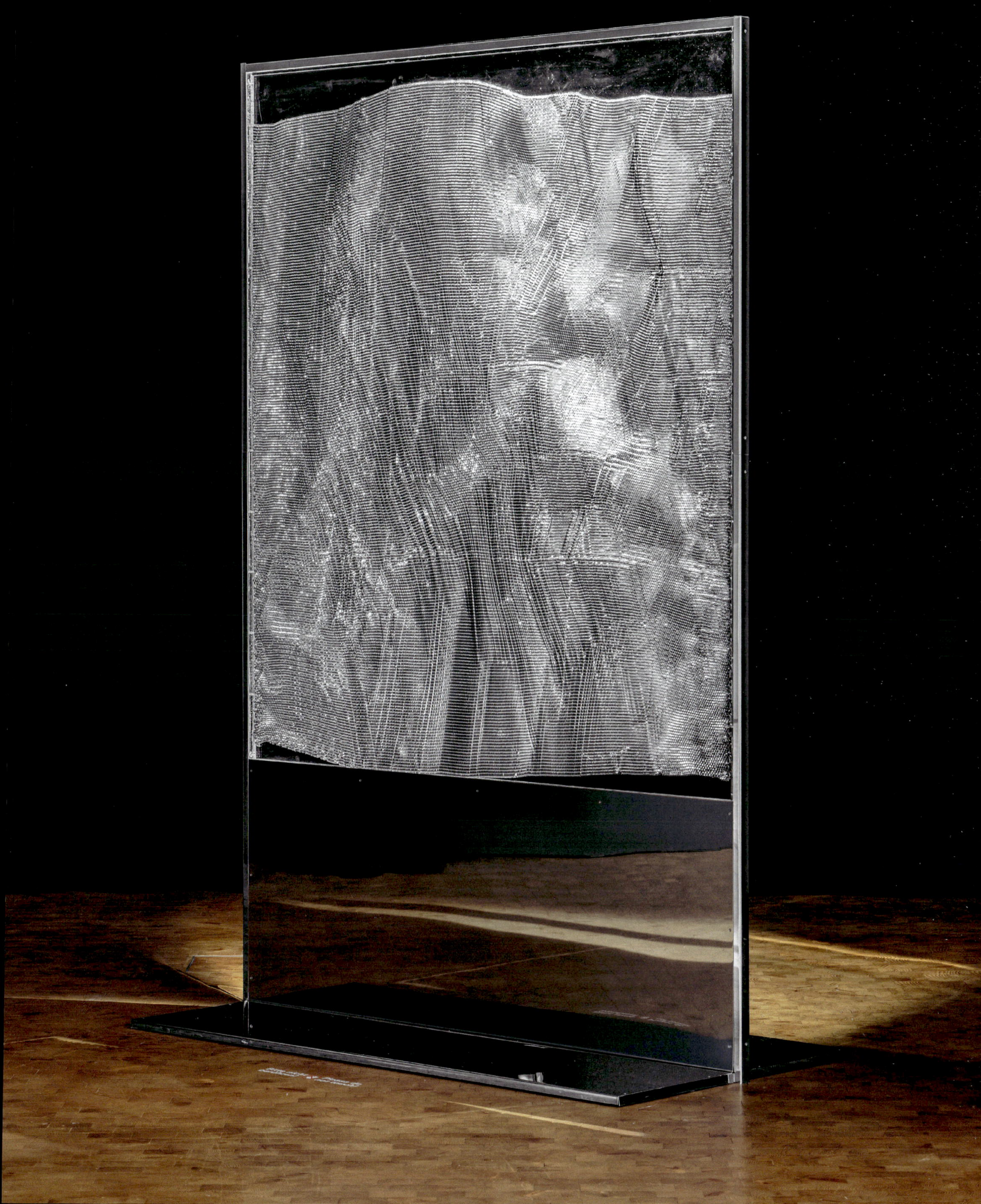

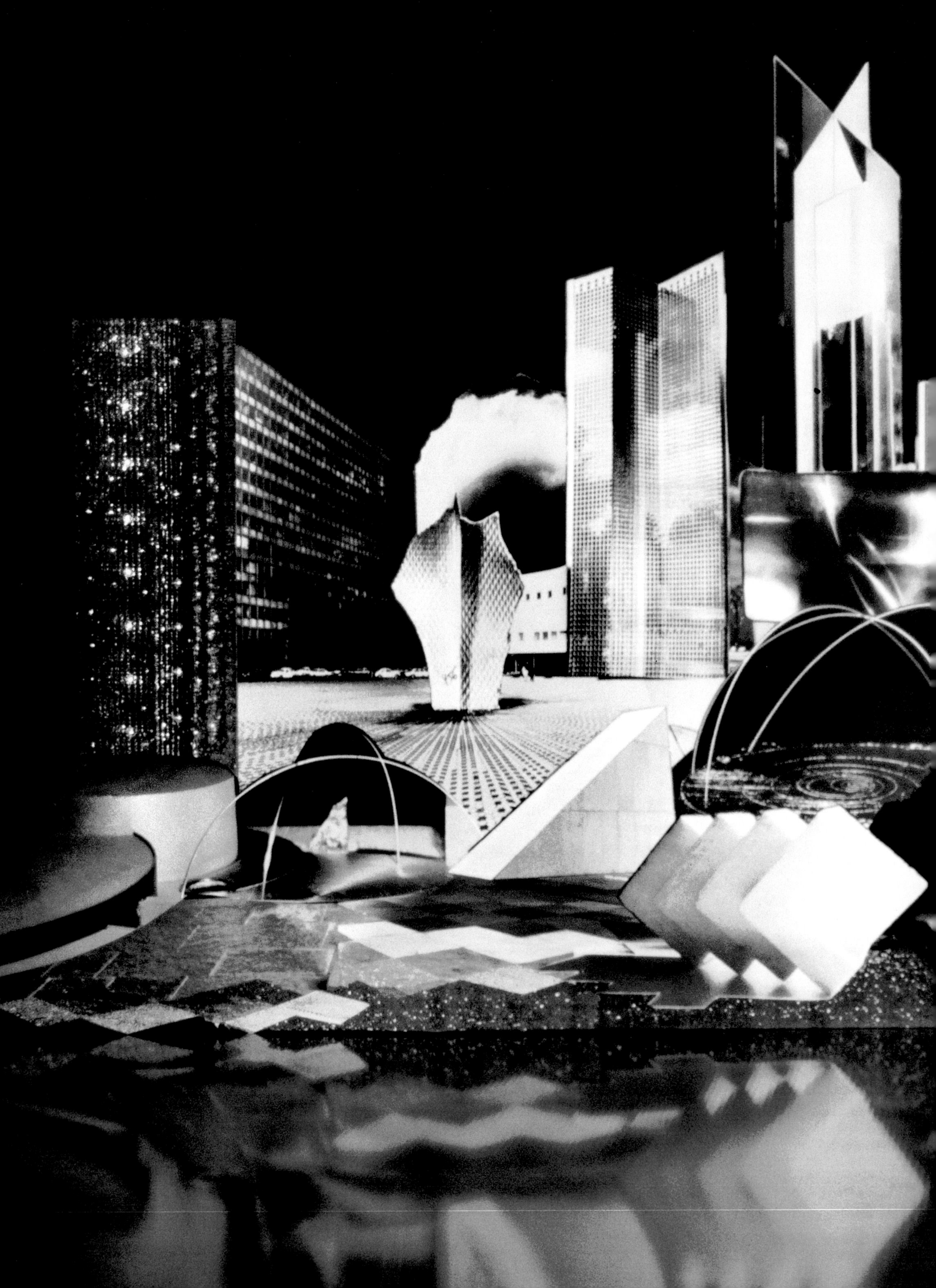

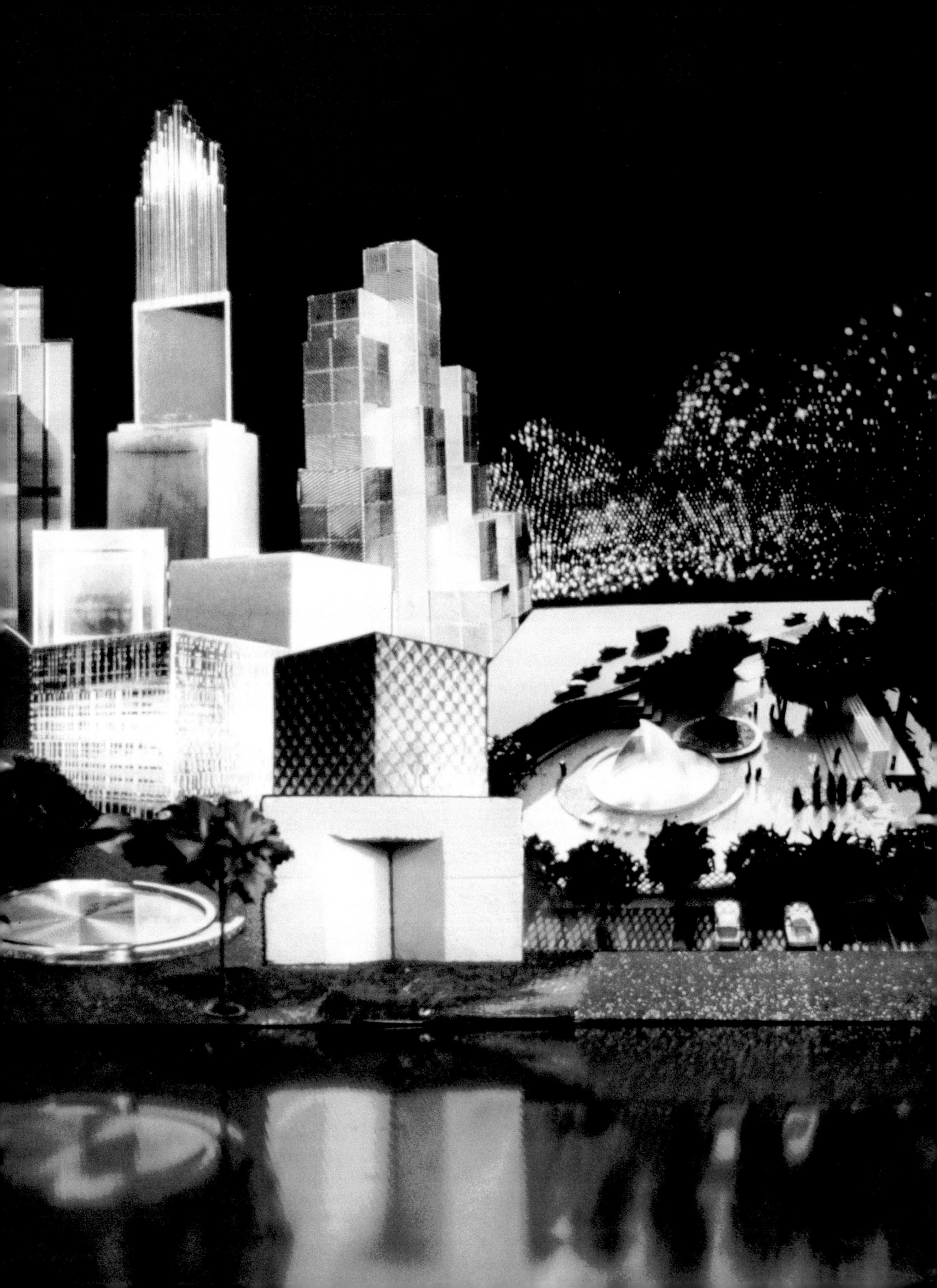

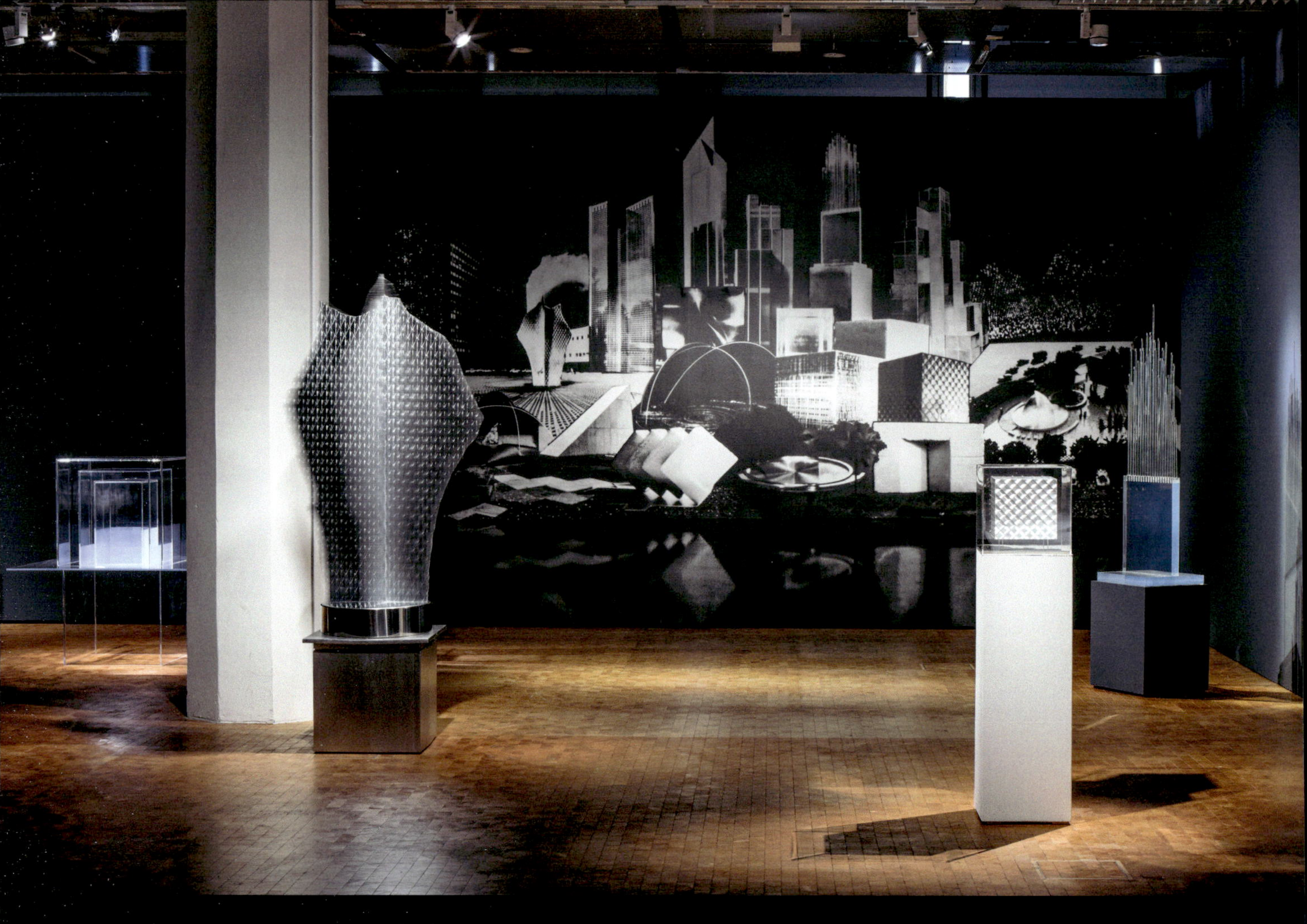

↑ *fig. 17* *Mack at ZKM*, exhibition view, ZKM | Karlsruhe 2023
→ *fig. 18* Heinz Mack, *Night-Light-Sculpture (Light Wing)*, 1970
→← *fig. 19* Heinz Mack, *Light-Ball*, 1965
→→ *fig. 20* Heinz Mack, *Optical Light*, 1964

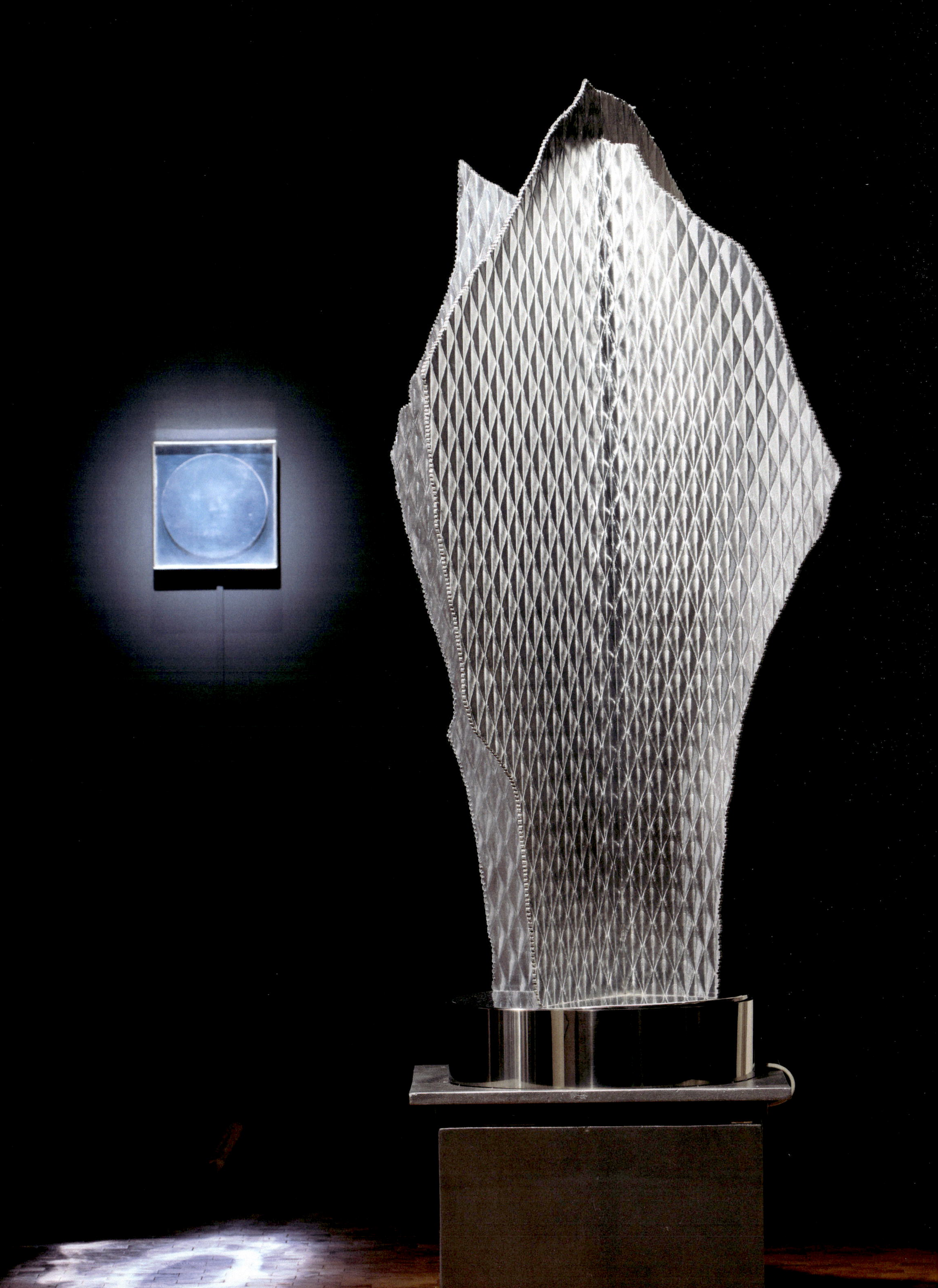

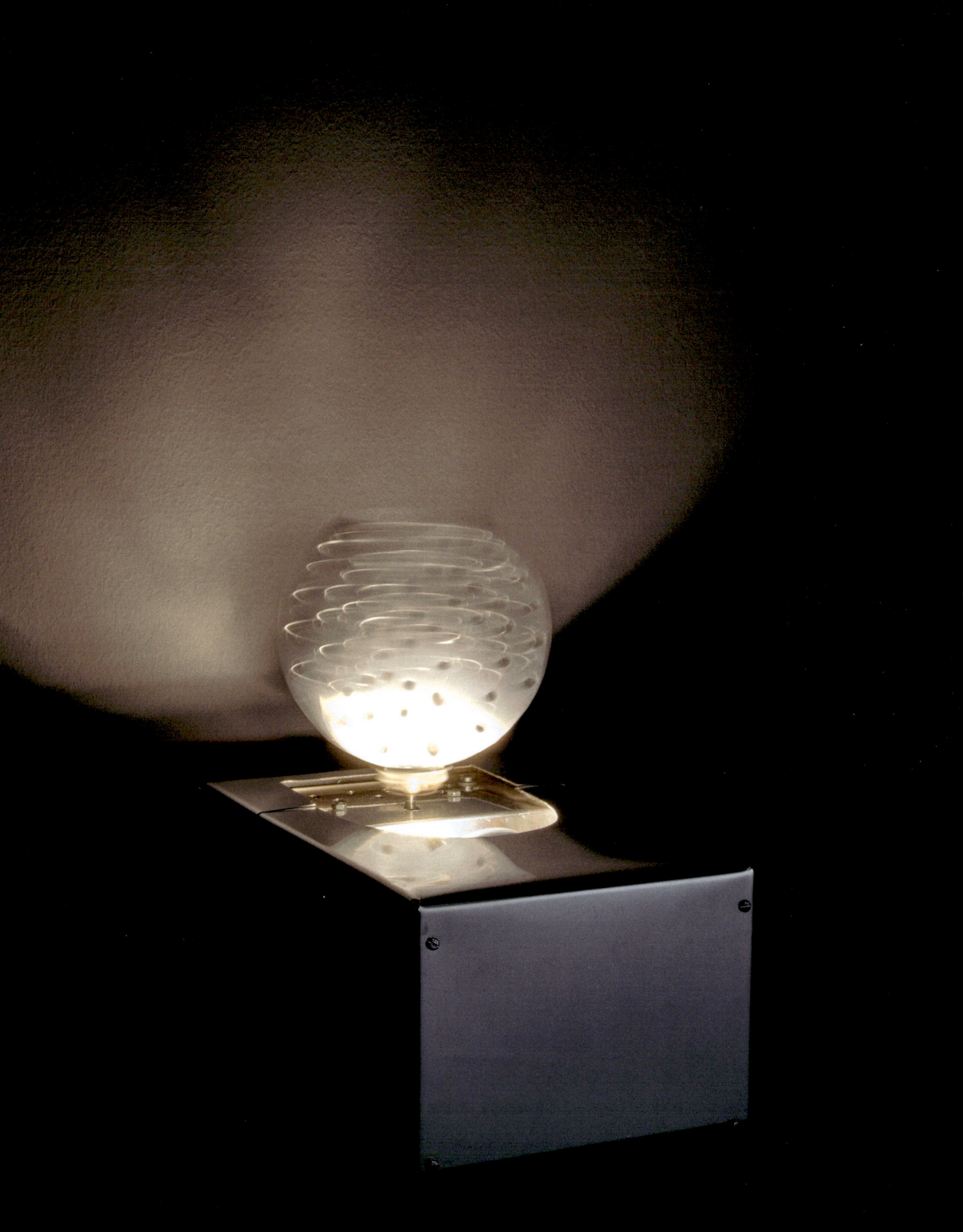

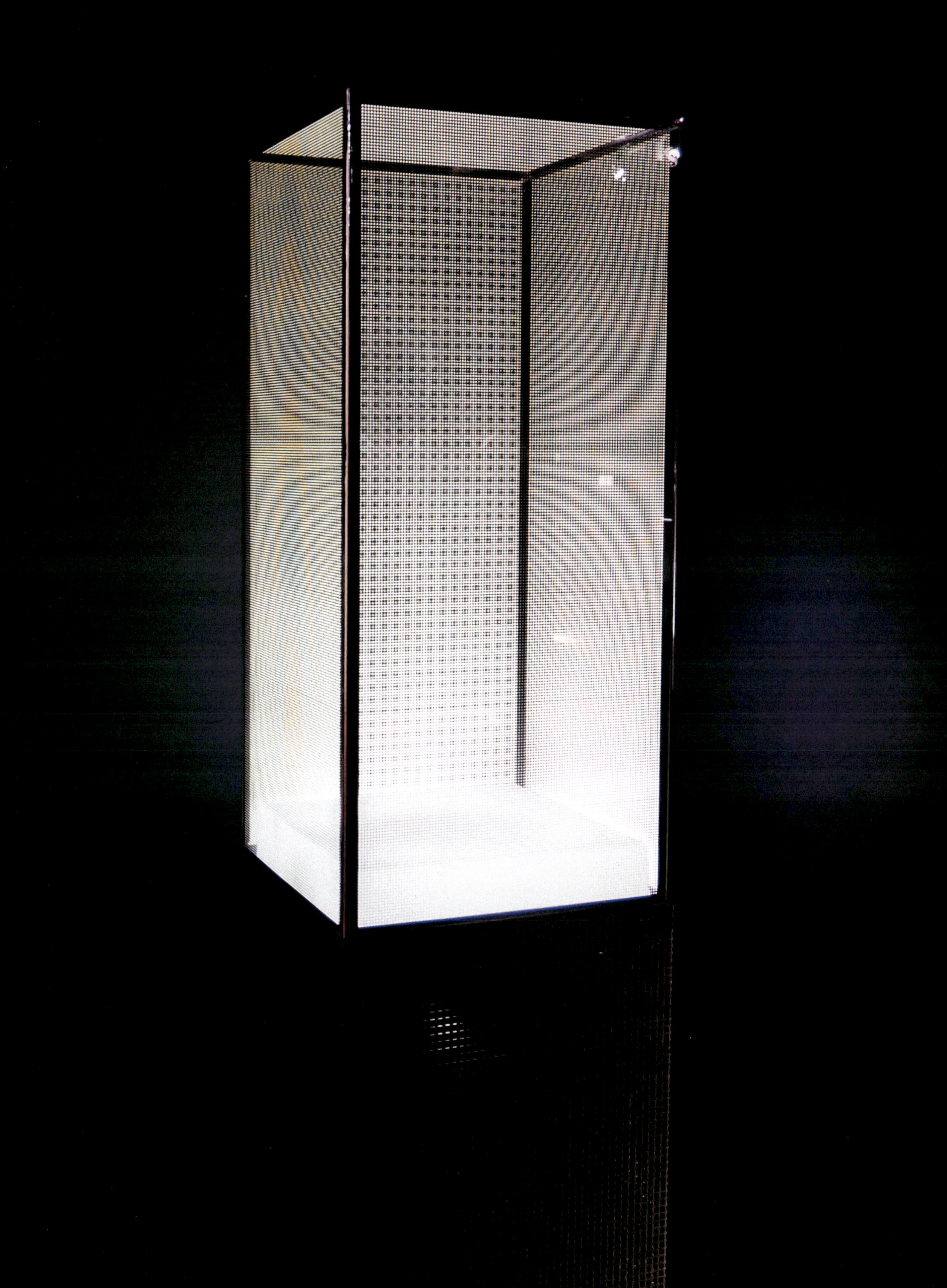

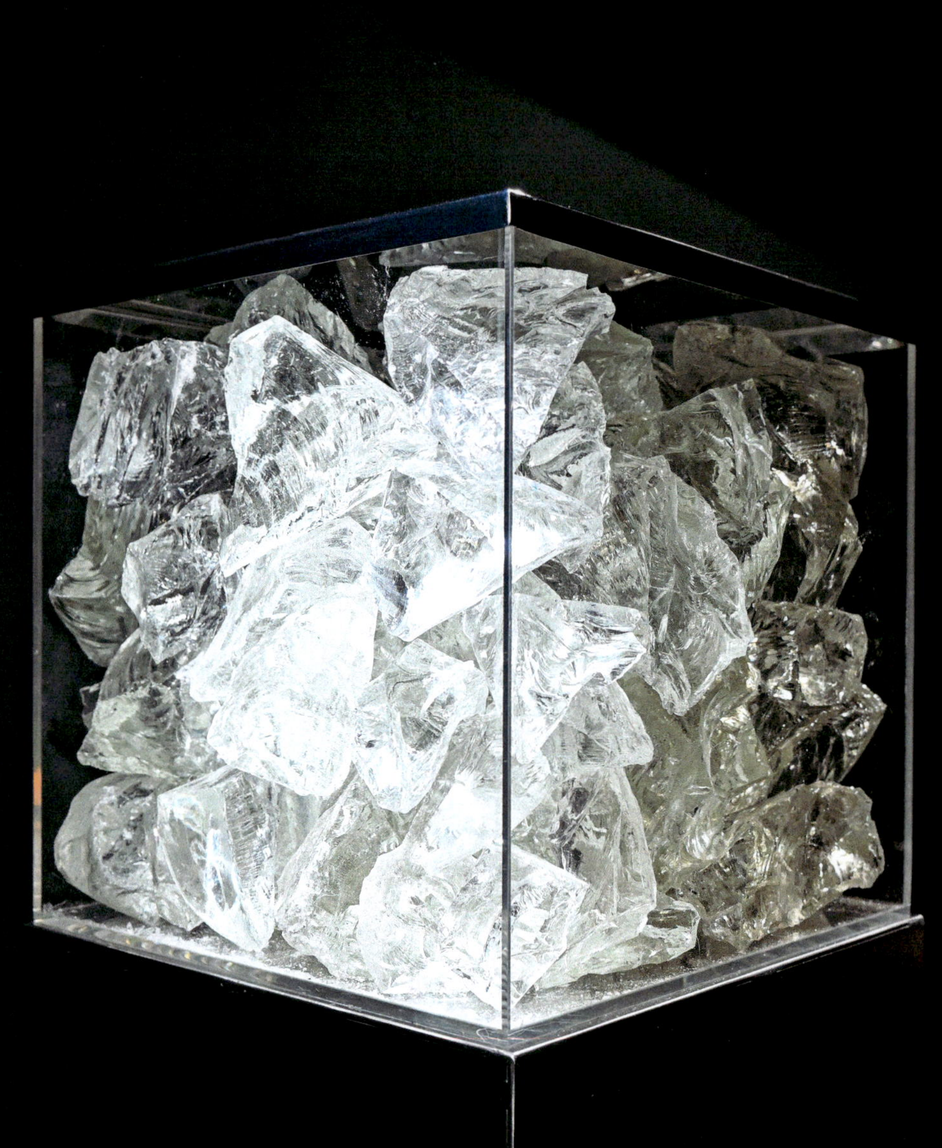

↑ *fig. 21* Heinz Mack, *Cube with Glass Chunks*, 2015 (idea: 1964)
→ *fig. 22* Heinz Mack, *The Shrine of the Void (Green and Yellow Version)*, 1968
→← *fig. 23* Heinz Mack, *Light Pavillion II*, 2006
→→ *fig. 24* Heinz Mack, *Very Little Cube in Silver*, 2020 (idea: 1974)

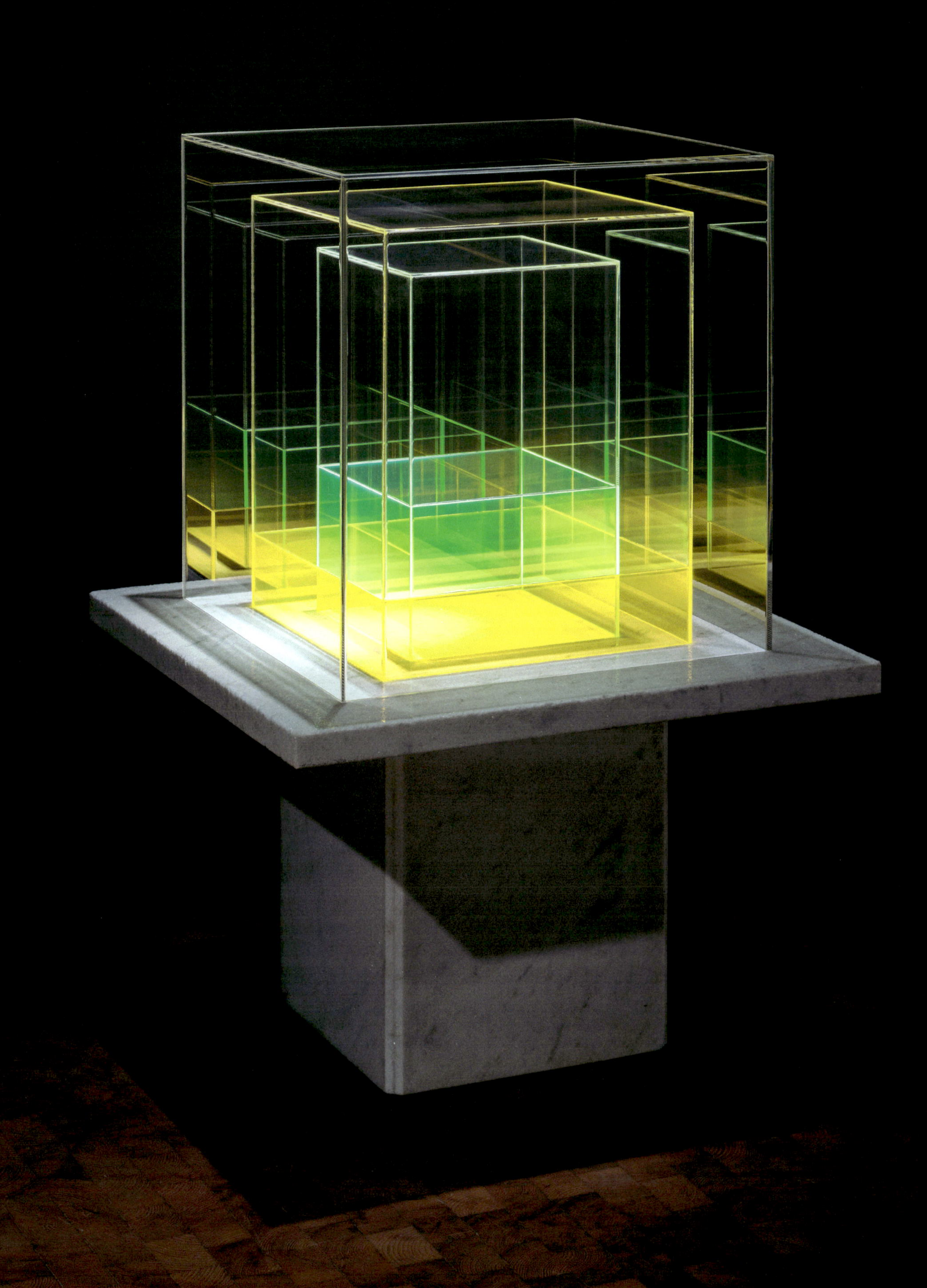

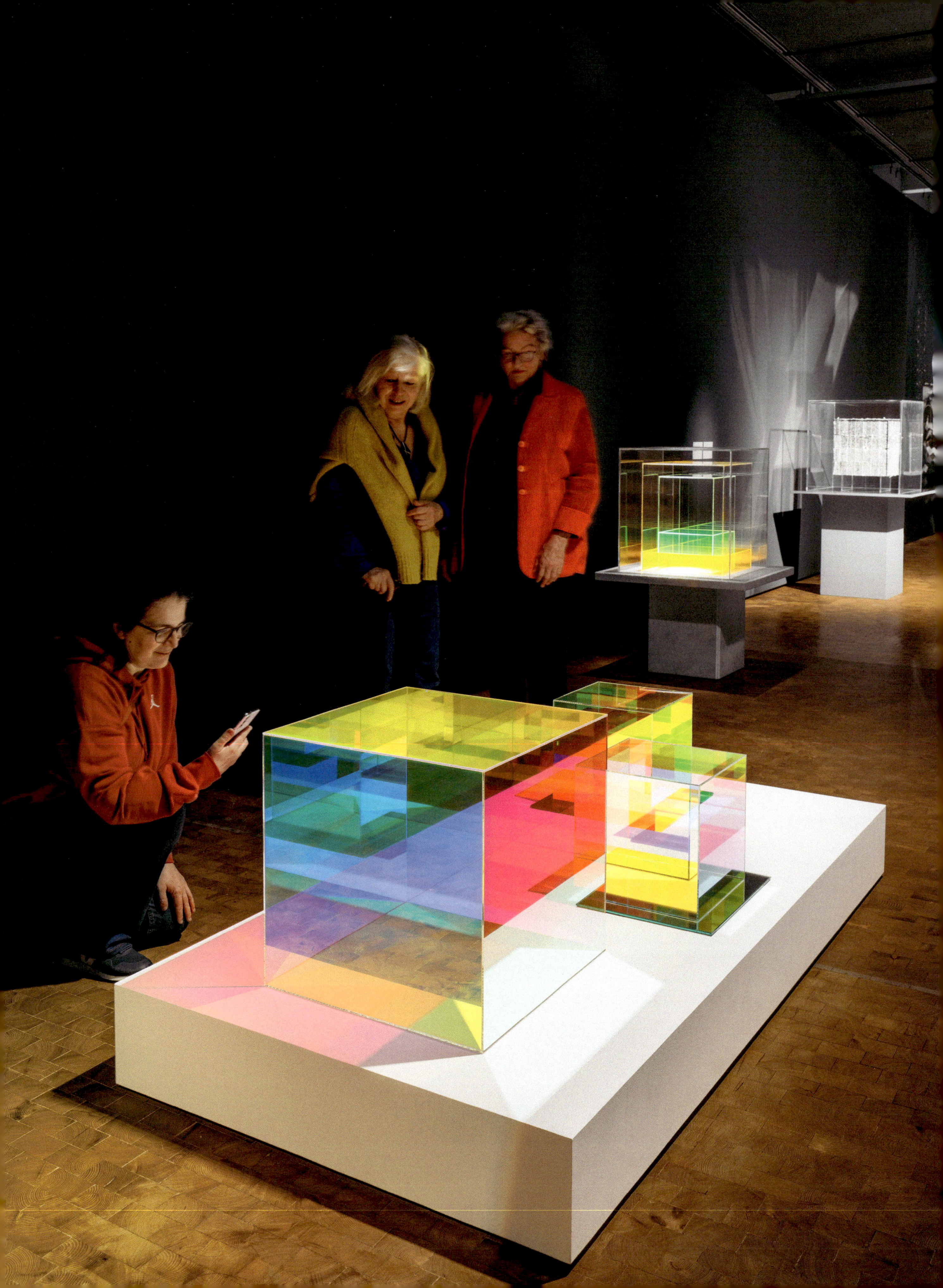

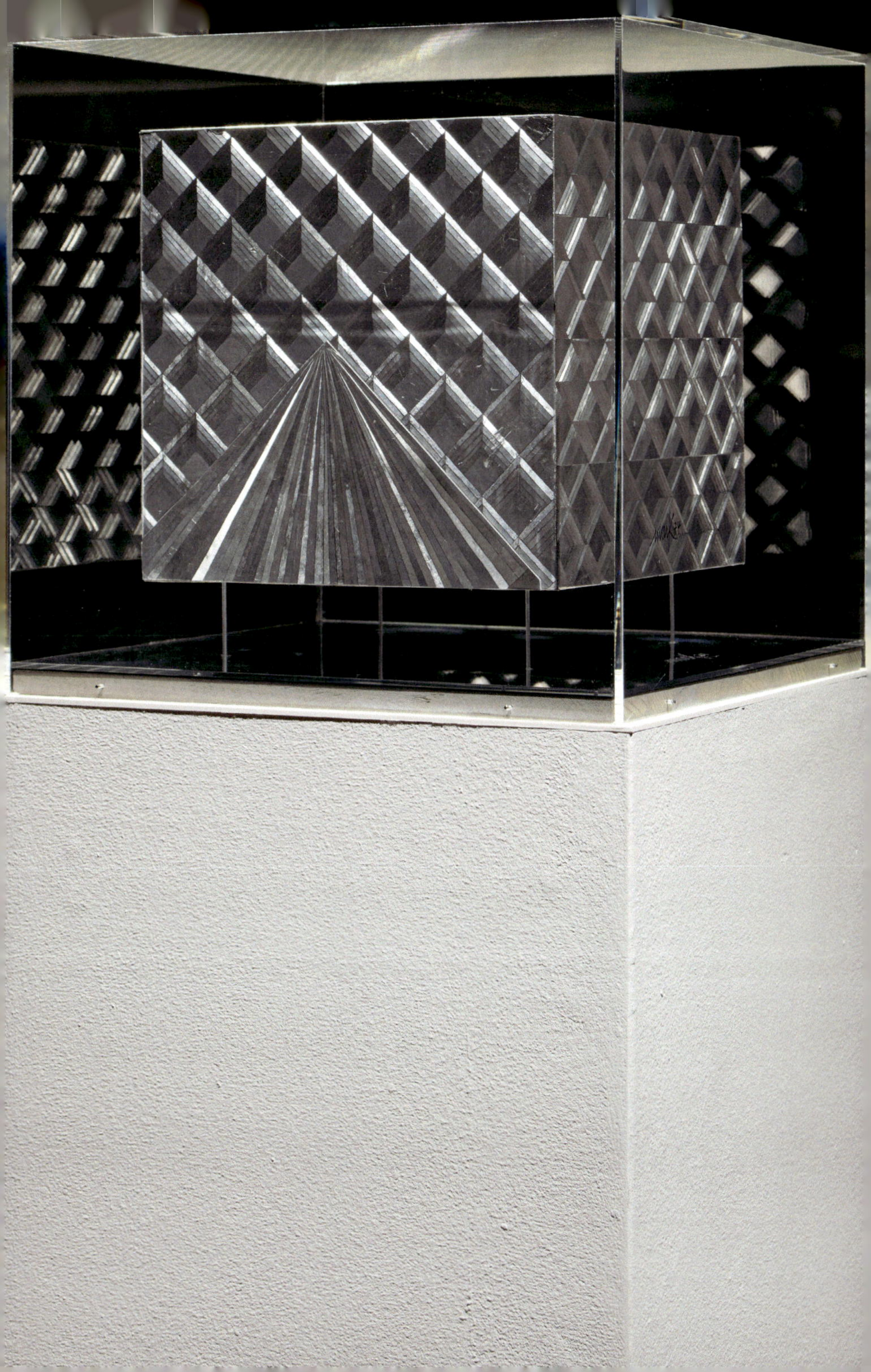

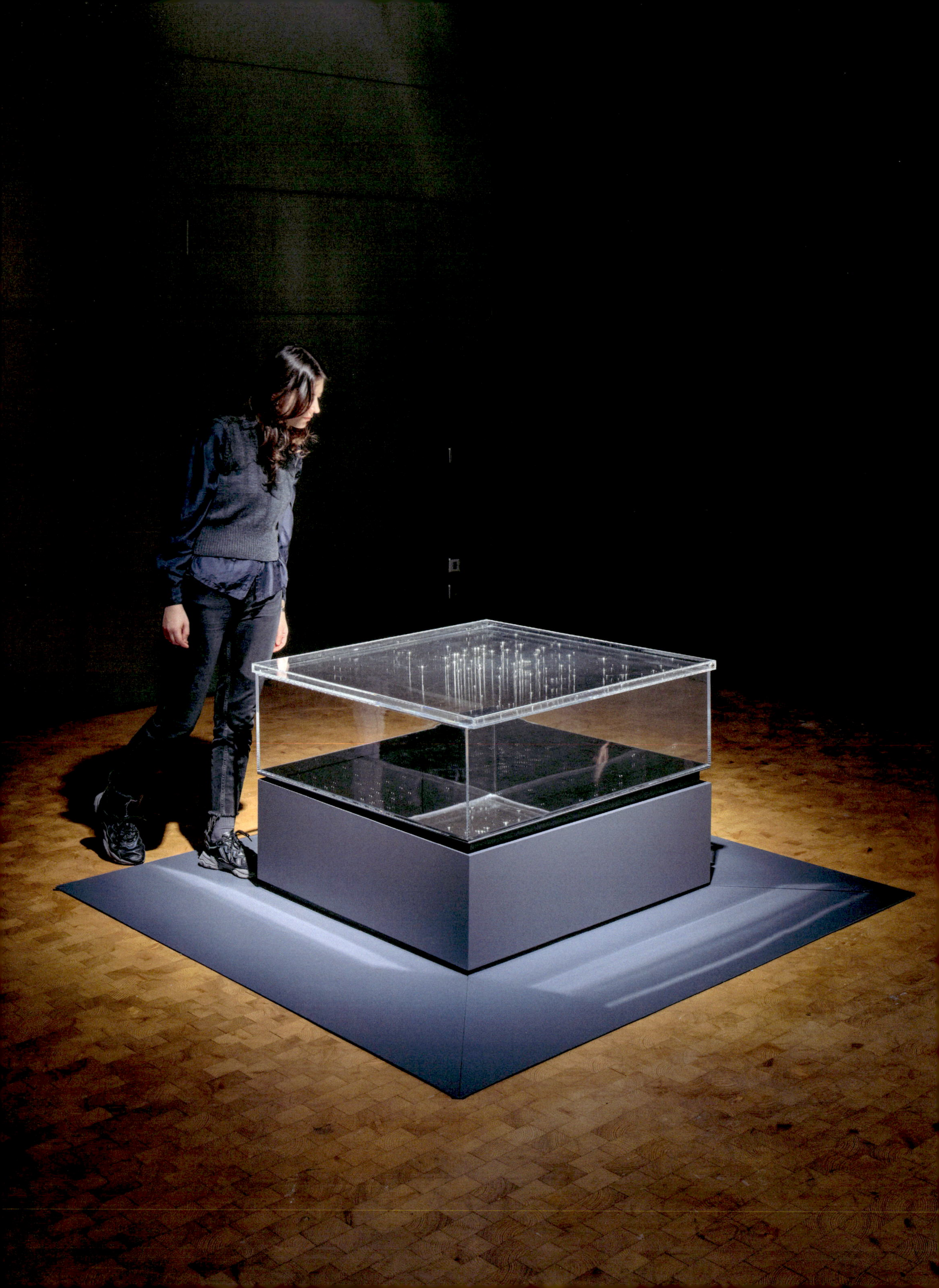

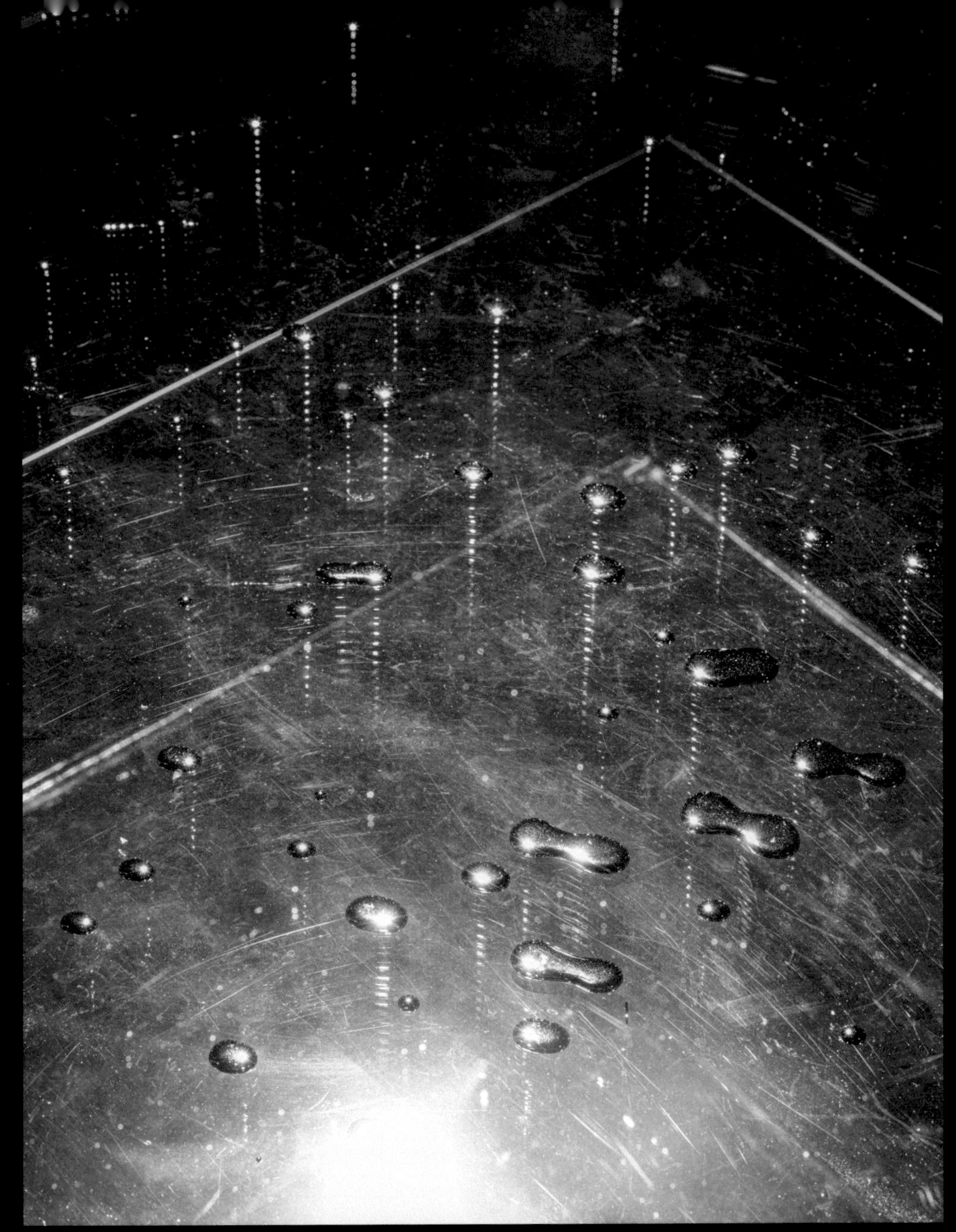

← *fig. 25* Heinz Mack, *Untitled*, 1970 (replica from 2023)
↑ *fig. 26* Heinz Mack, *Untitled*, 1970 (replica from 2023), detail

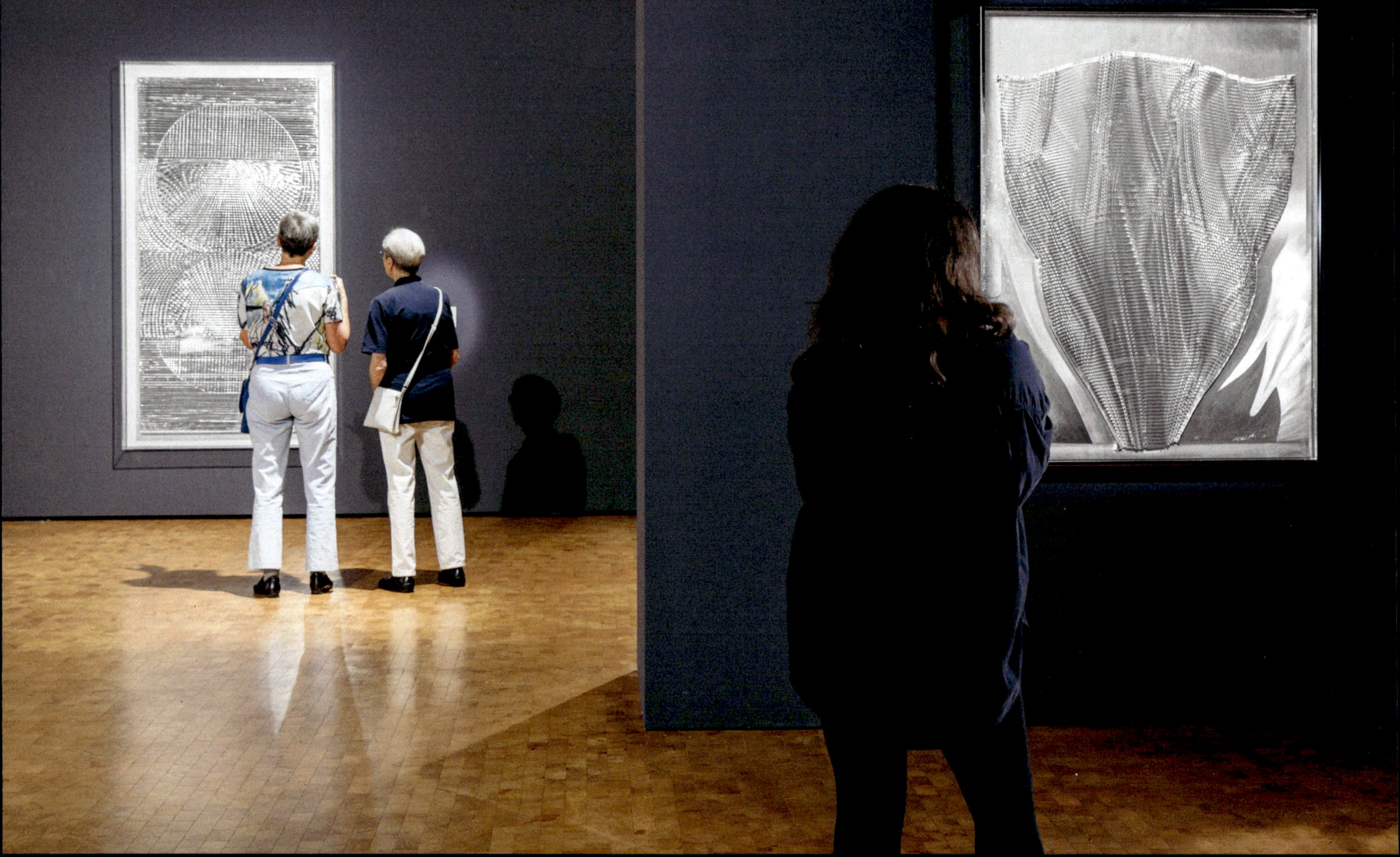

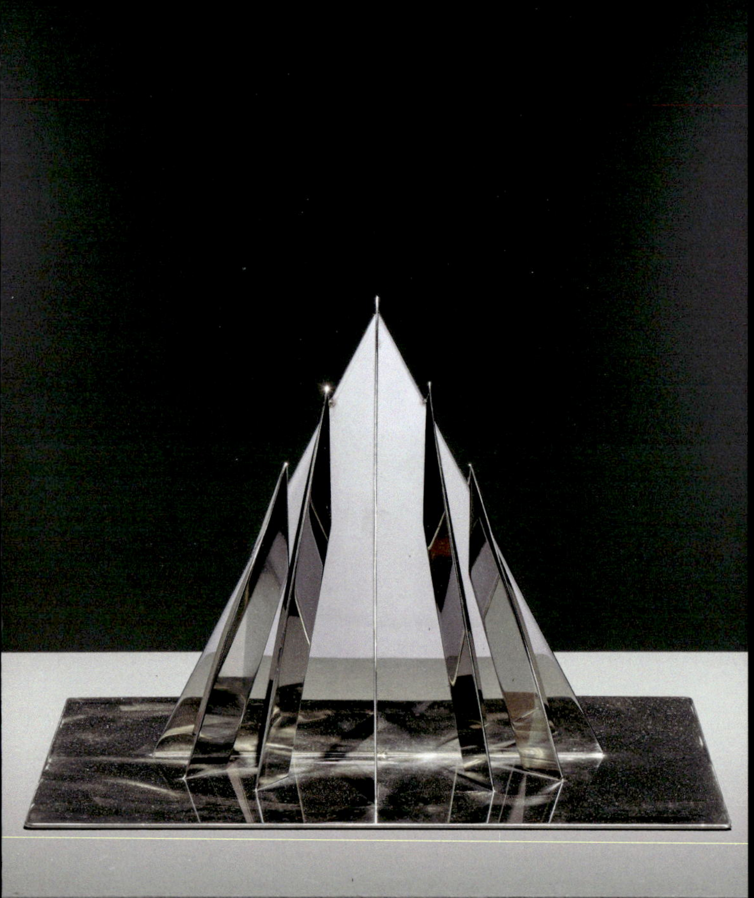

↑ *fig.* 27 left: Heinz Mack, *Light Relief (with Rotation)*, 1963
right: Heinz Mack, *Untitled*, 1964 (replica from 2017)

← *fig.* 28 Heinz Mack, *Wing Pyramid (Model for a Sacred Architecture)*, 1978 (idea: 1964)

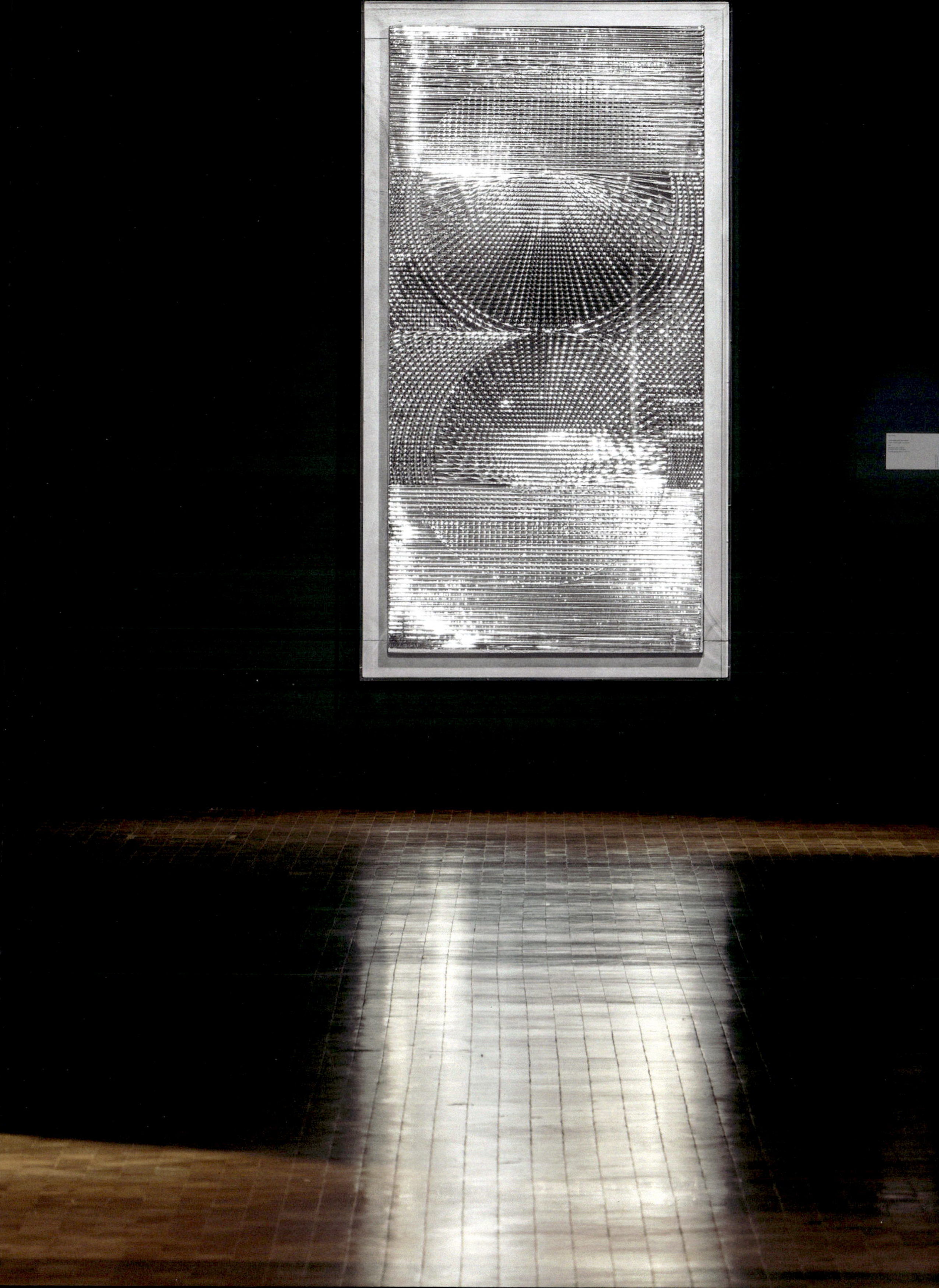

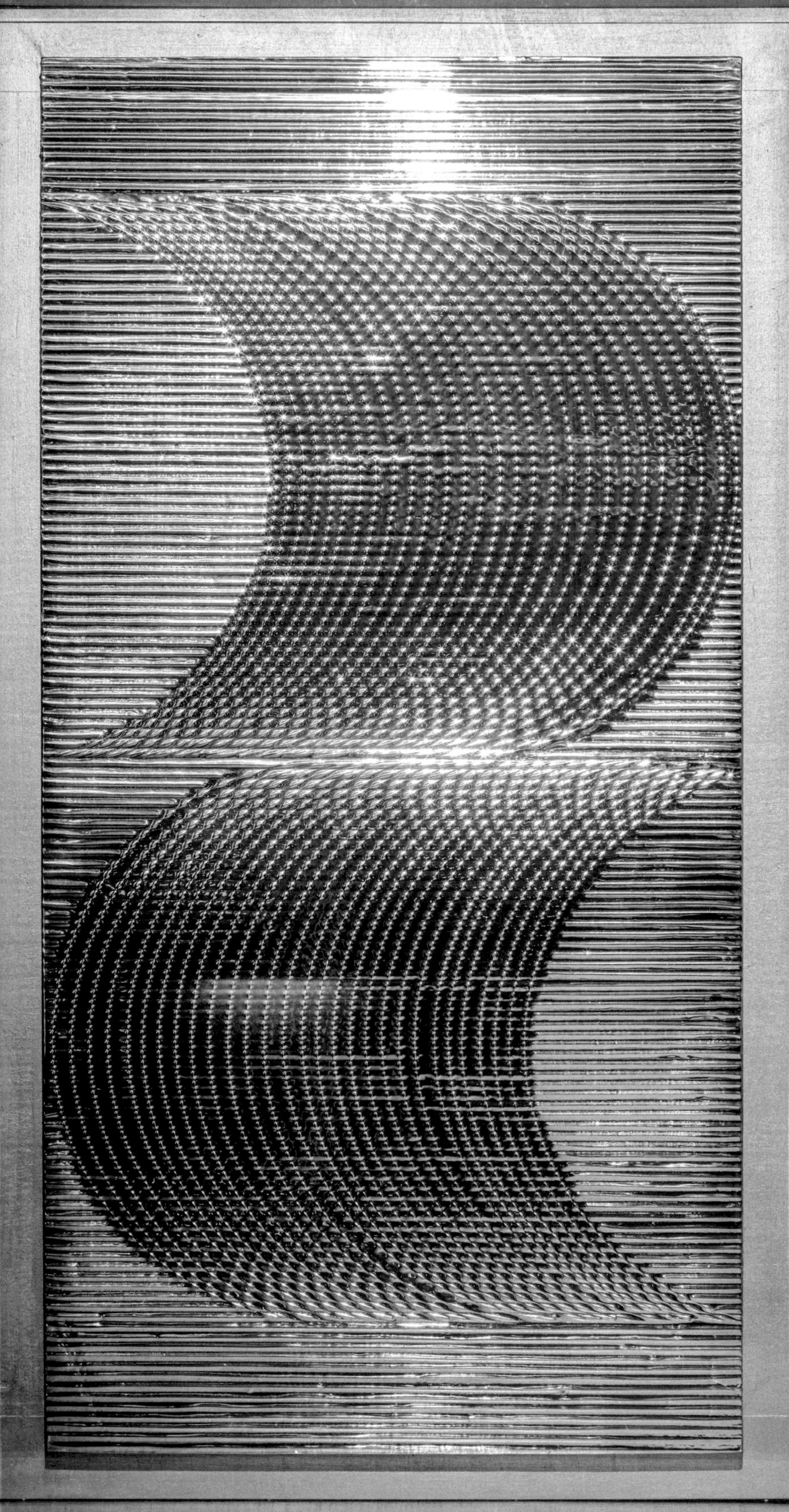

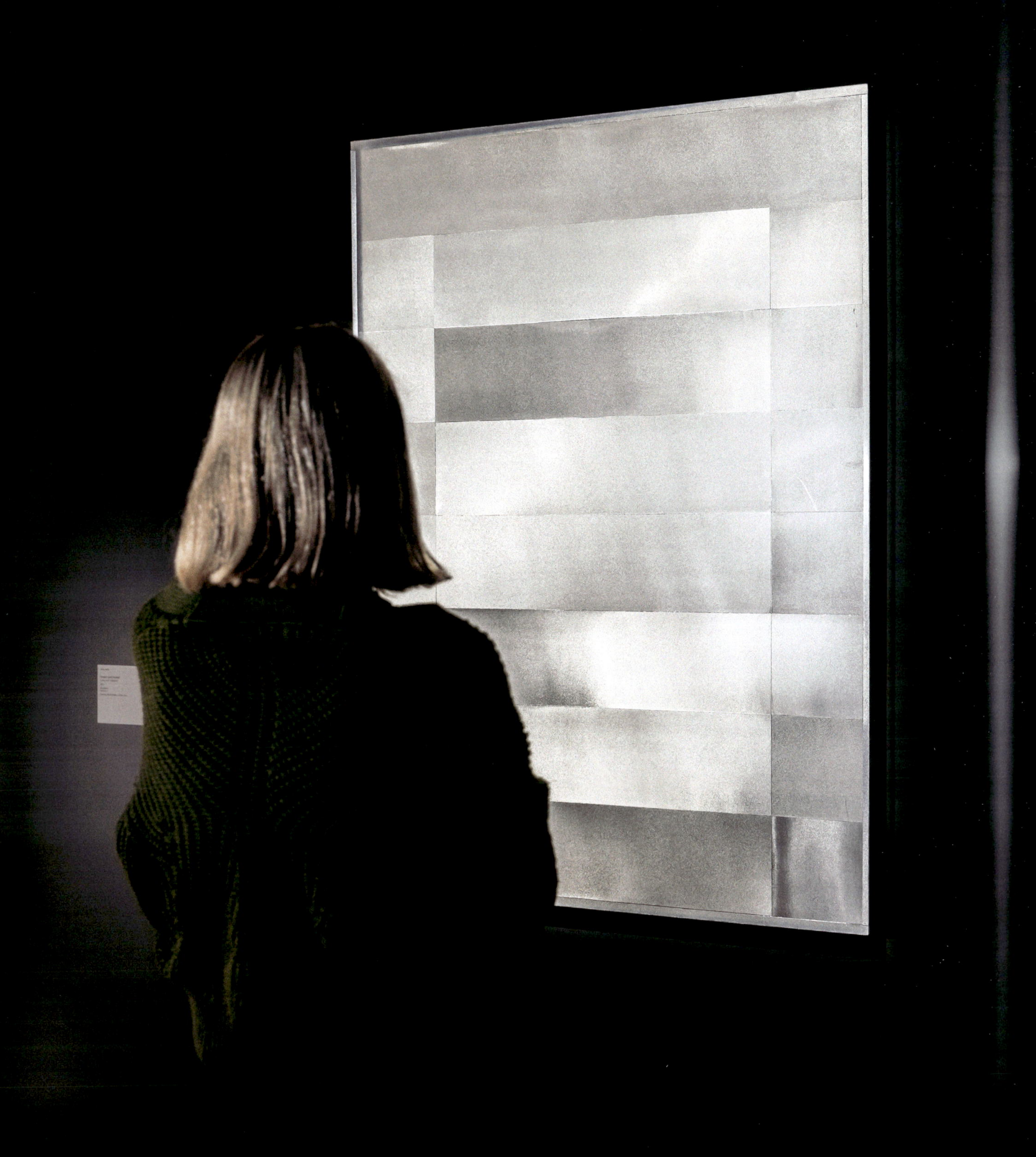

← *fig. 30* Heinz Mack, *The Dance (Light-Relief)*, 1963
↑ *fig. 31* Heinz Mack, *Law and Freedom*, 1973

→← *fig. 32* Heinz Mack, *Light Harp*, 1971
→→ *fig. 33* Heinz Mack, *Wind Chime for Light*, 1958

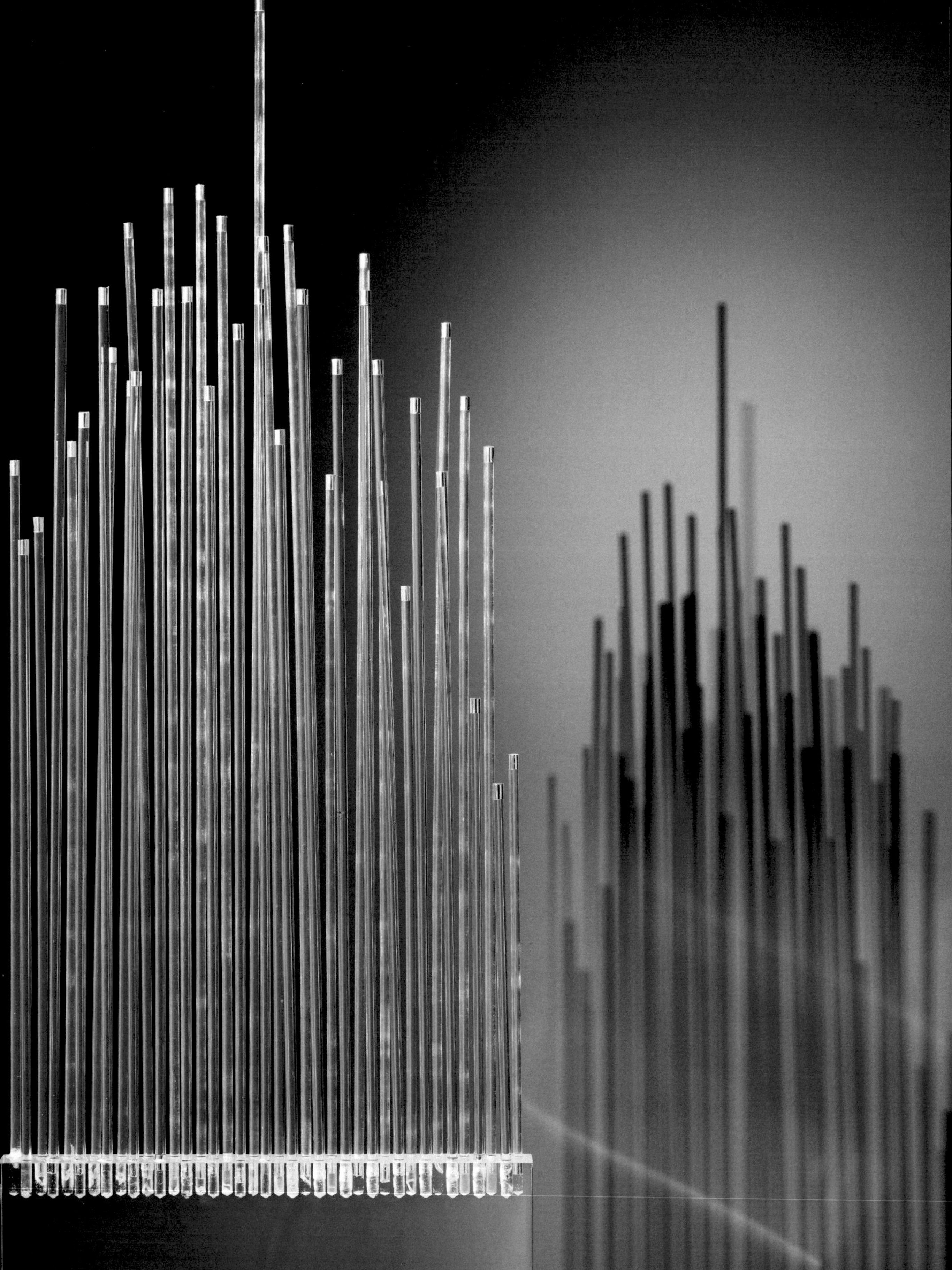

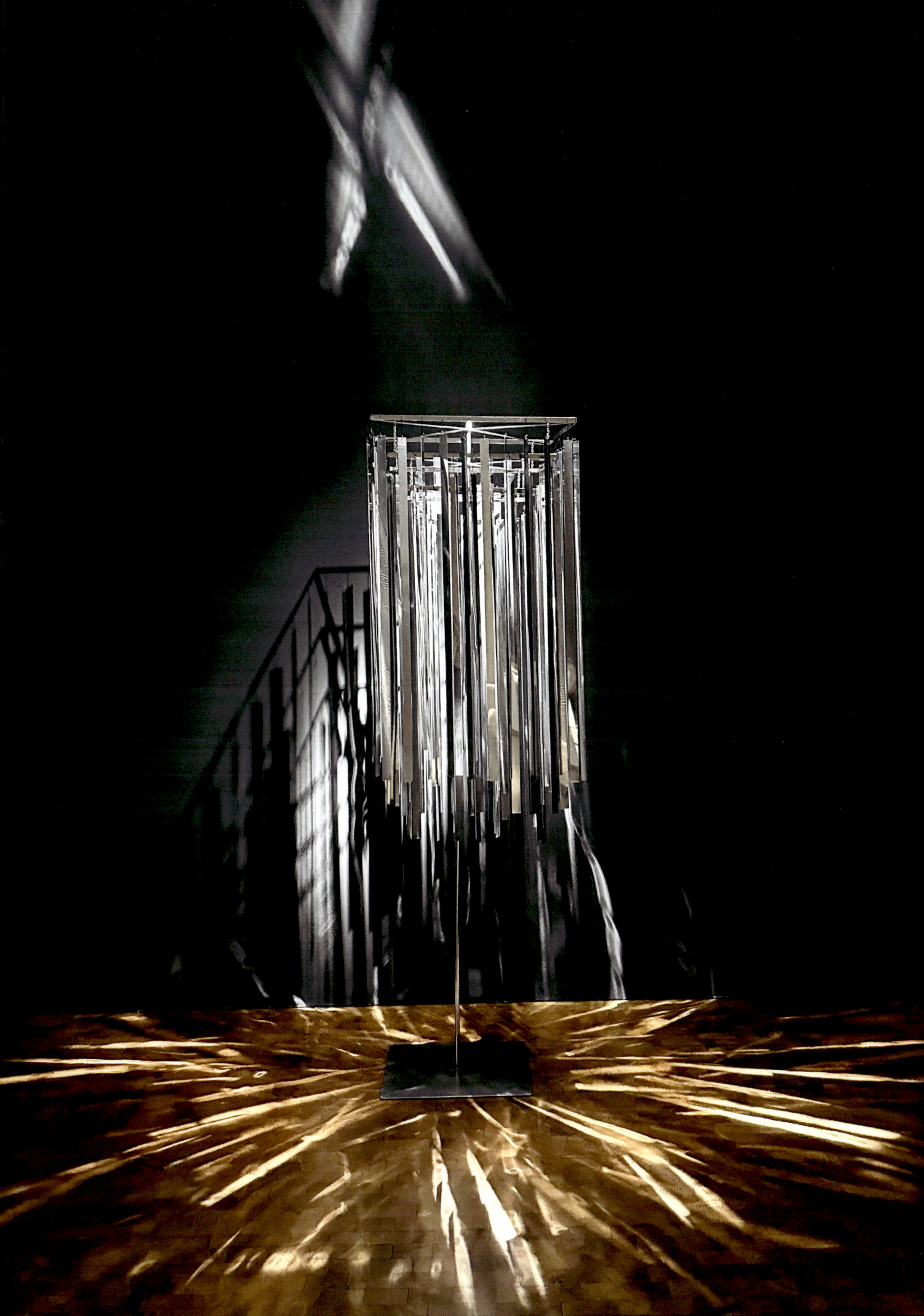

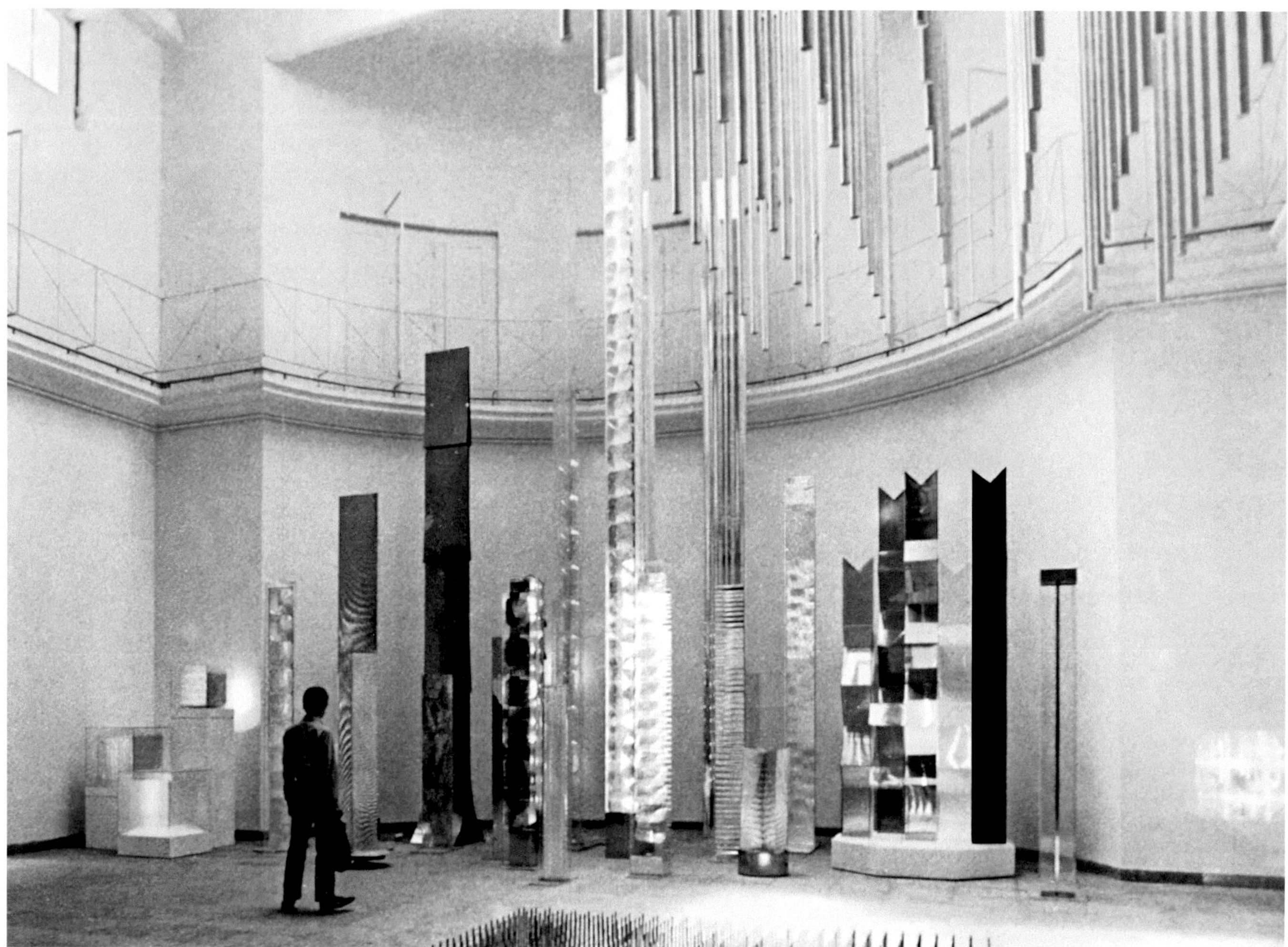

fig. 34 Heinz Mack, *Light-Steles*, exhibition view, German Pavillon at the XXXV. Venice Biennale 1970

Of Grand Ideas and the Proportionality of Means: Heinz Mack's Light Environment *Light – Movement – Space*

Heinz Mack's œuvre is closely linked to the concept of utopia.[1] Wieland Schmied even argues that "everything Heinz Mack does is inherently utopian and designed to implement the impossible."[2] Mack already formulated some of his most visionary ideas in his 1959 outline for the *Sahara Project*, when he imagined thirteen different stations for setting up his artworks in various endlessly vast settings. He sketches groups of light steles placed far out at sea or towering high above the desert. He envisions a mirror wall, an uninterrupted surface of mirrors 5 meters tall and extending over 100 meters across the desert sand. He plans *Artificial Suns* consisting of his kinetic light dynamos, also called rotors, measuring 50 to 100 meters in diameter and rotating slowly to project ever-changing light phenomena across the sky with their reflective surface structures. This manifesto, first published in 1961, is characterized by the spirit of its time; by the enthusiasm for technological innovations, by the optimism regarding the future which would overcome the "cultural graveyard" and the "vacuum" left behind by the horrors of the Second World War.[3]

figs. 146, 156

Heinz Mack was by no means the only one making these claims. The same ideas are reflected in the ZERO movement, which Mack founded together with Otto Piene in 1957 and which Günther Uecker joined in 1961. Together with their peers, such as Yves Klein, Piero Manzoni, Jean Tinguely, or Lucio Fontana, to name just a few, they dreamed of a radical new beginning which was based on the combination of art, nature, and technology and offered entirely new possibilities. And although ZERO was dissolved in 1966, the stated goals remain a driving force for Heinz Mack until today.

The interesting question is in how far large-scale, utopian undertakings such as the ones outlined in the plans for the *Sahara Project* were actually implemented. Fascinated with the topographic conditions of the desert, Mack traveled to the Sahara several times from 1955 onward. Thanks to its sheer vastness and unique lighting atmosphere, the desert offered ideal conditions for his work with light and space. Numerous photographs and films document Mack's interventions during his expeditions into the sandy and icy landscapes. These interventions, which only existed for as long as it took to document them, involve steles, cubes, and fans reflecting the light, sand reliefs and mirror walls in the desert, or the artist himself striding across the dunes in a silvery suit. In the ice desert of the Arctic, he placed floating objects on the water, let long strips of aluminum foil glide through the air, or had colorful weather balloons carry reflective nets that captured the sunlight. Heinz Mack, the light artist, uses these myriad reflective surfaces to create apparitions of light that seem to vibrate. Even though Mack was not able to bring all the stations of his *Sahara Project* to fruition, one cannot ignore that he made large parts of his utopian idea a reality – albeit, in some cases, in an abstract form. He succeeded in bridging the gap between utopia and reality. A gap that is conceptually inherent in the definition of utopia through

figs. 108, 123, 126, 140, 144, 231

figs. 189, 190, 191, 196, 201, 203 , 207

figs. 123, 200

figs. 185, 197

1 The term "utopia" is derived from the Ancient Greek words *ou* (not) and *tópos* (place). This concept of a "non-place" refers to something that can be imagined, but does not (yet) exist in reality.

2 Wieland Schmied, "Arbeit am Projekt der Modere. Über Heinz Mack und den Mythos vom Künstler als Konstrukteur neuer Welten," in: Wieland Schmied, ed., *Utopie und Wirklichkeit im Werk von Heinz Mack*, exh. cat. Liechtensteinische Staatliche Kunstsammlung Vaduz (Cologne: DuMont, 1998), 10–13, here 11. Translated from the German.

3 See ibid.

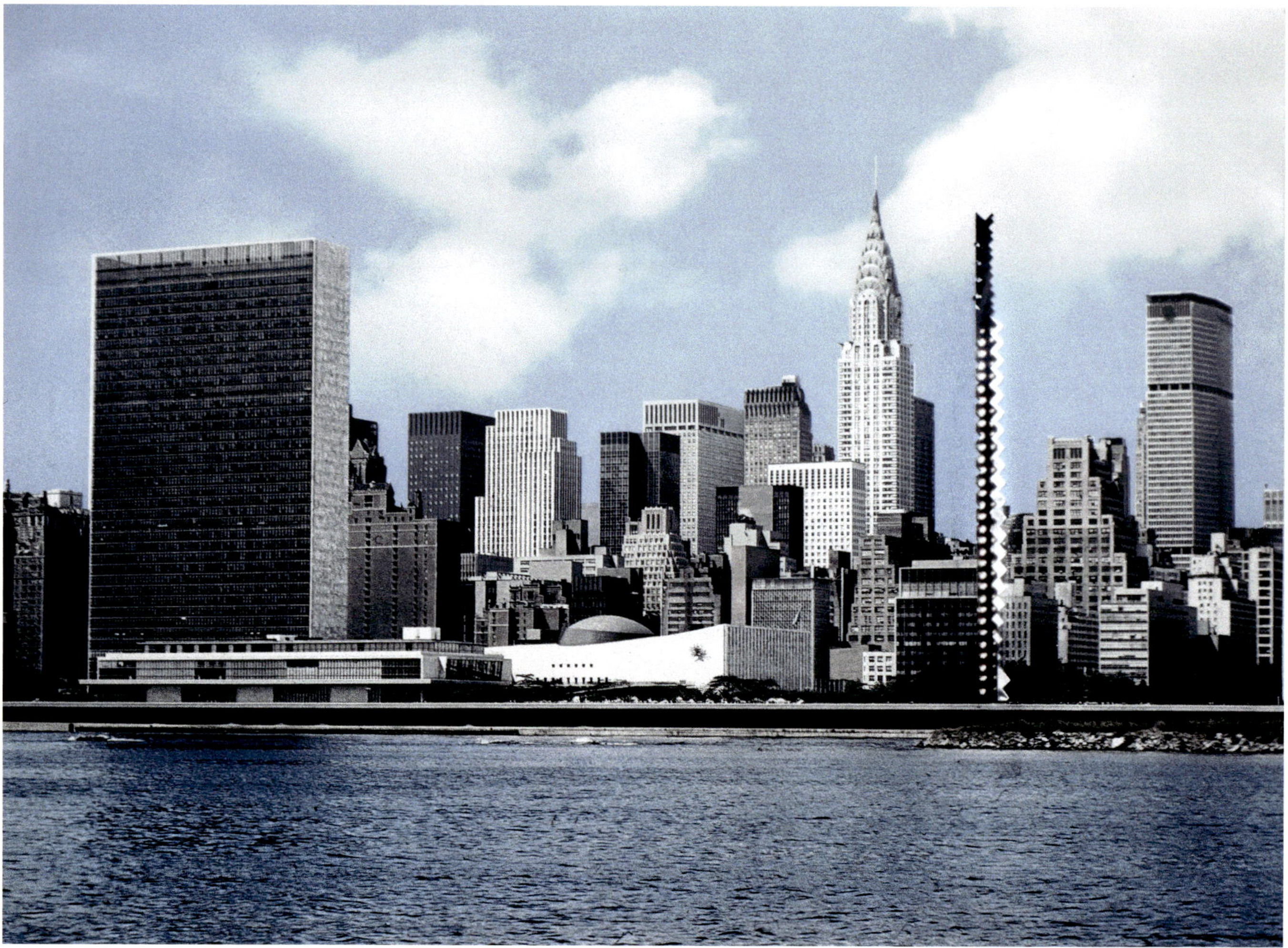

fig. 35 Heinz Mack, *The Sign of Peace*, 1974–1979, photo collage, not realized project for a 70 m high light stele in the UN park in New York

its discrepancy with reality, which it aims to change and improve. And yet, Mack's utopian designs did not remain confined to the realm of ideas. Actually implementing them continues to be the artist's motivation – even if this does not always pan out. He is thoroughly aware of the possibility of failure.[4] Many of his project ideas never proceed beyond the design stage. Especially when they involve public spaces, they are often faced with the limitations and boundaries of reality – whether in the form of regulatory or financial constraints. The 70-meter-tall stele *The Sign of Peace*, which the artist designed in 1974 as a gift to the UN at its headquarters in New York, could ultimately not be erected outside the building due to insufficient funding.[5]

fig. 35

Nevertheless, Mack is undeterred and continues to strive for the impossible and to "reach for the stars," as Wieland Schmied aptly puts it.[6] He remains firmly convinced that whatever is impossible may well become possible in the future. A 1978 article in which Mack describes how he imagines the world in the year 2000 is thoroughly optimistic and shows an unshakable faith in the potential of connecting art with science and technology.[7] And although our lives have turned out quite different in reality, many aspects of Mack's predictions have come true: Technological innovations have revolutionized almost all areas of life. Our daily lives are shaped by artificial intelligence. Life expectancy has

4 See ibid., 12.

5 See Schmied, *Utopie und Wirklichkeit*, 284, 285.

6 Schmied, "Arbeit am Projekt der Modere," in: Schmied, *Utopie und Wirklichkeit*, 13.

7 See Heinz Mack, "Kunst 2000," *Kunstforum*, no. 29 (1978): 46–55.

increased globally. And yet, we are still far from living without illness, without suffering, or without social injustice, let alone achieving total control of the weather, as Mack predicted.[8] In fact, the opposite seems to be the case: Environmental and humanitarian catastrophes are on the rise. The utopian future has transformed into a dystopian present. Many of our current prognoses for the future are grim.

But no matter how fantastic Mack's ideas may be, they are always aimed at transforming the world in its existing state, if primarily in an aesthetic sense.[9] The artist conceives utopianism as an "expansion of our visionary horizon," firmly convinced that "ideas can change the world." Driven by the search for beauty and always with a view to "expanding imagination" and refining perception, Mack views the impossible as a "horizon of new possibilities."[10]

Heinz Mack's large-scale perspective and ambition to achieve the impossible were defining characteristics for the exhibition *Mack at ZKM* from day one. The original plan was to present something unique, befitting the size of the available spaces in the former munitions factory, and never seen before: Mack's light environment *Light – Movement – Space*, which was realized for the first and only time at the 1970 German Industrial Exhibition in Berlin, was to be reconstructed at the ZKM. This *light plantation* is exemplary of Mack's extensive investigation of light, space, and motion, as well as his enthusiasm for technological innovations. According to the artist, some technical aspects of this installation could be solved much more elegantly today thanks to technological progress.[11] The reconstruction undoubtedly would have been an important contribution to the exploration and restoration of important artworks that have been lost to history. Unfortunately, it turned out that the complexity of the installation and the cost and effort of producing the special components and researching and manufacturing prototypes, implementing this project in a museum setting was neither possible nor justifiable. And so, Mack's observation from his 1970 remarks explaining the light space turned out to be true: "Why did I take part in an industrial exhibition? Because no museum or gallery could have given me the chance to realize the light space. I had all the artistic freedom I needed."[12]

figs. 36, 37, 38, 39, 40, 41

Mack's resentment of conventional art institutions, which can be seen in this quote, relates to several aspects. On the one hand, pragmatic issues such as insufficient funds and specific requirements dictated by the museums are limiting factors. On the other hand, it is connected to Mack's goal of claiming new spaces outside of the traditional cultural institutions, which Mack sees in the role of a dusty "cultural graveyard" concerned primarily with the preservation of art.[13] The artist sought to place his artworks into new contexts in order to see how these different environments – such as the polar sea or the desert – would affect their appearance and perception. He wanted to reach a different, broader audience and overcome the hierarchies and distances which traditional exhibition spaces tend to exacerbate. This is evident not only in his numerous works for public spaces, but also in his contributions to industrial and world exhibitions.[14]

The present publication, which accompanies and expands upon the exhibition *Mack at ZKM*, opens up a space of possibility which is not limited by the boundaries of reality and in which the proportionality of means is irrelevant. Against this background, this essay is

8 See ibid., 53, 54.

9 See Schmied, "Arbeit am Projekt der Modere," 12.

10 Heinz Mack, "Die Entfernung zwischen Utopie und Wirklichkeit," in: Schmied, *Utopie und Wirklichkeit*, 58–61, here 61. Translated from the German.

11 See Mack, "Kunst 2000," 46.

12 Heinz Mack, "Erklärung zum Lichtenvironment," (typoscript, Archive Heinz Mack, 1970). Translated from the German.

13 Mack, "Die Entfernung zwischen Utopie und Wirklichkeit," 58.

14 See Sabine Fabo, "Somewhere over the Rainbow: Light and Movement as Extension of the Experience of Space," in: Susanne Titz and Jee-Hae Kim, eds., *Mack. Kinetics*, exh. cat. Museum Abteiberg Mönchengladbach (Düsseldorf: Richter, 2011), 40–50, here 48.

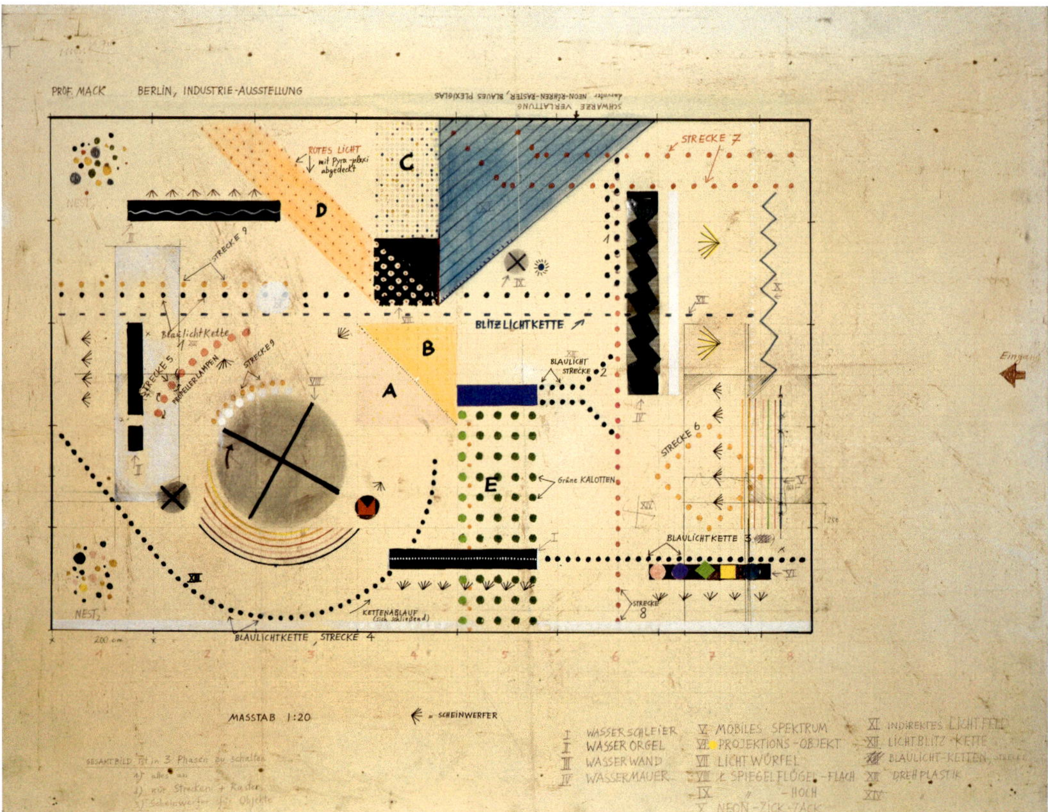

fig. 36 Floor plan for *Light – Movement – Space*, light environment at the Great Industrial Exhibition, 1970, Berlin

an invitation to explore the space of imagination and let the light environment *Light – Movement – Space* and those grand ideas from another time come to life once again.

An Environment for Light, Movement, and Space

In 1970, Heinz Mack was approached for an artistic contribution to the German Industrial Exhibition in Berlin, which was set to open later that year. He started by creating an exposé, which included an initial sketch of his design for the Hall of Honor – built in 1936 under National Socialism and connected to the Palais am Funkturm to serve as its entrance hall in 1956/1957 – as well as detailing his terms for a collaboration. Mack did not demand payment, but absolute artistic freedom. The organizers were to be responsible for implementing his design and bearing any and all cost. Working together closely with architect Hans Boventer, who was in charge of the exhibition section "Mensch und Technik – Kunst und Wissenschaft" [Human and Technology – Art and Science], the artist soon produced a detailed description of his light space. In August of 1970, Mack's engagement was officially confirmed by Berliner Ausstellungen GmbH – short notice, considering the exhibition was set to open on September 16 of the same year.

fig. 36

So what exactly does the light environment *Light – Movement – Space* entail? On a pedestal measuring 10 × 15 meters, Mack combined numerous sculptural works, many involving moving parts and water or light installations.[15] In addition to water and electrical lighting, the project involved mercury-coated plastic foils, lightweight mirrors,

15 The following descriptions are based on Heinz Mack's documents from the year of the exhibition ("Erklärung zum Lichtenvironment," "Detaillierte Baubeschreibung," "Exposé des Künstlers;" all 1970) as well as his 2022 "Arbeitspapier zum Lichtenvironment." All documents were provided by the Archive Heinz Mack.

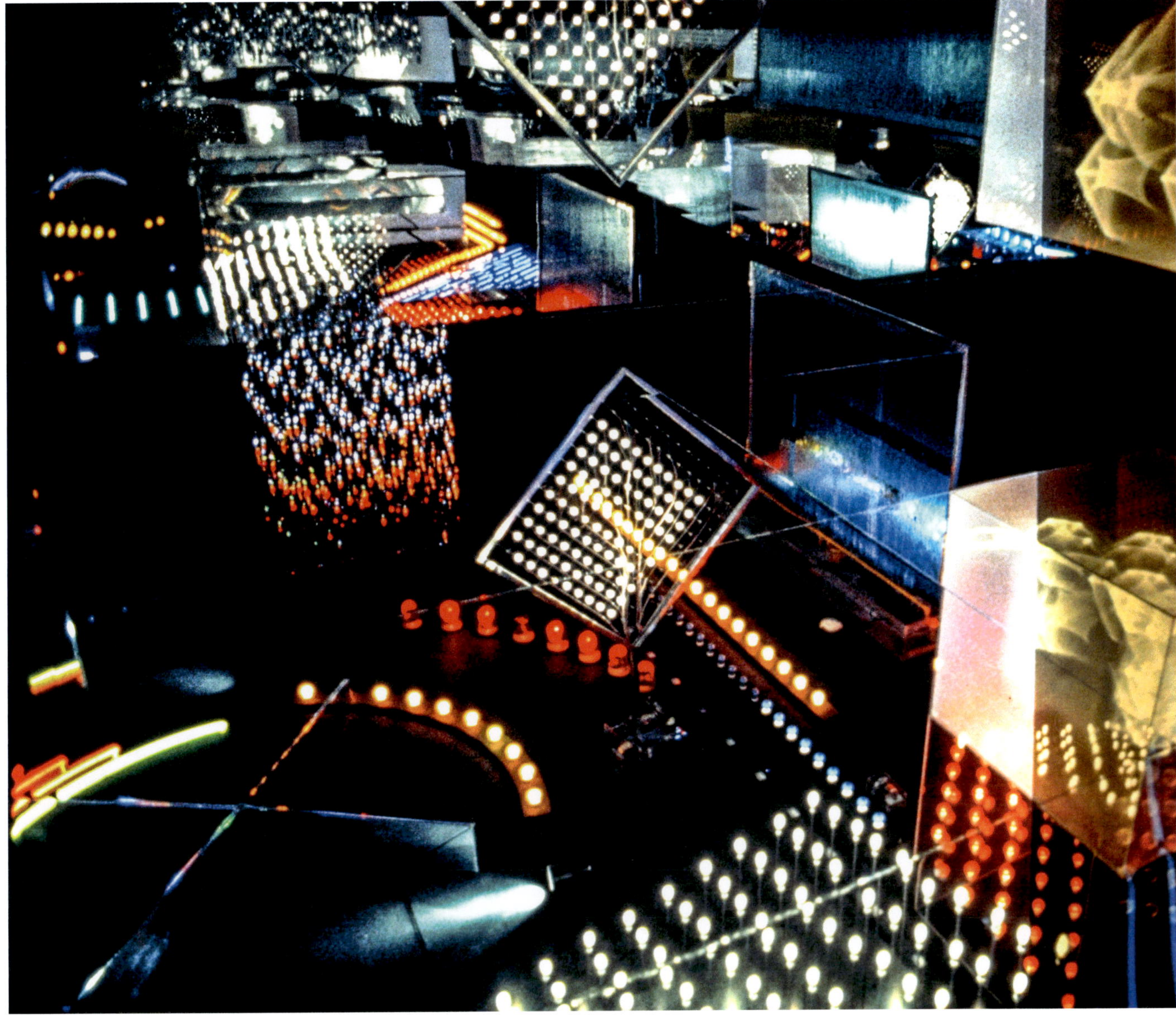

fig. 37 Heinz Mack, *Light – Movement – Space*, light environment at the Great Industrial Exhibition, 1970, Berlin

acrylic glass, polished stainless steel and aluminum, as well as motors that would set various parts of the installation in motion. The technical components of the installation, including lighting power supplies and control units as well as water pumps, the water supply, and the electrical turntable motors, were hidden from sight in the pedestal, which was only 30 cm high. Above all this, a mirror ceiling multiplied the visual effects of the environment infinitely. The entire room and all its windows were darkened in order to amplify the light effects of the installation. In contemporary photographs of the light environment, the space and its surroundings seem to dissolve altogether, disappearing in the multiplication of artificial light manifestations that overstimulate the senses.

figs. 37, 38, 40

The artist divided the installation into three groups: "Projects (I-XIV)" and "Surfaces (A-E)," which included various works and installations, and "Lines 1-8," a series of lighting circuits with different programming. One of the "Projects" was the so-called *Water Wall* (III). This was a paravent-like sculpture measuring approximately 2 × 3 meters,

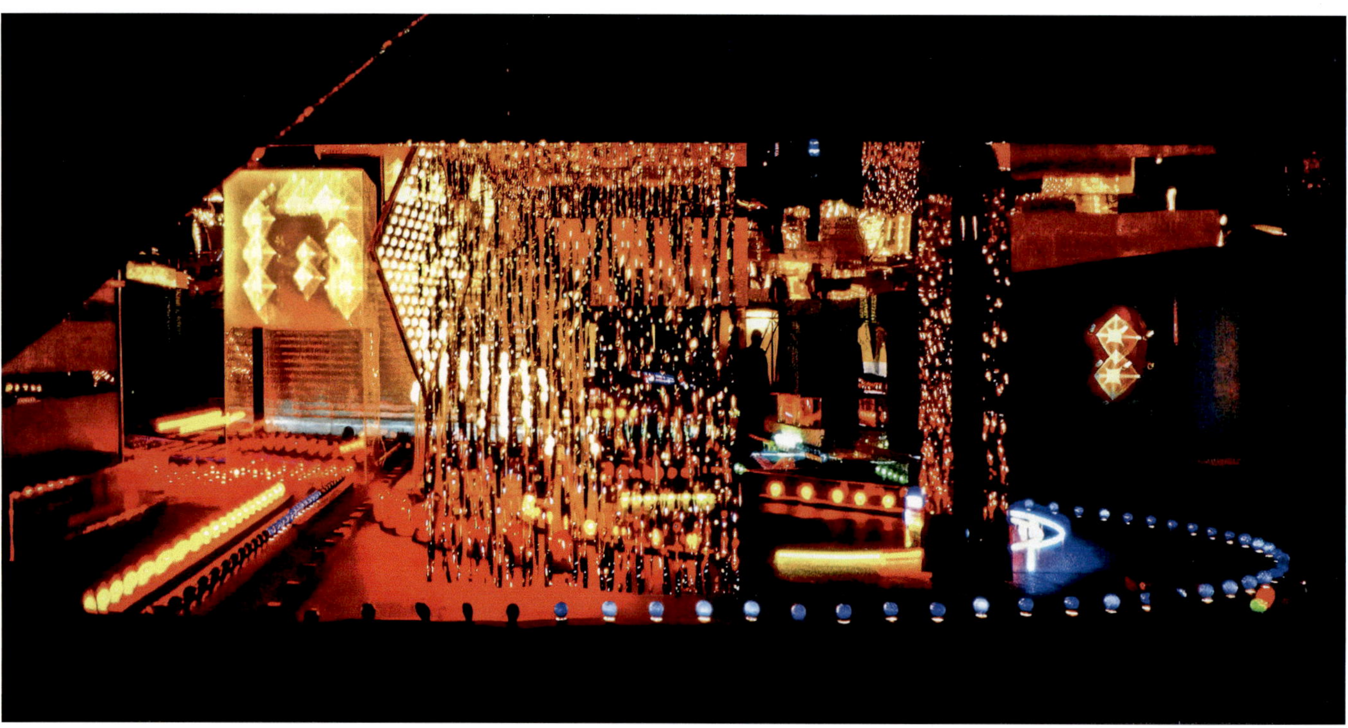

fig. 38 Heinz Mack, *Light – Movement – Space*, light environment at the Great Industrial Exhibition, 1970, Berlin

with a frame and feet constructed from aluminum square tube. Its entire surface was covered in thin aluminum sheets, each measuring 2 × 1 meters. The tubes of the frame also served as water pipes, enabling water to circulate within a closed system. Water was pumped into the upper tube, which had perforations to let the water drip across the shiny metal surfaces until it reached the bottom. Ten blue-tinted 150-Watt BEGA spotlights provided the necessary illumination.

fig. 39 Another project, the *Water Light Wall* (IV), consisted of a 180 × 400 × 60 cm acrylic glass wall rising from a water basin set into the pedestal, which featured another closed-loop water circulation system. Two vertical glass tubes led to the acrylic glass tub at the top of the wall. From there, the water flowed down ten zig-zagging outcrops on either side until it reached the basin at the bottom. An essential component of this project was its illumination using two 1000-Watt floodlights. In addition to these water installations, viewers could marvel at numerous neon pieces arranged on the pedestal – including the blue, *fig. 40* 5-meter-long *Neon Zigzag* (X), the *Rotation of the Rainbow* (VIII) comprising six neon tubes in the colors of the rainbow, and the *Lightning Chain* (XII), an array of lights programmed to produce a series of bright flashes. Furthermore, the installation included various (light-) kinetic sculptures, such as the light cube *Light Grid in Space* (VII), an acrylic glass cube with integrated electric lighting, or the stainless-steel stele *Mirror Wing* (IX), which slowly rotated on a turntable and reflected its brightly lit surroundings.

However, the display was not limited to the confines of the pedestal. The kinetic sculpture *Mobile Spectrum* (V) was suspended from a support structure. It comprised six tinted acrylic glass panes, each 3 meters wide. The artist had these panes suspended in equal distances of 20 cm and moving up and down independently using

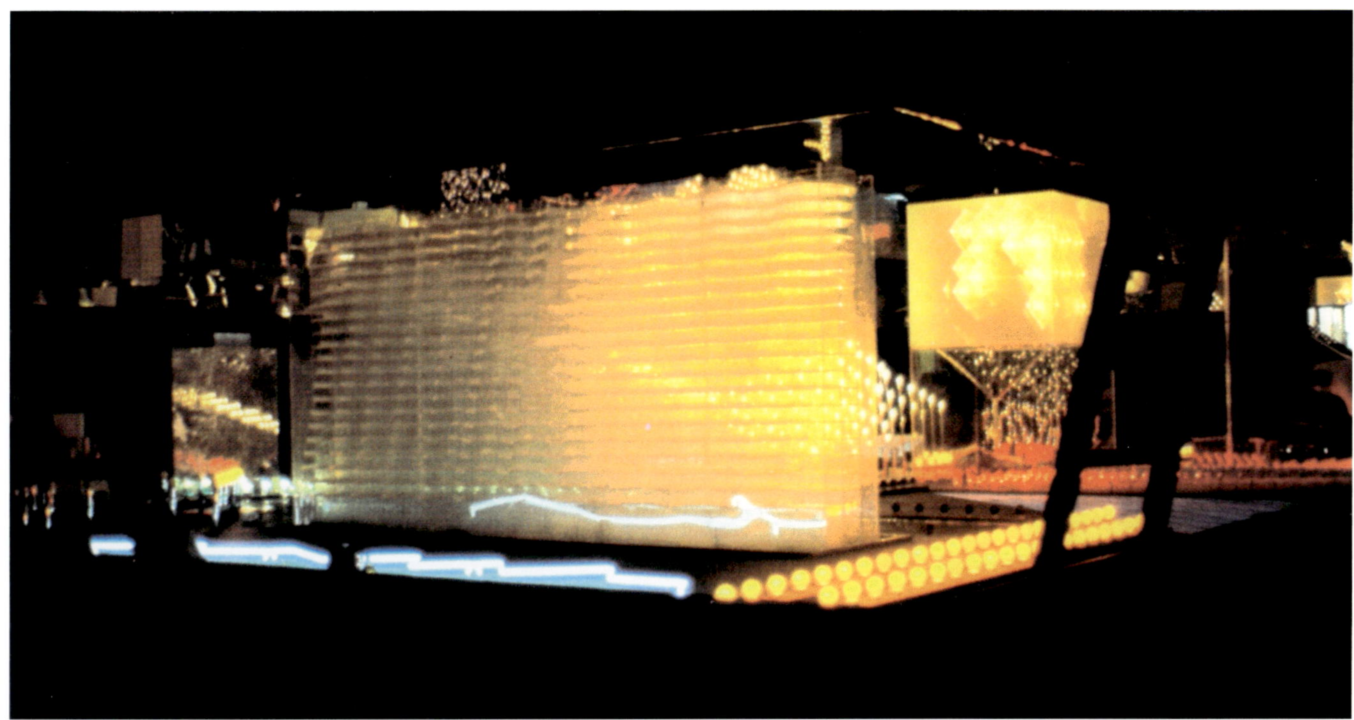

fig. 39 Heinz Mack, *Water Light Wall*, 1969–1970, part of the light environment *Light – Movement – Space* at the Great Industrial Exhibition, 1970, Berlin

electrical winches. This generated ever-changing visual intersections, which were amplified by the powerful illumination from six floodlights and twelve spotlights. *Surface AB* was formed by a square light sculpture titled *Chrome Bar Forest* (128 × 164 × 164 cm), which comprised 81 chrome bars of varying length topped with light bulbs. *Surface C*, *Surface D*, and *Surface E* featured control lights of different colors arranged in various patterns distributed throughout the pedestal. This array of surfaces was interspersed by the *Lines 1–8*, linear arrangements of lights in different colors that were programmed to follow specific illumination patterns. For instance, the curved blue chain of lights on *Line 4* followed a pattern that intensified from left to right and then dissolved in the opposite direction.

fig. 41

As this small selection of descriptions should demonstrate, the light environment *Light – Movement – Space* is a highly complex Gesamtkunstwerk, which not only combines contradictory elements such as electricity and water in ground-breaking ways, but also unites the key characteristics of Mack's artistic practice: Light, structure, movement, and color; mirror surfaces that dissolve not only the physical appearance of the sculpture but also that of its environment. Mack combined all of these elements in a dazzling potpourri of new technical materials and possibilities. By introducing real motion to his work through mechanical kinetics and creating a space which surrounds and captivates the viewers with its myriad lighting effects, Mack produces an extended experience of art.[16]

But how did art even begin to move, and what are the fundamental characteristics of kinetic artworks? These questions warrant a brief digression: Kinetics (from Ancient Greek *kinesis*, movement) are based on the suspension of the static nature of artworks. It is replaced with processes of movement which produce ever changing

16 See Fabo, "Somewhere over the Rainbow," 41.

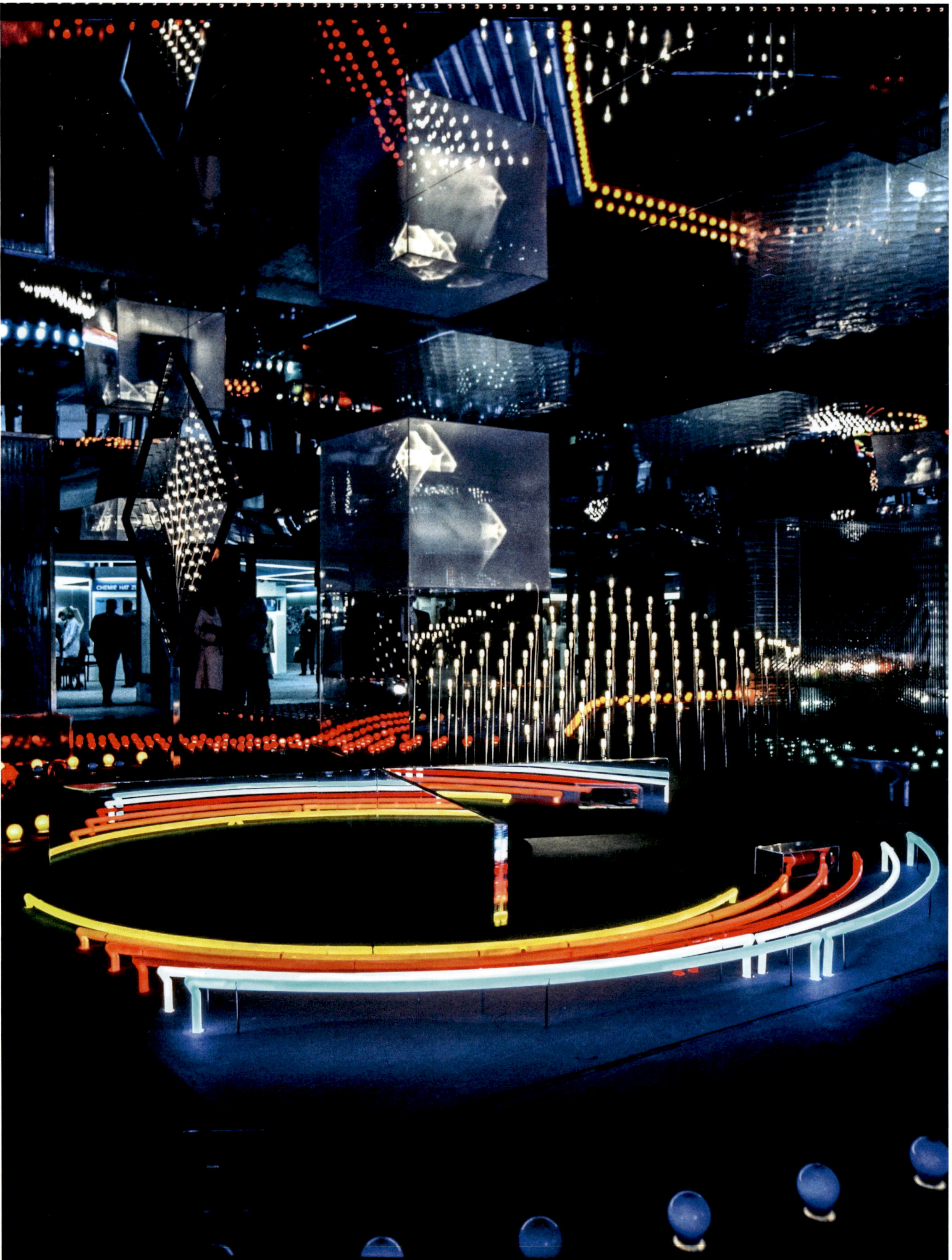

fig. 40 Heinz Mack, *Rotation of the Rainbow*, 1970, part of the light environment *Light – Movement – Space* at the Great Industrial Exhibition, 1970, Berlin

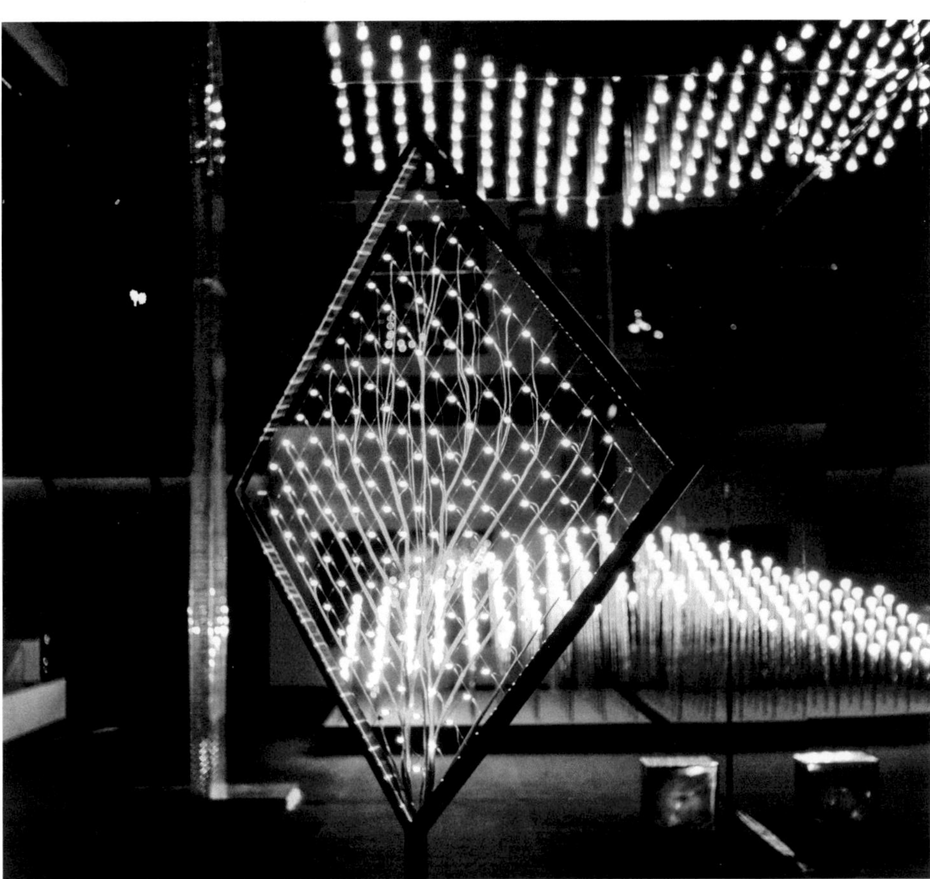

fig. 41 Heinz Mack, *Light Tree* and *Chrome Bar Forest*, 1969–1970, part of the light environment *Light – Movement – Space* at the Great Industrial Exhibition, 1970, Berlin

visual appearances and perspectives. Optical events step into the foreground. Historically, the development of kinetic art can be traced back to the dynamism of the futurists, who depicted multiple phases of movement in their paintings and sculptures at the beginning of the twentieth century. This led to the creation of motorized artworks which incorporated actual motion through mechanical means. Examples include Naum Gabo's *Kinetic Construction (Standing Wave)* (1919–1920), a metal rod protruding from a black base that is vibrated by a motor to create the appearance of a virtual volume, and Jean Tinguely's series *Constantes indéterminées* (from 1950 onward). Beginning in the 1930s, Alexander Calder designed various mobiles which were only set into
fig. 42 motion by air currents.[17] László Moholy-Nagy's *Light-Space-Modulator* (1930), a large "device used for demonstrating both plays of light and manifestations of movement,"[18] combines elements of movement with electrical lighting, which almost certainly was a source of inspiration for Heinz Mack.

Interactions with moving objects have always been a key element of Heinz Mack's artistic practice: In his early ZERO paintings, movement is hinted at by "dynamic structures," his light reliefs and light steles create the appearance of movement through vibrating reflections of light. His rotors, which he began designing in 1958, are the first works to include actual mechanical movement. These works are motorized apparatuses comprising a closed square box, in which one or more circular reliefs slowly rotate, sometimes in opposite directions.

17 Cf. Anina Baum, "From Light to Movement: Kinetic Sculptures by Heinz Mack," in: Titz and Kim, *Mack.Kinetics*, 94–98, here 95.

18 László Moholy-Nagy, "Light-Space-Modulator," http://www.medienkunstnetz.de/works/licht-raum-modulator/

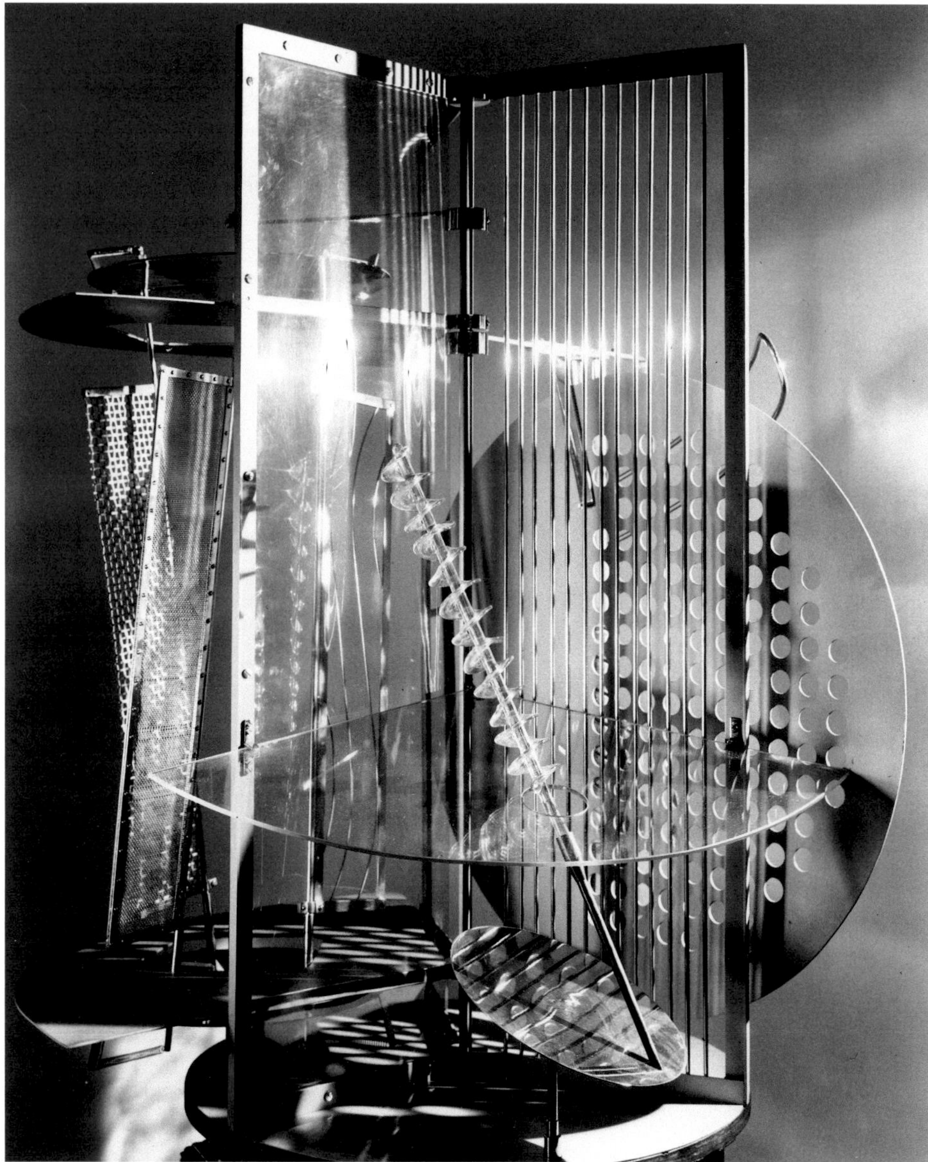

fig. 42 László Moholy-Nagy, *Light-Space Modulator*, 1930/2005

The view of the complex structures inside these contraptions is often obscured by translucent wavy glass panes, only letting distorted light reflections flash through to the outside world. With each rotation, these *light dynamos* generate new manifestations of light.[19]

Apart from making light and time visible using movement, Heinz Mack is also interested in expanding the perception of space. By utilizing new industrial materials – including stainless steel, aluminum, acrylic glass, honeycomb mesh from the aerospace industry, and Fresnel lenses[20] originally created for use in light houses and space telescopes – he creates new interactions with natural light, which is refracted and multiplied in never-ending variations. These shimmering and reflective surfaces are also characterized by their unique relationship to their spatial surroundings. They fragment, diffract, and multiply space. This can already be seen in Mack's early "instruments of light," such as the light steles, light cubes, or rotors, and the effects can be enhanced by positioning multiple works in the same room as an

19 See Baum, "From Light to Movement," 96, 97.

20 A Fresnel lens is a type of lens that uses less material than a conventional lens. This is achieved by dividing the convex geometry of the lens into multiple annular sections, resulting in a characteristic pattern of concentric ridges.

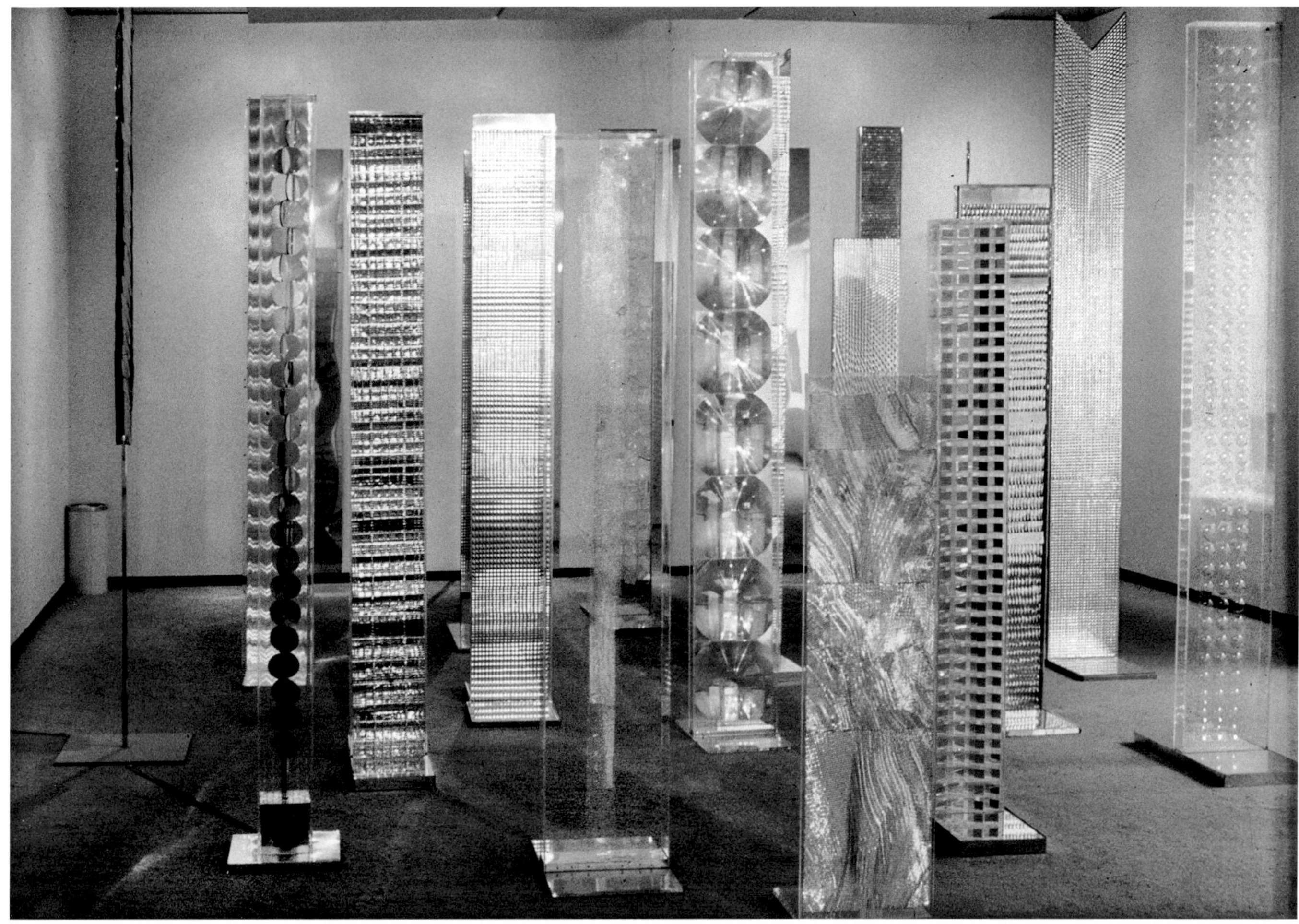

fig. 43 Heinz Mack, *Forest of Light*, 1966, exhibition view, Howard Wise Gallery, New York 1966

installation. Heinz Mack's first solo exhibition in New York, presented at the Howard Wise Gallery in 1966, was an impressive demonstration of this potential. Here, the *Forest of Light* was exhibited for the first time: an arrangement of 20 different light steles which mirrored not only the gallery space, but also the urban landscape of Manhattan. A similar spatial situation is achieved by the spiral arrangement of steles in the *Light Choreography* on display at the exhibition *Mack at ZKM*. Settings like these aim to directly involve the viewers as they walk around the artworks and have to actively adjust their perspective in order to perceive the different manifestations. And so, the activation of artworks, as discussed above in the context of kinetics, can also lead to an activation of the viewers. Contemplative immersion makes way for a reciprocal dialogue. This new relationship between artwork and recipient is a defining characteristic of art in the 1960s and 1970s.

figs. 43, 395

figs. 9, 10, 44

Rooted in the experimental practices of the futurist, surrealist, and dadaist movements, this period saw the development of several new art forms, from Conceptual Art and Actions to Performance Art as well as Land Art and Happenings, which not only called the traditional conceptions of art into question, but also aimed at forming an active connection between art and life. In this atmosphere, the environment in which a work of art exists becomes more and more significant. The term "environment" first gained traction in the late 1950s, when the American

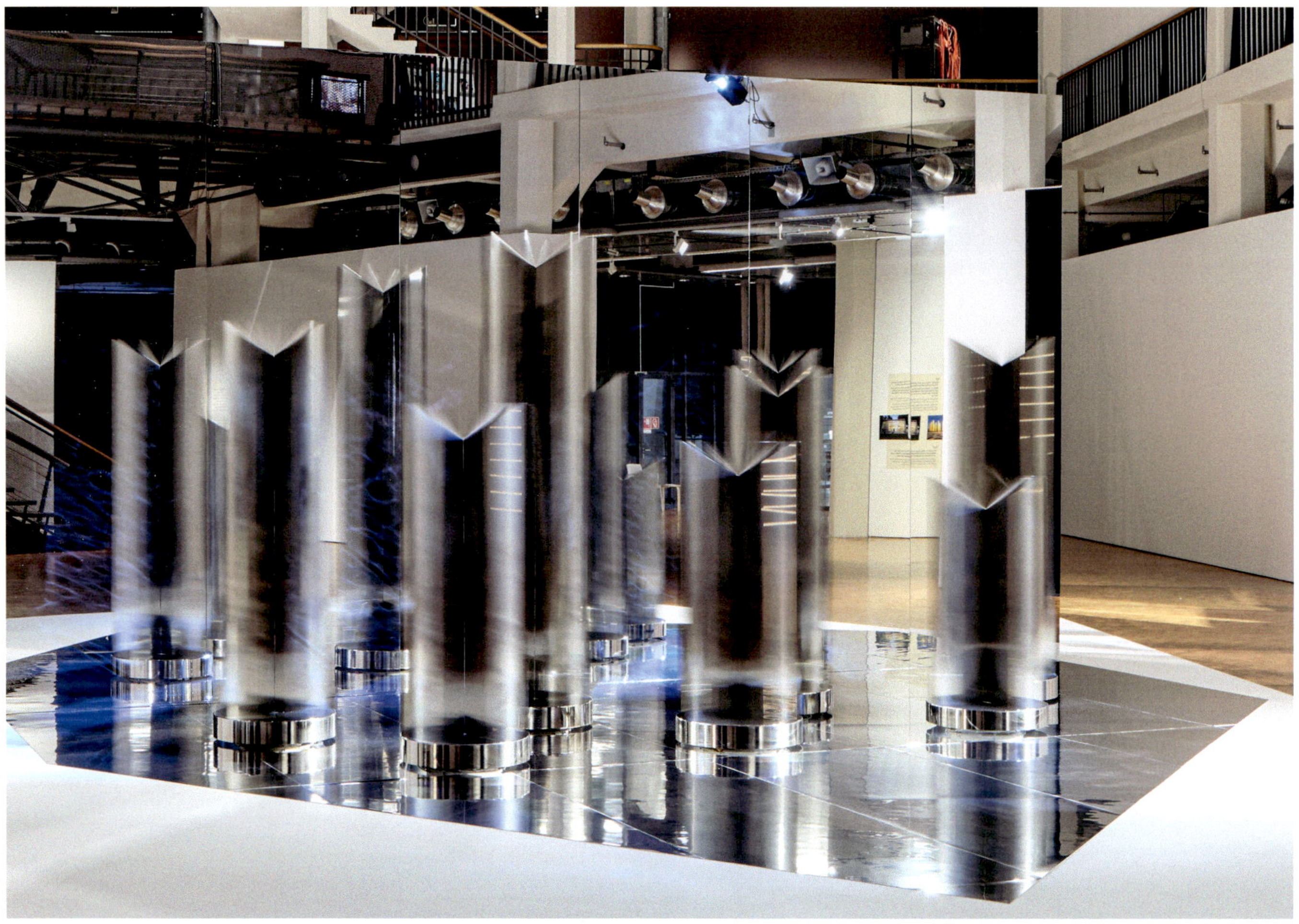

fig. 44 Heinz Mack, *The Mechanical Ballet*, 2015 (idea: 1966), kinetic ensemble, exhibition view, ZKM | Karlsruhe 2023

artist and inventor of the Happening Allan Kaprow used it for some of his works. It refers to spatial works which combine multiple components and media, and which can be entered by the audience and experienced from all sides. The immediate experience replaces pure observation. Kaprow invited his viewers to become part of their surroundings. The term is also used in the context of multi-medial art that utilizes light and sound. These multi-medial environments were often associated with mind-altering, psychedelic experiences – a stimulation of the senses not unlike the effects of certain drugs.[21]

This point takes us back to Heinz Mack. He also places the focus on a new experience of art and on honing the senses and expanding the perception of space. An environment which surrounds the viewer on all sides offers the perfect conditions to stimulate the visual, auditory, and even tactile senses. That is why the artist began exploring these art forms early on. In his 1960 exhibition *Hommage à Georges de La Tour* at Galerie Diogenes in Berlin, he presented a series of fire and phosphorus works, which brought the examination of light as seen in the paintings of French Baroque artist Georges de La Tour into reality. The glow of fires and candles, the strong contrasts between light and dark so typical of La Tour's paintings, were turned into visual and sculptural materials in their own right by Mack. He confronted the eyes of the viewers with an unreal after-image by having the candle-light

fig. 45

fig. 335

21 James Nisbet, *Ecologies, Environments, and Energy Systems in Art of the 1960s and 1970s* (Cambridge, MA: The MIT Press, 2014) 9, 15–18.

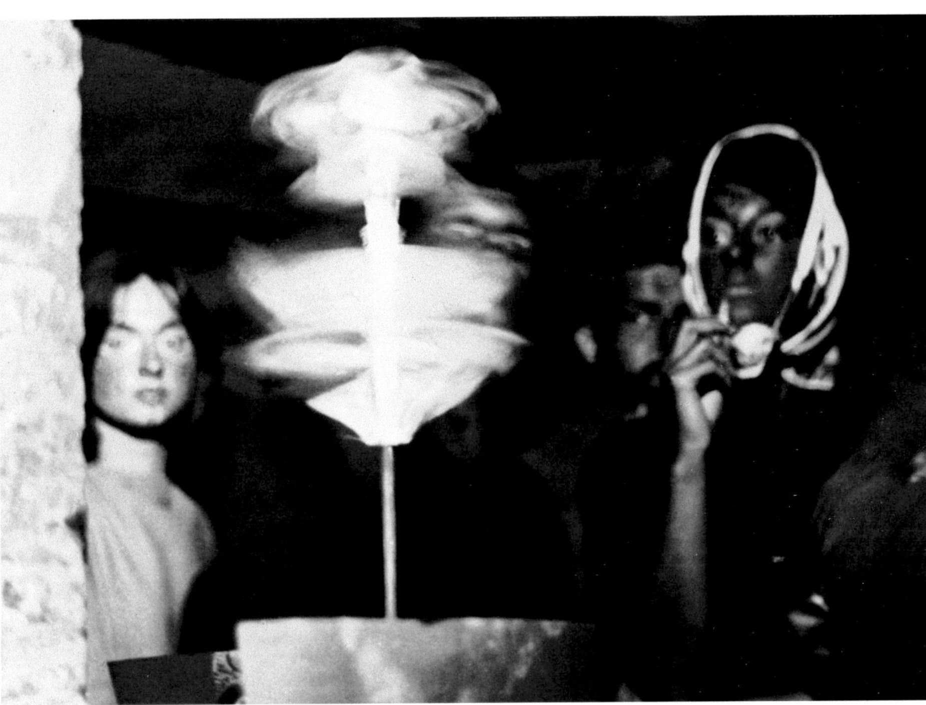

fig. 45 Heinz Mack, *Phosphorus Carousel*, 1960, exhibition view, first *Hommage à Georges de La Tour*, Galerie Diogenes, Berlin 1960

installation in the basement of the gallery suddenly extinguished by two performers wielding a wet tablecloth. Elsewhere, Mack placed a metal rod driven by a motor on a plinth and wrapped it in gauze soaked in phosphorus. The rotation of the rod produced a constantly changing, immaterial, centrifugal volume of light. During the opening of the exhibition, Mack ignited the gauze, creating a sparkling firework.

figs. 61, 62, 63, 64

As part of the same event, Mack also premiered his *Phosphorus Space*, which has been reconstructed for the ZKM exhibition. Various objects made from wood or aluminum move through a completely darkened room. These light sculptures—now painted with fluorescent paint instead of the original phosphorus—are illuminated by blacklight, creating an unreal and almost mystic atmosphere in the room. Their rotation dissolves form and materiality. All that remains are light traces in the darkness. This visual experience is accompanied by a computer-generated composition created by Götz Dipper specifically for this exhibition.

figs. 47, 55, 56, 57, 58, 59, 60

The entire situation feels like a staged performance; this can also be said of another reconstruction at the ZKM: *Ad Alta Potenza—16,000 Watts*. In a room completely covered in silver foil, five different mirror objects are illuminated by eight high-power beams. As the title suggests, this installation is geared towards maximizing the intensity of light. Some of the mirror objects slowly rotate in different directions. The silver surfaces of the wall elements reflect and diffract the bright beams of the floodlights, which creates a virtual expansion of the room. Movements are multiplied, generating a highly dynamic spatial effect. Inspired by the stage designs of Russian avant-garde artists El Lissitzky and Ljubow Popova as well as Bauhaus-artist Oskar Schlemmer, Heinz Mack creates a stage for light and movement. Both the *Phosphorus Space* and *Ad Alta Potenza* offer a purely frontal viewing perspective.

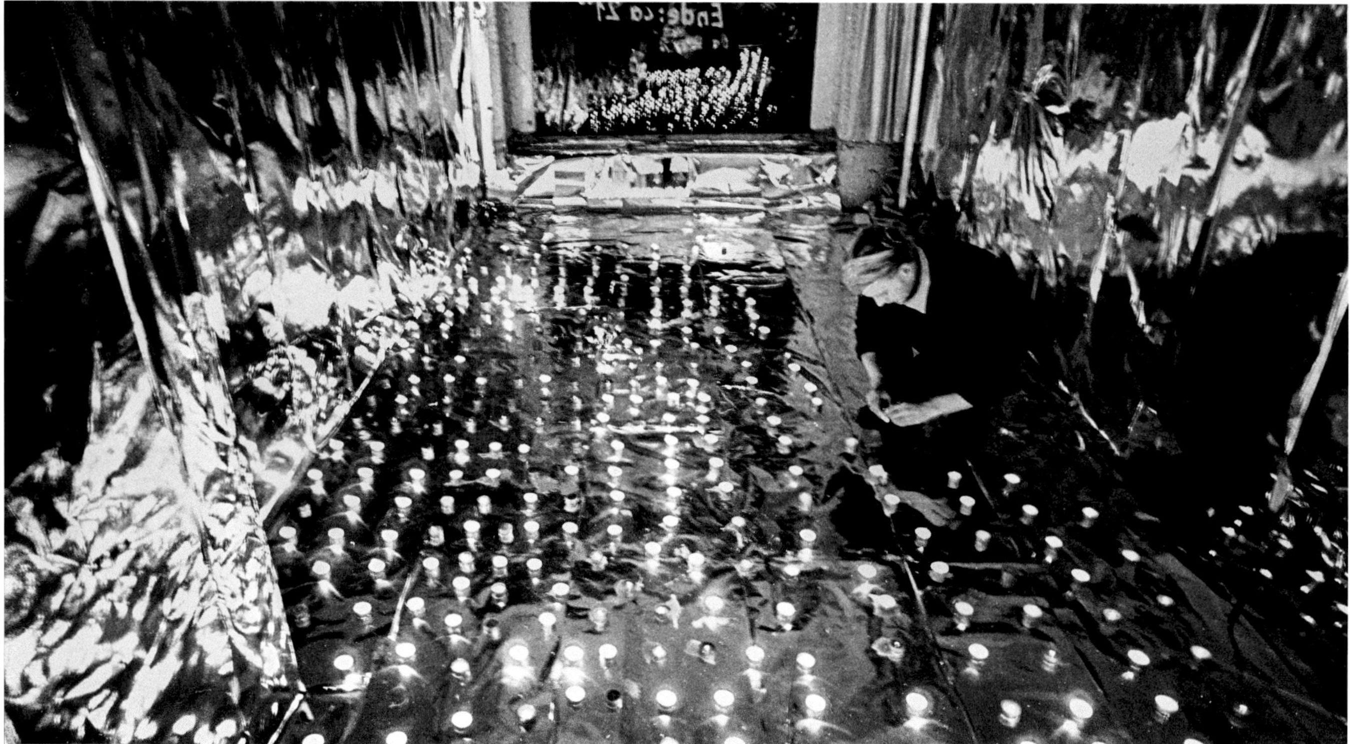

fig. 46 Heinz Mack at the second *Hommage à Georges de La Tour*, 1966, Galerie Schmela, Düsseldorf

Nevertheless, the striking visual impressions produced by these light spaces feel as though they completely encompass the viewer.

We can be quite certain that the 1970 light environment *Light – Movement – Space* would have had the same effect to an even greater degree. The technical and logistical implementation of the Berlin installation was extremely complex. Some of it was done by the artist himself; other components were handled by experts in electrical or mechanical engineering as well as plastics manufacturing.[22] This meant that the project was not planned purely on the basis of artistic considerations, but also required great technical adaptability from the various specialists who were involved in its realization. It was only possible thanks to the combination of different areas of expertise. The sheer scale of it all, the unforgiving schedule and the potentially hazardous juxtaposition of electricity and water posed a unique set of challenges. At the same time, new materials and electrical components had to be created and tested, especially in terms of lighting. To make this possible, major semiconductor and lighting manufacturers such as Philipps and Osram were brought into the fold in order to provide the greatest possible selection of interesting light sources.[23] This enabled the production of custom components at minimal cost, as several of the companies involved provided their specialists and material for free thanks to the advertising potential of the installation.

Heinz Mack's artistic vision, which transcended conventional dimensions and aimed to achieve the impossible, turned out to be an ambitious challenge for everyone involved, but it also offered a fitting scenario for celebrating the potential that exists at the intersection between art and industry, between art and technology. Could there ever be a better place for such an undertaking than an industrial exhibition?

22 See Mack, "Erklärung zum Lichtenvironment."

23 Hans Boventer, "Bauanleitung zum Lichtenvironment" (typoscript, Archive Heinz Mack, 1970).

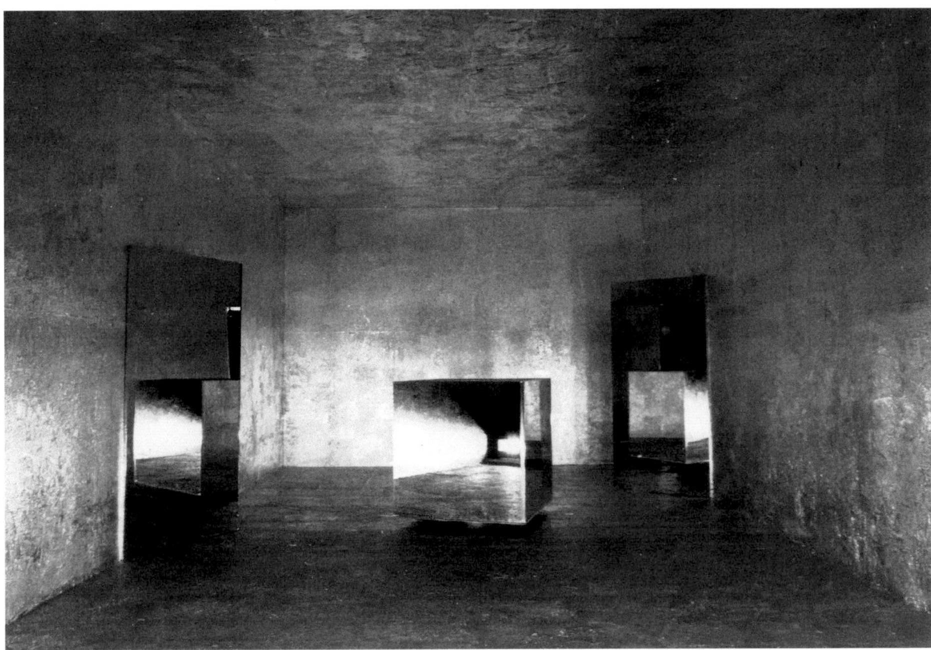

fig. 47 Heinz Mack, *Ad Alta Potenza – 16,000 Watts*, 1960, exhibition view, Galleria d'Arte Moderna, Bologna 1976

New Spaces for Art

In order to provide an adequate answer to this question, it is worth examining the history of industrial and commercial exhibitions. Around 1750, private business institutions began organizing industry fairs at regional and national levels. These events were primarily aimed at facilitating the exchange of information between trade, craft, and art. In addition to this transfer of knowledge, which was meant to benefit the economy of an entire nation, there was also a focus on increasing sales. For instance, the inaugural 1798 Paris National Exhibition with its 109 participating companies not only strengthened the French industrial sector, but also presented the entire country as a strong, confident, and ambitious nation. An effective model that would serve as a template for almost all subsequent industrial exhibitions. The desire for national image cultivation and the insatiable hunger for new markets, stoked by the industrial revolution and the relentless progression of early capitalism, soon drove the expansion beyond national borders. In the mid-nineteenth century, this led to the creation of new, international formats – the so-called world exhibitions.[24] The first such event, *The Great Exhibition of the Works of Industry of All Nations*, was held in London's Hyde Park in 1851. In the Crystal Palace, constructed from glass and iron specifically for this occasion, some 17,000 organizations from 28 countries presented their exhibits featuring raw materials, machines, products, and applied arts. This impressive display was one of the few world exhibitions that even generated a financial profit, inspiring an increasing number of international fairs in other cities – in London and Paris, but also in Vienna, Philadelphia, Sydney, Brussels and Antwerp, Chicago, Montreal, Osaka, or Hanover. The second ever world exhibition, held in 1855 under the title *Exposition universelle des produits de l'agriculture, et l'industrie et des beaux-arts de Paris*,

24 See Petra Krutisch, *Aus aller Herren Länder: Weltausstellungen seit 1851* (Nuremberg: Germanisches Nationalmuseum, 2001), 9–10.

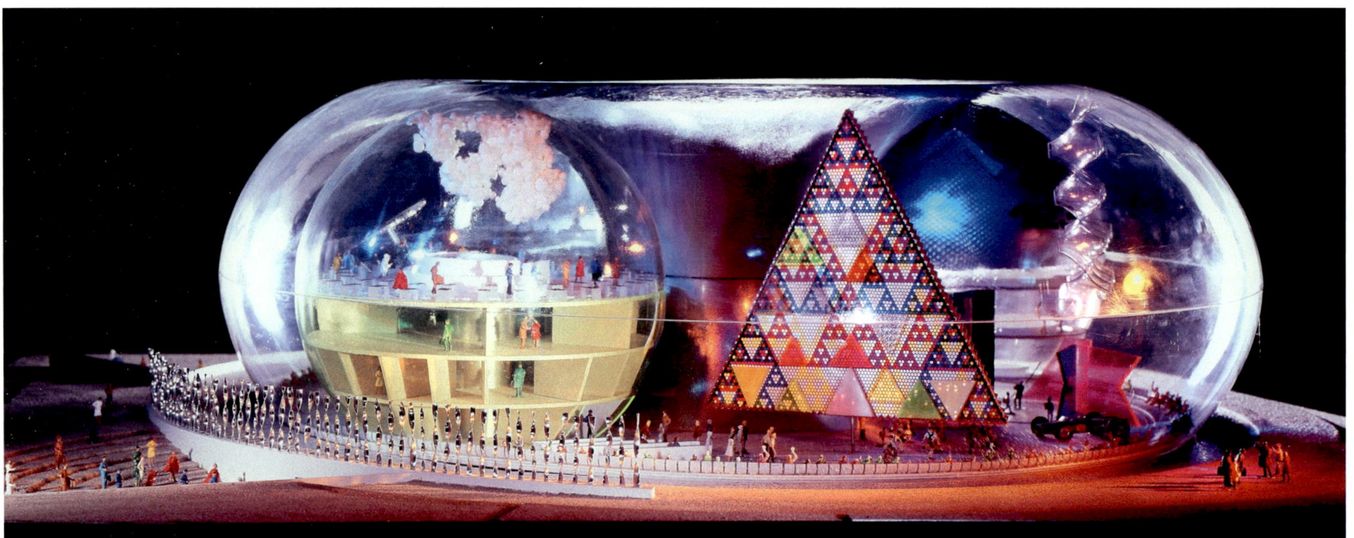

fig. 48 Horst H. Baumann, Gerhard Karsten, Wolfgang Körber and Heinz Mack, model for the construction of the German Pavilion at the Osaka World's Fair, 1970

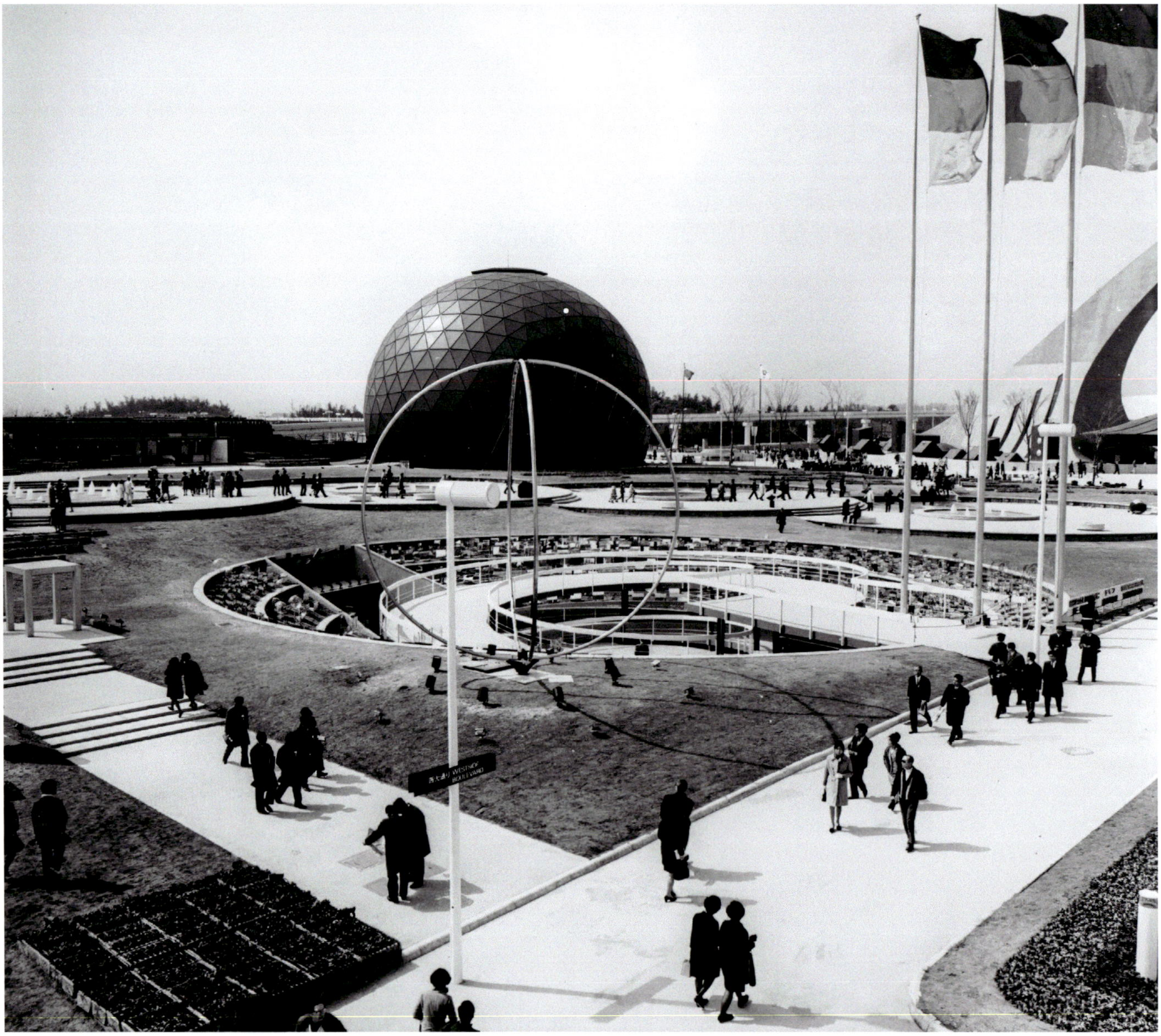

fig. 49 Design of the entrance spiral to the German Pavilion at the Osaka World's Fair, 1970

included a department dedicated to the fine arts. From 1889 onwards, entertainment and intercultural exchange continued to rise in significance. The major exhibitions offered ever more spectacular worlds of experience. They not only gave rise to monumental structures such as the Eiffel Tower in Paris (1889), but also to illusionist displays such as water and light shows as well as Ferris wheels and other fairground attractions. Around 1900, the establishment of a trade press moved the industry-specific exchange to other channels of communication and led to more exhibitions and fairs focusing on single sectors. Nevertheless, the format of world exhibition is still upheld to this day.[25] In 2025, a second world exhibition will be held in Osaka.

The golden age of the world exhibition was during the nineteenth and twentieth centuries. With their ambition of demonstrating progress and legitimizing what they showed as historically relevant, they stoked national pride and proclaimed the supremacy of Western industrial nations, whose economic power derived significantly from the exploitation of material and human resources in the occupied colonies. The technologically advanced way of life in the West placed itself above any and all other ways of life. This also led to members of indigenous populations being put on display at the world exhibitions. A propagandist strategy that degraded other cultures as "backward." And even if the world exhibitions of the twenty-first century no longer openly display such mechanisms of othering in their joyous, colorful, cultural-commercial mass spectacles, these problematic concepts still exist as internalized structures.

Compared to the institution of the museum, industrial and world exhibitions are inherently ephemeral. Time and again, exhibition halls are constructed amid entire urban landscapes, only to vanish again after a few weeks or remain as deserted ghost towns, mere shadows of their former glory. A world exhibition is an undertaking of immense cost, whose wastefulness is hard to justify in this day and age due to the environmental challenges and scarcity of resources. The same applies to industrial exhibitions. At the same time, the appropriation of artistic practice by commercial interests is tied to a popular marketing strategy, which in turn could be examined critically and called into question by artists.

In the 1960s and 1970s, a period characterized by economic upswings and technological euphoria, participating in the world exhibitions in Montreal (1967) and Osaka (1970) as well as the German Industrial Exhibition in Berlin (1970) offered an interesting and worthwhile opportunity for an artist such as Heinz Mack. The reasons may have been idealistic as much as they were pragmatic.

To reiterate, a world exhibition is a state-funded undertaking of immense cost and proportions. The German contribution in Osaka reportedly cost around 35 million German marks, with 11 million alone for the construction of the pavilion.[26] Such a highly subsidized exhibition can undoubtedly be lucrative for artists, who can take it as an opportunity to realize large-scale, cost-intensive projects. Of course, it is also a sign of great distinction when an artist is invited to exhibit their work to represent their entire nation. The fact that Mack was involved in two German contributions to world exhibitions in quick succession shows how important and representative his work was at the time.

25 Ibid., 26, 102, 113. See also: Thomas Schriefers, *Für den Abriss gebaut? Anmerkungen zur Geschichte der Weltausstellungen* (Hagen: ardenku, 1999), 15, 25, 27.

26 See Peter Brügge, "Warten auf ein deutsches Wunder," *Der Spiegel*, no. 13 (March 22, 1970).

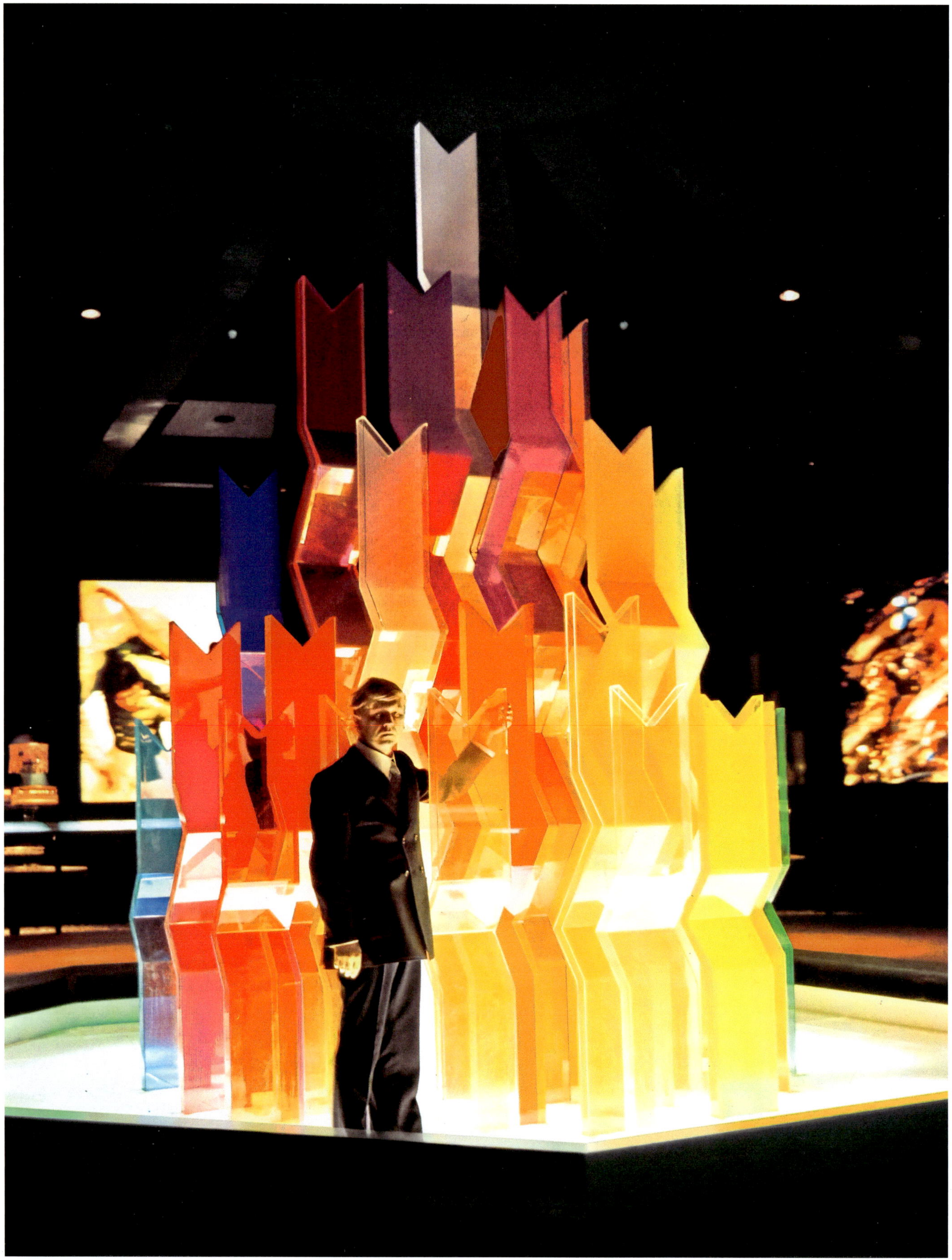

fig. 50 Heinz Mack, *Crown for the Color Spectrum*, 1969–1970, light sculpture for the Expo in Osaka

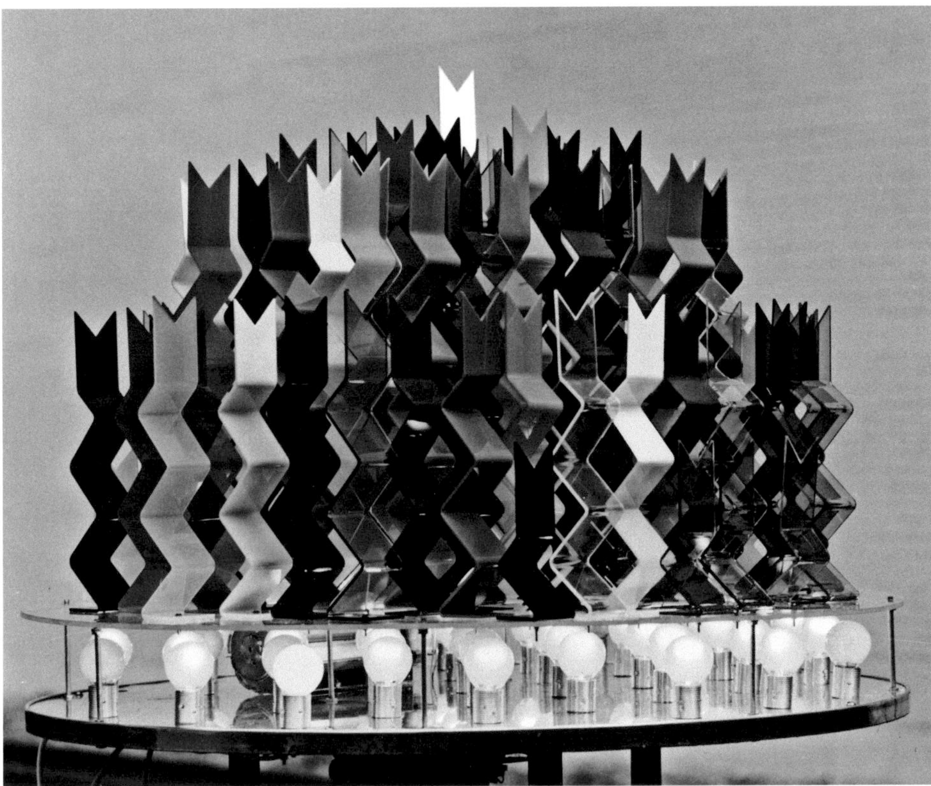

fig. 51 Heinz Mack, *Light and Color*, 1966, model, exhibited at the Montreal World's Fair, 1967

In Osaka, the federal government wanted him to bring attention to beauty and demonstrate that Germany was not only characterized by "efficiency and technology."[27] The German contribution to the world exhibition held in Japan from March to September of 1970 aimed to paint a new picture of Germany. Its theme "Gardens of Music" placed a strong focus on music and technology, aspiring to entertain the audience and emphasize the connection between culture and industry. Lacking information, technical difficulties, and general disorganization led to crowds ending up leaving the German pavilion more confused than impressed. The building designed by architect Fritz Bornemann boasted an imposing ultramarine dome rising 14 meters above the fairground and housing the world's first and only spherical auditorium, in which young composers of electronic music such as Karlheinz Stockhausen, Erhard Großkopf, and Eberhard Schoener demonstrated the technological possibilities of new music. Four additional exhibition halls were set below the ground. Here, visitors received general information about Germany oscillating between idyllic landscapes and technological progress, between science and art, not excluding sports and the Oktoberfest. The exhibits included the latest technical marvels in music, such as computers for generating music, electronic sound processing devices, and lighting consoles, alongside communication satellites and AV technology as well as medical and pharmaceutical innovations.[28]

fig. 48

fig. 49

At the center of the underground Hall D, Heinz Mack's *Crown for the Color Spectrum*, a 5-meter-tall kinetic sculpture made of colorful acrylic glass, almost seemed to be in flames thanks to its intense lighting from below. Mack had already presented a model for this sculpture at the 1967 world exhibition in Montreal. But this monumental sculpture

fig. 50

fig. 51

27 See Otto Heuser, "In 250 Spiegeln wird der Raum neu gefächert. Macks Idee zur Weltausstellung," *Westdeutsche Zeitung* (July 12, 1969).

28 See S. F., "Das Projekt Osaka. Die schönen Seiten der Deutschen / Weltausstellung 1970," *Frankfurter Allgemeine Zeitung* (June 26, 1969), 22; Peter Brügge, "Warten auf ein deutsches Wunder," *Der Spiegel*, no. 13 (March 22, 1970) and Lange William, "Expo 70 beginnt in Osaka," *Rheinische Post* (1970). All articles available in the Archive Heinz Mack.

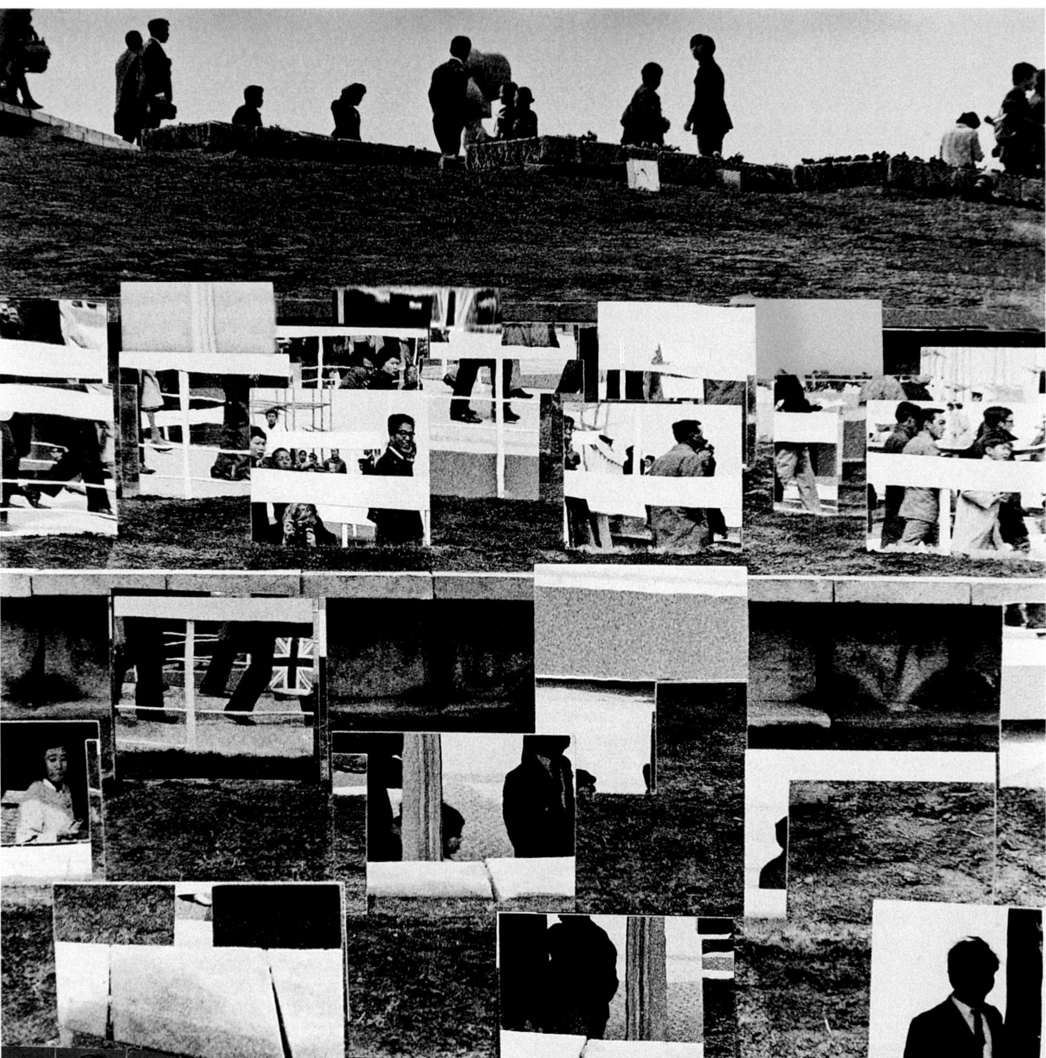

fig. 52 Heinz Mack, *Mirror Plantation*, 1970, in front of the German Pavilion at the Osaka World's Fair, 1970

was not his only contribution in Osaka. In front of the Expo Museum of Fine Arts, which housed 400 masterpieces from all around the world, Mack erected his 12-meter-tall *Light Stele*, which glowed from within. He was also involved in the landscaping of the area surrounding the German pavilion alongside landscape designer Walter Rossow. At the entrance to the pavilion, a spiral leading into the ground, Heinz Mack created his artificial garden – 250 mirrors in varying geometrical shapes up to 4.5 meters tall, made from highly polished stainless steel, with a total mirror surface area of 500 m². The effect of this *Jardin Artificiel*, a concept originally created for the *Sahara Project* in 1959, was astounding. The mirror plantation in Osaka created astonishing irritations: Fore- and background dissolved, nature blended into architecture and vice versa, and the concepts of near and far lost all meaning as the fragmented reflections produced ever-changing juxtapositions. Everything in the surrounding area was shattered into a kaleidoscopic effect, dissolved and reassembled anew in every instant. A successful implementation of Mack's artistic idea of immaterializing space and claiming new spaces for art.[29] Outside of the museum setting, his works interact directly with natural and urban landscapes, generating entirely new dialogues and

fig. 54

fig. 52

fig. 53

29 See Marianne Xhayet, "Spiegel-Garten geht nach Osaka," *Mönchengladbacher Stadtpost*, no. 158 (July 12, 1969) and Heinz Mack, "Spiegelformen plus einfache Geometrie," *Die Welt* (August 8, 1969). Both articles available in the Archive Heinz Mack.

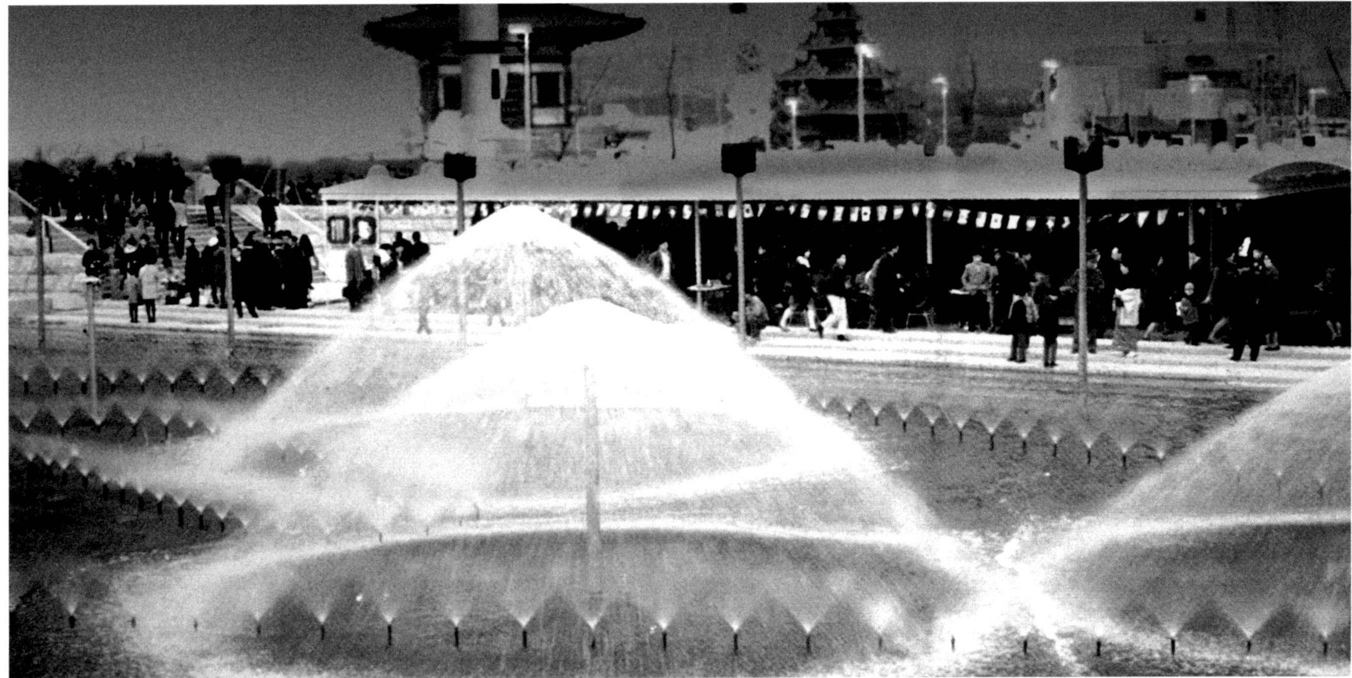

fig. 53 Heinz Mack, *Water Games*, 1970, fountain in front of the German Pavilion at the Osaka World's Fair, 1970

experiences. At the same time, integrated into a mass spectacle such as a world exhibition, they reach a large, broad audience which does not approach them with the expectations of typical art audiences.

Heinz Mack's contribution to the German Industrial Exhibition in Berlin (1970) was another resounding success in his effort to engage with the public: More than 300,000 people reportedly marveled at his light environment *Light – Movement – Space* in Berlin, without even explicitly knowing it was the work of an artist. The audience was fascinated – a "sensational success."[30] However, the art world hardly acknowledged it.

Looking Back and Looking Ahead

As a young, up-and-coming artist, Mack seized this opportunity to make his ambitious artistic vision a reality on a large scale. The light space could not have been realized in any conventional art institution. This was only possible under the unique conditions of the industrial exhibition. An event dedicated to showcasing the potency and progressiveness of industry. Furthermore, the industrial exhibition was equally suitable for Heinz Mack's work on a conceptual level. Following its motto "Human and Technology," the exhibition and its program of technological and scientific presentations was all about progress. Only a few voices raised critical tones by highlighting the influence which the industrial revolution and the latest technological developments had on the Earth. The majority of contributions were brimming with euphoria, heralding achievements such as "victory in the battle against hunger and poverty."[31] Optimistic prognoses which show that Mack's vision for the year 2000 is representative of the predominant attitudes of its time. Heinz Mack's artistic position is a beacon of optimism, faith in the future, and the coming together of art, science, and technology.

30 Mack, "Erklärung zum Lichtenvironment."

31 See *Mensch und Technik. Die technisch-wissenschaftlichen Vorträge. Deutsche Industrieausstellung Berlin 1970* (Berlin: Colloquium Verlag Otto H. Hess, 1971).

Of the aforementioned visions for the future, some have come to bear, at least in certain contexts. Other hopes remain entirely utopian, and new problems have surfaced. Still, large parts of the global population—which has grown significantly since 1970—are struggling with poverty and hunger, and the rift between the rich and the poor is getting wider and wider. Wars and violent conflicts are on the rise. Climate change has reached dangerous proportions, and its effects can be felt around the world, but especially in the Global South. All this has completely changed our perspective regarding the future and made us reevaluate the unconditional technophilia of the past.

And what became of Heinz Mack's light environment *Light—Movement—Space*? The light space has disappeared. Once the exhibition was over, after only ten days, it was dismantled. Only a few of its components can still be found in the artist's storage depot. An initiative of Berlin's Senate to purchase and maintain the work did not succeed at the time. Neither did the idea of Senator Rolf Schwedler, who wanted to transplant it to another prominent location where it could become a permanent installation surrounded by glass architecture.[32] The 1970 industrial exhibition spared no expense of resources and energy, just to generate an absolutely unique, ephemeral experience for one fleeting moment. An undertaking that might still be imaginable, but would be extremely hard to realize today, as it turned out during the preparations for the exhibition *Mack at ZKM*. Grand ideas like this are faced with new challenges and obstacles today. They have to be evaluated and deemed proportionate according to different criteria. This is not only due to limited financial means, especially when comparing a museum with entire industries, but also a different responsibility towards resources of any kind and a general shift in attitude towards the curation of exhibitions in this day and age.

And so, the light environment *Light—Movement—Space* remains a unique masterpiece of the past, which incorporated Mack's pioneering efforts at the interface between art and technology as well as the concepts of light, movement, and space. Nevertheless, Mack's optimism and his numerous grand ideas resonate throughout the ZKM exhibition, albeit without the reconstruction of the Berlin light space. Mack will always be a utopian, dreaming with open eyes[33] — a trait from which we can all learn something. His unshakable faith in beauty, in the potential of combining art, technology, and science, resonates through almost all of his works, from the multi-faceted light steles, reflective paravents, and magically vibrating rotors to his various stages for light and movement or his interventions in the Sahara and the Arctic. With his multi-faceted explorations of light, Mack stimulates our imagination and expands our perception. And we actually leave the exhibition with a renewed swing in our step. Mack counters the crises of our time with beauty and positivity. A visit to his cosmos rubs off on us, inspires us, gives us hope, and restores our faith in great ideas. Exactly what is needed in today's world, which so often seems hopeless.

Translated from the German by Dan Lawler.

32 See Mack, "Erklärung zum Lichtenvironment."

33 See Mack, "Kunst 2000," 51.

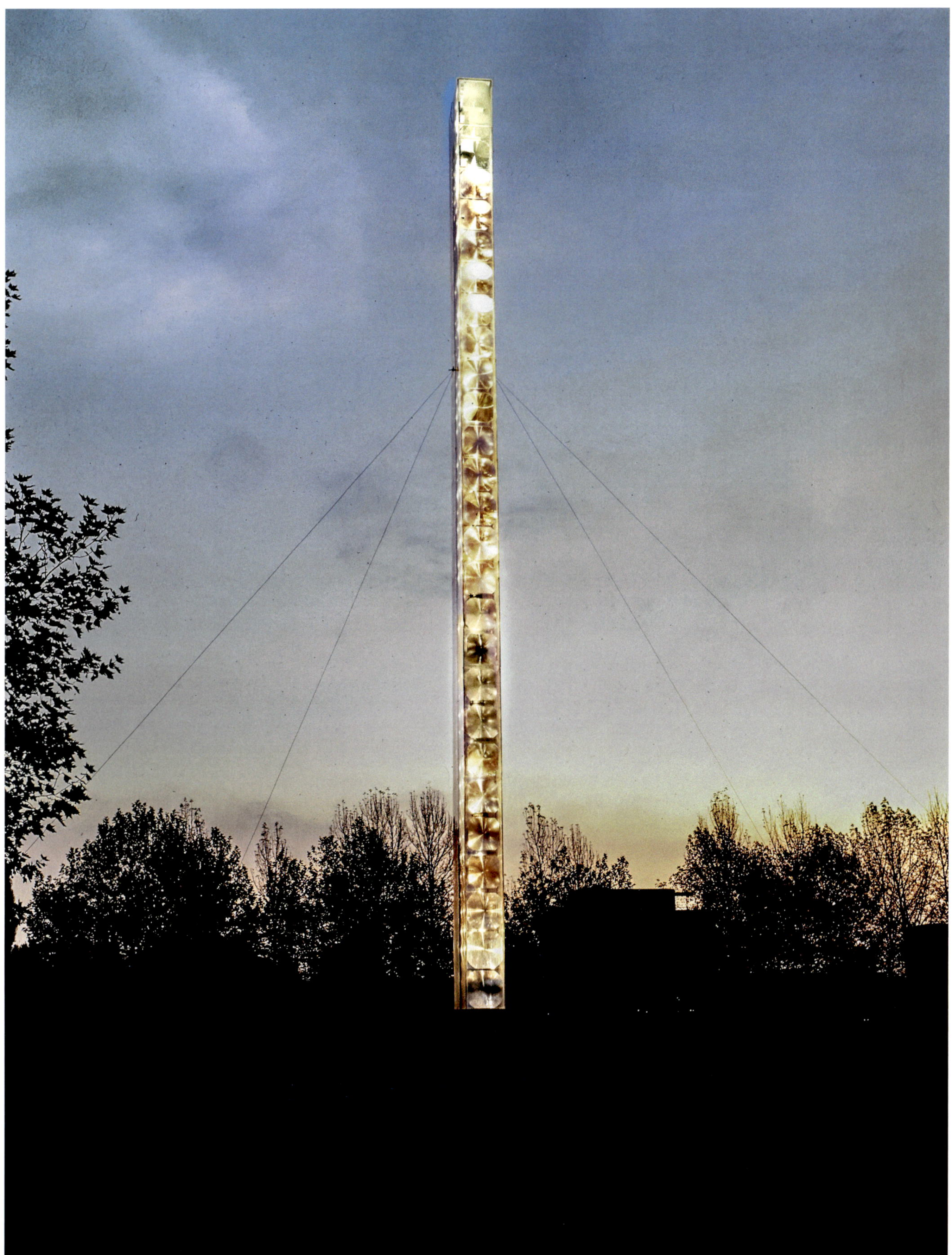

fig. 54 Heinz Mack, *Stele for the Sky*, 1970, public sculpture in front of the Expo Museum of Fine Arts, Osaka

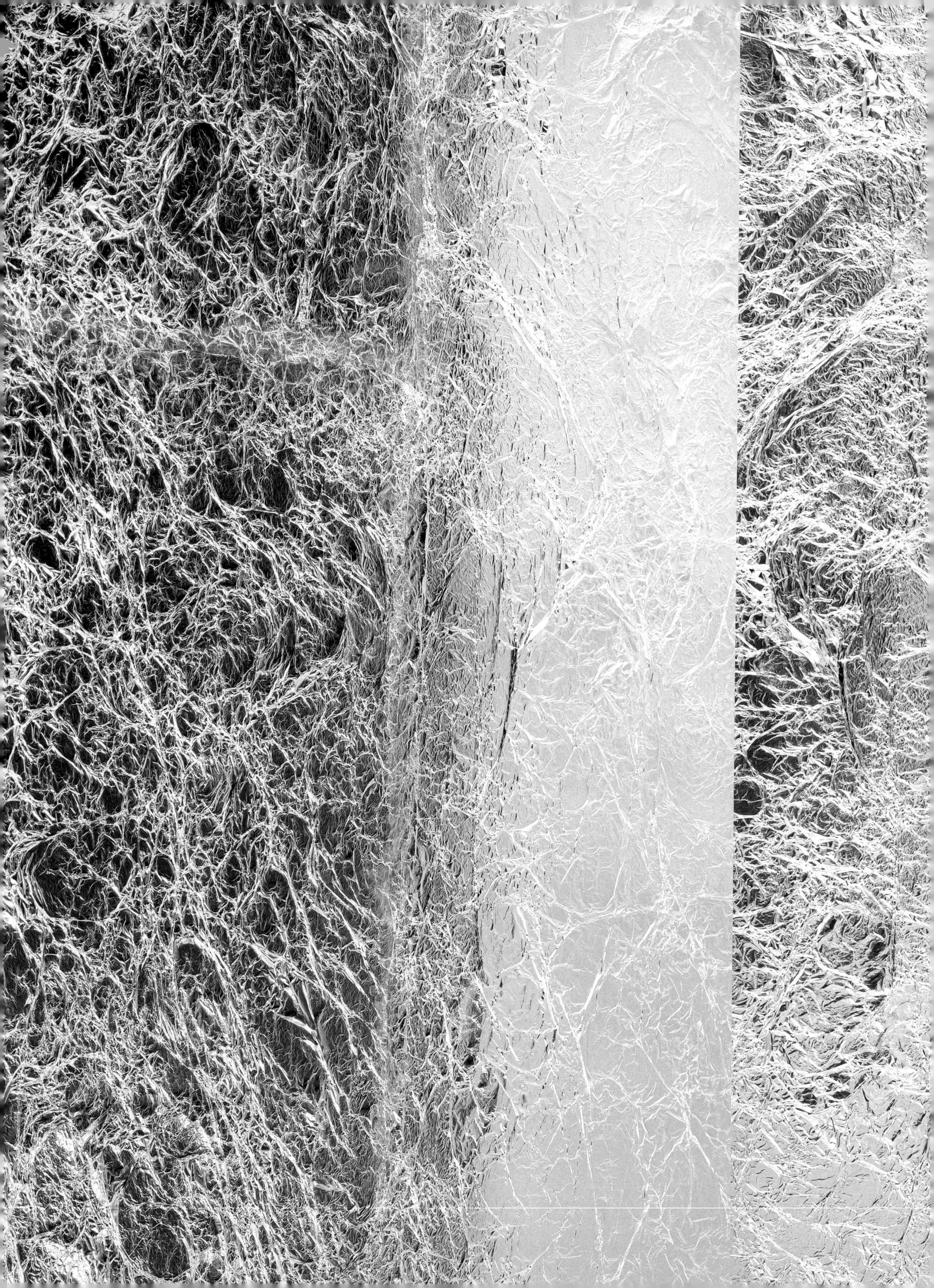

Ad Alta Potenza – 16,000 Watts

In a room completely lined with silver foil, five different mirror objects are illuminated by eight powerful spotlights. Some of them move slowly in different directions. The silver surfaces of the room reflect and refract the powerful beams, expanding the space virtually. The movements multiply and the spatial effect is extremely dynamic. The title *Ad Alta Potenza – 16,000 Watts* refers to the extreme light intensity emitted by this environment. Inspired by the stage designs of the Russian avant-garde artists El Lissitzky and Lyubov Popova as well as Bauhaus artist Oskar Schlemmer, Heinz Mack creates a stage, a showcase for light and movement.

Mack's original idea for this spatial installation, which he designed as a "reflector of light energy," dates from 1960. The first version of the work was created in 1976 for the opening exhibition of the Bologna art fair. In 2006, the installation was on show in the ZERO exhibition at the Museum Kunstpalast in Düsseldorf. Today, the work is owned by the ZERO foundation, Düsseldorf. For the current exhibition at the ZKM | Karlsruhe, it was restored, and a site-specific reconstruction was carried out thanks to the generous support of the Friends of the ZERO foundation.

← *fig. 55* Heinz Mack, *Ad Alta Potenza – 16,000 Watts*, 1976/2023 (idea: 1960), detail

*The quality of light, its beauty, is essentially a pure value of sensation, a creative act of freedom within the sphere of our sensibility.**

Works in the exhibition:
All works courtesy of the artist
unless otherwise noted

Ad Alta Potenza – 16,000 Watts
1976/2023 (idea: 1960)
Light environment: mirrors, silver foil, aluminum, wood, spotlights, motors
390 × 700 × 350 cm
ZERO foundation, Düsseldorf / donation Heinz Mack
Reconstructed in cooperation with ZKM | Karlsruhe, 2023
With kind support by the friends of the ZERO foundation
→ *figs. 47, 55, 56, 57, 58, 59, 60*

* Heinz Mack, "Light is not Light" (1964), originally published in: *Mackazin* (Frankfurt: Typos, 1967); reprinted in: *Mack. Life and Work 1931–2011* (Cologne: Dumont, 2011), 140. Translated from the German.

→ *fig. 56* Heinz Mack, *Ad Alta Potenza – 16,000 Watts*, 1976/2023 (idea: 1960)

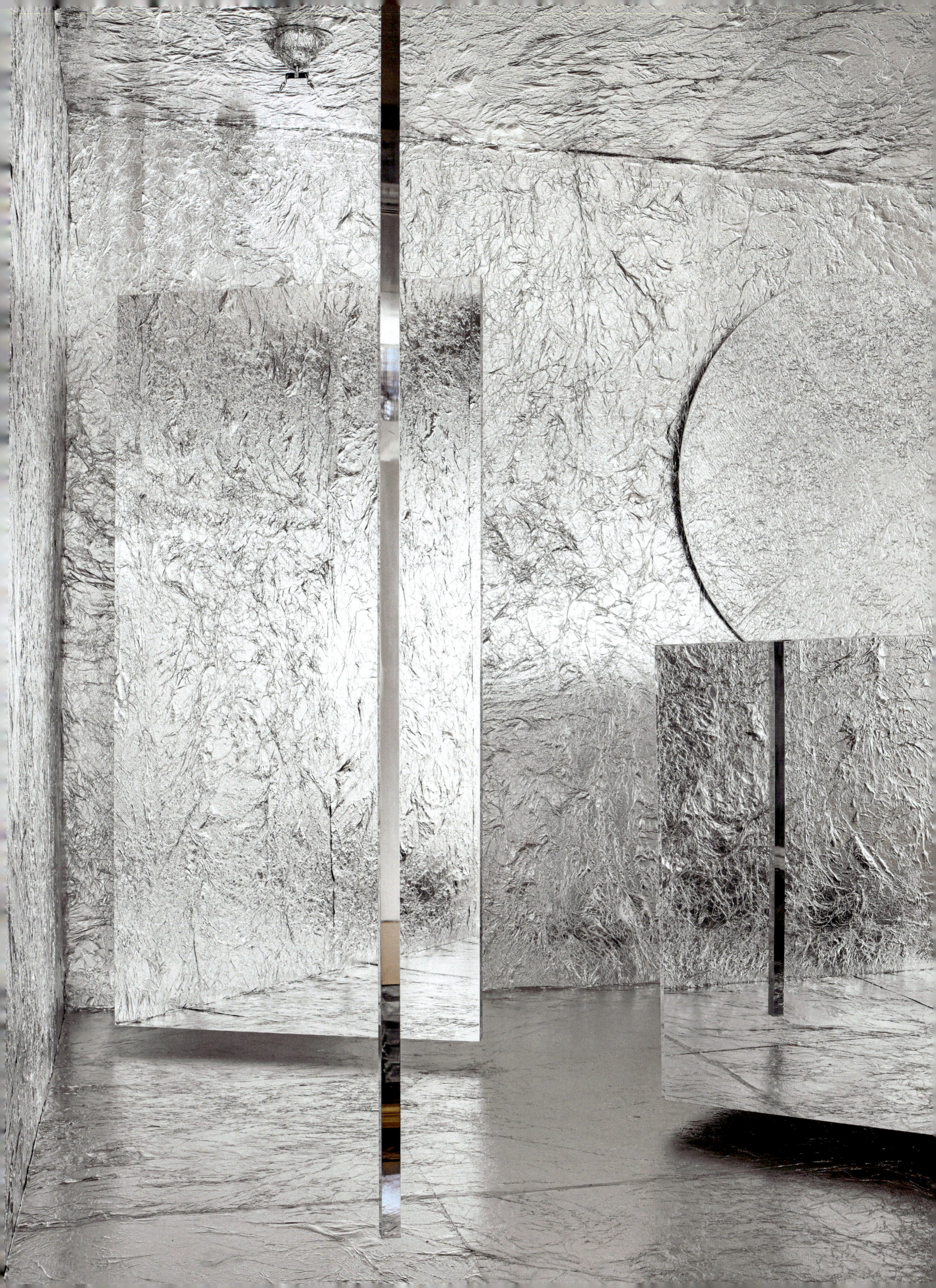

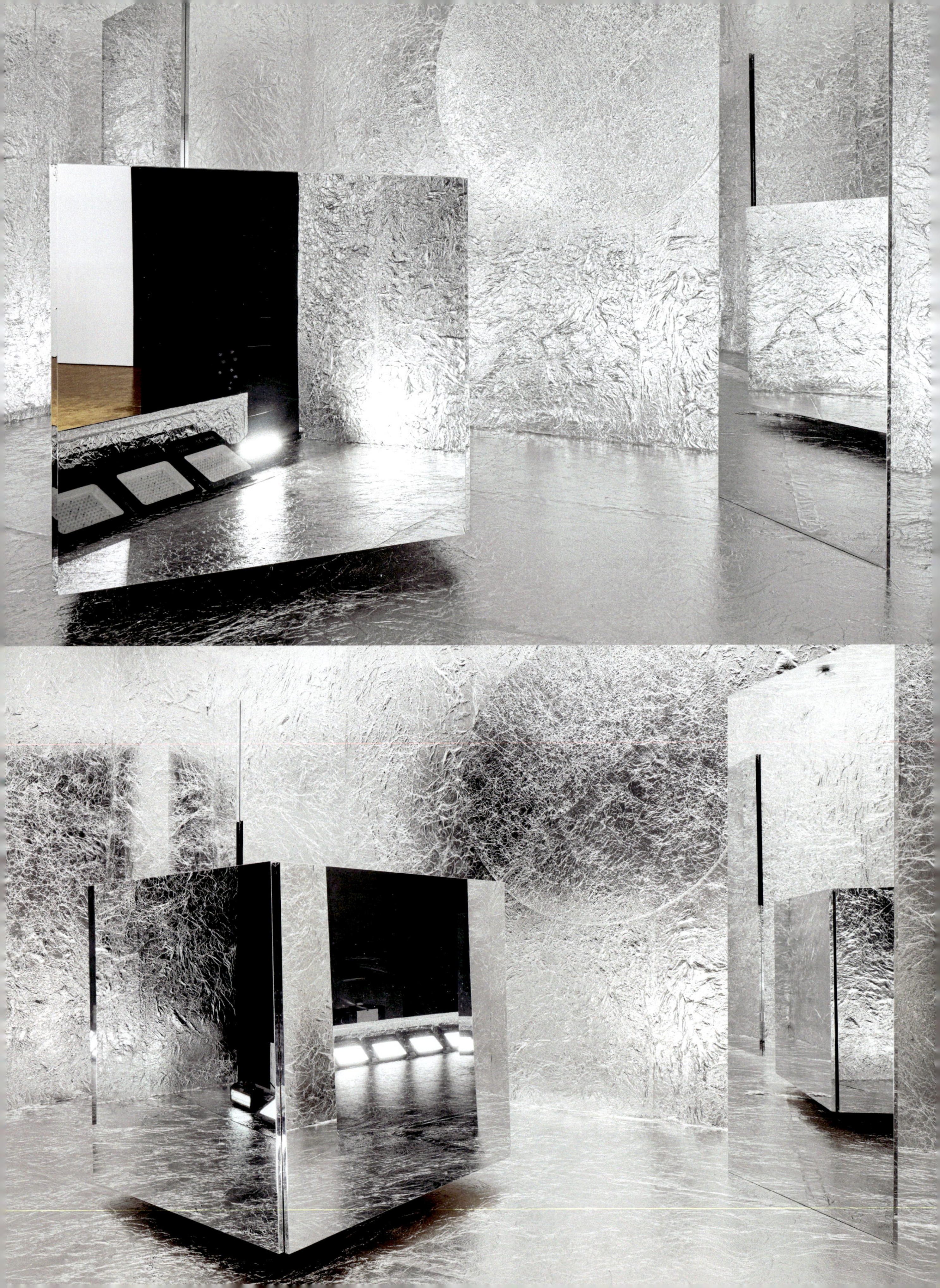

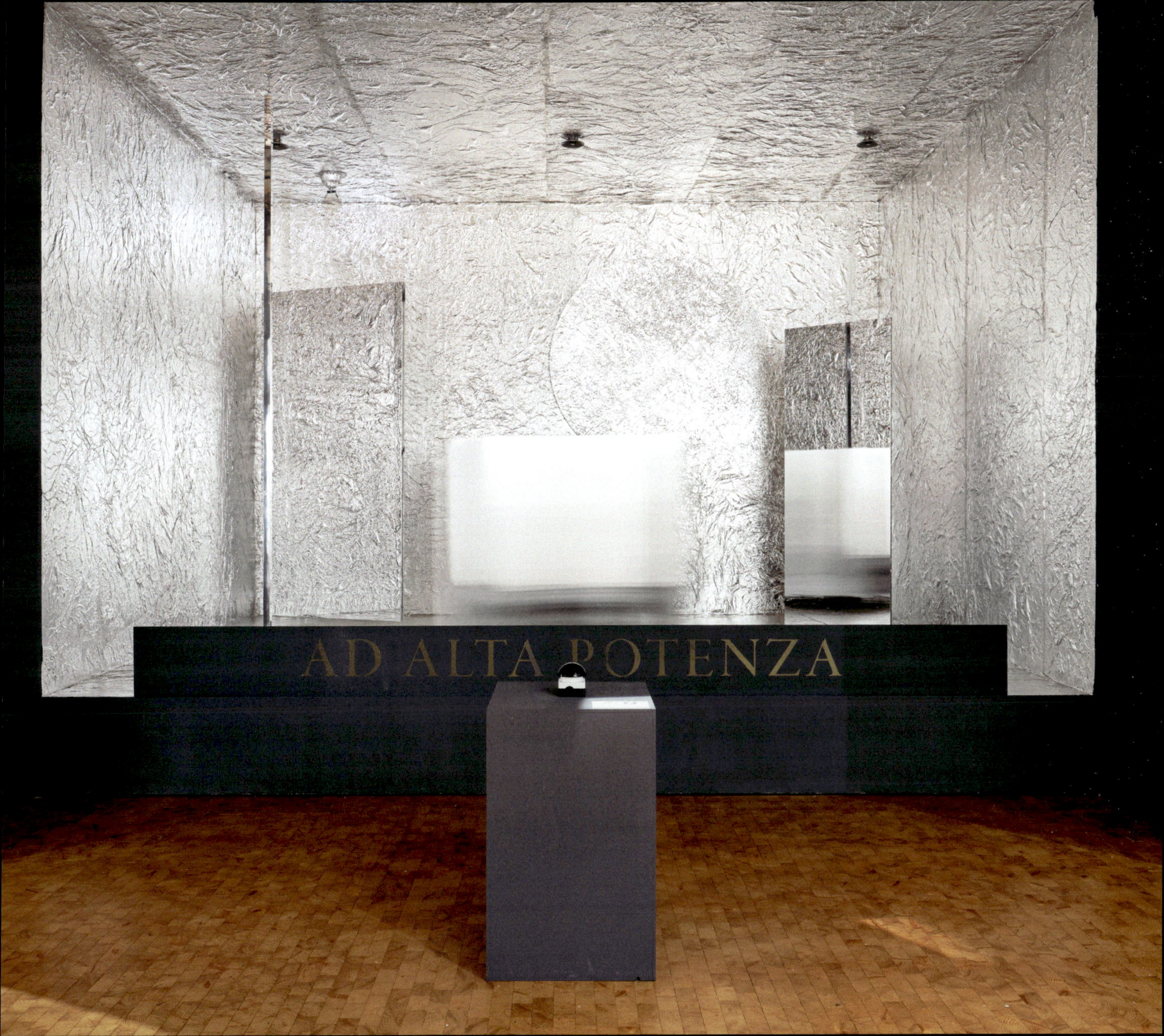
AD ALTA POTENZA

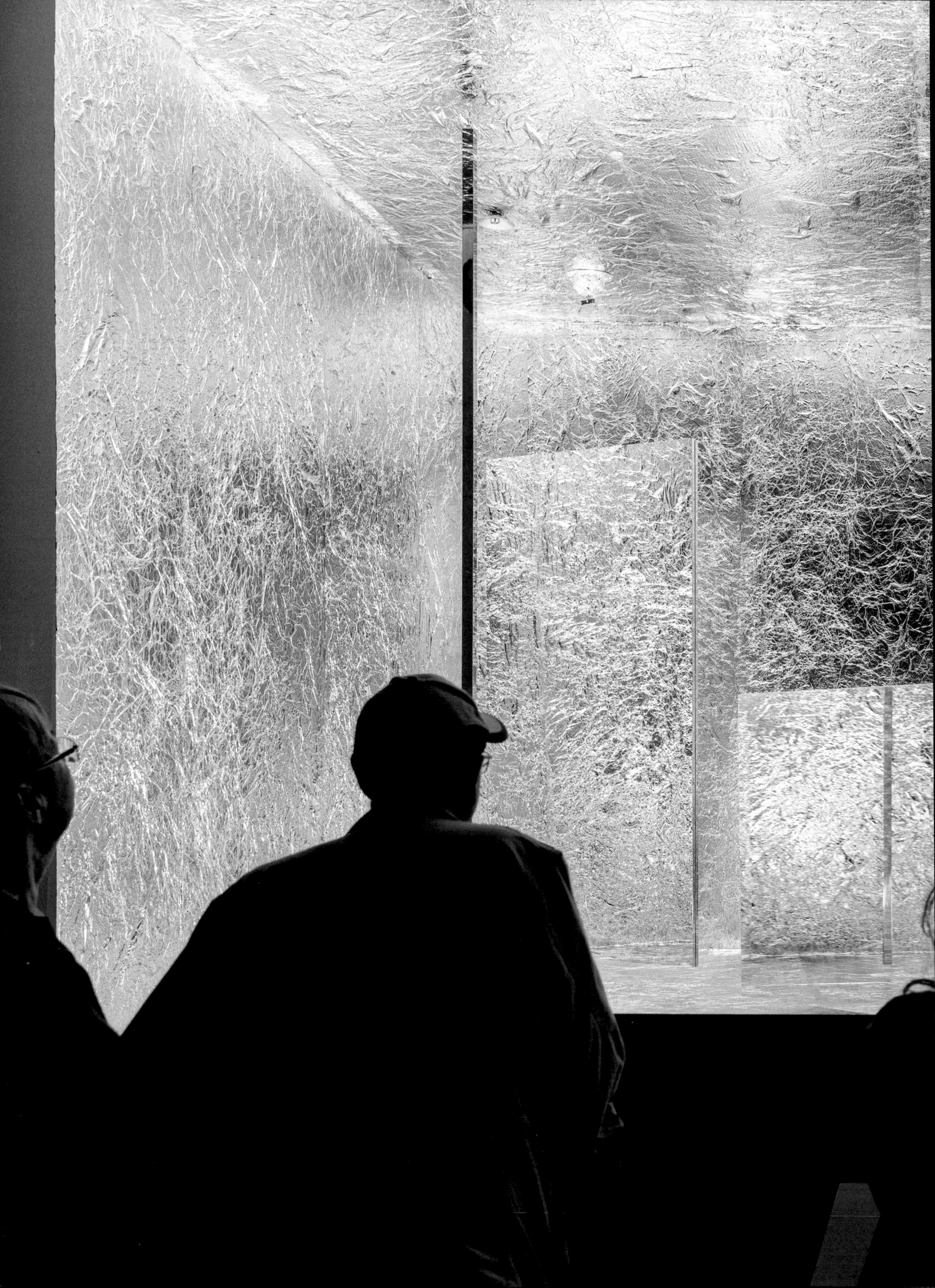

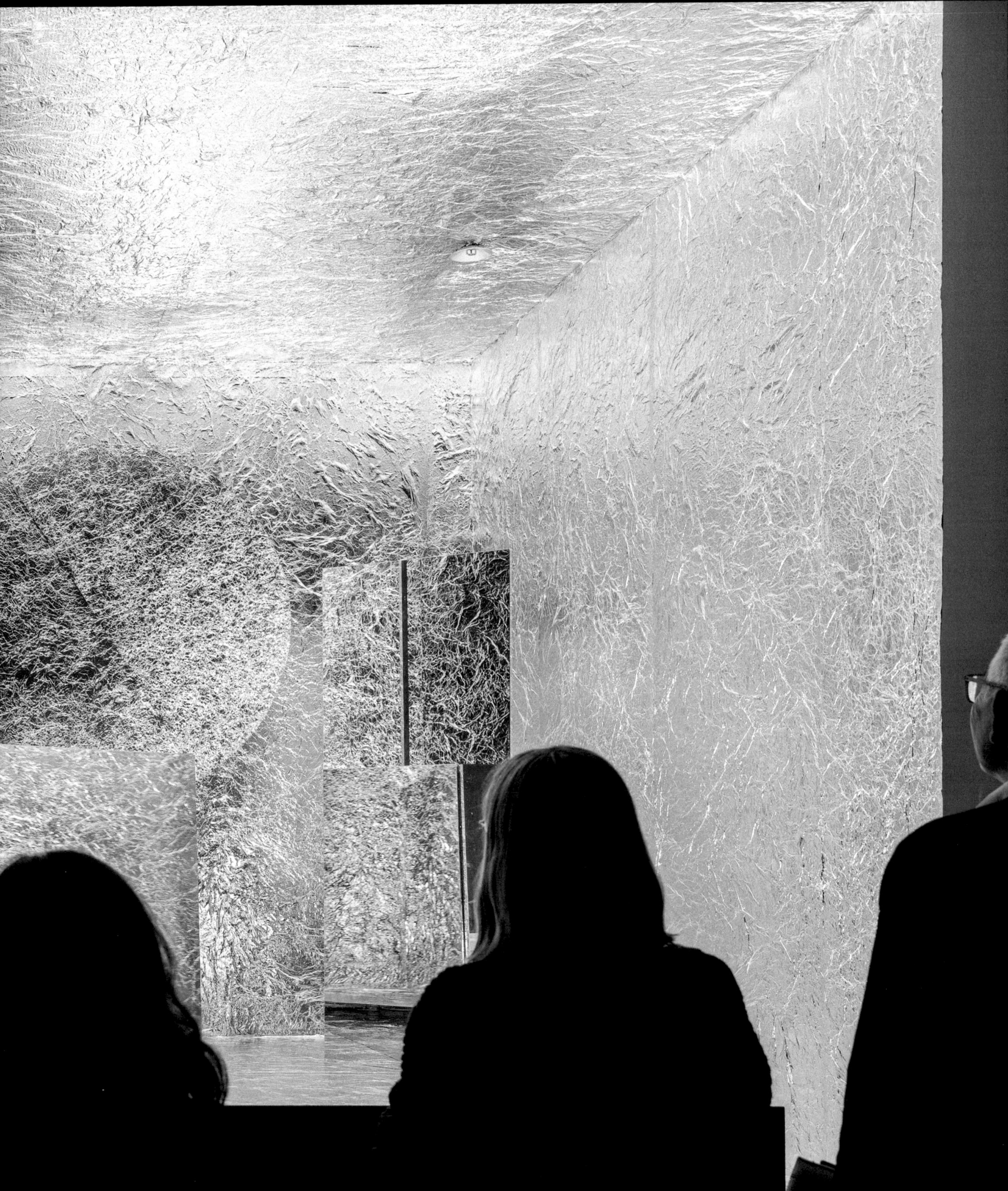

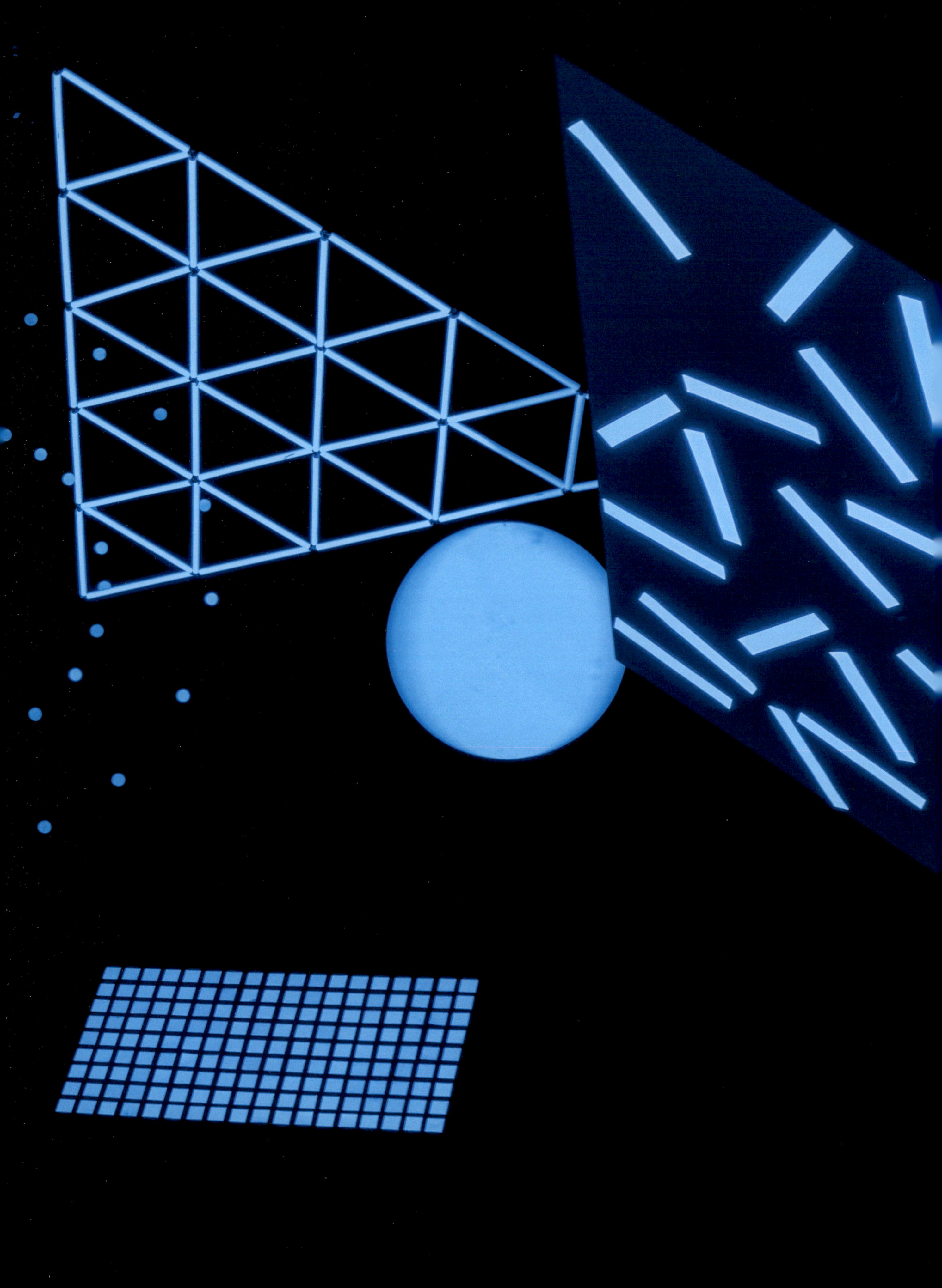

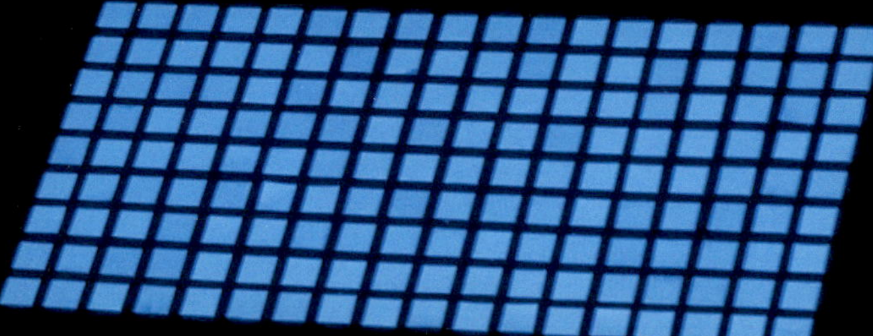

Hommage à Georges de La Tour

The centerpiece of this section of the exhibition is a reconstruction of the *Phosphorus Room*, which Heinz Mack created especially for his 1960 exhibition *Hommage à Georges de La Tour* at the Diogenes Gallery in Berlin, the only time it was shown. Georges de La Tour was a French baroque artist known for painting dramatic scenes illuminated by candlelight, with strong contrasts between light and dark. Mack picked up on this and developed the theme through fire and phosphorus sculptures. La Tour depicted the light of candles and the glow of fire in his works through imitating these visual effects in paint; over three hundred years later, Heinz Mack used light as the pictorial and sculptural material itself.

In the basement of the Berlin gallery, an installation was set up with 200 lighted candles, arranged in a perfect formation on a square mirror surface two meters across. On the opening night, two performers held up a wet white tablecloth over the area of burning candles, which they then dropped just as Mack proclaimed "ZERO." In the sudden darkness that followed, the audience witnessed an unreal afterimage.

The *Phosphorus Room*, by contrast, contained various constructions made of wood or aluminum, which glowed in the dark. Today, fluorescent paint is used instead of the original phosphorus. In the darkness, the painted structures become light sculptures, some of which are motor-driven and move slowly: their forms and materiality dissolve and reappear as traces of light draw the luminous structures out of the darkness. The visual events are accompanied by a computer-generated sound composition that was conceived especially for this exhibition. Mack's *Phosphorus Room* is understood as an early precursor of his light environments.

← *fig. 61* Heinz Mack, *Hommage à Georges de La Tour*, 1960/2023, detail

*Light is what gives space its sensuality, its atmosphere, its transparency. Light makes space lighter.**

Works in the exhibition:
All works courtesy of the artist
unless otherwise noted

Hommage à Georges de La Tour
1960/2023
Light environment: 9 fluorescent, partly kinetic sculptures, computer-generated sound
Reconstructed in cooperation with ZKM | Karlsruhe, 2023
Collection ZKM | Karlsruhe
→ *figs. 61, 62, 63, 64*

Components:

The Net Triangle
1960/2023
Wood, fluorescent paint
43 pieces of wood à 50 cm, perimeter 750 cm (250 + 250 + 250 cm)

The Propeller
1960/2023
Wood, fluorescent paint
230 × 190 cm

The Moving Hoops
1960/2023
Aluminum, black and fluorescent paint, motor
Ø ca. 80 cm, height 120 cm

The Moon
1960/2023
Wood, fluorescent paint, motor
Ø 100 cm

Checkered Grid
1960/2023
Wood, fluorescent paint, metal bracket
200 × 80 cm

Checkered Grid
1960/2023
Wood, fluorescent paint, metal bracket
150 × 70 cm

Large Checkered Field
1960/2023
Aluminum sheet, curved on a roller bench, fluorescent paint
180 × 135 cm

Wall Spiral
1960/2023
Fluorescent paint
Ø 270 cm

Large Side Wing
1960/2023
Wood, hinges, fluorescent paint
250 × 200 cm

Composition for the Phosphorus Room
2023
Computer-generated composition
Sound design: Götz Dipper

* Heinz Mack, *Sahara Project*, 1959 (typoscript, Archive Heinz Mack). Translated from the German.

→ *figs. 62, 63* Heinz Mack, *Hommage à Georges de La Tour*, 1960/2023, model

→→ *fig. 64* Heinz Mack, *Hommage à Georges de La Tour*, 1960/2023

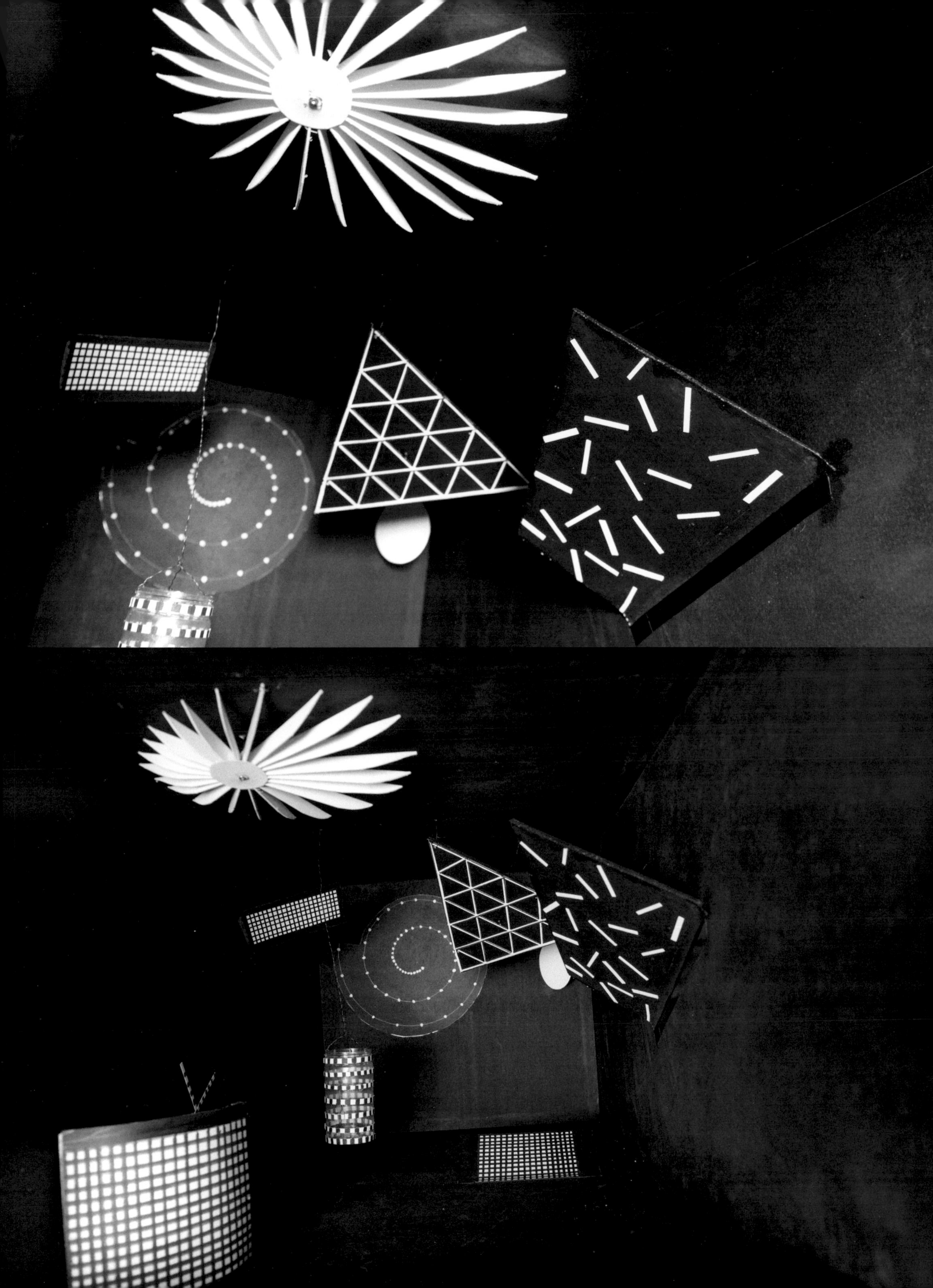

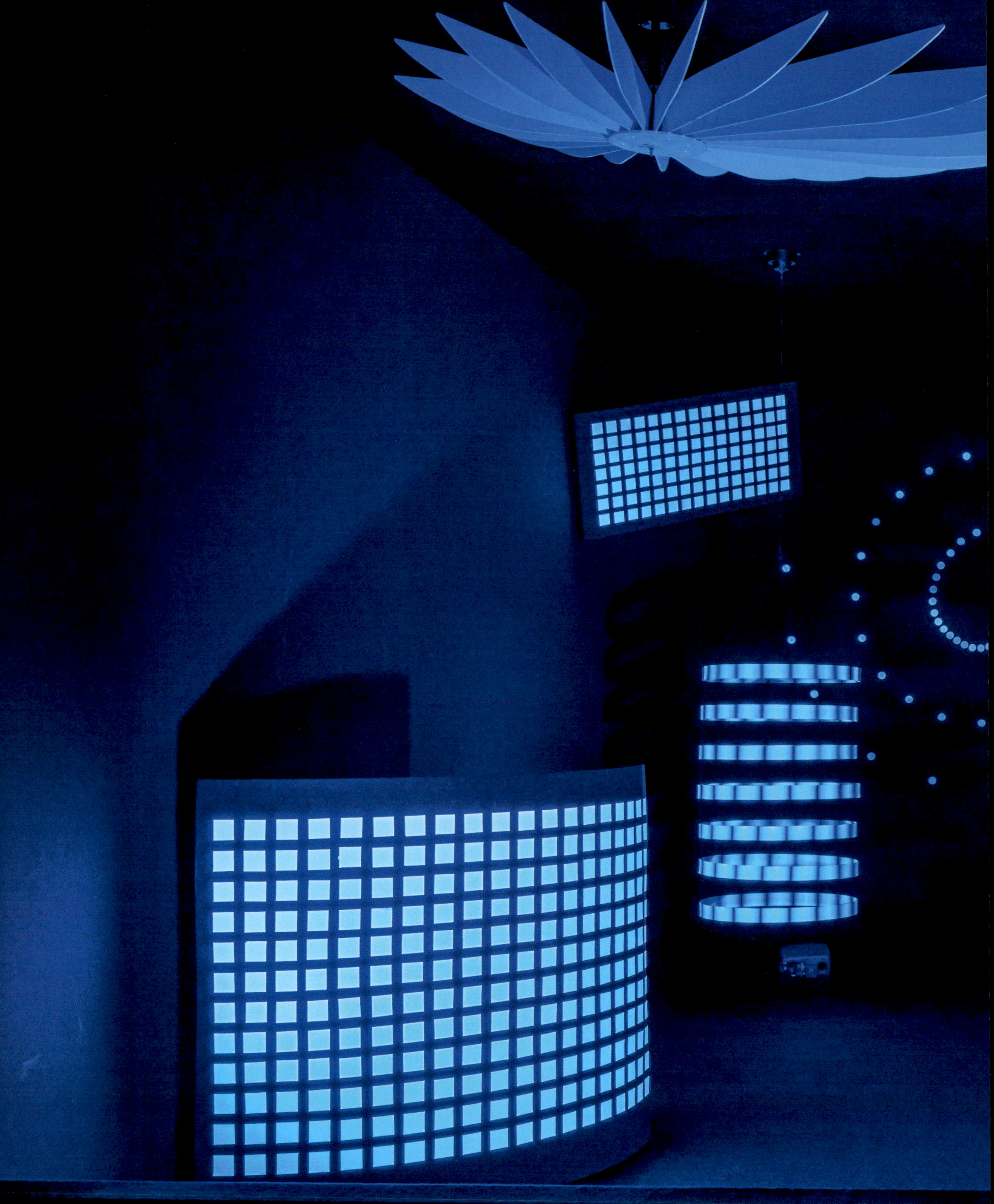

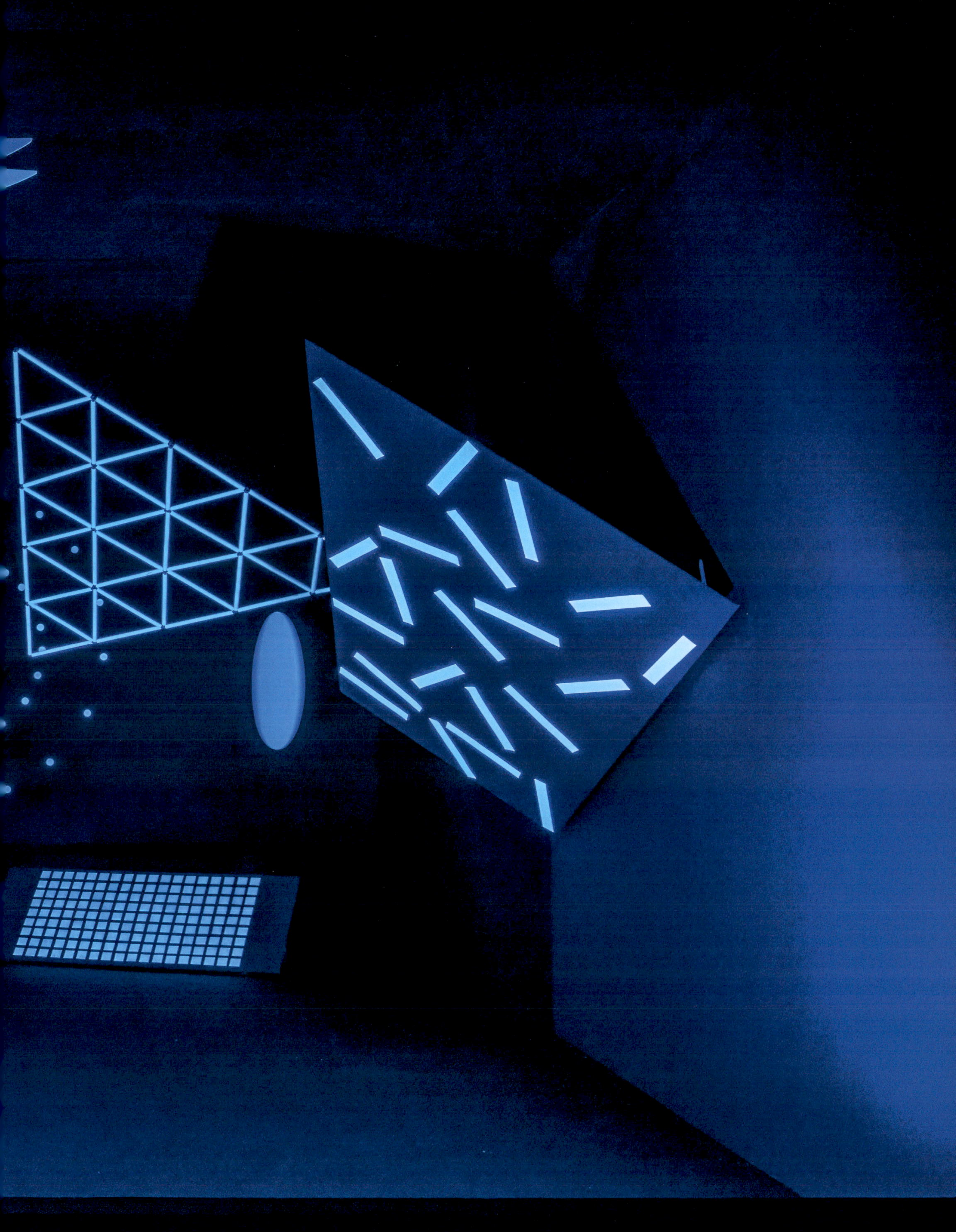

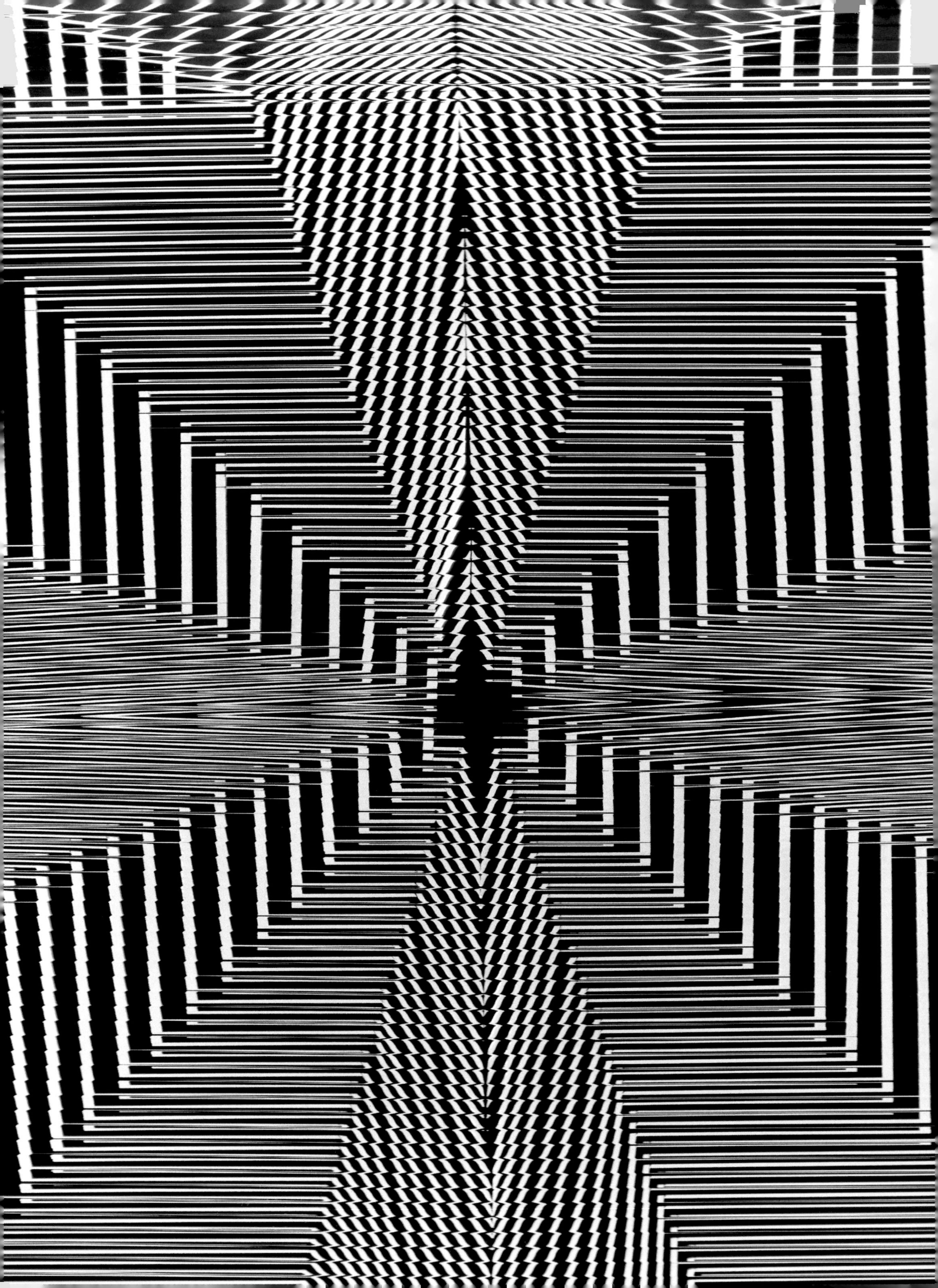

Cycle of Light

Engaging with movement is a fundamental theme in Mack's work. In the early ZERO paintings, dynamic structures suggest movement; in the light reliefs and light steles, the vibration of light on the surface acts virtually as an illusory visual movement. In the group of works called "rotors," which he created from 1958 onwards, Heinz Mack finally worked with real movement for the first time. These apparatuses consist of a square enclosed box in which one or more discs rotate slowly, sometimes in opposite directions. The circular reliefs are designed as complex structural fields, usually made of aluminum, stainless steel, wood, or plastic, and sometimes even paper. In the majority of these works, translucent corrugated glass panels obscure the view of the inner workings and create distorted reflections that flash out from within.

The various rotors, also known as *light dynamos*, are classified as belonging to the genre of kinetic art (*kinesis* is Ancient Greek for movement). Mack was not so much concerned with the movement as such, he was more interested in making light and time visible. The *light dynamos* generate new manifestations of light with each rotation. The continuous flow of movement is an invitation to linger and meditate. Here, Mack's immaterial materials – light, movement, and time – meet with physical sculptural materials and create an entirely new aesthetic experience.

← *fig. 65* Heinz Mack, *Kaleidoscope Rotor*, 2015 (idea: 1961), detail

*In my work I examine and strive for structural phenomena whose stringent logic I disturb or extend through aleatory interventions, in other words random actions. For if a creative process is completely determined, its results come across as undetermined, in fact positively chaotic in their arbitrariness, and thus they are the opposite of the intended stringency.**

Works in the exhibition:
All works courtesy of the artist
unless otherwise noted

Kaleidoscope Rotor
2015 (idea: 1961)
Rotor: wood, corrugated glass, electrical equipment, motor
154.5 × 154.5 × 50.5 cm, base 50 × 90 × 40 cm
→ *figs. 65, 66, 67*

Untitled
1970 (idea: 1960)
Rotor: aluminum, corrugated glass, stainless steel, wood, motor
151 × 151 × 43 cm, base 60 × 90 × 40 cm
→ *fig. 69*

Checkered Rotor
1967
Rotor: acrylic glass, aluminum, wood, stainless steel, motor
153.5 × 153.5 × 33.5 cm, base 60 × 125.5 × 35 cm
→ *figs. 71, 75*

ZERO Silver-Rotor
1960
Rotor: aluminum, corrugated glass, wood, stainless steel, motor
153.5 × 153.5 × 33.5 cm, base 70 × 120 × 30 cm
→ *fig. 73*

Castor and Pollux
1968 (replica from 2014)
Rotor: synthetic material, acrylic glass, aluminum, stainless steel, wood, motor
164 × 164 × 21 cm, base 50 × 100.5 × 42 cm
→ *fig. 68*

Rotor for Light Grid II
1968
Rotor: aluminum, wood, acrylic glass, stainless steel, motor
155 × 155 × 38 cm, base 60.5 × 121 × 38.5 cm
→ *figs. 70, 257*

White Lamella Rotor
1963
Rotor: wood, corrugated glass, motor
153 × 153 × 37.5 cm, base 60 × 100 × 30 cm
→ *figs. 4, 72, 76*

Mirror Rotor
1960
Rotor: wood, mirror glass, acrylic glass, motor
153 × 153 × 36 cm, base 60 × 90 × 40 cm
→ *figs. 74, 75, 253*

* Heinz Mack, "Structure," in: Heinz Mack, *Mack. Life and Work 1931–2011* (Cologne: Dumont, 2011), 480. Translated from German.

→ *fig. 66* Heinz Mack, *Kaleidoscope Rotor*, 2015 (idea: 1961)

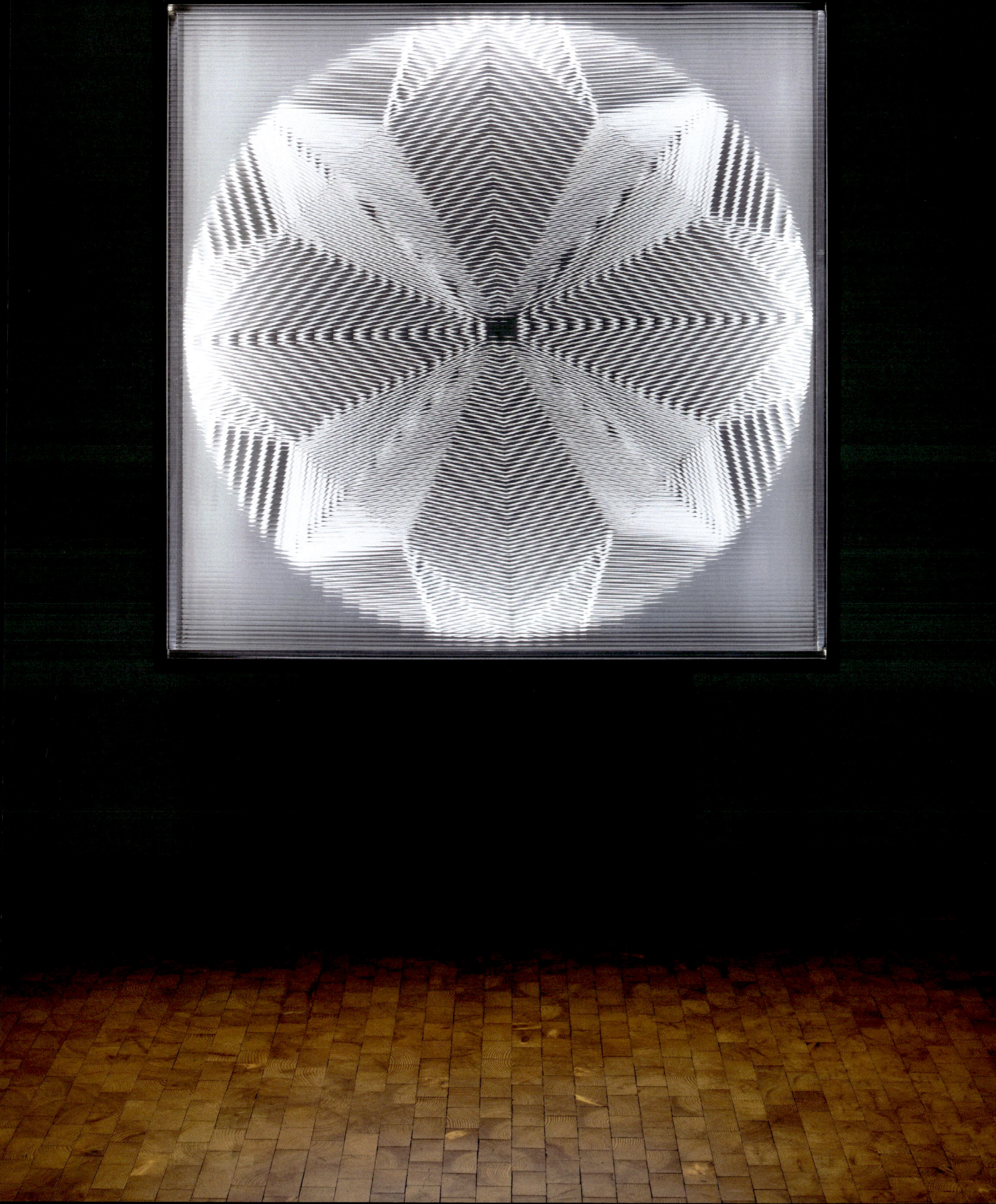

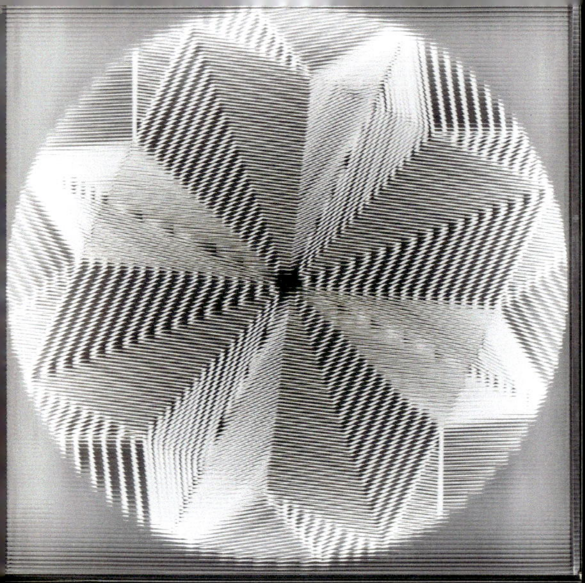

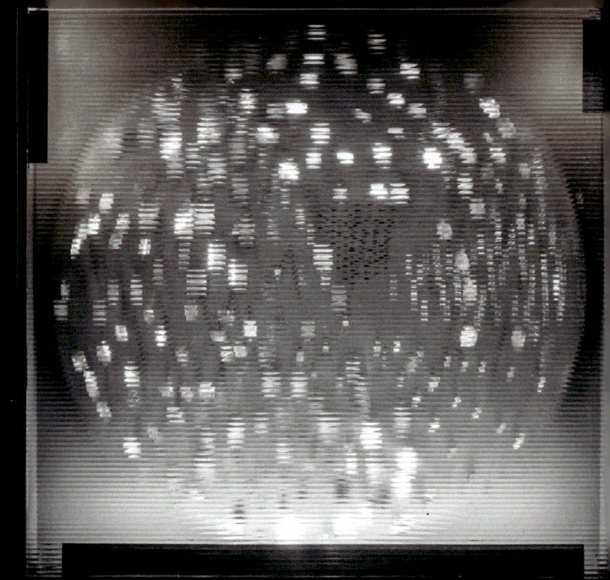

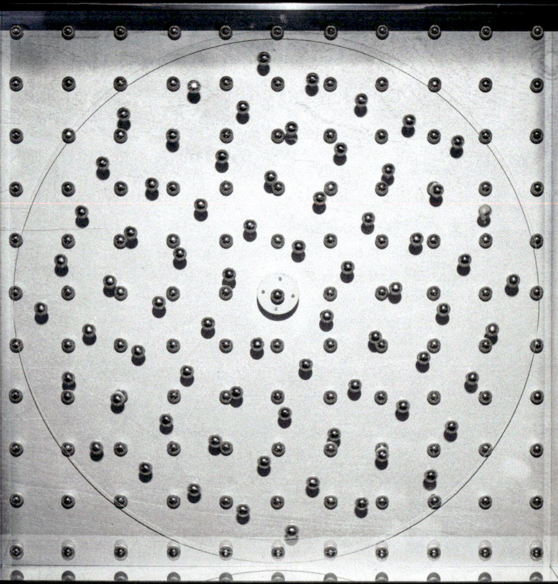

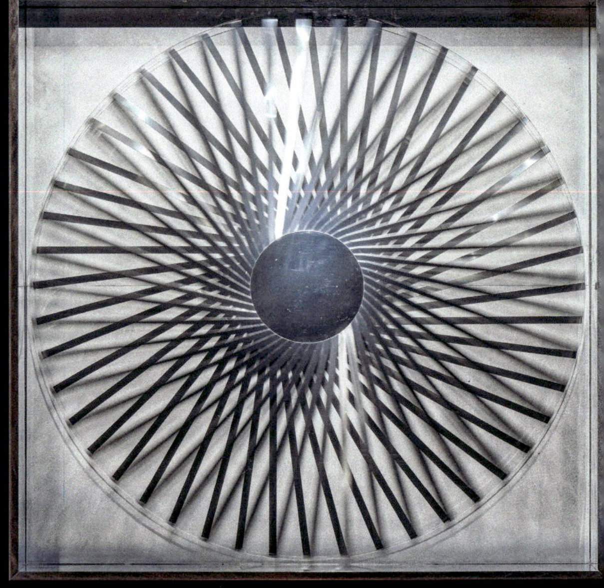

fig. 67 Heinz Mack, *Kaleidoscope Rotor*, 2015 (idea: 1961)
fig. 68 Heinz Mack, *Castor and Pollux*, 1968 (replica from 2014)

↑ *fig. 69* Heinz Mack, *Untitled*, 1970 (idea: 1960)
↓ *fig. 70* Heinz Mack, *Rotor for Light Grid II*, 1968

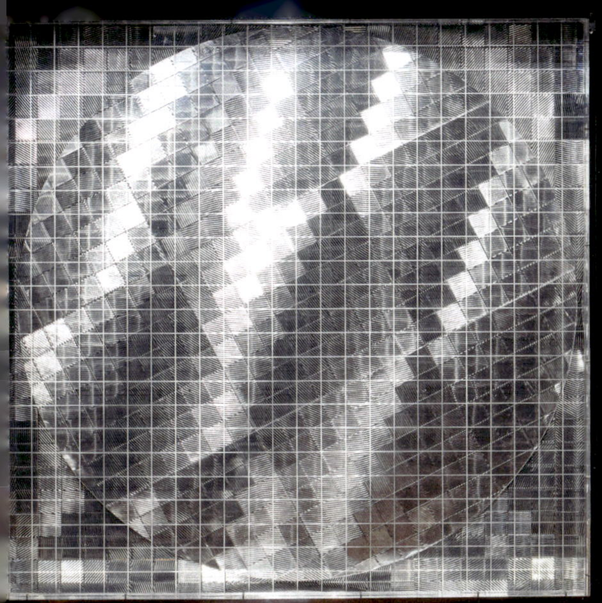

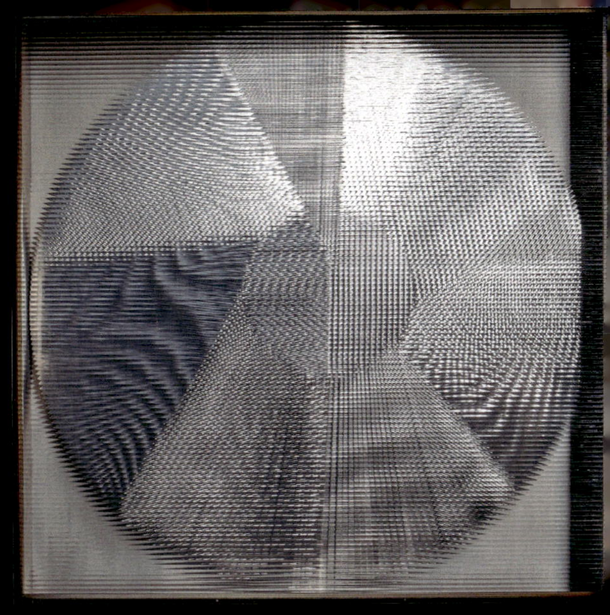

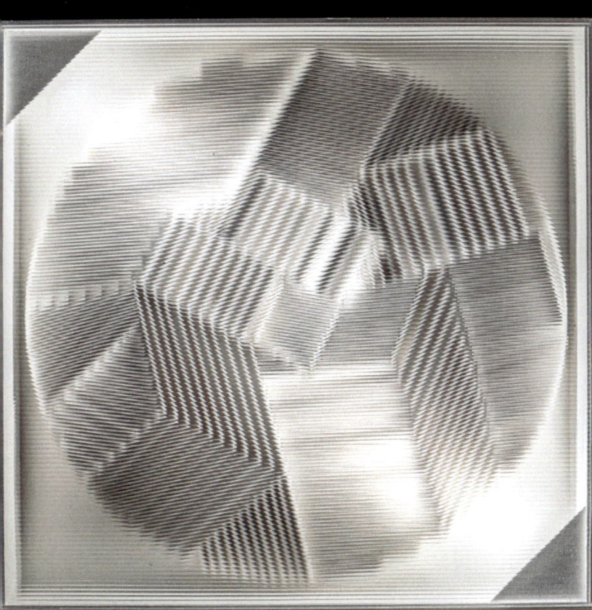

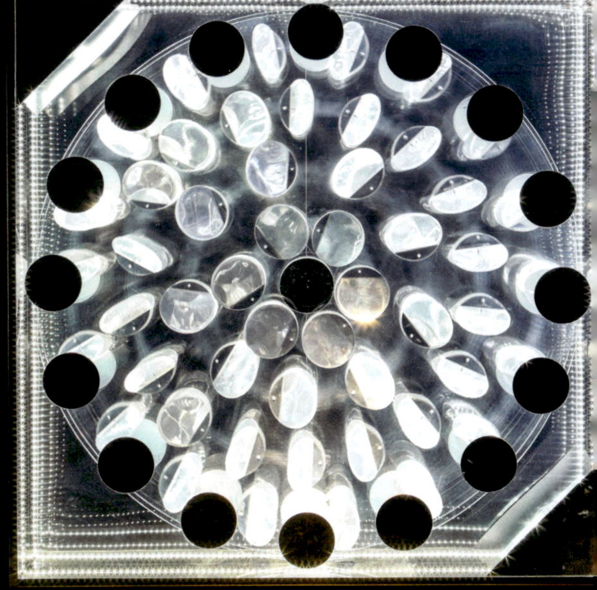

g. 71 Heinz Mack, *Checkered Rotor*, 1967
g. 72 Heinz Mack, *White Lamella Rotor*, 1963

↑ *fig. 73* Heinz Mack, *ZERO Silver-Rotor*, 1960
↓ *fig. 74* Heinz Mack, *Mirror Rotor*, 1969

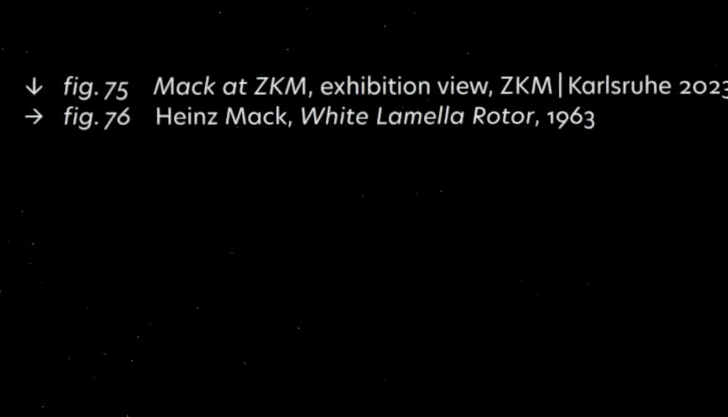

↓ *fig. 75* *Mack at ZKM*, exhibition view, ZKM | Karlsruhe 2023
→ *fig. 76* Heinz Mack, *White Lamella Rotor*, 1963

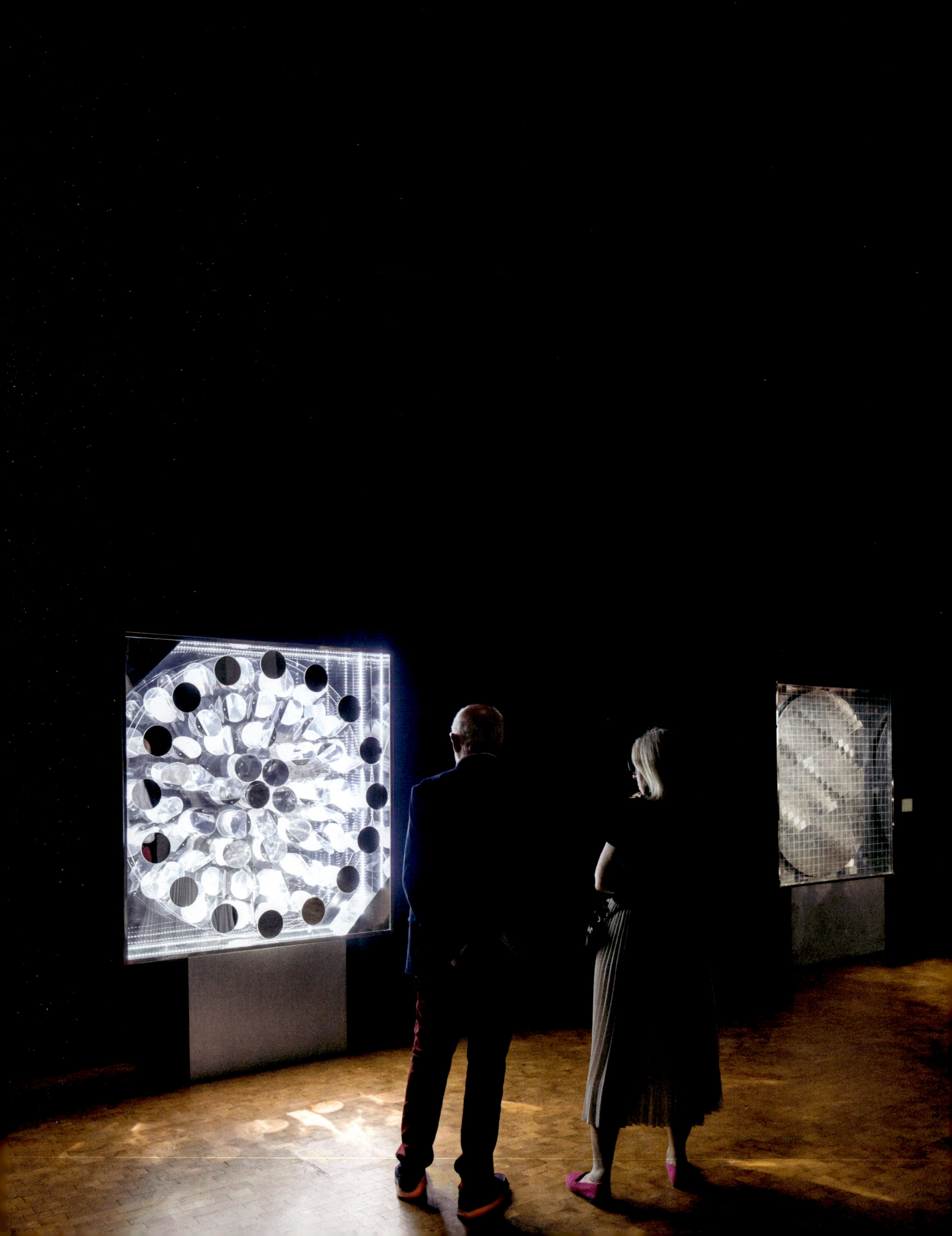

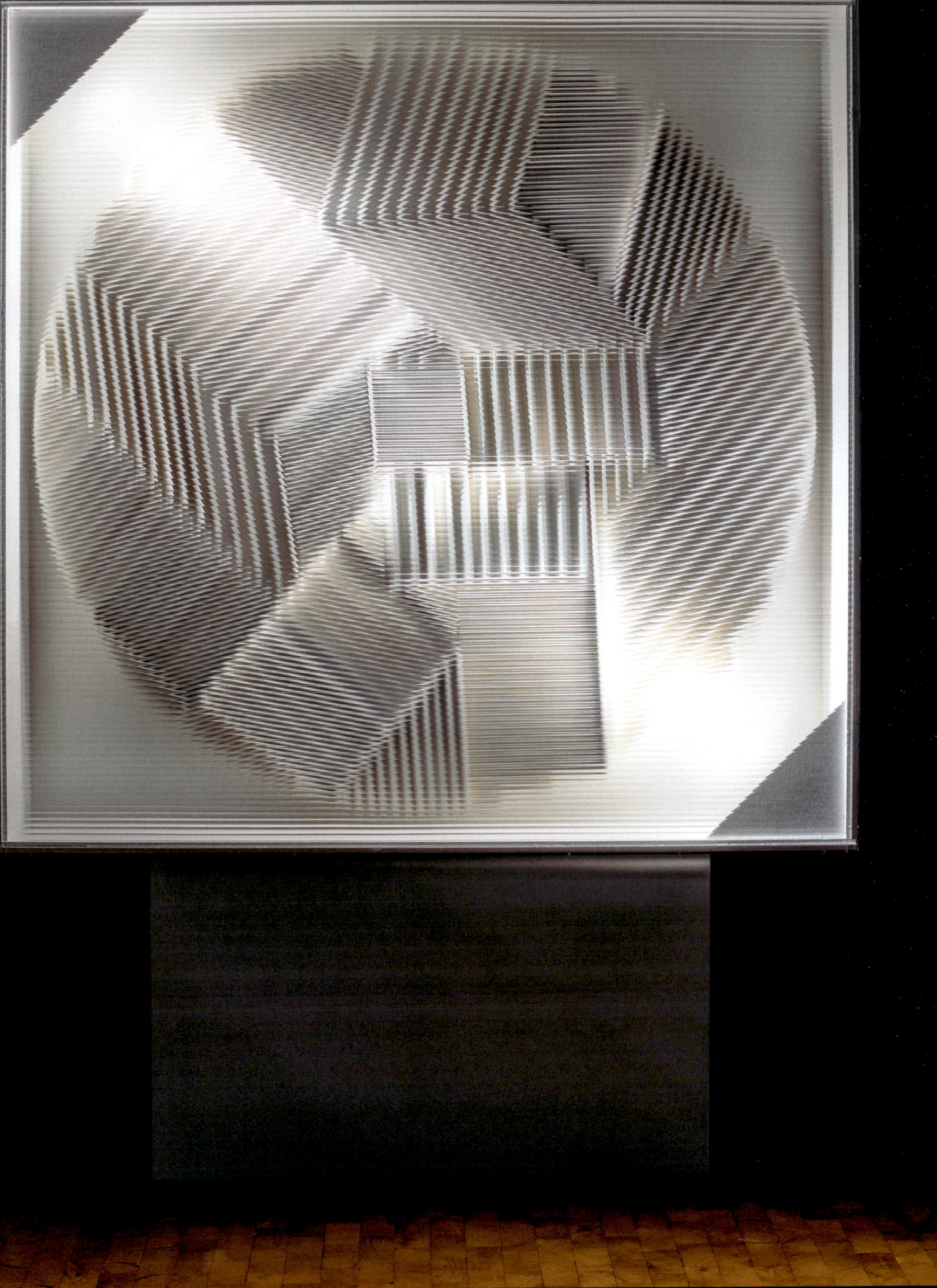

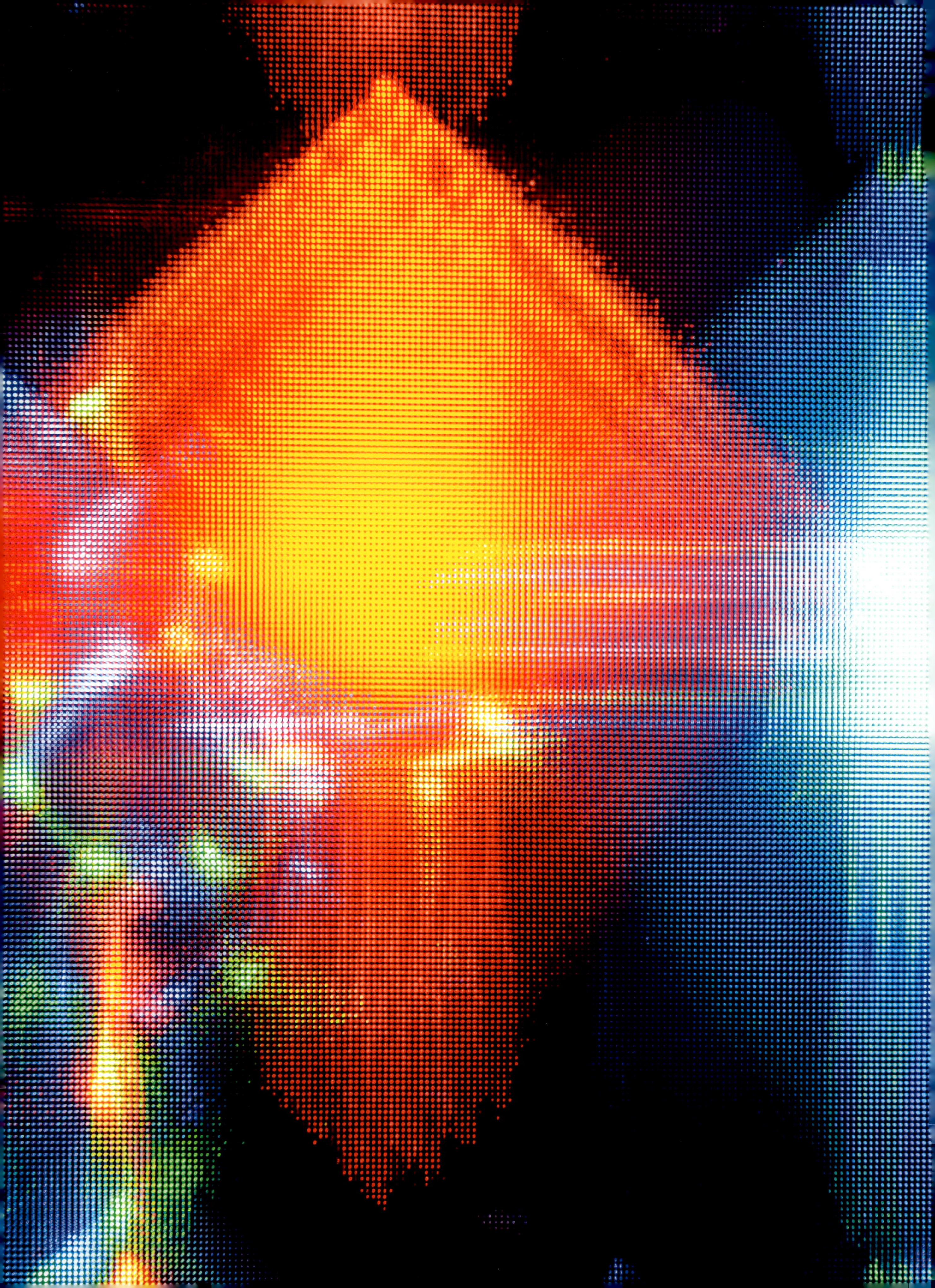

Small Light Orchestra

Sound travels through a medium as an acoustic wave and has a direct physical effect on the listener. This quality is also a characteristic of Heinz Mack's art. The artist is a music enthusiast and piano player. His works vibrate with dynamic structures, light, and color that let them appear almost musical. Mack used motorized rotors to create new light effects and later combined colored artificial light with real movement.

The artist employs electric light sources, housed inside black boxes or transparent acrylic glass cubes, that are trained directly on the viewers. Translucent screens and Fresnel lenses are used to optically distort the projection of light. Unlike the rotors, the motorized rotations of the kinetic light artworks are highly accelerated, creating a spectacular, futuristic effect.

This area of the exhibition presents a series of kinetic light works created in the period from 1960 to 2022. One of the highlights here is the *Cabinet of Light Treasures* (1964). Integrated into a mirrored display case are various shiny silver light objects, some of which are motorized, characteristic of the artist's early work. This small cabinet of wonders seems to glow from within. The contours of the objects dissolve and are lost in an immaterial appearance. The work utilizes all the essential elements of light kinetics. Mack's multifaceted repertoire evokes a sonorous concert of light.

← *fig. 77* Heinz Mack, *Light Screen – Dancing*, 2022, detail

*The line is a trace of time in space, as much as it is a trace of movement. In the line, time is on the run from itself. Time knows no standstill.**

Works in the exhibition:
All works courtesy of the artist
unless otherwise noted

Light Stars
2022
Light-kinetic sculpture: Pyra acrylic glass, wood, electrical equipment
57 × 57 × 57 cm
→ *fig. 100*

Light Wings – Moving
2022
Light-kinetic sculpture: Fresnel lenses, wood, electrical equipment
48 × 48 × 51 cm

Light Grid
2022
Light-kinetic sculpture: Pyra acrylic glass, wood, electrical equipment
50 × 50 × 50 cm
→ *fig. 89*

Light Space
2022
Light-kinetic sculpture: Fresnel lens, wood, aluminum, electrical equipment
48.5 × 48.5 × 50.5 cm
→ *fig. 87*

Light Box
1960 (replica from 2010)
Light-kinetic sculpture: wood, acrylic glass, electrical equipment
55 × 55 × 25.5 cm
→ *fig. 88*

Immaterial Appearance of a Transparent Sphere in front of a Cube
2022
Light-kinetic sculpture: acrylic glass, wood, electrical equipment
41 × 41 × 41 cm
→ *fig. 93*

Fire Ring
1960
Light-kinetic sculpture: acrylic glass, wood, electrical equipment
31.3 × 31.3 × 27 cm
→ *figs. 81, 82*

Space Corner (4 Phases)
2004 (idea: 1980–1992)
Light-kinetic sculpture: Fresnel lenses, electrical equipment, wood
49 × 54 × 54 cm
→ *figs. 84, 85, 86*

Untitled
1969
Light-kinetic sculpture: acrylic glass, wood, electrical equipment
40 × 51 × 36 cm, base 50 × 51 × 36 cm
→ *fig. 90*

Light Fan
2009
Light-kinetic sculpture: wood, Fresnel lens, electrical equipment, motor
53 × 40 × 40 cm
→ *figs. 79, 99*

Untitled
2005
Light-kinetic sculpture: wood, aluminum, Pyra acrylic glass, electrical equipment
49.5 × 32 × 32 cm

Kinetic Light Cube
1968/1977
Light-kinetic sculpture: electrical light radiator, acrylic glass, mirror, electrical equipment
70 × 70 × 70 cm, plate 0,6 × 90 × 90 cm
→ *figs. 92, 101*

Small Cascade of Colors
2022
Light-kinetic sculpture: aluminum, acrylic glass, neon tube, electrical equipment
71.5 × 18.5 × 8 cm, plinth Ø 25 cm
→ *fig. 91*

Light Symbol
2022
Light-kinetic sculpture: special lens, aluminum, wood, electrical equipment
47.5 × 47.5 × 46 cm
→ *fig. 102*

Light Screen – Dancing
2022
Light-kinetic sculpture: Pyra acrylic glass, wood, electrical equipment
50.5 × 50.5 × 52.2 cm
→ *fig. 77*

Electrical Sun
2010
Light-kinetic sculpture: wood, acrylic glass, electrical equipment
70 × 70 × 37 cm
→ *fig. 80*

Light Comb
2004
Light-kinetic sculpture: acrylic glass, glass, electrical equipment, wood
170 × 20 × 37 cm
→ *fig. 94*

Light Ladder
2010 (idea: 1970)
Light-kinetic sculpture: aluminum, electrical equipment, stainless steel
400 × 50 × 12 cm, plinth 17 × 80 × 80 cm
→ *fig. 162*

Cabinet of Light Treasures
1964
Light-kinetic sculpture: acrylic glass, aluminum, wood, electrical equipment
185 × 67 × 56 cm
Private collection
→ *figs. 2, 78*

Untitled
2022 (idea: 1970)
Light-kinetic sculpture: Fresnel lenses, acrylic glass, wood, electrical equipment
61.5 × 61 × 61 cm
→ *fig. 83*

* Dieter Honisch, "Interview mit Heinz Mack," in: Dieter Honisch, *Mack. Skulpturen 1953–1986* (Düsseldorf: Econ, 1986), 119. Translated from the German.

→ *fig. 78* Heinz Mack, *Cabinet of Light Treasures*, 1964

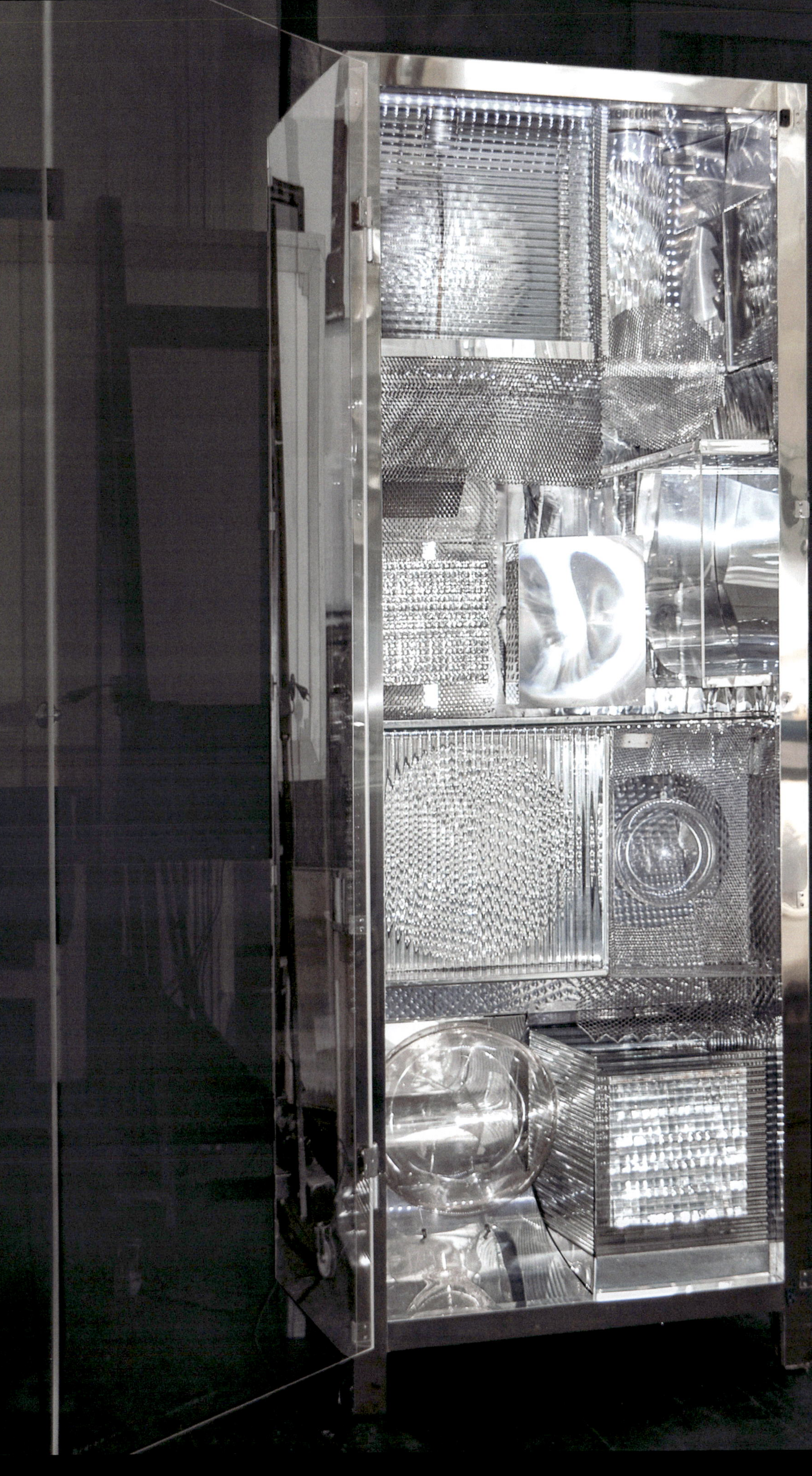

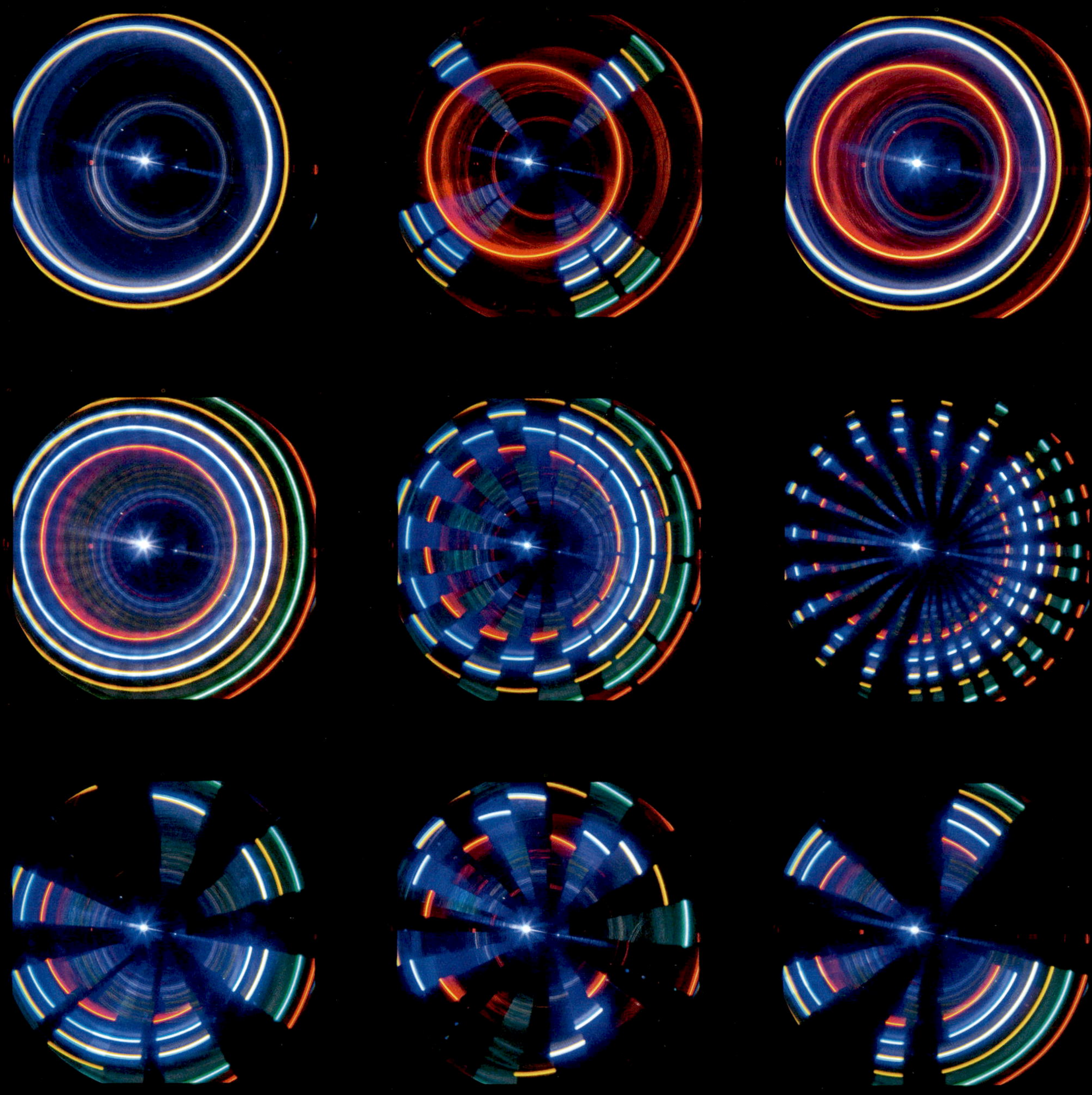

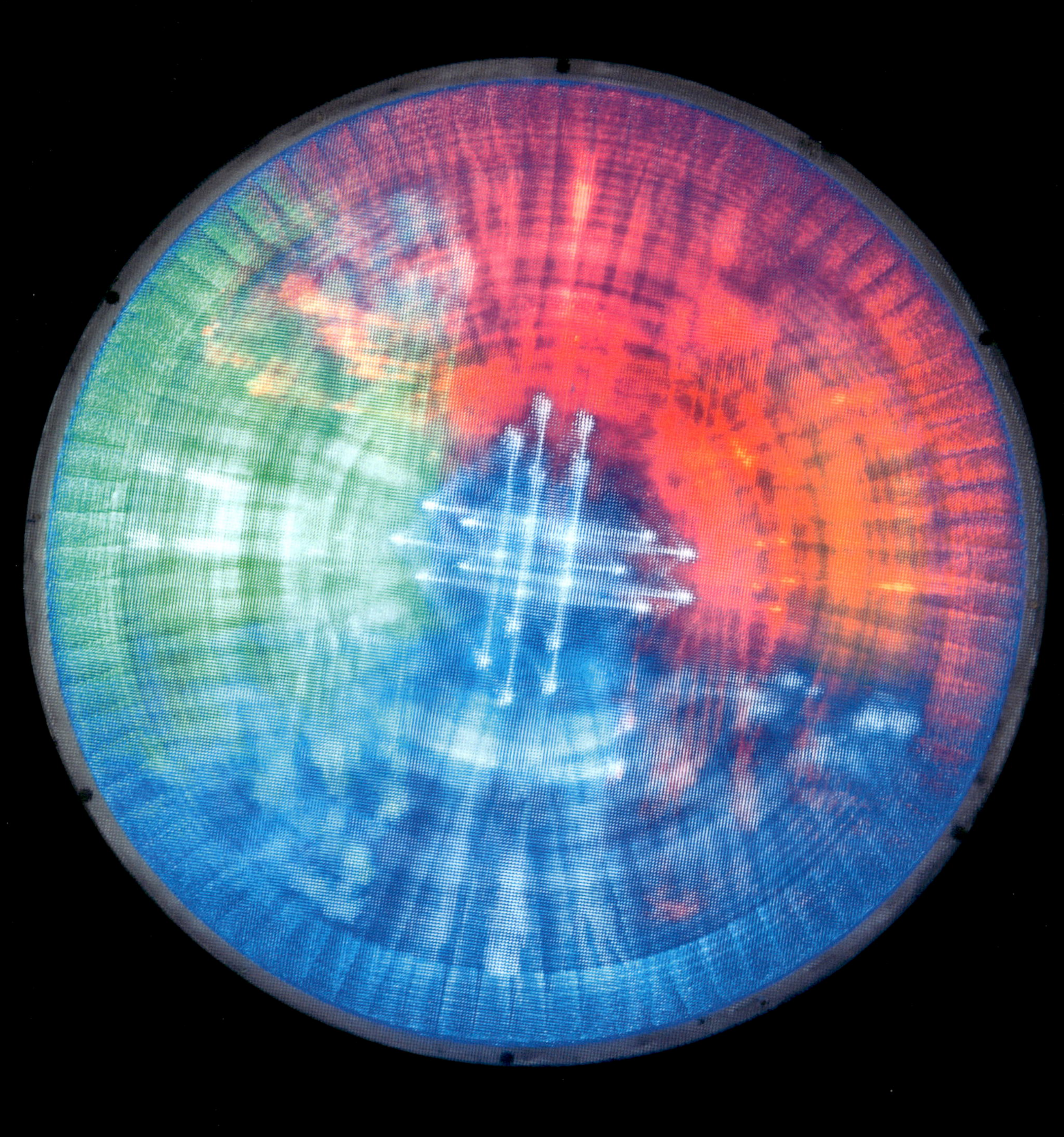

← *fig. 79* Heinz Mack, *Light Fan*, 2009
↑ *fig. 80* Heinz Mack, *Electrical Sun*, 2010

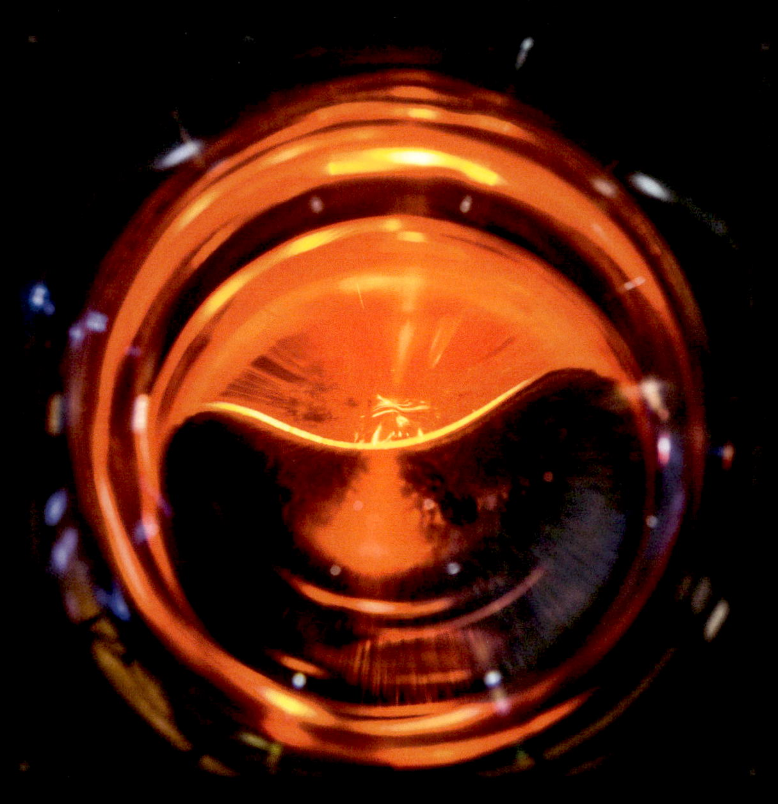

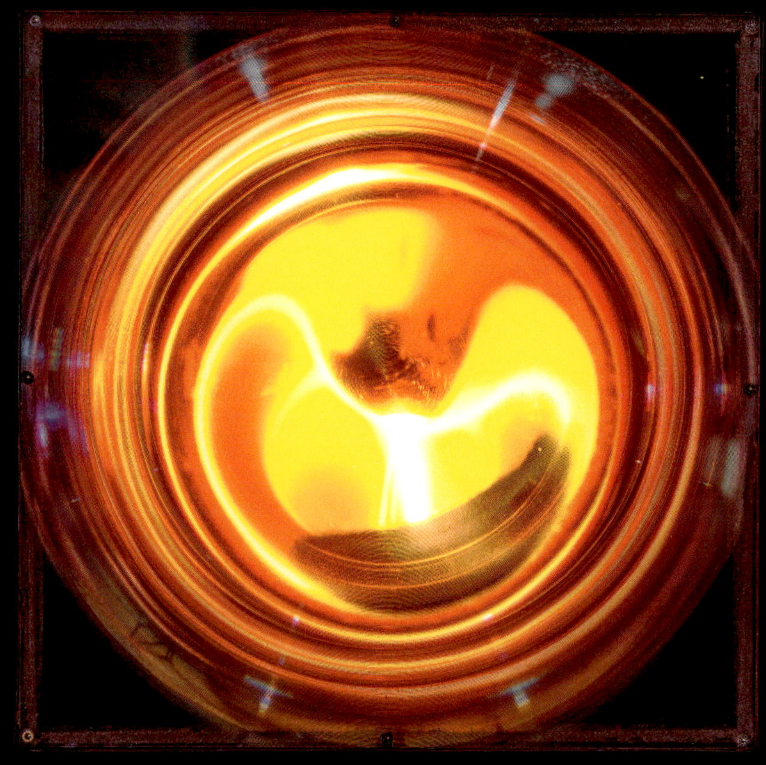

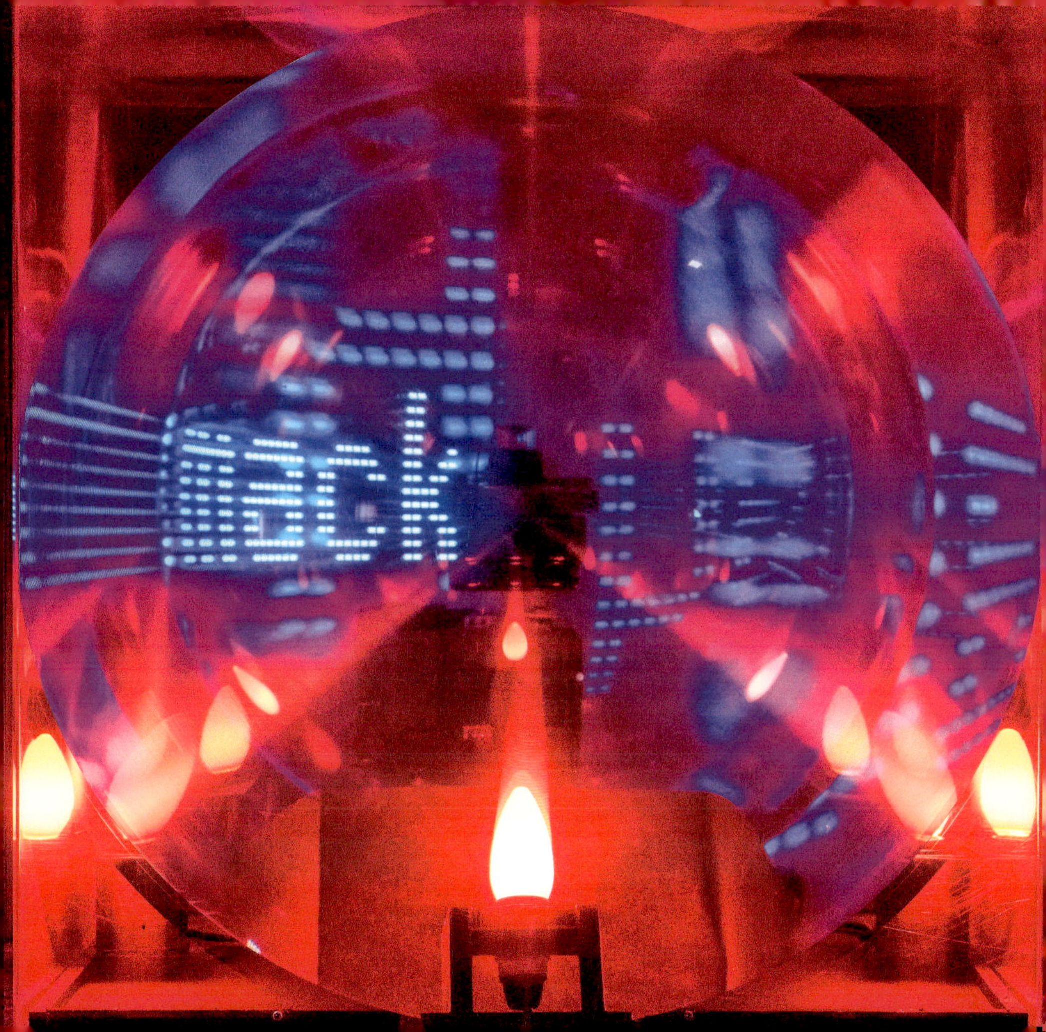

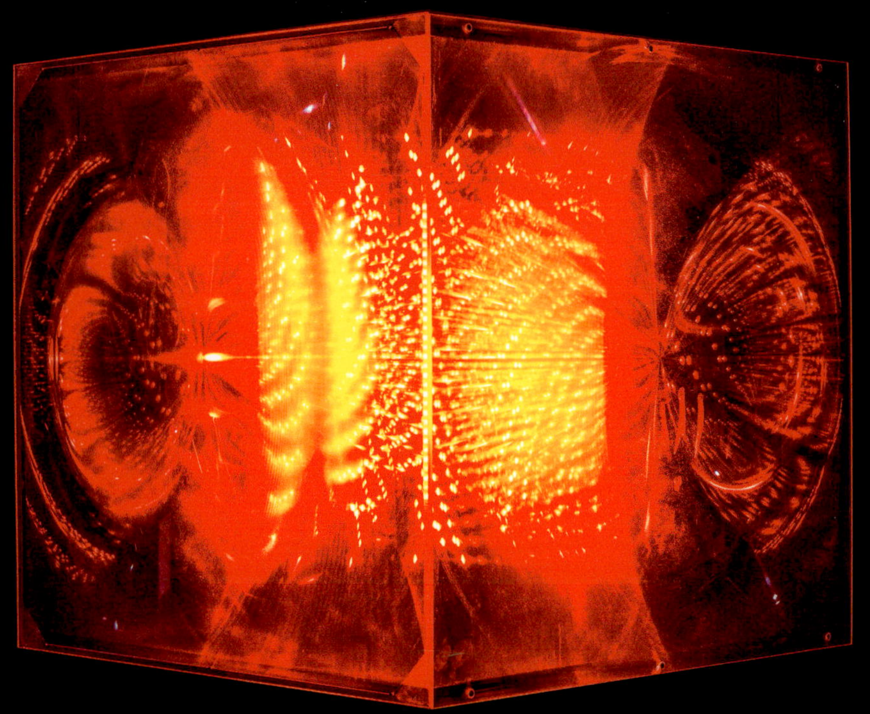

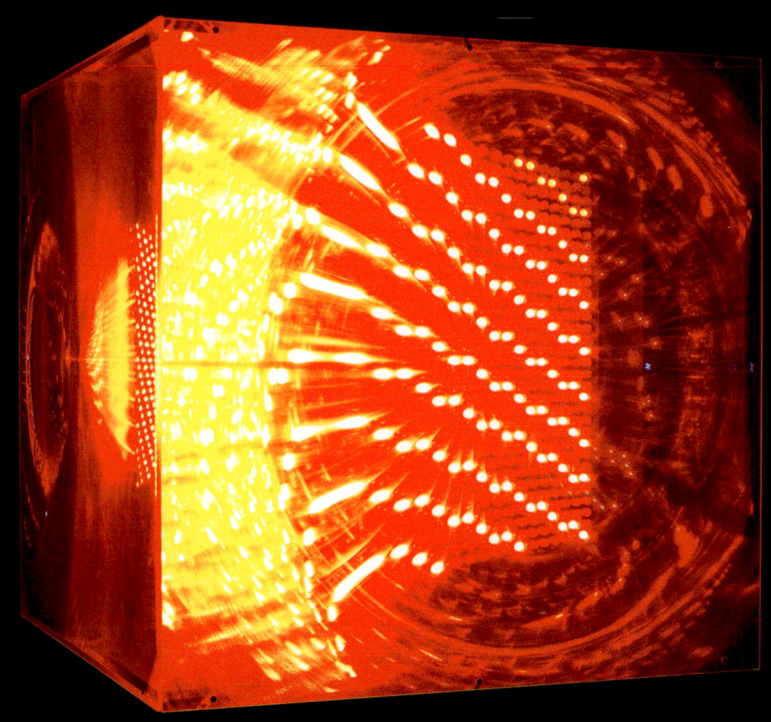

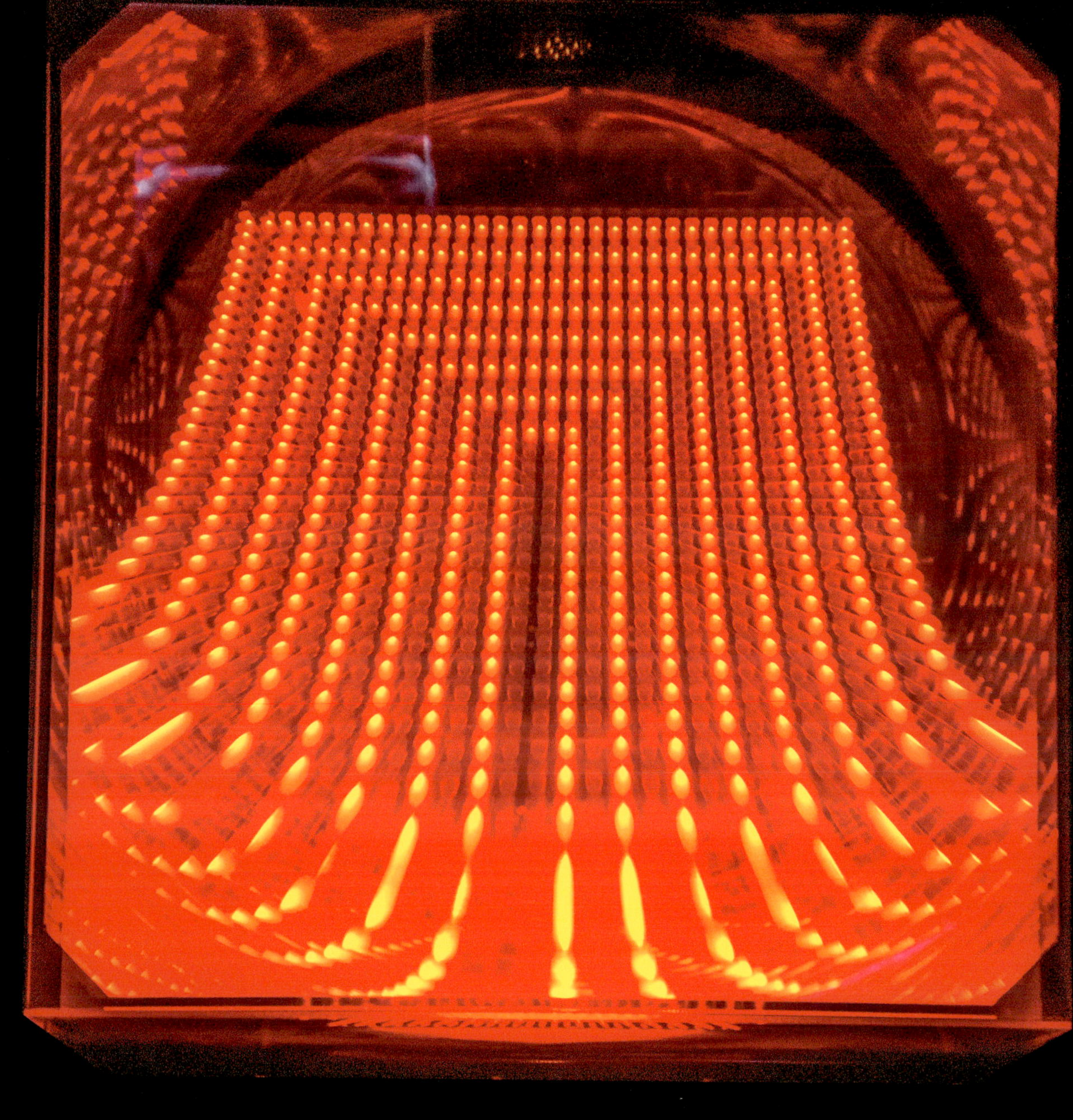

figs. 84, 85, ↑ *fig. 86* Heinz Mack, *Space Corner (4 Phases)*, 2004 (idea: 1980–1992)

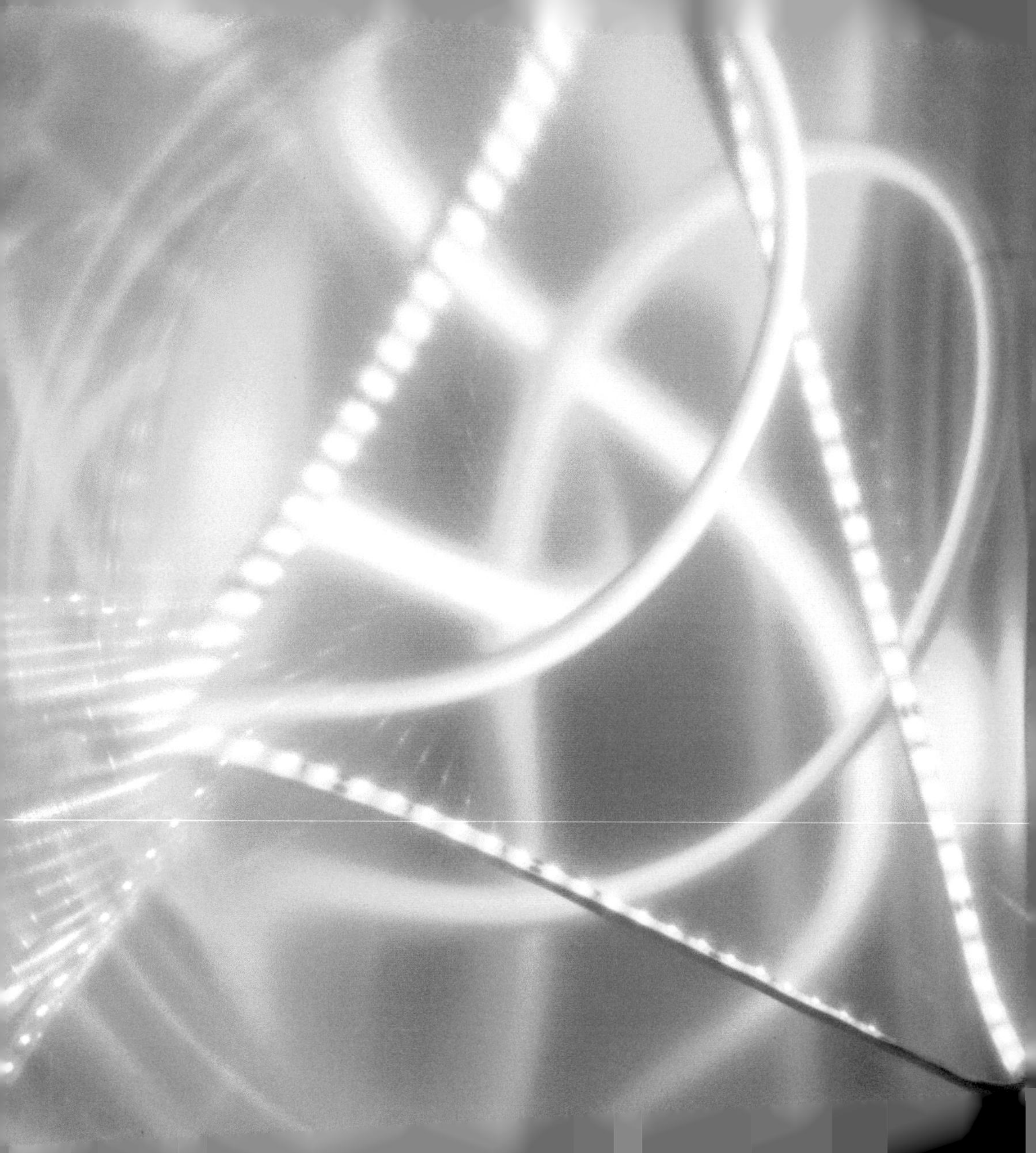

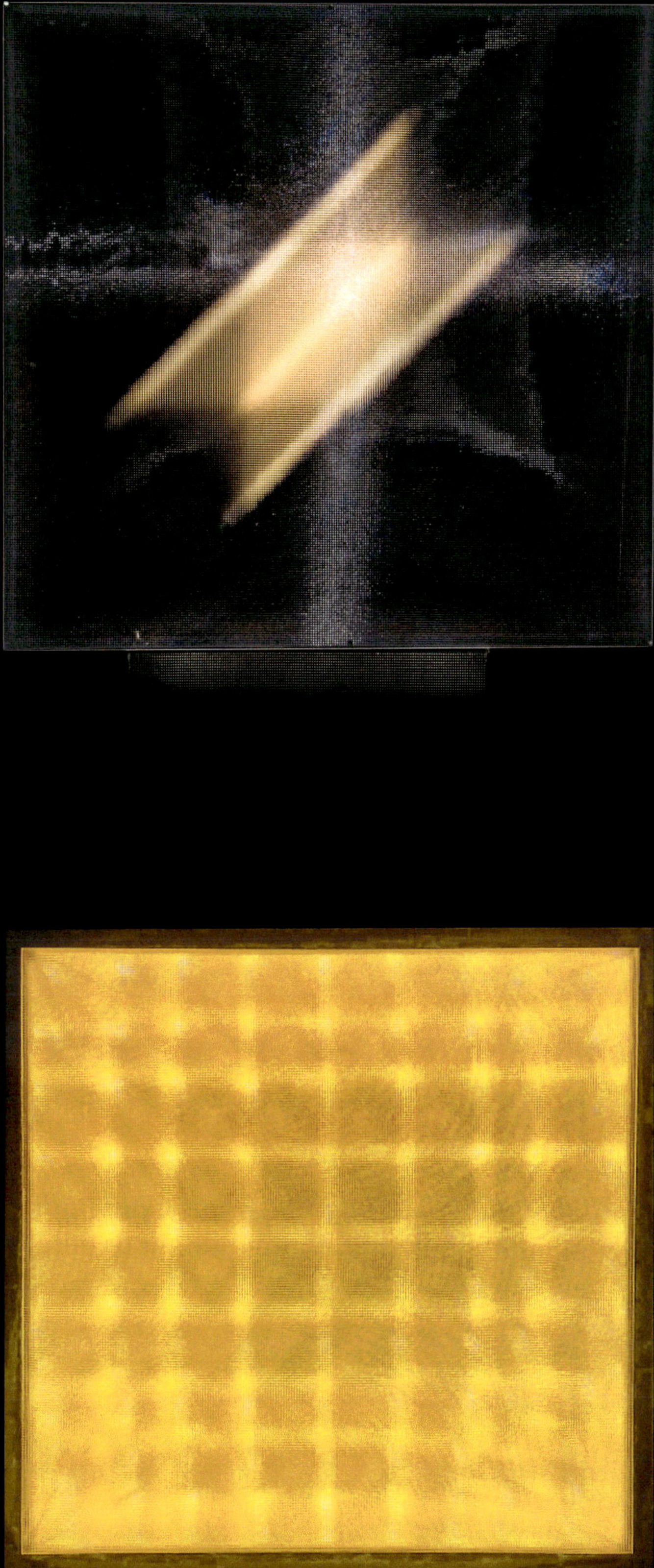

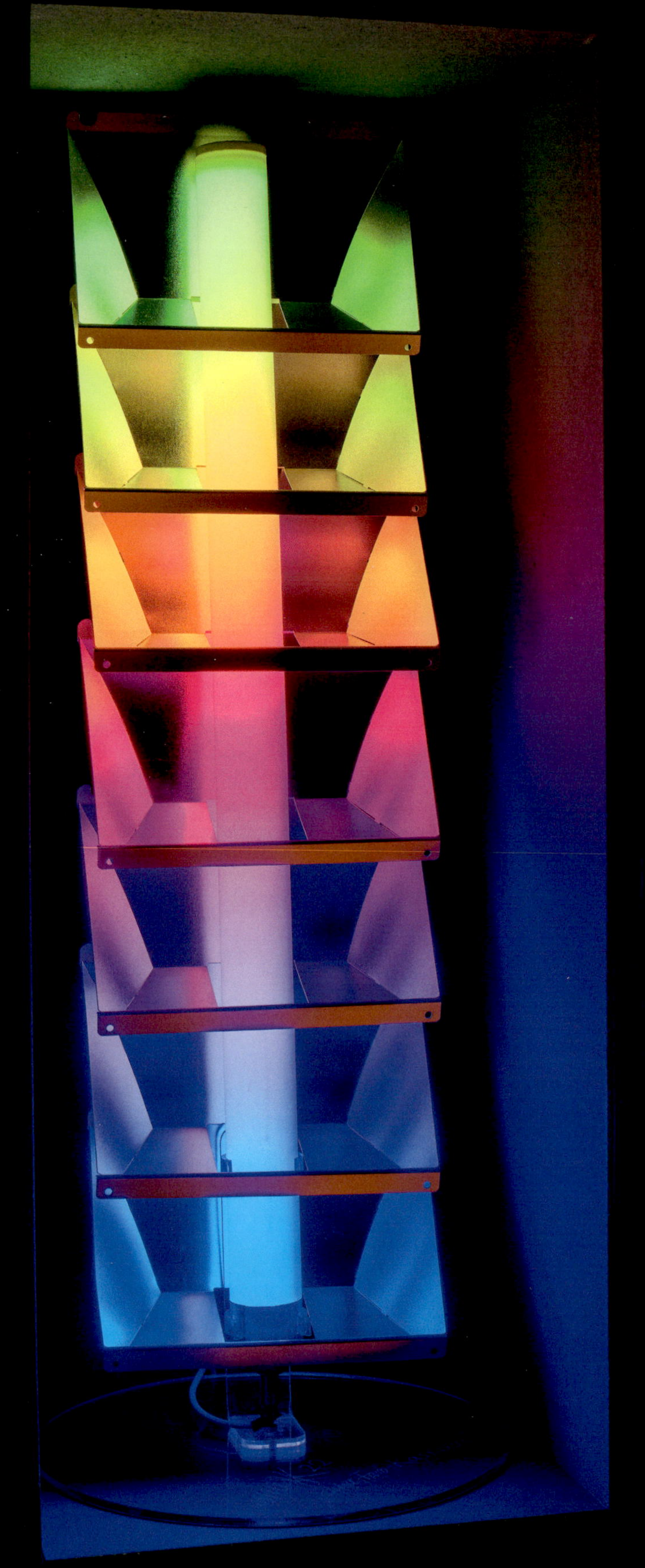

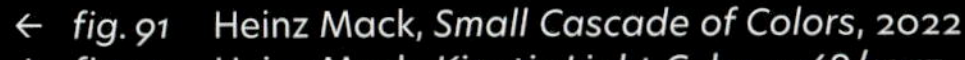

← *fig. 91* Heinz Mack, *Small Cascade of Colors*, 2022
↓ *fig. 92* Heinz Mack, *Kinetic Light Cube*, 1968/1977
→← *fig. 93* Heinz Mack, *Immaterial Appearance of a Transparent Sphere in front of a Cube*, 2022
→→ *fig. 94* Heinz Mack, *Light Comb*, 2004

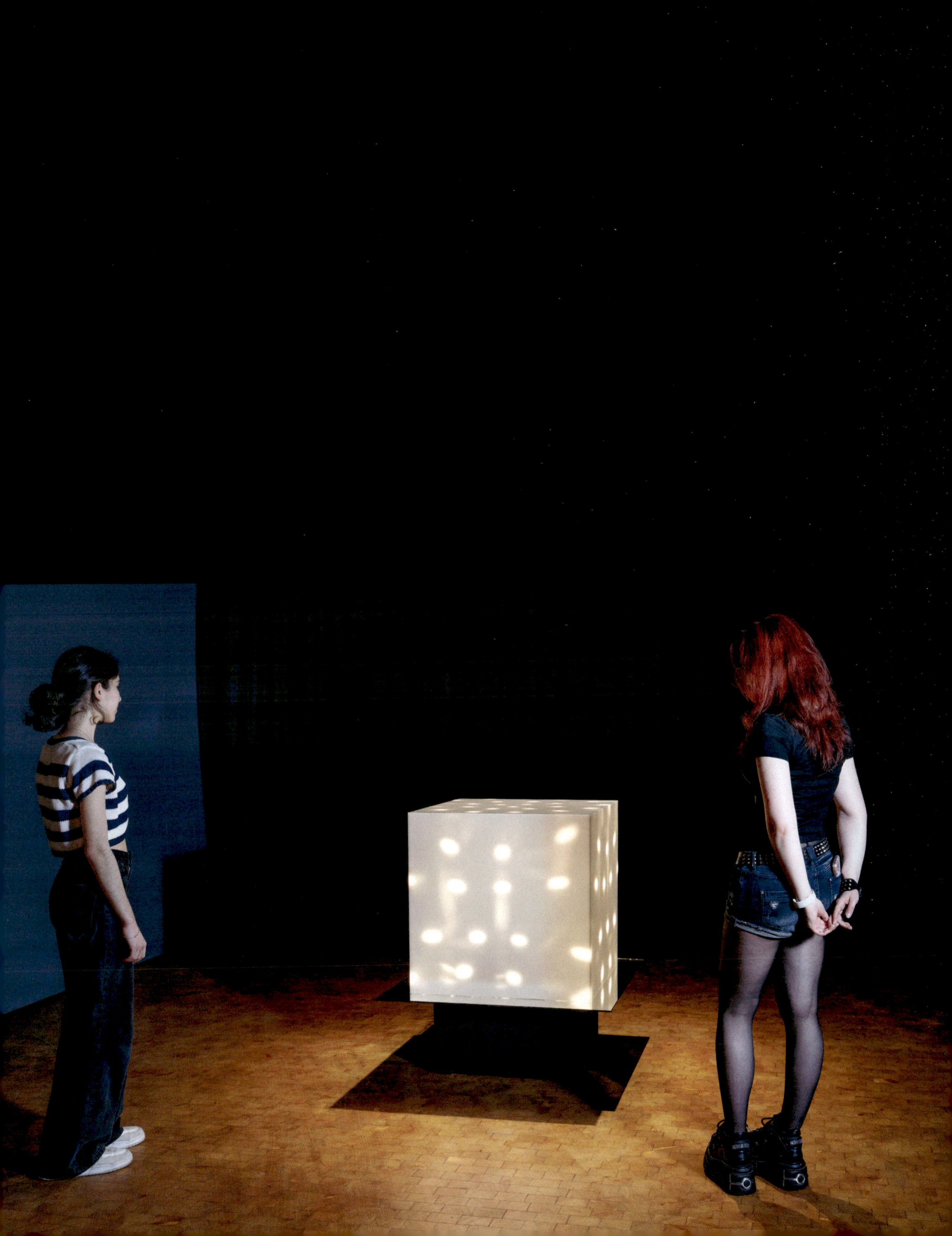

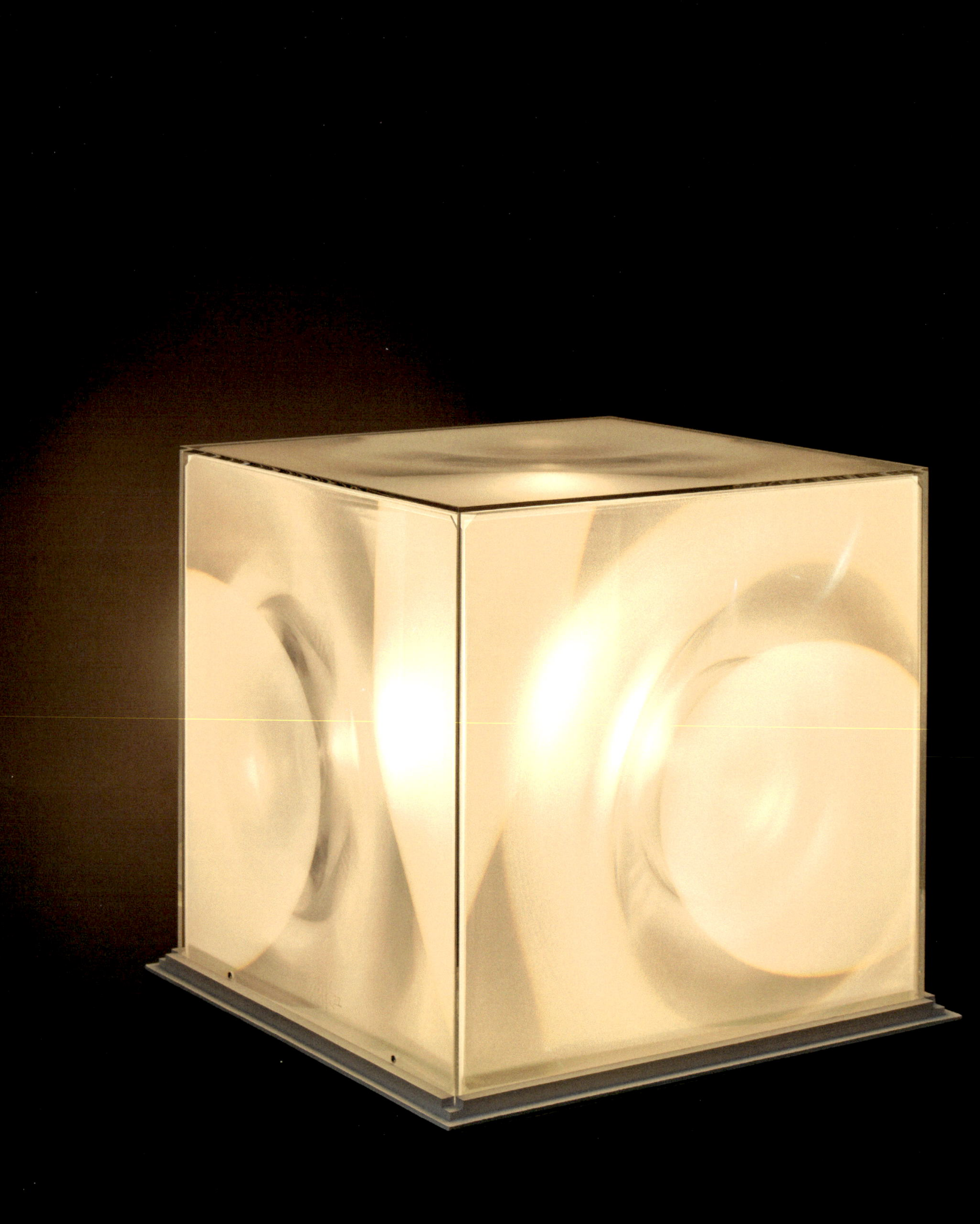

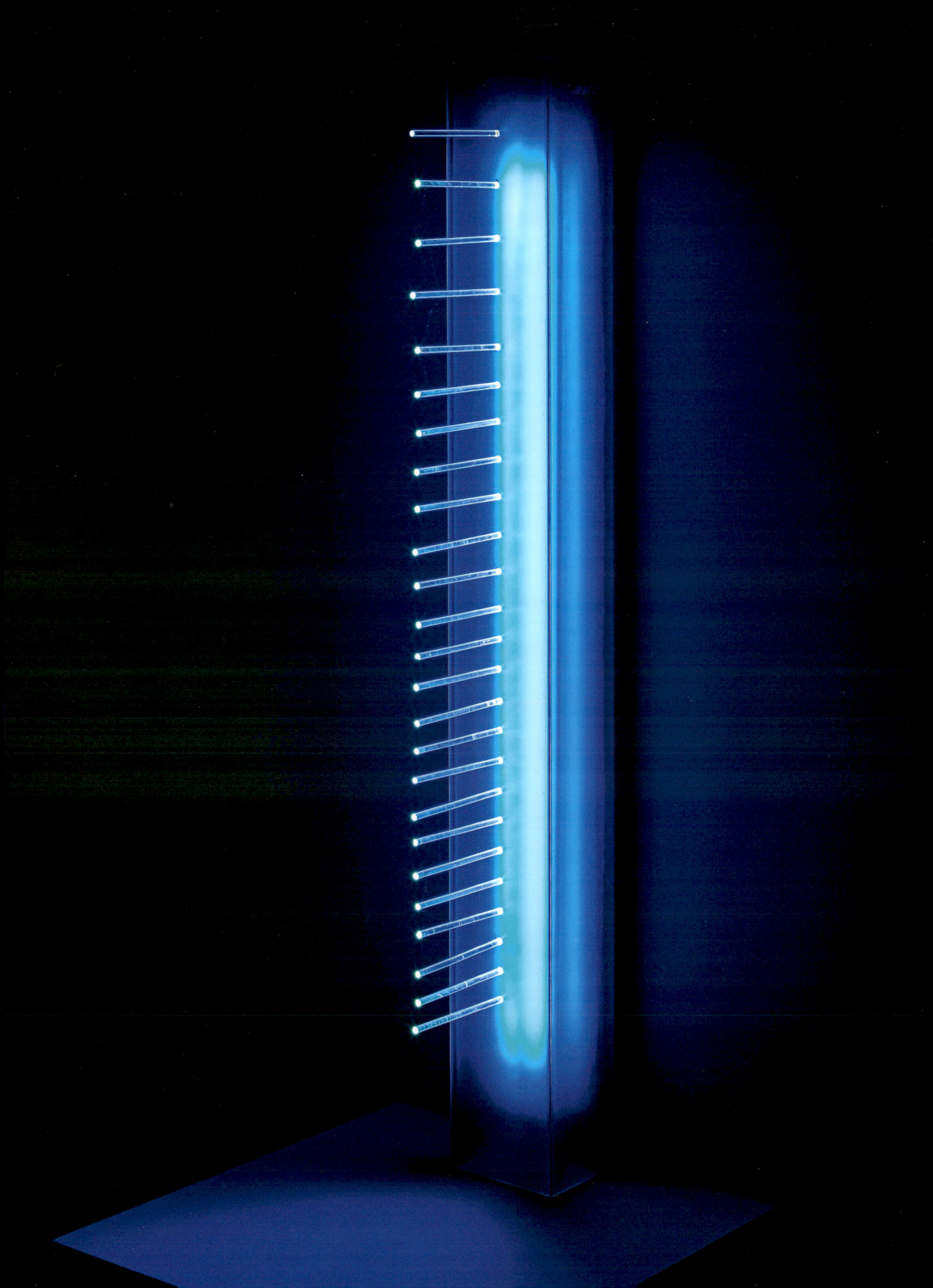

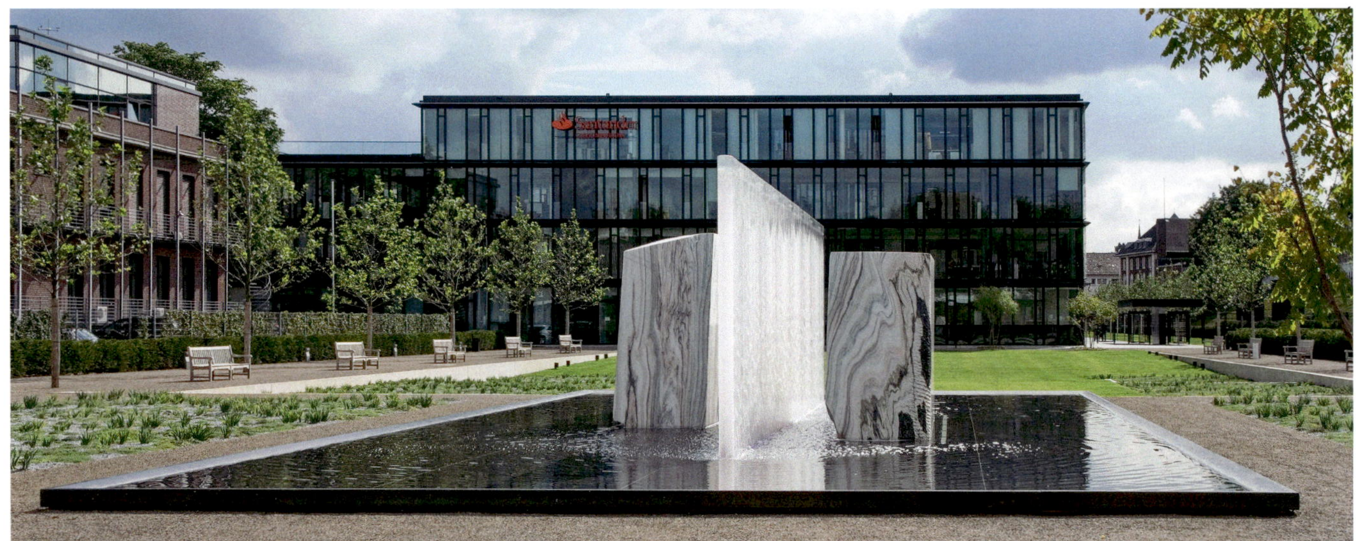

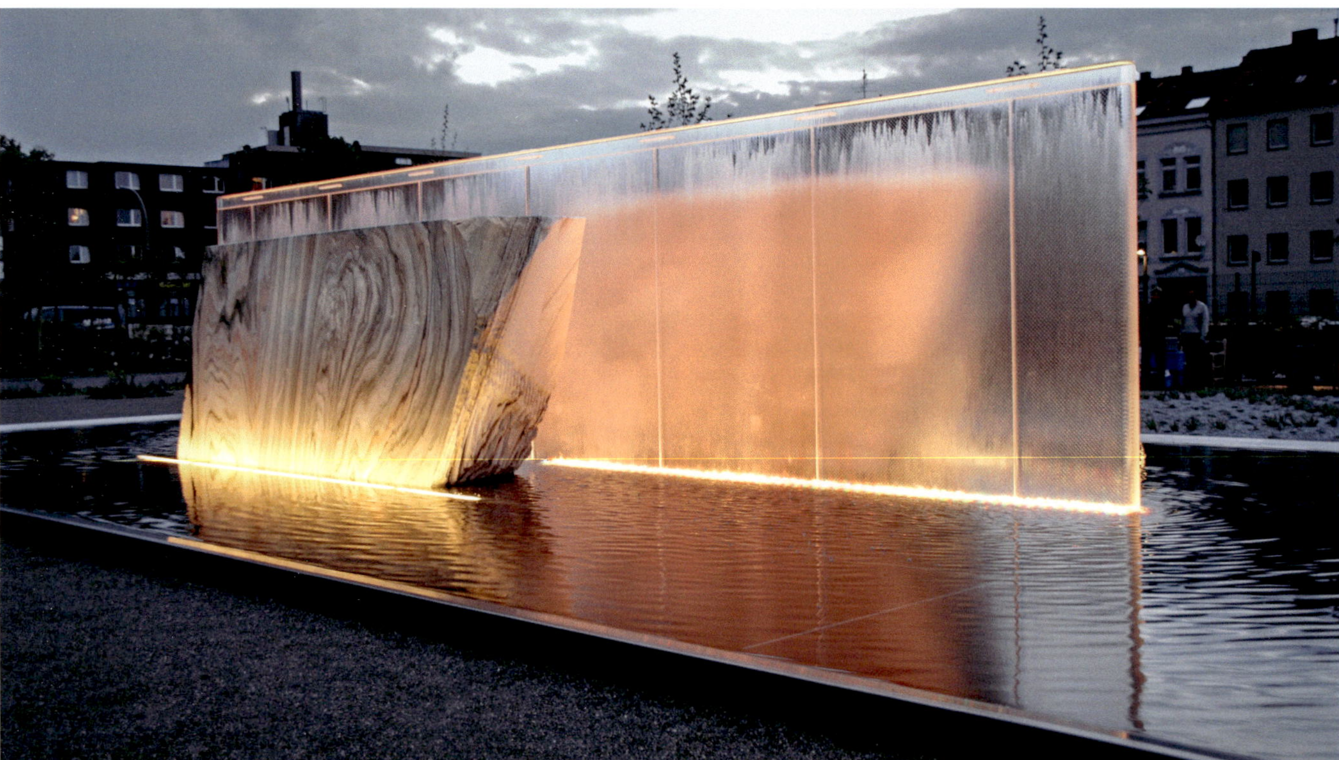

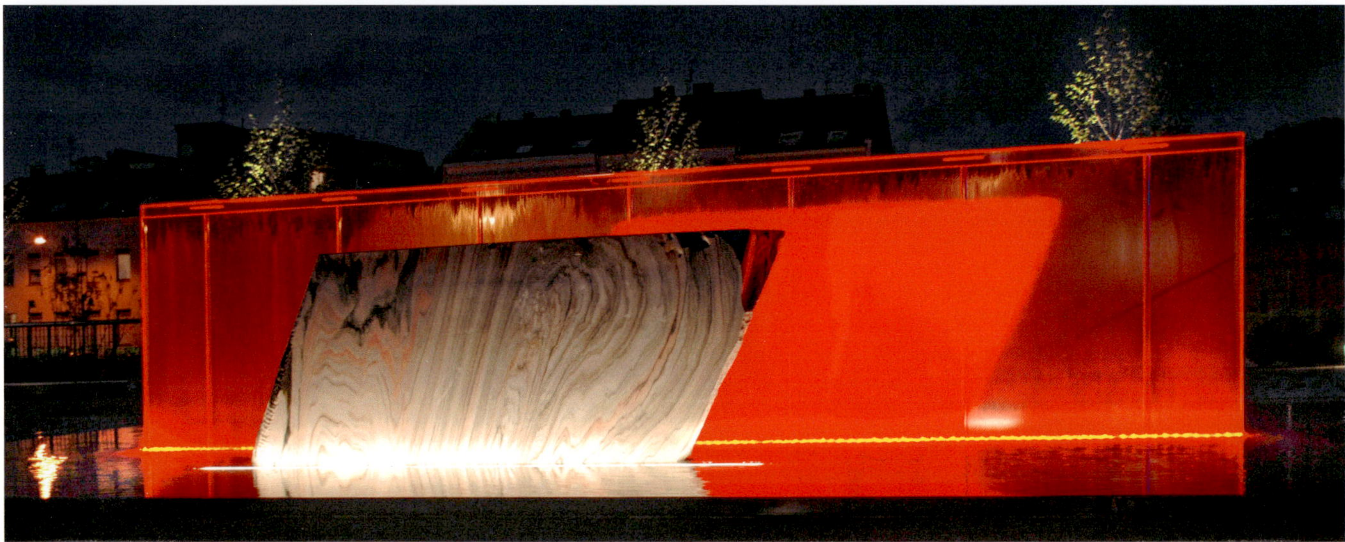

figs. 95, 96, 97 Heinz Mack, *Stone Water Glass Sculpture*, 2007, fountain, marble, acrylic glass, water and lighting technology, 3.2 × 20 × 10 m, Santander Consumer Bank, Mönchengladbach

The Four Elements in the Art of Heinz Mack

The *Stone Water Glass Sculpture* and Light

figs. 95, 96, 97

In 2007, Heinz Mack created the *Stone Water Glass Sculpture* for Santander Bank's landscaped gardens in Mönchengladbach.[1]
A 20 × 10-meter shallow water basin forms the base for three mighty structures that tower more than three meters above the water level: two vividly veined blocks of marble weighing 45 and 47 tons from the Sölker quarry in the Dachstein Mountains in Austria, between them a acrylic glass wall measuring 13 × 3.7 meters. The water is pumped up inside the glass wall, creating a curtain of water flowing over both sides of it. As this curtain of water flows down, always the same and yet always new, it appears youthful, light, weightless, transparent, even immaterial: the water playing with lightness. Contrasted to this are the two marble blocks that flank it, heavy and domineering, ancient and absolutely opaque: solemnly sublime. The piece as a whole seems to be designed according to the archetypical phenomenon of polarity. Yet the filigree veining of the stone blocks also looks almost like it is flowing, indeed the stone seems like a record of the fluid dynamics that existed 350 million years ago. The marble therefore acquires something of the fluid quality of water, a memory of the Earth's primordial state, when what later became rock formations were still moving, fluid aggregates. The water basin, on the other hand, appears to take on the function of a plinth, a stone base structure that supports the weight of architectural structures or sculptures. Polarity is therefore not a contradiction in Mack's work, but rather a dynamic forcefield, with one pole always taking on the qualities of the other. The affinities between stone, water, and light follow the principle of transformation, metamorphosis. This corresponds to the transformative powers of the elements in ancient philosophy.

Mythology and natural philosophy must always be kept in mind when thinking about Mack's work. Water, for example, calls to mind the philosopher Thales of Miletus, who viewed it as the primordial basis of all existence: the world generated from a single element.
The image of the fluid, once molten rock also recalls the philosopher Heraclitus, who believed the world had been created from fire. Or it invokes the seismic and marine god Poseidon, who was not just lord of the waters, but also of the subterranean world. It was he who dramatically brought the solid rock to life during an earthquake. In the depths of Poseidon's kingdom, the fire awaits, from which living creatures are protected by the Earth's cooled crust, although deadly streams of lava still frequently erupt from volcanoes. In many cultures, stone mountains are not seen as dead, but alive, and revered as holy places. Fire, fluids, solids, storms, and light form permanent or temporary ensembles on the smallest and largest scale: that is the mighty interplay of the elements, which speaks no language, yet sometimes leaves us speechless. That is their sympoiesis. Mack is an artist of stone, water, fire, and air in the modern age. They form separate spheres and at the same time work together in the global spheres of planet Earth. They enable the existence of the ecosphere and biocoenosis, the evolution of all terrestrial life forms. Mack connects to these archaic dimensions of the lithosphere,

1 Heinz Mack, *Mack. Kunst für die Santander Consumer Bank Mönchengladbach. Eine Dokumentation* (Mönchengladbach: Atelier Mack / Santander Consumer Bank, 2007).

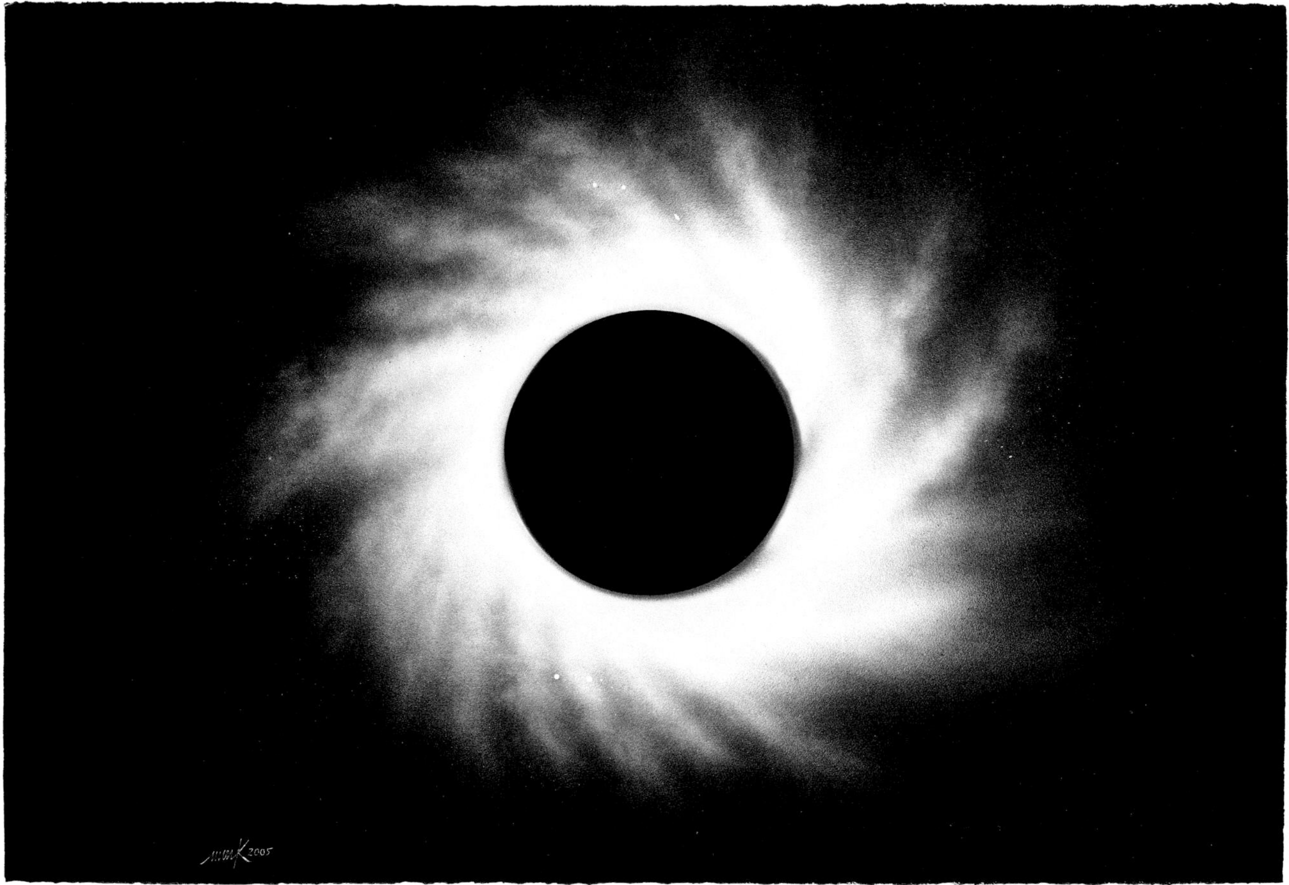

fig. 98 Heinz Mack, *Untitled*, 2005, spray paint on cardboard, 76,5 × 111 cm

the atmosphere, the hydrosphere, and the sphere of fire, and knows how to draw a unique aesthetic aura from each of them.

The surface of the water basin becomes a game of mirrors with the three objects, but also the surrounding space, the gardens, the sky, and the clouds. Reflective pools of water were a classic effect used in the parterre of the French formal garden. Here, the water flowing down the acrylic glass wall works with the refraction and semitransparency of the light. When night falls, the bright-white base color of the marble contrasts with the ambient light, and the color black, that primordial phenomenon of darkness, dominates the space. Blackness is not a personification, but an abstraction of Nyx, of the nocturnal realm of absence and the mother of death, as described by Hesiod. For Mack, black is a color and therefore a phenomenon of light. This can be seen in his use of black light and shadows in his installations.[2] In early natural philosophy, like in the Bible, black is often understood as the state prior to creation, before "appearances" enter the world with the god Phanes (the luminous one). From the union of night and darkness (Nyx and Erebos) the day and the ether are born, making it possible for celestial light to illuminate the material world. Beliefs like these were held by the Orphics. Phanes, the god of light, is not only responsible for the diaphanous, that which shines through, but for everything that can become or seeks to become a "phenomenon": the "bright" world as a whole. These are the philosophical ideas about light that underlie not only the *Stone Water Glass Sculpture*, but all of Mack's œuvre.

2 Cf. Heinz Mack and Hubertus Schoeller, eds., *Mack. Licht im Schwarz*, exh. cat. (Düsseldorf: Galerie Schoeller, 2001); Helmut Friedel, ed., *Heinz Mack. Licht Schatten*, exh. cat. Museum Frieder Burda (Munich: Hirmer, 2015).

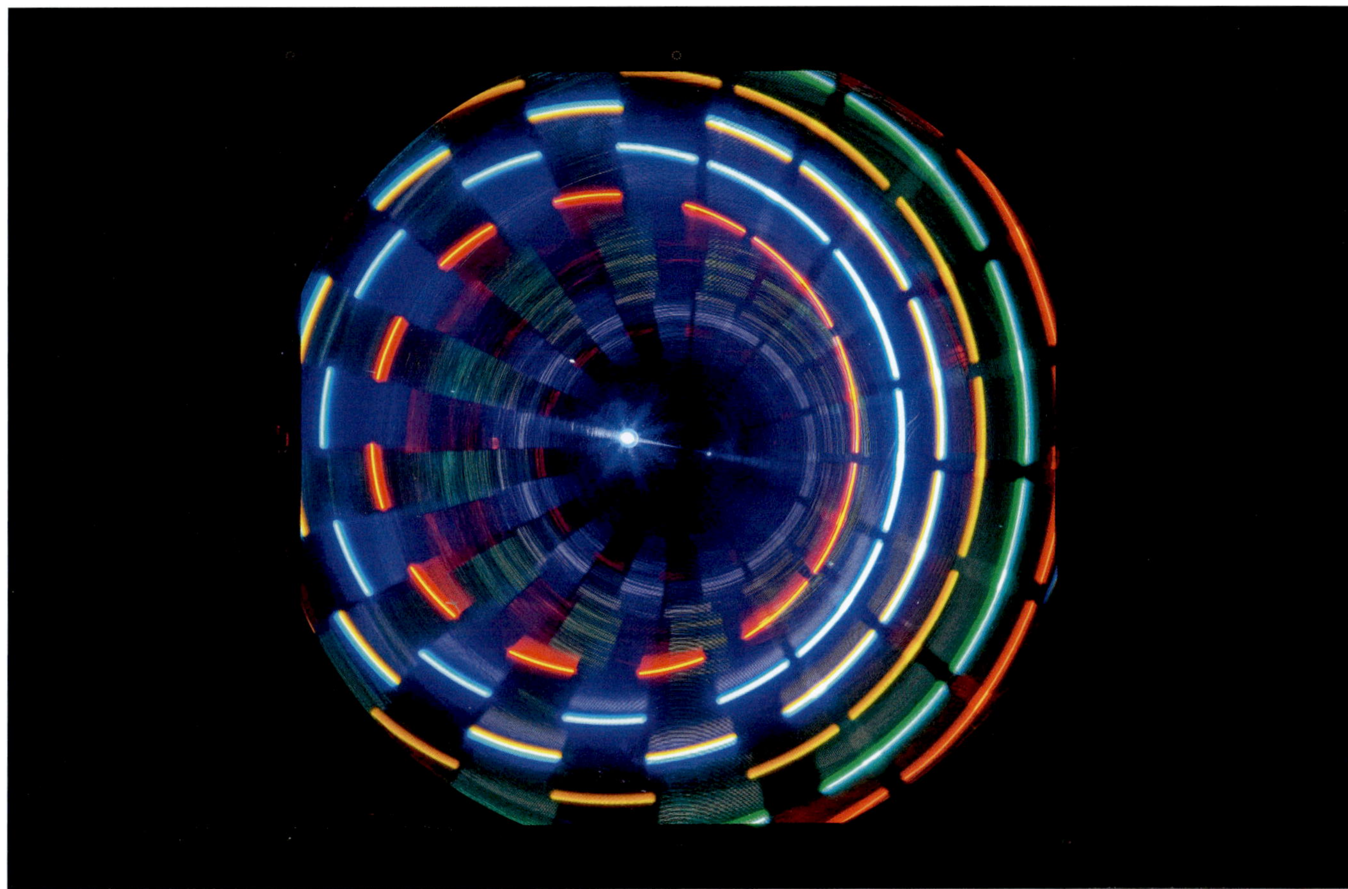

fig. 99 Heinz Mack, *Light Fan*, 2009, exhibition view, ZKM | Karlsruhe 2023

Even before his technical work on matter, Mack is a light artist. There are very few artists as aware of the constituitive function of the color black as Mack: "Black is black light, white is white light. [...] Black is an extremely beautiful color."[3]

figs. 98, 247

In its cosmic, solar, and terrestrial, for us natural, dimension, light acquires something additional in its technical form – at least after fire had been mastered and the first use of man-made light. The legacy of Prometheus triumphs in the immense significance of artificial light. Primordial light is the primary medium of Mack's art, the light of nature's creation, which gives allows him to use artificial light as well as artificial colors. This also has anthropological significance: the human being coevolves with technology and is therefore inventor and *technite*, a *homo faber*, a tool-making animal (and of course an *animal symbolicum* too).

It thus comes as no surprise that technical light appears in all of Mack's work; and in the *Stone Water Glass Sculpture* too. Mack installed thin strips of LED lights in the water at the feet of the marble blocks and the acrylic glass wall, which illuminate the sculpture through the water. The carefully chosen sequences of colors are digitally controlled. The blocks of marble and the wall of water become surfaces upon which abstract moving images are projected. The color valency of the marble and the curtain of water continuously change. Their luminosity is strengthened or weakened depending on the weather and the color of the sky on a particular day, the largest existing screen for the light effects of the elements.

3 Cf. Mack, Schoeller, *Licht im Schwarz*, 17; this also contains a poem by Mack about the color black (1977), 130. See also: Max Raphael, *Die Farbe Schwarz: Zur materiellen Konstituierung der Form* (Frankfurt am Main: Suhrkamp, 1983); Hartmut Böhme, "Magie, Metaphysik und Ästhetik des Weißen und des Schwarzen in Literatur und Kunst," in: Monika Wagner and Helmut Lethen, eds., *Schwarz-Weiß als Evidenz* (Frankfurt am Main: Campus, 2015), 17–46; Ingeborg Flagge, Peter Cachola Schmal and Ulrike Brandi, eds., *Das Geheimnis des Schattens: Licht und Schatten in der Architektur*, exh. cat. Deutsches Architektur-Museum Frankfurt am Main (Tübingen: Ernst Wasmuth, 2002).

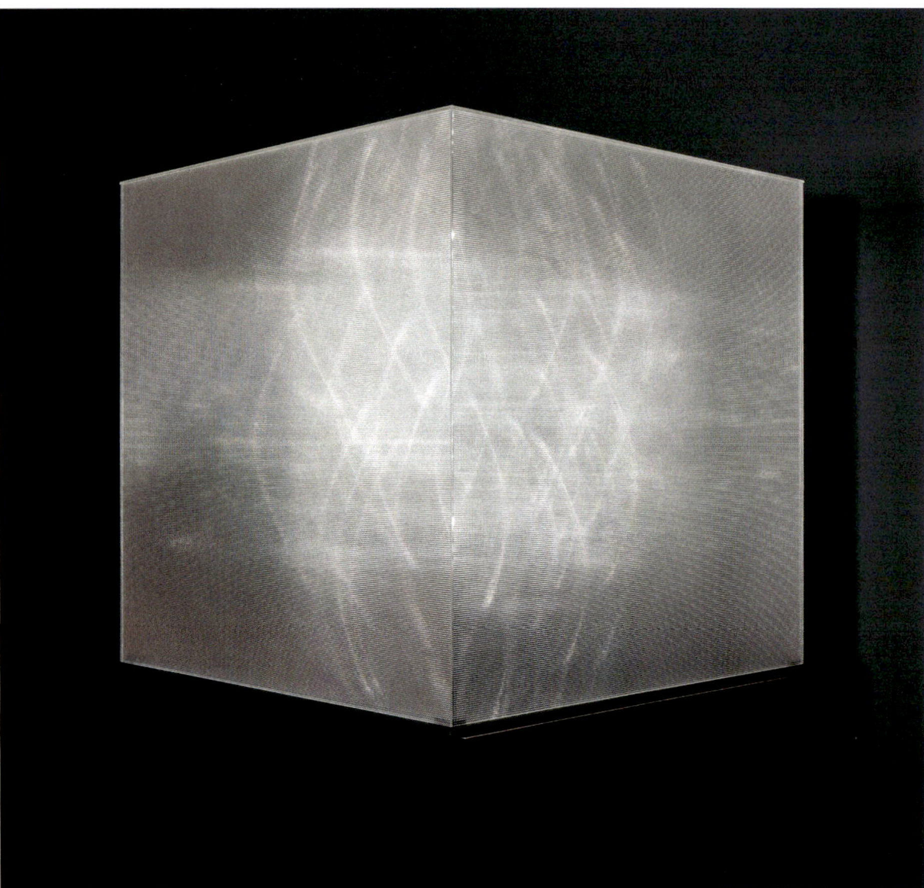

fig. 100 Heinz Mack, *Light Stars*, 2022, exhibition view, ZKM | Karlsruhe 2023

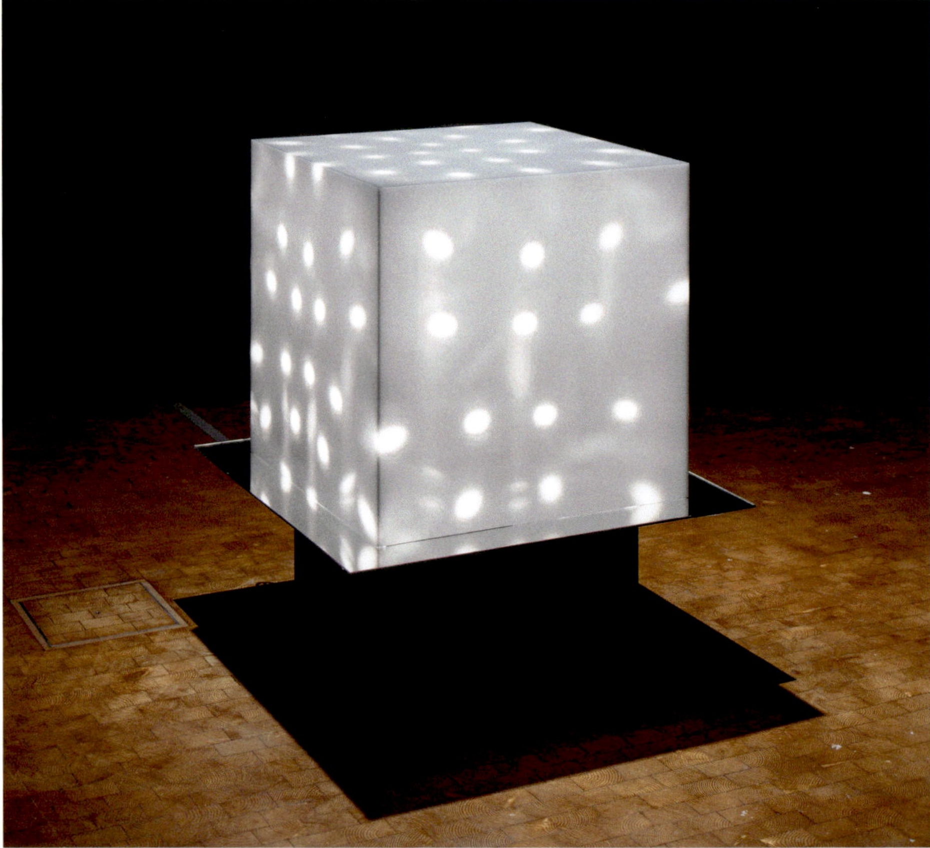

fig. 101 Heinz Mack, *Kinetic Light Cube*, 1968/1977, exhibition view, ZKM | Karlsruhe 2023

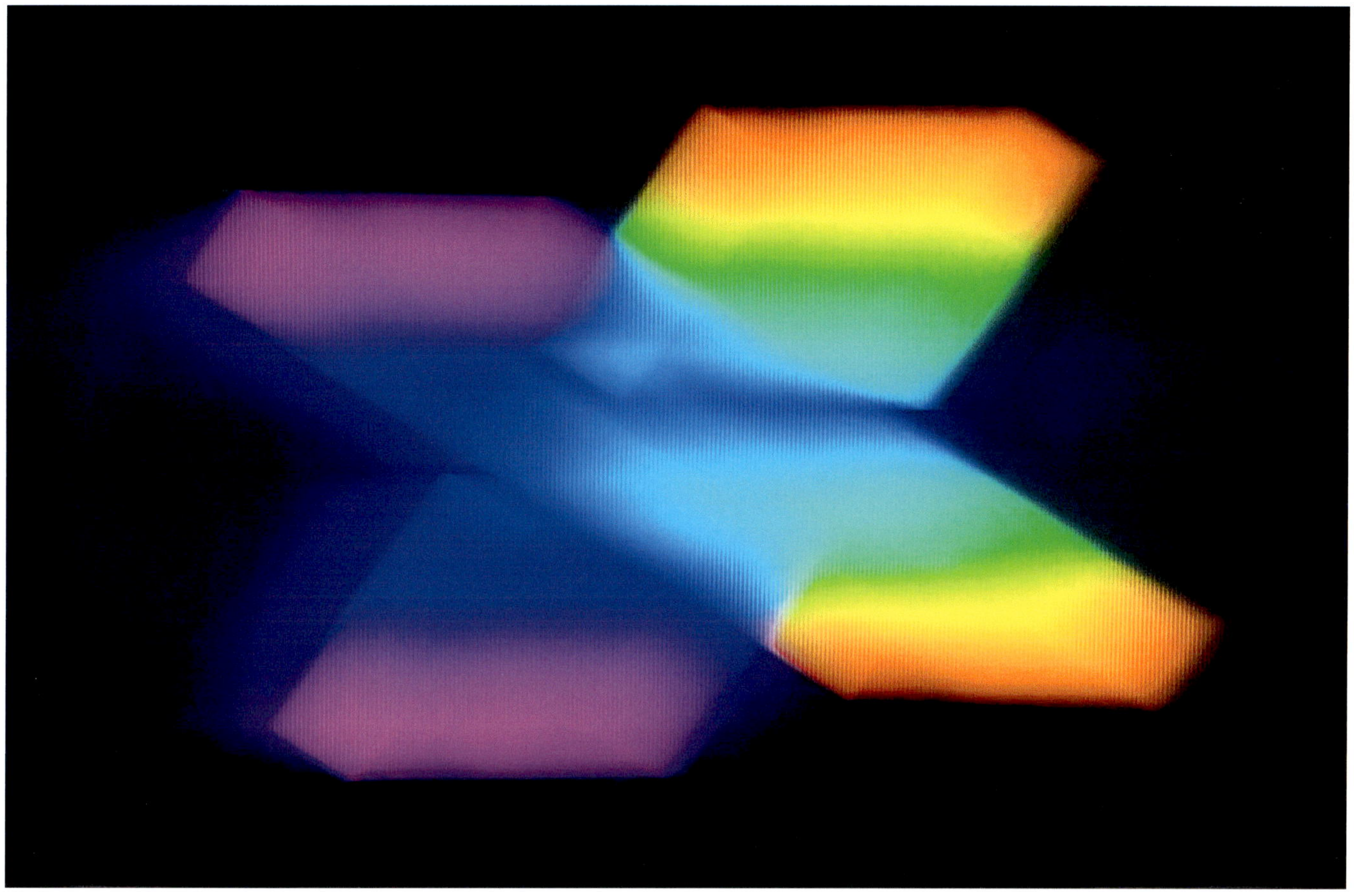

fig. 102 Heinz Mack, *Light Symbol*, 2022

figs. 38, 79, 88, 89, 94, 99, 100, 101

Works like *Light Stars*, *Light Cone*, *Light Wall*, *Light Window*, *Light Relief*, *Light Grid*, *Light Rain* or kinetic walls of light are just as much an integral part of Mack's formal language since the 1960s as light rotors and light steles. At the same time – and this is true since his expeditions to the desert and the Arctic – Mack never appears as a solitary, absolute subject in his works. On the contrary, light, sky, weather, geological formations, substances, and materials, in other words the entire theater of the elements become the artist's co-creators. The autonomy of art that has been fetishized since the Renaissance is shared between the artist, the ether, and the elements in Mack's work. This creates a new economy of aesthetic productivity, a kind of artistic sharing economy. The artist makes use of the aesthetic surplus of light, materials, and the elements for mutual gain, namely an idealistic, but also aesthetic, and perhaps even ecological one. Conversely, the mute stones, materials, and elements receive attention and are placed in a setting that gives them value, weaving completely novel networks and performances between things and people.

fig. 102

We can see that Mack is an artist who allows the materiality of the elements and things to interact with each other. With an awareness of the history of the earth and sky, he turns every local arrangement of objects into a cosmic-aesthetic work of art, but an abstract one, without the semantics that were developed in religions, cultures, rituals, and metaphysics. Mack creates purely aesthetic rituals that allow us to experience what Hans Blumenberg has called the "absolute metaphor"

fig. 103

of light. Light is pure presence: ZERO. In this way, the fifth element is doubly brought into play. On the one hand, it emerges through the performative power of light, which enables all things to appear in the first place or plunges them into blackness. On the other, through our eyes, light constitutes the sensual world, the *mundus sensibilis*, for itself and for us. Furthermore, the refraction of light creates the universe of colors — through the medial in-between of turbid light[4] or the refractive index of objects. The infinite variability and expressiveness of colors are celebrated in the *Stone Water Glass Sculpture* — especially at night.

Empty Spaces — Signals of Art

We can now understand why, when Mack was defining his style and especially his relationship to spacetime between the 1960s and the 1990s, he preferred spaces devoid of objects, far from the big cities with their plethora of things, people, and sensory stimuli. Consequently, Mack organized expeditions to the African and Arabian deserts and to the Arctic.[5] He experiences and depicts these places as pure spaces of silence and absence, into which he implants works of art that are extremely ephemeral in character. In the desert, everything is blown away and slowly erased by the wind, is buried and preserved without a trace in the middle of nowhere. It was the aesthetic qualities of emptiness and abstraction that the ZERO artist was seeking in these extreme places. Only an empty space without a function allows the elementary quality of light to be experienced. At the most fundamental level of perception, it leads to a structure that is as abstract as it is self-reflexive: the seeing of seeing. In this 're-flection,' the phenomena of the world encounter the dynamics of perception and consciousness. Precisely in their meaningless emptiness — at the zero point of art, this uncanny "nothing at all" (*nullum*) and "non-being" (*non esse*) — the desert and the Arctic teach the young artist tough lessons that still influence his art today.

At the same time, these natural spaces allow the artist unprecedented gestures of self-affirmation, oscillating between the experience of the tininess of the self and boundless ambition. The desert and Arctic are as generous as they are merciless, sumptuous and ascetic, sublime and abstract. For Mack, they are the archetypes of space. Mack *must* explore them in order to create a viable theoretical and aesthetic basis for the ZERO movement. However, with hindsight it can be said that these spaces of emptiness and their associated transgressions of the subject constitute the starting point and limit of Mack's aesthetic.

In 1976, for example, Mack had himself photographed from a distance by Thomas Höpker in the Grand Erg Occidental, Algeria's vast sea of sand, wearing a silver suit and posing like an antenna. Nothing but the endless, disorientating rhythm of the dunes. Beneath the sun, the light reflected back from the dunes; and shadows that are outlined as sharply as they can only be in the desert. The photographs show no sign of civilization, no traces of the expedition team or its equipment. Only a tiny Mack in the distance, standing on the ridge of a dune transmitting optical signs with his raised signal flags. Silent distress calls? Triumphant beacons of the self? Perhaps Mack is only a dwindling memorial to human vanitas and the illusion of reason. Occasionally, in his

4 This phrase is derived from Goethe, in German: "das Trübe." Mack is not only familiar with the history of the philosophy of light, but also Goethe's color theory: cf. Barbara Steingießer, ed., *Taten des Lichts. Mack & Goethe*, exh. cat. Goethe Museum Düsseldorf (Berlin: Hatje Cantz, 2018). Furthermore, like Goethe, Mack also has a deep knowledge of geology, cf. Wolf von Engelhardt, *Goethe im Gespräch mit der Erde: Landschaft, Gesteine, Mineralien und Erdgeschichte in seinem Leben und Werk* (Weimar: Hermann Böhlaus Nachfolger, 2003); Hartmut Böhme, "Stein-Reich. Zur Theorie des Erhabenen aus dem Blick des Menschenfremdesten," in: idem, *Natur und Figur: Goethe im Kontext* (Paderborn: Brill, 2016), 85–133.

5 An accompanying program text on the desert and Arctic expeditions was published as "Das Sahara-Projekt" (1959). Reprints appeared in, amongst others, Wieland Schmied, ed., *Utopie und Wirklichkeit im Werk von Heinz Mack*, exh. cat. Liechtensteinische Staatliche Kunstsammlung Vaduz (Cologne: DuMont, 1998), 16–21 and in Uwe Rüth, *Mack. Licht der Wüste, Licht des Eismeeres*, exh. cat. (Marl: Skulpturenmuseum Glaskasten Marl, 2001), 8–11. Cf. Sophia Sotke, *Mack. Sahara: From ZERO to Land Art — Heinz Mack's Sahara Project* (Munich: Hirmer, 2022), 24–54.

figs. 104, 126

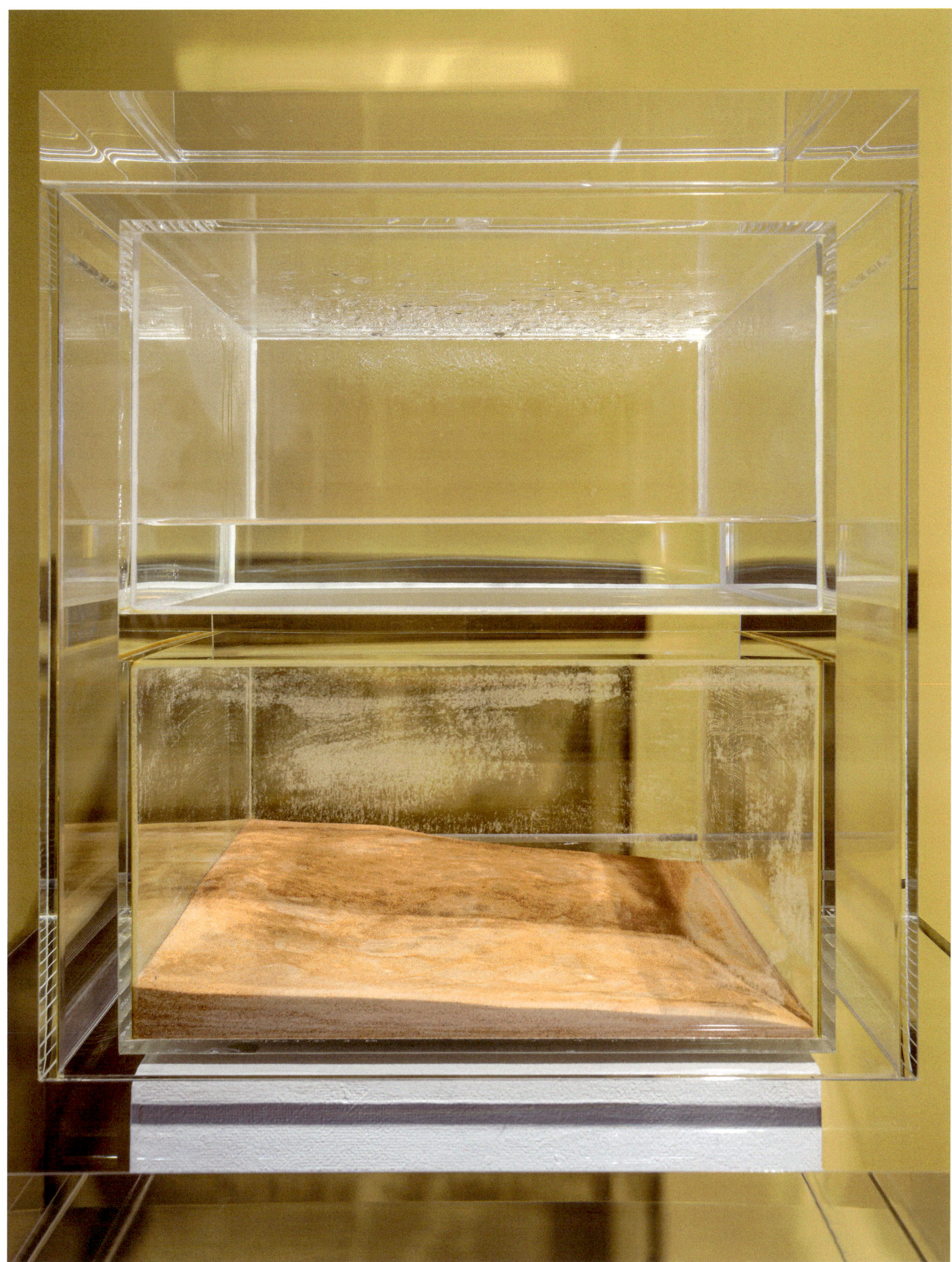

fig. 103 Heinz Mack, *The Sea Above the Desert*, 1967/1968, exhibition view, ZKM | Karlsruhe 2023

fig. 104 Heinz Mack in a silver suit with reflectors, Grand Erg Occidental, Algeria, 1976, photo: Thomas Höpker

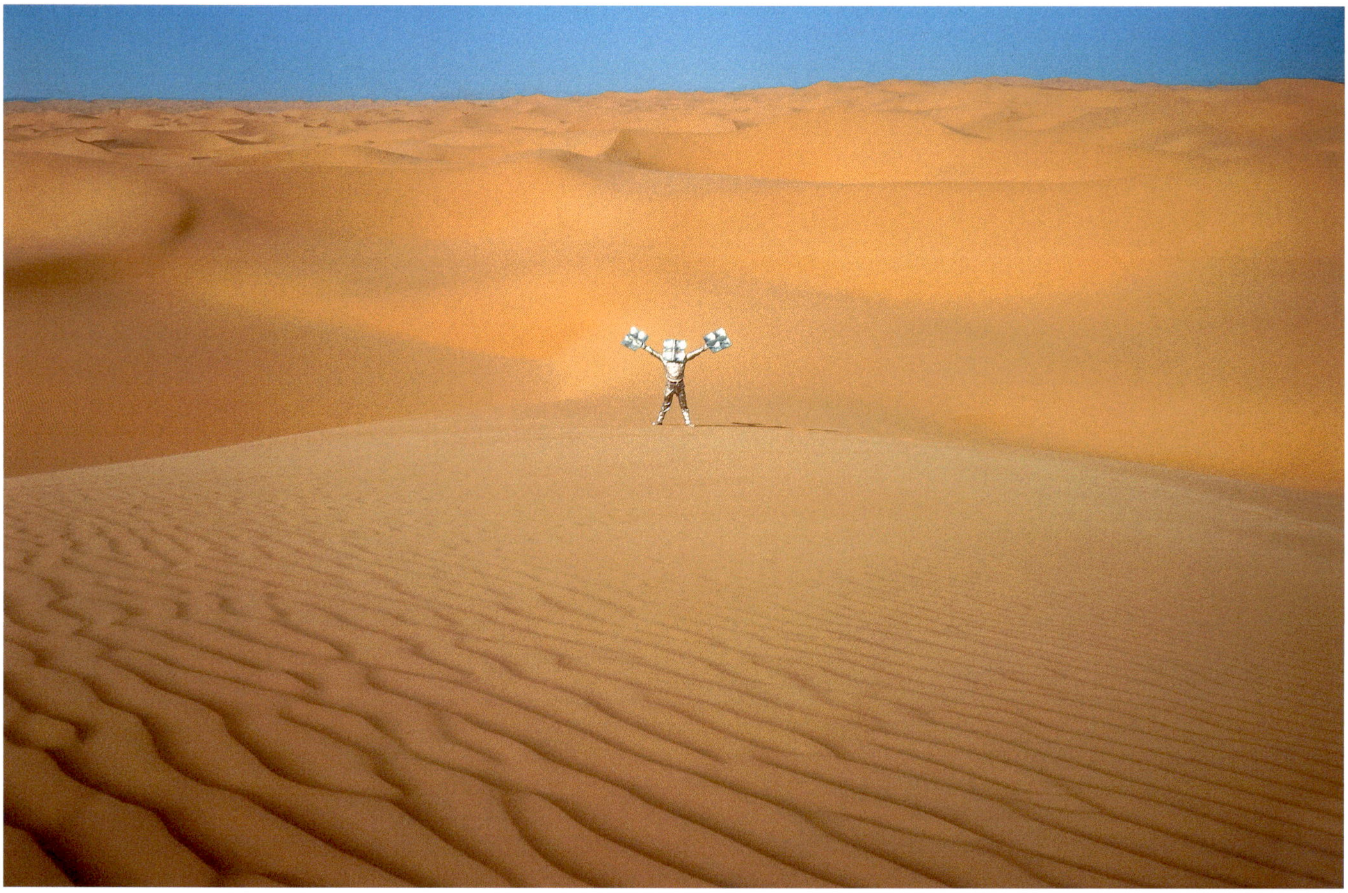

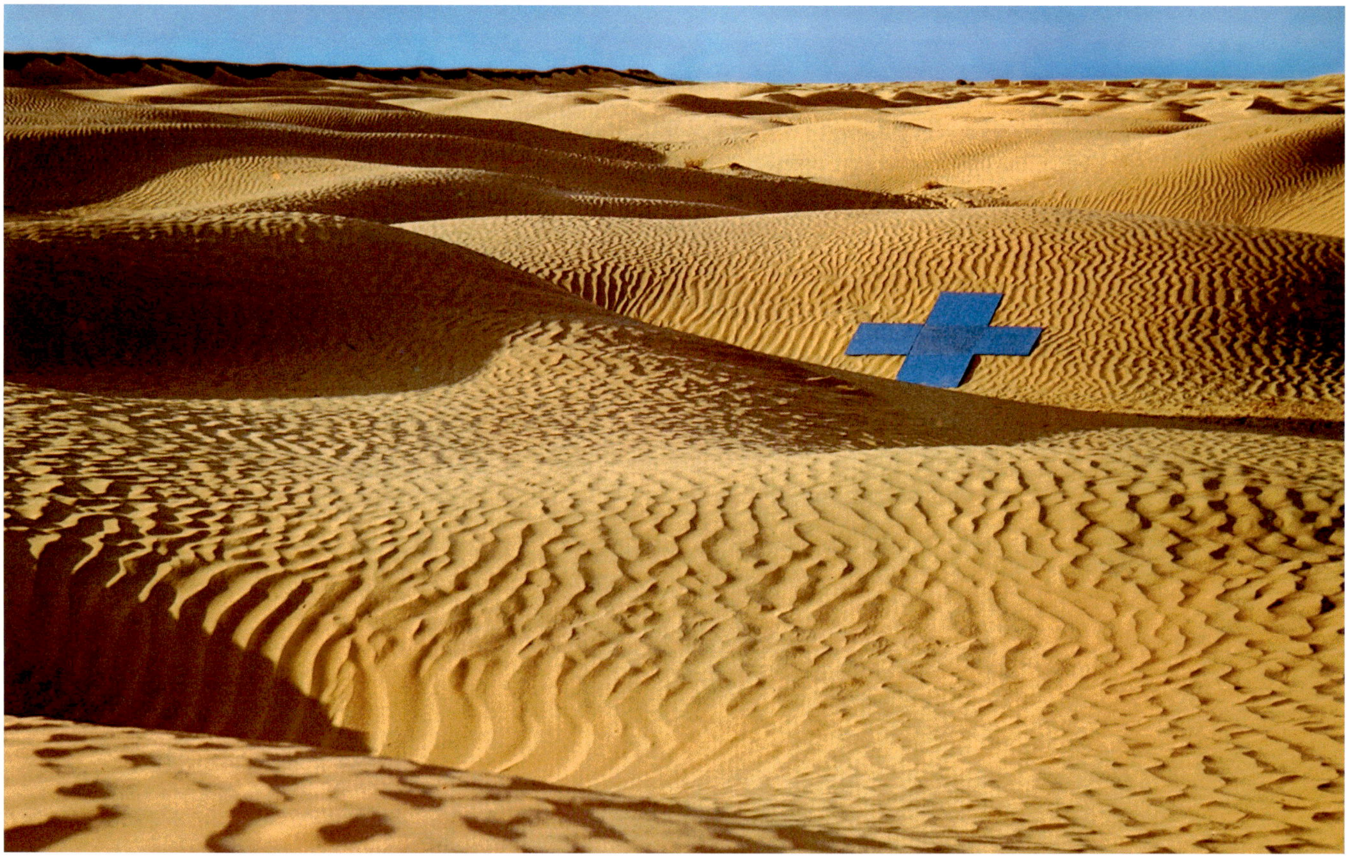

fig. 105 Heinz Mack, *The Cross of the South*, 1976, aliminum, 500 × 500 cm, photo: Thomas Höpker

fig. 106 Heinz Mack, *Great Space Arrow*, Grand Erg Occidental, Algeria, 1976, aluminum, lengh 8 m, aluminum, photo: Thomas Höpker

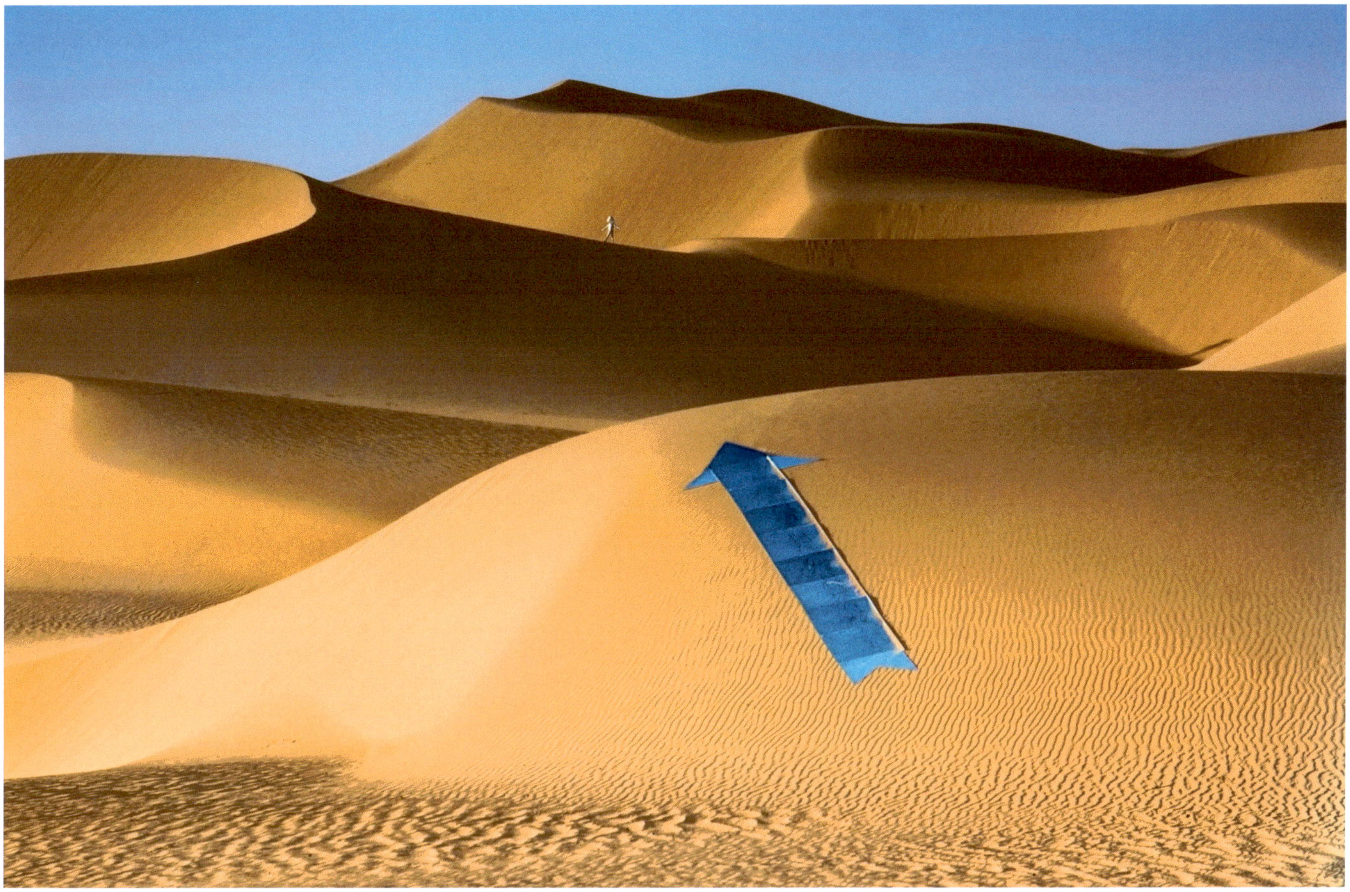

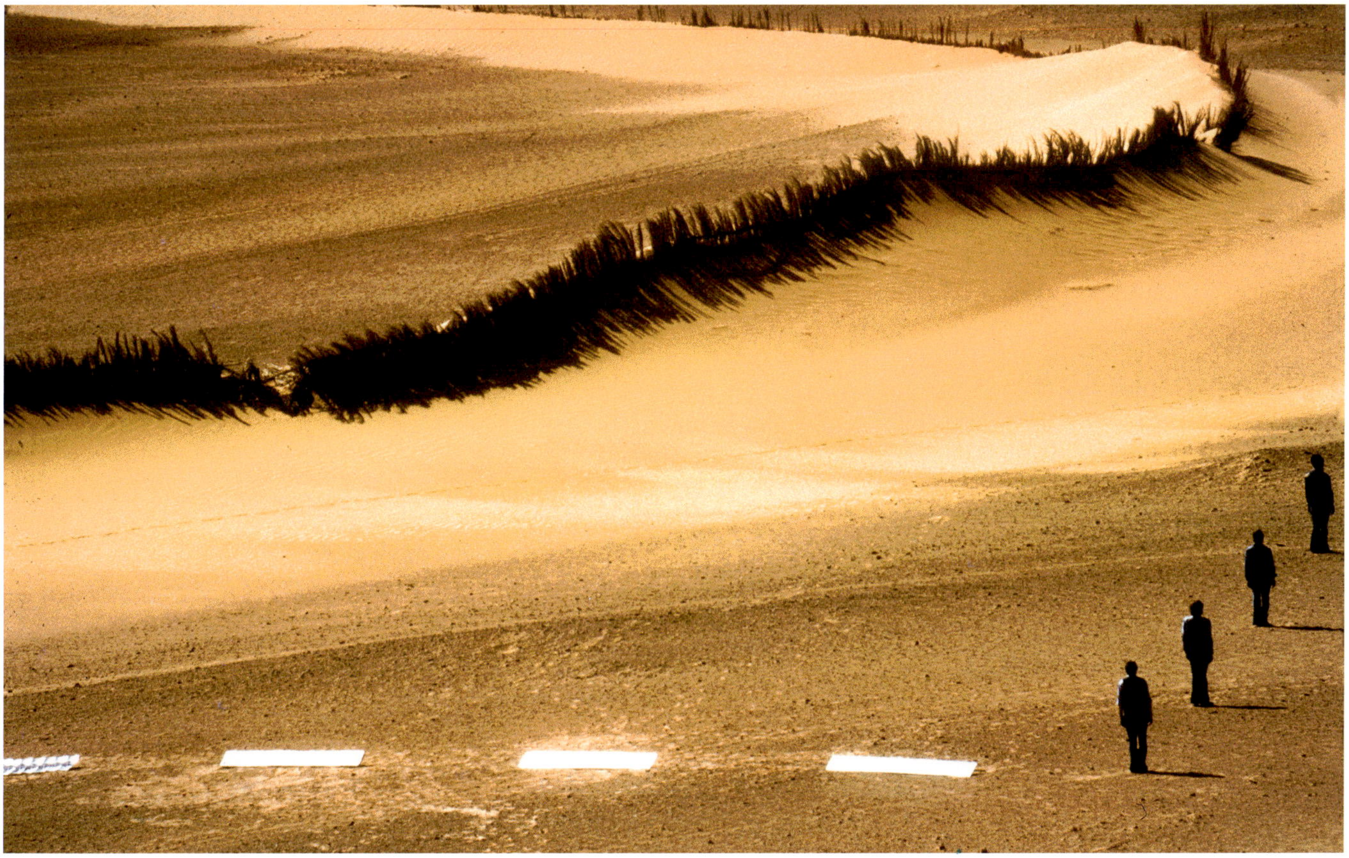

fig. 107 Heinz Mack, *Scale of the Desert*, Grand Erg Occidental, Algeria, 1976, aluminum reflectors, 56 × 220 cm each, photo: Thomas Höpker

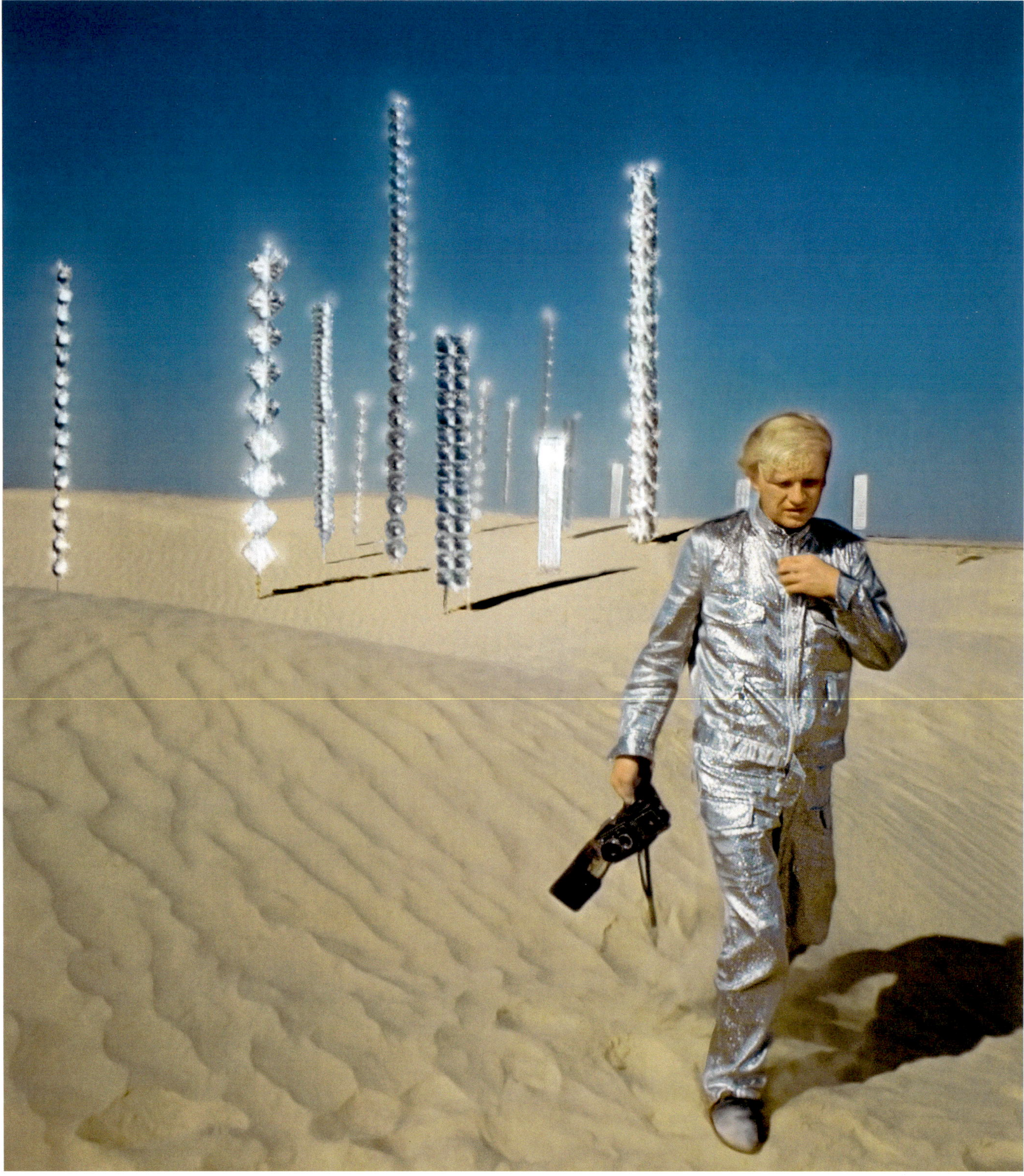

fig. 108 Heinz Mack during the filming for *Tele-Mack* in the Tunisian desert, 1968, photo: Edwin Braun

silver overalls, Mack looks like a lost space traveler on an alien planet. Yet Mack, as tiny as he may seem, adopts a powerful stance in the endless sea of sand: *I am here*. Iconically, this figure of the self lost in the infinite corresponds to another action, in which colored weather balloons were released in front a huge iceberg. Once again, these are signals sent from a tiny figure standing on the plateau of an enormous iceberg – in the same antenna pose as in the desert. It is the same stance, wavering between triumphant and lost, self-aggrandizing and self-diminishing, that we encounter in a photo of the 24-year-old artist, taken when he visited the Tunisian desert for the first time in 1955.

figs. 127, 143

fig. 134

fig. 106

figs. 107, 182

figs. 108, 140, 141, 153

Mack also worked with light steles in the desert; in 1967 he created a plantation of mirrors, which, like a solar field, pulled the blue light of the sky down onto the sand; or he stuck rows of mirrors or shards of mirrors into the sand, so as to carry out upside-down experiments. He turned fan- or flower-shaped aluminum webs into "artificial gardens" in the arid sea of sand. He scored, raked and scraped a 25 × 5-meter field into the soft wave patterns of the sand, as though it were a meditative Zen garden or a message to the gods above. He placed a red and white aluminum reflector strip measuring 56 by 2.2 meters in the Grand Erg Occidental, invoking the linear scales familiar to us from cartography and suggesting that this might be the start of a scale measurement of the desert. This is also reminiscent of the 15-metre-long, aluminum *Great Space Arrow* mirroring the blue sky that Mack positioned in the sand of the finely grooved slope of a dune, also in the Grand Erg Occidental. As a signal for direction, this arrow is absurd in the desert, but it points exactly toward the tiny figure of Mack in the distance in his silver outfit. In another piece, he tracked the changing rays of light in the desert with a descending line of reflective aluminum rods; in reality an impossible project and yet a self-conscious marking of the empty space and a model for countless light steles, which are an archetypal form in Mack's work. Of course, he also erected these light steles in the desert.

Ephemeral Signatures and Dynamic Structures

These projects are almost always about actions of implanting or of signification.[6] They are culturally constituitive acts of scoring and marking spaces of archaic barrenness. Mack undertakes expeditions to the ends of the earth and to the genesis of culture. He places testimonies to almost archaic cultural activities right in the middle of these inhospitable landscapes of sand and ice. Nonetheless, the sublime and dangerous vastness of the desert leaves space for hominisation. Considering the environmental catastrophes caused by technical culture today, it is remarkable that Mack does not perform any gestures of power, but rather interprets the disappearing traces of the primary acts of culture. Although they are all markings, scorings, drawings made by humans, the traces of the work have faded away. It is as though the thingly significations of art – the arrow, the artificial garden, the raked grid pattern, the light steles, the weather balloons – are not of this world at all. It is as though these works are not images made by hand, but *acheiropoíeta* that have fallen from the sky. This is the word that was used for icons and holy images, from which all traces of their "manufacture" had been erased: images not of this world, but yet appearing in

6 The light experiments in the Wahiba Desert from 1968–97 are particularly impressive, cf. Schmied, *Utopie und Wirklichkeit*, figs. 27–34. Here too the honeycomb aluminum and thousands of small prisms are important for breaking and reflecting the light. The *Jardin Artificiel* also consists of objects planted into the sand, a mixture of extreme artificiality and natural phenomena like light, sand, wind, and ice working together that is typical of Mack.

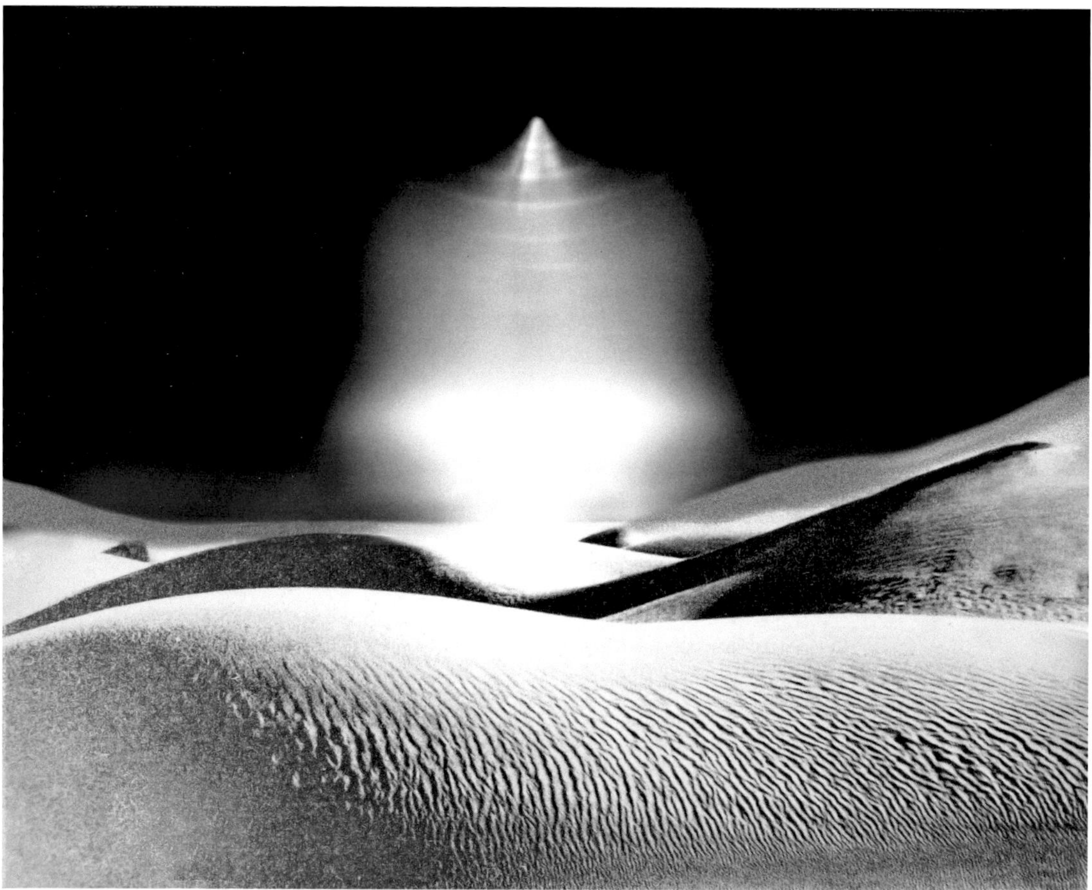

fig. 109 Heinz Mack, *Virtual Volume*, 1963, photo collage

it through some mysterious act of image creation. Mack's signatures – all these works are the artist's suprapersonal signatures – are erased from his works. In full knowledge that the objectified works, no doubt personifications of the artist, will disappear in the desert sand anyway. That is a powerful, perhaps even depressing lesson of nature.

It is the camera that attempts to prevent the accelerated disappearance of art works and other human relics with documentary images. The images of Mack's work are not, however, documents of the installations as they "really" were in the desert and the ice, but rather stylized pictures taken by professional photographers like Thomas Höpker and Lothar Wolleh or Mack himself, or filmed for *Tele-Mack*. They created the iconic images of these expeditions, which are all documents of Mack's intended aesthetic.

It is not for this reason alone that all of Mack's works are only made possible by technology. On the one hand, we see the metamorphic and powerful dynamics of nature and the elements, on the other, art in its formative creativity. In the digital control of the play of light, we might recognize the *quinta essentia*, which was once the divine, immaterial element that enveloped everything and held it together in a mathematical form. The successor to this subtlest of manifestations of ancient spirit exists today in the universe of signs operating in media technology: signs that are processed by mathematics and the algorithms of image and language. This makes not only knowledge and technical action possible, but also communication. In Mack's work, attention must

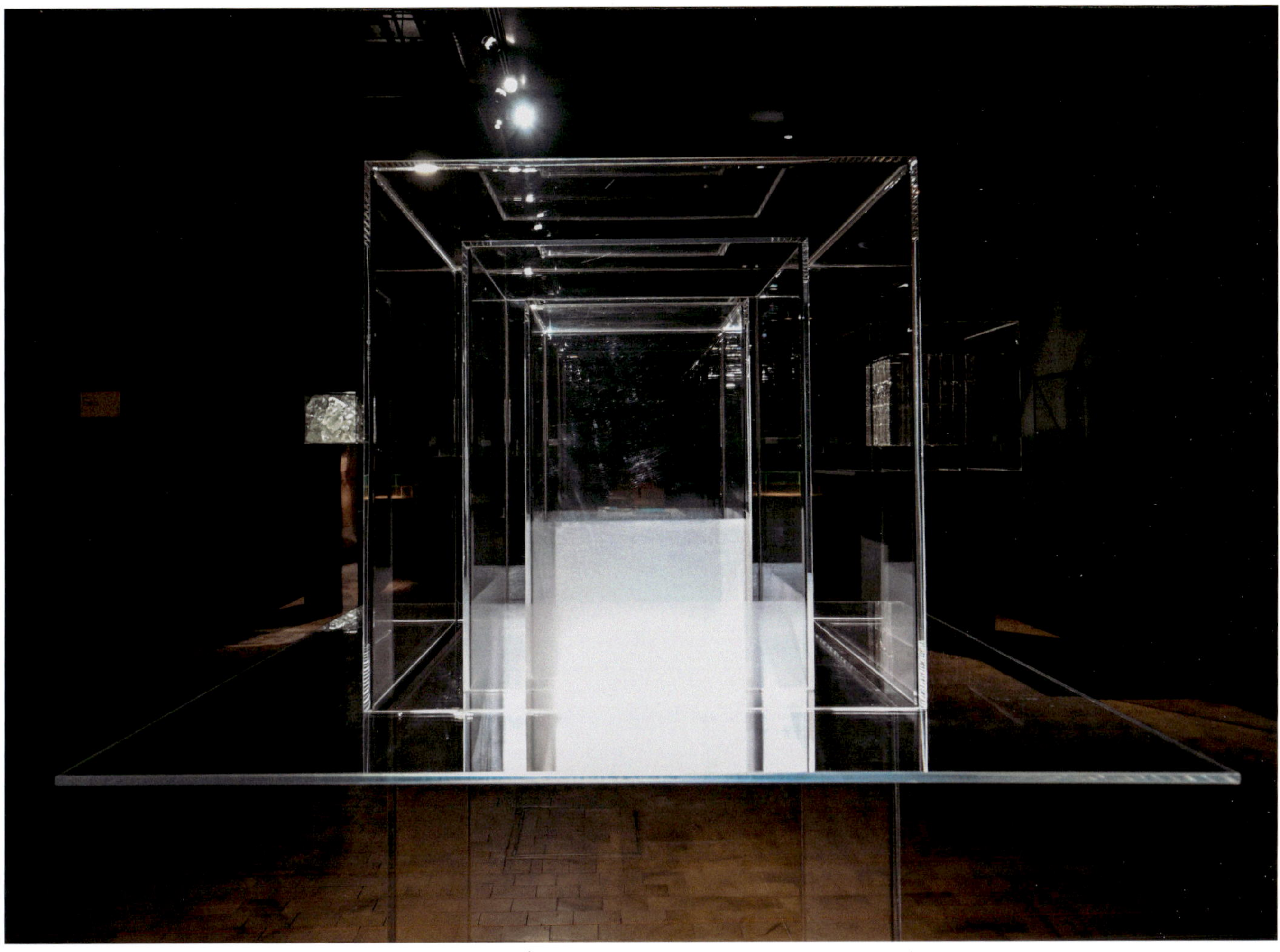

fig. 110 Heinz Mack, *Untitled*, 2020, cube, exhibition view, ZKM | Karlsruhe 2023

always be paid to the technical, mechanical and digital aspects. Only the technology, often hidden, enables the material objects to interact with the elements and the ether.

figs. 238, 240, 245, 247, 261, 264

In his work, mathematics – the ether of modernity – is always at play. As early as 1957, Mack made dynamic, structured grids, which resemble circuit boards for electronic components (printed circuit boards, stripboards), like complex barcodes or music scores, in his studio in Düsseldorf. Scored lines as code stretch from the earliest mathematics on Babylonian notched tablets all the way to the optoelectronic barcodes that organize our world of commodity-things and their logistics today. The first experiments with this technology were only carried out a few years *after* Mack's dynamic, structured grids. Nowadays the barcodes and the QR-codes are ubiquitous, but Mack had already been experimenting with geometric, mathematical patterns in his reliefs for decades, with spherical light refractions, with polished stainless steel or anodized aluminum foil, which is dynamically structured by light, folds, and perforations. His work with light refraction and geometric figures, one could argue, is mathematics implemented in art. In any case, Mack's forms are geometry transformed into art, expressions of the immaterial spirit in material language.[7]

fig. 111

7 Albrecht Dürer believed that geometry was the ideal path to aesthetic knowledge, because it revealed "art in nature." Cf. Albrecht Dürer, *Schriftlicher Nachlass*, ed. Hans Rupprich, 3 vols. (Berlin: Deutscher Verein für Kunstwissenschaft, 1956–69), here vol. I, 106; I,145–6.; III, 168–9 III, 295–6.

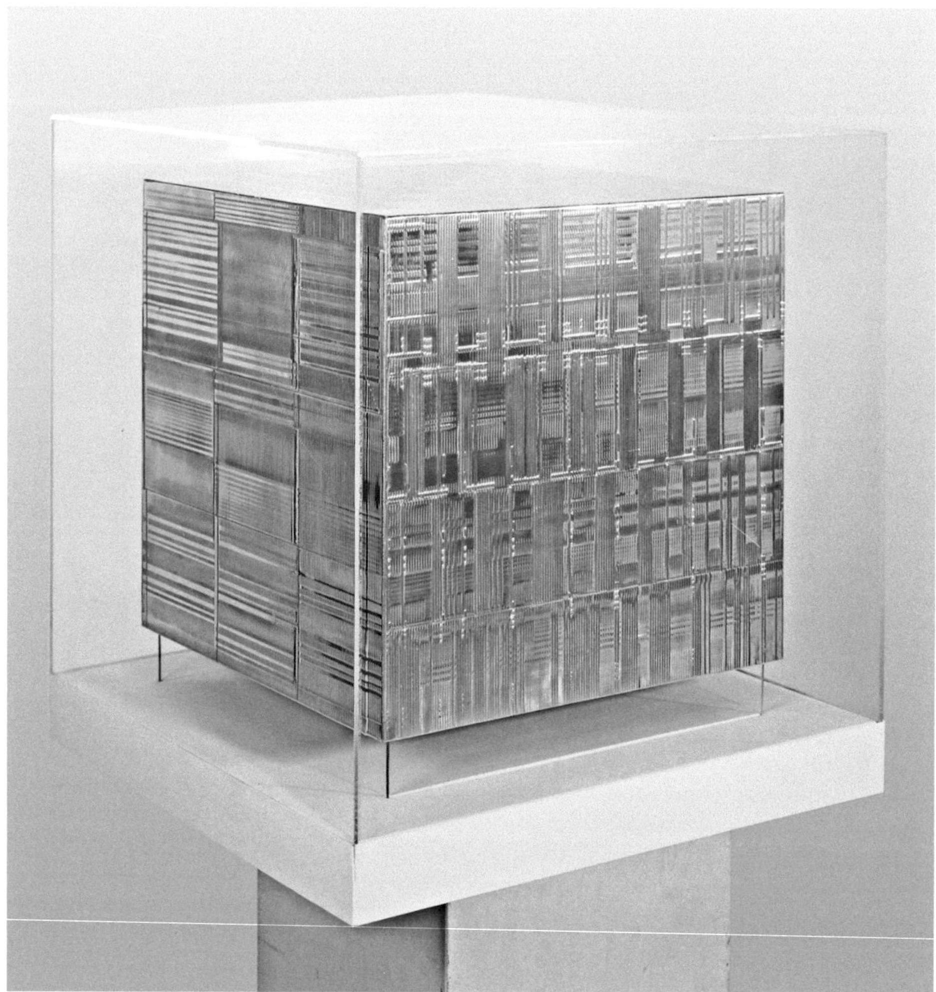

fig. 111 Heinz Mack, *Kaaba*, 1958, cube: aluminum, wood, acrylic glass, 70×65×65 cm

In the Middle Ages, the god-artist (*deus geometra*) is the creator whose symbol is the mathematical compass, with which the world of materialized forms, i.e. earth and space, are created.[8] The Platonic solids that underlie all existence are geometric constructions that are calculated mathematically. Johannes Kepler[9] and Isaac Newton also pursued this idea, the latter portrayed by William Blake naked at the bottom of the sea and equipped with a compass (1795/1805). It would be worth attempting to identify the "Platonic solids" that become the immaterial building blocks of Mack's work, and thus also of his construction of the world. The stele as *axis mundi* (cf. the *Endless Column* by Constantin Brancusi, 1937/38) is also a primal form in Mack's work, just like the circle, spiral, triangle, ray of light (the line), etc. It is no coincidence that one of his ephemeral pieces with metallic acetate film in the Algerian desert is called *Dream of the Geometrician* (1976): nothing, and that is already everything, but the marking of a line in the empty landscape of the dunes. The geometrician dreaming in forms of elementary geometry here is Mack himself. The scored clay tablets from Babylon, however, are one of the earliest forms of writing and counting. Mack was already referring to them as "dynamic structures" in the 1950s. He knows that they laid the groundwork for the mathematical algorithm, but also for kinetics. Algorithms

fig. 112

8 *Bible moralisee. Codex Vindobonensis 2554 der Österreichischen Nationalbibliothek*, ed. Reiner Hausherr (Graz: Aveda, 1992). Cf. Friedrich Ohly, "Deus Geometra. Skizzen zur Geschichte einer Vorstellung von Gott," in: *Tradition als historische Kraft*, ed. Norbert Kamp and Joachim Wollasch (Berlin/New York: De Gruyter, 1982), 1–42.

9 Johannes Kepler, *Mysterium Cosmographicum* (Tübingen, 1596), caput II, tabula III.

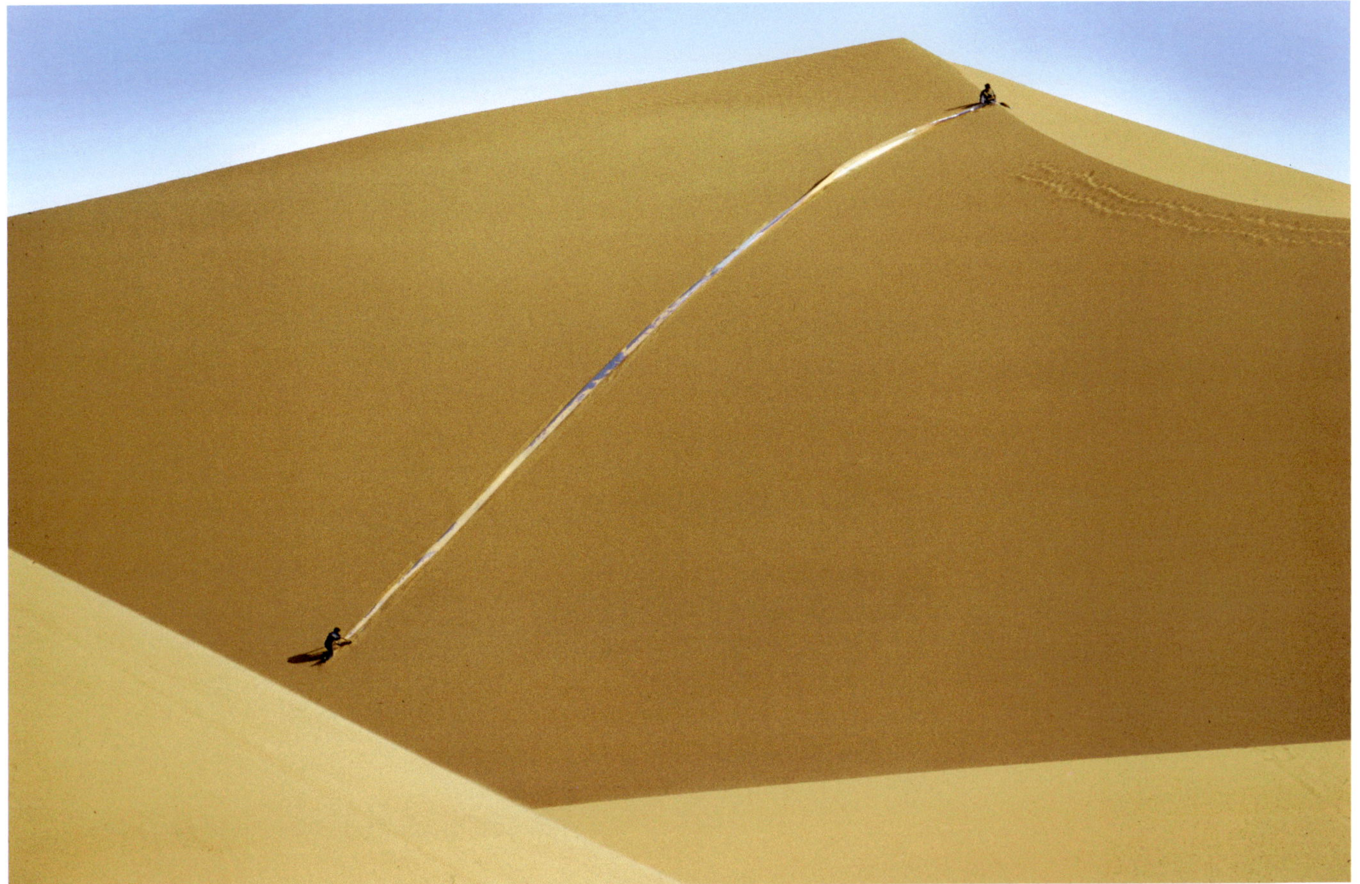

fig. 112 Heinz Mack, *Dream of the Geometrician*, Grand Erg Occidental, Algeria, 1976, aluminum foil, lengh ca. 200 m, photo: Thomas Höpker

are translated into many of Mack's light pieces, especially the electronic, mechanical installations, and into kinetic objects, inherent to which are an invisible mathematics. The explicit reference to ether in Mack's art is most evident in his highly technical installations.[10]

Towards an Aesthetic Theory

Once again, it is no coincidence that Mack gives one of his perfect light reliefs the title *The Sea I (Light-Relief)* (1963): a fine mesh of aluminum with horizontal grooves is framed by a silver-plated wooden panel and covered with acrylic glass. The honeycomb structure of the aluminum changes with the light. Every groove is individualized by tiny irregularities. Again, we see how Mack combines heterogeneous materials sympoietically. It is precisely this sympoiesis of the heterogenous that Mack calls "structure": "Structure is a comprehensive system, in the sense of a strict order. It is a programmatic concept that refers to the overall makeup of a system of relationships, into which all parts are integrated and have the function of supporting and revealing the ordering system."[11] The mesh with its horizontal grooves creates the formal unity of the material multiplicity. The title *The Sea I (Light-Relief)* gives it an elemental twist that associates the piece with natural philosophy. Is the sea, the hydrosphere, number "I" in the tetrad of the elements? A hidden reference to Thales? Or is the "I" only a playful wink at Albrecht Dürer's *Melencolia I* (1514), of which there was no continuation either?

10 The *ether as quinta essentia* is the first, eternal, ageless, unchanging and inviolable entity, revolving around itself and forming the sphere of the sky (*tò proton soma*). The ether is thus most closely related to light and the mathematical structure of the universe. This is why Mack's light art is a descendant of the theory of ether.

11 Heinz Mack, "Structure" (2010), in: Susanne Titz and Jee-Hae Kim, eds., *Mack. Kinetics*, exh. cat. Museum Abteiberg Mönchengladbach (Düsseldorf: Richter, 2011), 299–300, here 299. Cf. also Heinz Mack, "The New Dynamic Structure," ibid., 19–21, also in: Raphael Gatel, Grègoire Robinne and Matthieu Poirier, eds., *Mack. Spectrum 1950–2016*, exh. cat. Galerie Perrotin, Paris (Paris: Éditions Dilecta, 2016), as an insert, n. p.

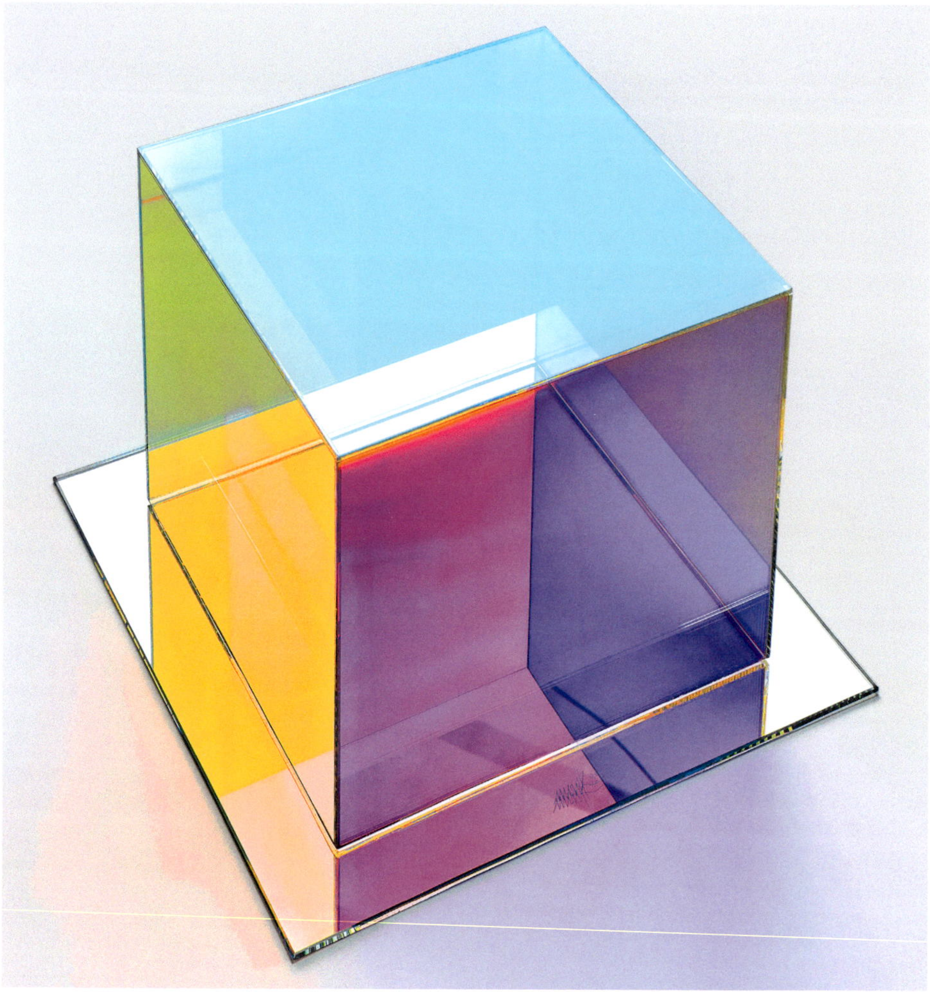

fig. 113 Heinz Mack, *Light Pavillion I*, 2006, cube

With the concept of "dynamic structure," Mack clearly found his guiding aesthetic principle very early on. First and foremost, this means a wholeness based on the integration of heterogenous parts. As innovative as ZERO art is and as contemporary as Mack's artistic sensibility, the link to classical and Renaissance aesthetic theories is also unmistakable. Leon Battista Alberti used the terms *concinnitas/ integritas* for what Mack called wholeness: symmetry, order, harmony, elegance, mathematical transparency, totality, and integrity. It is important to note that Mack understands "dynamic structure" as a force or capacity (*dynamis*) that operates both in art *and* nature, in the macro- *and* microcosm. "Structure" demonstrates *dynamis* and *energeia*, potency and action, i.e. the capacity for realization.[12] In Alberti's aesthetic, whether Mack follows it deliberately or not, there are further aspects to wholeness that can all be viewed as part of Mack's "dynamic structure": cohesion (*cohesio*), harmony (*consensus*), number and relationship (*finitio*), arrangement (*collocatio*), connection (*nexus*), and agreement (*compactum*).[13]

These characteristics can easily be identified in Mack's light reliefs, e.g. in the *The Dance (Light-Relief)* (1963) or in the desert experiments with the *Jardin Artificiel* (1968–97). Two further concepts are important: symmetry and repetition. The furrows, grooves, scores,

figs. 3, 30, 115

fig. 116

12 Mack, "Structure," 300.

13 Leon Battista Alberti, *On Painting*, ed. and trans. Rocco Sinisgalli (Cambridge: Cambridge University Press, 2011) and idem., *De Re Aedificatoria. On the Art of Building in Ten Books*, trans. Joseph Rykwert, Robert Tavernor and Neil Leach (Cambridge, MA: MIT Press, 1988), here IX, 5. See also: Robert William Tavernor, *Concinnitas in the Architectural Theory and Practice of Leon Battista Alberti* (Cambridge: Cambridge University Press, 1985); Anthony Grafton, *Leon Battista Alberti. Baumeister der Renaissance* (Berlin: Hill & Wang Pub, 2002).

fig. 114 Heinz Mack, *The Sea I (Light-Relief)*, 1963, aluminum on wood, silver bronzed, acrylic glass, 214 × 115 × 10 cm

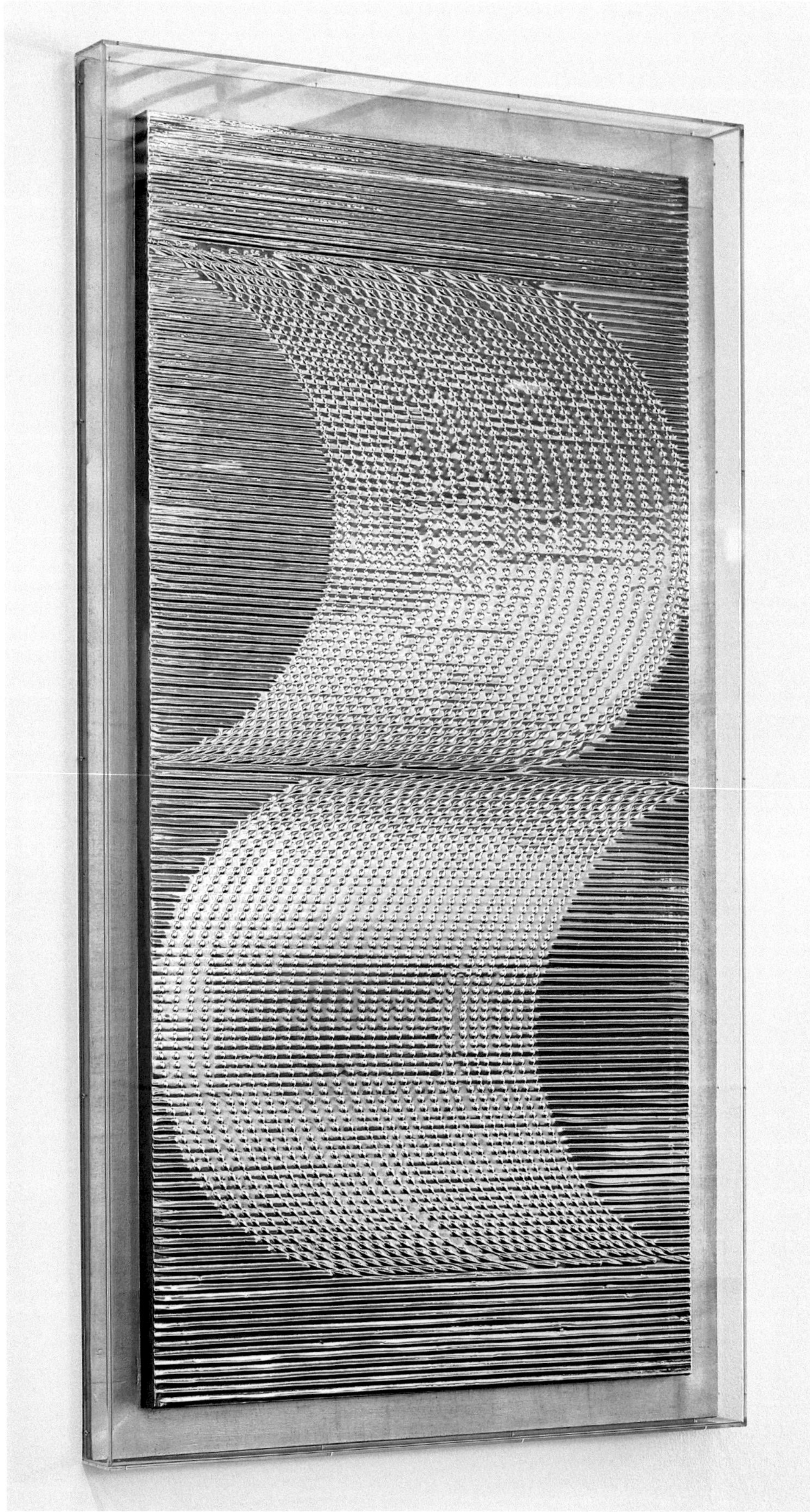

fig. 115 Heinz Mack, *The Dance (Light-Relief)*, 1963, light relief

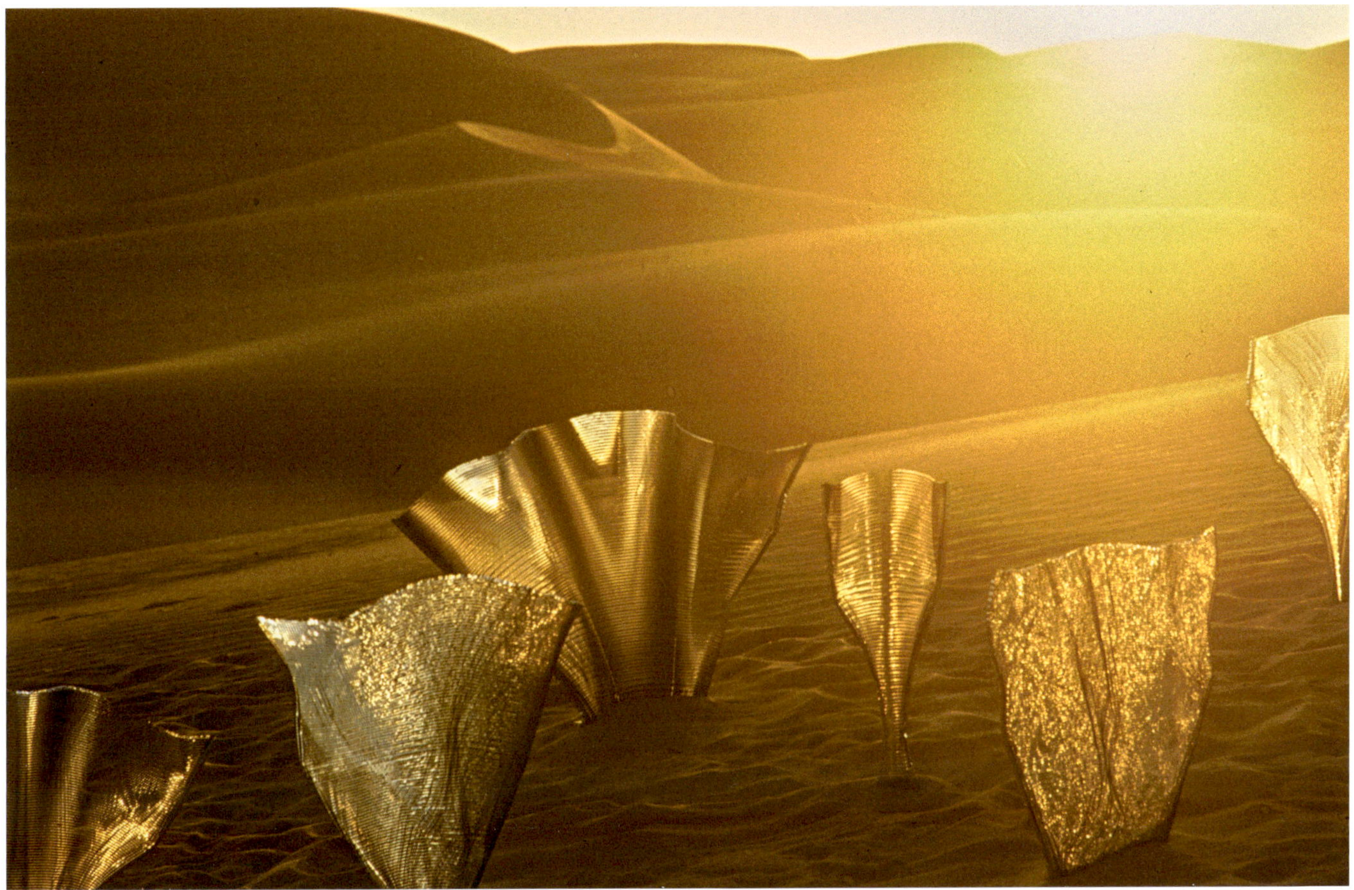

fig. 116 Heinz Mack, *Light Fans*, Grand Erg Oriental, Tunisia, 1968, light sculpture, photo: Edwin Braun

lamellae, folds, serrated lines, which are arranged symmetrically, in parallel, or according to a geometric pattern, always occur in multiples. Repetition and minimal deviation, identity and difference, organize the reliefs and most of Mack's other groups of works. The symmetry produces relations, correspondences, similarities, and self-references (of images to themselves): every point has a corresponding equivalent in precisely one other point. Similarity and repetition produce seriality. Many types of series can be identified in Mack's work (e.g. the steles), each generated according to the same pattern of production and yet open to variation. If ornamentation or arabesques are created in the process, they nonetheless all obey the principle of infinite repetition.

figs. 13, 43, 117

This must be balanced by an equally infinite variability, so as to avoid, as Mack writes, idle states, boredom, or overwhelmingness. Here the temporality of the relief becomes a criteria: it makes a difference to the whole whether the repetition is holistically integrated through rhythm, arrangement, and relationship (*finitio*), or whether it veers towards empty time, boredom, and tedium. Mack, who is musically highly educated, also identifies this ambiguous relationship in music.[14] For example, in his famous *Bolero,* Maurice Ravel develops an intricate pattern of notes consisting of repetition and variation, a more radical version of which can be found, according to Mack, in twelve-tone music, or in Cubism and Structuralism in visual art. Johann Sebastian Bach's *The Art of Fugue* should also certainly be mentioned here.

fig. 118

14 A seminal work on this is: Magdalena Zorn, "Das Klingen sehen. Musikalität im Werk Macks," in: Van den Valentyn, *Heinz Mack*, 58–61; the section "Rhythmus auf dem Grund der Leere" is particuarly important.

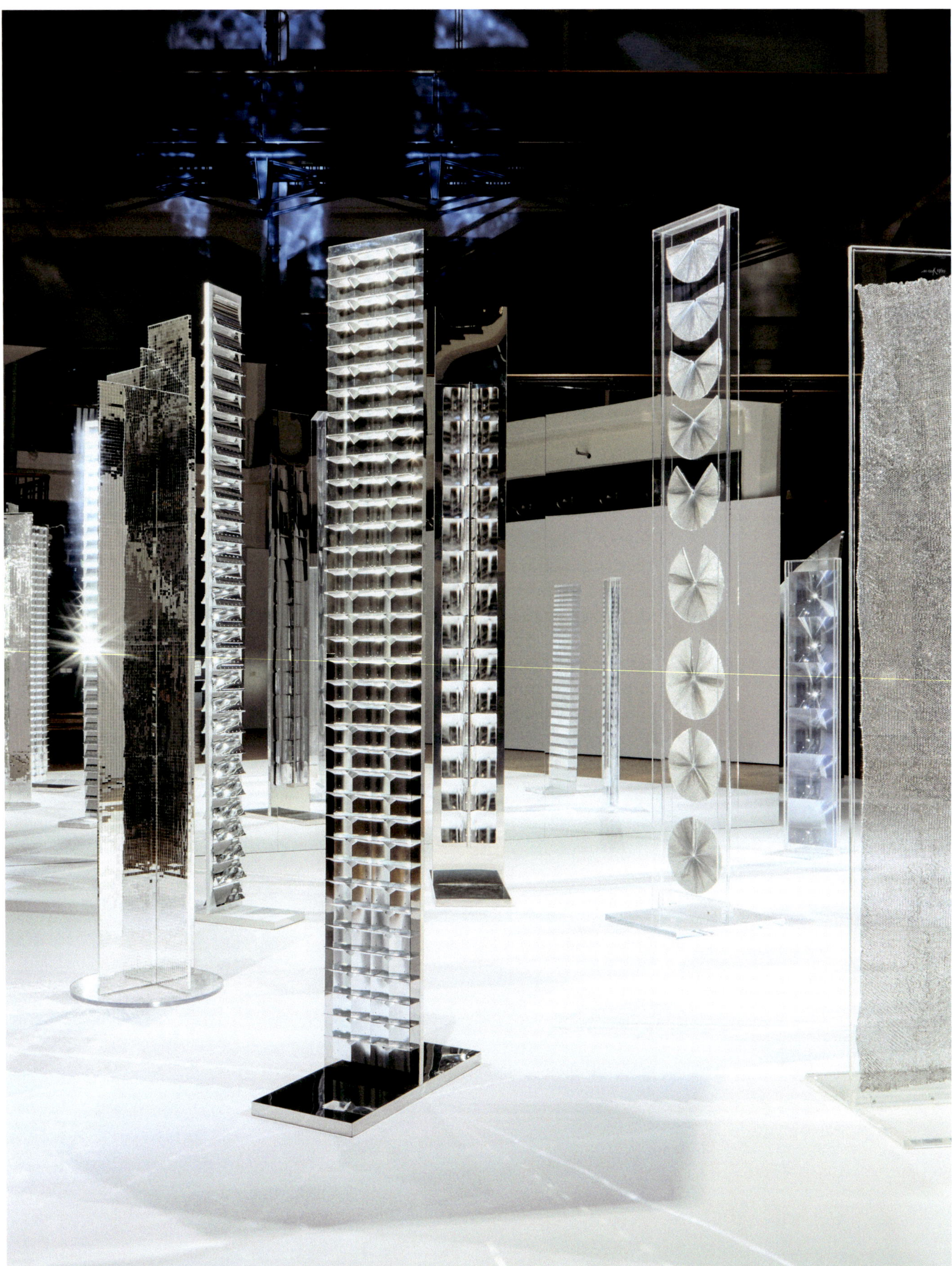

fig. 117 Heinz Mack, *Light Steles*, 1964–2020, installation view, ZKM | Karlsruhe 2023

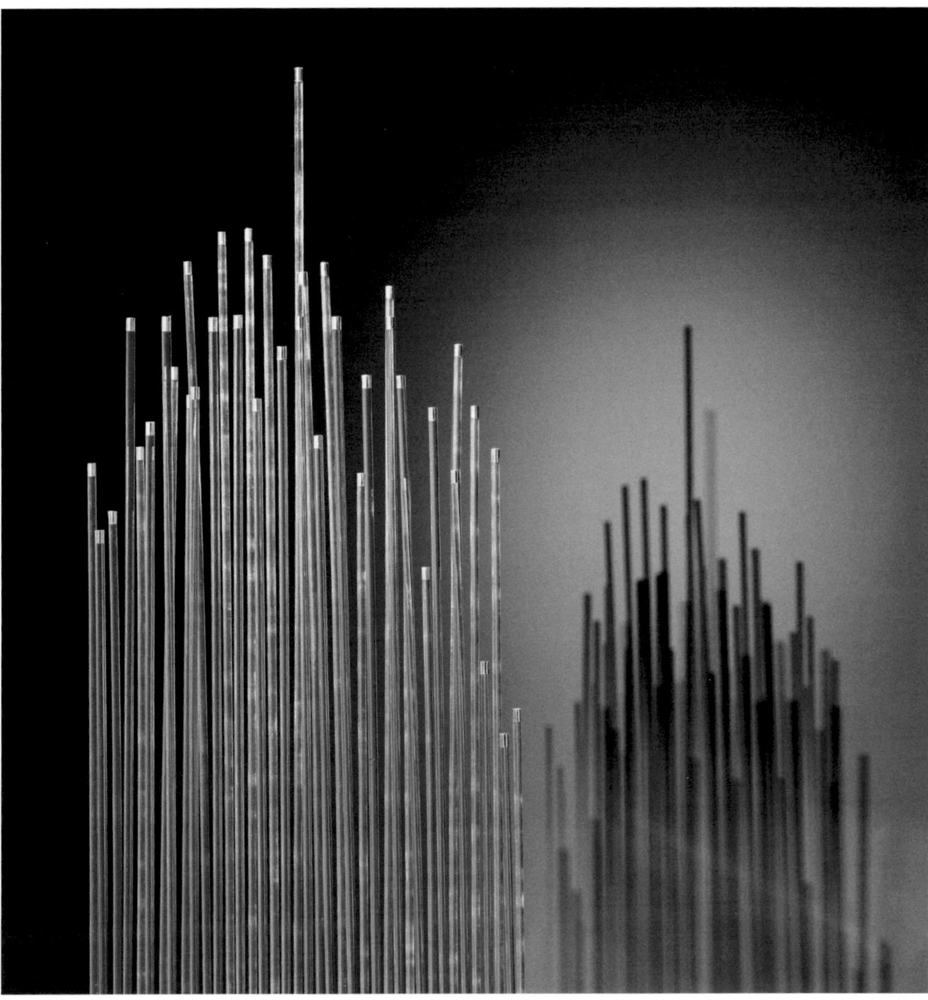

fig. 118 Heinz Mack, *Light Harp*, 1971, light sculpture, installation view, ZKM | Karlsruhe 2023

Fire and Air

Earth, water, and light have been the main focus of my observations thus far. But what about the elements of fire and air? According to Ancient Greek teachings, these are the opposites to water and earth and unlike these do not tend to move downwards, but upwards. In the *Stone Water Glass Sculpture*, the marble and water represent weighty heaviness and downward flow, in other words *gravitas*; light is the surrounding element, illuminating, diaphanous, and refractory. Where are the elements of air and fire to be found in Mack's work?

figs. 95, 96, 97

Let us take a look at the expedition to Greenland in 1976: Mack placed burning pitch torches on a square, wooden construction in an extremely rugged, icy landscape under the dim sky. He then sent the torch structure out into the endless Arctic Ocean as the *Fire Raft*. The appearance of the barely moving sea is reminiscent of his dynamic structural grids or the delicate ripples in the sand in the desert's sea of dunes. Icebergs on the horizon, horizontal windows in the sky letting the light into the image: golden pathways on the blue-silvery, shimmering waters of infinite calm. The fire, water, air, and light interact with each other, linked to each other by reflections and shades of color. The man-made raft carrying fire is reminiscent of Pyrophoros, the fire-carrier,

fig. 196

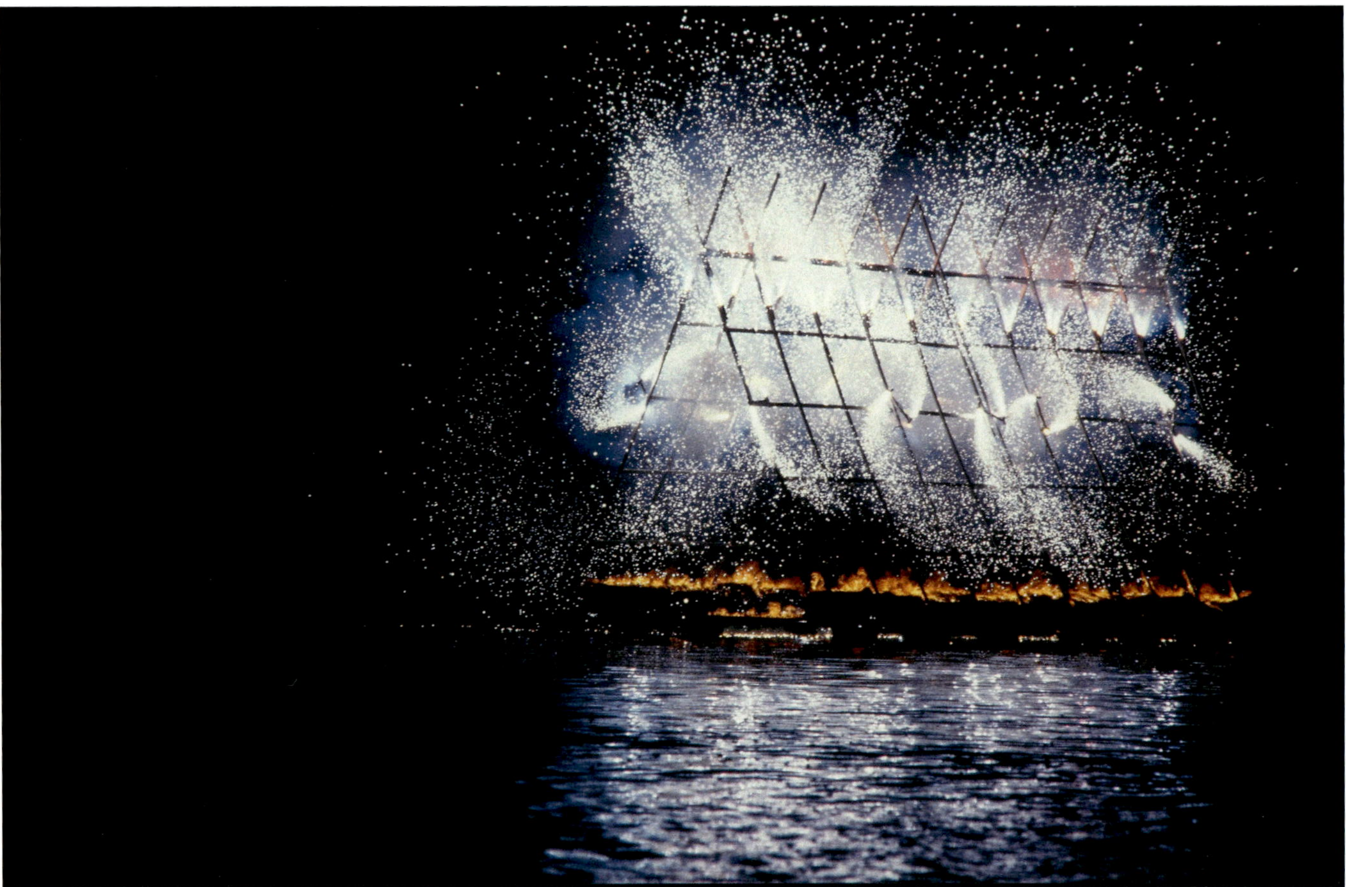

fig. 119 Heinz Mack, *Fire Ship*, Stuttgart 1979, pyrotechnics, wooden construction, c. 10 × 18 × 8 m, idea: 1963, realizations: 1968 for *Tele-Mack*, 1978–79 for light festivals in Essen, Duisburg and Stuttgart, 2010 for the Düsseldorf harbor

as Prometheus was also called. The Arctic fire installation also quotes the *Fire Ship*, which Mack burned in the Tunisian desert in 1968. Whenever a fire breaks out in a piece of art (and often destroys it in the process), it is an homage to Prometheus, who gave humanity the capacity for culture when he gave them fire.

fig. 119

In one of Mack's photographs, fire becomes a pure symbol, but also one devoid of meaning: he photographs the sun over the Sahara and one can almost feel its mercilessly burning flames. Mack also experimented with a slowly turning solar rotor, on whose surface the setting sun was reflected. Just above the horizon of the wavy, sandy ground of the desert, the reflected image of the sun appears in flashes, almost like the sudden flash of light at the beginning of creation. Between 1968 and 2010 in Essen, Duisburg, Düsseldorf, and Stuttgart, Mack produced a fire raft similar to the one sent out into the Arctic Ocean.[15] His experiments with light and fire in the desert established the paradigm for all of Mack's future light and kinetic pieces.

figs. 121, 122

On the almost motionless surface of the icy sea around Greenland, Mack and his team installed a seven-meter-high *Sail without Wind and Ship – The Secret of the Arctic* (1976) in front of a huge, jagged iceberg. How can this sail, the traditional emblem for the power of moving air, keep itself afloat on the water? It is an absolute sail. Mack had adopted a similar pose in his astronautical silver suit on a hill near the Kebili Oasis, holding up an eight-meter-long, metallic acetate

fig. 200

15 Cf. also the Stuttgart Festival of Lights, 1979, in: Titz and Kim, *Kinetics*, 242–7.

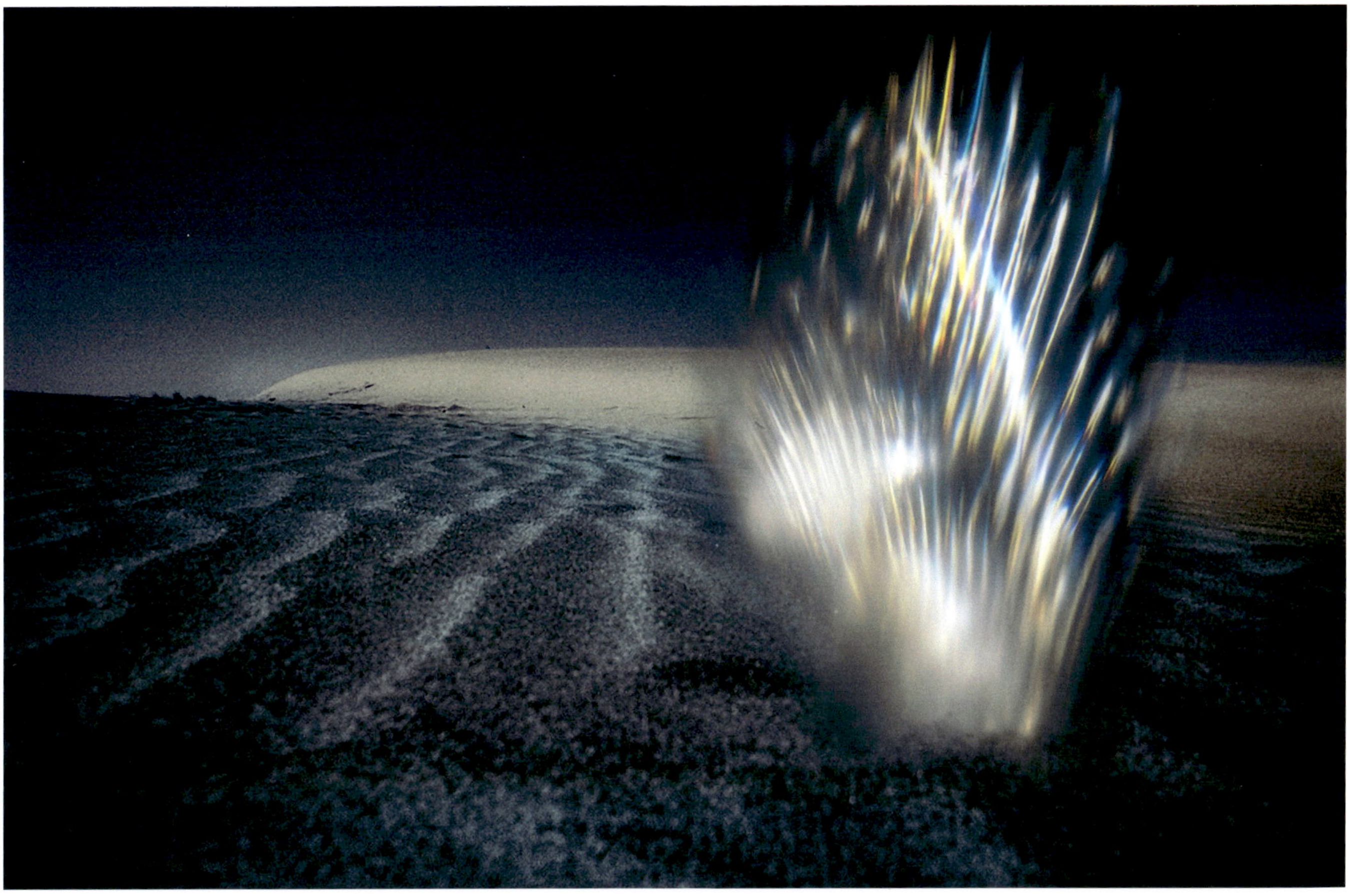

fig. 120 Heinz Mack, *Fire and Light Experiments in the Desert*, 1968, photo collage

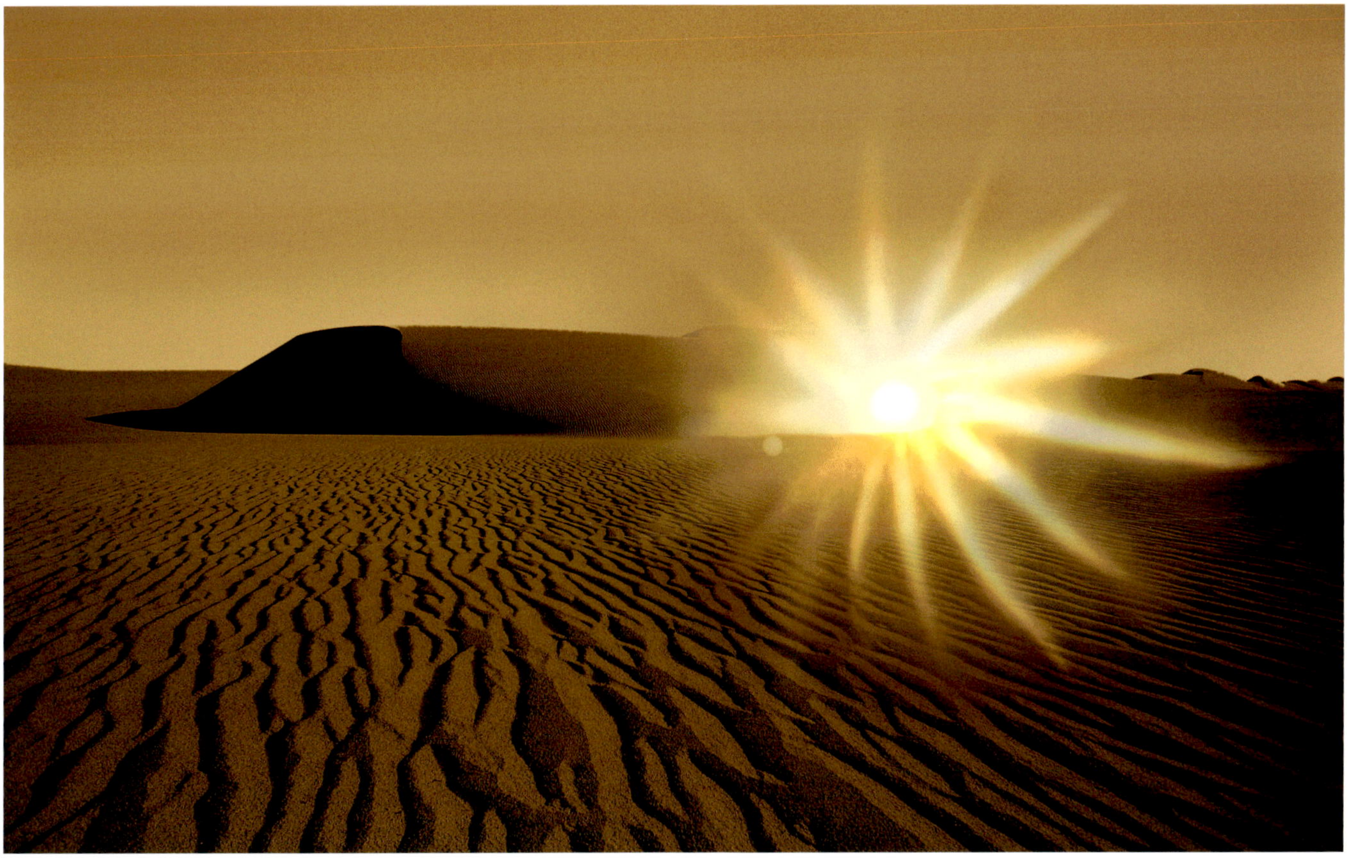

fig. 121 Heinz Mack, *Fire and Light Experiments in the Desert*, 1968, photo collage

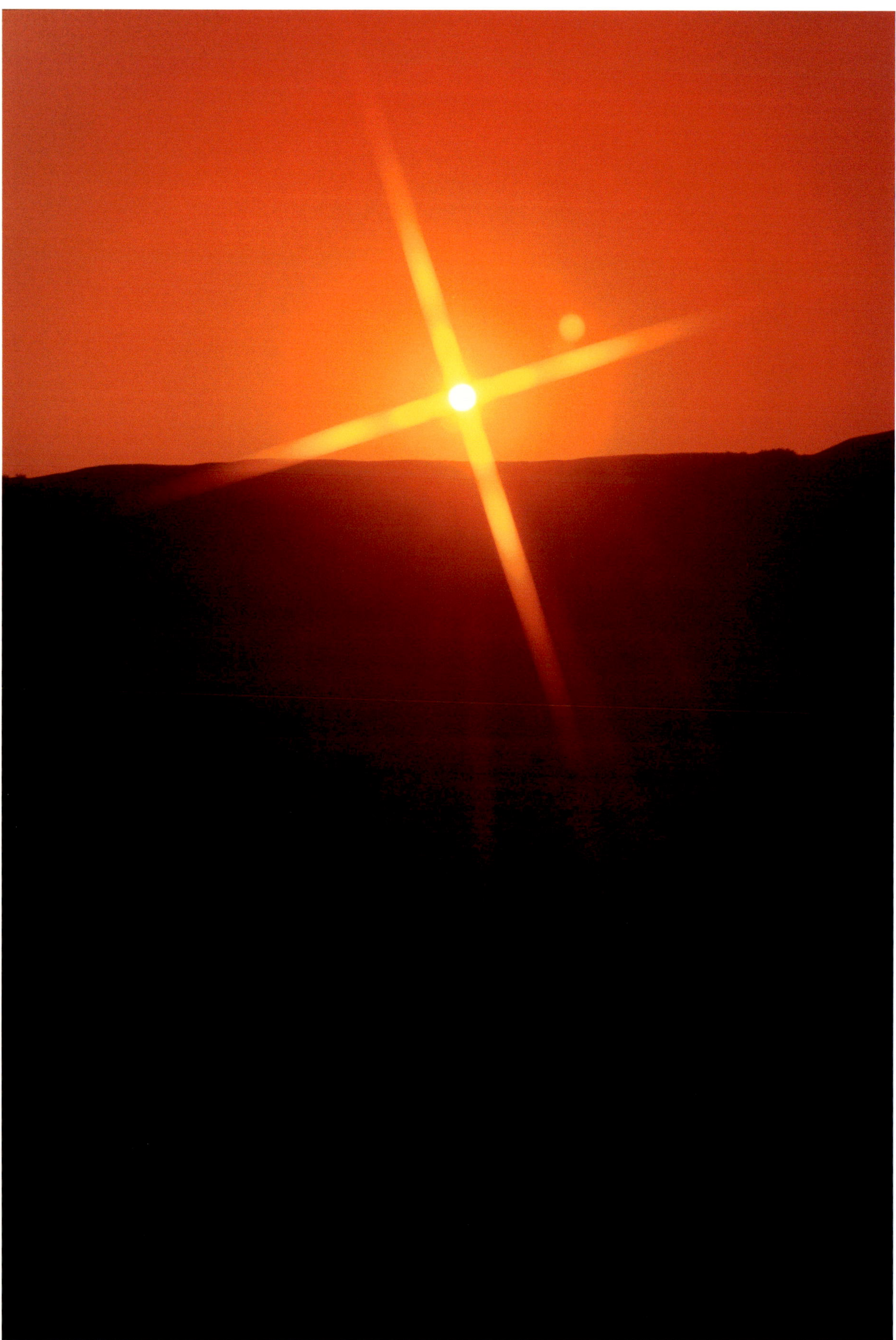

fig. 122 Heinz Mack, *Star, Space, Horizon*, 1970, photographic experiment

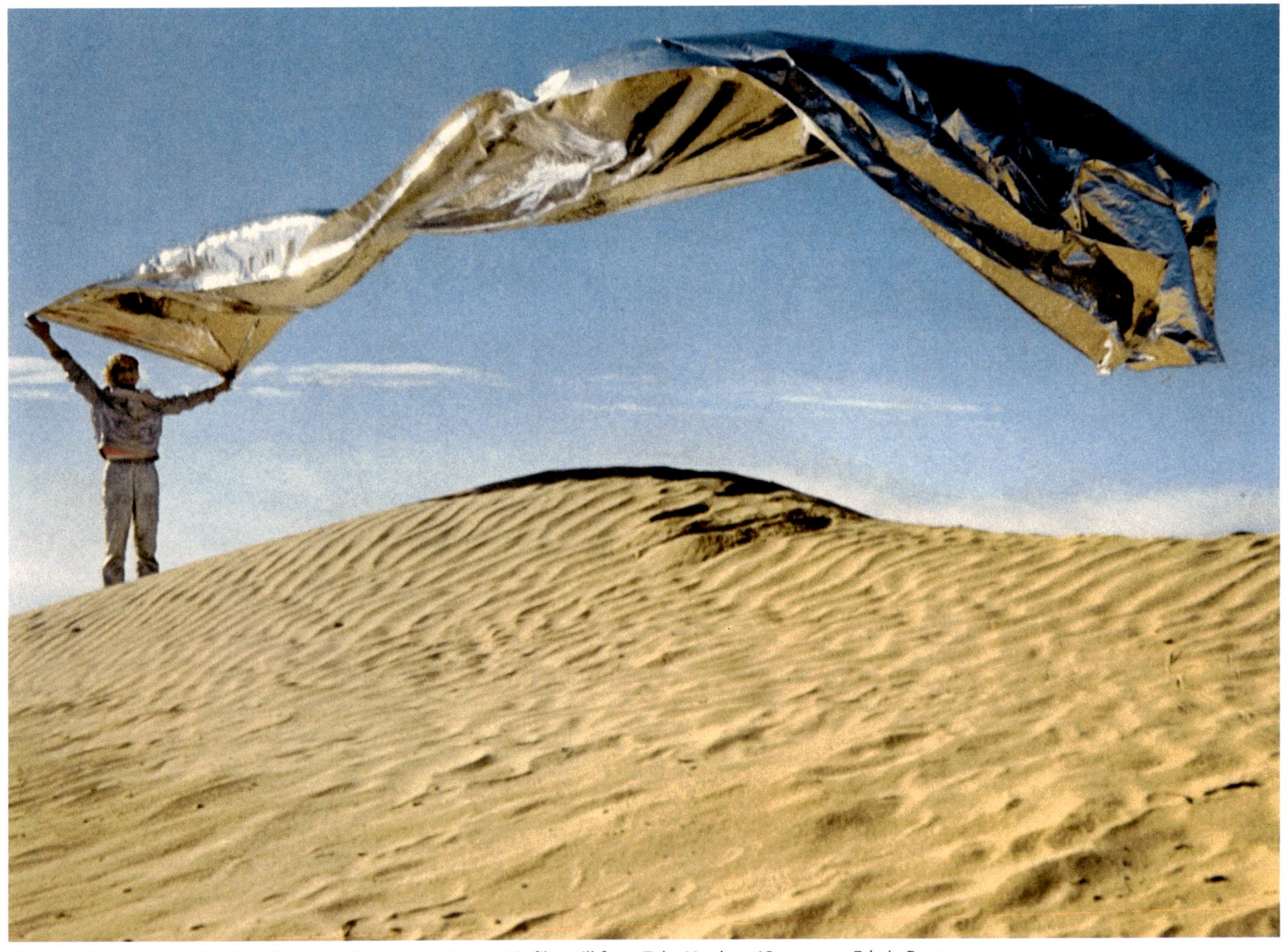

fig. 123 Heinz Mack with silver flag, Kebeli Oasis, Tunisia, 1968, film still from *Tele-Mack*, 1968, camera: Edwin Braun

fig. 123

sheet, which fluttered in the desert wind like a weather flag. Both actions had to grapple with the same problem in representing the element of air: moving air, wind, and storms appeal to the ear, but not the eye.

Wind and storms can also be felt on the skin, sometimes one even has to struggle to keep one's balance and stay upright. Air also conveys sensations of heat and cold. Combined with rain, hailstones, or snow, the potentially icy cold and stormy air can develop such force that we must fear for our ability to assert ourselves or even survive. In a hurricane we have to fight to breathe, for the breath of life. We start to panic. Of course, clouds, those wonderful airships of our imagination, are endlessly playful visualizations of air and its movements – yet clouds almost never appear in Mack's work. Nonetheless, he has an elementary approach to the air, namely in his two archetypes of space, the desert and the Arctic Ocean. The desert with its characteristic patterns in the sand – the endless ridges of the dunes and the fine-grained rhythm of the grooves in the sand – is a geomorphological artist of form *par excellence*. For an artist so aware of form and so sensitive to kinetic patterns like Mack, it must be an aesthetic validation that the ripples in the sand are formed by the same physical force in both the ocean and the desert: the water currents and the wind. Water and air, or the sea, sand, and wind, therefore correspond to each other in how their patterns are formed. In the sea and the desert, currents of water and air reveal their unique power to shape the environment, sometimes gentle and constant, sometimes stormy and unbridled. "Vis superba formae" – the proud power of form, as Goethe once quoted. This power to create form is also intrinsic to the very elements that do not possess a fixed form themselves: water and air.

fig. 124

In 1972, Mack developed the idea of a *Water Cloud* and created a sculpture out of air and water, illuminated at night, in the Olympic Park in Munich. In it, the elements celebrated a joyous marriage in the shooting and spraying jets of water, weaving delicate aerosol veils or falling back down into the water. 74,000 liters of water a minute sprayed through 98 nozzles into the sea of air, the two elements united against their nature (*para physin*) in one ephemerous *coniunctio*. Technology and art work, as Aristotle knew, not with nature, but against it. The elements fused by Mack, although separate by nature, cannot be permanently joined – but can, like an oxymoron, temporarily overcome their contradictions, just as it was possible for fire and ice to coexist on the raft.

The Obsolescence and Relevance of the Theory of the Elements

The cathedral is the art of light in stone and glass. Dürer's landscape watercolors demonstrate a new kind of "aquatic" brushstroke. William Turner's paintings are studies of light and water. Landscape art has depicted the atmosphere of landscapes created by the interplay of the elements and light since the seventeenth century. Friedrich Hölderlin's language also pursues a poetry of the current. Friedrich Nietzsche's philosophy follows a wind rose of thought. Landscape painting reached its peak when painters learned to portray the hazy fragrance of distance, air. Art around 1800 was a new stage in the discovery of nature. This is evident in exhibitions from the last few decades, for example *Water, clouds, light and stones. The Discovery of Landscape in European Painting around 1800* (Mittelrhein-Museum Koblenz, 2002), *Expedition Kunst. The Discovery of Nature from C. D. Friedrich to Humboldt* (Hamburger Kunsthalle, Hamburg, 2002) or *Nature unleashed. The Depiction of Catastrophe since 1600* (Hamburger Kunsthalle, Hamburg, 2018).[16]

The latter focused on the destructive side of nature, which Goethe also emphasized in his weather studies. Along with their integrative power, the destructive side of the elements, which is deeply rooted in collective memory, has never been suppressed. Consecutive major disasters are particularly terrible. For example, in 1775 an earthquake in Lisbon was followed by a tsunami, fires, and social anomie. These kinds of cascades still happen to this day, as in Japan in 2011, when an undersea earthquake caused a tsunami, which resulted in both massive flooding and the nuclear reactor meltdown in Fukushima, which triggered mass migration and made entire regions uninhabitable due to radioactive contamination.

There is no doubt that we must still contend with the four classical elements and the *quinta essentia* culturally, artistically, and in practical terms for our lives today. One might say that atomic explosions and catastrophic nuclear meltdowns represent the "dirty" side, so to speak, of the once sublime and divine ether/light. On the other hand, the natural sciences have *uno sono* almost totally dismantled the theory of the elements: it has been declared irrelevant.

16 The original titles of these exhibitions are translated from the German: *Wasser, Wolken, Licht und Steine. Die Entdeckung der Landschaft in der europäischen Malerei um 1800* (Mittelrhein-Museum Koblenz, 2002), *Expedition Kunst. Die Entdeckung der Natur von C. D. Friedrich bis Humboldt* (Hamburger Kunsthalle, Hamburg, 2002) or *Entfesselte Natur. Das Bild der Katastrophe seit 1600* (Hamburger Kunsthalle, Hamburg, 2018).

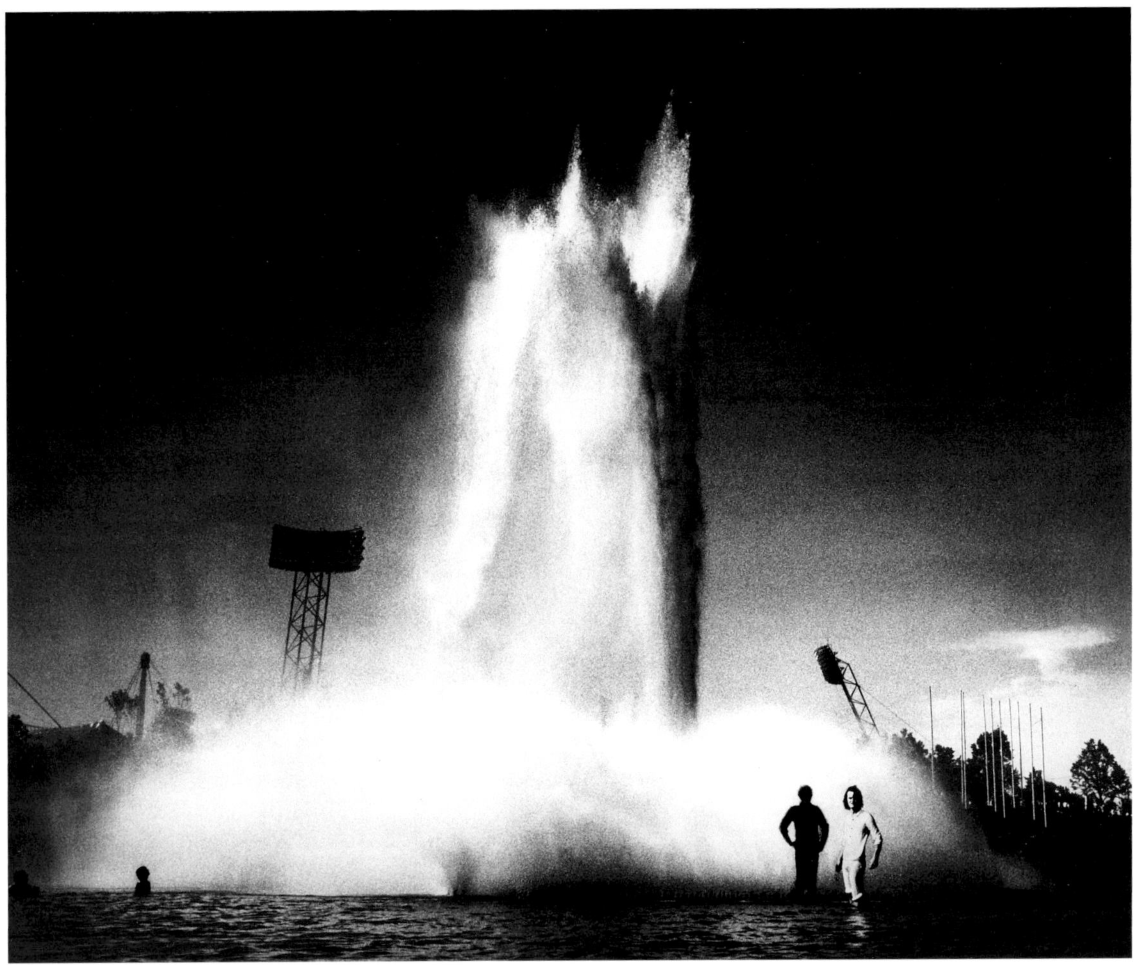

fig. 124 Heinz Mack, *Water Cloud*, 1971-1972, Olympic Park, Munich, water games, height: 8 – max. 36 m, photo: Lothar Wolleh

However, when one sees how an artist like Mack, who is familiar with the sciences and technology, has been using science and the elements as a distinguishing mark of his art for more than six decades, one must ask whether this should be taken seriously not just aesthetically, but also epistemologically. Can Mack's art (but also some land art and nature writing) be viewed as a rehabilitation of the theory of elements in public, urban spaces and museums? Could this become a force in its own right in the discourse of political ecology and the Anthropocene? After all, many important parameters used to explain our entering the new geological era of the Anthropocene are of a planetary nature and therefore also belong to the philosophy of the elements.

To conclude, I will therefore ask whether the elements, 200 years after their liquidation, are fundamental for ecological discourse today. Of course, this cannot mean simply reproducing the theory of elements. What matters is their epistemological transformation. We have already seen how Mack transforms the elements into the idiom of art. By making them innovative, experimental, critical, interventional, disruptive, he overcomes their ancient character. There is never any one-to-one equivalence in Mack; otherwise, he would no longer be a modern artist. But what is precisely interesting is that Mack, as a representative of an avantgarde that seeks to rethink art from the ground up (ZERO), makes use of the traditions of natural philosophy and the elements.

Ecology is a science where the four categories of the elements, despite being rejected by the modern sciences, become applicable again. Perhaps the liquidation of the elements was a mistake that has in fact contributed to today's ecological disasters? Is the persistent presence of the elements in the field of art a sign of that? Are the elements a kind of mirror, in which the arts and ecology are reflected in each other? Has the wholeness and singularity of nature been lost along with the elements? Do we only become aware of the elementary in nature again when natural disasters occur—earthquakes, volcanic explosions, floods, tsunamis, typhoons, periods of drought, desertification, soil karstification, burning forests, melting glaciers, and receding ice caps? Added to this are energy crises, famines, and mass migration, species extinction and the catastrophic overexploitation of resources which were once the "worthy gifts" of the elements.

In our technical world, the elements seem to have been pushed to the edge of civilization's perception. Nature, bodies, elements, but also animals, plants, and the climate are no longer simply a given. They are becoming artificial in the sense that they are put under protection, or even must be produced. In short: they are not the sacrosanct foundation of existence, but aspects of individual and biopolitical planning.

Of course, there is also an optimistic perspective on our globe, molded by technologies, machines, and technomorphic practices. The ill-equipped human being can compensate using reason. As Cicero writes: "Men are given the compensation of reason to make up for what they lack in nature."[17] Because the human being is born into the world less capable than animals, they have the opportunity to escape the constraints of nature. Nature was described as *physis*, i.e. as that which germinates. The function of the elements is therefore to secure the order of the living sustainably. As *stocheia*, the elements, similar to musical notes, are the "links" of a world that is one whole and possesses one aesthetic form. By virtue of the elements, nature contains an autopoietic structure that attracts appreciation and admiration from humans, but also respect and fear. Despite this dichotomy, the theory of the elements roughly corresponds to what "cosmos" means: ornate order.

These ideas no longer fit into the modern conception of nature. According to Immanuel Kant, nature is the order of appearances, governed by laws, that is produced by the mind. Nature is what can be technically made out of it and with it. We understand nature as technomorphous, according the model of the human being themselves as a technical agent. Kant even speaks of a "technology of nature": nature itself operates like a technology that we have developed. Thus, according to Kant, there can be a "fitting together" of nature, technology, and man, a harmonization of the antagonistic processes and practices of these three entities.

Faced with the planetary exploitation of nature, we must develop a critique of anthropocentrism. Goethe saw this as a self-deception, whereby the human being relates everything that exists to himself: "Man is accustomed to value things to the extent that they are useful to him, and since he is disposed by temperament and situation to consider himself the crowning creation of Nature, why should he not believe that he represents also her final purpose?"[18]

17 Cicero, *Der Staat / De re publica*, ed. Rainer Nickel (Mannheim: Artemis & Winkler, 2010), 219. Translated from the German.

18 Johann Wolfgang von Goethe, *Goethe's Botanical Writings*, trans. Bertha Mueller (Honolulu: University of Hawaii Press, 1952), 82.

This *anthropocentric* view of nature is responsible for the centuries of delay in producing a *biocentric* one. Nature is governed by a diverse democracy of existence: "[...] in the universe nothing is up nor down, everything demands the same rights in a common middle point."[19] Nature is not a service provider set up for the human being, based on which one can assume that "everything in existence exists for his own sake, exists only as a tool and auxiliary instrument for his own life."[20]

Nature is in its very essence a creator of form. This limits the utilitarian exploitation of nature. Yet form, as immaterial as it may be, is bound to substance, to the elements of fire, water, earth, air. Light is what allows things to appear in the first place and at the same time is the medium of the immaterial. Light is thus the primal form of art. Light and matter are the conditions of the physiognomic world of forms, which speak to us, sometimes attracting, sometimes repelling us, sometimes destructive, sometimes generative, sometimes giving, sometimes taking. What the play of the elements shows is what the evolutionary biologist Josef H. Reichholf calls "the expressive diversity of living nature" or referring to Adolf Portmann "the 'self-expression' of life".[21]

We are also strangers to this understanding of the elements today. Science is produced in the absence of the subject and its sensory, historical concreteness. Since neither the object studied nor the subject studying it appear in the natural sciences as a living being with needs, we never ask how useful for life, agreeable, and healthy the knowledge we attain is.

The elements do not just represent an inexhaustible reservoir of symbols, metaphors, images, and turns of phrase in European culture. Rather: each age also speaks the language of its technology. Today's semantic extensions of language are describing the world of the immaterial flow of data: this language separates subjects from the sphere of matter and bodies, it therefore separates subjects from nature. This cultural trend is not new, but rather continues to pursue the age-old desire to overcome the corporeal and transform the self into a super-ego.

The ecological crises today show the limits of research into ecosystems that proposes that ecological problems should be solved with precisely the same technology that caused them. The ecological approach asks: which nature do we want? This turns nature into a project that treats processes of nature and the requirements of culture equally. Nature, therefore, is not a primal origin behind us, but rather is in front of us. It is still ahead of us, as catastrophe, paradise, home, culture-nature.

We have, and this is the primary message of ecohumanism, only this *one* earth. The fact that we are but a tiny corner of existence in space is a consequence of the Copernican experience. It establishes the geopolitical dimension of the Anthropocene. Anthropocene does not mean a new spiral in Earth engineering, but instead civilization adapting to the finite dimensions of people on this Earth. Mack preceded his Sahara project with the following statement:

"...You ask: Can the project also be realized? ... I answer: Yes!"

Translated from the German by Anna Galt.

19 Johann Wolfgang von Goethe, *Sämtliche Werke. Briefe, Tagebücher und Gespräche*, Frankfurt Edition [= FE], vol. 24: *Schriften zur Morphologie* (Frankfurt am Main: Suhrkamp), 614. Translated from the German.

20 Goethe, *Goethe's Botanical Writings*, 82.

21 Josef H. Reichholf, *Der Ursprung der Schönheit: Darwins größtes Dilemma* (Munich: C. H. Beck, 2011), 18. Translated from the German.

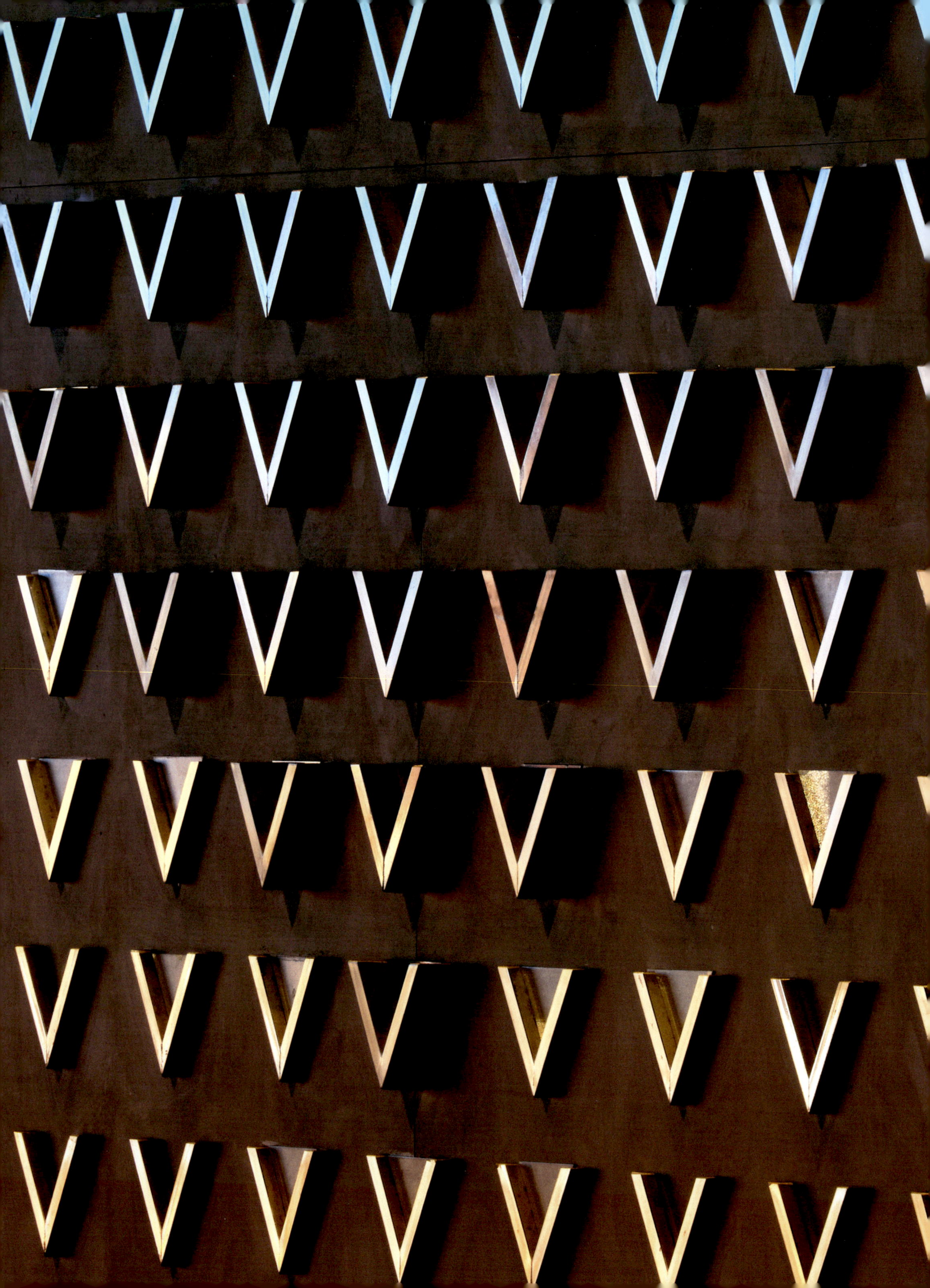

Silence of the Sahara – New Reservations for Art

The *Sahara Project* condenses Heinz Mack's work and also ZERO's basic idea of claiming new spaces for the visual arts. The artist has visited the Sahara several times, and he is utterly fascinated by its topography. The desert offers ideal conditions for working with light and space in their purest form.

In a first outline for the *Sahara Project* in 1959, Mack sketched thirteen different locations for the installation of his works in the desert that combined to form an artificial garden, a *Jardin Artificiel*. In 1968, the artist was able to partially realize his plan when he traveled to Tunisia with a small team from the German broadcasting corporation Saarländischer Rundfunk to create the film *Tele-Mack*. In 1976, another expedition was undertaken, with the photographer Thomas Höpker, to Algeria and the Grand Erg Occidental. There, Mack placed light-reflecting steles, cubes, and fans, sand reliefs and walls of mirrors in the desert sand dunes. The *Sahara Project* is one of the first artworks in European art conveyed exclusively by media; the actions and objects were only accessible to the public through images. The presentation in the atrium of the ZKM attempts to reconstruct the light phenomena that resulted from the interaction of the works with the blazing sun.

Heinz Mack is considered a pioneer of Land Art in Europe. This art movement, which emerged towards the end of the 1960s, produced artistic works interacting directly with the natural environment.

In the context of today's human-made climate catastrophe, the *Sahara Project* raises new, existential questions and at the same time points to possible solutions. For example, the large walls of reflectors and the extensive plantations of plates that the artist conceived 65 years ago anticipate the solar power plants now being built in the great desert regions. Heinz Mack's works, which capture and redirect light, represent an artistic utopia that has since become reality with today's photovoltaic technology; that is, with the conversion of light energy into electrical energy by means of solar cells.

← *fig. 125* Heinz Mack, *The Seasons of the Desert*, 1974/1976, detail

*I wish we would visit these immeasurable natural spaces to make the second immeasurable space, the space of art, a reality within them. This artificial space I call the preserve of art; in this preserve, which will ultimately become a total one, art shall find a new freedom. The goal of the Sahara Project is to set this liberation in motion.**

*I place light objects in the open space expecting that the light and the space will fall on these objects to fill them with light and space.***

Works in the exhibition:
All works courtesy of the artist
unless otherwise noted

Water Cross in the Sand
1972
Floor sculpture: acrylic glass, colored liquid, sand
5 × 354 × 354 cm
→ *figs. 128, 397*

***Caravan*, Grand Erg Occidental, Algeria**
1976
Light box
580 × 378 × 10 cm
Photo: Thomas Höpker
Collection ZKM | Karlsruhe
→ *figs. 127, 128, 139*

Sahara Relief
2011 (idea: 1976)
Ensemble: stainless steel, sand
91 stainless steel elements à 33 × 33 × 47 cm
→ *figs. 128, 137, 138, 139*

The Seasons of the Desert
1974/1976
Light reliefs: wood, aluminum, steel, canvas
2 panels à 285 × 337 × 6 cm
→ *figs. 125, 128, 137*

Golden Cube
1968
Cube: brass, acrylic glass
100 × 90 × 90 cm, plinth 7.5 × 30 × 30 cm, plate 1 × 100 × 100 cm
→ *figs. 128, 139*

Golden Cube
2004
Cube: aluminum, acrylic glass
50 × 50 × 50 cm, plinth 9 × 30 × 30 cm
→ *figs. 128, 136*

Transparent Light Cube
1960
Cube: acrylic glass, crystal glass, marble
90 × 92 × 92 cm, plate 3 × 130 × 130 cm
→ *figs. 128, 137, 139*

The Sea Above the Desert
1967/1968
Cube: acrylic glass, glass, sand, water
40 × 35 × 35 cm, plate 3 × 50 × 50 cm
→ *figs. 103, 168*

Sand Table
1972
Sculpture: acrylic glass, Sahara sand
110 × 110 × 52 cm
→ *figs. 130, 131*

The Islands – Sand Relief
1974
Relief: sand, aluminum, wood, acrylic glass
103 × 173 × 11.5 cm
→ *figs. 129, 133*

The Desert in Me
1963
Relief: Sahara sand, wood, acrylic glass
161 × 100 × 10 cm
→ *fig. 132*

Sand Relief
1956/1957
Relief: sand, cardboard, gold bronze, acrylic glass
61 × 64 × 11.2 cm

Large Sand Relief
1962/1970
Relief: Sahara sand, wood, acrylic glass, stainless steel
107 × 144.5 × 17 cm
→ *fig. 135*

Sand Relief - Sand Waves
1958
Relief: sand, plaster, synthetic resin, wood, acrylic glass
131.4 × 31.5 × 6.5 cm

The Artist in the Grand Erg Occidental, Algeria
1976
Photo print
Photo: Thomas Höpker
→ *fig. 126*

***Large Sand Relief*, Grand Erg Occidental, Algeria**
1976
Light box
46 × 65 × 11.4 cm
Photo: Thomas Höpker
→ *figs. 131, 134*

***Topology of Space*, Grand Erg Occidental, Algeria**
1976
Light box
46 × 65 × 11.4 cm
Photo: Thomas Höpker
→ *figs. 131, 166*

***City of Light in the Desert*, Grand Erg Occidental, Algeria**
1976
Light box
46 × 65 × 11.4 cm
Photo: Thomas Höpker
→ *fig. 131*

* Heinz Mack, *Sahara Project*, 1959, typoscript, Archive Heinz Mack. Translated from the German.
** Heinz Mack, 1966.

→ *fig. 126* Heinz Mack, The Artist in the Grand Erg Occidental, Algeria, 1976, photo: Thomas Höpker

→→ *fig. 127* Heinz Mack, *Caravan*, Grand Erg Occidental, Algeria, 1976, photo: Thomas Höpker
→→ *fig. 128* *Mack at ZKM*, exhibition view, ZKM | Karlsruhe 2023

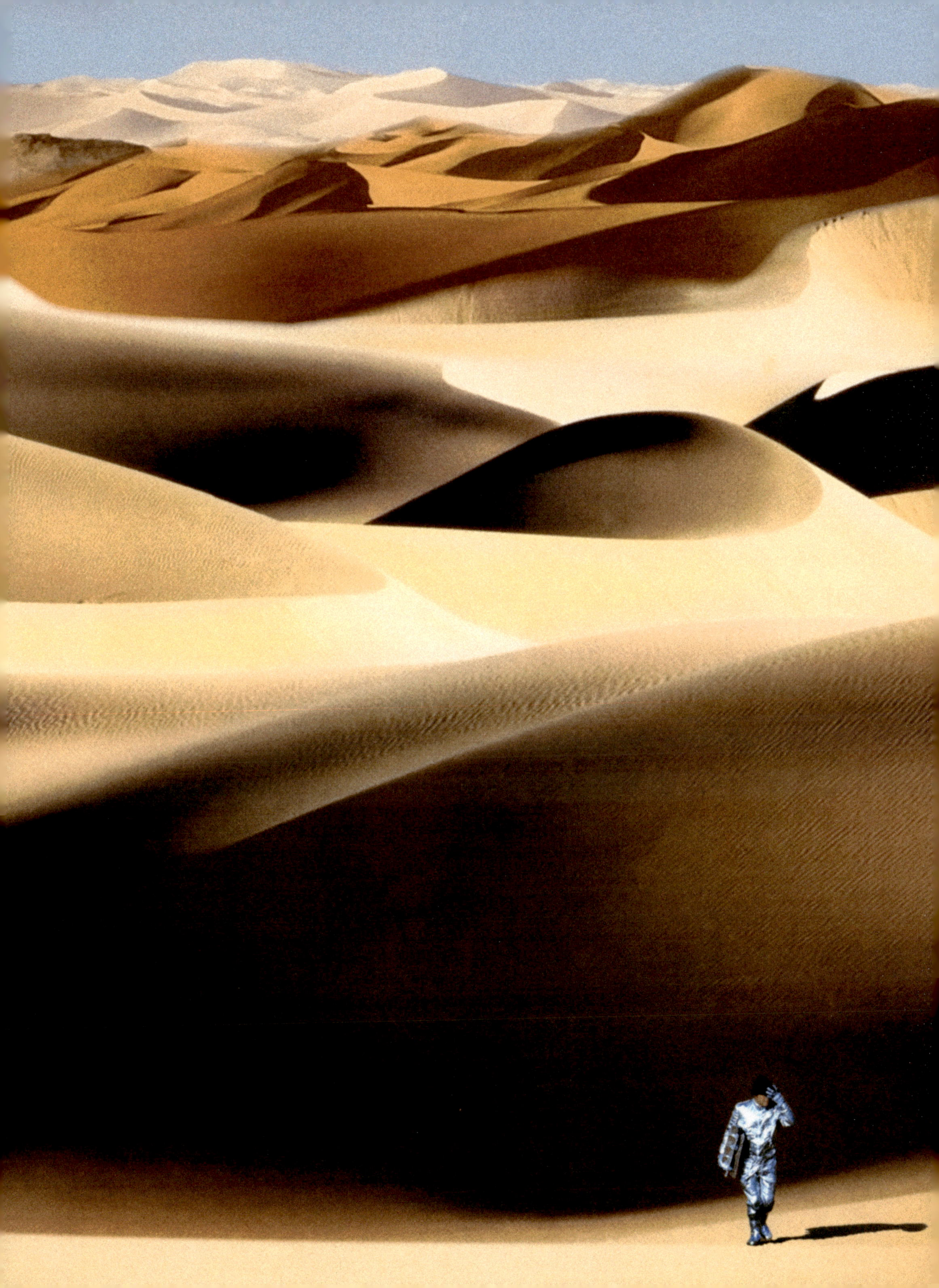

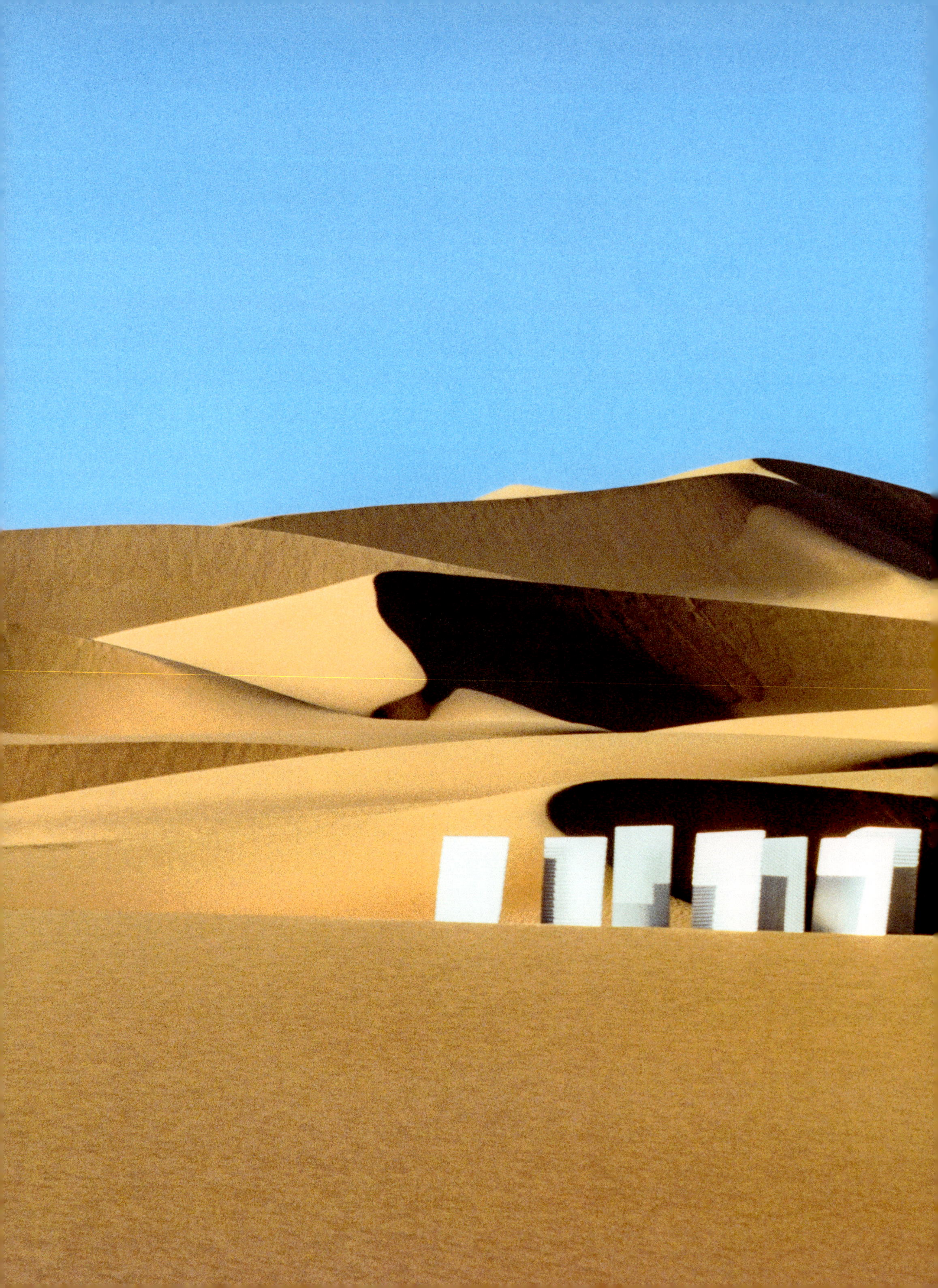

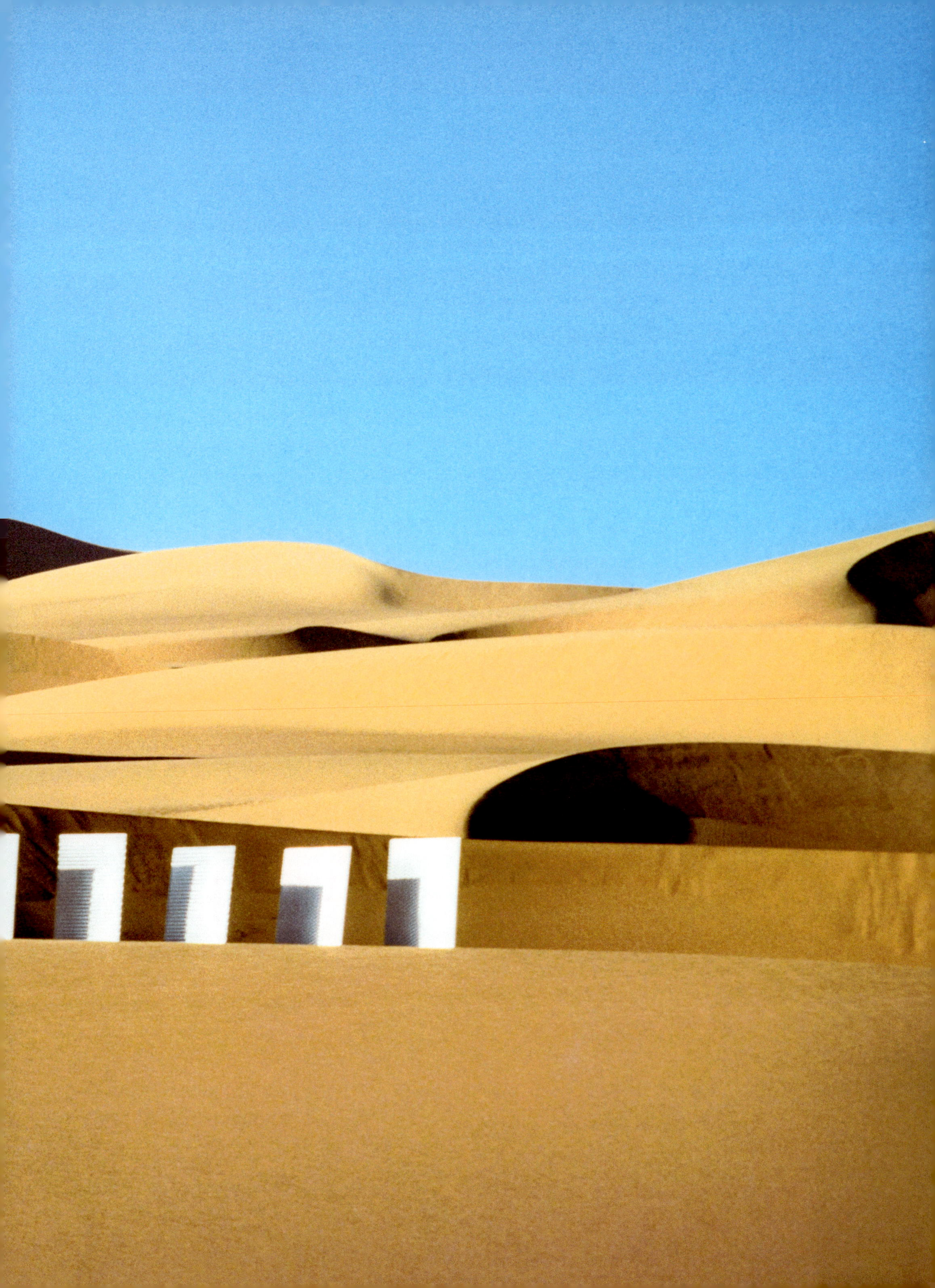

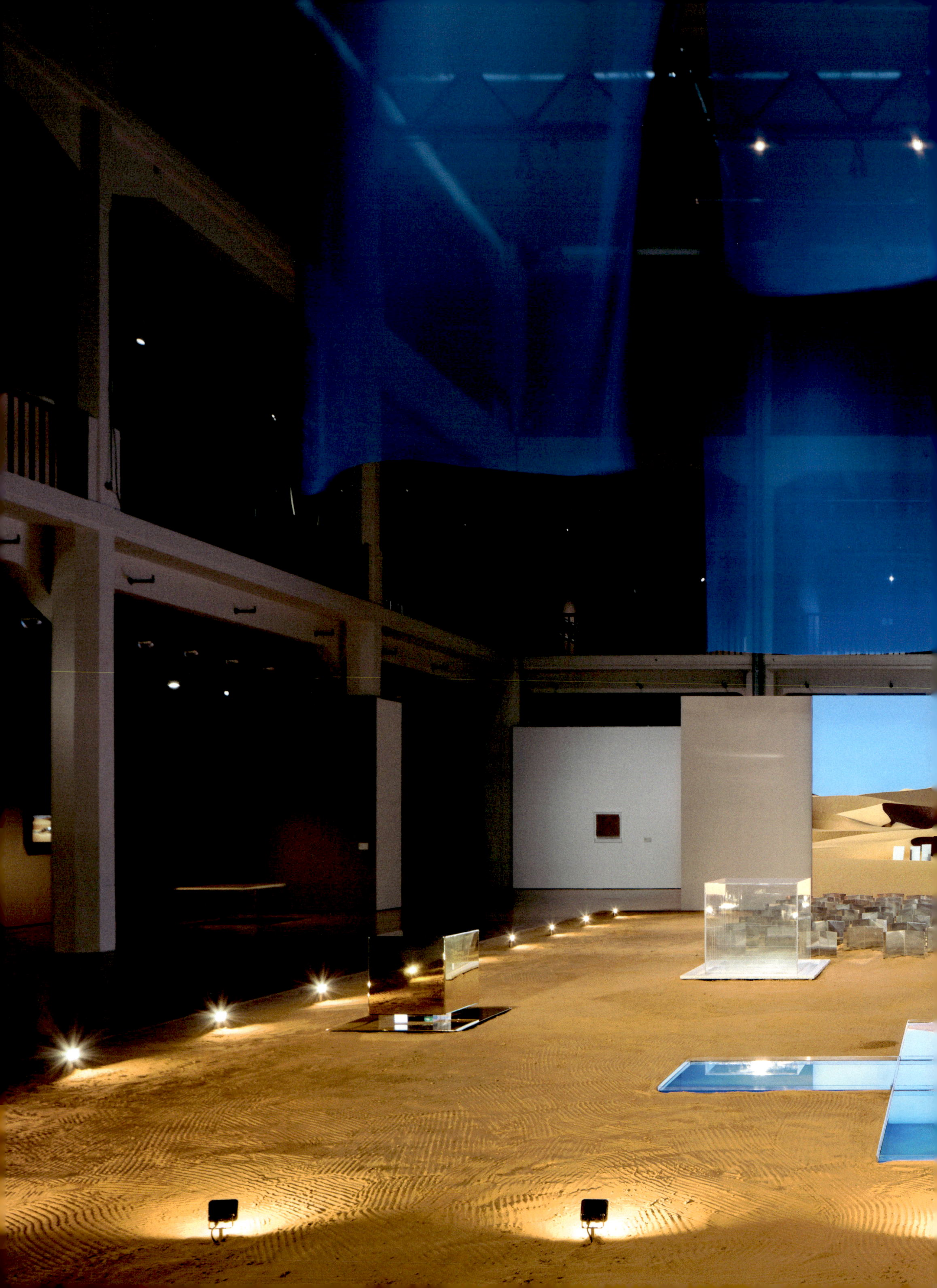

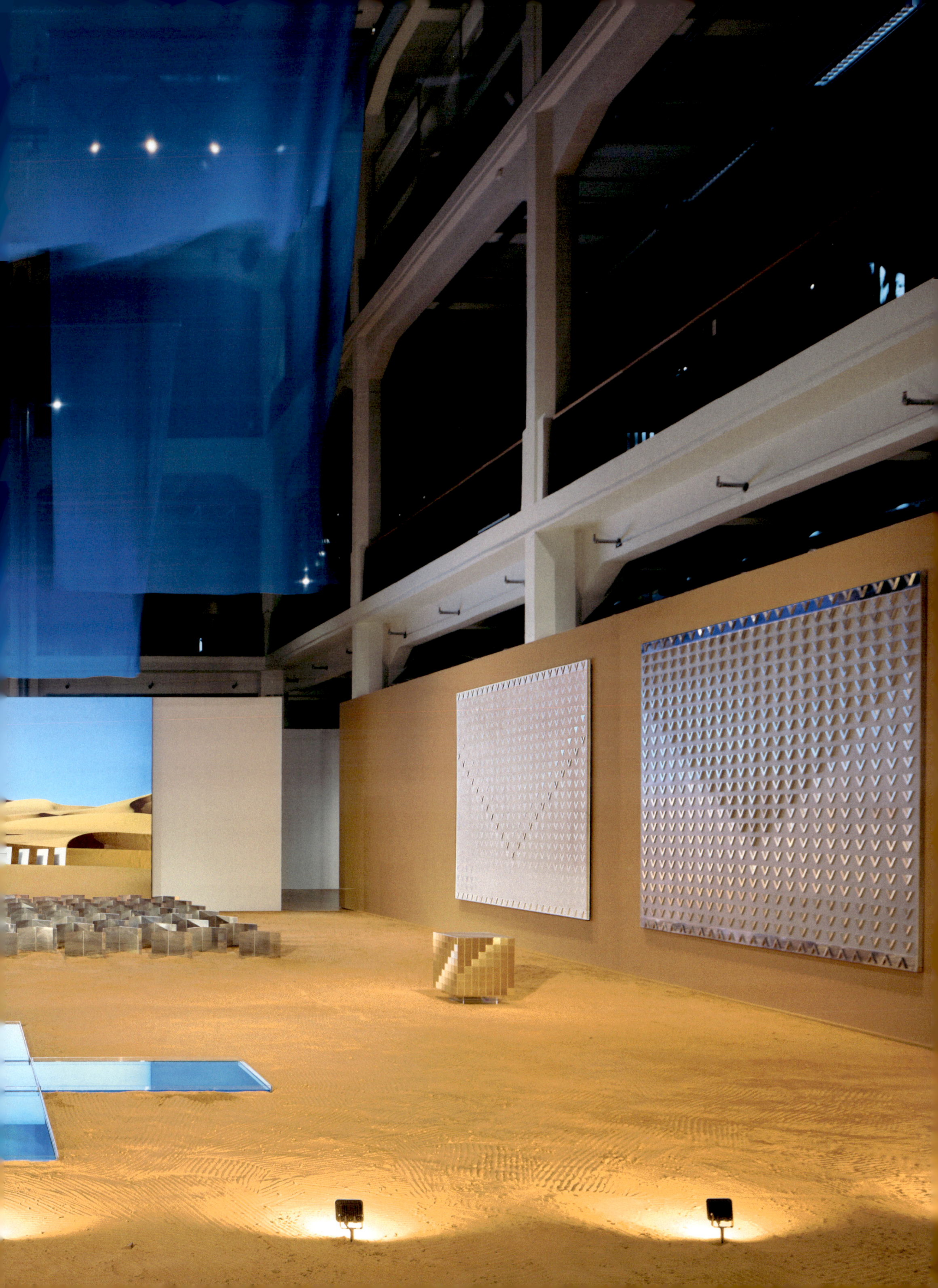

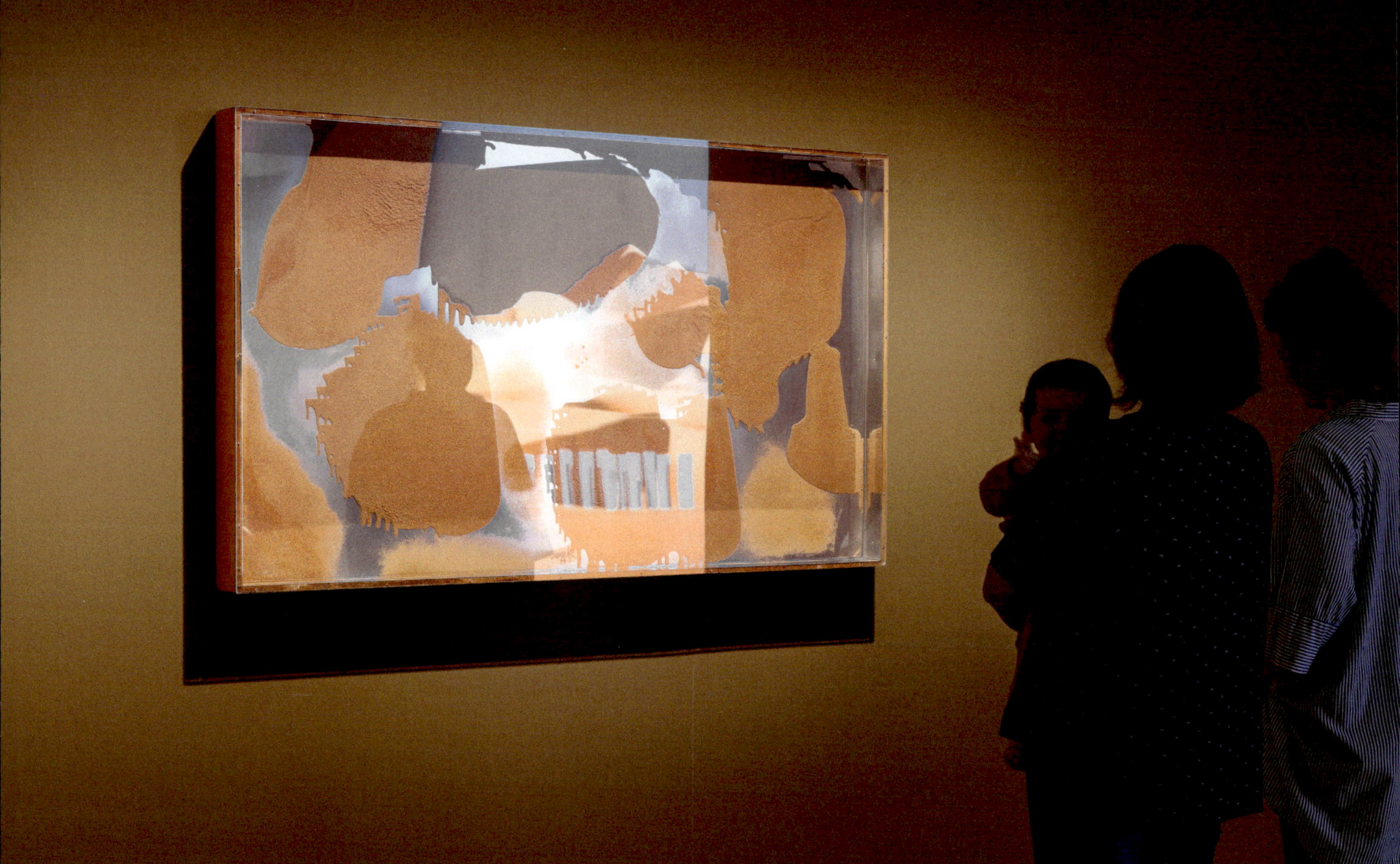

↑ *fig. 129* Heinz Mack, *The Islands – Sand Relief*, 1974
↗ *fig. 130* Heinz Mack, *Sand Table*, 1972, detail
→ *fig. 131* *Mack at ZKM*, exhibition view, ZKM | Karlsruhe 2023

→← *fig. 132* Heinz Mack, *The Desert in Me*, 1963
→↗ *fig. 133* Heinz Mack, *The Islands – Sand Relief*, 1974
→→ *fig. 134* Heinz Mack, *Large Sand Relief*, Grand Erg Occidental, Algeria, 1976, photo: Thomas Höpker

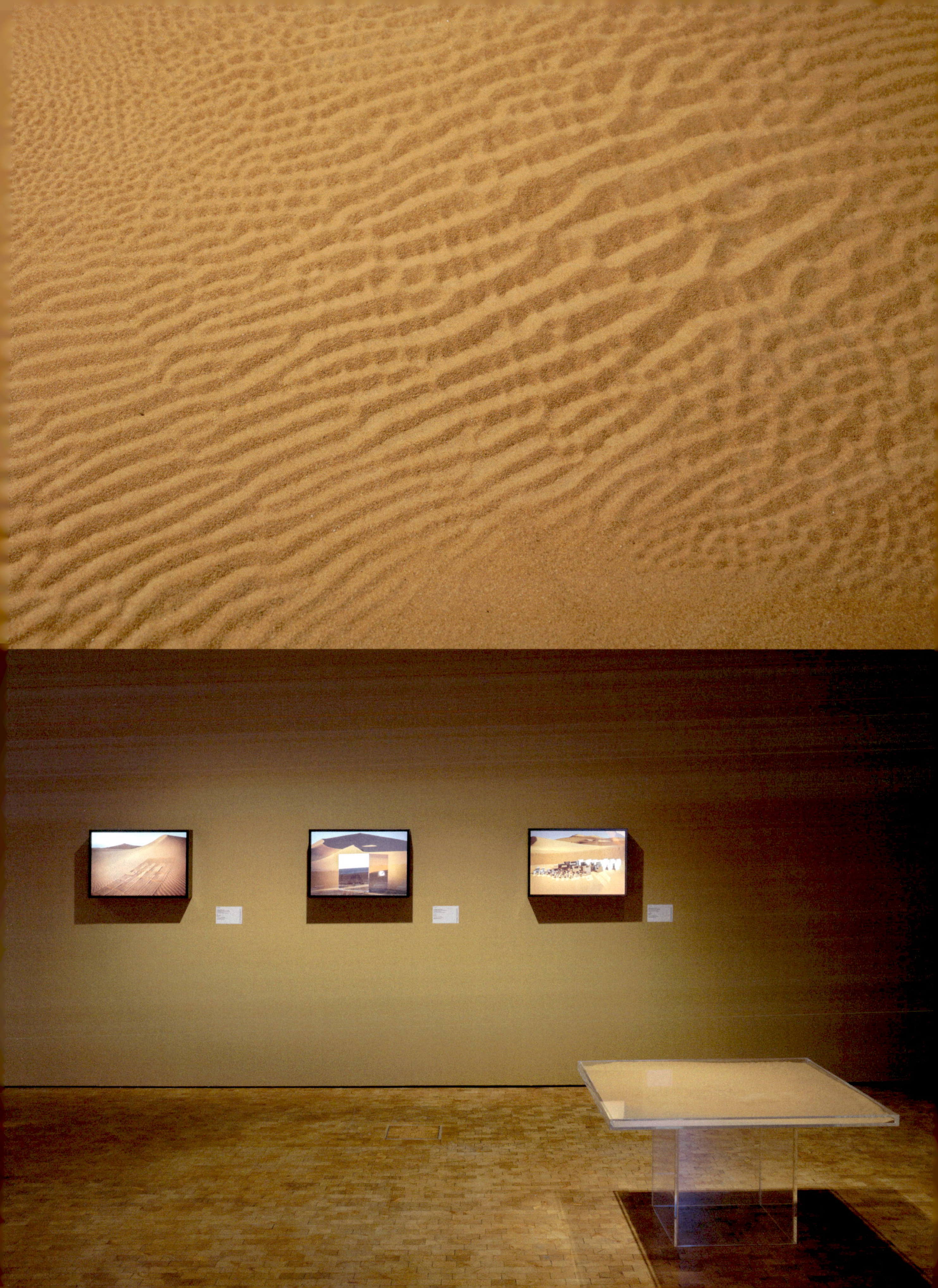

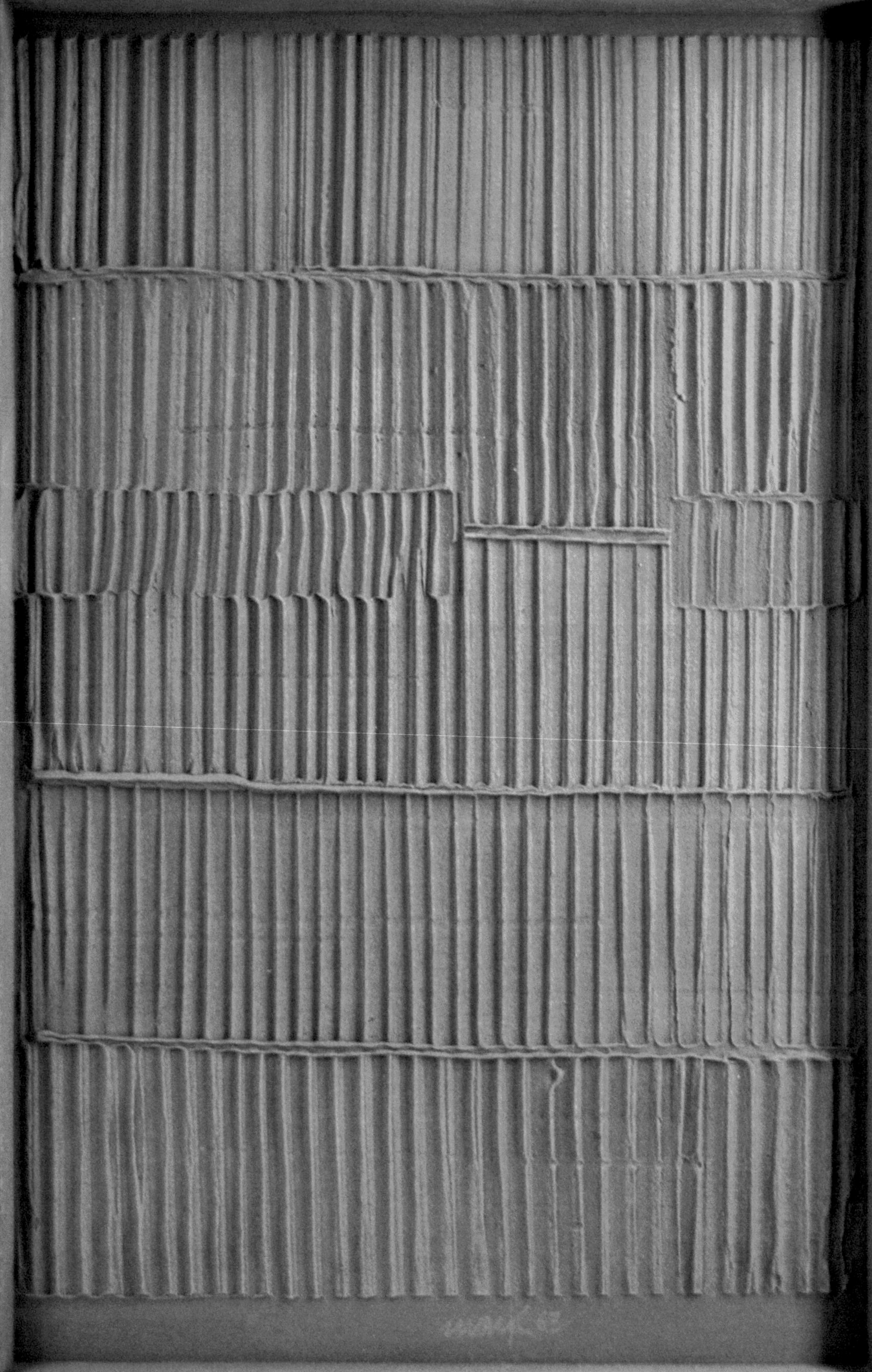

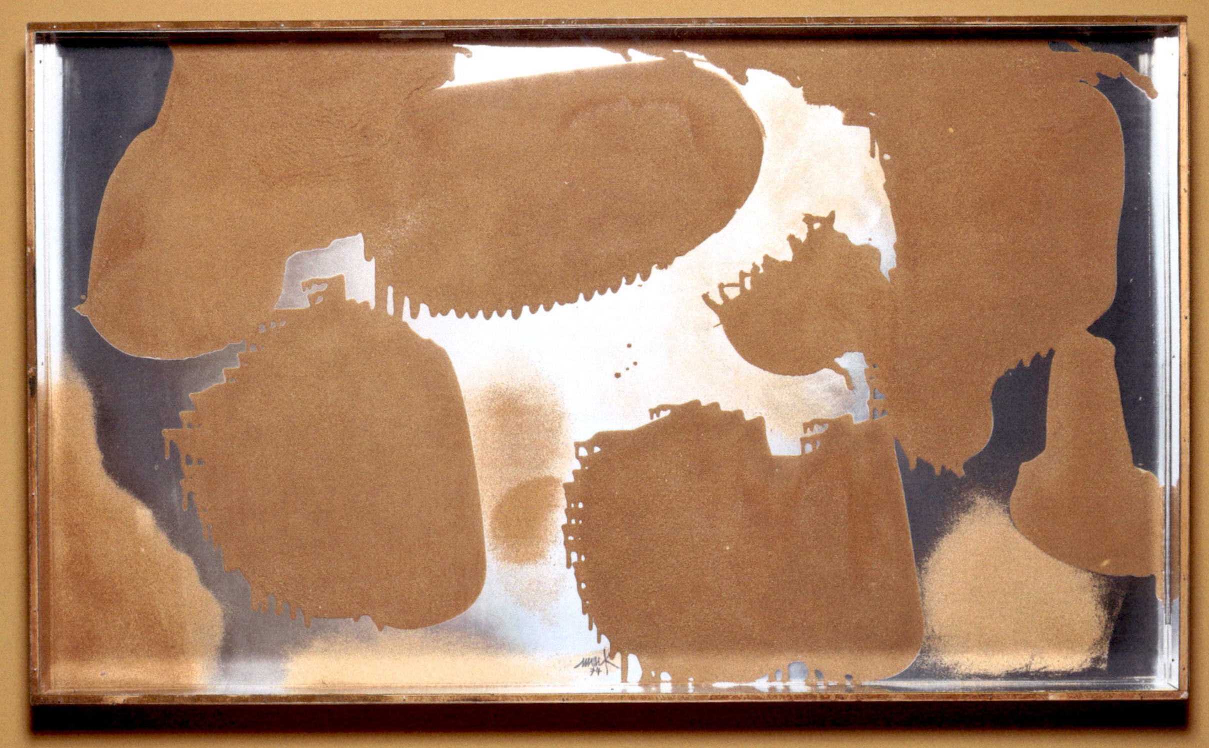

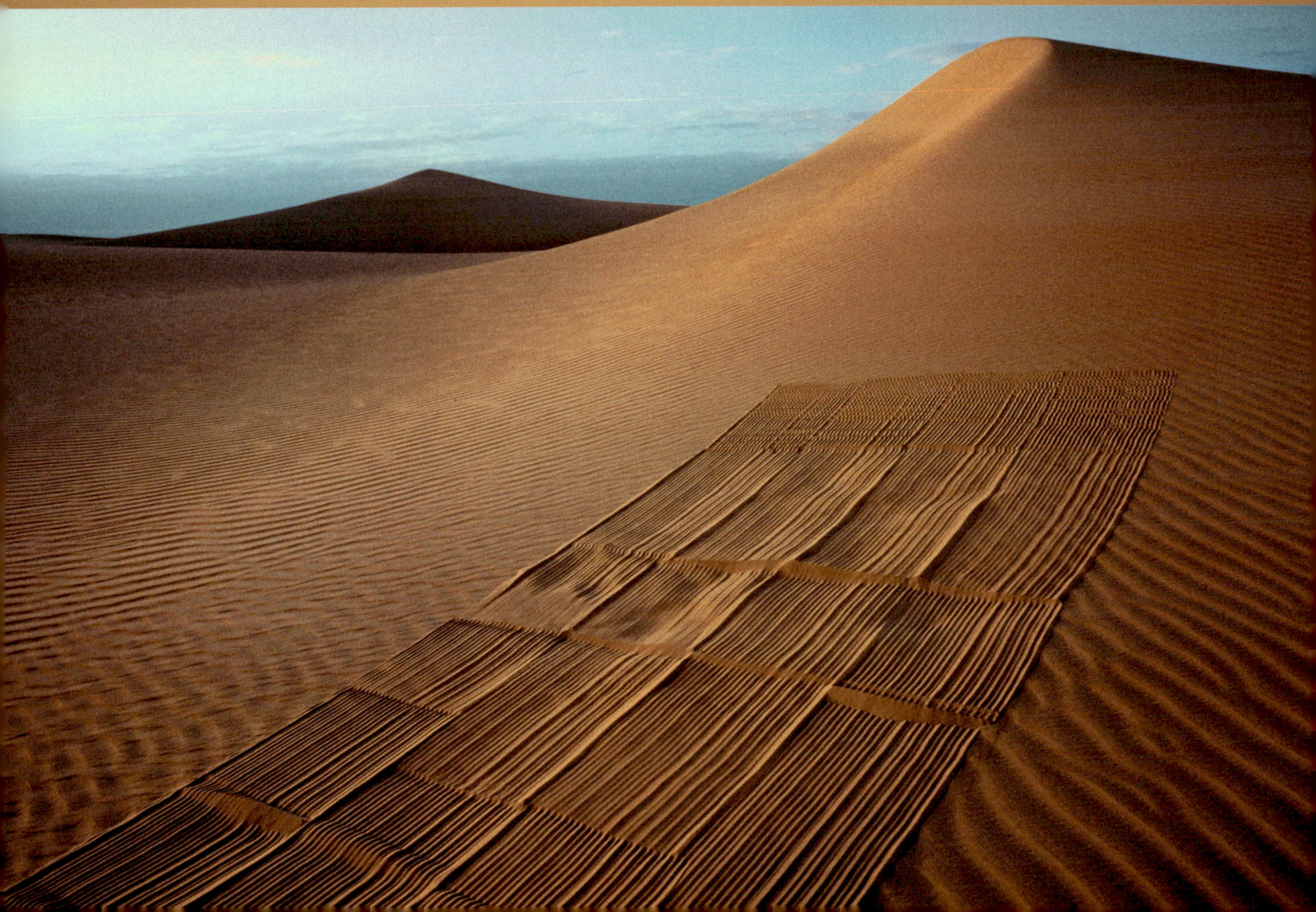

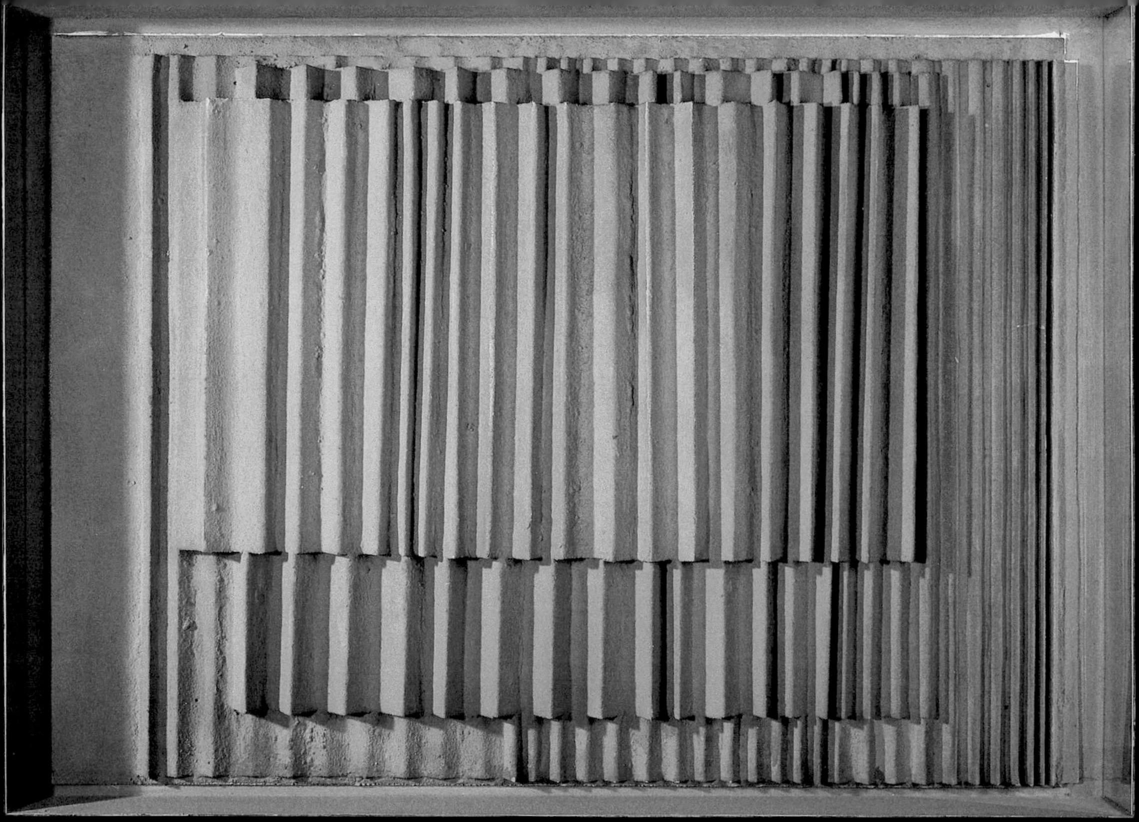

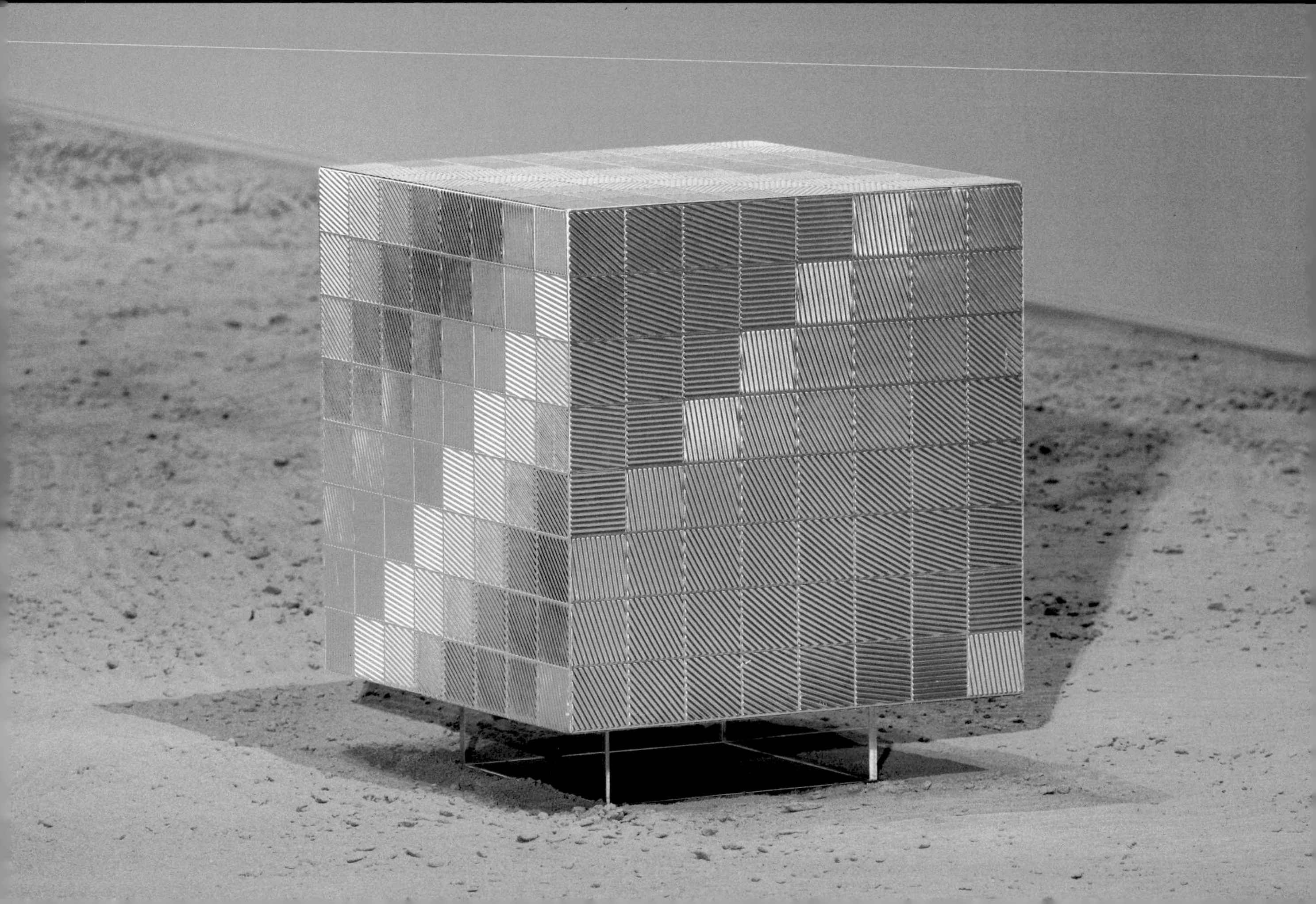

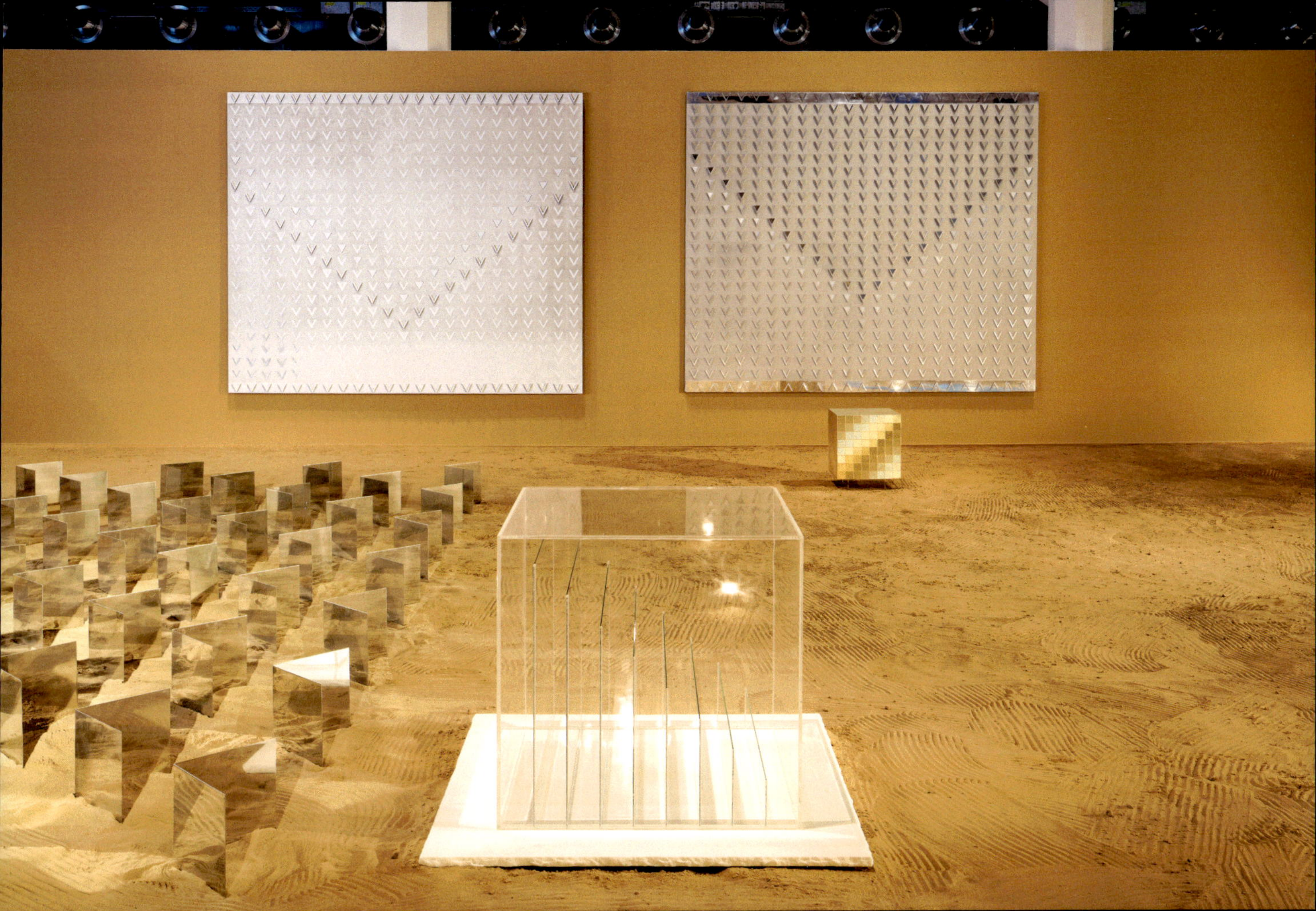

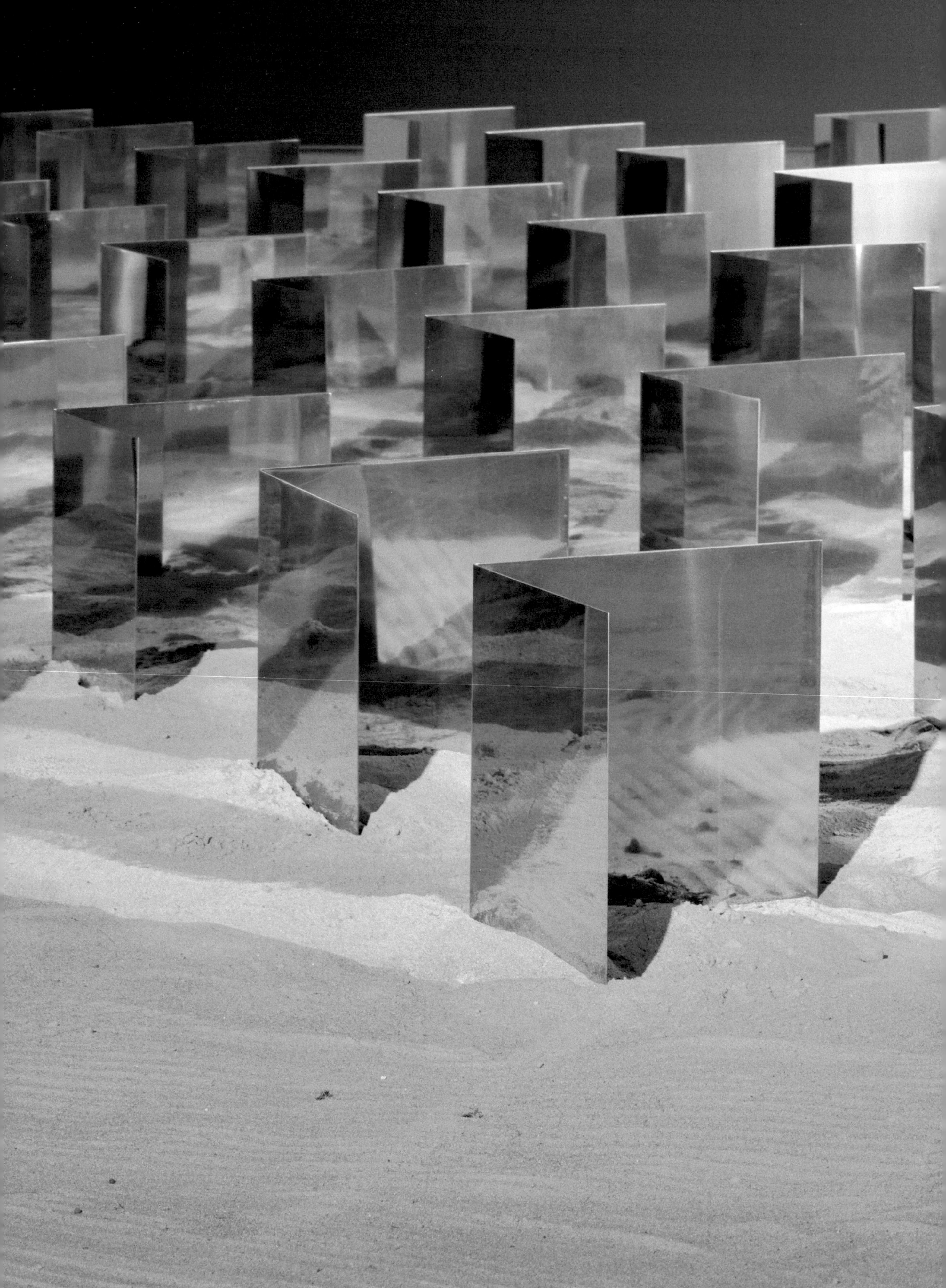

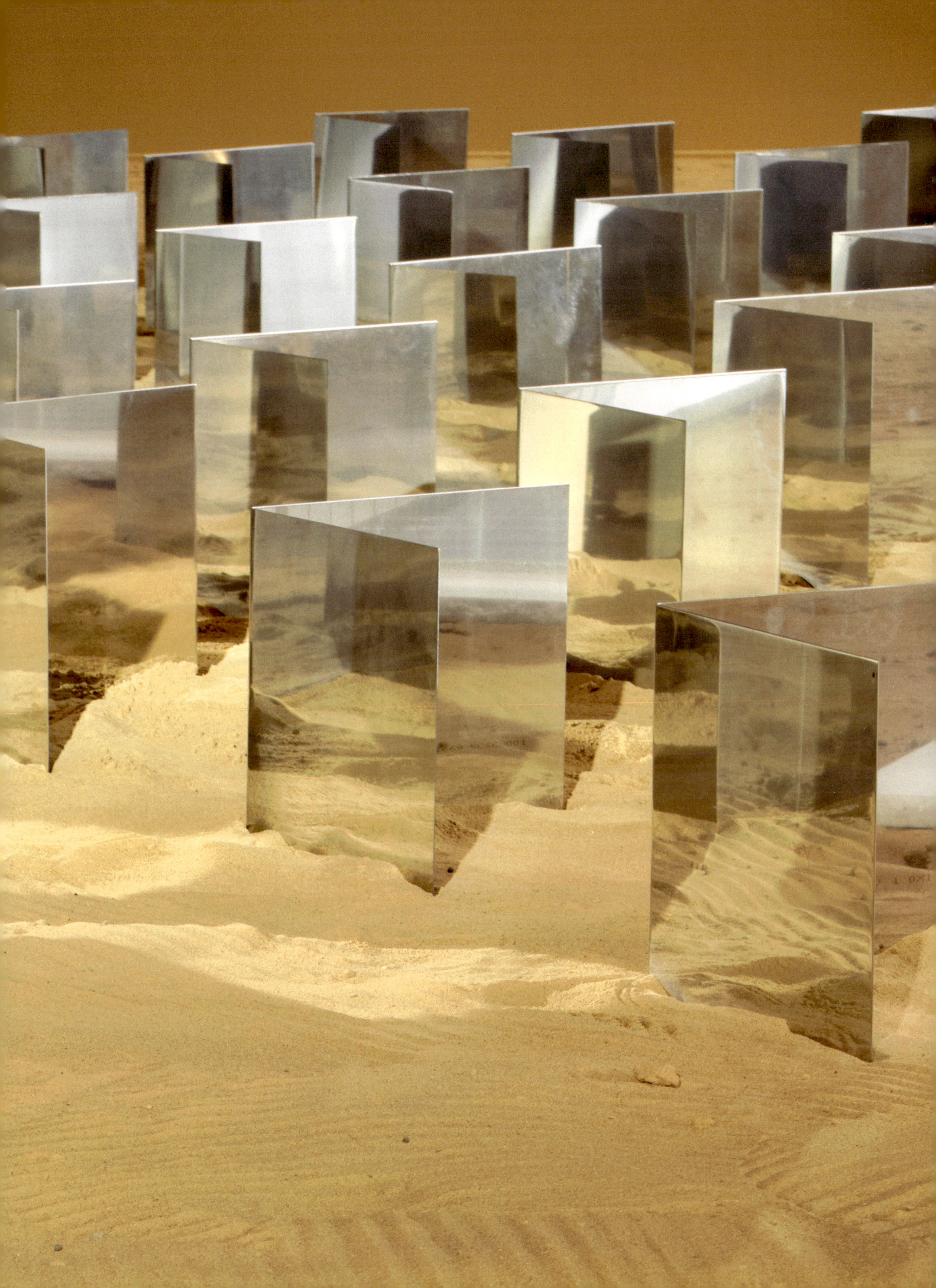

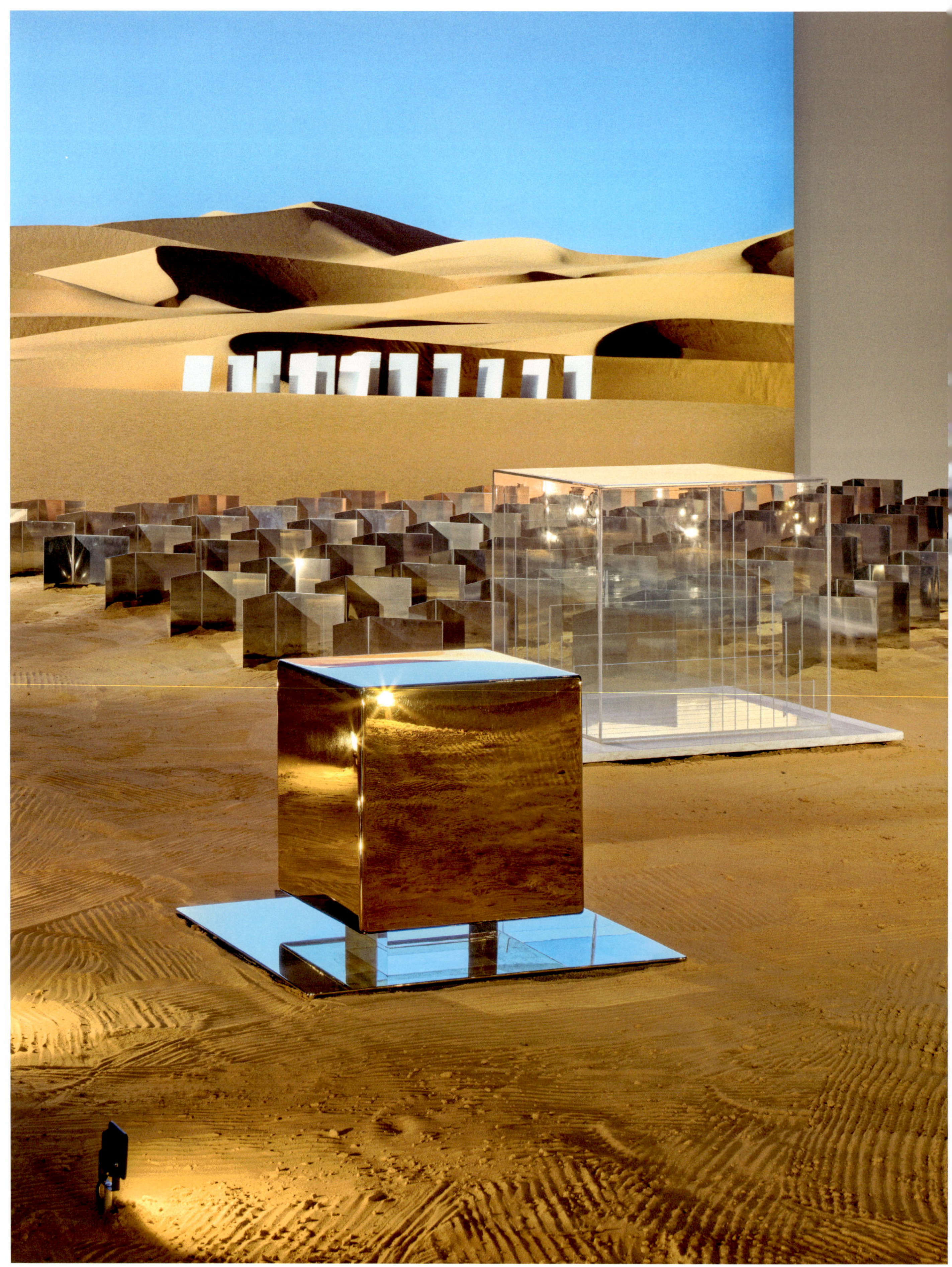

fig. 139 *Mack at ZKM*, exhibition view, ZKM | Karlsruhe 2023, foreground: Heinz Mack, *Golden Cube*, 1968

Light, Energy, Cosmos: Heinz Mack's *Sahara Project* as a Vision for the Twenty-First Century

In 1976, Heinz Mack walks across the Grand Erg Oriental – the largest sea of sand in the Sahara. He is on an "expedition into the artificial gardens" and has come to Algeria to carry the ideas of his *Sahara Project* into the desert. In the Timimoun oasis, to where he has traveled with the photographer Thomas Höpker and a team, he notes in his sketchbook: "Our senses are alert; and our work is to capture the light; we are hunters and adventurers, chasing the fast, fleeting light, setting traps for it, with the help of technical instruments. ... Then our instruments break the light down into its spectral colors, revealing its pure cosmic energy."[1]

Mack positions twelve mirrored reflectors in the Algerian desert sand. Their metallic surfaces reflect the dazzling light of the glistening desert sun and throw it back into the golden space of the desert. Mack had written down the idea for this *Light Plantation* in his legendary text *Sahara Project* in 1959. It is based on the idea that works of art that capture, collect, and amplify light on their surface become vibrating "light phenomena"[2] in a vast, light-flooded space like the Sahara. The artist sees his sculptures as "objects of light in space"[3] and light as a creative material, comparable to the paint used by a painter. In the Sahara, "a cloak of intense light"[4] would outshine the materiality of his technical constructions made of aluminum, stainless steel, and mirrored glass. And so he laid out his rows of reflective metal in the desert to bring out the dazzling light of the sun on their surface.

figs. 127, 138, 139, 143

Formally, Mack's *Light Plantations* – conceived sixty-five years ago in the *Sahara Project* and realized in the African desert during the 1960s and 70s – anticipate the solar farms that are being realized today in deserts and other regions of the world. The focus on light and space, which emanates from the *Sahara Project* and runs like a thread through Heinz Mack's entire œuvre, reveals an artistic attitude towards nature and technology that gains relevance in the light of the human-made climate catastrophe. Likewise, the comparative examination of contemporary art and renewable energy raises the question of the aesthetic dimension of modern technologies: Shouldn't artists – just like engineers – be involved in the design of solar power plants? Taking into account the current state of research in solar technology, such a collaboration – theoretically outlined for the first time in this essay – could take the ideas of Heinz Mack's *Sahara Project* into the twenty-first century. As co-authors, an engineer and an art historian, we have tentatively realized this in this text.

The *Sahara Project*, 1959

Heinz Mack conceived the *Sahara Project* in 1958, after he had already traveled to the Sahara twice, and documented it in writing the following year. In it, he designed a *Jardin Artificiel* consisting of thirteen stations, in other words an artificial garden in which his sculptural objects interact with the space and light of the desert. For Mack, the concept of the

1 Heinz Mack, quoted in Henri Nannen, ed., *Mack. Expedition in künstliche Gärten*, photography by Thomas Höpker (Hamburg: Gruner+Jahr, 1977), unpaginated. Translated from the German.

2 Heinz Mack, *Das Sahara-Projekt*, 1959 (typoscript, Archive Heinz Mack), 2, translated from the German. First English translation in *ZERO*, vol. 3 (1961), recent translation in Sophia Sotke, *Mack. Sahara: From ZERO to Land Art – Heinz Mack Sahara-Project 1959–1997*, trans. Gérard Goodrow (Munich: Hirmer 2022), 24–54.

3 Heiner Stachelhaus, *ZERO: Mack, Piene, Uecker* (Düsseldorf: Econ 1993), 82, quoted from Sophia Sotke, *Mack. Sahara: From ZERO to Land Art – Heinz Mack Sahara-Project 1959–1997*, trans. Gérard Goodrow (Munich: Hirmer 2022), 24.

4 Mack, *Sahara-Projekt*, 3.

Jardin Artificiel is linked to the demand for a purely artistic design of our landscape spaces.[5] The *Sahara Project* refers to open natural spaces of great dimensions in which the "inventory" of the civilized world has not yet spread – the artist includes not only the desert, but also the Arctic, the sky, and the seas.[6] "In such spaces, the clarity of light and the fullness of the silence are forever expanding. ... It is my wish that we should visit such immense natural spaces in order to realize that they have within them a second immense space, the space of art. I call this artificial space the preserve of art."[7]

In this "preserve," art can find a new freedom, far away from civilization and cultural institutions. In the stations of his *Jardin Artificiel*, Mack describes the preserve as "gardens that no gardener has yet dreamed of,"[8] and indeed the artificial vegetation initially seems like a dream that can hardly be realized. Mack's artificial garden thus lies somewhere between utopia and reality. In this respect, the desert is to be understood as a "non-place" in the sense of the Ancient Greek *ou tópos*, from which the term utopia is derived.[9] What seemed like a utopian dream in 1959 is now a *de facto* reality – not realized by artists with the aim of creating an artificial design, but rather implemented by engineers and technicians to produce renewable energy. The visionary quality of Heinz Mack's *Sahara Project* becomes evident when one takes a closer look at the individual stations of the *Jardin Artificiel*.

The Light Steles

The *Sahara Project* is based on the idea of "a vibrating light stele in a desert," as Mack describes in the first station of the project, titled "The Light Steles." A stele consists of an upright shaft with mirrored reflectors mounted vertically. In the *Sahara Project*, Mack writes that when the sunlight is multiplied in the reflectors and thrown back into the space of the desert, the intensity of the light can outshine the materiality of the technical construction.[10]

"It must be possible to vibrate a powerful apparition of light in such a way that its intensity necessarily demands a new environment, the expansion of which no longer conforms to the classical rules of measure, volume, and proportion."[11]

The artist had already suspected in 1959 that the space of the desert was particularly suitable for creating a vibrating light effect, but it was not until 1967 that he recognized the spatial quality of the Sahara itself, when he first provisionally and experimentally erected a bronze column in Tunisia. He noticed that the light of the sun immediately "accepted" the sculpture and increased its visibility. The column became a sublimation of light, its material immaterialized, so to speak. Mack observed how the size of the column changed with the vastness of the desert; the optical dimension no longer corresponded to the physical dimension. At a greater distance, the column would sometimes appear larger, or it would appear smaller as one approached it. In 1967, the artist realized that in the Sahara, the balance between real, virtual, and optical scales was suspended.[12]

In 1968, Mack traveled to the Tunisian desert again, this time with a film crew from Saarländischer Rundfunk (SR) to shoot scenes for the film *Tele-Mack*. During the filming, he wore a silver jumpsuit that

5 See Nannen, *Mack*.

6 Mack, *Sahara-Projekt*, 1–2.

7 Mack, *Sahara-Projekt*, 1.

8 Mack, *Sahara-Projekt*, 1–4.

9 The term "utopia" is composed of the ancient Greek *ou* (not) and *tópos* (place), literally meaning "non-place"; see Heinrich Schmidt, *Philosophisches Wörterbuch*, new revision by Georgi Schischkoff (Stuttgart: Kröner, 1991), 749.

10 Mack, *Sahara-Projekt*, 3, see Sotke, *Mack. Sahara*, 25.

11 Mack, *Sahara-Projekt*, 2.

12 See Michael Beck and Ute Eggeling, eds., *Mack. The Sky Over Nine Columns* (Düsseldorf: Beck & Eggeling 2014), 50–51.

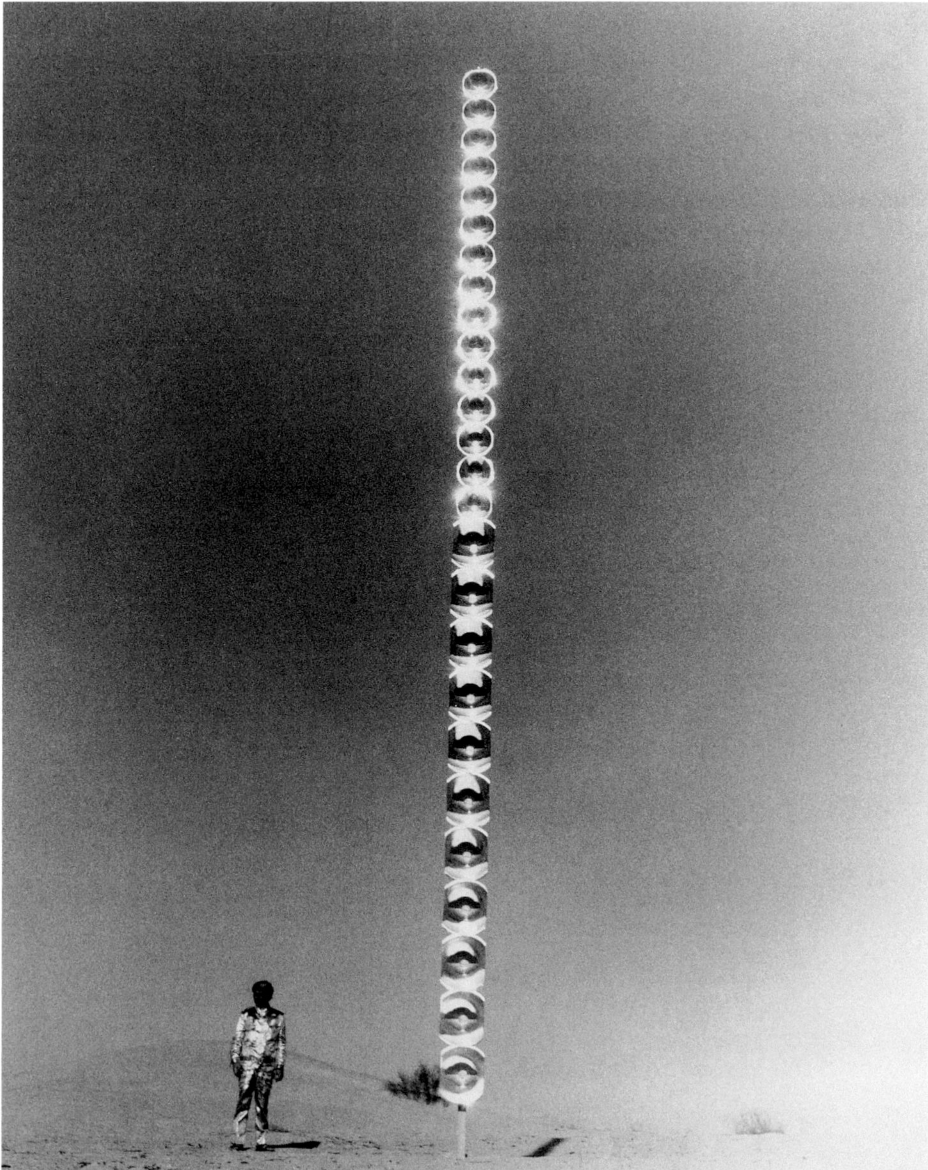

fig. 140 Heinz Mack next to his eleven-meter-high light stele in the Sahara, east of the Kebili oasis, Grand Erg Oriental, Tunisia, film still from *Tele-Mack*, 1968, camera: Edwin Braun

fig. 231

fig. 140

turned him into a reflective light object, visible from afar in the open desert landscape. East of Kebili, he erected an eleven-meter-high stele made of aluminum reflectors, which in the glittering light of the sun was transformed into an immaterial light phenomenon.

"It was only when the first silver stele, eleven meters high, was installed and the African sun got caught in the focus of its twenty-six light reflectors that our eyes saw more than even our boldest assumptions had expected; these are those moments of pure fascination in which all thought is suspended."[13]

fig. 108

During the filming of *Tele-Mack*, a group of eight other steles was erected around this light stele. They seemed to glow from within, even though their only source of light was the desert sun, which was reflected, refracted, focused, and dispersed on their metallic surfaces. Mack had described this grouping of steles in the *Sahara Project* as "widely visible beacons of the preserve."[14]

13 Heinz Mack, "Sahara: 1968," in Margit Staber, *Heinz Mack. Eine Monografie* (Cologne: DuMont, 1968), 94–95, here 94, quoted from Sotke, *Mack. Sahara*, 27–28.

14 Mack, *Sahara-Projekt*, 3.

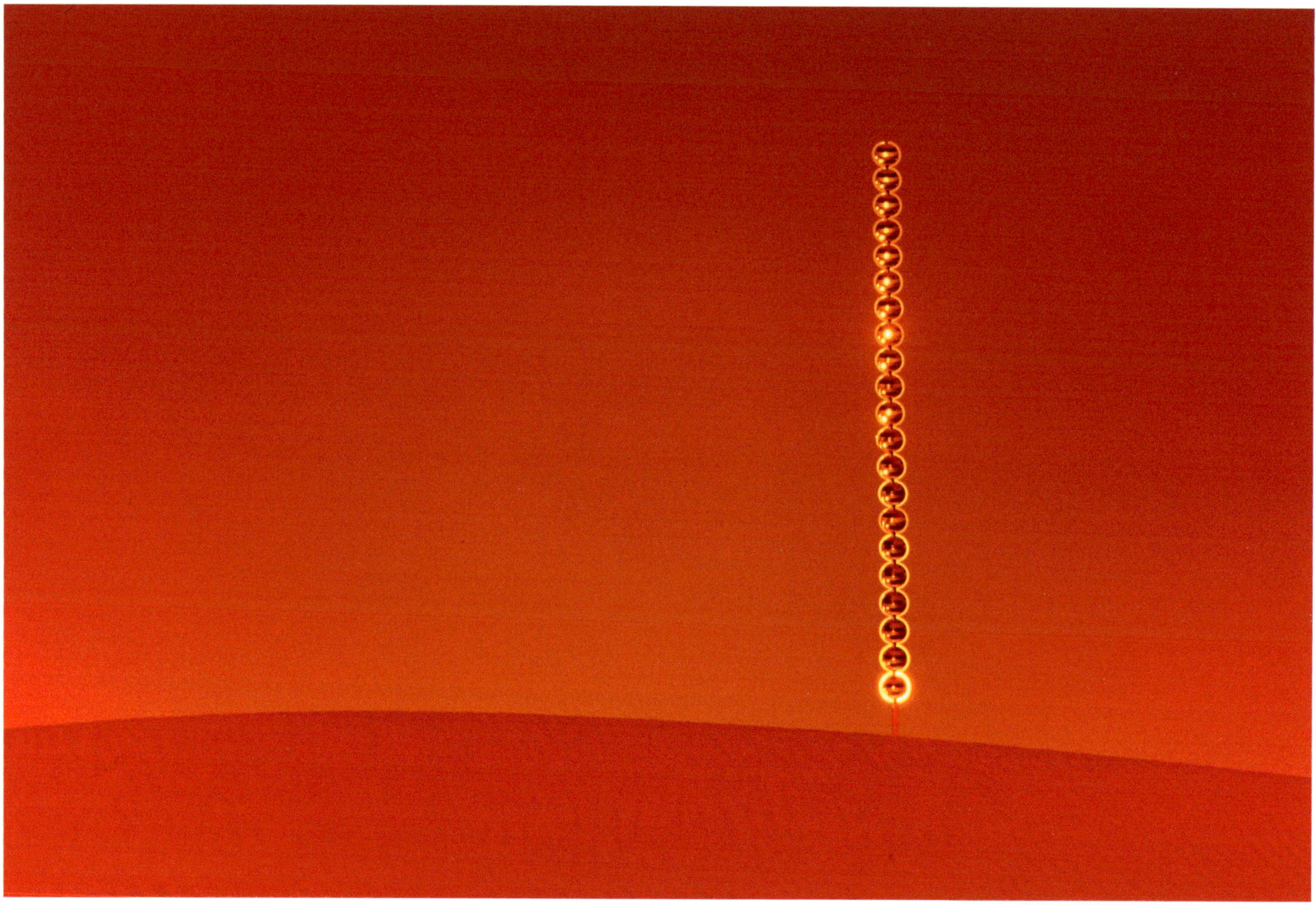

fig. 141 Heinz Mack, *Large Stele in the Wahiba Desert*, 1997, aluminum reflectors, anodized, height: 14 meters, Wahiba desert, Oman

fig. 141

Finally, in 1997, Mack traveled to the Wahiba Sands in Oman and created a fourteen-meter-high light stele consisting of twenty-one aluminum reflectors that was braced and held in place by thin nylon ropes. He positioned the stele on the crest of a high sand dune and waited for dusk to take the perfect photograph. During the sunset, which lasts only a few minutes in the desert, Mack was able to photographically capture a completely distinctive, uniquely beautiful light phenomenon. The setting sun was found again in each of the twenty-one reflectors, multiplied many times over as a red ball of light as the sky and sand turned red.[15] "The light column growing towards the sky, illuminated by the glistening sun of the desert, leading upwards as a flickering, vibrating, and dematerialized vertical movement in a flowing rhythm, is truly a worthy continuation of Brâncuși's idea of the *Endless Column*," judged Uwe Rüth. According to Rüth, rarely has a photograph captured a work as convincingly as the photograph of the *Large Stele* from 1997 standing in the red evening light of the Wahiba desert. "Only those who have seen this light for themselves have an idea of the uniqueness, the fascination of the sensual experience of having seen this work there."[16]

The photo of the *Large Stele in the Wahiba Desert*, to which Uwe Rüth refers here, also brings to light the media aspect of the *Sahara Project*. Mack brought the mirror reflectors into the desert, installed his light stele there, and photographed it at a moment when it literally

15 Sotke, *Mack. Sahara*, 100–108, esp. 104.

16 Uwe Rüth, "Heinz Mack und sein Sahara-Projekt," in idem, *Mack. Licht der Wüste, Licht des Eismeers*, exhib. cat. (Marl: Skulpturenmuseum Glaskasten, 2001), 17–62, here 34, quoted from Sotke, *Mack. Sahara*, 104.

appeared "in the best light," with the setting sun reflected in each of its reflectors. He then dismantled the *Light Stele*, which had only briefly become a visually experienceable reality in the Wahiba.[17] Today's viewers can only experience the work through photographic reproductions.

As early as 1959, Mack and other ZERO artists had considered staging an exhibition without an audience "in favor of a pure, ideal situation." During a car trip to Antwerp with Yves Klein and Otto Piene, he considered placing large sculptures in the Sahara or Antarctica "that would correspond to the dimensions of the landscape" and could only be viewed "from the air." With the help of meteorologists, geologists, and physicists specializing in optical phenomena, the idea was to investigate the scientific conditions under which mirages occur.[18]

"We were motivated by the hope that it should be possible to create an artistically generated mirage and thus spread out an ensemble of numerous light phenomena in the large, open natural environment, creating a completely immaterial spatial image."[19]

When *Tele-Mack* was broadcast on Westdeutscher Rundfunk (WDR) in 1969, Mack declared: "The film is thus neither a reportage nor a document of an art exhibition; rather, it is itself an exhibition. The premiere and the duration of the exhibition are identical."[20] The idea was to create an exhibition that would no longer take place in a museum or gallery but would appear exclusively and only once on television. "All the objects that I will show in this exhibition can only be made known to the public through television and will also be destroyed by me in the end," Mack said.[21] Although he was generally positive about the technical reproducibility of his desert action in the film *Tele-Mack*, he also reflected on the disadvantages of the medium: "The beauty of such light forms is non-verbal and silent, but it is repeatable and transferable through the medium of 'film,' even if the special conditions of film will distort this beauty."[22]

According to Wolfgang Ullrich, however, Mack actually succeeded in translating the optical effect of his seemingly immaterial works in the desert into the medium of film. The light-reflecting surfaces of his objects created very different impressions depending on the time of day and the weather. "Most importantly, it allowed for effects that made the material seem immaterial," Ullrich writes. "Mack made sure to maximize the photogenic potential: precisely because there were no viewers on site, it was all about producing strong images."[23]

This takes the "work of art in the age of its mechanical reproduction"[24] to a new level, where it exists as an ephemeral event only at the moment of its technical reproduction. In this sense, projects such as *Tele-Mack* and Gerry Schum's *Fernsehgalerie* (Television Gallery) are part of the media-related Land Art of the 1960s.[25] Gerry Schum argued that technical reproduction and mass media had ushered in a new era in the history of visual art, one that could reach a much wider audience. The existence of the work of art was shifting "from a real object as point of departure to the photographic representation. The photograph becomes the actual art object," Schum claimed.[26] The broadcast of their films on television thus had a social significance for both Schum and Mack, allowing them to reach a wider audience that might not have found their way to an art exhibition.[27]

17 See Sotke, *Mack. Sahara*, 104–108.

18 Heinz Mack, "Biographische Notiz," undated, Vorlass (promised bequest) Heinz Mack, ZERO foundation, Düsseldorf, mkp.ZERO.1.IV.Eigene Texte, translated here from the German; see Sotke, *Mack. Sahara*, 40.

19 Mack, *Biographische Notiz*.

20 Quoted in Eo Plunien, "Silberstelen in der Sahara," *Die Welt* (January 23, 1969), Archive Heinz Mack, quoted from Sotke, *Mack. Sahara*, 69.

21 Quoted in Barbara Hess, "Abendschau. Drei Filme über Kunst," in Ulrike Groos, Barbara Hess, and Ursula Wevers, eds., *Ready to Shoot: Fernsehgalerie Gerry Schum*, exhib. cat., Kunsthalle Düsseldorf, Casino Luxembourg, and Museu de Arte Contemporânea de Serravalves Porto (Cologne: Snoek 2003), 9–21, here 19, quoted from Sotke, *Mack. Sahara*, 69.

22 Mack, *Sahara: 1968*, 94. Translated from the German.

23 Wolfgang Ullrich, *Raffinierte Kunst: Übung vor Reproduktionen* (Berlin: Wagenbach, 2009), 88–89. Translated from the German.

24 See Walter Benjamin, *The Work of Art in the Age of Mechanical Reproduction* [1935], trans. J. A. Underwood (London: Penguin, 2008).

25 For more on Schum, see: Groos, Hess, Wevers, *Ready to Shoot*.

26 Quoted in Ullrich, *Raffinierte Kunst*, 83; Gerry Schum, "Introduction to the Broadcast. Fernsehgalerie Berlin Gerry Schum" [1969], in Groos, Hess, Wevers, *Ready to Shoot*, 67–69, here 68.

27 See Sotke, *Mack. Sahara*, 69.

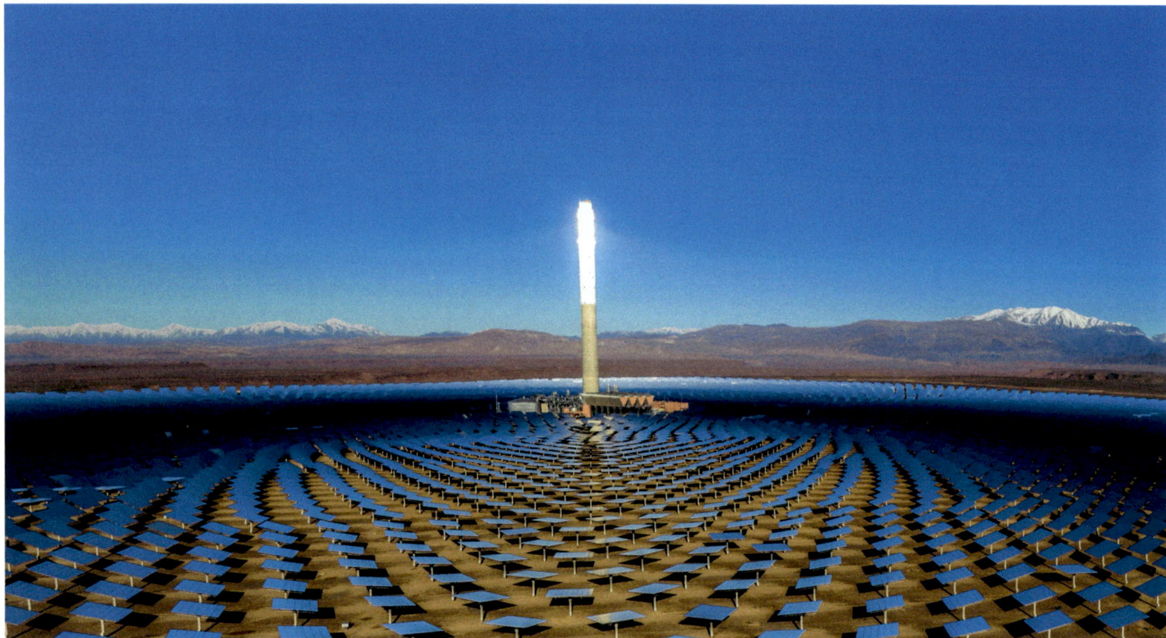

fig. 142 The Noor Solar Complex, Ouarzazate, Marocco

fig. 142

Mack's light steles are also a surprising anticipation of the world of the twenty-first century in a completely different way. In their inherent relationship with the sun, whose light is reflected by highly polished aluminum, they bear a striking resemblance to today's solar power plants in the desert, whose solar towers concentrate sunlight from mirrored reflectors and convert it into heat or electricity. Today, Morocco is home to one of the world's largest solar power plants with millions of heliostats, mirrors that automatically adjust to the sun's rays. The Noor solar complex in Ouarzazate has three solar storage power plants, two with mirrors in the form of a parabolic trough and one with a solar tower power plant.[28] The dazzling sunlight is concentrated at the top of the 240-meter-high Ouarzazate tower. Norman Rosenthal has already pointed out the formal similarity between this technological architecture and Mack's light steles in the desert: "It is a profound case of an artist who anticipates the scientist – his utopia of half a century ago a reality today."[29]

Various technologies are used today to harvest the sun's energy. It is important to distinguish between two basic types of energy conversion from sunlight: conversion to heat and conversion to electricity. When sunlight is used to generate heat, mirror systems are used to capture the sun's rays and direct them onto an absorber. The focused solar rays generate temperatures of up to 1000 degrees Celsius in the absorber materials.[30] This thermal energy is then used, for example, to contribute directly to the surrounding heat supply via storage tanks or to drive a turbine, which can be used to generate electricity. These systems are implemented on a variety of scales, from rooftop systems for domestic water heating to large-scale solar power plants in desert regions.[31] Because this technology typically uses tracking mirrors, it requires sufficient direct sunlight throughout the year, making regions of the world with little cloud formation the most suitable.

28 See Britta Klagge, Matthias Naumann, and Sören Becker, *Energiegeographie: Konzepte und Herausforderungen* (Stuttgart: Eugen Ulmer, 2021), 283–285.

29 Norman Rosenthal, "Heinz Mack: An Artist of Union," in Çağla Özbek, ed., *Mack. Sadece Işik ve Renk / Just Light and Colour*, exhib. cat. (Istanbul: Sakıp Sabancı Müzesi, 2016), 24–35, here 29.

30 See Deutsches Zentrum für Luft- und Raumfahrt e.V. (DLR), Institut für Solarforschung, ed., *Solarthermische Kraftwerke – Wärme, Strom und Brennstoffe aus konzentrierter Sonnenenergie* (Cologne: DLR, 2021).

31 See "Kalifornien: Weltgrößtes Solarkraftwerk hat Betrieb aufgenommen," *spiegel online* (February 15, 2014), www.spiegel.de/wirtschaft/unternehmen/kalifornien-weltgroesstes-solarturm-kraftwerk-geht-in-betrieb-a-953685.html.

The Light Reliefs

Since the ZERO period, Heinz Mack has been using industrial materials whose surfaces reflect light in a special way. The first light relief was created in 1957, when the artist stepped on a sheet of aluminum foil lying on a sisal carpet and observed how an immaterial relief of light manifested itself above the surface. "When I picked up the foil, the light had the opportunity to vibrate," Mack recalls.[32]

"My metal reliefs, which I prefer to call *light reliefs* ... require light instead of color in order to come to life. Polished to a mirror finish, a slight relief structure is enough to shake the tranquility of light and set it vibrating. The potential beauty of these structures would be a pure expression of the beauty of light."[33]

figs. 30, 115

Here, the picture surface no longer functions as a mere carrier of a representation but becomes the site of an actual event that unfolds between the work and the viewer in interaction with light and space. Somewhat later, materials such as aluminum mesh, acrylic glass, mirrors, and optical lenses found their way into his œuvre. As Ulrike Schmitt notes, the use of "innovative, non-art materials" was typical of the artists of the ZERO movement.[34] By using these reflective, distorting, or transparent materials, they sought to immaterialize their works.

"It is no longer the artist alone who generates the form, but the materials themselves, in interaction with the forces and energies that act upon them, creating independent constellations that change over time ... In this respect, the works are to be understood as surfaces of modulation and articulation: Light and shadow are their actual materials."[35]

In the tenth station of the *Jardin Artificiel*, the light reliefs are integrated into the *Sahara Project*. As panels of highly polished metal positioned freely in the desert sand, facing skyward, the actual articulation of the light unfolds through the relief structures embossed into them. As Mack describes: "it is thus not the metal relief that manifests itself, but rather the relief of light that outshines the materiality of the metal."[36] The direct involvement of light is even more obvious here than in the light steles. And with regard to today's solar power plants in the desert, the visual correspondence between the light plantations standing upright in the sand and today's photovoltaic panels is obvious. A closer look at the various realizations of this tenth station in the desert reveals an astonishing series of visionary anticipations.

fig. 143

fig. 127

For example, the *Safrane Mirror Plantation* consisted of twenty concave crystal mirrors that Mack placed as an ensemble in the Tunisian desert in 1967. Similar to the *Caravan* illustrated above, the mirrors were installed in a serial arrangement. The elements of the *Safrane Mirror Plantation* rose diagonally into the sky, mirroring its blue color on their concave surfaces and becoming resistances to the light that they threw back into the space. According to Mack, the artistic intention of such mirror plantations was always "to irritate and intensify the artificial appearance of an already artificial nature through mirroring."[37] Using mirror reflectors, Mack erected large lattice chains and structural surfaces in the desert, on which the light flickered and glowed, blending in with the material construction. The reflectors function as concave mirrors that capture the sunlight. As early as 1976, Mack was already thinking about using electronically controlled

32 Heinz Mack, "Die Ruhe der Unruhe," in *ZERO*, no. 2 (1958), unpaginated; Vorlass (promised bequest) Heinz Mack, ZERO foundation, Düsseldorf, mkp.ZERO.1.VII.139, quoted from Dieter Honisch, *Mack. Sculptures, 1953–1986* (Dusseldorf: Econ, 1987), 12. Translated from the German.

33 Mack, *Ruhe der Unruhe*. Translated from the German.

34 Ulrike Schmitt, *Der Doppelaspekt von aterialität und Immaterialität in den Werken der ZERO-Künstler: 1957–67*, PhD diss., University of Cologne, 2013, 12, quoted from Sotke, *Mack. Sahara*, 112.

35 Schmitt, *Der Doppelaspekt*, 12.

36 Mack, *Sahara-Projekt*, 6, quoted from Sotke, *Mack. Sahara*, 40.

37 Nannen, *Mack*. Translated from the German.

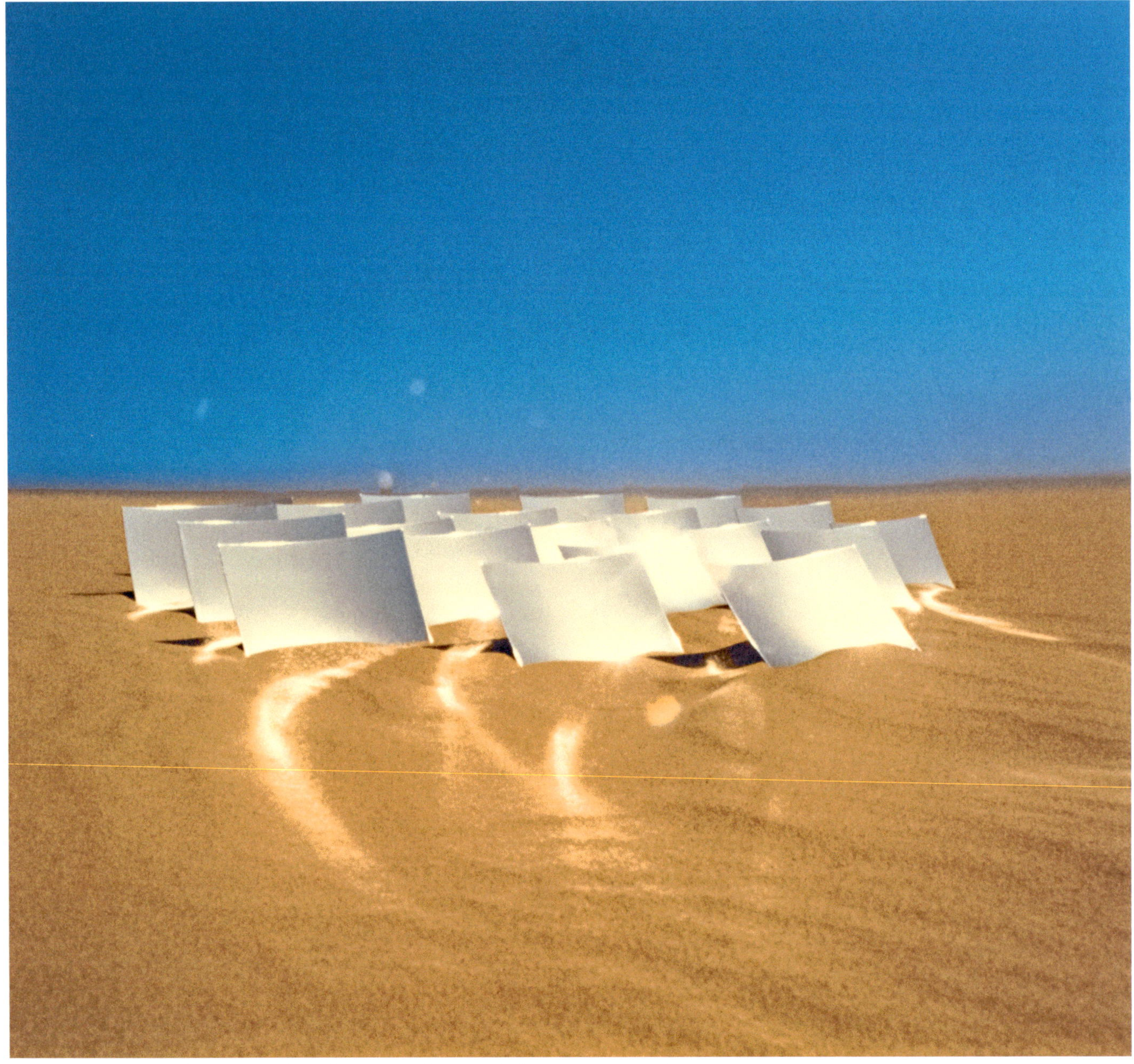

fig. 143 Heinz Mack, *Safrane Mirror Plantation*, 1967, Tunisia, crystal mirrors, 50 × 50 cm each

sensors to align them so that they always catch the sun's rays at the best angle.[38] It is only a small step from this artistic utopia to today's technical realization for energy production.

Photovoltaic (PV) modules are used to convert sunlight into electricity. The flat, rectangular modules are made of semiconductor materials that use photons to directly generate electrons so that an electric current can flow.[39] Different materials are used in today's PV modules, and depending on the chemical element, the modules have different degrees of efficiency, i.e., they generate different amounts of electric power per surface area. Most PV modules are made of silicon, a non-toxic material that is the second most abundant chemical element on Earth after oxygen. Today, silicon PV modules achieve efficiencies of ~27%.[40]

38 Nannen, *Mack*.

39 See Adolf Goetzberger, Bernhard Voß, and Joachim Knobloch, *Sonnenenergie: Photovoltaik – Physik und Technologie der Solarzelle* (Stuttgart: Teubner, 1997).

40 See Fraunhofer Institute for Solar Energy Systems (ISE), *Photovoltaics Report* (Freiburg im Breisgau: ISE, 2023).

Other PV semiconductor materials, such as gallium arsenide-based compounds, can achieve significantly higher efficiencies of up to 47%,[41] but are correspondingly more complex to manufacture and therefore more expensive, and some are toxic and rare.

Due to their significantly lower manufacturing costs, printed PV modules are a possible alternative. Here, the semiconductor material, which consists of organic-inorganic compounds, is applied in the liquid phase process and then dried. Although these modules have a significantly lower efficiency (~17%),[42] they offer other advantages. They are produced on flexible substrates and can therefore be applied to many surfaces with different geometries. In addition, printed PV modules are very light weight and, depending on the design, can be realized translucent.

The applications for PV technologies today go beyond traditional rooftop systems. In Germany, large PV parks are now mostly located along railroads and expressways. However, new developments show that such large PV power plants can also be excellently combined with agricultural use if the design is adapted accordingly. In addition to generating electricity, this Agri-PV technology offers protection for plants or even livestock under the solar roofs. Floating PV systems can now also be installed on inland lakes. Photovoltaic modules have a special design when they are installed in façades or as window replacements in buildings, on car roofs or on tents. Integrated photovoltaics are currently experiencing an encouraging surge in development as the demand for clean energy sources and the need for multiple uses of space and area on urban as well as agricultural land continue to grow.

Energy and Cosmos

figs. 108, 123, 140, 144, 231

In the film *Tele-Mack*, the artist, dressed in a silver jumpsuit, walks through a labyrinth of light reflectors erected in the sand dunes, each consisting of four concave aluminum elements. In each one, the desert sun is reflected as a glistening ball of light on a blue firmament, multiplied many times over in Mack's *Jardin Artificiel*. A cosmic aspect emanates from works such as this, linking Mack's actions in the desert to the celestial bodies of our universe. Here – as later in the Wahiba desert – the artist entered into a dialogue with the star closest to Earth, whose radiation is the basic prerequisite for life on our planet. He also appears in his silver jumpsuit, which is reminiscent of NASA's space suits. Just a few months before the images of the first moon landing on July 20, 1969 went around the world, the "Silver Mack"[43] could be seen on German television screens in May 1969 in a similarly barren desert landscape. There, he installed various sculpturesmade of so-called honeycomb netting – a flexible, light, and strong aluminum mesh developed for aaerospace applications which, like a honeycomb, consists of a multitude of regular hexagons and refracts the light many times like small glass prisms. The artist used tension and pressure to deform this mesh into fan- and wing-like structures.

The fact that the *Sahara Project* came to fruition in the intellectual atmosphere of the "Space Age" – and even more specifically in the period between Sputnik 1, the first artificial satellite to go into orbit in 1957, and the moon landing of Apollo 11 in 1969[44] – becomes

41 Fraunhofer Institute, *Photovoltaics Report*.

42 Andreas Distler, Christoph J. Brabec, and Hans-Joachim Egelhaaf, "Organic Photovoltaic Modules with New World Record Efficiencies," *Progress in Photovoltaics* 29, no. 1 (January 2021), 24–31, https://doi.org/10.1002/pip.3336.

43 "Hans Emmerling im Gespräch mit Anette Bosetti," in Jürgen Wilhelm, ed., *Mack im Gespräch* (Munich: Hirmer, 2015), 55–62, here 56. Hans Emmerling is the director of the film *Tele-Mack*.

44 See also Thomas Kellein, *Sputnik-Schock und Mondlandung: Künstlerische Großprojekte von Yves Klein zu Christo* (Stuttgart: Hatje, 1989), 51ff.

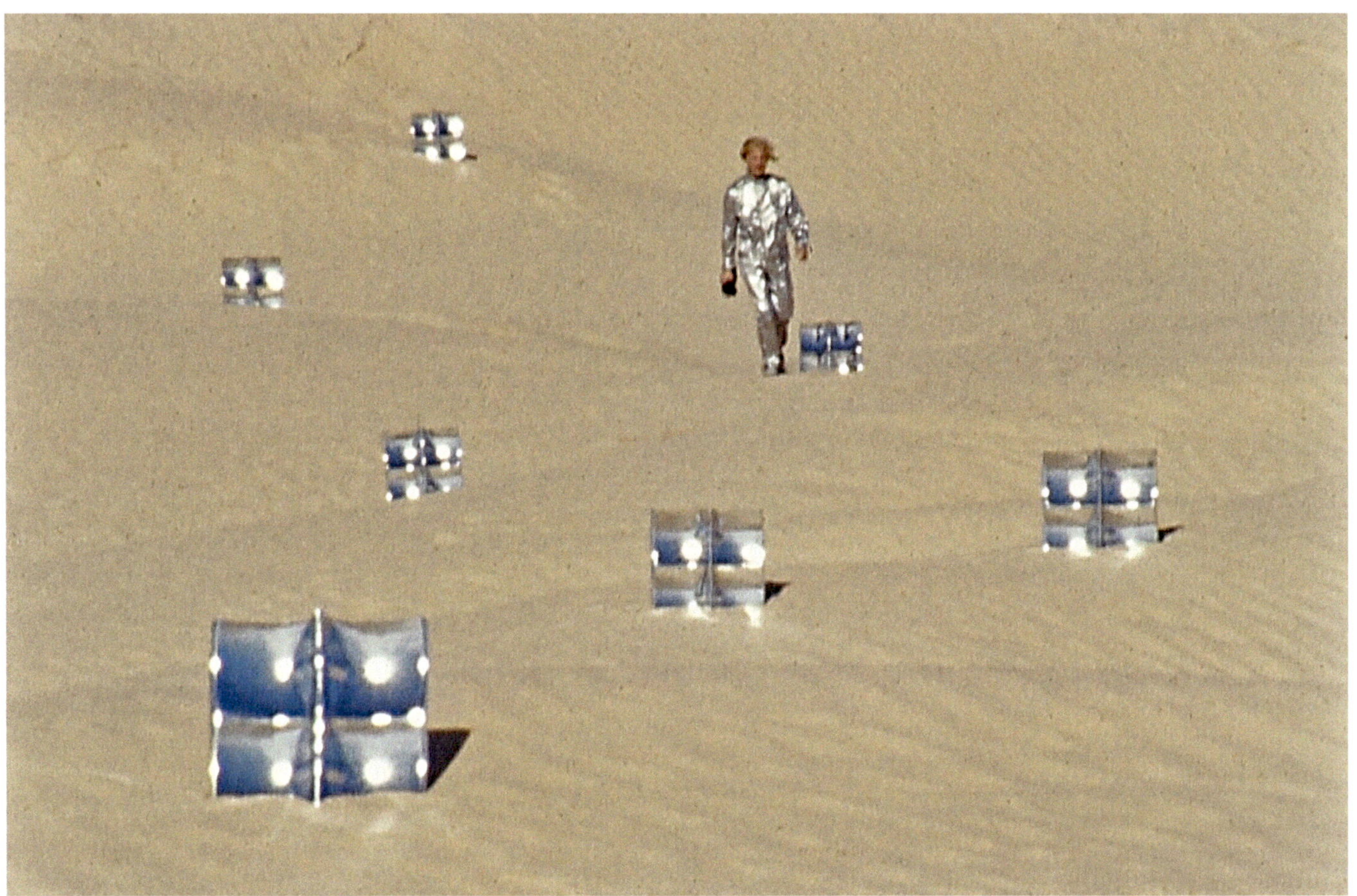

fig. 144 Heinz Mack with light reflectors in the Sahara, east of the Kebili oasis, Grand Erg Oriental, Tunisia, film still from *Tele-Mack*, 1968, camera: Edwin Braun

especially clear when one considers Mack's collages, his visualized imaginings, and his unrealized projects in this context. In the *Sahara Project* collages, virtual volumes spread out across the night sky as immaterial phenomena of light. The *Light Project for the Southern Algerian Desert* (dated 1962–63) shows the artistic imagination of celestial bodies moving in circles over the Sahara. In this collage, stars and planets glow like a mirage in the night sky. Mack also imagined new means of transportation for natural spaces like the Sahara, as "flying architectures" over the desert. These should "not be left by the tourists of the new millennium, so that large parts of the preserve, such as the artificial gardens, are no longer entered."[45] With this in mind, Mack collaged a disc-shaped metal structure into the night sky over the Sahara as a flying object "for a new, primarily optical tourism, rich in imagination, with new rituals."[46]

fig. 145

Station 12: The Artificial Suns

The idea of floating immaterial light phenomena in the desert sky also comes from the *Sahara Project* and its twelfth station, *The Artificial Suns*. Mack wrote in the *Sahara Project* that the slowly rotating light formations of his dynamos would only gain their actual energy when their disc diameter was fifty to one hundred meters. He wanted "the open dimension of a large disc of light, the changing structures of movement of which continually exchange, lose, and find each other

45 Mack, quoted in Nannen, *Mack*. Translated from the German.

46 Nannen, *Mack*. Translated from the German.

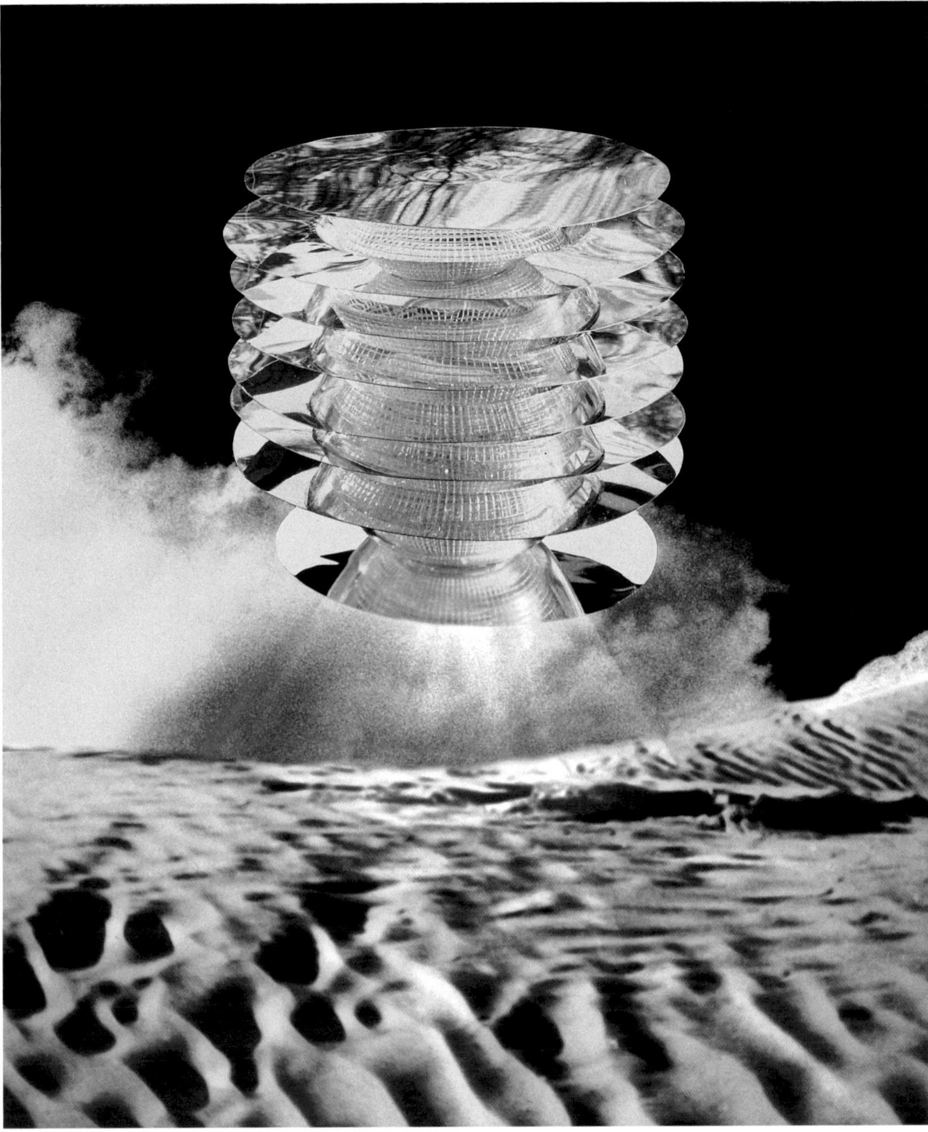

fig. 145 Heinz Mack, *Untitled*, 1968, photo collage

again, in a 'state' of continuous transition." The phenomenon of the mirage is intended to create the impression "that these artificial suns become apparitions of the sky."[47]

Circular, light-kinetic rotors or dynamos have been a symbol of the ZERO movement since 1958 and continue to be part of Mack's sculptural œuvre to this day. His idea of a dynamic, constantly changing appearance is more evident in this group of works than in any other.[48] The appearance of the rotors is determined by one or more circular discs rotating at a slow speed, sometimes in opposite directions, behind a translucent, often grooved glass surface. The slow movement, together with the reflection of light, produces constantly changing light phenomena, creating virtual images of the slow movement of light in a state of constant transformation.[49] Here, movement takes the place of form, and in the continuum, beginning and end become interchangeable. For Mack, the rotors have something of the equanimity and serenity of ancient Indian philosophy "in the sense of the Buddhist doctrine of eternal recurrence as expressed in the circular form."[50]

47 Mack, *Sahara-Projekt*, 7, quoted from Sotke, *Mack. Sahara*, 43.

48 See Honisch, *Mack. Sculptures*, 16.

49 For more on the *Rotors*, see: Robert Fleck and Antonia Lehmann-Tolkmitt, *Heinz Mack: A Twenty-First Century Artist*, trans. Gérard Goodrow (Munich: Hirmer, 2019), 47ff.

50 Heinz Mack, quoted in Yvonne Schwarzer, *Kunst Portrait: Das Paradies auf Erden schon zu Lebzeiten betreten: Ein Gespräch mit dem Maler und Bildhauer Heinz Mack* (Witten: ars momentum, 2005), 2, quoted here from Sotke, *Mack. Sahara*, 43.

The Arctic Sun (1964) shows a rotor disc floating in the sky over the Arctic Sea. This visualizes the monumental idea of showing an artificial sun as a light source over the ice desert, which, however, was never realized in this form. Mack did, though, travel to Greenland, where he realized parts of his *Jardin Artificiel* in the Arctic. This "expedition into artificial gardens" took place in 1976 and was documented by Thomas Höpker. The name Mack is synonymous with utopia, wrote Wieland Schmied: "Everything Heinz Mack does is conceived as utopia, is designed to achieve the impossible. Everything he does is conceived on a grand scale and demands realization on a gigantic scale."[51] This is especially true of the *Sahara Project* and its twelfth station, which are located somewhere between utopia and reality. "Utopia, the emptiness of the non-place that is to be filled, is like the desert in which any human scale is lost," Uwe Rüth formulated.[52] The *Sahara Project* is decisively characterized by the immeasurable vastness of the desert into which it was projected. The monumentality of the space determines the artistic ideas, which can unfold on a freer, larger scale because they are not bound to the museum context.

fig. 146

A Project for the Twenty-First Century

Since its conception in 1959, the *Sahara Project* has had a decisive influence on Mack's sculptural work, while at the same time retaining its intended immanence. This includes a visionary quality that has lost none of its relevance more than sixty years after its formulation. Mack, who has also been described as a "twenty-first century artist,"[53] expressed many ideas in the *Sahara Project* that were ahead of their time. For example, the ideas of a monumental light stele and a plantation of mirror reflectors in the desert have long since become reality in energy technology.

On the coasts of the world's oceans, huge parks of wind turbines have been erected to generate energy – they are reminiscent of Mack's enormous rotors, which he designed as "artificial suns" with a diameter of more than fifty meters.[54] In addition to the offshore wind farms, these power plants are now located in the Sahara, particularly in Morocco, which is now leading the way in North Africa in its transition to renewable energies, not only solar but also wind power.[55]

Since Mack did not receive any funding from private sponsors or public institutions for his *Sahara Project*, many of the ideas in it have only been realized in an experimental and rudimentary form. With today's technology, however, it would be possible not only to realize the ideas of the *Sahara Project*, but also to combine them with the actual production of renewable energy. In the face of the climate crisis, which scientists and activists consider to be the most pressing problem of our time, artists like Heinz Mack could also be involved in the aesthetic design of future technologies and the ideas of the *Sahara Project* could be further developed in the twenty-first century: "But no artistic imagination will suffice ... if art gives up its immanent claim to change the world – for the better."[56]

Translated from the German by Gérard Goodrow.

51 See Wieland Schmied, "Arbeit am Projekt der Moderne: Über Heinz Mack und den Mythos vom Künstler als Konstrukteur neuer Welten," in idem, ed., *Utopie und Wirklichkeit im Werk von Heinz Mack*, exhib. cat., Liechtensteinische Staatliche Kunstsammlung, Vaduz (Cologne: DuMont, 1998), 10–13, here 11. Translated from the German.

52 Rüth, *Heinz Mack*, 20. Translated from the German.

53 Fleck, Lehmann-Tolkmitt, *Heinz Mack*.

54 Mack, *Sahara-Projekt*, 7; see also: Sotke, *Mack. Sahara*, 139.

55 See Klagge, Naumann, Becker, *Energiegeographie*, 279; see also "Sahara Desert Wind Farms: A Learning Curve to Scale-Up," *Saharawind*, https://saharawind.com/en/sahara-desert-wind-farms-a-learning-curve-to-scale-up.

56 Heinz Mack, quoted in Schmied, *Utopie und Wirklichkeit*, 9, quoted here from Sotke, *Mack. Sahara*, 139.

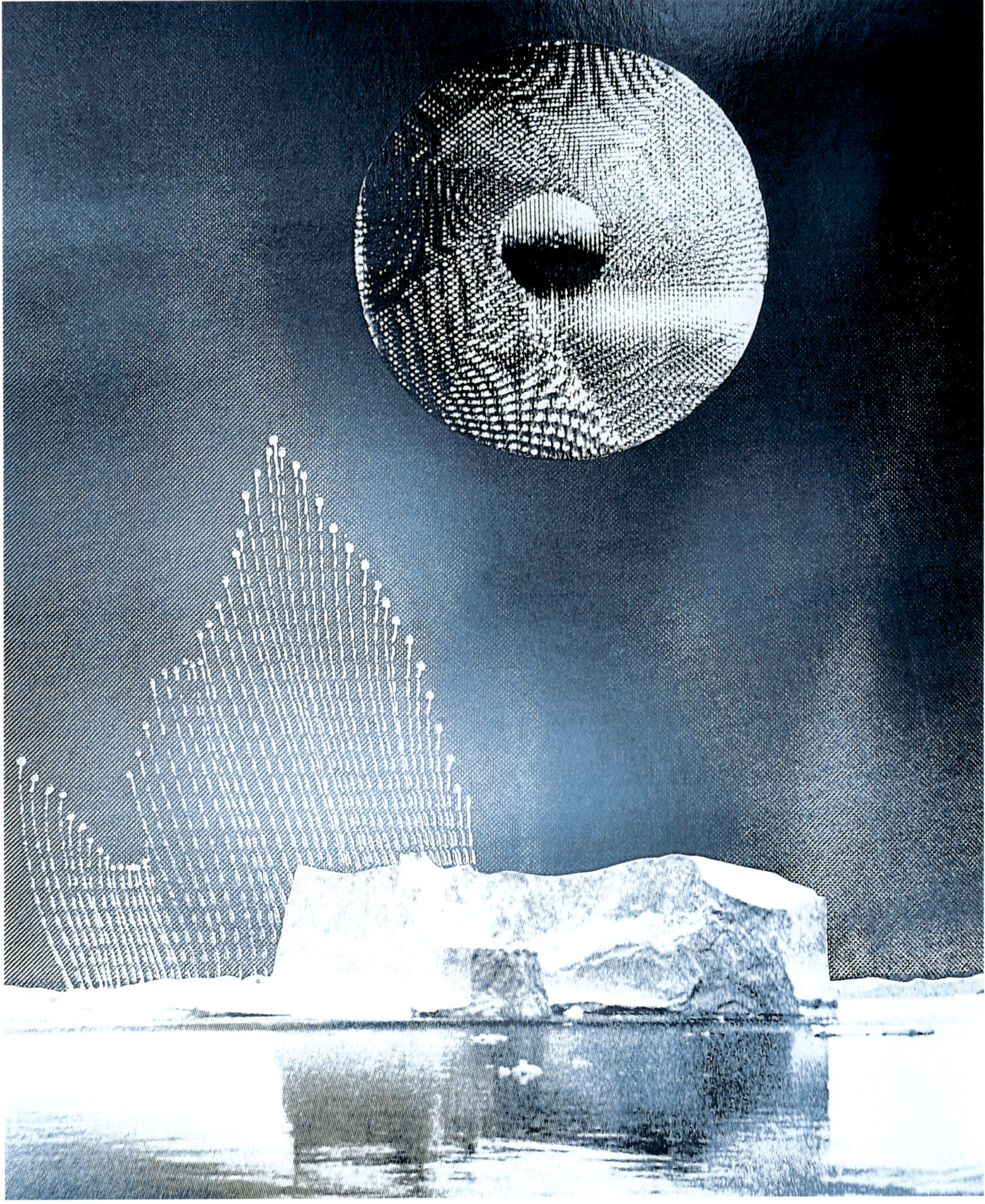

fig. 146 Heinz Mack, *Arctic Sun*, 1964, photo collage

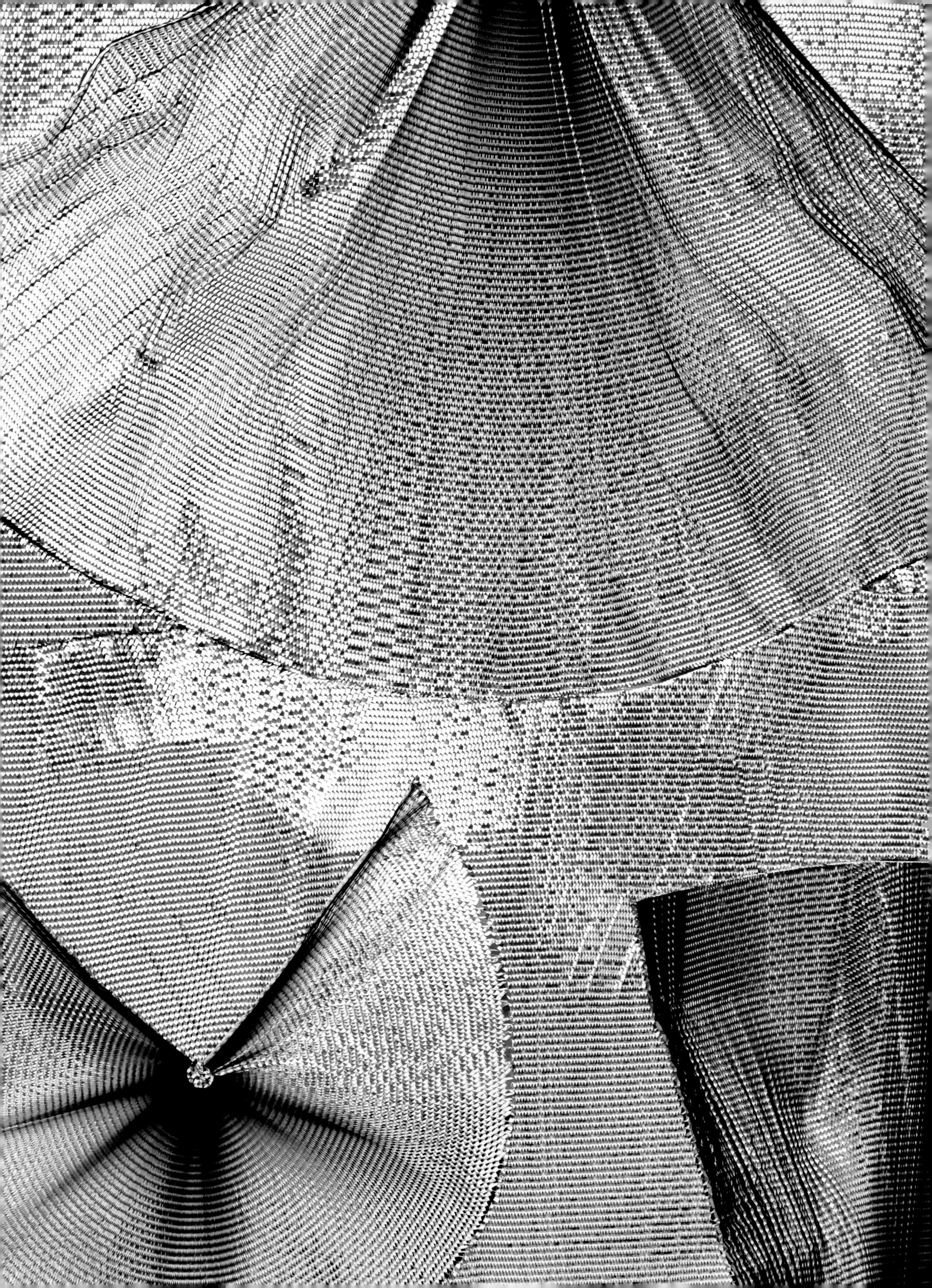

November 30, 2023 – April 21, 2024

Jardin Artificiel: The ZKM as guest at EnBW with Heinz Mack's *Sahara Project*

Since the 1950s, Heinz Mack has been striving to create a new harmony between humankind, nature, and technology. Throughout this time, he has used natural elements in his artworks, such as light, fire, air, water, and sand, as creative means of expression. Working with kinetic principles as well as new industrial and chemical materials, Mack developed his expanded concept of sculpture. Light, movement, structure, and color are central to his practice. His works are made as "instruments of light," connecting with the surrounding space and interacting directly with viewers.

The *Sahara Project*

In 1959, the artist conceived the idea of a *Jardin Artificiel*, an artificial garden that would include thirteen different locations for the installation of his works in the desert. The endless expanse of the desert landscape and its unique lighting atmosphere offered ideal conditions for working with light and space in their purest form. Since 1955, the artist has visited the Sahara several times. After first experiments with light in the Algerian and Moroccan deserts in 1962, he was able to partially realize his plan in 1968, when he was in Tunisia with a small team from Saarländischer Rundfunk [Saarland Broadcasting Corporation] to create the film *Tele-Mack*. In 1976, another expedition was undertaken, with the photographer Thomas Höpker, to Algeria and the Grand Erg Occidental. Mack placed light-reflecting steles, cubes, and fans, sand reliefs and walls of mirrors in the desert sand dunes. Their reflective surfaces caught the sunlight and amplified it, creating downright vibrating light phenomena.

← *fig. 147* Heinz Mack, *The Garden in the Garden*, 1979–1980, detail

Since the actions were only accessible to the public via images, the *Sahara Project* is one of the first artworks in European art conveyed exclusively by media. At the same time, it made Heinz Mack a pioneer of Land Art. This art movement, which emerged towards the end of the 1960s, produced artistic works interacting directly with the natural environment.

The *Sahara Project* in Our Time

In the context of today's environmental crisis, the Sahara Project has new, existential resonance. Mack's large banks of reflectors and the extensive plantations of plates were conceived 65 years ago, anticipating the need for new ecological thinking and preempting solar plantations and solar power plants now being built in the great desert regions. Heinz Mack's works, which capture and redirect light, represent an artistic utopia that has since become reality with today's photovoltaic technology.

Mack at EnBW

The exhibition in the foyer of the EnBW head offices approaches Mack's monumental *Sahara Project* through photographs, collages, and sculptural objects as well as previously unpublished video footage. At the same time, one can follow how artistic utopias manifest themselves in reality, how they can anticipate and shape social discourses. The presentation coincides with the exhibition *Mack at ZKM* at the ZKM | Karlsruhe (September 16, 2023 – April 14, 2024).

*Space was no longer space; time was no longer time; mass no longer mass; all relationships and proportions no longer applied.**

*We will have to create new experiential spaces, a kind of artificial garden which people will visit in order to escape the bleakness of our urban landscapes.***

Works in the exhibition:
All works courtesy of the artist unless otherwise noted

The Garden in the Garden
1979–1980
Light sculpture: three parts, aluminum, acrylic glass, stainless steel
175 × 525 × 3 cm
→ *figs. 7, 147, 148, 149*, cover

Untitled (paravent with two wings)
1972
Light sculpture: Aluminum, acrylic glass
305 × 205 cm
→ *fig. 150*

***Light Stele*, Kebeli Oasis, Tunisia**
1962
Photo collage: digitally transformed, ink jet print
47 × 30.5 cm
→ *figs. 152, 153*

Fata Morgana
1968
Photo collage: digitally transformed, ink jet print
37.5 × 32 cm
→ *figs. 152, 154*

Virtual Volume
1963
Photo collage: digitally transformed, ink jet print
32 × 39 cm
→ *figs. 109, 152*

Untitled
1968
Photo collage: digitally transformed, ink jet print
39 × 32 cm
→ *figs. 145, 152*

***Light Fans*, Grand Erg Oriental, Tunisia**
1968
Photo print
Photo: Edwin Braun
→ *fig. 116*

Heinz Mack in a silver suit with reflectors, Grand Erg Occidental, Algeria
1976
Light box
46 × 65 × 10 cm
Photo: Thomas Höpker
→ *fig. 104*

***Great Space Arrow*, Grand Erg Occidental, Algeria**
1976
Light box
46 × 65 × 10 cm
Photo: Thomas Höpker
→ *fig. 106*

My House in the Desert
1997 (idea: 1960)
Light box
46 × 65 × 10 cm
→ *fig. 174*

***Ksar*, Grand Erg Occidental, Algeria**
1976
Photo print
Photo: Thomas Höpker
→ *fig. 155*

***Light Reflectors*, Wahiba Sands, Oman**
1997
Photo print
→ *figs. 149, 151*

***Large Stele in the Wahiba Desert*, Oman**
1997
Light box
125 × 188 × 20.5 cm
→ *fig. 141*

Recordings of the *Sahara Project*
1976
16 mm film (digitized), color, silent
18:09 min
Camera: Fritz Bagel

* Heinz Mack, "Mack zu diesem Buch", in *Mack. Kunst in der Wüste. Bilder zum Sahara-Projekt* (Munich: Josef Keller, 1969), 10. Translated from the German.
** Heinz Mack, *Lecture at the Academy of Fine Arts, Stuttgart*, 1977, (typoscript, Archive Heinz Mack). Translated from the German.

→→ *fig. 148* Heinz Mack, *The Garden in the Garden*, 1979–1980

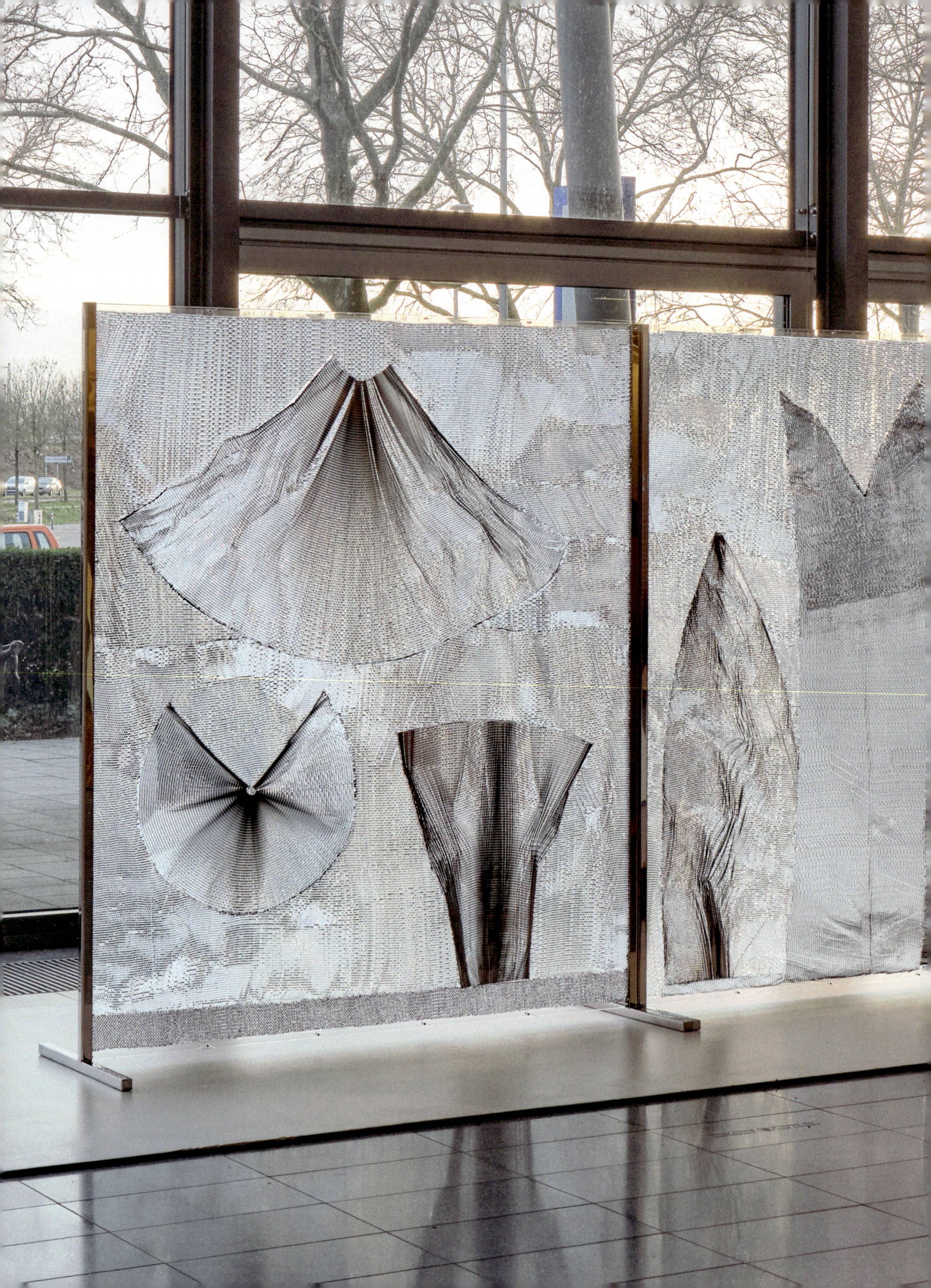

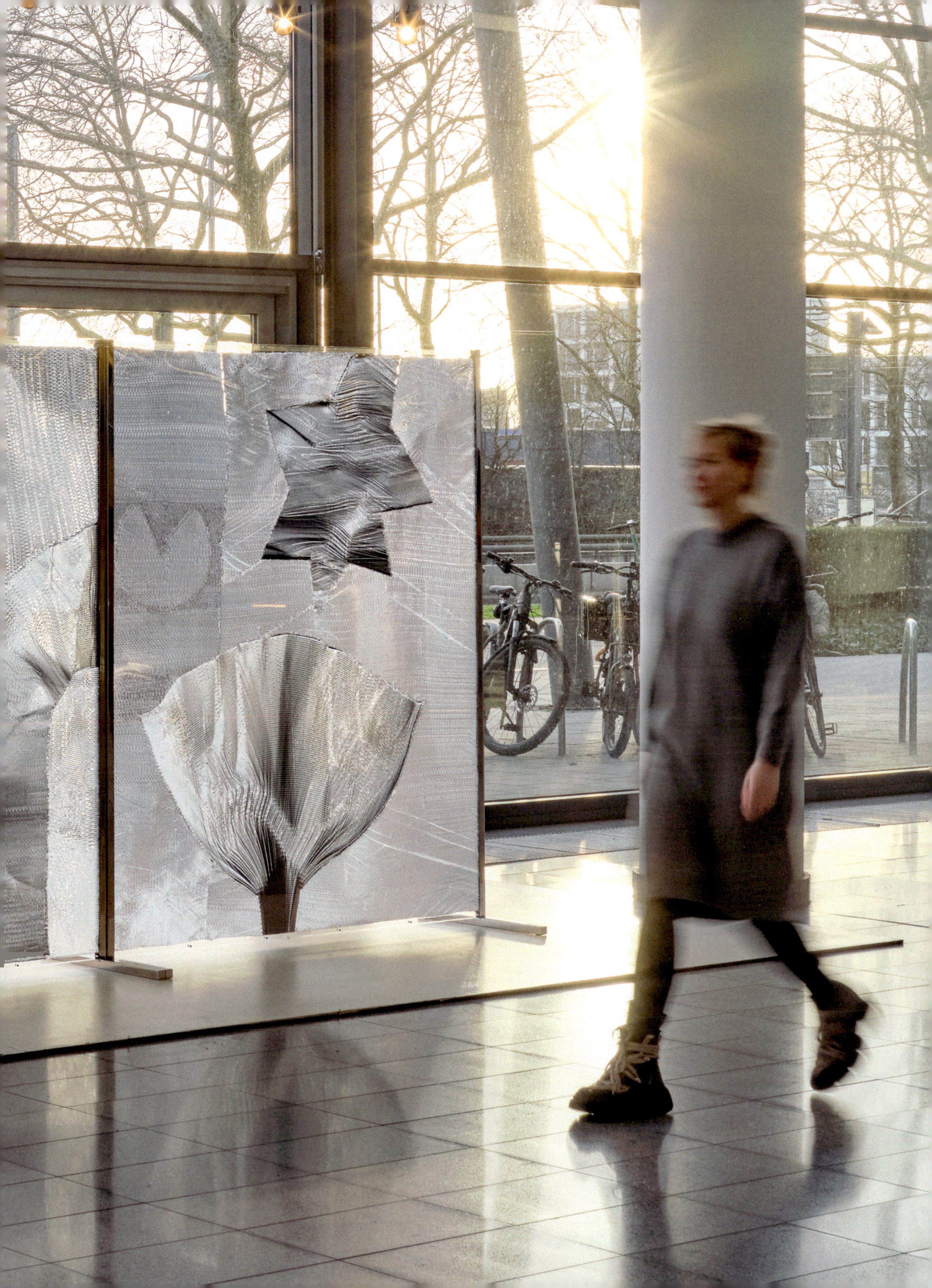

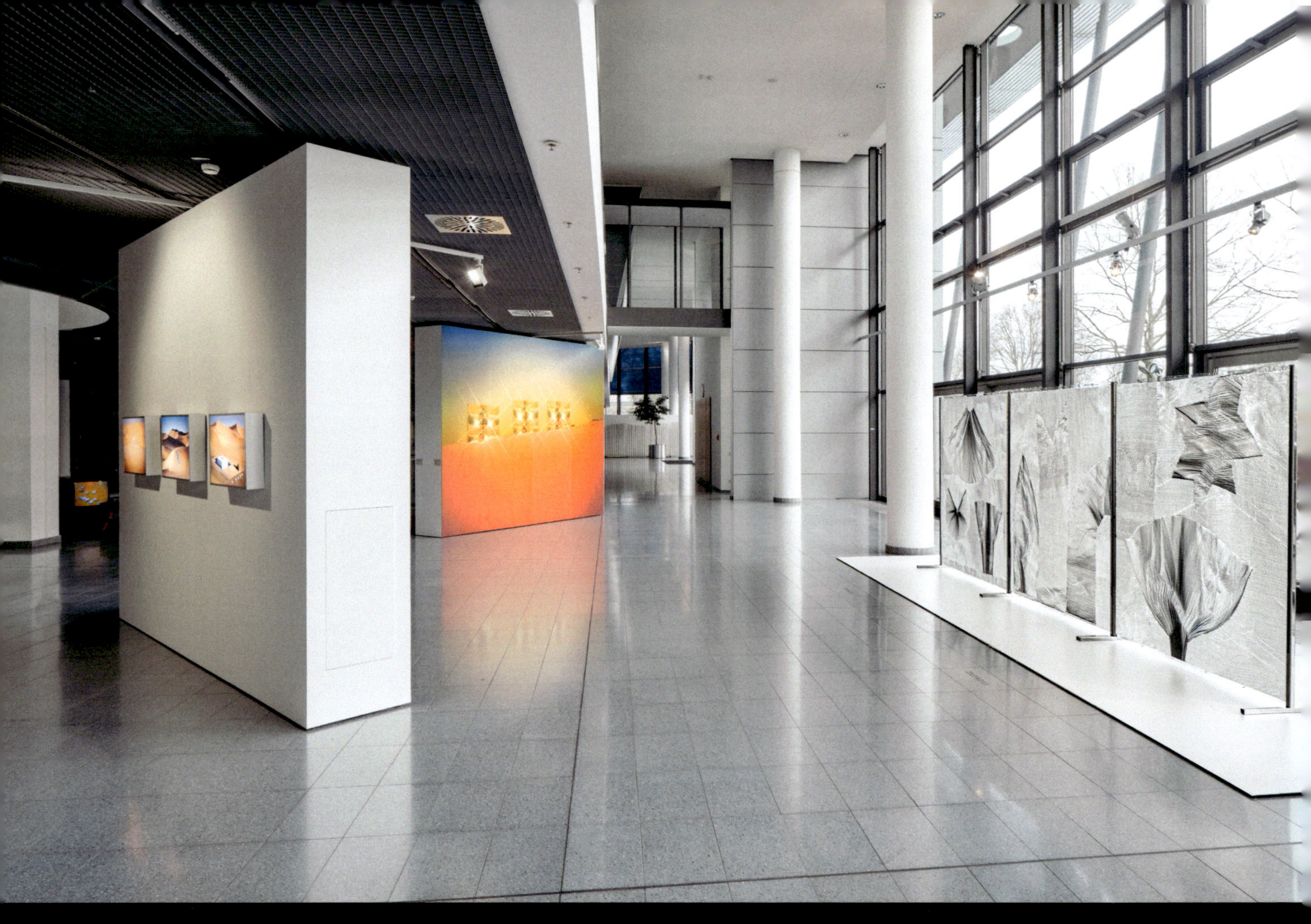

↑ *fig. 149* *Jardin Artificiel. The ZKM as guest at the EnBW with Heinz Mack's* Sahara Project, exhibition view, EnBW Karlsruhe 2024

→ *fig. 150* Heinz Mack, *Untitled (paravent with two wings)*, 1972

→→ *fig. 151* Heinz Mack, *Light Reflectors*, Wahiba Sands, Oman, 1997

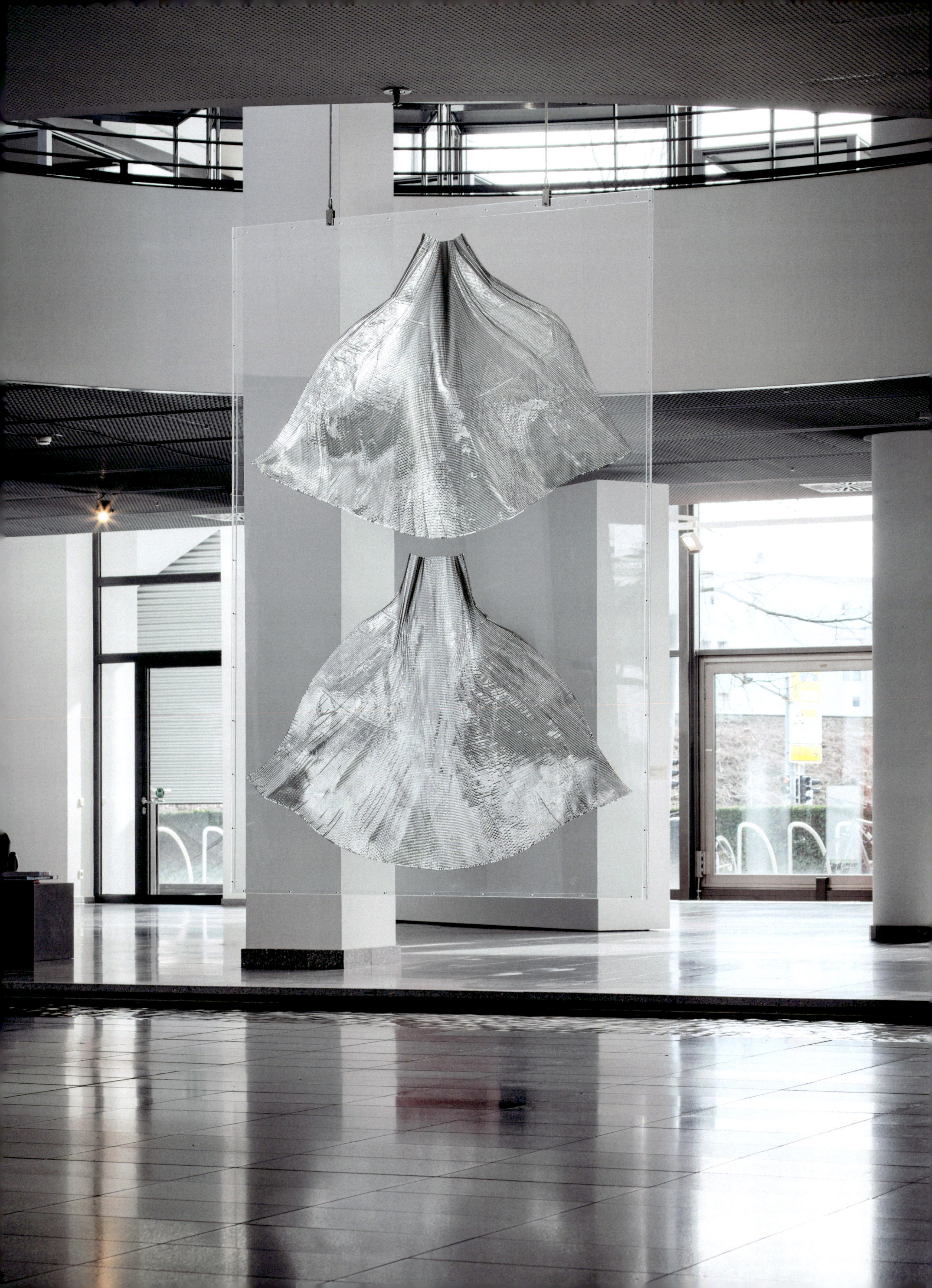

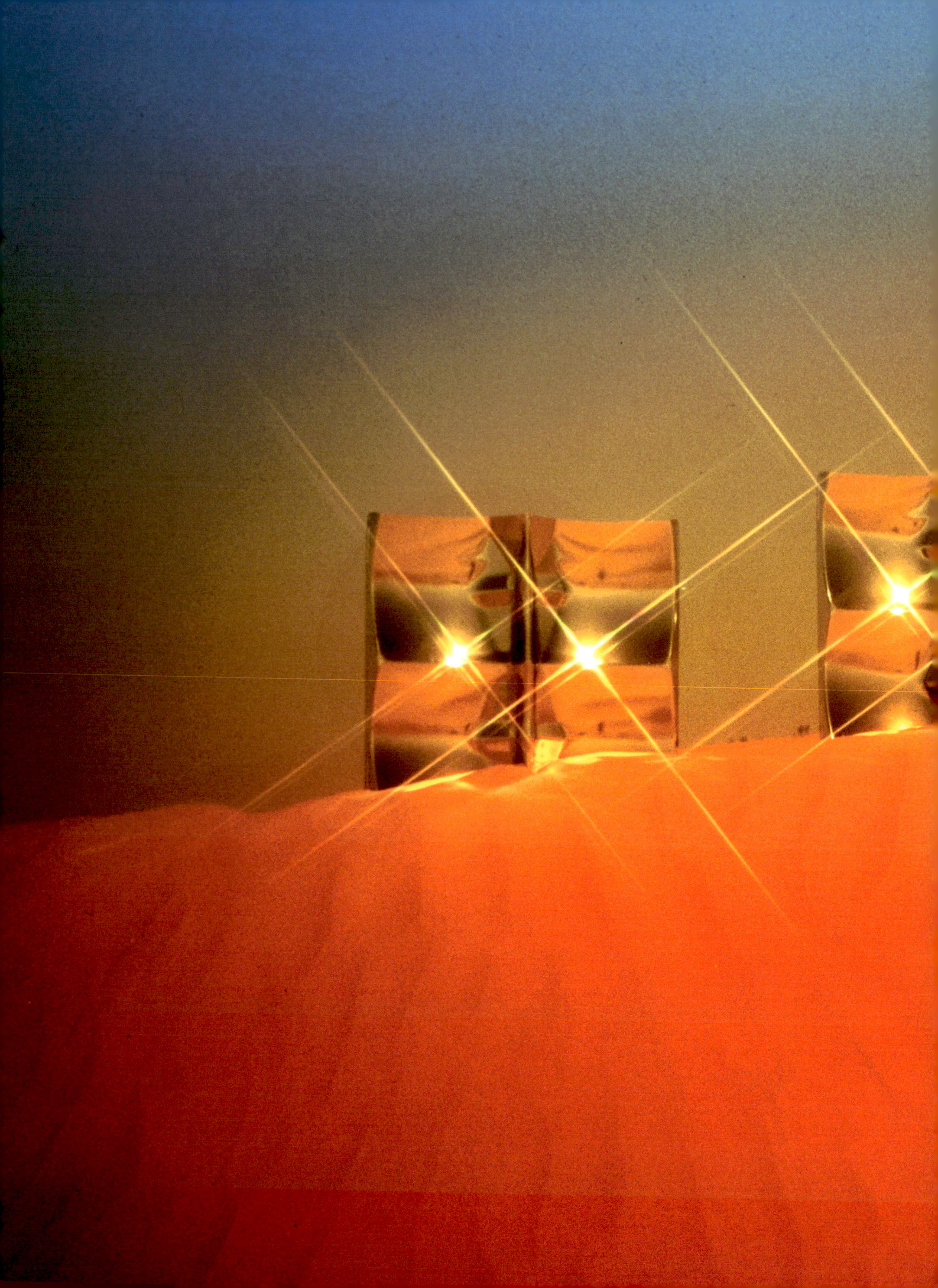

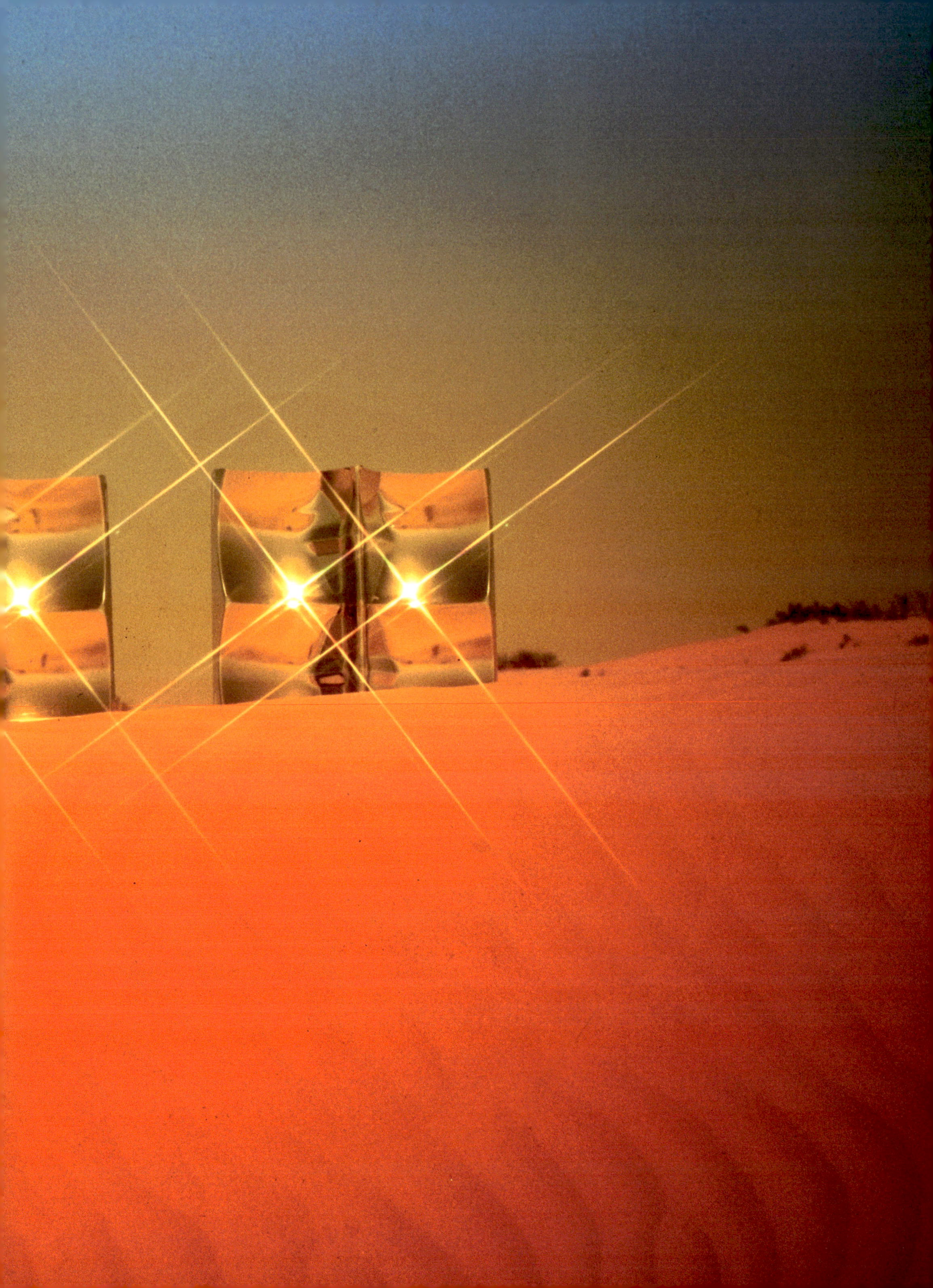

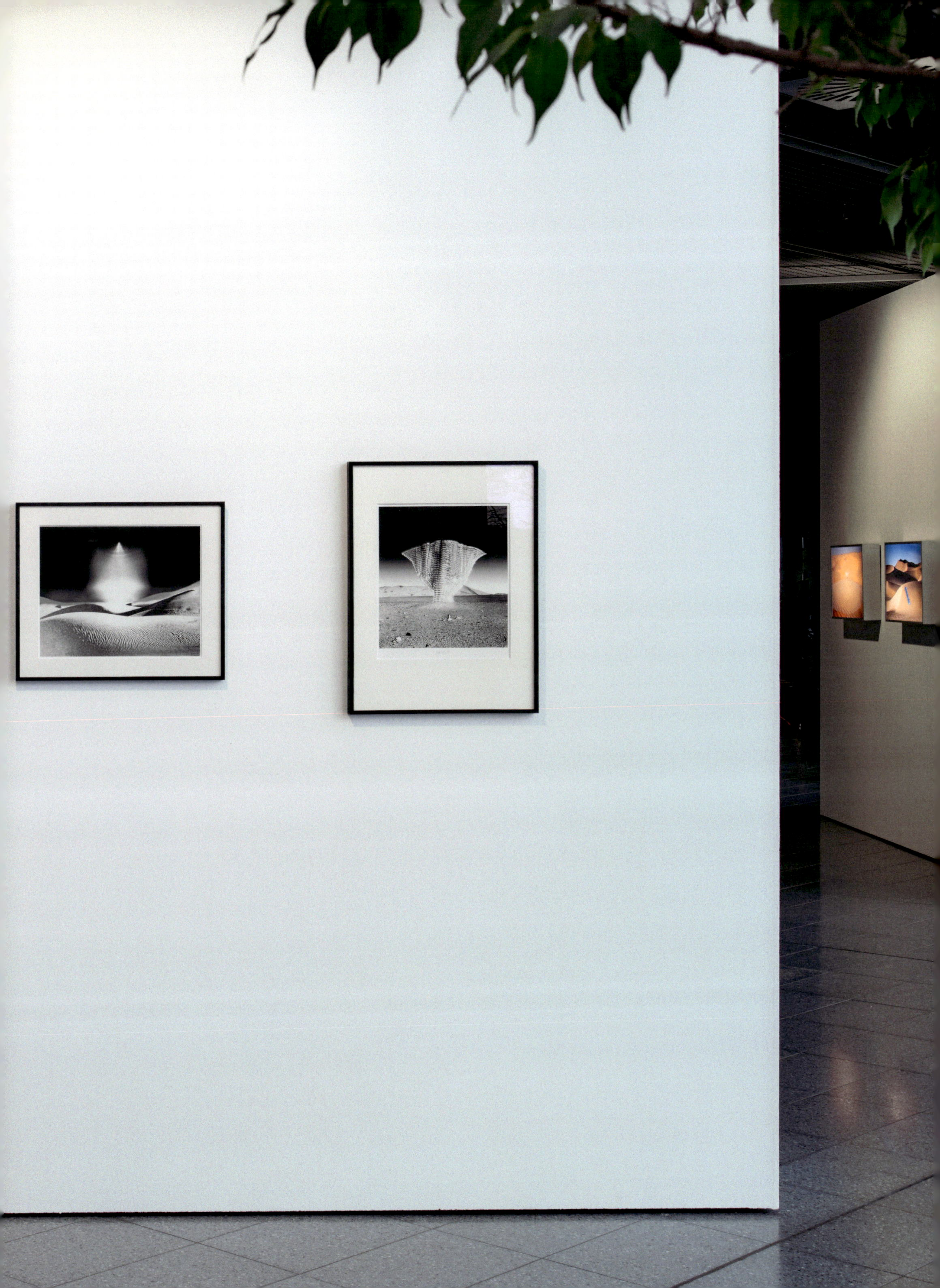

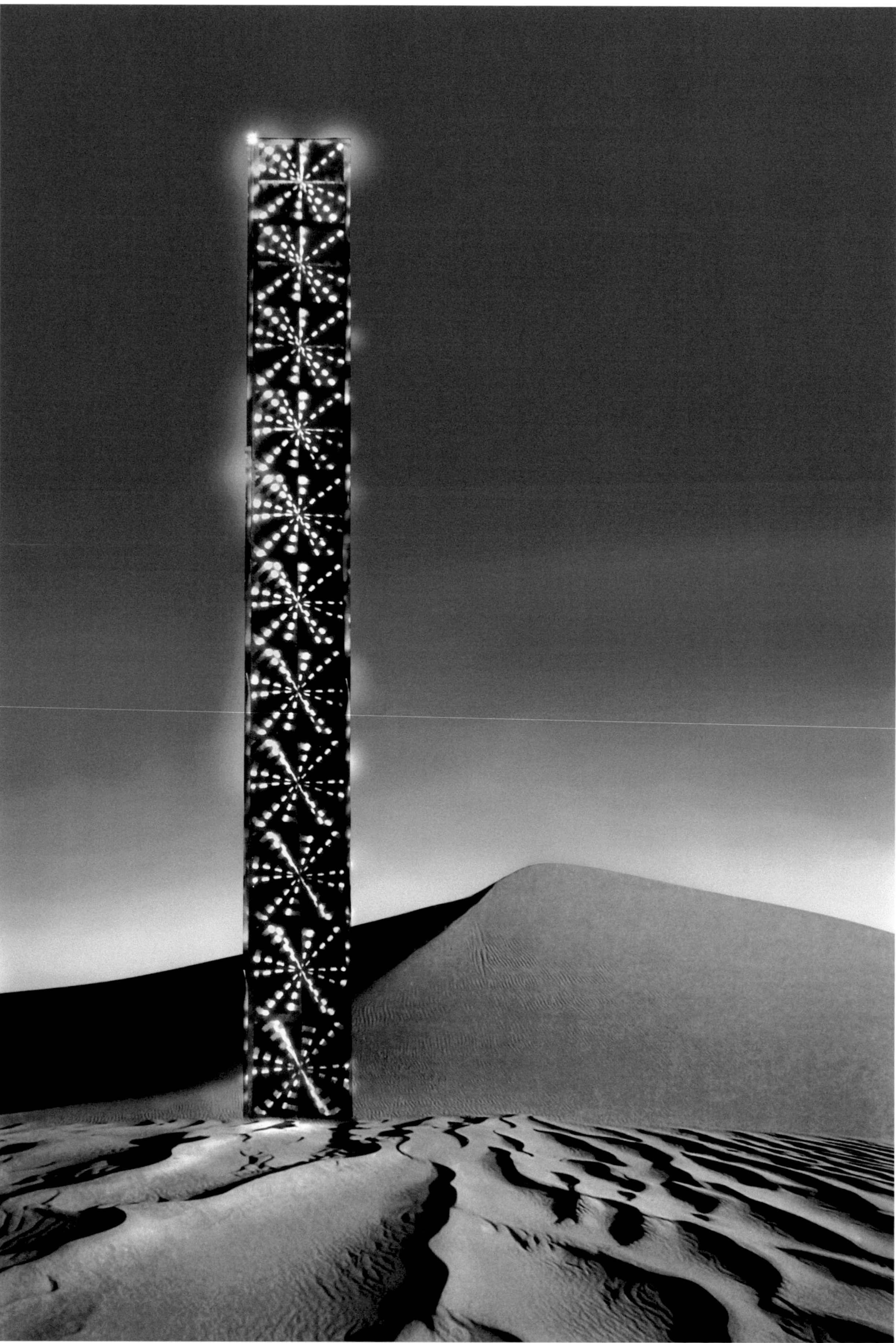

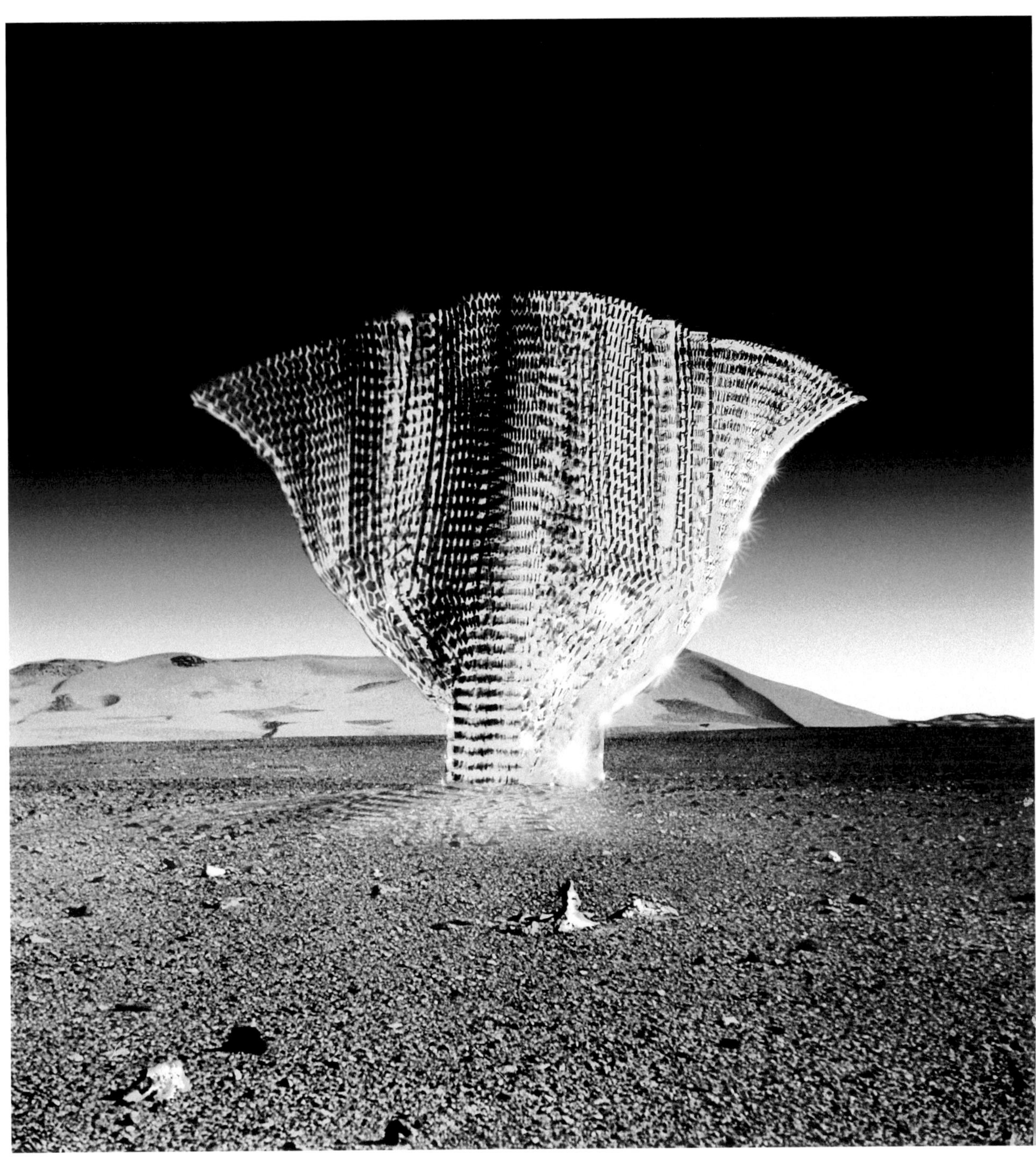

←← *fig. 152* *Jardin Artificiel. The ZKM as guest at the EnBW with Heinz Mack's* Sahara Project, exhibition view, EnBW Karlsruhe 2024
← *fig. 153* Heinz Mack, *Light Stele*, Kebeli Oasis, Tunisia, 1962

↑ *fig. 154* Heinz Mack, *Fata Morgana*, 1968
→→ *fig. 155* Heinz Mack, *Ksar*, Grand Erg Occidental, Algeria, 1976, photo: Thomas Höpker

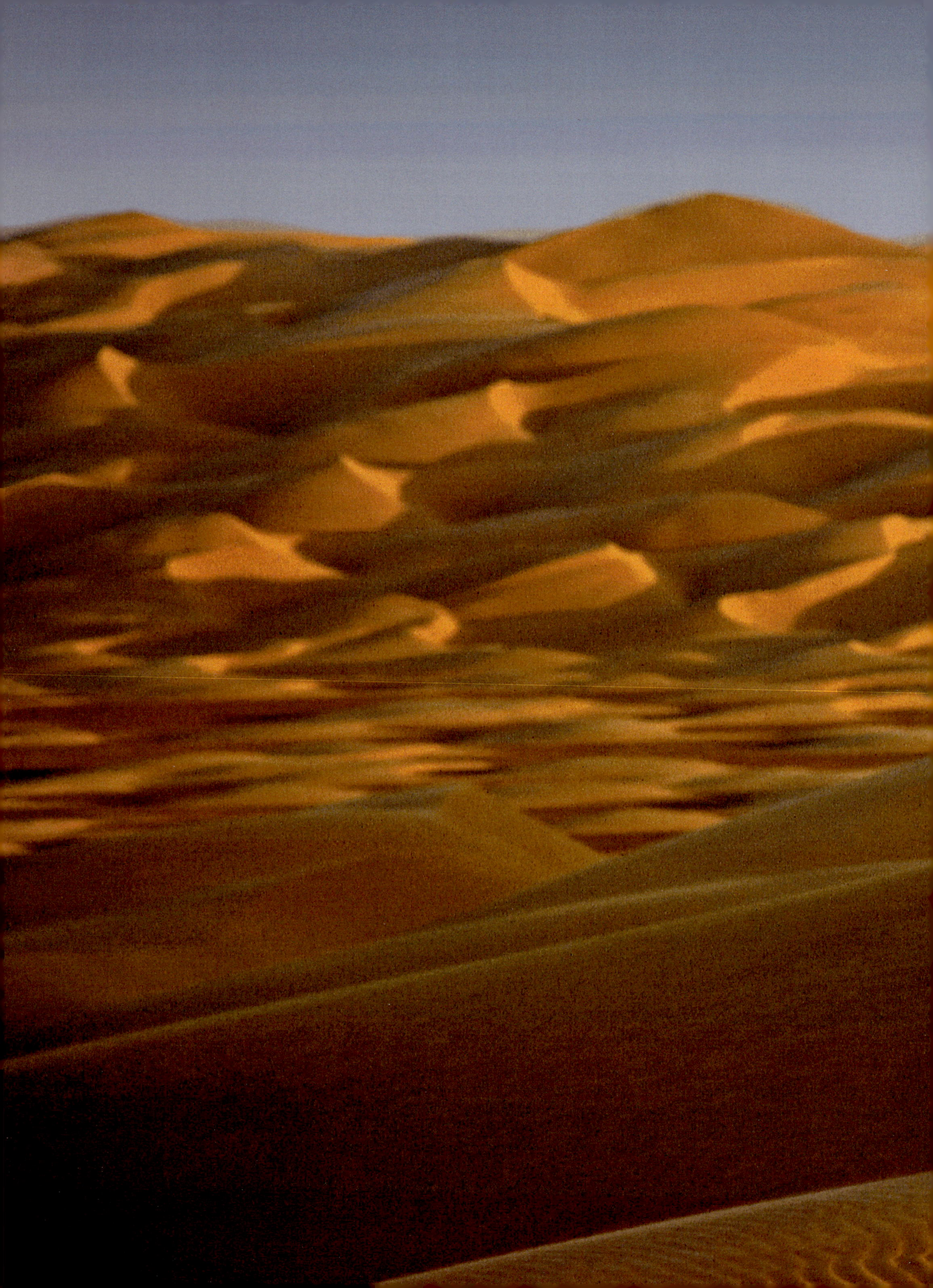

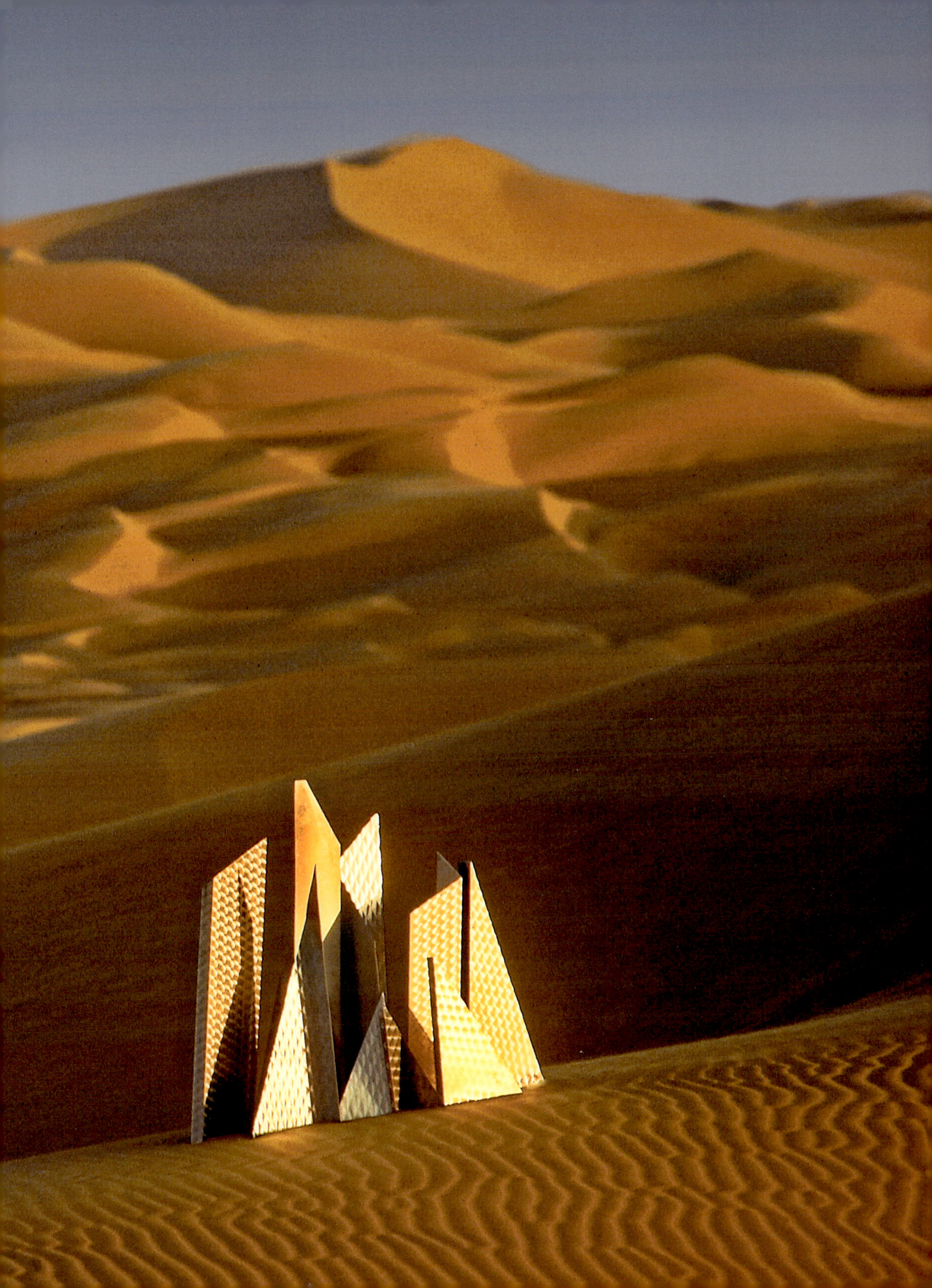

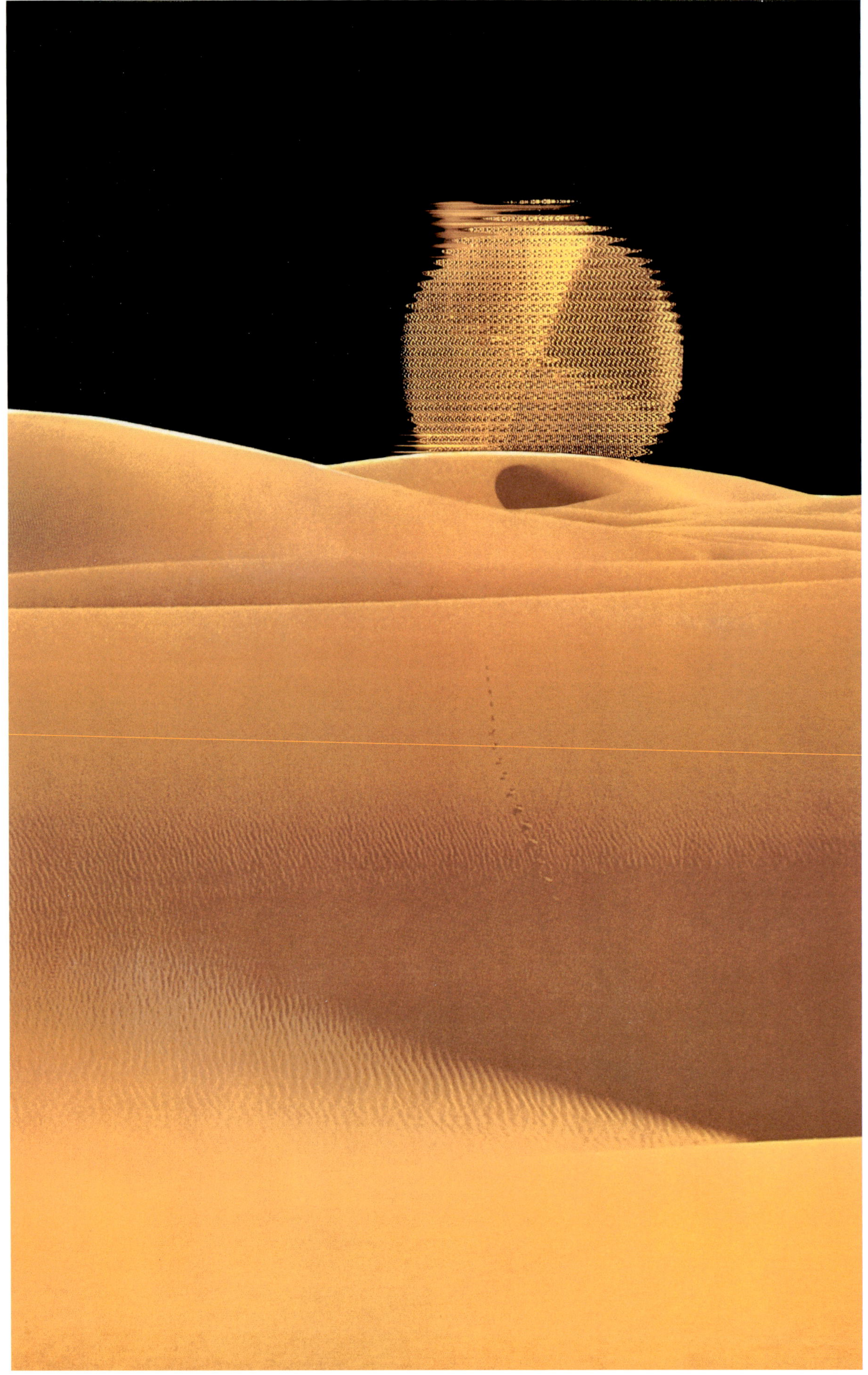

fig. 156 Heinz Mack, *Sun Rotor*, Tunisia, 1968, photo collage

An Artist in the Twenty-First Century: Heinz Mack in the Mirror of Contemporary Positions

Reviewed in the context of today, the works of Heinz Mack still radiate a certain timelessness. For this reason, Mack, who was born in Lollar, Hesse in 1931, is often referred to as "a twenty-first century artist." In their monograph of the same title, published in 2019, Robert Fleck and Antonia Lehmann-Tolkmitt[1] attribute this above all to a reawakening of interest in the figure of the artist and the ZERO movement he is associated with since the 2000s, which has manifested itself in numerous exhibitions and publications and has since subjected Mack's work to a reconsideration. In 2015, for example, the German magazine *art* boldly referred to the ZERO movement, which Heinz Mack founded together with Otto Piene in Düsseldorf in 1957, as "Germany's coolest artist group."[2] Looking at ZERO through the "eyes of contemporary artists"[3] is important in order to gain new perspectives on the work today, as also the art historian and curator Daniel Birnbaum, who was involved in a comprehensive and highly acclaimed retrospective in New York, Berlin, and Amsterdam in 2014/15, repeatedly emphasizes.[4] In his artistic œuvre, also beyond ZERO, Heinz Mack anticipated many themes that are still being addressed by artists today. A direct comparison of contemporary positions, however, has not yet been made. The referential frame from which today's artists draw is, of course, immensely diverse and subject to the most varied influences and parallel developments.[5] Nonetheless, it is precisely the joy of experimenting with new materials, the investigation of space and its perception, and the interdisciplinary, exploratory approach of his artistic practice that make Heinz Mack's work connectable to this day and also represent a relevant source of inspiration for subsequent generations of artists.

Artistic affinities can be found among current contemporary positions, whose working methods, choice of materials, and understanding of art show fascinating parallels to those of Heinz Mack and who may have more or less, consciously or unconsciously, oriented themselves toward the artist's work. Mack's work with light as a creative medium and his exploration of natural resources have often been compared to the work of contemporary artists such as Alicja Kwade, Carsten Höller, or, most frequently, Ólafur Elíasson.[6] Although Elíasson himself considers any influence to be rather "minimal,"[7] both formal and conceptual parallels can certainly be drawn between the Danish-Icelandic artist's work and Mack's. Elíasson's interest in collaborative, scientifically oriented working methods also shows similarities to ZERO's self-image as a global network that served as a nucleus for experimental and critical art.[8]

Heinz Mack has always been interested in the effect of light in all its facets. The exploration of space and time and their subjective perception is the central concern of his artistic-experimental practice. As "instruments of light",[9] his sculptures, installations, steles, and objects mirror, refract, and reflect light, thus elevating it to the status of an artistic object in itself. Depending on the incidence of light and the viewing position, new manifestations emerge, rhythmizing the surface and giving

1 Robert Fleck and Antonia Lehmann-Tolkmitt, *Heinz Mack. A Twenty-First Century Artist*, trans. Gérard Goodrow (Munich: Hirmer, 2019).

2 See the cover and lead story of the March 2015 issue of *art: das Kunstmagazin*: "ZERO. Deutschlands coolste Künstlergruppe."

3 Mattijs Visser in conversation with Daniel Birnbaum, "ZERO heute. Geschichte wiederholt sich nicht, aber sie reimt sich," in Dirk Pörschmann and Margriet Schavemaker, eds., *ZERO*, exh. cat. Martin-Gropius-Bau, Berlin (Berlin: König, 2015), 233–40, here 235. Translated from the German.

4 See Pörschmann and Schavemaker, *ZERO*.

5 See Visser and Birnbaum, "ZERO heute," 240.

6 See, for example, Fleck and Lehmann-Tolkmitt, *Heinz Mack*; Visser and Birnbaum, "ZERO heute."

7 Visser and Birnbaum, "ZERO heute," 234.

8 See Visser and Birnbaum, 237.

9 See p. 21 of this volume.

figs. 9, 159

it an immaterial effect. The physical presence of the viewer is directly incorporated into Mack's works through reflections, and at the same time constitutes the work as such.

fig. 157

The effects of space, color, and light also play a fundamental role in Ólafur Elíasson's work. Like Mack, he deals intensively with the connection between nature, technology, and art. To this end, he works across genres and in a variety of media, creating sculptures, kinetic installations, Land Art, and multi-sensory environments, whose proximity to works like the *Light Space (Hommage to Fontana)* that Heinz Mack, Otto Piene, and Günther Uecker presented at documenta III in 1964, has already been pointed out.[10]

In particular, Elíasson's spectacular stagings of natural phenomena, simulated by technological means, address aspects of perception and allow viewers to enter immersive worlds. His studio resembles a laboratory in which scientists, theorists, and designers from a wide range of disciplines work together to develop, produce, experiment, archive, research, and publish projects.[11] In initiatives such as the Institut für Raumexperimente (Institute for Spatial Experiments) at the Berlin University of the Arts (2009-2014), an experimental educational and research project on knowledge production and collective working methods, and the Studio Other Spaces (since 2014, together with the architect Sebastian Behmann), Elíasson is dedicated to exploring the "spatial, historical, ecological, social, and emotional parameters of a site and its users."[12] Thanks to his extensive teaching activities, Elíasson's former students, such as Julius von Bismarck and Julian Charrière, also derive new approaches from their interdisciplinary practice. The artists often reflect on contemporary perceptual phenomena in relation to the direct effects of climate change due to human influences.

fig. 204

fig. 158

One of Elíasson's best-known installations, *The weather project*, which in 2003 bathed the industrial architecture of the Tate Modern in London in glistening, artificially generated sunlight, is a good example of this. Opposite the entrance to the former turbine hall, a brightly lit semicircular screen hung high up on the wall. Two hundred monofrequency lights mounted behind the semitransparent material of the semicircular surface provided immense luminosity. Mirrored panels mounted on the ceiling created a flickering image of the semicircular disc, completing the appearance of the surface into an intensely glowing orange-yellow circle that gave the impression of an artificial setting sun. Fog that was let in from the sides of the hall further enhanced the atmospheric effect of the space. The light from the artificial sun had a truly magical appeal. The reflection of the events in the hall added a surreal dimension to the experience, blurring the boundaries between above and below, reality and illusion.

The exhibition caused a sensation and attracted many visitors. The participatory elements of *The weather project* also fostered a shared reception: The exhibition was accompanied by a media campaign and a discussion among Tate staff members about the influence of the weather on our social lives. In a survey, for example, 90% of staff said they discussed the weather with other people at least once a day, 44% said they did so even three times a day. Other questions focused on the general mood associated with different temperatures and weather phenomena, as well as economic or health factors ("9. Do you think

10 See Daniel Birnbaum, "Zero aus heutiger Sicht," in Heike van den Valentyn and Tiziana Caianiello, eds., *Lichtraum (Hommage à Fontana): der documenta-Beitrag von Heinz Mack, Otto Piene und Günther Uecker 1964* [*Spot on*, no. 4], exh. cat. (Düsseldorf: Museum Kunstpalast, 2009), unpaginated.

11 See Studio Olafur Eliasson, "About Studio Olafur Eliasson," https://olafureliasson.net/studio, accessed March 11, 2024.

12 Studio Other Spaces (SOS) was founded by Ólafur Elíasson and Sebastian Behmann in 2014. See Studio Other Spaces, "About Us," https://www.studiootherspaces.net/about-us, accessed March 11, 2024.

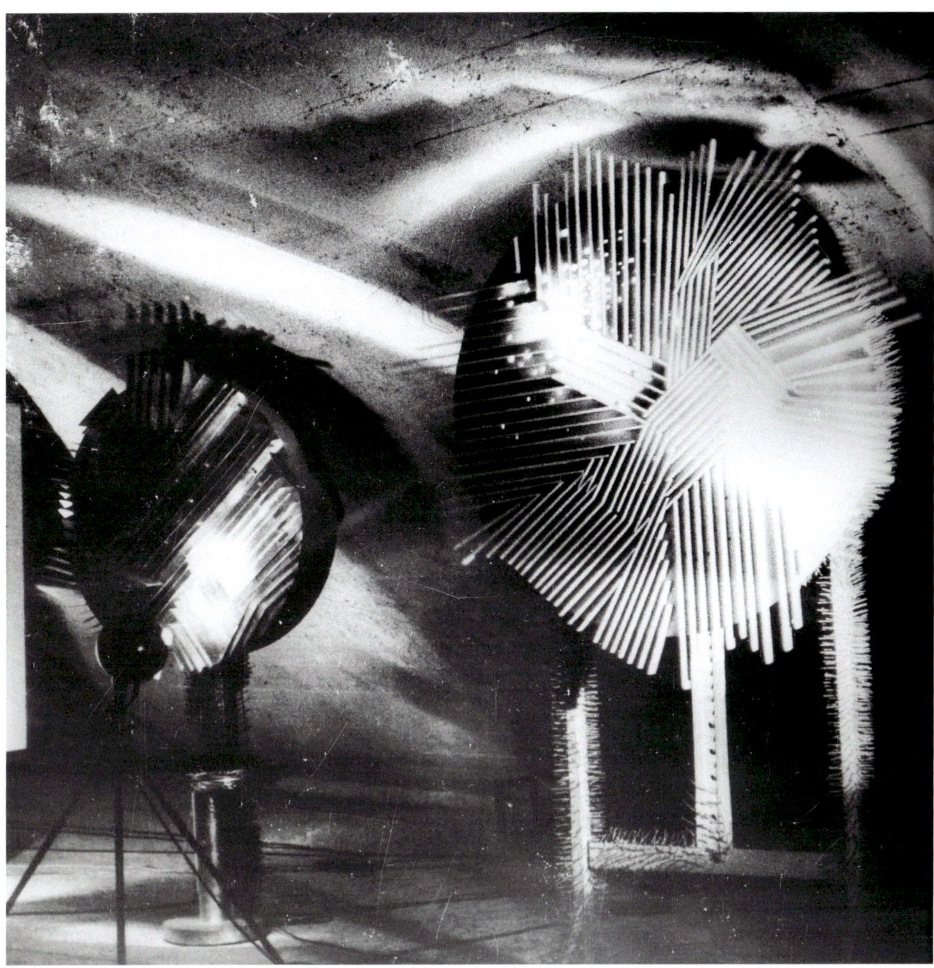

fig. 157 Heinz Mack, Otto Piene, and Günther Uecker, *Light Space (Hommage to Fontana)*, 1964, exhibition view, documenta 3, Kassel, 1964

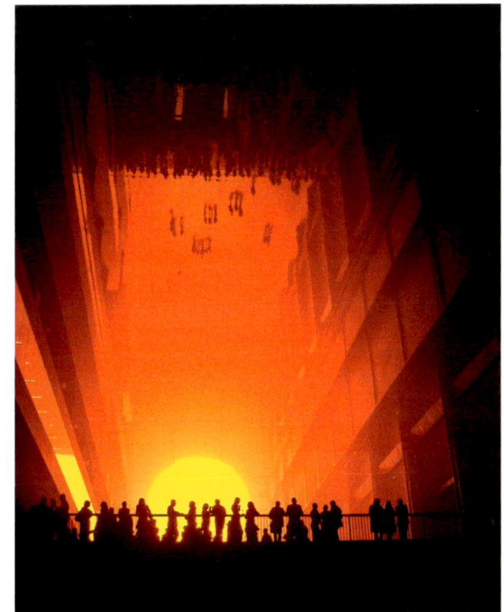

fig. 158 Ólafur Elíasson, *The weather project*, 2003, monofrequency lights, projection foil, haze machines, mirror foil, aluminum, scaffolding, 26.7 × 22.3 × 155.44 m, installation view Tate Modern, London, 2003

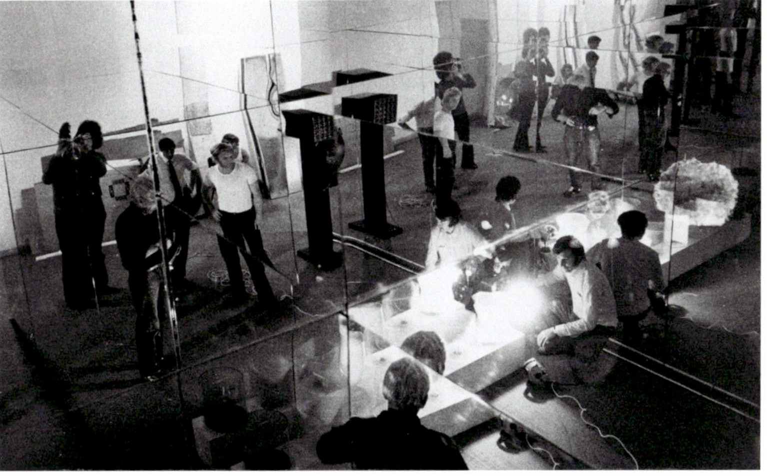

fig. 159 Heinz Mack, *Mirror Cabinet*, 1972, Kunsthalle Düsseldorf

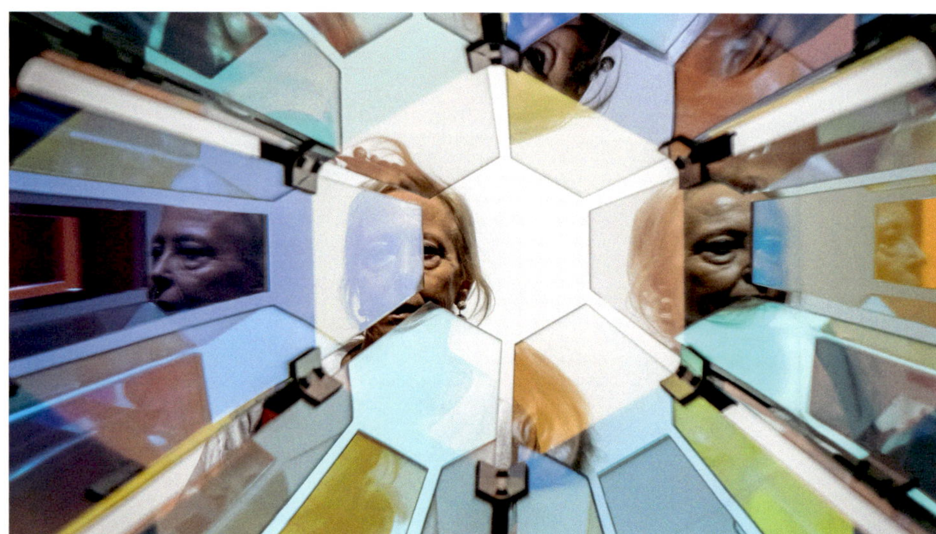

fig. 160 Ólafur Elíasson, *Colour spectrum kaleidoscope*, 2003, color-effect filter glass, stainless steel, 180×75×200 cm, installation view *Olafur Eliasson: Nel tuo tempo*, Fondazione Palazzo Strozzi, Florence, Italy, 2022

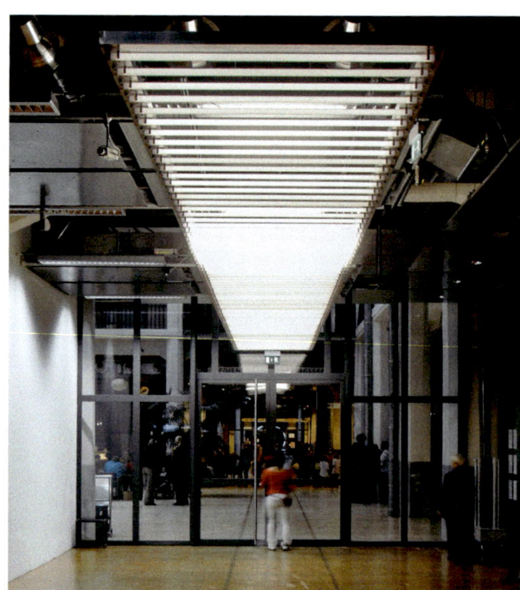

fig. 161 Olafur Eliasson, *Lichtwelle*, 2001, exhibition view, *Masterpieces of Media Art from the ZKM Collection*, ZKM | Karlsruhe 2004

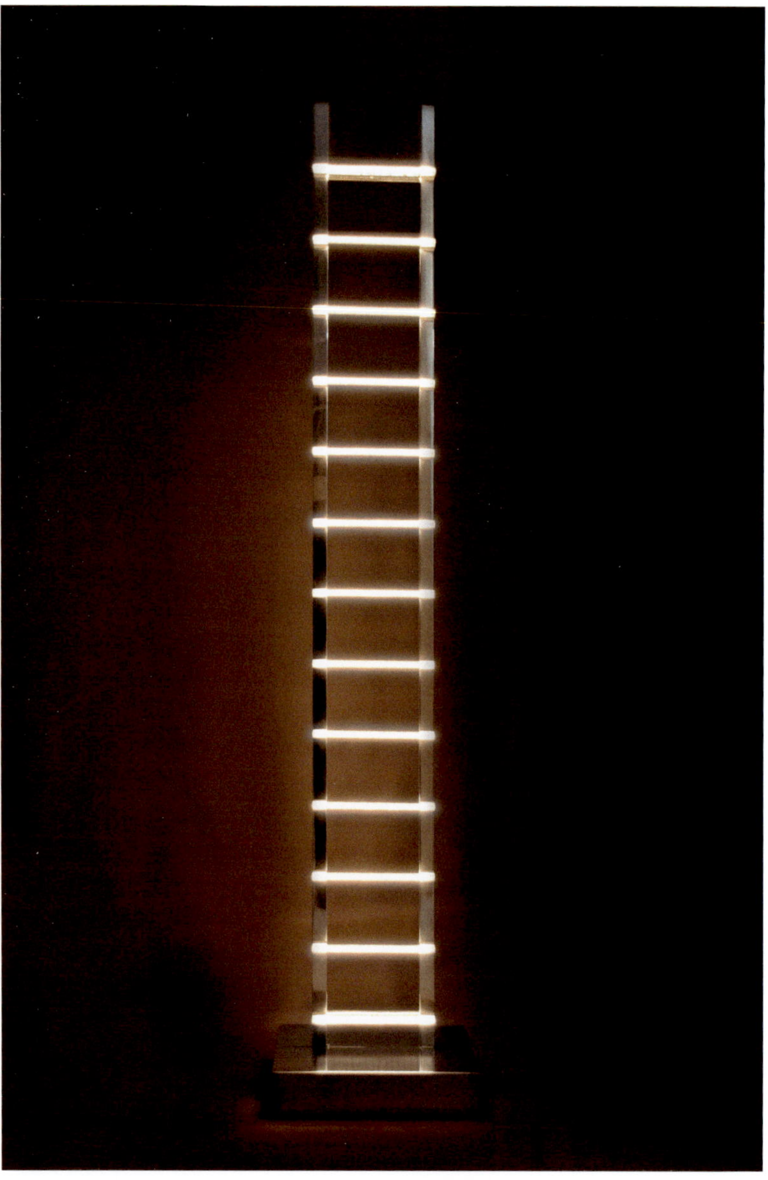

fig. 162 Heinz Mack, *Light Ladder*, 2010 (idea: 1970), light-kinetic sculpture

that the weather or climate in any way impacts on your salary?", "11. In which season do you think you eat the healthiest?").[13]

The weather project achieved its spectacular illusory effect through a very simple technical construction that was easily recognizable upon closer inspection.[14] Heinz Mack's light-kinetic works also radiate a certain mysticism precisely because of the often very simple technical construction hidden from the viewer which thus gives them a particularly futuristic effect. Unlike Mack, however, Elíasson makes a point of revealing the underlying technology: "I believe that in order to achieve a challenging engagement with art that avoids the manipulation of the viewer, every part of the construction behind the presentation of art must be made a transparent part of that presentation."[15] The awareness of the artificiality of the work not only allows reflection on the perception of reality, but also makes its constructedness visible.[16] In this way, the mirrored ceiling serves not only as an optical illusion, but at the same time can be understood as a bridge to the self-perception and self-awareness of emancipated spectators.[17] The mirror is deliberately held up to them. The perception of their own reflection confronts the viewers with their own gaze and tears them away from the usual detached attitude.[18] As early as 1961, Mack described the function of reflective surfaces in his art: "In approaching the mirror, viewers are confronted with a situation in which they inevitably encounter themselves."[19] Passing through this Lacanian mirror stage,[20] such a new visual experience, triggered by Elíasson's spectacular staging, can also unleash an emancipatory potential.

By artificially isolating natural phenomena such as the weather, reproducing them technologically, and bringing them back into the urban and institutionalized reality of everyday life, Elíasson not only reflects on the immense sublimity of nature, but also draws our attention to its vulnerability and the acute threat to natural resources posed by human behavior. The work reflects our relationship with the weather and possible co-dependencies in the mirror of current technological solutions to the problem of increasing climate change, such as climate engineering. On closer inspection, the apparently staged technological victory over the sun also carries threatening, dystopian associations.[21]

Reflective surfaces that demand (self-)reflection on the part of the observer also find actual application in the work of the artist Monica Bonvicini. Using the same formal means as Heinz Mack, Bonvicini's works refer to the cool material aesthetics of Minimal Art, which is, however, ironically and strikingly counteracted in the artist's work by unusual, sometimes brute elements and their surprising use. In doing so, she addresses issues of power and representation, gender roles and mechanisms of exclusion that are reflected in the aesthetics and functionality of architecture and designed space. Patriarchal hierarchies and their social construction are expressed through the use of cold, non-natural materials such as glass, steel, chrome, mirrored surfaces, and artificial light.

Bonvicini's work *Don't Miss a Sec'.* (2004) consists of a pavilion that is completely mirrored inside and out and has already been exhibited in various public spaces. With its smooth walls reflecting the urban environment, the architecture is reminiscent of the reduced surface aesthetics of Minimal Art, to which Heinz Mack's works can also be

13 "Tate Weather Monitoring Group Survey. Survey conducted among Tate staff April 2003," in Susan May, ed., *Olafur Eliasson. The Weather Project*, exh. cat. Tate Modern, London (London: Tate Publishing, 2003), 59–95 (quotation on 63f.).

14 See Hans Dickel, *Natur in der zeitgenössischen Kunst. Konstellationen jenseits von Landschaft und Materialästhetik* (Munich: Silke Schreiber, 2016), 48f.

15 Olafur Elíasson, "Museums Are Radical," in: May, *Olafur Eliasson*, 130–139, here 138.

16 See Susan May, "Meteorologica," in: May, *Elíasson. The Weather Project*, 16–28, here 17f.

17 See Jacques Rancière, *Le spectateur émancipé* (Paris: La fabrique éditions, 2008).

18 See Dickel, *Natur in der zeitgenössischen Kunst*, 46.

19 Heinz Mack, "The Sahara Project," in: *ZERO*, nr. 3 (1961), unpaginated. Translated from the German.

20 Jacques Lacan, "The Mirror Stage as Formative of the *I* Function as Revealed in Psychoanalytic Experience" (1948), in idem, *Écrits*, trans. Bruce Fink in collaboration with Héloïse Fink and Russell Grigg (New York and London: W. W. Norton, 2006), 75–82.

21 See Dickel, *Natur in der zeitgenössischen Kunst*, 49ff.

figs. 164, 165

attributed, and which some of his early works even anticipate.[22] But there is more behind the façade: The cube houses a fully functional stainless steel toilet with an integrated washbasin. From the inside, the walls look like windows, offering a 360° view of the outside. People inside the cube can therefore observe what is happening on the street and at the same time relieve themselves undisturbed without being seen. The walls of the pavilion are so-called two-way mirrors. The mirror effect is created by a special coating of metal oxide and is intensified when the rooms separated by the glass wall are illuminated with different levels of brightness. Part of the light is reflected by the thin film on the glass surface, while the rest is transmitted to the other side. The darker room is thus optically shielded. These mirrors, also known as float glass, are familiar from interrogation rooms in police procedurals. The use of such a material is highly reminiscent of Heinz Mack's experimental use of various transparent materials, such as acrylic glass coated with mercury or certain minerals, which alternate between transparency and iridescent reflections. Bonvicini also explicitly refers to artists such as Dan Graham, who has repeatedly used float glass in his architectural sculptures and pavilions in public spaces.[23]

figs. 23, 113, 163, 171, 406
fig. 167

As noted above for the work of Heinz Mack, it can also be said of Bonvicini's work that only the physical presence of the viewer defines the nature of the work and at the same time creates a new spatial experience.[24] However, the role of the spectator is challenged even more consistently than with Mack and other representatives of Minimal Art. The work explicitly provokes the viewer to relate and to behave to it in some way. Whether gazing at one's own reflection in passing or observing the outside world from within, the work's title instructs viewers not to miss a second of what is happening, not even while pursuing intimate needs by actually using the toilet inside. However, the practical utility implied in Bonvicini's work seems rather questionable. The contradictory nature of the installation, through the illusionistic use of the interrogation mirror, creates uncertainty and discomfort rather than making us want to follow the artist's invitation without hesitation. This confrontation of the audience with its own behavioral conventions is an essential element of Bonvicini's artistic practice.[25] The work draws attention to the distinction between private and public space and the regulations to which each is subject.

fig. 164

This example also demonstrates that the purity of the materials used here and the formal abstraction of the work can no longer do justice to Minimal Art's aspiration to emancipate the work from its representational function. While the Minimal Art of the 1960s was still characterized by a reduction of content in favor of surface design and its immediate aesthetic effect, in Bonvicini's works material and form and their cool aura are almost overloaded with symbolic meaning. However, the dissonance between the appearance of the object and its effect is by no means a discrepancy for Bonvicini, but rather establishes a new definition of beauty in the work of the contemporary artist. For Bonvicini, aesthetic judgment arises precisely from the tension between the classical, elementary form and the power structures it implies—symbolized in *Don't Miss a Sec'.* by the contradiction between inside and outside. From this, in turn, a critique of the formation of the canon can be derived: "how to keep working with what responds to the canon of

22 See Dieter Honisch, *Mack—Skulpturen 1953–1986* (Düsseldorf: Econ, 1986), 154ff.

23 See Monica Bonvicini, "to be able to see beauty again," in *Kunstforum International*, no. 286 (2022) [*Das Schöne—Plädoyer für ein eigensinniges Phänomen*, ed. Martin Seidel], 138–39, here 139.

24 See Vanessa Joan Müller, "Der involvierte Betrachter. Monica Bonvicinis Kunst der Konfrontation," in Rein Wolfs, ed., *Monica Bonvicini. Both Ends*, exh. cat. Kunsthalle Fridericianum, Kassel (Cologne: Walther König, 2010), 142–45, here 144.

25 See Müller, 144f.

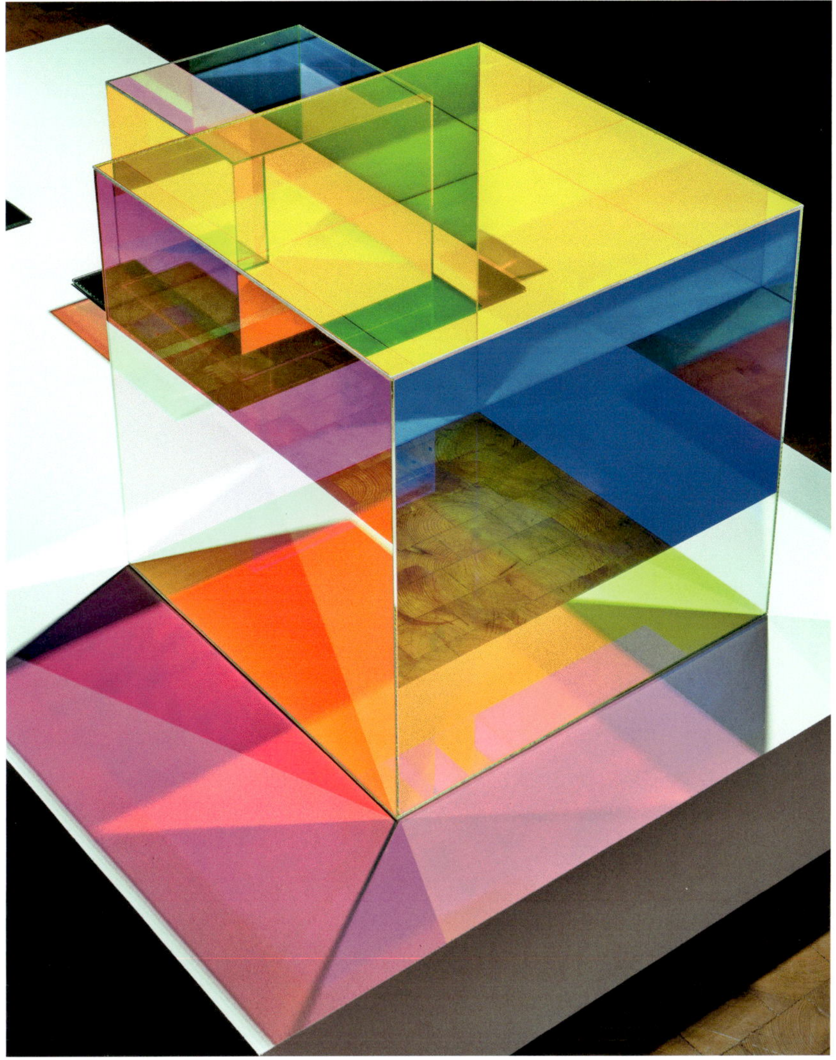

fig. 163 Heinz Mack, *Light Pavillion II*, 2006, cube, exhibition view, ZKM | Karlsruhe 2023

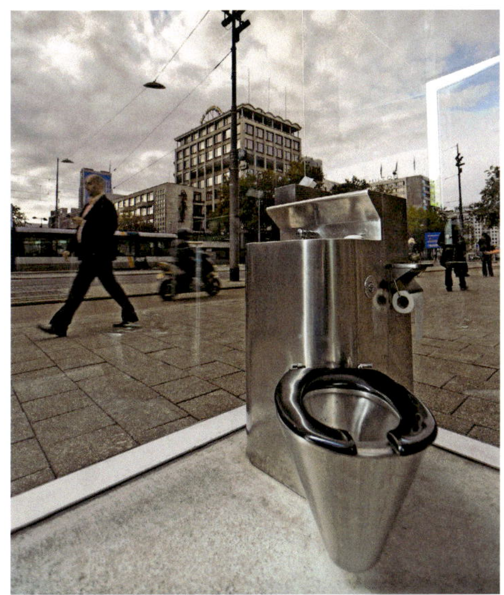

fig. 164 Monica Bonvicini, *Don't Miss a Sec'.*, 2004, inside view

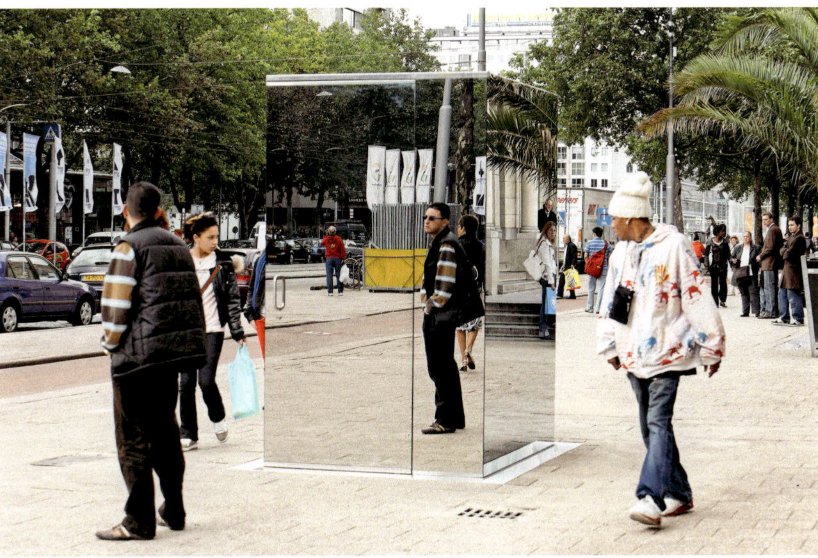

fig. 165 Monica Bonvicini, *Don't Miss a Sec'.*, 2004, two-way mirror glass structure, stainless steel toilet unit, concrete, aluminum, fluorescent lights, milk-glass panels, outside view

fig. 166 Heinz Mack, *Topology of Space*, Grand Erg Occidental, Algeria, 1976, photo: Thomas Höpker

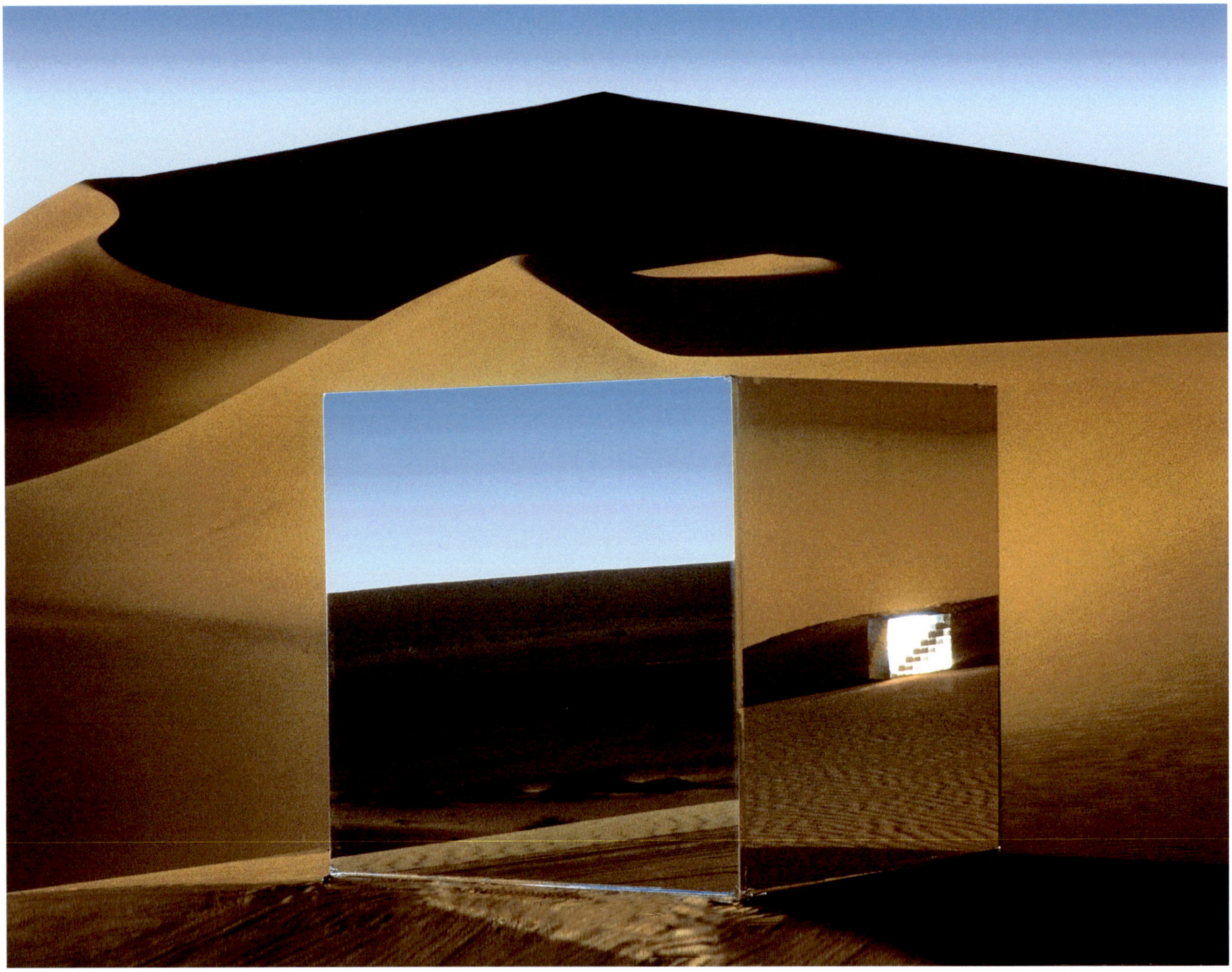

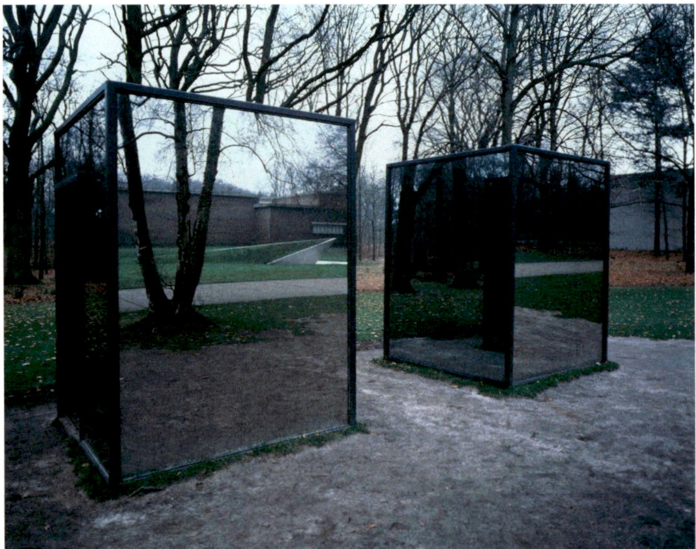

fig. 167 Dan Graham, *Two Adjacent Pavilions*, 1978–81, installation view, Kröller-Müller Museum, The Netherlands

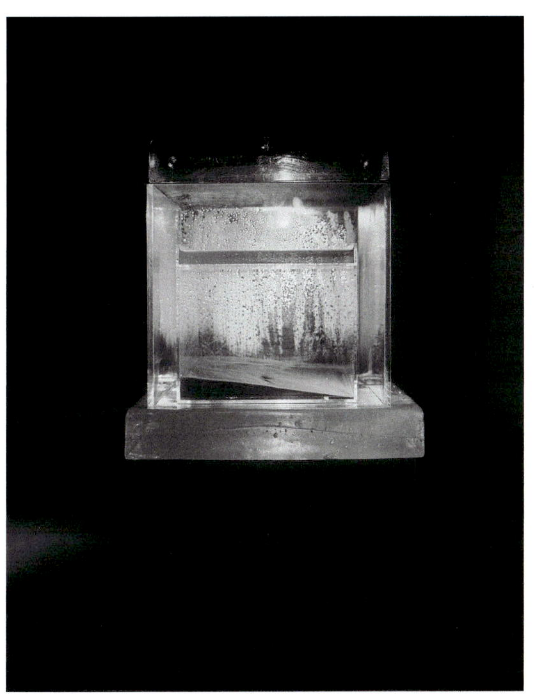

fig. 168 Heinz Mack, *The Sea Above the Desert*, 1967/1968

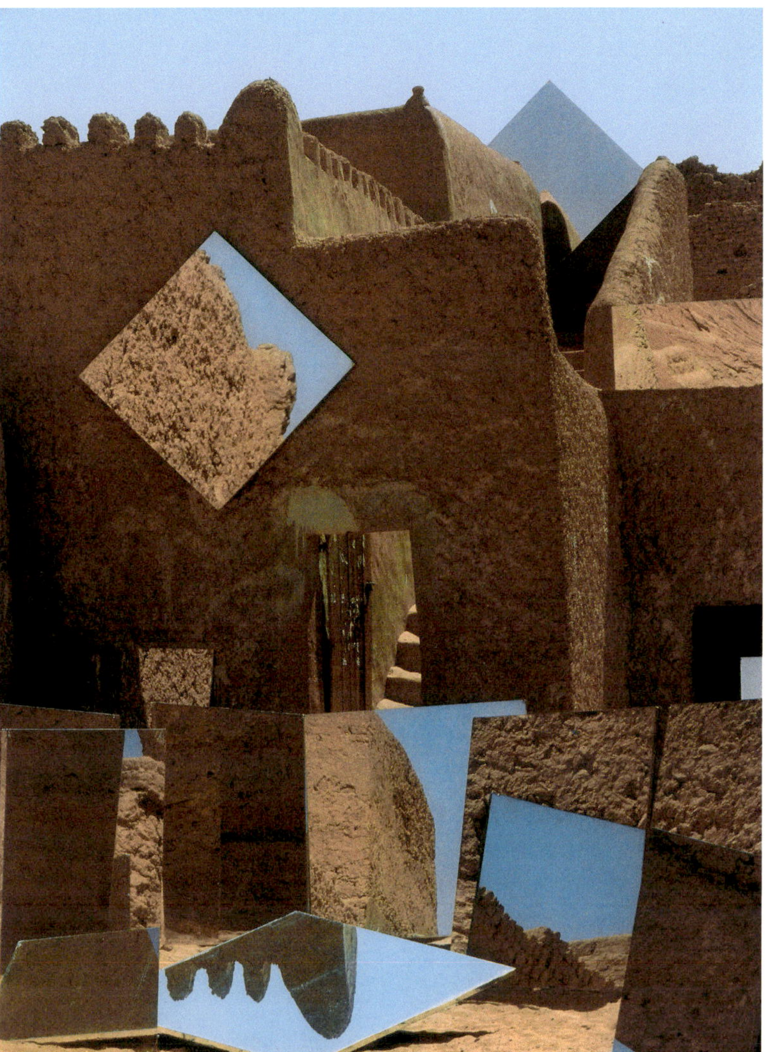

fig. 169 Heinz Mack, *Mirror Environment in a Southern Algerian Village*, 1976, photo: Thomas Höpker

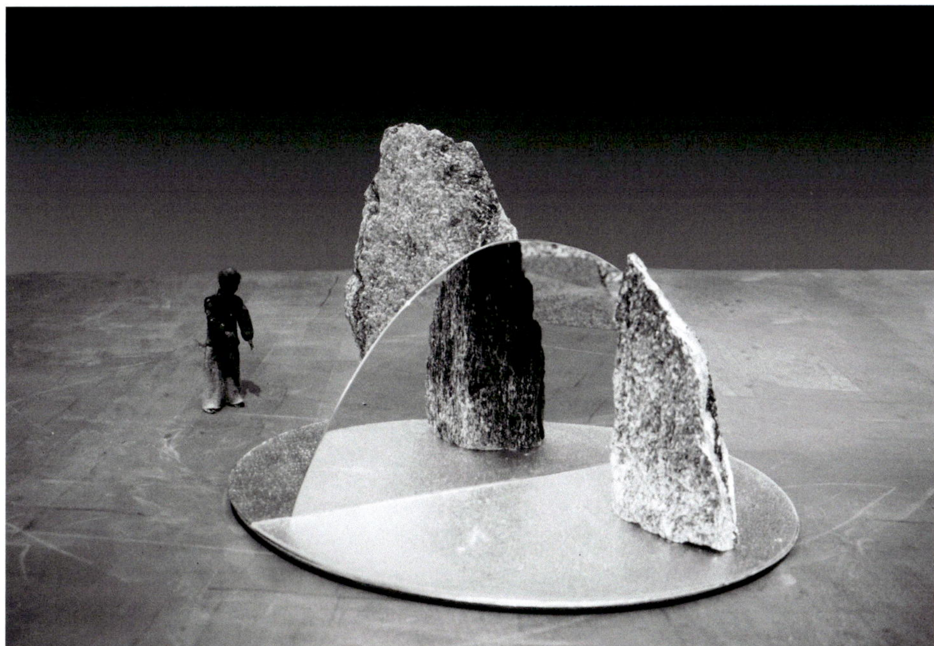

fig. 170 Heinz Mack, *Model for a Square Design*, 1980–1983, stainless steel, granite

fig. 171 Heinz Mack, *Design for Glass Architecture*, 1968–1997, mineral vapor-coated glass, max. height: 100 cm

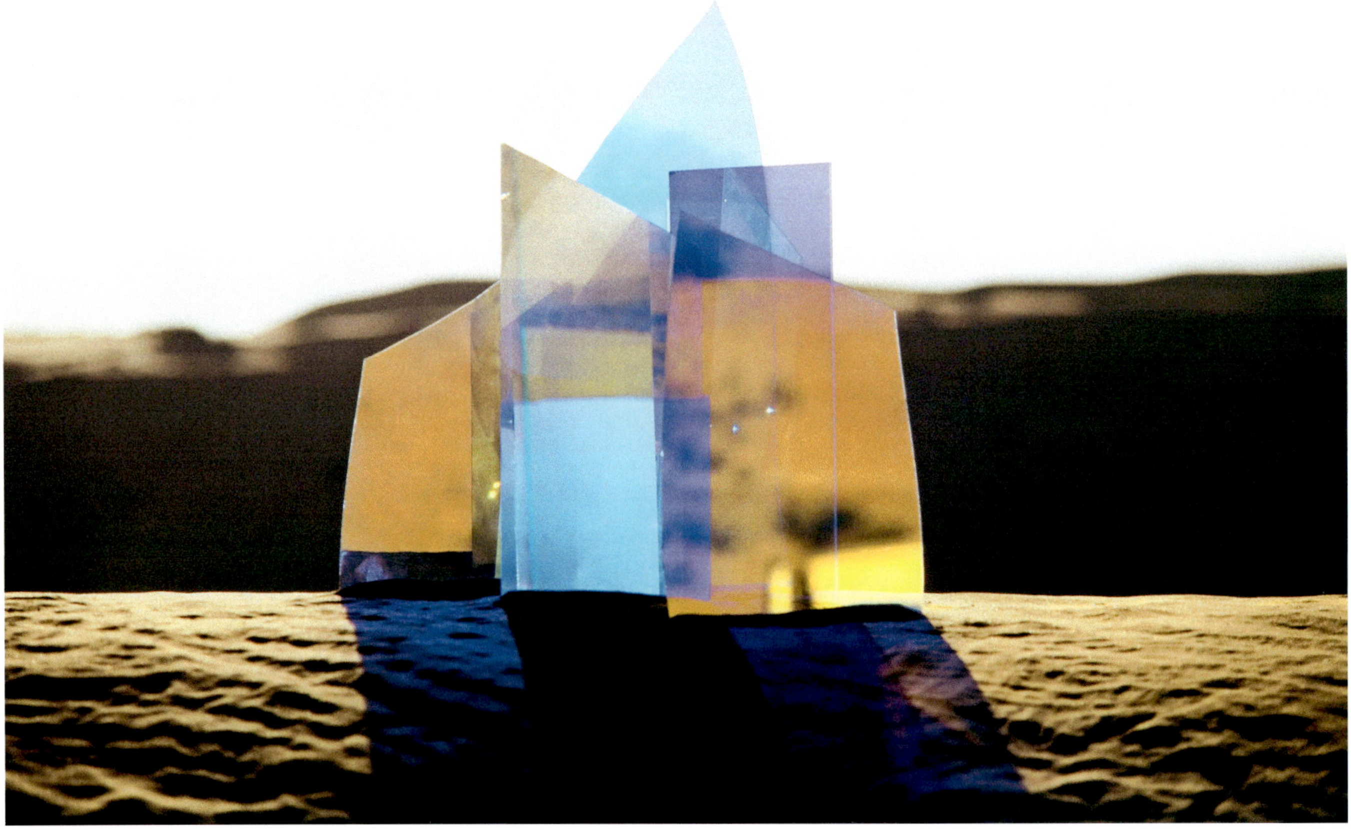

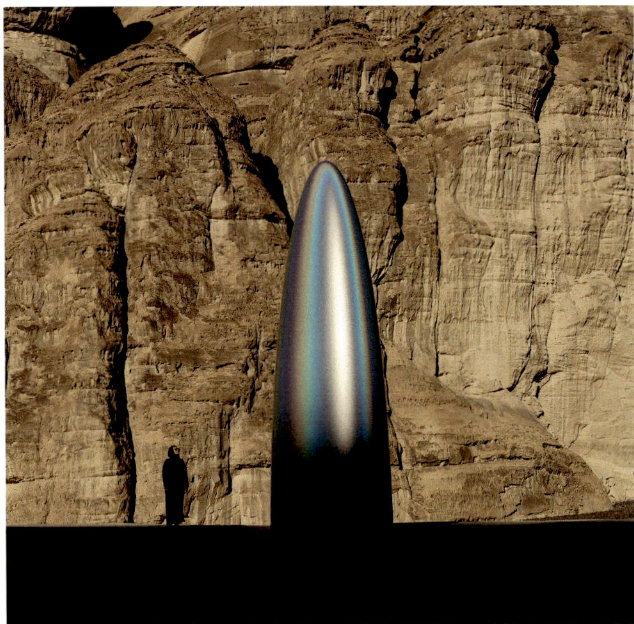

fig. 172 Gisela Colón, *The Future Is Now*, 2020, site-specific installation at Desert X, Al-Ula, Saudi Arabia, *Parabolic Monolith Iridium*, engineered aerospace carbon fiber, 762 × 244 × 305 cm

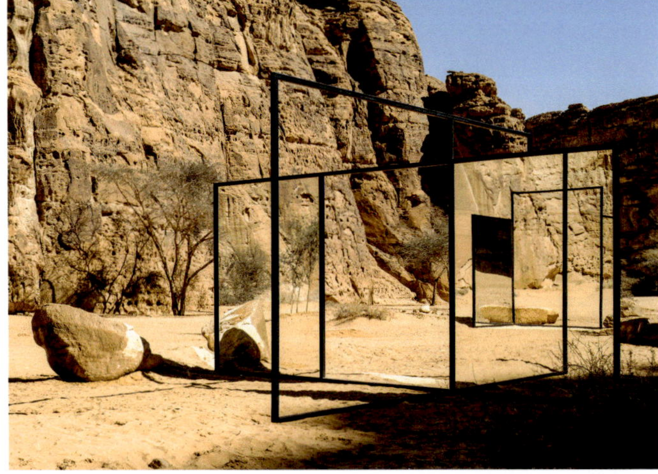

fig. 173 Alicja Kwade, *In Blur*, 2022, site-specific installation at Desert X, AlUla, Saudi Arabia

beauty? Who defines these canons and why should we just follow, blindly? Many of my works explore the friction between aesthetic and violent power dynamics; I see beauty in these unexpected elements flirting and clashing with each other at the same time."[26]

Urban space is of fundamental importance in the work of both, Monica Bonvicini and Heinz Mack. Mack's artistic exploration of space and light always includes considerations of architectural solutions: "I have always described a large part of my works as models, namely models for larger realizations that should be set up in urban and rural areas as a visible expression of our time."[27] Mack's numerous works in public spaces assert themselves against the architecture of the postwar era.[28] Like Bonvicini's glass pavilion, they open up a dialogue with urban life, which is, however, destabilized by the work's disruptive presence.

figs. 95, 96, 97, 361, 362, 363, 364, 366, 370, 378, 400, 401, 402, 403

Heinz Mack's artistic ambitions went far beyond the urban space: "But tomorrow, in our search for a new dimension of art, we will also have to look for new spaces in which our works will take on an incomparable appearance. Such spaces are the sky, the sea, the Antarctic, the deserts. In them, the preserves of art will rest like artificial islands."[29] Heinz Mack's early experimentation with natural and site-specific resources such as sand, light, wind, and heat made him a pioneer of Land Art in Europe.[30] In 1961, he published the idea of the *Sahara Project*, first formulated two years earlier, for the realization of new "preserves of art"[31] in harmony with nature.[32] The goal of this ambitious, utopian concept was not only to leave the institutional spaces previously assigned to art and to open up new artistic terrain, but also to extend the realms of experience in the encounter with space and light: "It must be possible to set a strong light phenomenon in vibration in such a way that its intensity necessarily requires a new environment, the extent of which no longer corresponds to the classical rules of proportion. The aim here is to make light visible in light and light visible in space."[33]

figs. 104, 105, 106, 107, 112, 134, 143, 144, 155, 166, 169, 177, 178, 179, 316, 320

In the 1960s, at around the same time as Mack's first efforts to realize the *Sahara Project* with light experiments in the desert, the movement of Earth and Land Art emerged in the United States. Artists such as Michael Heizer, Nancy Holt, and Robert Smithson created art in nature that referred to the outdoor space and its natural conditions and went into a reciprocal relationship with the landscape as artistic material. Heinz Mack's works in the Sahara, and later also in the Arctic, should certainly be seen as part of this historically significant artistic movement.[34]

figs. 185, 189, 190, 191, 196, 197, 198, 200, 201, 203, 207

Today, Land Art is an innate part of the artistic repertoire and is also represented institutionally as a matter of course.[35] This can be seen in the numerous Land Art biennials and public sculpture parks around the world, which are often created with the aim of culturally enriching rural regions. One particular project that has been presenting site-specific, contemporary works specifically in desert regions since 2017 is the Desert X Biennial, which is run by a Californian non-profit organization. Its stated mission is to produce exhibitions "that respond meaningfully to the conditions of desert locations, the environment and indigenous communities; promoting cultural exchange and education programs that foster dialogue and understanding among cultures and communities about shared artistic, historical, and societal issues;

26 Bonvicini, "to be able to see beauty again," 139.

27 Heinz Mack, "Vortrag in der Akademie der Bildenden Künste, Stuttgart," typescript (Archive Heinz Mack, 1977). Translated from the German.

28 See *Mack. Ars urbana: Public-Space Art 1952–2008* (Munich: Hirmer, 2007).

29 Mack, "The Sahara Project." Translated from the German.

30 See Sophia Sotke, *Mack. Sahara: From ZERO to Land Art – Heinz Mack's Sahara Project*, trans. Gérard Goodrow (Munich: Hirmer, 2022).

31 Mack, "The Sahara Project."

32 See Sophia Sotke, *Das Sahara-Projekt von Heinz Mack im internationalen Kontext von ZERO und Land Art, 1959–1976*, PhD diss. University of Cologne, 2020.

33 Mack, "The Sahara Project." Translated from the German.

34 See Sotke, *Mack. Sahara*.

35 Of course, Land Art also had to assert itself institutionally from the very beginning, if only for the sake of funding its projects. Documentation for the subsequent communication of ephemeral, site-specific works was therefore an integral part of artistic practice right from the beginning of the movement. See Anne Hoormann, "Land Art," in: Hubertus Butin, ed., *Begriffslexikon zur zeitgenössischen Kunst* (Cologne: Snoek, 2014), 241–245, here 243.

and providing an accessible platform for artists from around the world to address ecological, cultural, spiritual, and other existential themes."[36] The first Desert X Biennials were held in Coachella Valley, California. In 2020, an additional location was added in the desert oasis of Al-Ula in Saudi Arabia, which is now also held every two years.

Located in the mountainous region of the Hejaz in northwestern Saudi Arabia, the oasis is situated in an area of exceptional geological and archaeological importance. Since probably the middle of the second century BCE, Al-Ula has served as a trading town on the historic Incense Route. This road from Oman through western Saudi Arabia to the Mediterranean – one of the oldest trade routes in the world – was used to transport frankincense and myrrh from southern Arabia, and spices and gems from India and Southeast Asia to Europe by dromedary. The nearby archaeological site of Hegra, an ancient Nabataean city, is a UNESCO World Heritage Site with impressive rock tombs. Not far away are Islam's two most important holy sites, Mecca and Medina, which were already important to pre-Islamic civilizations. Today, the region around Al-Ula is being revitalized primarily through a variety of cultural activities. In addition to Desert X, the oasis regularly hosts exhibitions and festivals, including music festivals and desert raves, light shows and video installations, and a citrus festival.[37]

Time and again, the artistic positions presented at the biennial reveal such clear parallels and references in form and content to the works of Heinz Mack that he is obviously an important point of reference for today's artists, and a comparison of the works highlights interesting nuances and differences between the generations.

fig. 172

Gisela Colón's monumental sculpture *The Future is Now* (2020), for example, almost seems to pay homage to Mack's light steles in the Sahara. Standing alone in the landscape, surrounded by the massive rock formations of the Saudi desert that date back many millions of years to the Precambrian era, the nine-meter-high monolith looks like the testimony of an extraterrestrial intelligence placed on Earth. With its mysteriously iridescent surface, the futuristic-looking phallic stele clearly stands out from its natural surroundings. The artist works with a variety of innovative materials, such as carbon fiber, which is used in aerospace technology and creates different surface effects depending on the incidence of light.[38] Colón's "light apparition" reaching for the sky evokes a variety of associations and, according to the artist, should be interpreted primarily as a symbol of a future that she describes as post-Anthropocene. Mankind plays a rather subordinate role in her vision of a new structure between the Earth and the cosmos.[39] The harmonization of nature and technology expressed in her work and the striving for a connection between heaven and earth are an almost ideal continuation of Heinz Mack's utopian work.[40]

fig. 173

Entitled *Sarab*, the second exhibition at Al-Ula in 2022 featured several commissioned works dedicated to the themes of mirage and oasis, with particular reference to events and histories specific to the desert.[41] These included the installation *In Blur* by the German artist Alicja Kwade. Several black metal frames, some with mirrored surfaces, set into the rocky gorge, blend harmoniously into the structure of the landscape. Depending on the viewer's position, the reflection and inversion of the geological formations creates new framings, compositions,

36 Desert X, "About," https://desertx.org/about/about, accessed March 13, 2024.

37 Royal Commission for AlUla, "Experience AlUla," https://www.experiencealula.com/en, accessed March 13, 2024.

38 See Desert X, "Gisela Colón. The Future is Now," https://desertx.org/dx/desert-x-alula-2020/gisela-colon, accessed March 13, 2024.

39 See Desert X, "Gisela Colón."

40 See Wieland Schmied, ed., *Utopie und Wirklichkeit im Werk von Heinz Mack* (Cologne: DuMont, 1998).

41 See Desert X, "Desert X 2022 AlUla, Saudi Arabia February 11 – March 30," https://desertx.org/dx/desert-x-alula-2022, accessed March 13, 2024.

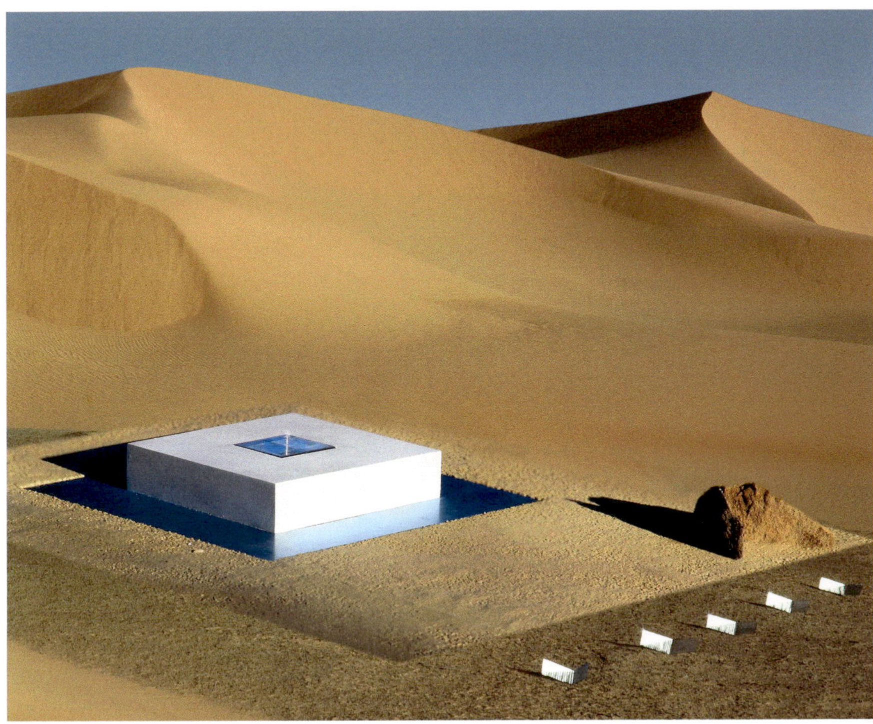

fig. 174 Heinz Mack, *My House in the Desert*, 1960/1997, model (see station 9 of the *Sahara Project*)

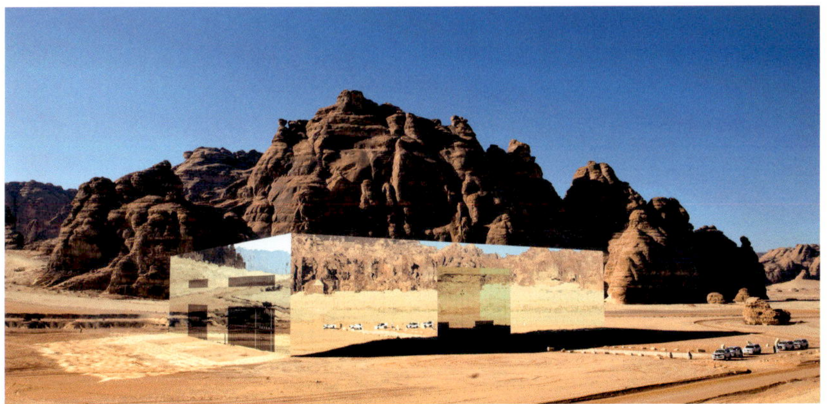

fig. 175 Gió Forma Architects and Black Engineering, Maraya Concert Hall, 2017, multi-purpose theatre, entertainment, and conference venue

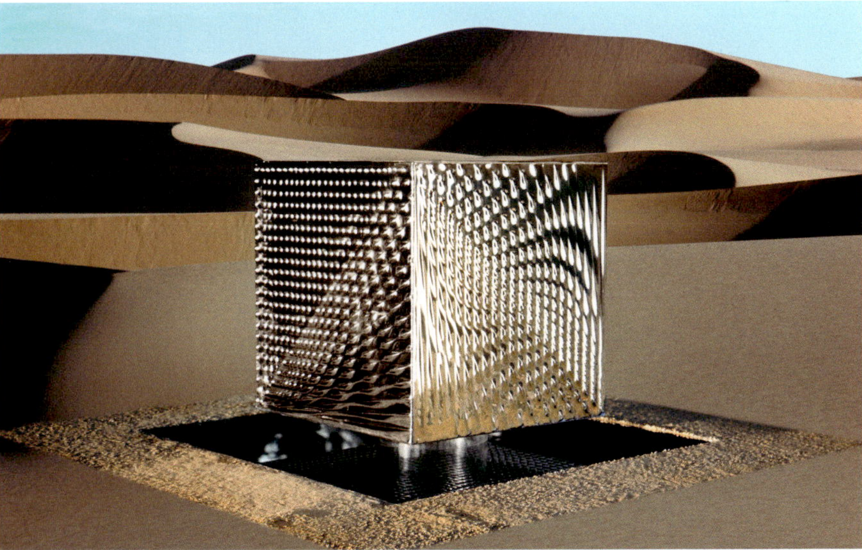

fig. 176 Heinz Mack, *Silver Cube from the Sahara Project*, 1959, aluminum, wood, 45 × 45 × 45.5 cm

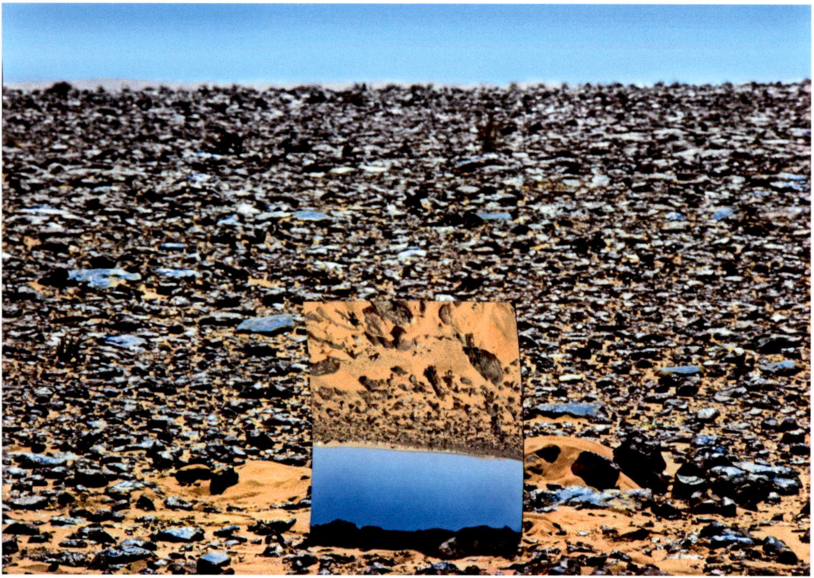

fig. 177 Heinz Mack, *Mirror between Sky and Desert*, Tunisia, 1967, coated glass, 70x70 cm

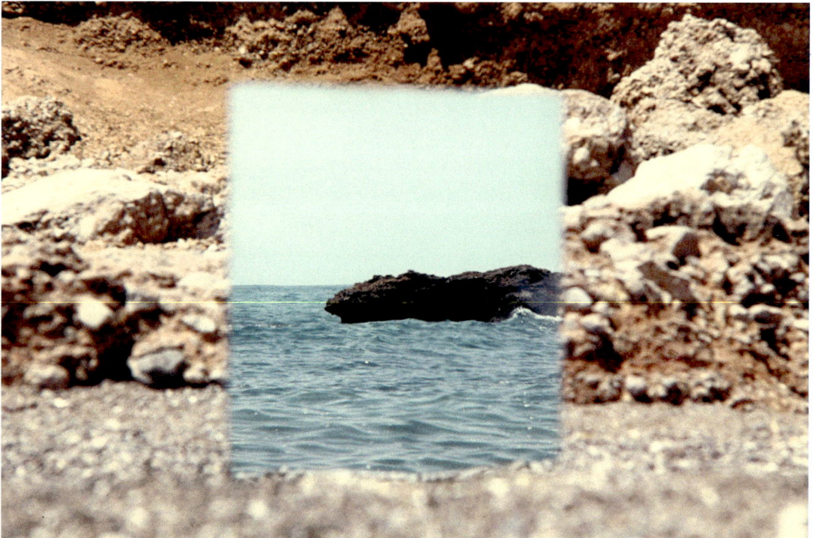

fig. 178 Heinz Mack, *Mirror between Sky, Earth and Sea*, Ibiza, 1963, crystal mirror, 100 × 100 cm

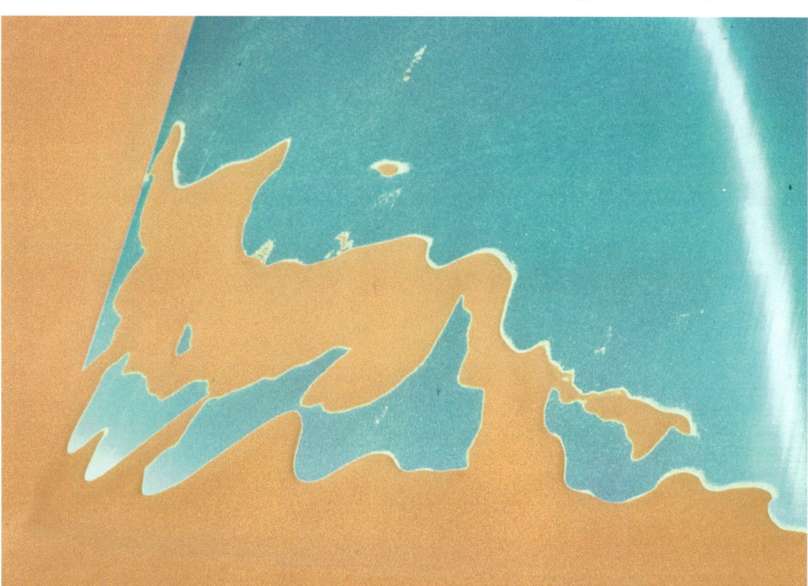

fig. 179 Heinz Mack, *Mirror in the Desert, Reflecting the Sky*, 1976, Grand Erg Occidental, Algeria, photo: Thomas Höpker

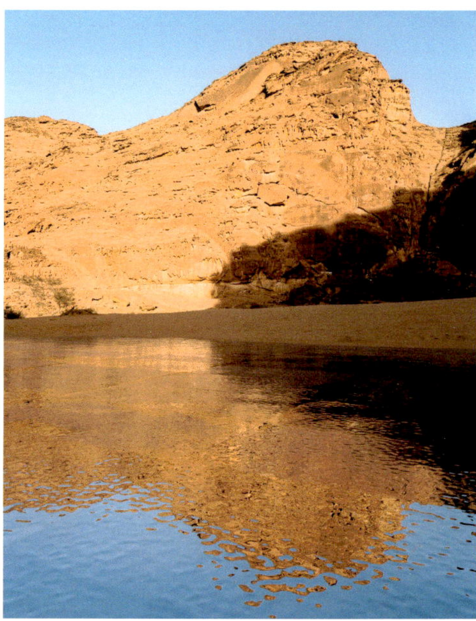

fig. 180 Abdullah Al Othman, *Geography of Hope*, 2022, site-specific installation at Desert X, Al-Ula, Saudi Arabia

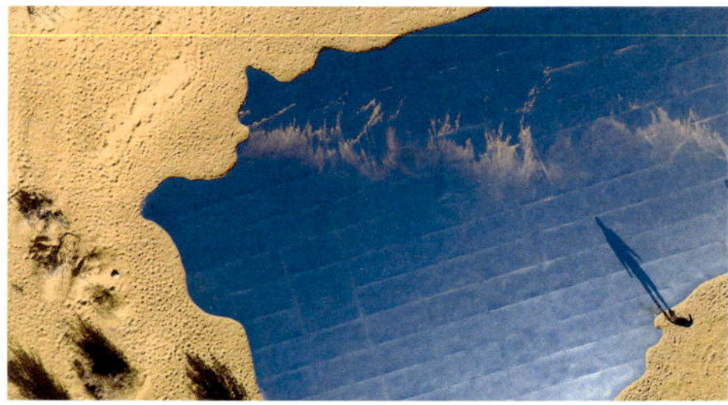

fig. 181 Abdullah Al Othman,, *Geography of Hope*, 2022, detail

and overlays. In this way, the work emphasizes the subjectivity of perception while at the same time enhancing the aspects of the landscape. The reflection of light and the multiple reflections of the desert landscape create an almost mirage-like effect.[42] Addressing aspects of the perception of space and time, Kwade's works contain both natural elements and industrially produced materials, whose materiality and heaviness cancel each other out in complex arrangements – formal and thematic elements that are also typical of Heinz Mack's work.

figs. 180, 181

Abdullah Al Othman's installation titled *Geography of Hope* is also characterized by reflective surfaces that deceive the eye and play with perception. The numerous embossed stainless steel plates laid flat on the ground shimmer in the light due to their irregular and undulating surface structure, creating the impression of a natural lake in the desert in which the sky is reflected. Here, it is not only about the tension between reality and illusion or the aesthetic impression of a supposedly empty and uninhabited natural space, but the desert is rather understood as a social and cultural space with a moving history. The title of the work refers to the hope of the desert dwellers associated with the mirage and the idea of finding water at a long-awaited oasis. [43]

The Desert X Biennial is a prime example of how the field of art is intertwined with political, social, economic, and ecological factors. Funded by the Royal Commission for Al-Ula, the exhibition project in the oasis is part of the comprehensive measures implemented by Saudi Crown Prince Mohammed bin Salman under the umbrella of his "Vision 2030." In 2019, the royal family announced extensive social and economic reforms as part of the multibillion-dollar plan to wean the country off its dependence on the oil industry. This structural transformation has already included improvements in the social status of women, such as the granting of driver's licenses and the gradual abolition of guardianship laws or the restrictions of the "Mutawa" religious police. However, much remains to be done in other areas, as Saudi Arabia under Mohammed bin Salman is also responsible for numerous human rights violations, such as restrictions on freedom of assembly, censorship, torture and mass executions, the forced relocation of local populations to make way for the techno-futuristic city of Neom, or the internationally controversial military offensive in Yemen, which has particularly affected the civilian population.[44] Outwardly, however, efforts are being made to promote and showcase the country's culture in order to make Saudi Arabia attractive to non-Muslim tourists, who have only been allowed to travel the country since the end of 2019.[45]

In the run-up to the first Desert Biennial in Saudi Arabia, a controversy arose among the participating artists and the organizers about the ethics of realizing such a project on behalf of the Saudi government. Those involved in Desert X hope that the international exhibitions will at least initiate a dialogue across cultures and national borders. It remains to be seen, however, how openly this dialogue can continue to be conducted in the future and whether it is able to also have an effect at a political level.[46]

In addition to these recently developed projects that contribute to the enhancement of the region around Al-Ula, there is another outstanding cultural institution in the area that bears striking analogies to Heinz Mack's work. The Maraya Concert Hall, designed by the

42 See Desert X, "Alicja Kwade: In Blur," https://desertx.org/dx/desert-x-alula-2022/alicja-kwade, accessed March 13, 2024.

43 See Desert X, "Abdullah AlOthman. Geography of Hope," https://desertx.org/dx/desert-x-alula-2022/abdullah-alothman, accessed March 13, 2024.

44 See Aliki Kosyfologou, "Vision 2030. Internationale Modernisierungsnarrative, Gesetzesreformen und innere Widersprüche in Saudi-Arabien," Rosa Luxemburg Stiftung, June 22, 2021, https://www.rosalux.de/news/id/44568/vision-2030#_ftnref1, accessed March 13, 2024.

45 See Sabine B. Vogel, "Saudi-Arabien als neues Zentrum der Kunst im Nahen Osten?" in *Kunstforum International*, no. 281 (2022), 298–303.

46 See Vivian Yee, "Saudi Politics Unsettle an Exhibition," in *The New York Times*, February 12, 2020, C1, https://www.nytimes.com/2020/02/11/arts/design/Desert-X-AlUla-saudi-arabia.html, accessed March 13, 2024.

fig. 175

German-Italian architecture and design studio Gió Forma, is a venue for concerts, theatrical performances, conferences, and gastronomy.[47] The rectangular building, which is completely mirrored from the outside, is undoubtedly reminiscent of Heinz Mack's cubic sculptures and architectural designs.

figs. 136, 137, 139, 163, 166, 176

In the nearby sixty-five-square-kilometer Wadi AlFann (Valley of the Arts), commissioned works by famous artists will soon be created and installed on behalf of the Royal Commission. Land Art pioneers Agnes Denes, Michael Heizer, and James Turrell are the first to be featured alongside the two Saudi artists Ahmed Mater and Manal AlDowayan.[48] AlDowayan, who is also representing Saudi Arabia at the 2024 Biennale di Venezia, is known for her critical approach to state policies regarding the social and political status of women in Saudi society.[49] Artists working in the context of these tense relations are therefore also increasingly taking on a social role and responsibility—whether through their institutional representation or by maintaining a critical stance within it.

Heinz Mack's profound influence on younger generations of artists is certainly most evident in the field of Land Art, although it is by no means limited to this genre. A vivid example of the cross-genre and global perception of Mack's work is provided by the Beijing-based video artist and sculptor Yu Honglei. In his double-screen video *En Route* (2016), the artist follows Heinz Mack's tracks in the desert by directly integrating scenes from the film *Tele-Mack* (1968/69) into the fragmented narration of the video. In 1968, Mack traveled to Tunisia together with the film director Hans Emmerling and a small team from the German broadcaster Saarländischer Rundfunk. While filming *Tele-Mack*, he was able to realize parts of his extensive *Sahara Project* in the Tunisian desert. The film documents Mack's work; but as an artistic essay, it also finds its own contemporary formal language in keeping with the zeitgeist. The *Sahara Project* is thus one of the first works of European art to be conceived in terms of the media, as the ephemeral actions in the desert could only be made accessible to the public through images conveyed by the media.[50] In 1969, the film was broadcast for the first time on German public evening television.[51] It began with a spectacular car scene in which Mack was seen in a moving convertible—according to the artist, a tactic to motivate the saturated television audience to continue watching.[52] In Honglei's video, we also follow a car at the beginning as it races through a barren desert landscape. However, in the side-view mirror, instead of the actual landscape behind, we see excerpts from *Tele-Mack*. By montaging different shots in the image, Honglei creates surreal doublings and displacements.[53] Inspired by Lawrence Weiner's *Blue Moon Over* (2001), he presents a road movie composed of multiple accumulated and rearranged visual and audio elements, including footage of desert rallies, overlaid with Weiner's striking aphorisms and minimalist visual signs. This mixing and sampling into a digital assemblage creates a unique visual language that freely uses and deploys the information it finds, seemingly transcending geographical boundaries.[54] Honglei's work is characterized by its processual nature, through which the contexts of meaning are revealed only gradually and fragmentarily. This open, non-linear narrative structure, in which space and time are blurred, is not only reminiscent of ZERO, but also a reflection of the perception and knowledge gained from navigating digital space.

fig. 184

figs. 108, 123, 231

47 See Johannes Stühlinger, "Spiegel unserer Zeit," in *ubm magazin.*, https://www.ubm-development.com/magazin/spiegel-unserer-zeit/, accessed March 13, 2024.

48 See Royal Comission for AlUla, "Wadi AlFann," in *Living Museum*, 2023, https://www.livingmuseum.com/en/arts/art-in-the-landscape/wadi-alfann, accessed March 13, 2024.

49 See National Pavilion of Saudi Arabia | La Biennale di Venezia, "Artist Manal AlDowayan," 2024, https://saudipavilion.org/art/60th-international-art-exhibition/manal-aldowayan/, accessed March 13, 2024.

50 See Fleck und Lehmann-Tolkmitt, *Heinz Mack*, 61.

51 See Sotke, *Das Sahara-Projekt*, 152.

52 Personal statement by the artist in a conversation with the author, 2023.

53 See Giulia Bini, Sabiha Keyif, and Philipp Ziegler, eds., *Hybrid Layers*, exh. cat. (Karlsruhe: ZKM | Karlsruhe, 2017), 22.

54 See Bini et al.

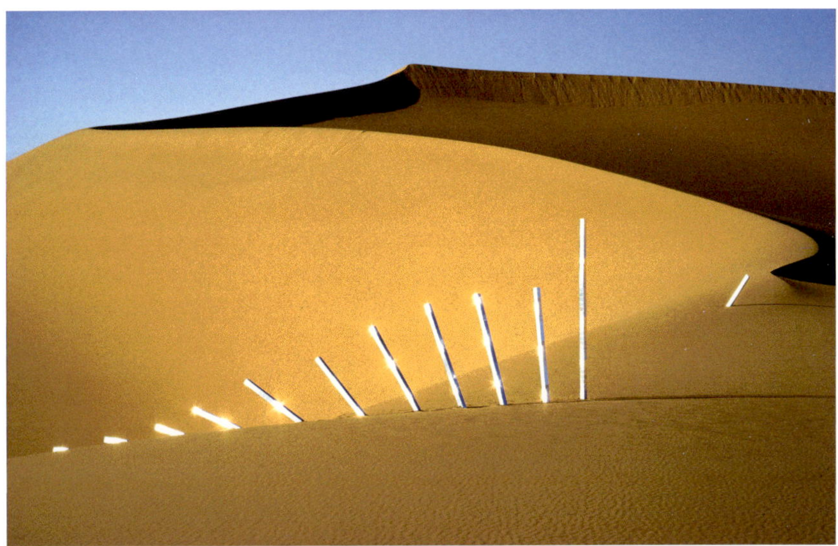

fig. 182 Heinz Mack, *Declination of Light Beams*, Grand Erg Occidental, Algeria, 1976, aluminum, ca. 2 × 8 m, photo: Thomas Höpker

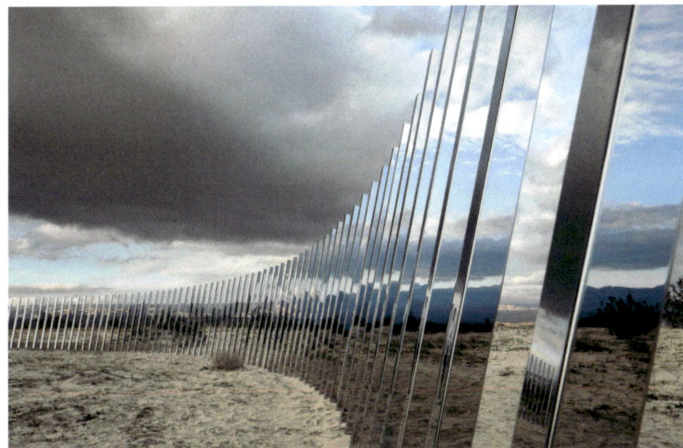

fig. 183 Philip K. Smith III, *The Circle of Land and Sky*, 2017, site-specific installation at Desert X 2017, Palm Springs, USA

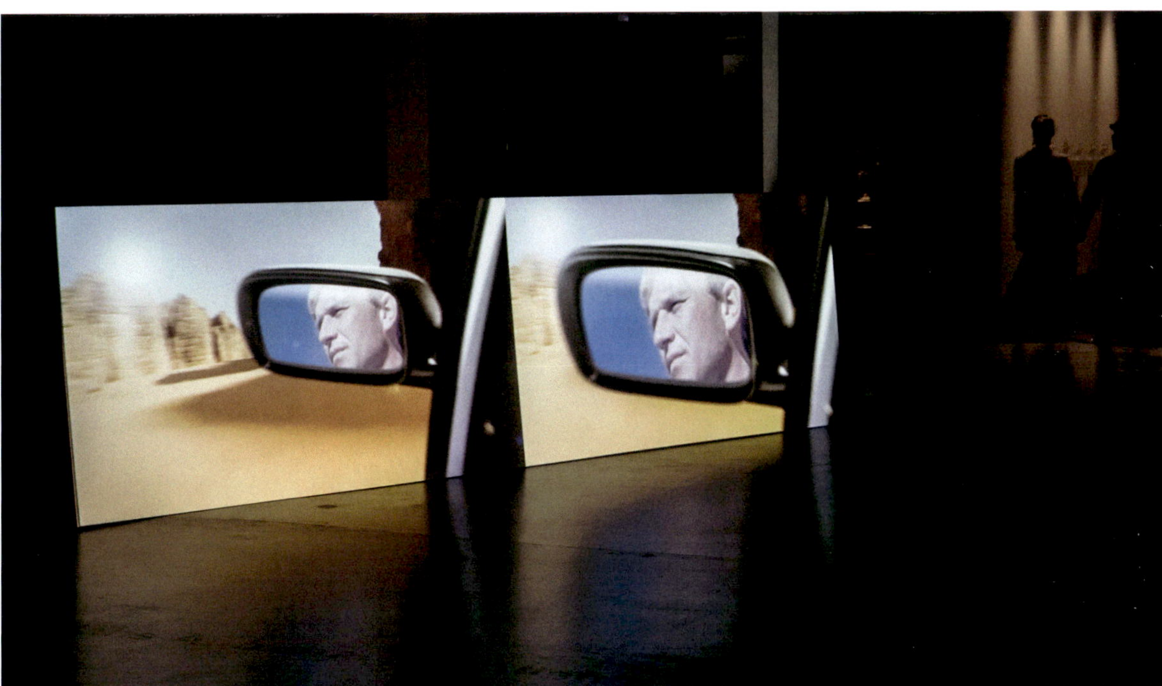

fig. 184 Yu Honglei, *En Route*, 2016, video, exhibition view, *Hybrid Layers*, ZKM | Karlsruhe 2017

fig. 185 Heinz Mack, *Balloons Are Sent Into the Sky From the Boat*, Greenland, Arctic 1976, photo: Thomas Höpker

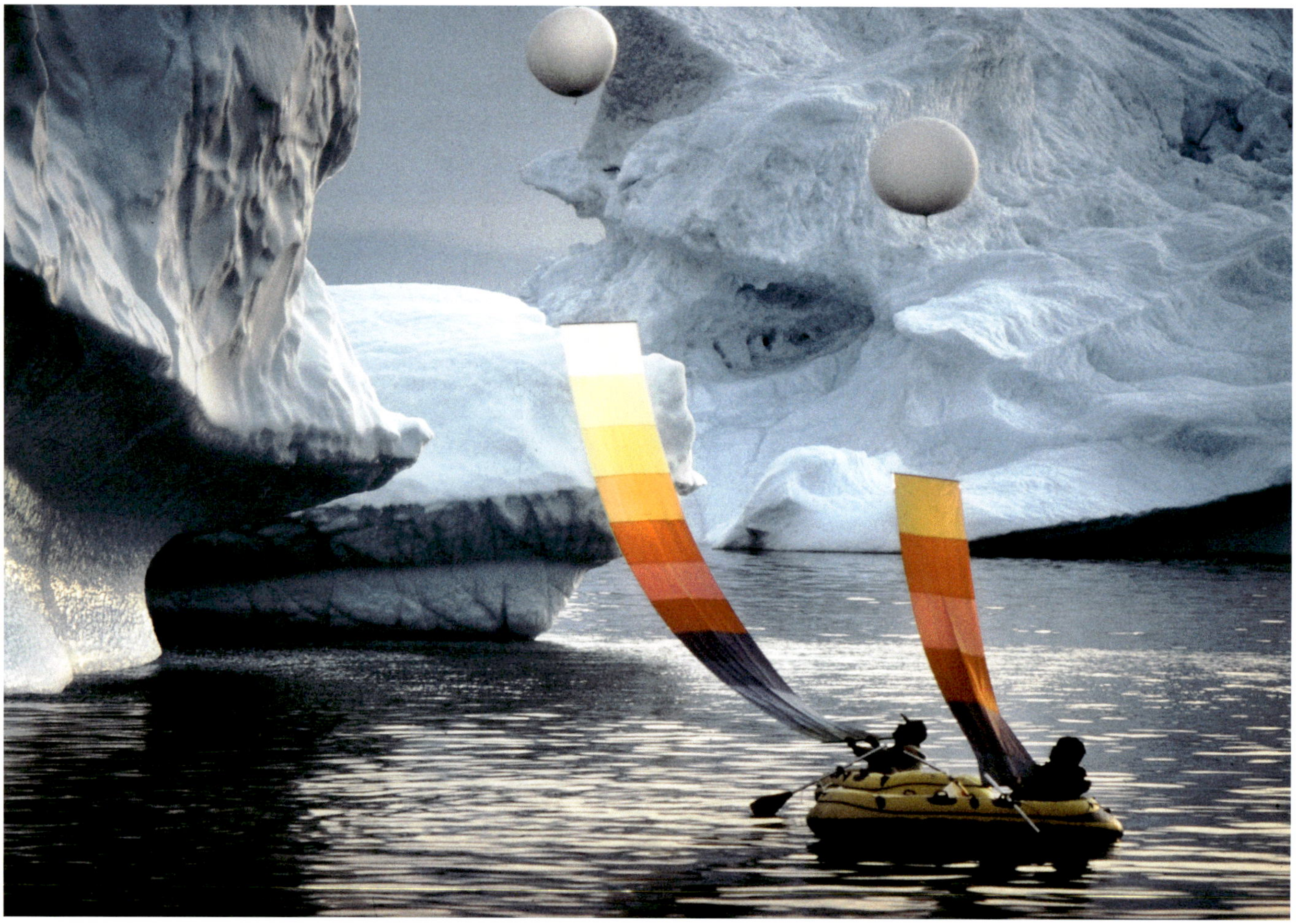

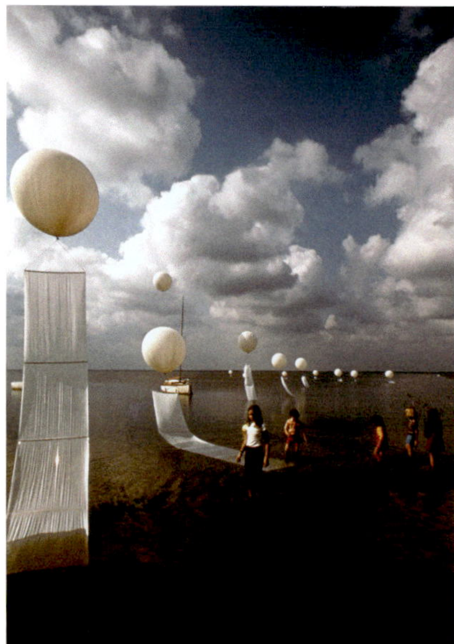

fig. 186 Soun-Gui Kim, *Situation plastique III – Octobre à Bordeaux*, 1973, 16 mm film, MMCA Collection Seoul

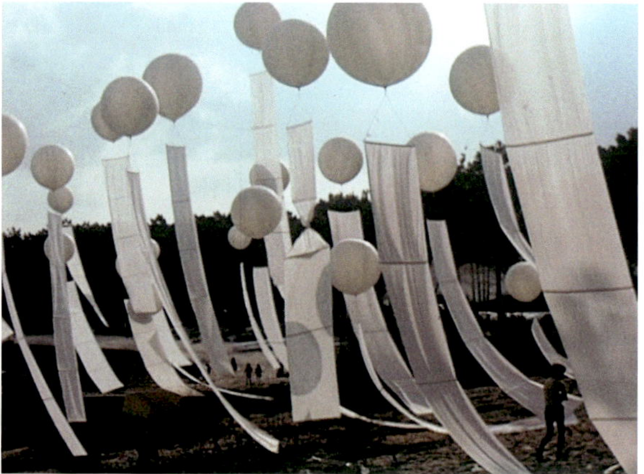

fig. 187 Soun-Gui Kim, *Situation plastique III – Octobre à Bordeaux*, 1973, 16 mm film, MMCA Collection Seoul

The work demonstrates the multifaceted possibilities that arise for artists in the twenty-first century, in a globally networked world where everything is ubiquitously accessible. Images from and evidence of everyday culture can be effortlessly appropriated and interwoven with those of art history, creating ever new references. Through the continued use and interpretation by subsequent generations of artists, Heinz Mack's works also appear in a new light, and the context and meaning of his art also change.[55] This openness of meaning towards visual culture also reflects the self-image of contemporary art. The exemplary positions described here take up Mack's artistic work, his formal strategies, and his utopian concepts in a variety of ways, reinterpreting them and testifying to a heightened awareness of socio-political problems against the backdrop of the "Capitalocene."[56] While the generation of ZERO artists still hoped for a "brave new world" and tried to realize it through the means of art, today's artists are confronted with the disheartening consequences of political, economic, and ecological developments in the crisis-ridden capitalist society of the twenty-first century and are critically examining the future that lies ahead of them. The optimism and pioneering spirit associated with ZERO's utopian attitude are difficult to sustain today.[57] Perhaps it is simply time to dream together again?

Translated from the German by Gérard Goodrow.

55 See Visser and Birnbaum, "ZERO heute," 235f.

56 The term "Capitalocene" is a critical further development of the "Anthropocene" as a geological era that is influenced by human activity. It emphasizes that the ecological effects are particularly shaped by the political and economic power relations and inequalities in the context of global capitalism, under the influence of which humans act. See Jason W. Moore, ed., *Anthropocene or Capitalocene? Nature, History, and the Crisis of Capitalism* (Oakland: PM Press, 2016).

57 See Dirk Pröschmann and Margriet Schavemaker, "Rendezvous mit einer vergessenen Avantgarde," in Pörschmann and Schavemaker, *ZERO*, 15.

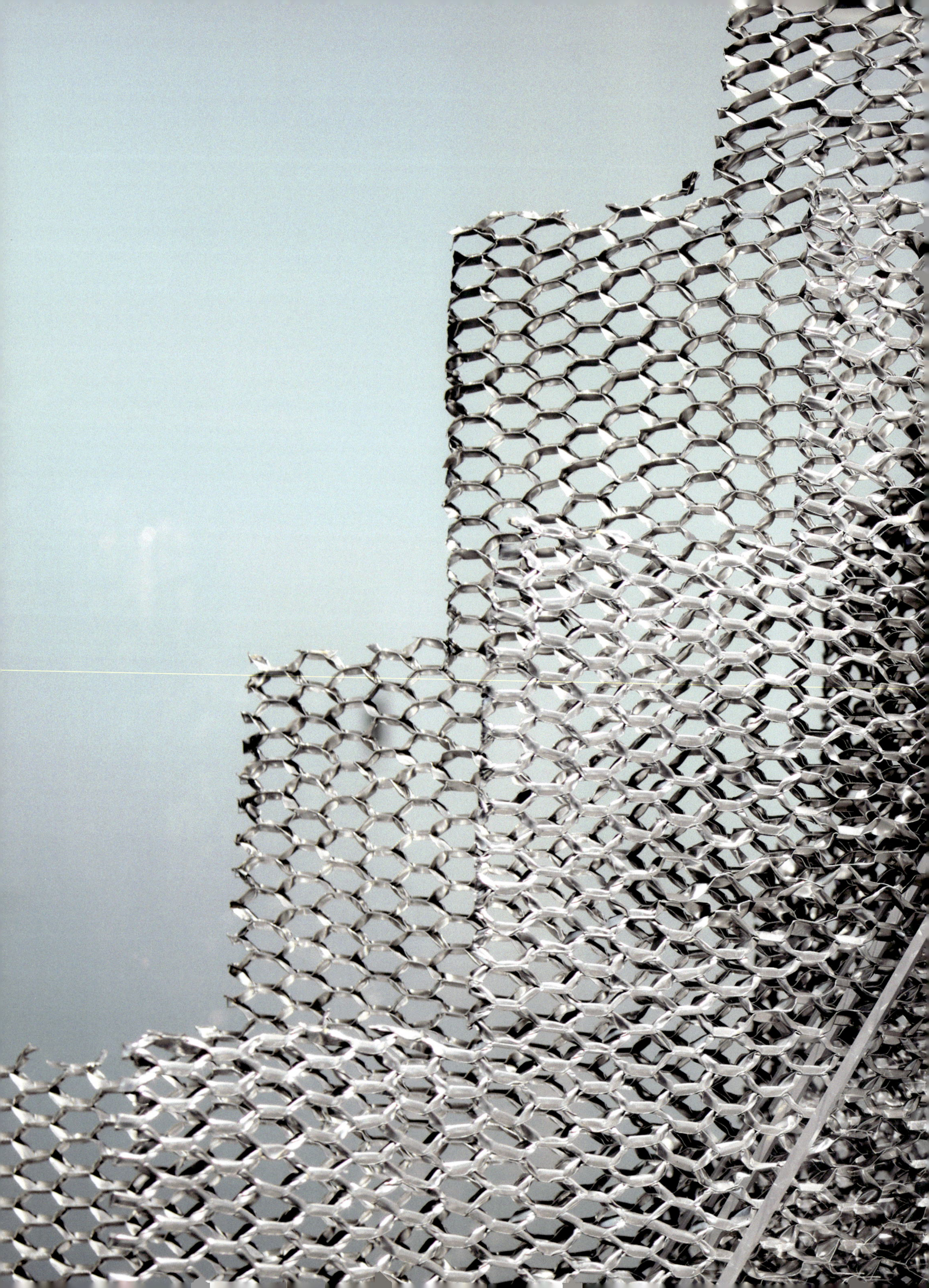

Light of the Sea of Ice – Expedition to the Arctic

For Heinz Mack, the ideas expressed in the *Sahara Project* were not exclusively tied to the desert. He repeatedly stated that it could be implemented in all the wide open natural spaces of the Earth. These included also the sky, the sea, and the icy landscapes of the Arctic or Antarctica, whose vastness and apparent placelessness fascinated him. In 1976, Mack traveled to the Algerian Sahara together with photographer Thomas Höpker, and also for the first time to the Arctic Circle in Greenland.

The white ice desert, like the Sahara, is characterized by monochromaticity, overwhelming scale, and boundlessness. Here, too, light is preeminent; according to the artist, its mood is veritably melancholic. Amid the snow and ice, Mack staged his light objects and performed various actions. He made objects float on the water, lengths of aluminum foil hover in the air, and colored weather balloons rise into the sky with light-reflecting nets that caught the sunlight. Mack also played with the antithetical elements of fire and water: The *Fire Raft* carries torches across the Arctic Ocean. In a previously unpublished image, the construction with its flares stands on an iceberg surrounded by clouds of black smoke. Here, the artist experimented with the forces of the elements: although the fire melts the ice, at the same moment it runs the risk of being extinguished by the water it has produced.

The resulting field reports and Höpker's photographic documentation, gave rise to a comprehensive report that was published in *Stern* magazine that same year by journalist Axel Hecht, who had also traveled with the group. In 1977, the lavishly illustrated book *Mack. Expedition in künstliche Gärten* [Expedition in artificial gardens], photography by Thomas Höpker, edited by Henri Nannen, was published.

← *fig. 188* Heinz Mack, *Arctic Pyramid*, 2020 (idea: 1976), detail

Tomorrow, however, we will have to seek out new spaces in our search for a new dimension of art; spaces in which our works will achieve incomparable appearances. These spaces include: the sky, the ocean, the Antarctic, the deserts. There, the preserves of art will rest as artificial islands. *

Works in the exhibition:
All works courtesy of the artist
unless otherwise noted

Arctic Pyramid
2020 (idea: 1976)
Light sculpture: aluminum, acrylic glass, stainless steel, wood
55 × 66 × 68 cm, cover: 66 × 71 × 71 cm
→ *fig. 188*

***Ice Crystal Sculpture*, Greenland, Arctic**
1976
Light box
45 × 65 × 11.5 cm
Photo: Thomas Höpker
→ *fig. 189*

***Colored Weather Balloons Over an Iceberg*, Greenland, Arctic**
1976
Photo print
Photo: Thomas Höpker
→ *figs. 193, 197*

***Pascal's Triangle*, Greenland, Arctic**
1976
Light box
65 × 45 × 10 cm
Photo: Thomas Höpker
Collection ZKM | Karlsruhe
→ *fig. 190*

The Steles in the Sea
circa 1960
Light box
166 × 135 × 19.5 cm
→ *figs. 192, 194*

***Fire Raft*, Greenland, Arctic**
1976
Light box
45 × 65 × 10 cm
Photo: Thomas Höpker
Collection ZKM | Karlsruhe
→ *fig. 196*

***Light Prisms in the Arctic (Model for a Floating Research Station)*, Greenland, Arctic**
1976
Light box
45 × 65 × 10 cm
Photo: Thomas Höpker
Collection ZKM | Karlsruhe
→ *fig. 191*

***Balloons Are Sent Into the Sky From the Boat*, Greenland, Arctic**
1976
Light box
45 × 65 × 10 cm
Photo: Thomas Höpker
Collection ZKM | Karlsruhe
→ *fig. 185*

***The Fire Raft in the Iceberg*, Greenland, Arctic**
1976
Light box
45 × 65 × 10 cm
Photo: Thomas Höpker
Collection ZKM | Karlsruhe
→ *figs. 195, 208*

***Dream of the Navigator*, Greenland, Arctic**
1976
Light box
45 × 65 × 11.5 cm
Photo: Thomas Höpker

* Heinz Mack, *Sahara Project*, 1959, typoscript, Archive Heinz Mack. Translated from the German.

→ *fig. 189* Heinz Mack, *Ice Crystal Sculpture*, Greenland, Arctic, 1976, photo: Thomas Höpker, detail

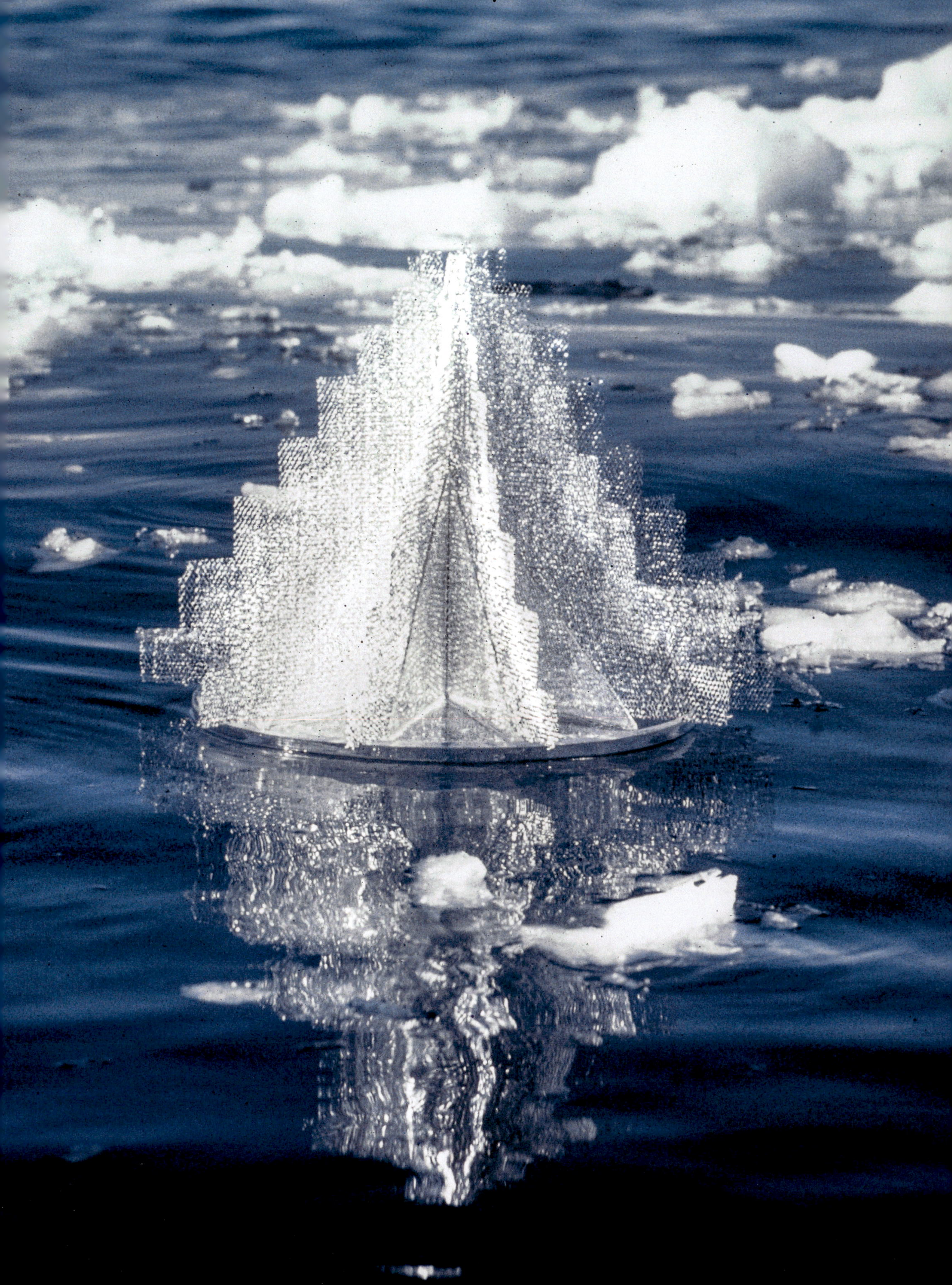

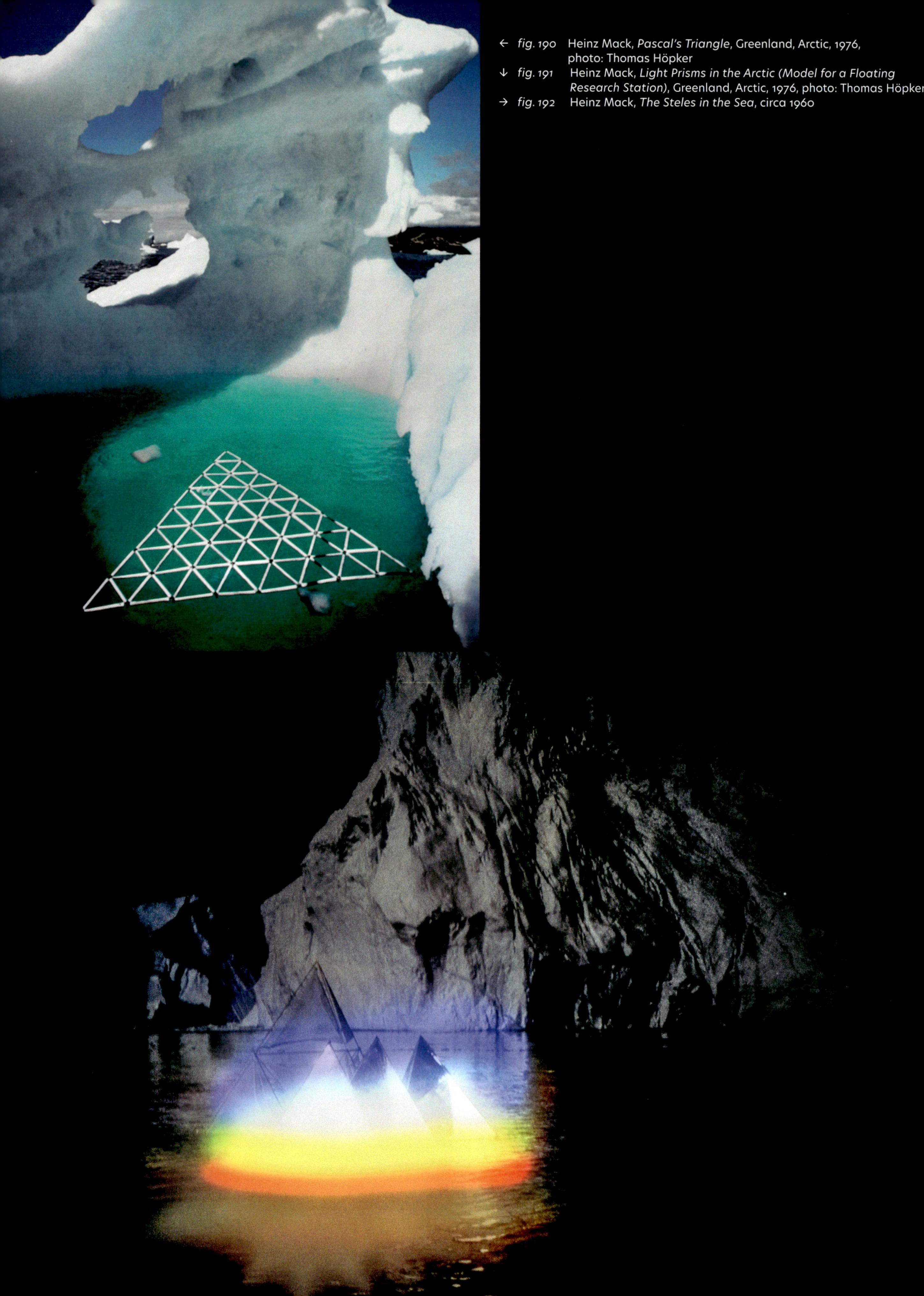

← *fig. 190* Heinz Mack, *Pascal's Triangle*, Greenland, Arctic, 1976, photo: Thomas Höpker
↓ *fig. 191* Heinz Mack, *Light Prisms in the Arctic (Model for a Floating Research Station)*, Greenland, Arctic, 1976, photo: Thomas Höpker
→ *fig. 192* Heinz Mack, *The Steles in the Sea*, circa 1960

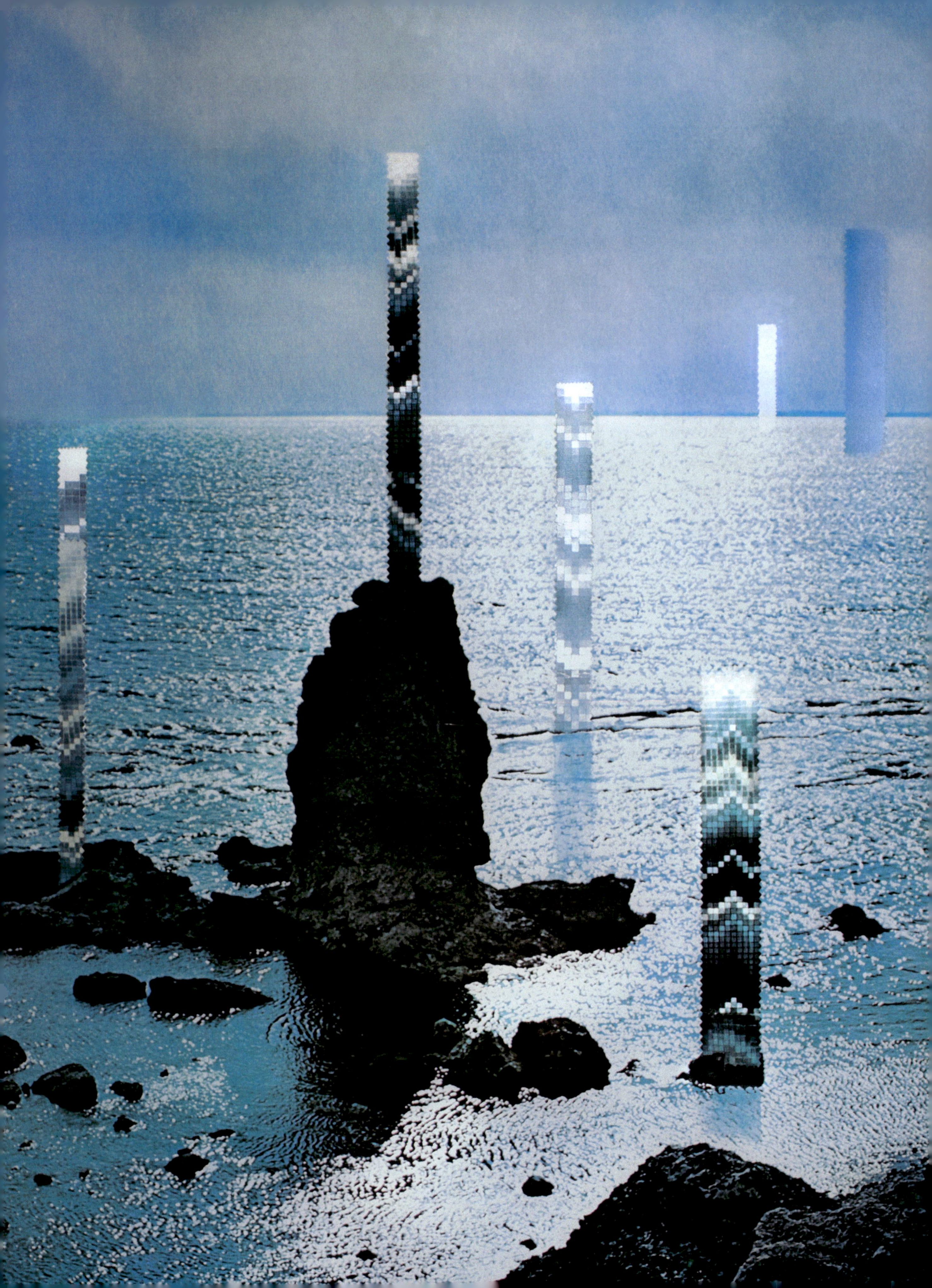

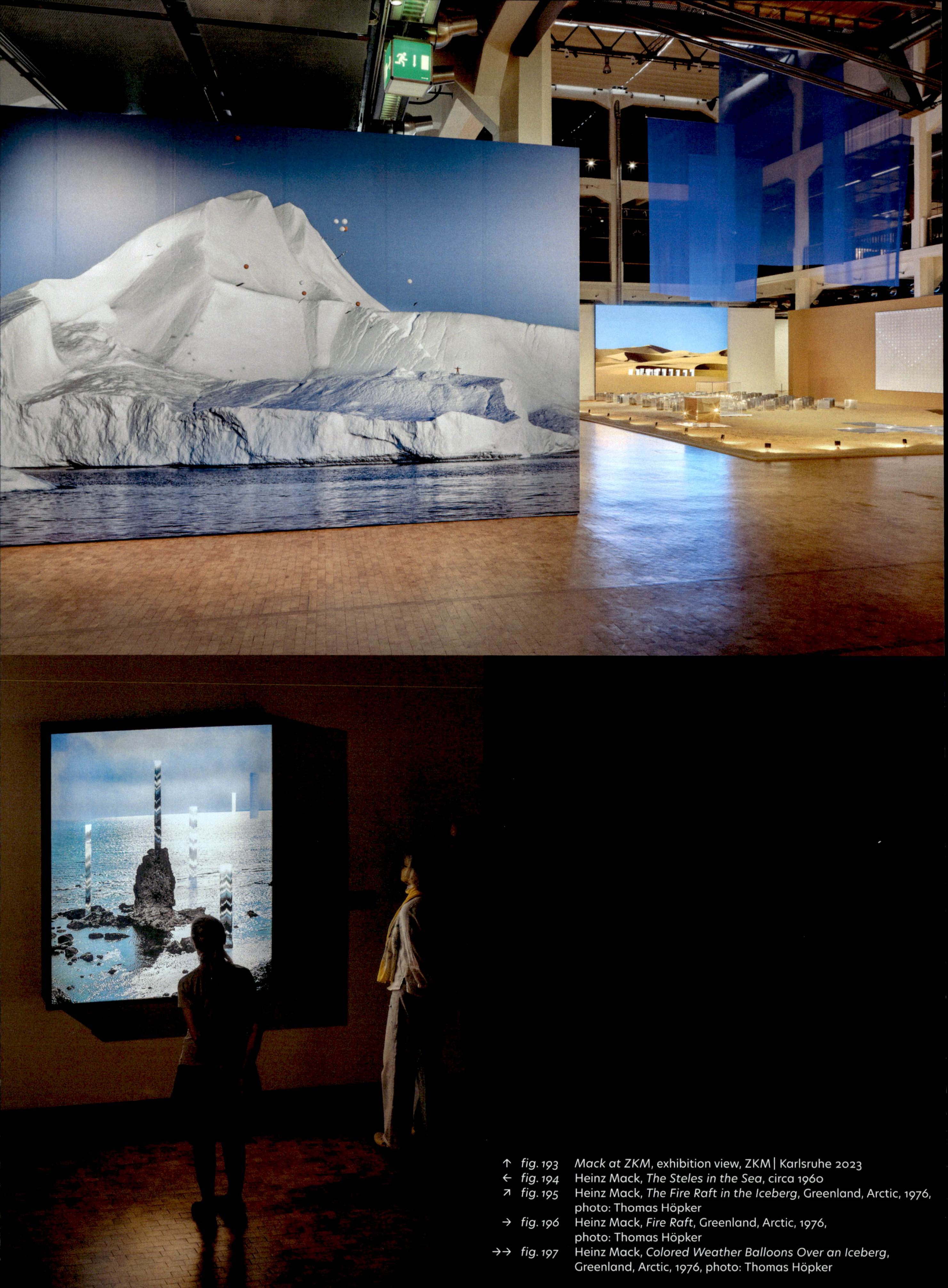

↑ *fig. 193* *Mack at ZKM*, exhibition view, ZKM | Karlsruhe 2023
← *fig. 194* Heinz Mack, *The Steles in the Sea*, circa 1960
↗ *fig. 195* Heinz Mack, *The Fire Raft in the Iceberg*, Greenland, Arctic, 1976, photo: Thomas Höpker
→ *fig. 196* Heinz Mack, *Fire Raft*, Greenland, Arctic, 1976, photo: Thomas Höpker
→→ *fig. 197* Heinz Mack, *Colored Weather Balloons Over an Iceberg*, Greenland, Arctic, 1976, photo: Thomas Höpker

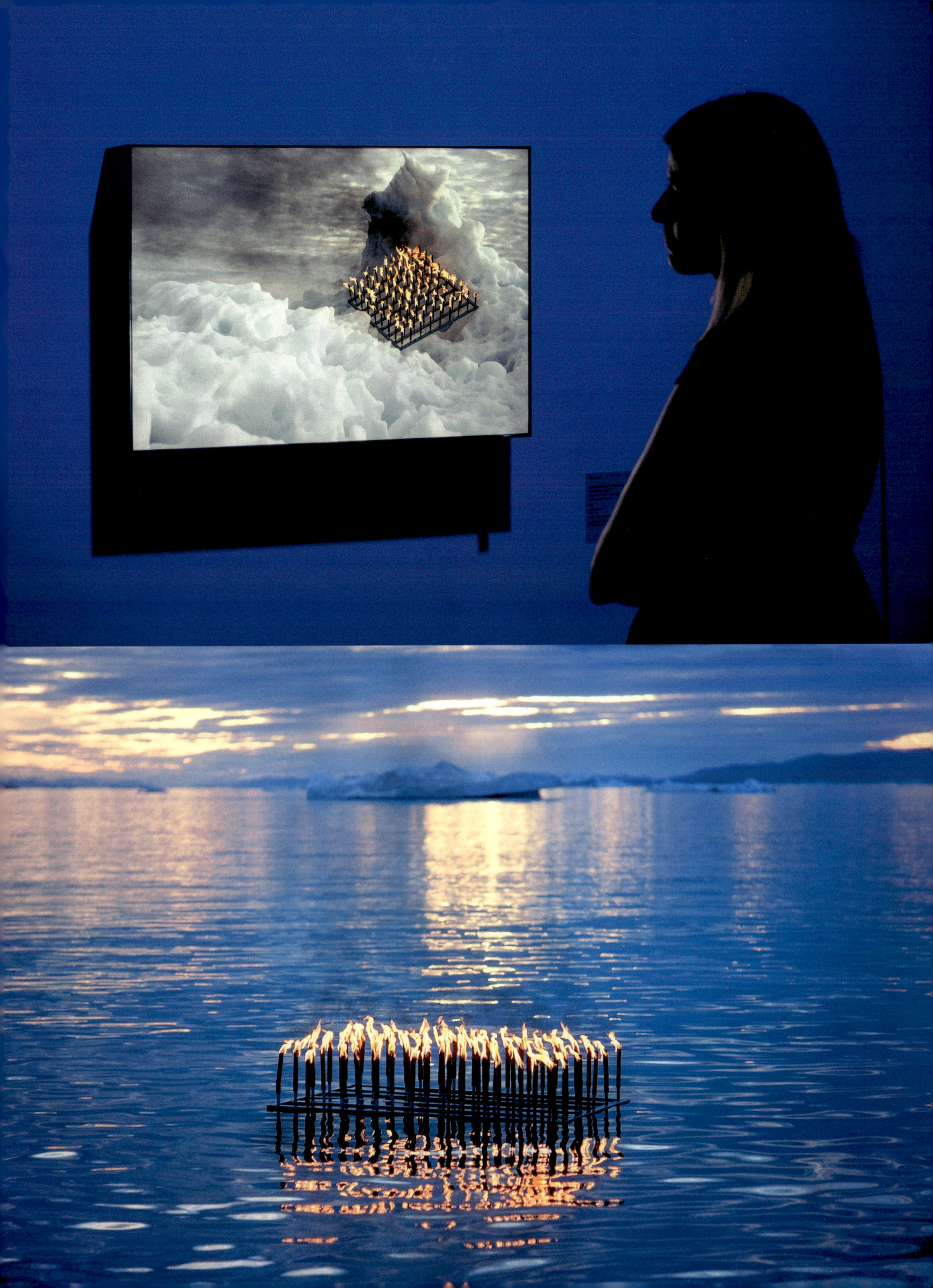

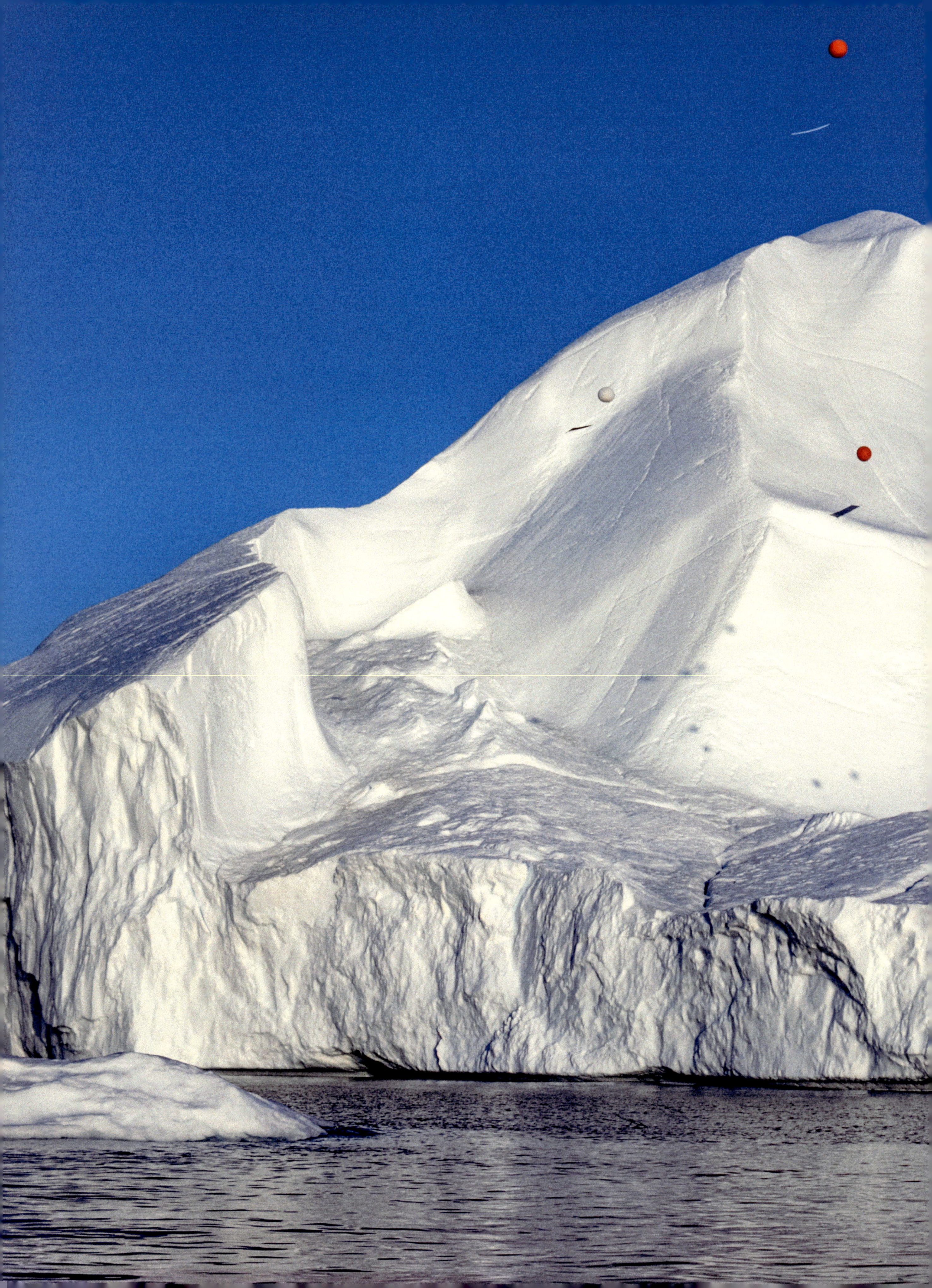

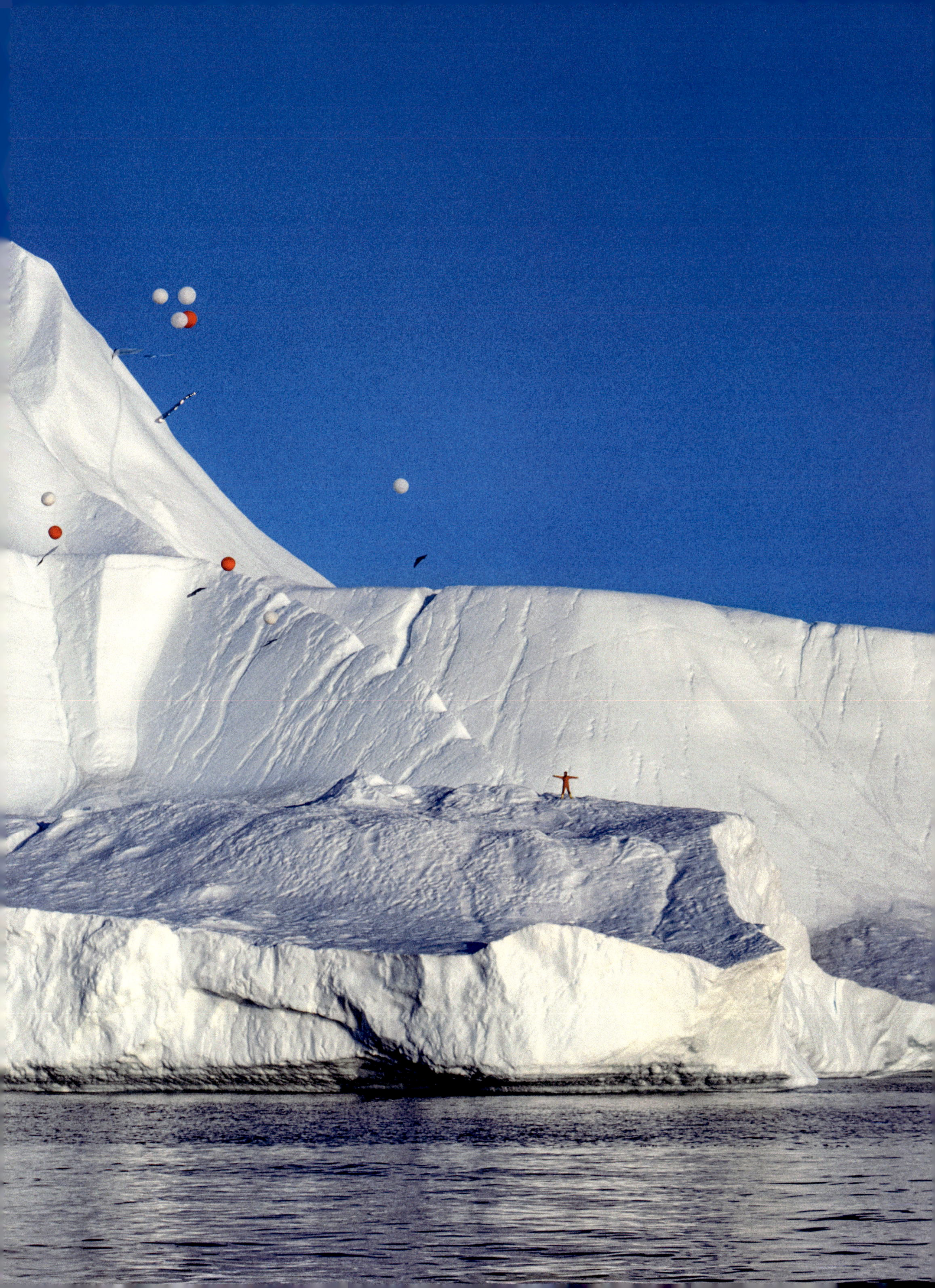

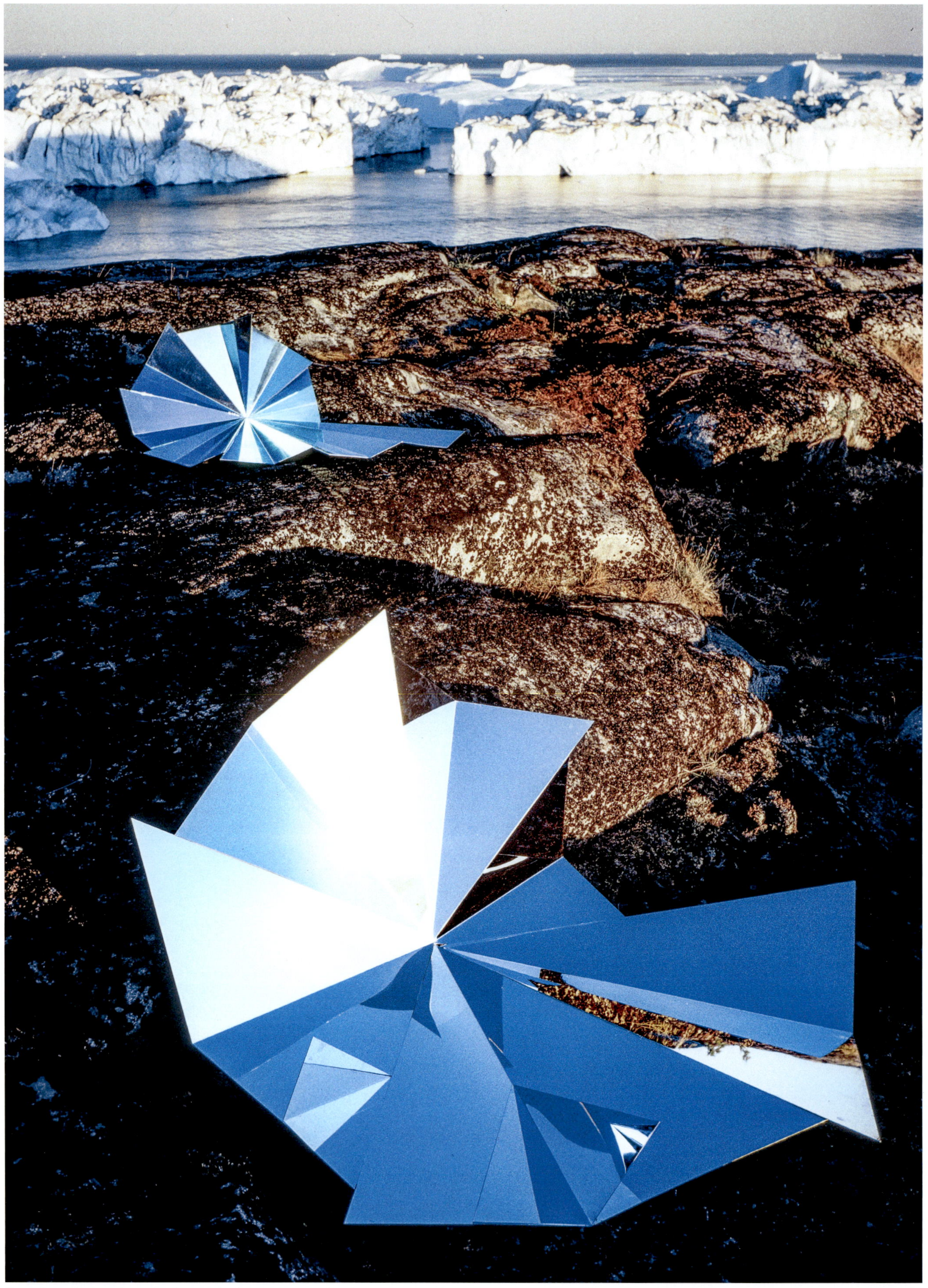

fig. 198 Heinz Mack, *Light Flowers in the Arctic*, Greenland, Arctic, 1976,, aluminum, Ø ca. 250 cm, photo: Thomas Höpker

Too Beautiful to Be True? Heinz Mack's Arctic Art

A Shift in Attitude

Looking back, the way Heinz Mack envisioned the year 2000 and the future beyond that in a lecture in 1978 is quite touching. The realization that many of his predictions did not come true can make us feel sentimental. What great optimism allowed Mack to assert that "infectious diseases will no longer exist" and that "cancer will be defeated by the year 2000"? And how much faith in progress did it take to claim that life expectancy would already be "somewhere around 150 years by the year 2025"? What sort of experiences nourished his conviction that a "complete solution of the energy problem" could be expected, with certainty, by the year 2000? Mack even heralded "total control over the weather. We will have sunshine wherever we want sunshine, we will have rain wherever we want rain." As a result of these fantastic developments, he concluded, humanity would "be characterized by an entirely new attitude towards life."[1]

In contrast to the freedom and quality of life that Heinz Mack envisioned for future generations, we now often look back to the 1970s as a much happier and more carefree time, when people were curious about a future that seemed to promise spectacular achievements. Instead, we have had to accept that much of that progress has simply not occurred, and even concede that individual freedoms have come under threat as the comfort zone of the West can no longer be taken for granted. Older generations see defining characteristics of their lives called into question, while younger generations are confronted with feelings of resignation, grief, and anger in the face of mounting pessimism. They no longer associate the future with freedom, but with loss; for them, it is not some perfect future, but the future perfect – characterized by what *will have been*, i.e., what will no longer be.

From this perspective, not only Mack's rosy predictions, but also some of his works seem like relics of a bygone era. Sensing the sheer optimism in which these works are rooted can feel especially disenchanting in retrospect. Some may also feel envy towards the older generation's perceived freedom, or even anger at how that freedom and carefree lifestyle will incur even greater cost from future generations. Where decisions used to be guided by the maxim of enabling a better life for one's children, the perception that parents and grandparents had it much easier is increasingly taking hold. And even those who manage to stave off such negative thoughts may find the things that were possible in the era of unfettered optimism hard to believe.

Aesthetical Experimentation

Perhaps the most astonishing work in Mack's œuvre, from today's perspective, is his 1976 Arctic project. Here, the shift in attitude from boundless optimism to downright fear regarding the future is the most palpable. Today, any mention of the Arctic suffices to conjure up images of melting glaciers, rising water levels, and the resulting mass displacements. The Arctic is no longer associated with untouched

1 Heinz Mack, "Kunst 2000," *Kunstforum*, no. 29 (1978): 46–55, here 53, 55. Translated from the German.

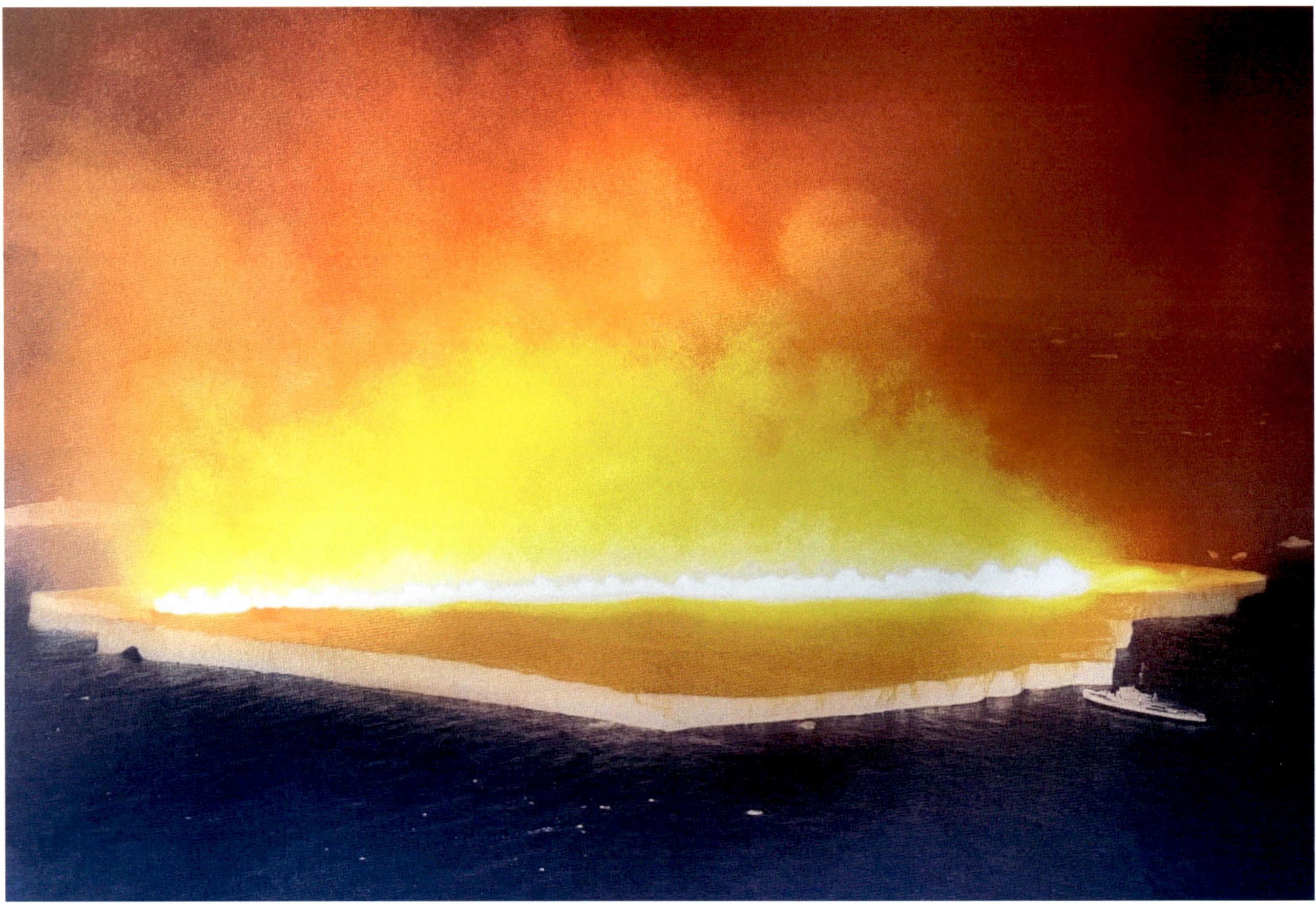

fig. 199 Heinz Mack, *Fire Ridge (Project)*, 1975, photo collage

nature and boundless adventure, but with a dangerous tipping point for the global climate. These are the associations borne in mind when we look at photographs of Mack's expeditions to the far north today and read his statements about the art projects he implemented there, and even more so about the ones he did not. In that 1978 lecture, he also described a plan that involved using a helicopter to airlift large snow blowers onto a 500-meter long floating iceberg, where they were to carve out a huge furrow. "This furrow was to be filled – from the helicopter – with combustible material, gasoline dyed with chemicals to burn red; the idea being that this huge white iceberg would float in the blue ocean, burning with a gigantic ridge of red and yellow fire."[2]

fig. 199

What an undertaking! Torching an entire iceberg using fossil fuels and chemicals, just to create spectacular imagery? Mack even approached NATO to help make his plan a reality, but to no vail. However, he speculated that a new consumer society might make something like this possible in the future.[3] In all of his grandiose plans, Mack never had to worry that such a wasteful use of resources might face harsh criticism – for him, any reaction to his work in the Arctic other than curiosity and enjoyment of its beauty would have been unfathomable. He got to experience firsthand the overwhelming and sublime light, colors, and shapes of the Arctic's untouched natural landscape. In an interview with Dieter Honisch, he described the challenges posed by that "infinite expanse" and its "all-encompassing brightness" with awe.[4]

2 Ibid., 54. Translated from the German.

3 Ibid.

4 "Gespräch mit Heinz Mack," in: Henri Nannen, ed., *Mack. Expedition in künstliche Gärten*, photography by Thomas Höpker (Hamburg: Gruner + Jahr, 1976).

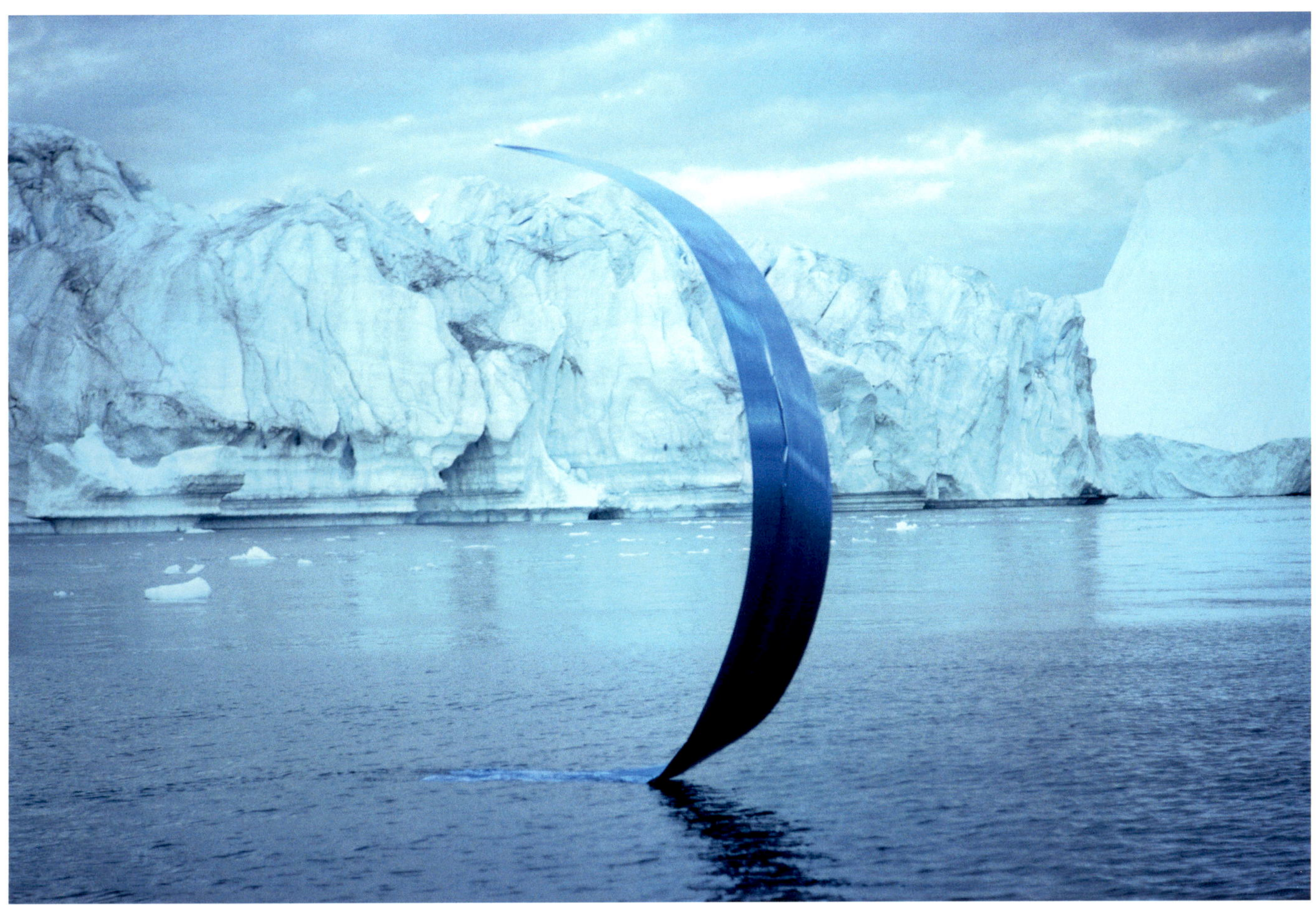

fig. 200 Heinz Mack, *Sail without Wind and Ship – The Secret of the Arctic*, 1976, Greenland, Arctic, mercury vapor-coated foil, max. height 7 m, photo: Thomas Höpker

Much like he did for his *Sahara Project*, which he had been pursuing since the late 1950s and which came to partial fruition on several occasions in the 1960s and 1970s, Mack brought a range of materials and objects on his Arctic expedition in order to expose them to the local conditions. In what ways do aluminum steles glisten in the all-encompassing brightness of the Arctic desert? How do sails and balloons react to the extreme cold? What are the effects of mirrors surrounded by ice? How can fire burn on ice floes? These were some of the questions guiding Mack's work in the Arctic. They imbued his artistic exploits, implemented with the help of his team as well as photographer Thomas Höpker and journalist Axel Hecht, with an air of scientific experimentation. A tight schedule (the Arctic expedition only lasted three weeks[5]) and unpredictable, changing weather conditions made the inherently difficult work in the extreme environment even more challenging. Furthermore, the success of the expedition would only become apparent after its completion, when the photographs and film footage could be developed and viewed.

figs. 185, 189, 190, 191, 198, 201, 203

figs. 200, 207

figs. 196, 208

In fact, photographic documentation is all that remains of the endeavor. Although there was talk of creating lasting installations in the Arctic, not unlike Land Art, and establishing a form of art tourism that would involve presenting those installations from aircraft, Mack quickly abandoned these ideas. Only a single floating work of art was left behind "as a token of gratitude or a sacrifice to the Arctic sea,"[6]

5 See Axel Hecht, "Sahara und Arktis," in: Nannen, *Expedition in künstliche Gärten*.

6 Uwe Rüth, "Heinz Mack und sein Sahara-Projekt," in: *Mack. Licht der Wüste. Licht des Eismeeres*, exh. cat. (Marl: Skulpturenmuseum Glaskasten, 2001), 17–62, here 48, 33. Translated from the German.

the intention being to emphasize, rather than violate, the extreme natural landscape. At the same time, the fact that Mack's pieces were only temporarily set up for the camera made them "untouchable, unharmed, invulnerable" and meant they existed purely as "visual sensations."[7] And because Mack's work in the Arctic can only be experienced through films and photographs, they are purely immaterial events. There is no risk of disappointment or disturbing the "enchantment of the photogenic" by getting too close to them.[8] As a result, these works come closer to Mack's understanding of beauty as "a manifestation of angels"[9] than any tangible objects. And because the images do not reveal what exactly they depict, how a lighting effect or other phenomenon was created, or any sense of scale, Mack's works become all the more mysterious; there is an even greater freedom of association and more fuel for imagination than if it were possible to reconstruct what materials and techniques the artist used on site.

We can surmise that Mack's non-invasive approach to the uninhabited Arctic and Saharan realms was primarily motivated by aesthetic and artistic reasons. He was following the Romantic tradition in seeking out the beauty and purity of nature and viewing art as that instance which does not aim to "jealously conceal" its qualities, but to adopt them as its material in order to expand our imagination.[10]

In 1976, renowned German editor Henri Nannen published the seminal volume *Mack. Expedition in künstliche Gärten* [Mack. Expedition to Artificial Gardens], comprising some 200 pages of Thomas Höpker's photographs of Mack's artworks: A varied mix of images from the Sahara and from the Arctic, with ever-changing objects placed in the respective landscapes. The objects serve as amplifiers; they exaggerate the sublime effect of an iceberg, the brightness of the sky, or the vastness of the sea. And because the steles, cubes, or balloons do not introduce narrative or symbolic elements to the images but merely serve as abstract objects, they prompt the viewer to perceive the landscape primarily as an interplay between shapes and colors. The landscape and the objects interact freely and playfully as though performing on a vast stage, even improvising with the most powerful forms of nature as though everything were movable and weightless.

Liberation from Meaning

This marks the fulfillment of Heinz Mack's ambitions for the *Sahara Project*, which he outlined in 1959 (and revised in 1961). He spoke of a "preserve of art" and speculated that, in a natural reserve far from civilization, art would "find a new freedom." This freedom was linked to "Zone ZERO" and thus conceptualized as a rejection of any prescribed meaning – a tabula rasa or zero point, making space for "our limitless expectations." The last sentence of this text, much of which almost reads like a manifesto, was: "Only if we have the courage to realize the total preserve [of art], we can expect that beauty will gain a new radiance in this world."[11]

Mack's close conceptual link between beauty and freedom is reminiscent of Friedrich Schiller's philosophy of art, while the experiments he conducted in the Sahara and in the Arctic and the resulting images already presuppose the accomplishments of abstract art and

7 Heinz Mack, "Zwischen Tag und Traum," in: Wieland Schmied, ed., *Utopie und Wirklichkeit im Werk von Heinz Mack* (Cologne: Dumont, 1998), 55. Translated from the German.

8 Wolfgang Ullrich, *Raffinierte Kunst. Übung vor Reproduktionen* (Berlin: Wagenbach, 2009), 88. Translated from the German.

9 "Gespräch mit Heinz Mack."

10 Mack, "Kunst 2000," 48. Translated from the German.

11 Heinz Mack, "Das Sahara-Projekt," in: Schmied, *Utopie und Wirklichkeit*, 17–21, here 17, 21. Translated from the German.

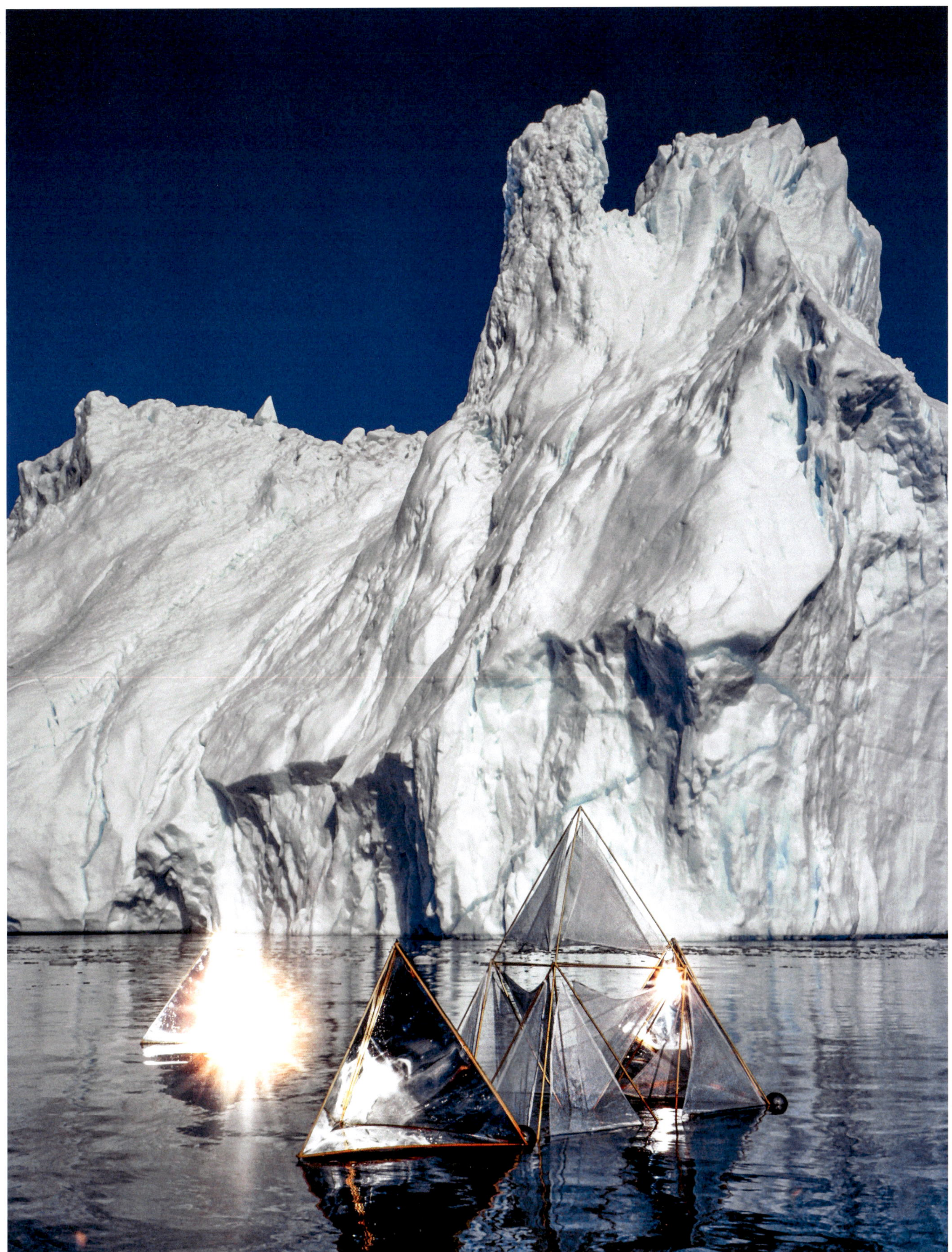

fig. 201 Heinz Mack, *Light Prisms in the Arctic (Model for a Floating Research Station)*, Greenland, Arctic, 1976, photo: Thomas Höpker

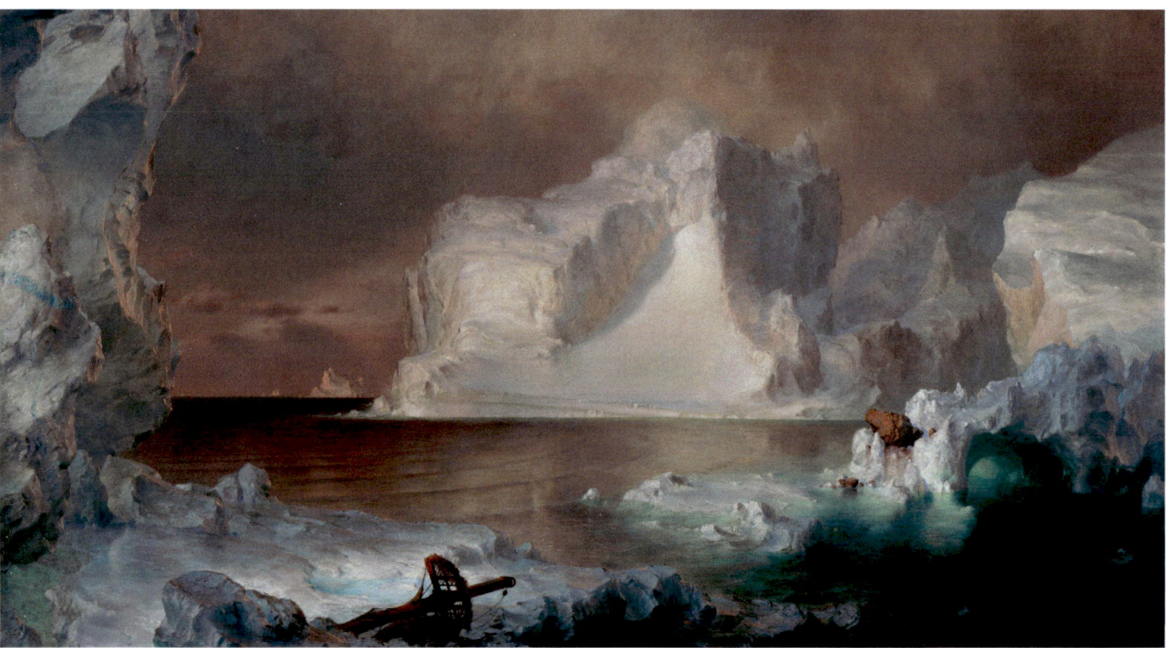

fig. 202 Frederic E. Church, *The Icebergs*, 1861, oil on canvas

the idea that there could be something like a first or last image – before or after any compulsion to convey meaning. In that same vein, cultural theorist Hartmut Böhme refers to Mack's Arctic art as "liberation from meaning," describing it as "nothing but a phenomenon, an apparition of light."[12]

As a result, this art is imbued with a sense of radicalism that outbids and rejects all previous works of art involving the Arctic. Although depictions of the icy landscapes of the far north date back to the sixteenth century, they are almost always found within the genre of marine painting. Here, the ice served as a backdrop for lurid hero worship through popular anecdotal themes such as whaling and shipwrecks, usually in service of "emphasizing the indomitable [human] daringness to cross boundaries."[13]

But even as the rise of landscape painting transformed the sublime Arctic into a desirable motif during the nineteenth century, it still required the inclusion of accessories that imbued the respective image with a certain dramatic significance. Even Caspar David Friedrich's painting *Eismeer* (1824), arguably the most famous example of this genre, still includes a shipwreck. This left no choice but to associate the natural scenery with death, and to read the painting as a heavy-handed admonition for humans to rein in their curiosity and hubris and stay within their rightful – god-given – boundaries.

A particularly striking example of how much less freedom than Heinz Mack nineteenth-century artists had in their depiction of the Arctic is the US-American painter Frederic Church. Unlike Friedrich, Church had firsthand experience traveling to the polar region, which lent great credibility to his paintings involving Arctic imagery. Especially his 1861 work *The Icebergs* is a masterpiece of nuanced coloring, a milestone in the history of depicting icebergs. When it was shown in New York and Boston, accompanied by a professional media campaign, it was met with admiration – but also caused alienation. Many thought

12 Hartmut Böhme, "Tote Natur? Stein und Petrefakt, Wüste und Arktis als Dimensionen der Kunst im Anthropozän," *Kunstforum International* 258 (2019): 97–105, here 99. Translated from the German.

fig. 202

13 Dirk Tölke, *Eislandschaften und Eisberge. Studien zur Motiv- und Bildgeschichte von Eisformationen und polaren Szenerien in Gemälden und Graphiken des 16. bis 20. Jahrhunderts* (Diss., RWTH Aachen University, 1995), 64. Translated from the German.

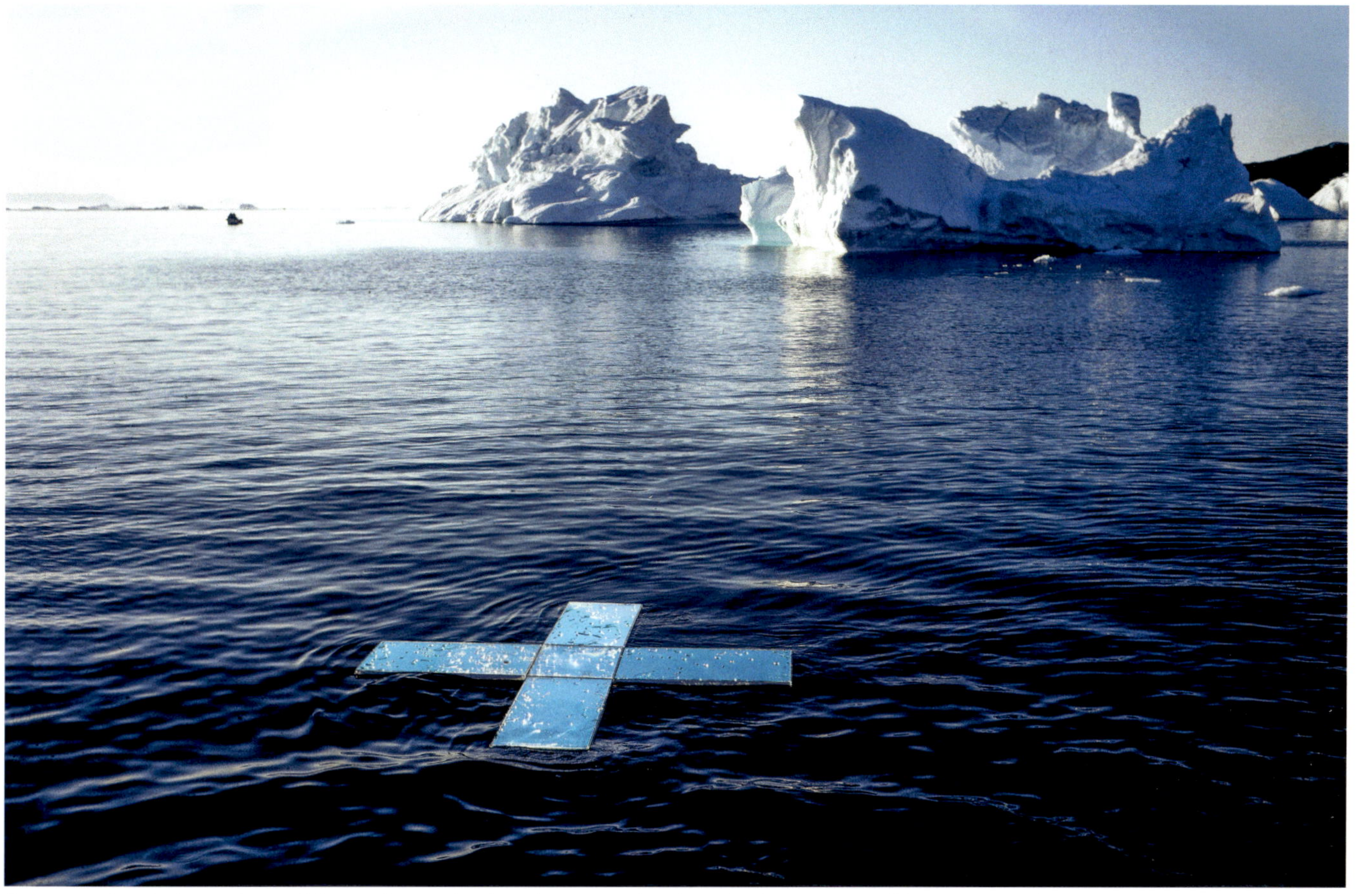

fig. 203 Heinz Mack, *The Cross of the North*, Greenland, Arctic, 1976, enclosed acrylic glass container filled with colored water, 10 × 250 × 250 cm, photo: Thomas Höpker

that Church's depiction of the frosty-sublime landscape, devoid of any traces of human presence or stories, left something to be desired. Their yearning for entertainment, spectacle, or morality went unfulfilled, and the painting was not sold. A significant career setback for Church, who had previously enjoyed stellar commercial success. He managed to have the painting exhibited again a year later in London – and even found a buyer – but only after caving to the tastes of the broader public and adding a broken ship's mast to the front and center. This indication of a deadly tragedy reaffirmed the image of the Arctic as a dangerous place – instead of continuing to show it as a place of uniquely idiosyncratic beauty, as he had originally intended.[14]

In comparing Church's painting with one of the photographs of icebergs from Mack's Arctic expedition, which shows a cruciform assembly of plastic troughs floating in the foreground,[15] it becomes obvious that the two artists convey entirely different images. Unlike Church, Mack does not force us to equate the Arctic with death. While the cross does allow for this connotation, it is so clearly staged as an abstract shape, in bright shades of blue that evoke happiness and freshness, that other associations are every bit as plausible, if not more so. And even if one sees the cross as a reference to the innumerable depictions of shipwrecks in the Arctic, this does not serve to revive some past meaning, but rather to remember it and thus mark it as belonging in the past. As such, Mack's cross is an element that, instead of limiting the freedom of interpretation, enhances it.

fig. 203

14 See Eleanor Jones Harvey, "The Tip of *The Icebergs*," in: Eleanor Jones Harvey, *The Voyage of the Icebergs. Frederic Church's Arctic Masterpiece*, exh. cat. (Dallas: Dallas Museum of Art, 2002), 45–69.

15 See Sophia Sotke, *Mack. Sahara* (Munich: Hirmer, 2022), 90.

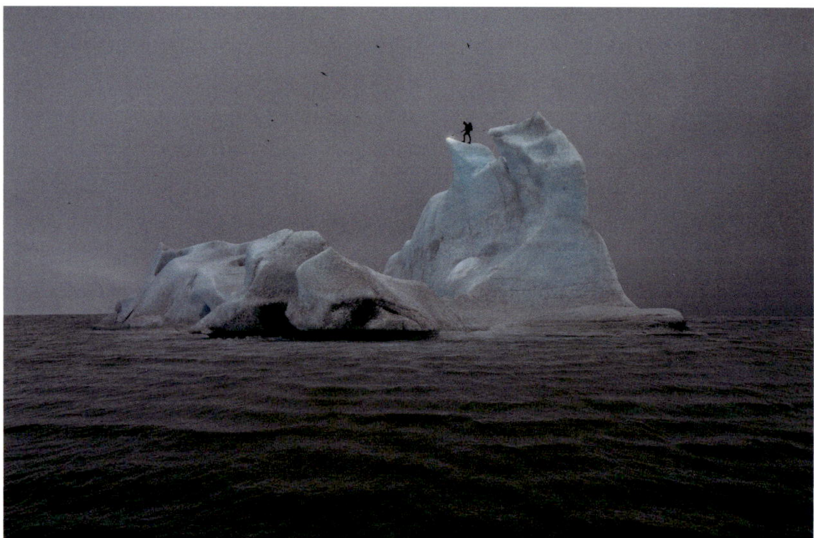

fig. 204 Julian Charrière, *The Blue Fossil Entropic Stories III*, 2013

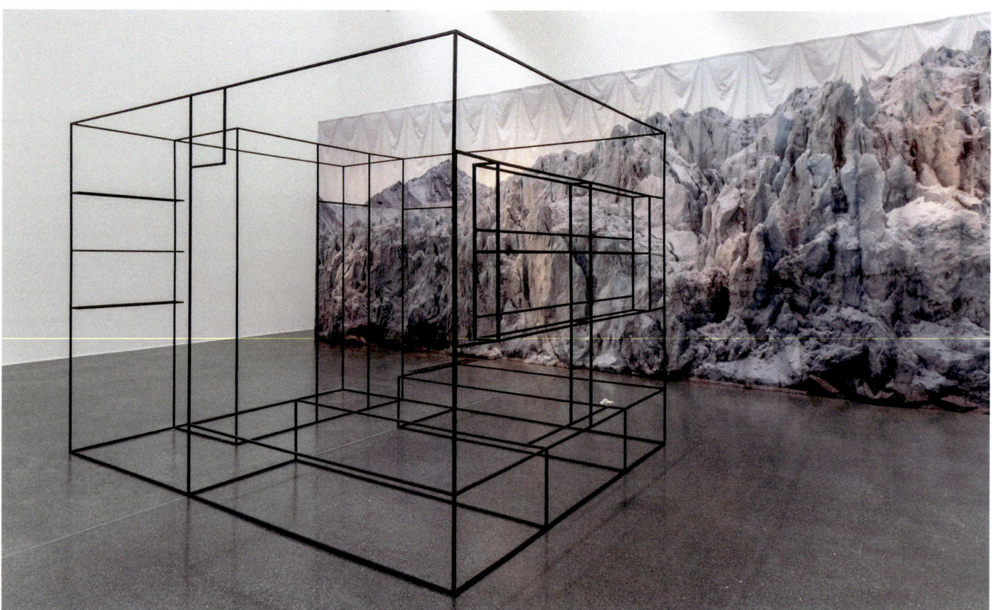

fig. 205 Lena von Goedeke, *Full Fathom Five*, exhibition view, Dortmunder U 2019

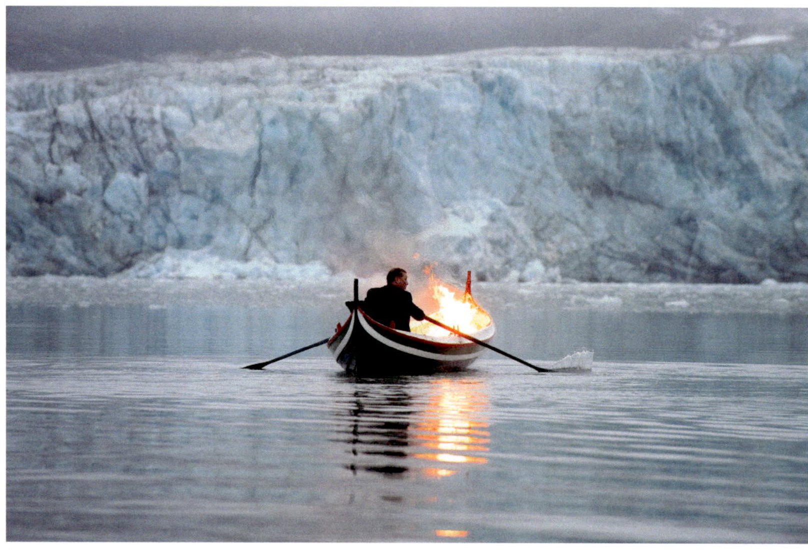

fig. 206 Stein Henningsen, *The Boat*, performance, 2021

After Freedom

It was Heinz Mack's program to look at the Arctic freely – unburdened by any semantic presuppositions – and to share this freedom, born from the spirit of the ZERO movement, with his audience. This makes it truly exceptional: as much as a zero point had been reached when Mack left behind any and all heroic-dramatic stories of conquest and failure, even contradicting the common conception of "hostile unfettered forces of nature," and, to quote art historian Wieland Schmied, virtually decreeing "all traces of tragedy banished from art," the motif has since been once again charged with dark and heavy significance.[16] It is even doubtful whether any other motifs are as strongly associated with certain topics today as the Arctic.

The presence of ecological issues, which now dominate the entirety of Arctic iconography, started taking hold a few years before Mack's Arctic expedition in projects initiated by Lawrence Weiner, Iain and Elaine Baxter, and Harry Savage on a 1969 journey to the Arctic documented by art theorist Lucy Lippard, who accompanied the group of artists.[17] Where they addressed the dangers of oil extraction in the region and the general fragility of the local ecosystem,[18] today climate change, global warming, and melting glaciers have become the central issues.

fig. 204

For instance, when Julian Charrière scaled an iceberg in Iceland for his 2013 work *The Blue Fossil Entropic Stories* and melted the ice with a gas torch, this should not be interpreted as some smaller version of Mack's plan to put a gigantic ridge of fire across an iceberg and create an aesthetic phenomenon never seen before, but as a "shockingly visual intervention" to raise awareness for the dangers of climate change.[19] Charrière also joined an expedition to Greenland which gathered climate change data for scientific purposes, and he initiated a collection of essays from various disciplines negotiating the climate crisis to accompany a film project about several glacier fields (*Towards No Earthly Pole*, 2019).[20] In 2017, he was also invited to the first (and, to date, only) *Antarctic Biennale*, which took place across twelve different locations in the southern polar region. Much like Mack's *Arctic Project*, the interventions and installations – around twenty in total – of this event were not intended for an on-site audience, but only documented in various media. However, this was motivated primarily by ecological rather than aesthetical considerations: the organizers did not want to encourage any additional tourism, and almost all contributions dealt directly with climate change in some form.[21]

fig. 205

In recent years, global climate change has brought the Arctic, the Antarctic, and other glacier regions into the focus of many more artistic projects, with especially the Arctic garnering an unprecedented amount of attention. To name a few examples: Lena von Goedeke creates installations, videos, and photographs that illustrate the realization that the extreme ecosystem of the Arctic and the human beings traveling there are threatening each other's existence; photographer Georg Sailer shows the Arctic as a landscape shaped by economic and military interests; Icelandic photojournalist Ragnar Axelsson documents the changes that have taken place in the Arctic over the last few decades, often with a sentimental gaze; Stein Henningsen performs with

fig. 206

16 Wieland Schmied, "Arbeit am Projekt der Moderne. Über Heinz Mack und den Mythos vom Künstler als Konstrukteur neuer Welten," in: Schmied, *Utopie und Wirklichkeit*, 10–13, here 10–11.

17 See Lucy R. Lippard, "Art within the Arctic Circle," *The Hudson Review* 22, no. 4 (1969/1970): 665–74.

18 See ibid., 666, 669.

19 Ann-Katrin Günzel, "Der Blick auf die Welt oder: Der lange Weg durch die Landschaft," *Kunstforum International* 284 (2022): 50–69, here 53.

20 See Dehlia Hannah, ed., *Julian Charrière. Towards No Earthly Pole* (Milan: Mousse Publishing, 2021).

21 See http://nadimsamman.com/the-antarctic-biennale.

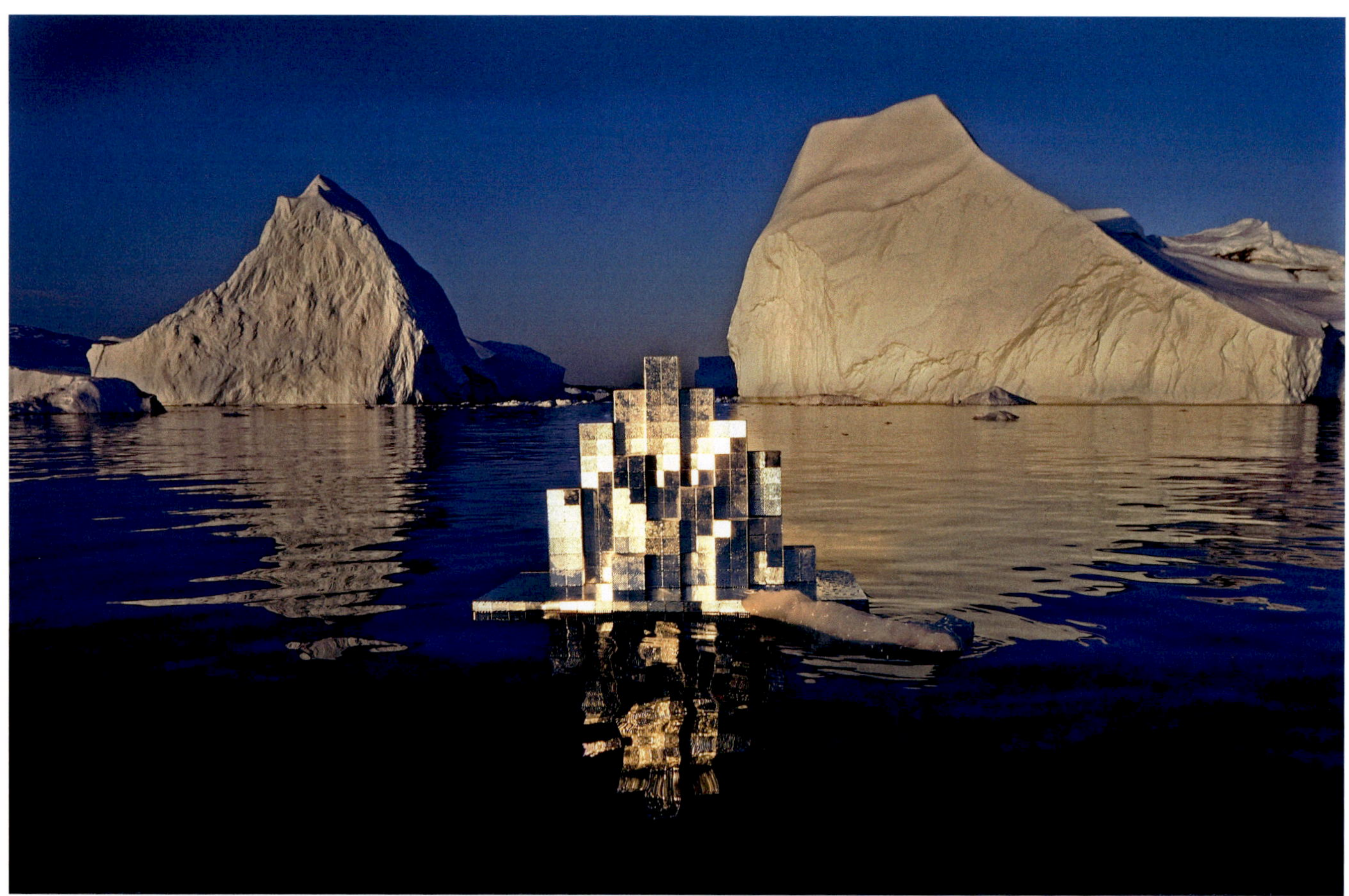

fig. 207 Heinz Mack, *Light Architecture (Model for a Floating Research Station in the Arctic)*, 1976, aluminum, 94 × 140 × 80 cm, photo: Thomas Höpker

fire and ice; Mariele Neudecker builds miniaturized Arctic landscapes in display cases, as if they were already historic relics. The boom of Arctic-related art is further fueled by initiatives such as the scholarship program "The Arctic Circle," which was established in 2009 and provides multiple artists and scientists with residencies on a vessel embarking on expeditions to the far north every year to facilitate their projects and interdisciplinary exchange.[22]

A Second Career for Heinz Mack's *Arctic Project*?

Apart from the question whether the amount of Arctic travel involved in these artistic projects exacerbates the issues at hand, there are also discussions about which kinds of imagery might be best suited to increase the general public awareness for the climate crisis. Should we attempt to capture the traces and auspices of the impending catastrophe seismographically, or would it be better to tell the most dramatic stories of loss? Or could existing images of ice and the Arctic illustrate what is under threat from the expected rise in temperature if it is not slowed down and continues to reshape landscapes around the world, including those of the far north? Might those images in the Romantic tradition, which express the sublime nature of those vast, desolate, white landscapes and frozen structures, receive new significance and urgency through the climate change discourse? Could they even be at the beginning of a second career?

22 See https://thearcticcircle.org/program.

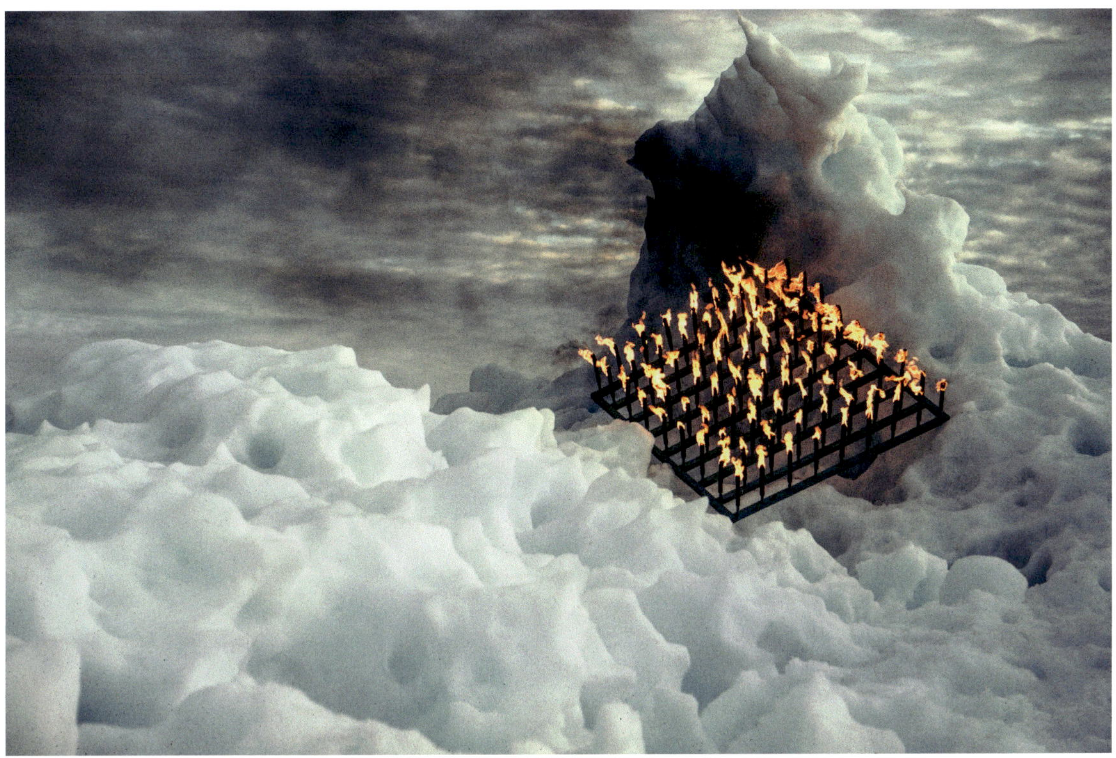

fig. 208 Heinz Mack, *The Fire Raft in the Iceberg*, Greenland, Arctic, 1976, photo: Thomas Höpker

Sublime images like those created by Friedrich, Church, and Mack, which strive to be timeless and isolated from concrete events, could indeed make it easier to view nature as something for which humanity bears responsibility. While facing the vast, hostile landscape might make us feel infinitely small and insignificant, it can also convey a sense of some higher order that would be violated by interfering with this landscape or even damaging it irreversibly. What is more, facing the sublime allows us to feel part of a greater whole – and thereby appreciate that the destruction of that greater whole also directly affects us.

In her investigation of a similar argument, art historian Birgit Schneider also warns that an aesthetic of the sublime can be trapped in a "logic of the spectacle," which places the audience in a state of overwhelmed passive awe – and therefore fails to help motivate humans to act or change their existing behaviors.[23] Her colleague Anne Hemkendreis, who is generally more open to a renaissance of the sublime, also states her concern that depictions of vast and empty landscapes could nourish fantasies of purity, which are inherently aggressive and rooted in colonial traditions of conquest: "sublime icescapes often reiterate colonial perspectives."[24]

While Heinz Mack's *Arctic Project* is indeed characterized by a search for "pure natural space,"[25] his objects approached that space with a certain variety and playfulness. Mack used it as the foundation for interventions that were meant to impress, but not to intimidate, his remote audience. But while the colorful lights of the resulting photographs may have inspired viewers to embark on their own journeys and seek out new experiences in the 1970s, the same images seem like relics of a bygone light-heartedness today. As a result, it is almost impossible to abstain from assigning meaning to these objects. Is the *Fire Raft* a

23 Birgit Schneider, "Sublime Aesthetics in the Era of Climate Crisis? A Critique," in: T. J. Demos, Emily Eliza Scott, and Subhankar Banerjee, eds., *The Routledge Companion to Contemporary Art, Visual Culture and Climate Change* (New York: Routledge, 2021), 263–73, here 272.

24 Anne Hemkendreis, "Who owns the Arctic? Polar Heroism and Climate Change in Mariele Neudecker's Tankwork *Cook and Peary* (2013)," *Inquiries into Art, History, and the Visual* 4 (2022): 893–916, here 908.

25 Rüth, "Heinz Mack und sein Sahara-Projekt," 31.

figs. 196, 208
figs. 185, 197
figs. 192, 207

monument after all? Are we not forced to think of surveillance when we see weather balloons, to think of the oil rigs of the fossil fuel era when we see pillars rising from the ocean?

But as much as Mack's images from the Arctic have become burdened with negative associations, they still show a beautiful dream – it has merely turned from a prophecy to an illusion. From today's perspective, the things we see in these images of the Arctic are too good to be true. This in turn also makes it easier to leave behind all those expectations that were once tied to it, allowing the pictures of Mack's Arctic experiments to help us more consciously bid that promised future farewell. Contemplating it could even be a spiritual exercise.

Ultimately, the images could contribute to the "metamorphosis" diagnosed by French philosopher Bruno Latour in his final years. In his book *After Lockdown: A Metamorphosis* (2021), Latour analyzes how the knowledge of ecological mechanisms and the expectation of catastrophic events changes human perception and requires us to modify our understanding of ourselves. Based on his impressions from the pandemic and its brutal lesson that one's behavior could have direct and potentially lethal consequences for others, but also as a result of the growing presence of climate change, Latour describes how he realized he had "undergone an actual metamorphosis," writing: "I still remember how, before, I could move around innocently taking my body with me. Now I feel like I have to make an effort and haul along at my back a long trail of CO2 that won't let me buy a plane ticket and take off, and that now hampers my every movement, to the point where I hardly dare tap at my keyboard for fear of causing ice to melt somewhere far away."[26]

The metamorphosis thus consists in no longer perceiving oneself as an autonomous, free individual, but experiencing life from within a network of dependencies and causalities. This is quite a painful realization. Latour speaks of a "nightmare" – and of the desire to "go back to what I was before: free, whole, mobile"[27] – at the same time, he understands that it will not be possible to carry on as before. All the more important, he concludes, to develop techniques to perceive this metamorphosis as more than just loss. In order to develop curiosity for what it might be like to exist in such a closely knit network with completely different life forms and no longer have to feel the impotence of individuality, it is first necessary to break ties with the old way of life. To have been "free, whole, mobile" is all well and good as a memory of the past, but it should also be recognized as an unfulfillable maxim of life; only then can we look back at that past without bitterness.

In this sense, Heinz Mack's Arctic art offers an excellent contribution. Furthermore, it could also make sense to heed one of the prophecies for the year 2000 which the artist made in the late 1970s. He was certain that there would be "a monument, [...] a kind of sacred architecture" – a "glass cube" measuring 50 × 50 × 50 meters. In Mack's vision, this cube would contain "nothing but pure ozone, pure air."[28] What could be a better monument to climate change and environmental protection? A relic from a time in which we still believed purity was achievable, and a memorial for a time in which our hopes for a good ecological future have been buried?

fig. 209

Translated from the German by Dan Lawler.

26 Bruno Latour, *After Lockdown: A Metamorphosis* (Cambridge: Polity Press, 2021), 2–3.

27 Ibid., 3.

28 Mack, "Kunst 2000," 55.

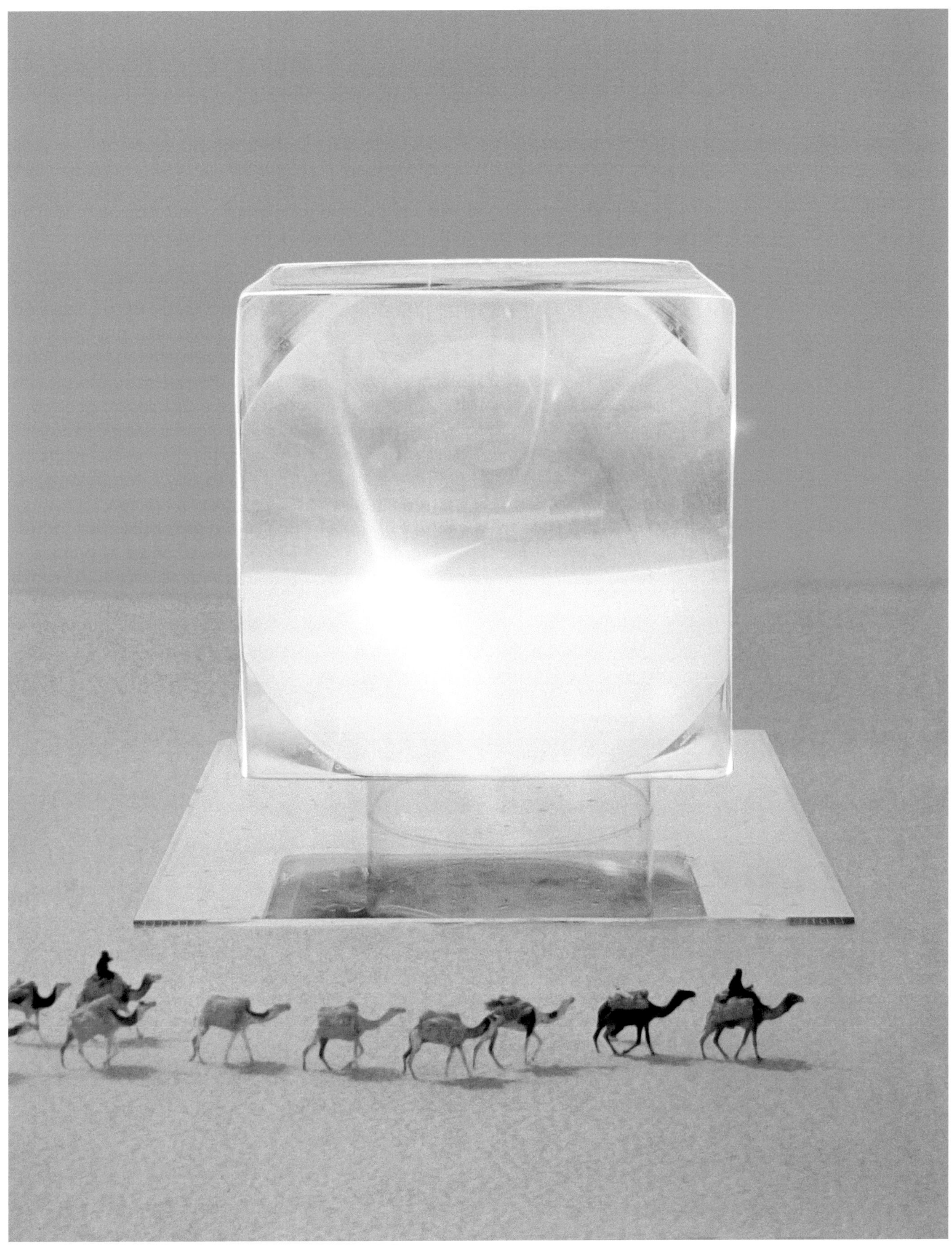

fig. 209 Heinz Mack, *Design for the Symposion*, 1960, photo collage, 48,5 × 33 cm

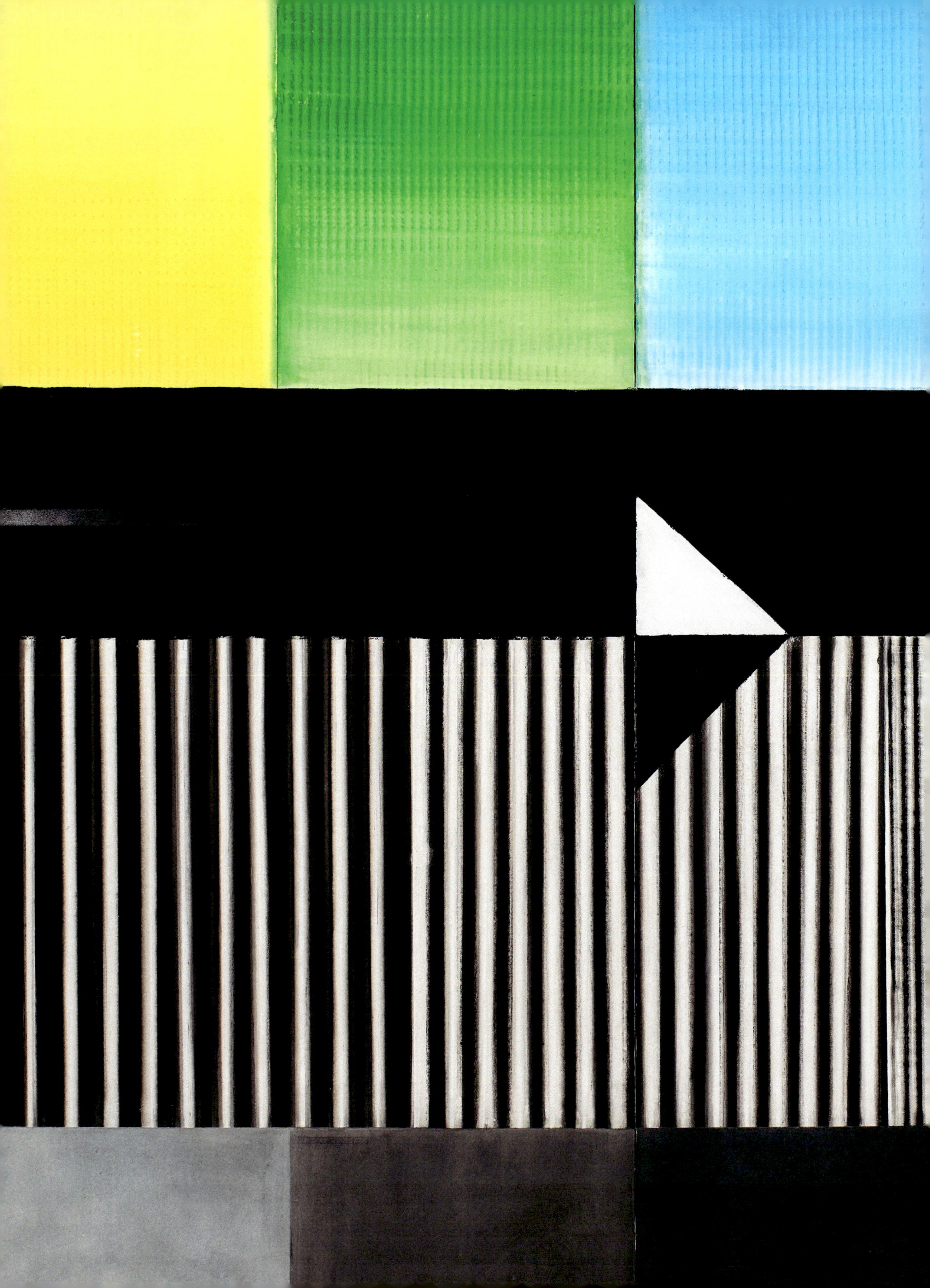

Chromatic Constellations

For the exhibition at the ZKM | Karlsruhe, Heinz Mack has created the site-specific installation *Crown of Flags* for the Subspace of the ZKM glass cube. Many lengths of fabrics in various sizes and colors form a crown hanging from the ceiling. Fans equipped with timers set the textile banners in motion, while spotlights make the colors glow. The work is aligned above a circular platform, an architectural feature that was originally designed to show sculptures from the ZKM Collection.

Flags waving in the wind, using the air as a creative element, are recurring motifs in Mack's work. They can be found in numerous works in public spaces, from sculptural installations to experimental interventions in the Sahara as well as in the Arctic. The term "crown" evokes associations with a corona (Latin for crown), which describes light phenomena, haloes, around the sun or moon that result from the diffraction of light waves.

The exploration of light and color is a central objective of Heinz Mack's artistic practice. He determines the composition of the colors through an ordering system that he finds intuitively. The respective incidence of light determines the intensity, purity, luminosity, and radiance of the colors. The *Crown of Flags* visualizes such phenomena and at the same time creates a fascinating interplay of color, light, and movement that fills the space.

← *fig. 210* Heinz Mack, *Big Light Spectrum, Color Spectrum – A Tribute to Johann Wolfgang von Goethe*, 1982, detail

I have a passionately vital relationship to color — Dionysus supports me in this. Occasionally, Apollo visits me in my studio and sees to it that the color is filled with light and finds its form. *

Works in the exhibition:
All works courtesy of the artist
unless otherwise noted

Big Light Spectrum, Color Spectrum – A Tribute to Johann Wolfgang von Goethe
1982
Painting: pigment, wax crayon,
synthetic resin on wood and paper
304 × 404 × 12 cm
→ *figs.* 210, 212

Crown of Flags
2023
Installation: textile, wood construction,
wide beam spots, fans, timer
Ø 6.7 m, lengths of fabric, 37 cm wide,
50 to 320 cm long
Produced in cooperation with ZKM | Karlsruhe
→ *figs.* 211, 213, 214

* Heinz Mack quoted from Walter Smerling and Eva Müller-Remmert, eds., *Mack. Apollo in my studio*, exh. cat. Museum Küppersmühle, Duisburg (Cologne: Wienand, 2015), 40.

↗ *fig.* 211 Heinz Mack, *Crown of Flags*, 2023, exhibition view, ZKM | Karlsruhe 2023

→ *fig.* 212 Heinz Mack, *Big Light Spectrum, Color Spectrum – A Tribute to Johann Wolfgang von Goethe*, 1982

→→ *figs.* 213, 214 Heinz Mack, *Crown of Flags*, 2023, exhibition view, ZKM | Karlsruhe 2023

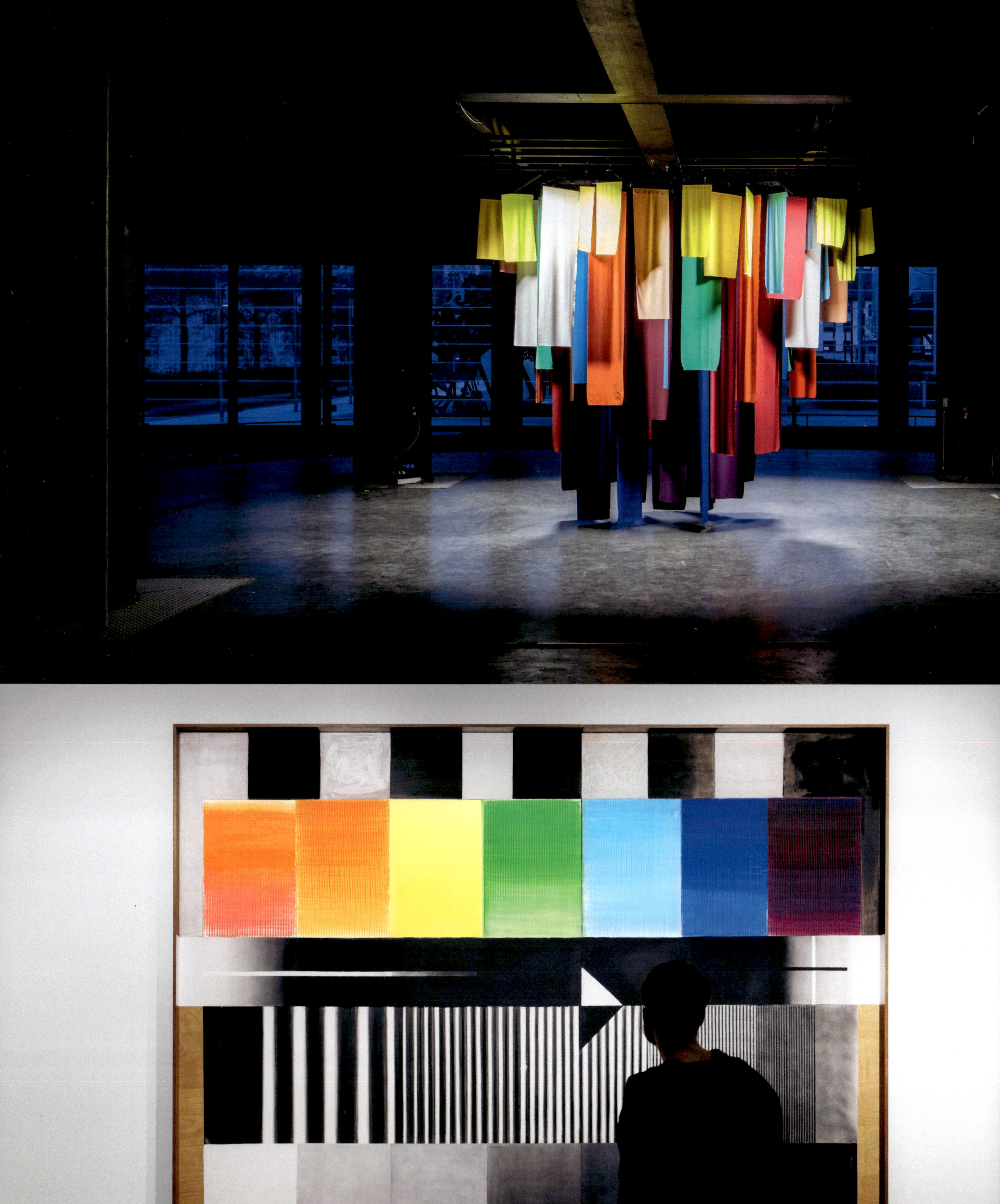

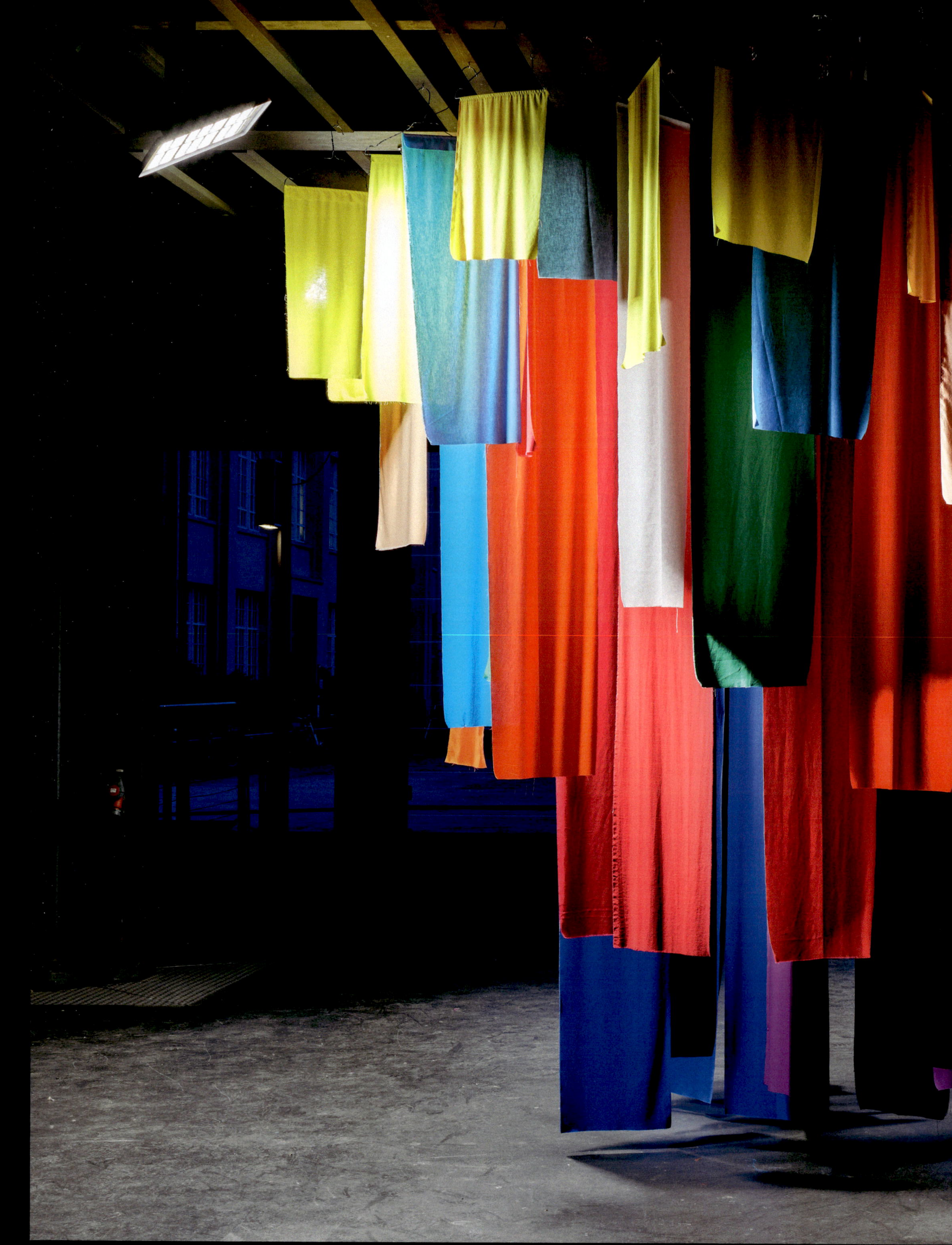

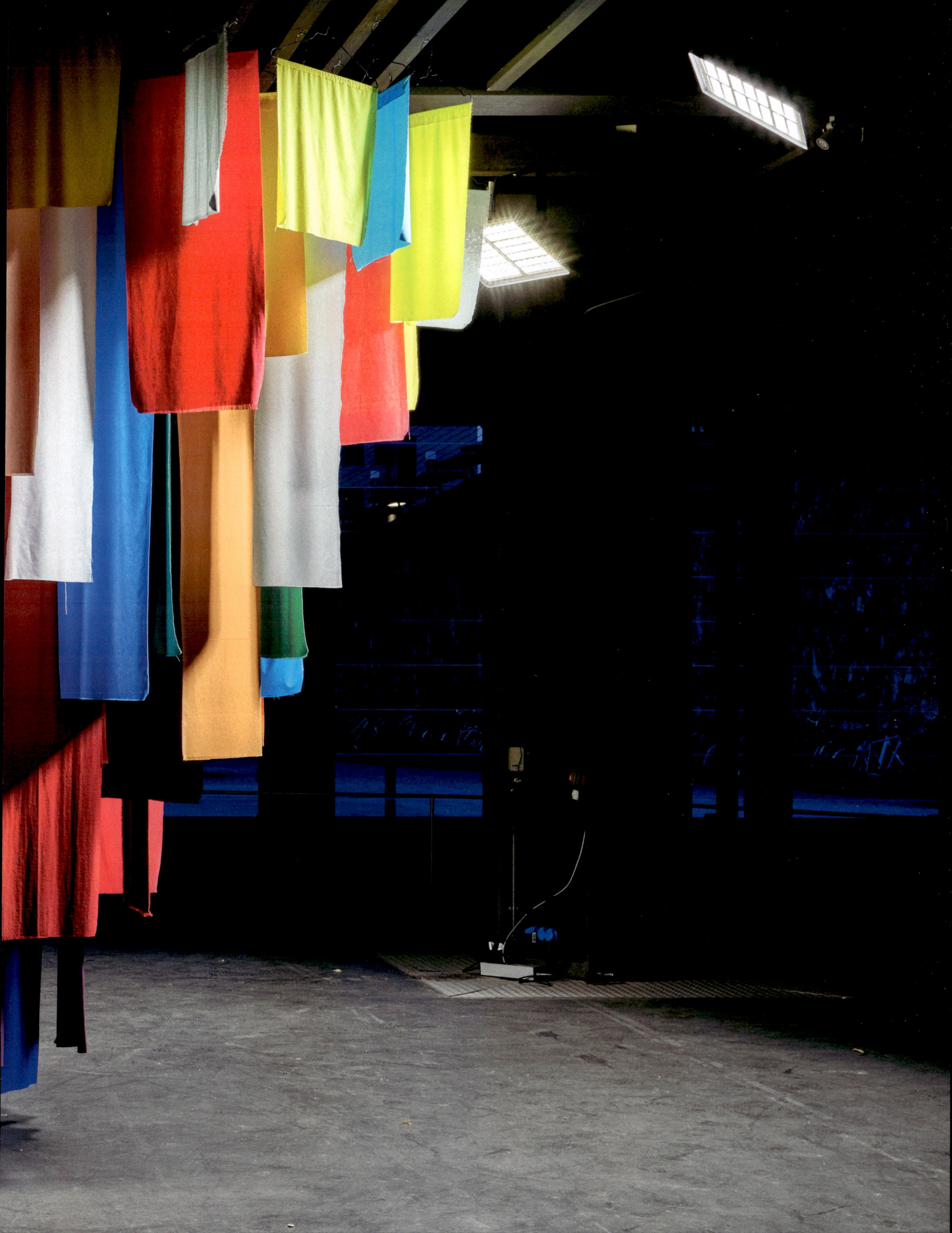

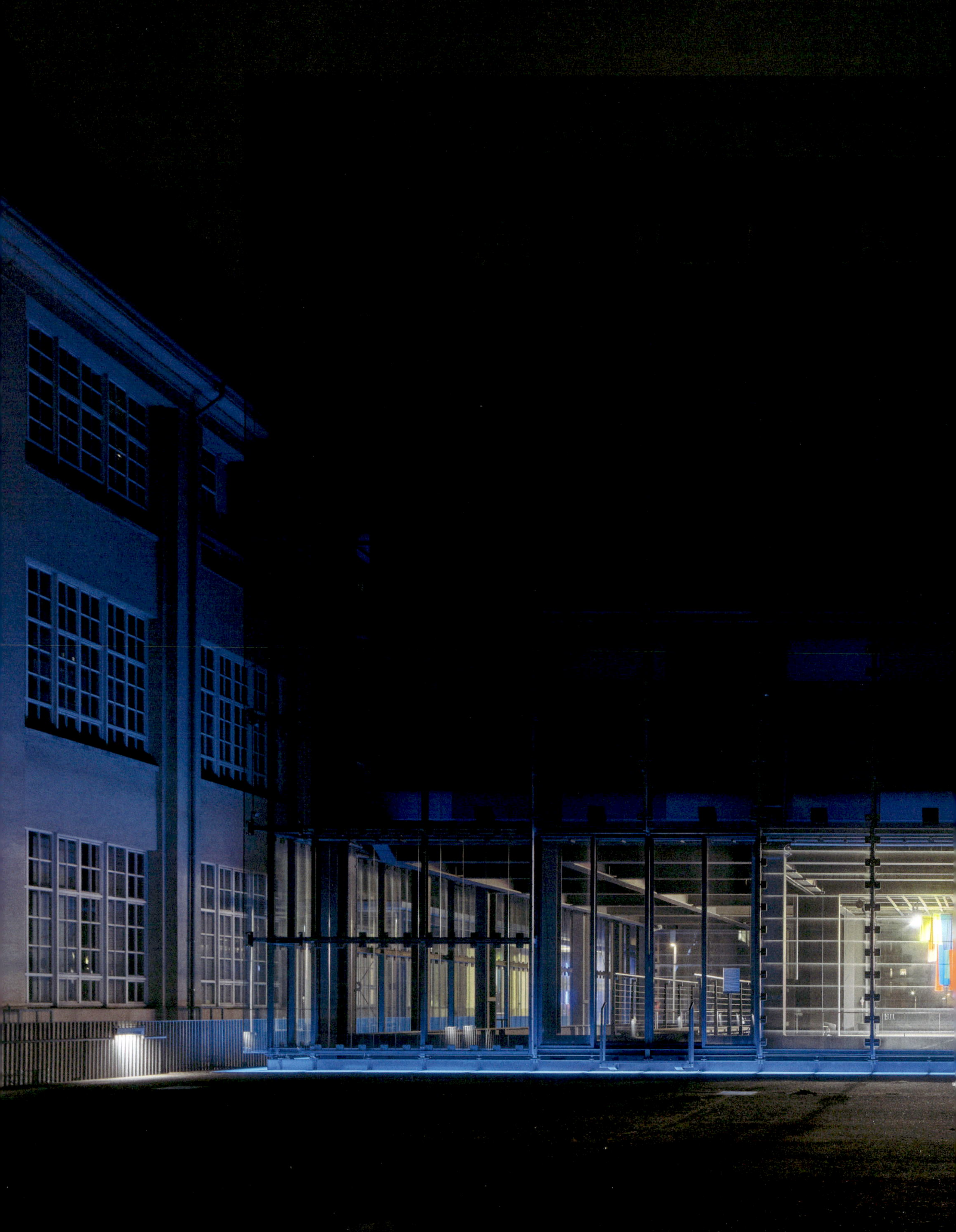

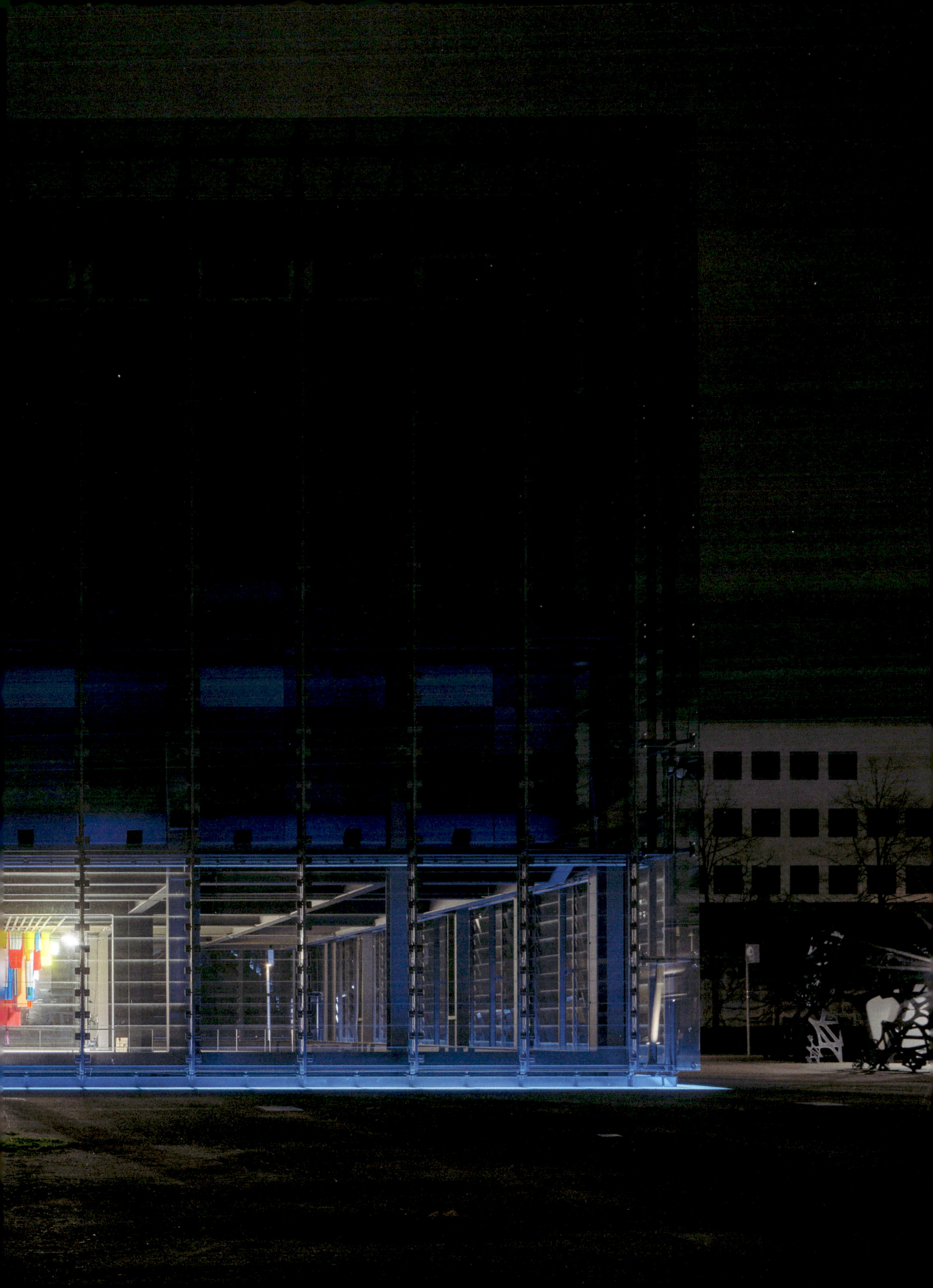

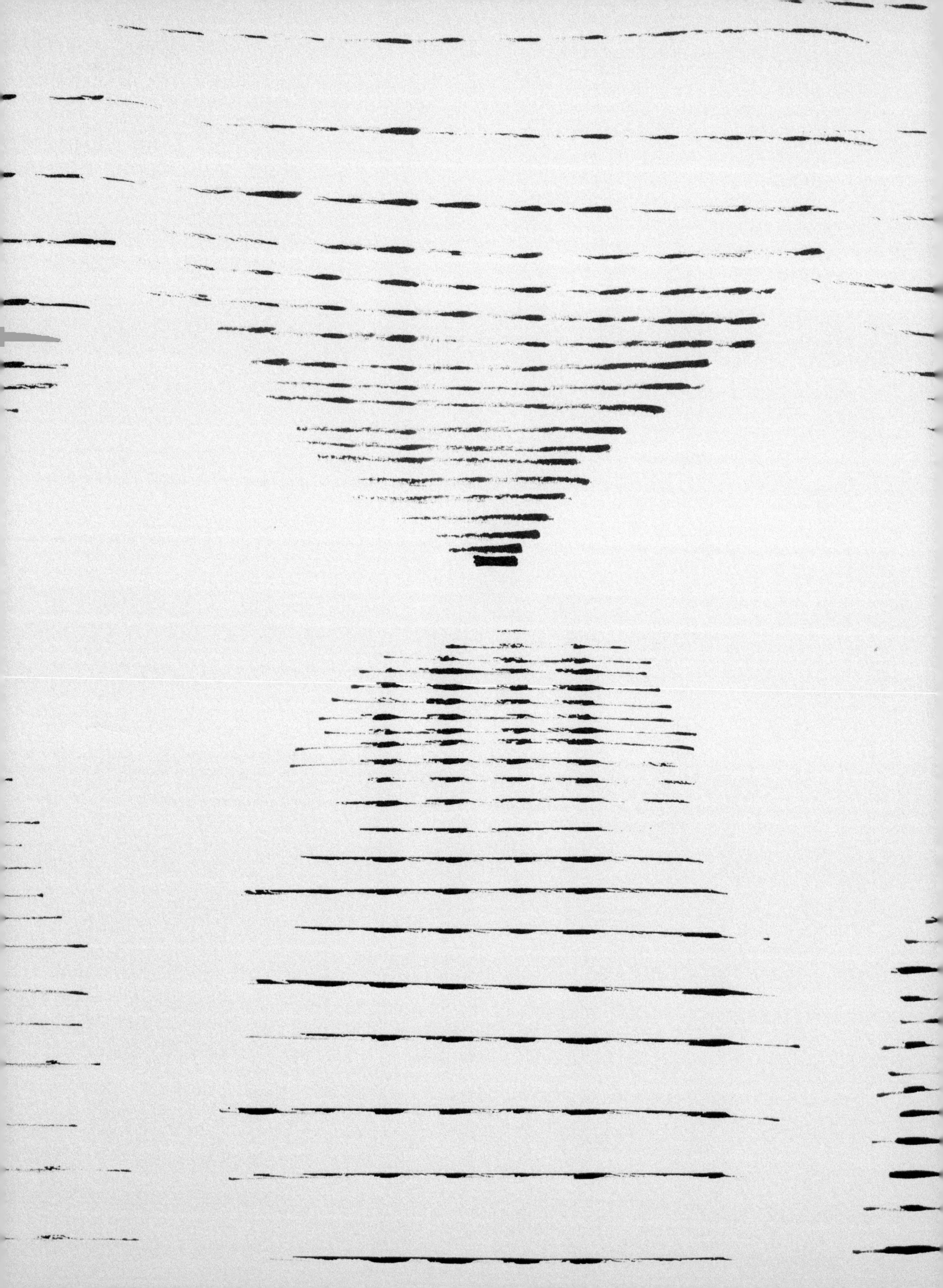

The Repose of Restlessness

When Heinz Mack left the Düsseldorf Art Academy in 1953, the German art scene was dominated by abstract Informalist painting. In keeping with the artistic new beginning demanded by the ZERO group, Mack soon broke away from this color-intensive, subjective art. In his paintings and graphic works, he replaced traditional composition with simple two-dimensional structures which he called "structural zones." He filled the surface with similar pictorial elements, using very little color. Mack's monochrome surfaces almost seem to vibrate due to their dynamic structure.

Just like his steles with their clear-cut geometry, Mack's serial arrays have a connection to Minimal Art. This era-defining art movement from the United States in the 1960s also avoided traditional compositions in favor of repeated forms in geometric sequences and often used industrial materials. In the design of his surfaces, however, Mack works intuitively and is open to irregularities.

In his reliefs made of wood, paper, or plaster, Mack puts three-dimensional structures on the surface, building out beyond the conventions of the flat plane. Color gradations are no longer necessary here, as real light becomes the constitutive factor. The incidence of light and the casting of shadows produce dynamic rhythms, creating an expression of continuous movement and vibration. Thus, the reliefs can be understood as "instruments of light."

In addition to a selection of early ZERO paintings, reliefs, and drawings, this section of the exhibition also features several white marble sculptures. Mack sees himself primarily as a sculptor, and in the last 20 years, the artist has increasingly turned to creating sculptures made of stone, some of monumental size.

← *fig. 215* Heinz Mack, *Untitled*, 1957, detail

*The restlessness of the line: it wants to become surface; the restlessness of the surface: it wants to become space. This restlessness is what guides a painter's sensibility. Lines, surfaces, and spaces must continually blend into each other, cancelling out each other in that dialectal sense that our language allows. If this integration is kept visible, a painting begins to vibrate, and our eye can find rest within restlessness.**

Works in the exhibition:
All works courtesy of the artist
unless otherwise noted

Rhythmic Progression of a Cube
1996 (idea: 1977)
Sculpture: marble, wood
29 × 55 × 35 cm, base 93 × 28 × 28 cm
→ *figs. 227, 228*

White Marble Stele
2012
Sculpture: marble
284 × 25 × 9.5 cm, plinth 11.5 × 60 × 60 cm

Untitled
1958
Relief: synthetic resin, sawdust, pigments, cardboard, wood
83 × 95 × 7 cm

White Relief
1959
Relief: synthetic resin, wood, acrylic glass
88 × 71 × 4.5 cm
→ *fig. 220*

Untitled
1955
Relief: wood
79 × 56 × 12 cm
→ *fig. 224*

Elementary Stone Block
2017
Sculpture: marble, wood
60 × 37 × 37 cm, base 100 × 28.5 × 34 cm
→ *figs. 226, 228*

4 FREQUENCIES
1959
Painting: synthetic resin on canvas
132 × 194 cm

Structure Dynamic Blanc
1958
Painting: synthetic resin on canvas
111 × 89 cm
→ *fig. 228*

Untitled
1957/1958
Painting: synthetic resin and cork on nettle
101.5 × 117 cm
Private Collection
→ *fig. 219*

White Rhythm
1960
Relief: synthetic resin, wood, acrylic glass
90 × 100 × 9 cm
Private collection

Design for Wall Relief
1956
Relief: wood
70 × 92 × 7 cm
→ *fig. 223*

White Relief Trail
1959
Relief: synthetic resin, wood, acrylic glass
87 × 67.5 × 7.5 cm
→ *fig. 222*

White Relief
1964
Relief: synthetic resin, plaster, burlap, wood, acrylic glass
126 × 85.5 × 9 cm
→ *fig. 221*

Wall Relief
1955–1957
Relief: wood
110.5 × 79 × 12.5 cm
→ *fig. 225*

For Étienne-Jules Marey
1969
Drawing: India ink applied to paper with reed pen, framed
139 × 103.5 × 6 cm
→ *fig. 218*

For Étienne-Jules Marey
1969
Drawing: India ink applied to paper with reed pen, framed
139 × 103.5 × 6 cm

For Étienne-Jules Marey
1969
Drawing: India ink applied to paper with reed pen, framed
139 × 103.5 × 6 cm

The Movement of Water
1958
Drawing: India ink with reed pen on Schoeller paper, framed
73 × 54.5 × 5 cm
→ *fig. 217*

Untitled
1957
Drawing: India ink applied to paper with reed pen, framed
73 × 54.5 × 5 cm
→ *figs. 215, 216*

Untitled
1957
Drawing: India ink applied to paper with reed pen, framed
59 × 74 × 5 cm

Untitled
1957
Drawing: India ink applied to paper with reed pen, framed
59 × 74 × 5 cm

Untitled
1958
Drawing: India ink applied to paper with reed pen, framed
59 × 74 × 5 cm

* Heinz Mack, "Die Ruhe der Unruhe," *ZERO*, nr. 2, 1958. Translated from the German.

→ *fig. 216* Heinz Mack, *Untitled*, 1957

→← *fig. 217* Heinz Mack, *The Movement of Water*, 1958
→→ *fig. 218* Heinz Mack, *For Étienne-Jules Marey*, 1969

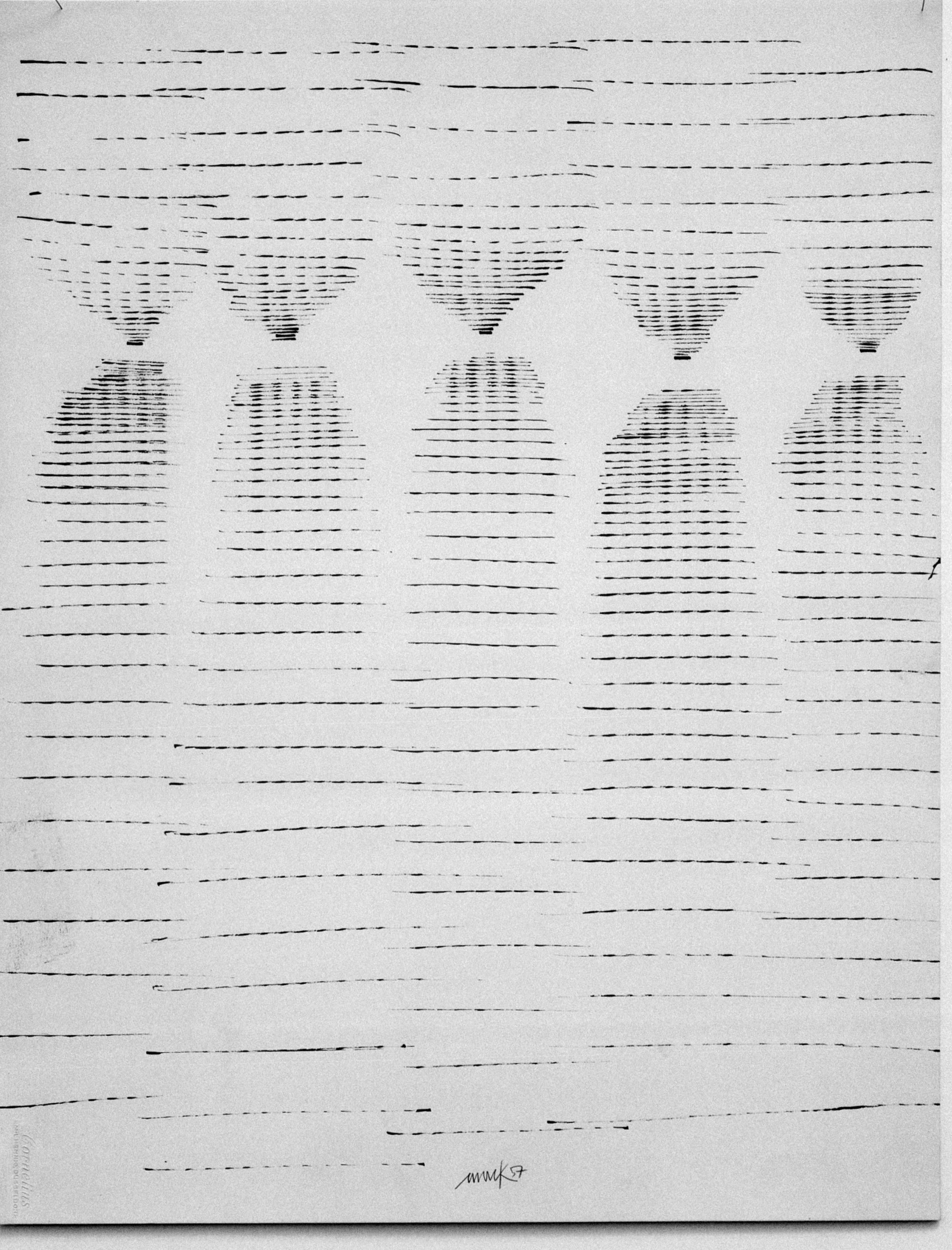

mack 58

„DIE BEWEGUNG DES WASSERS"

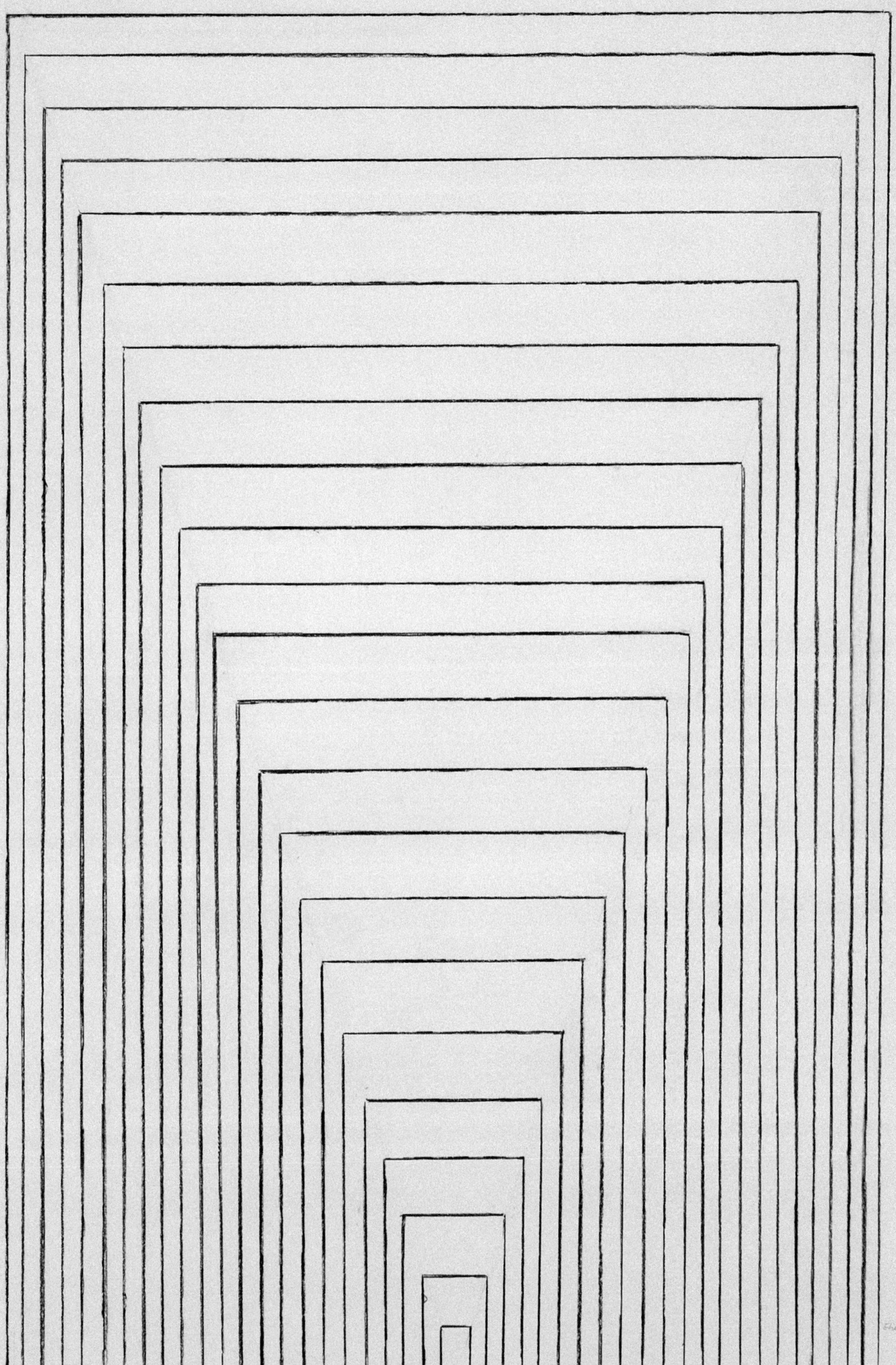
für
Etienne Jules Marey

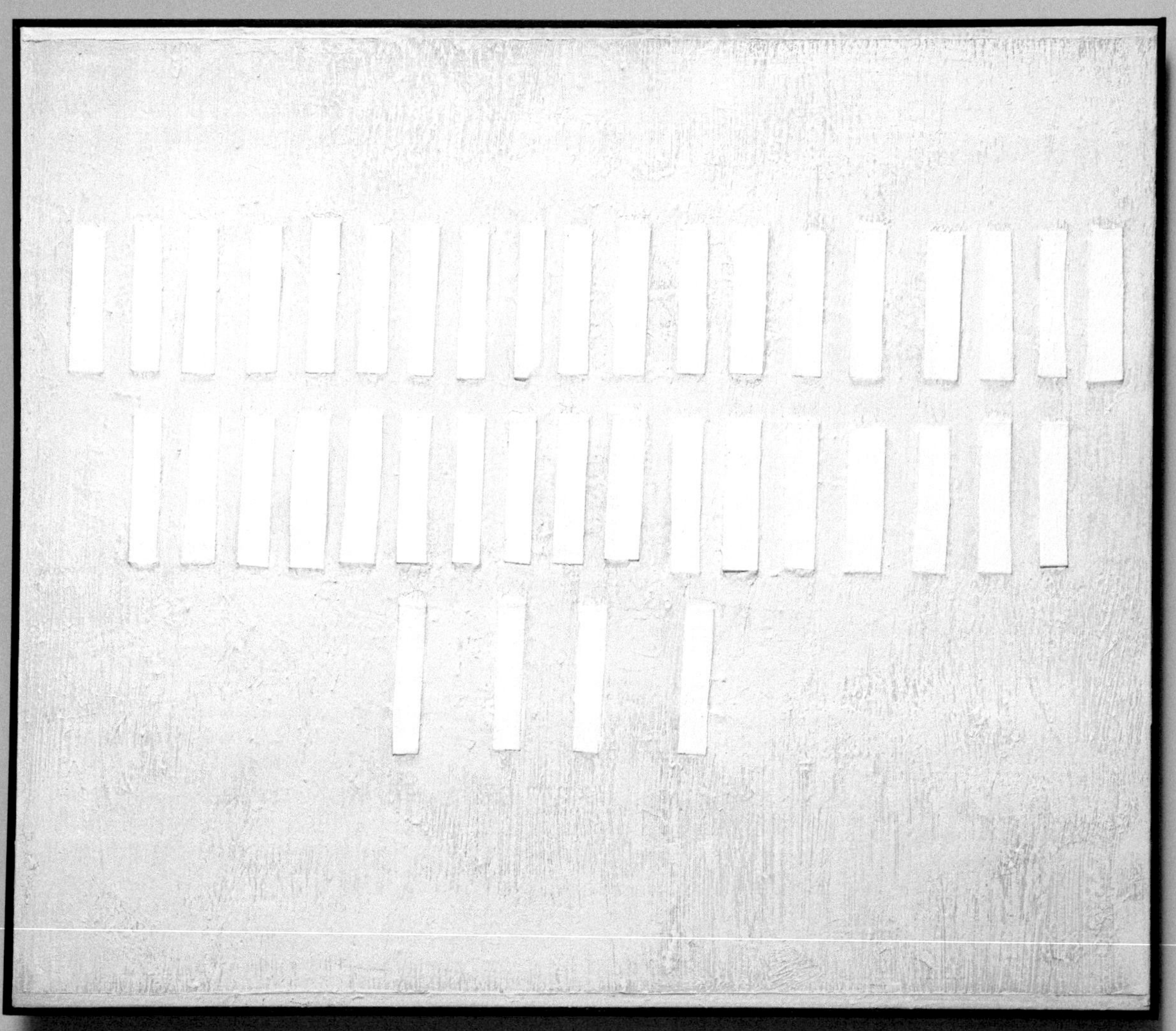

↑ *fig. 219* Heinz Mack, *Untitled*, 1957/1958
→ *fig. 220* Heinz Mack, *White Relief*, 1959

→← *fig. 221* Heinz Mack, *White Relief*, 1964
→→ *fig. 222* Heinz Mack, *White Relief Trail*, 1959

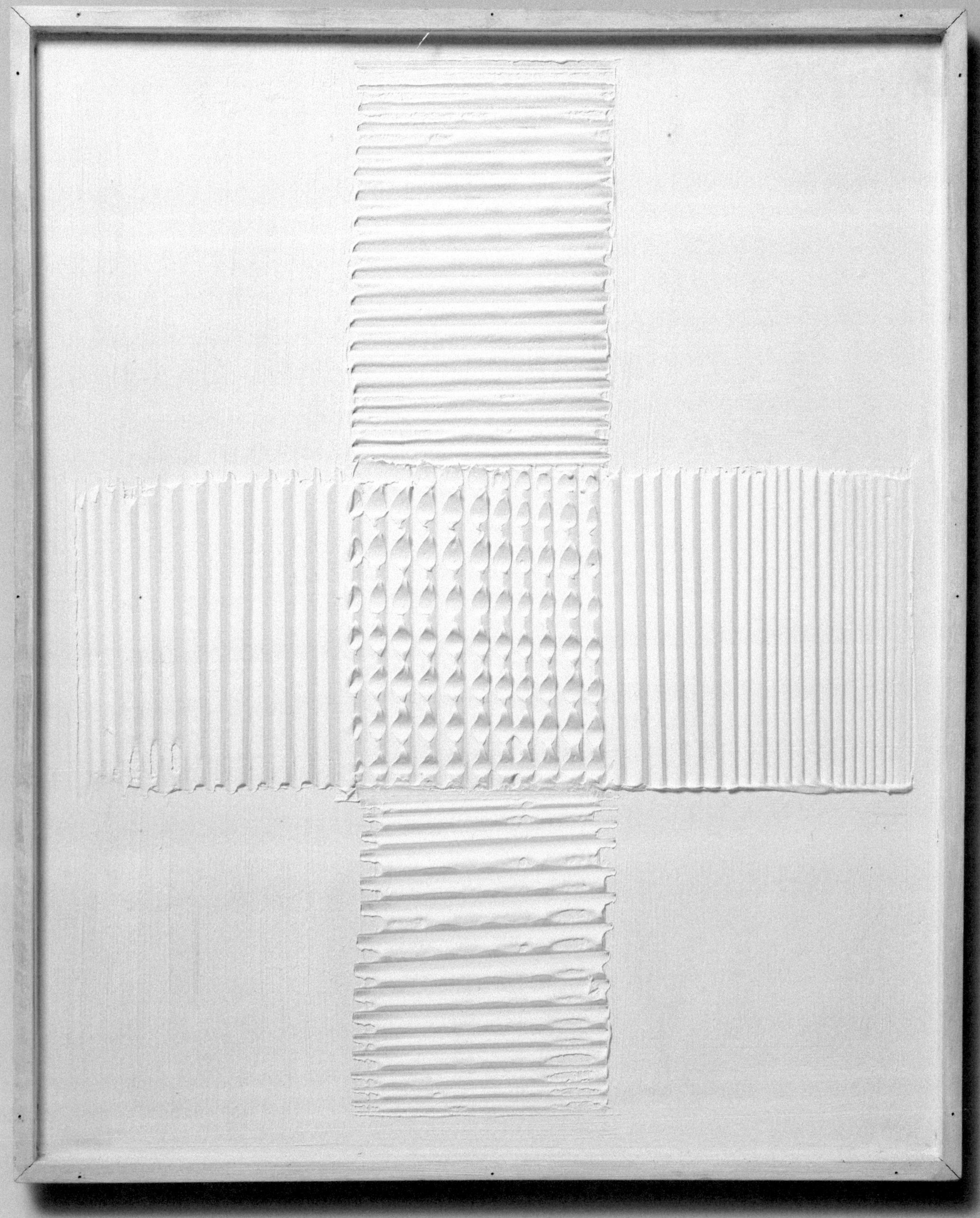

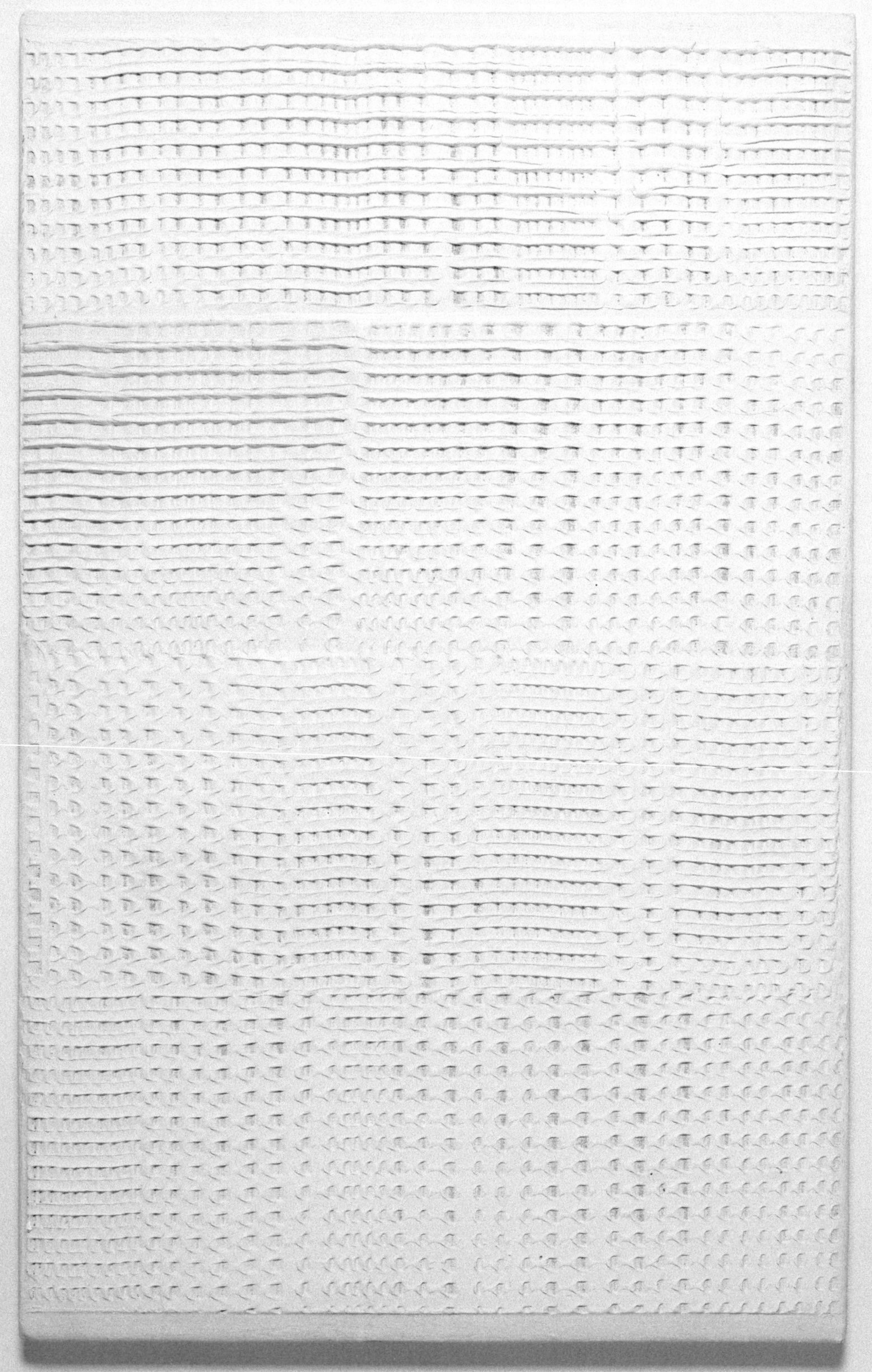

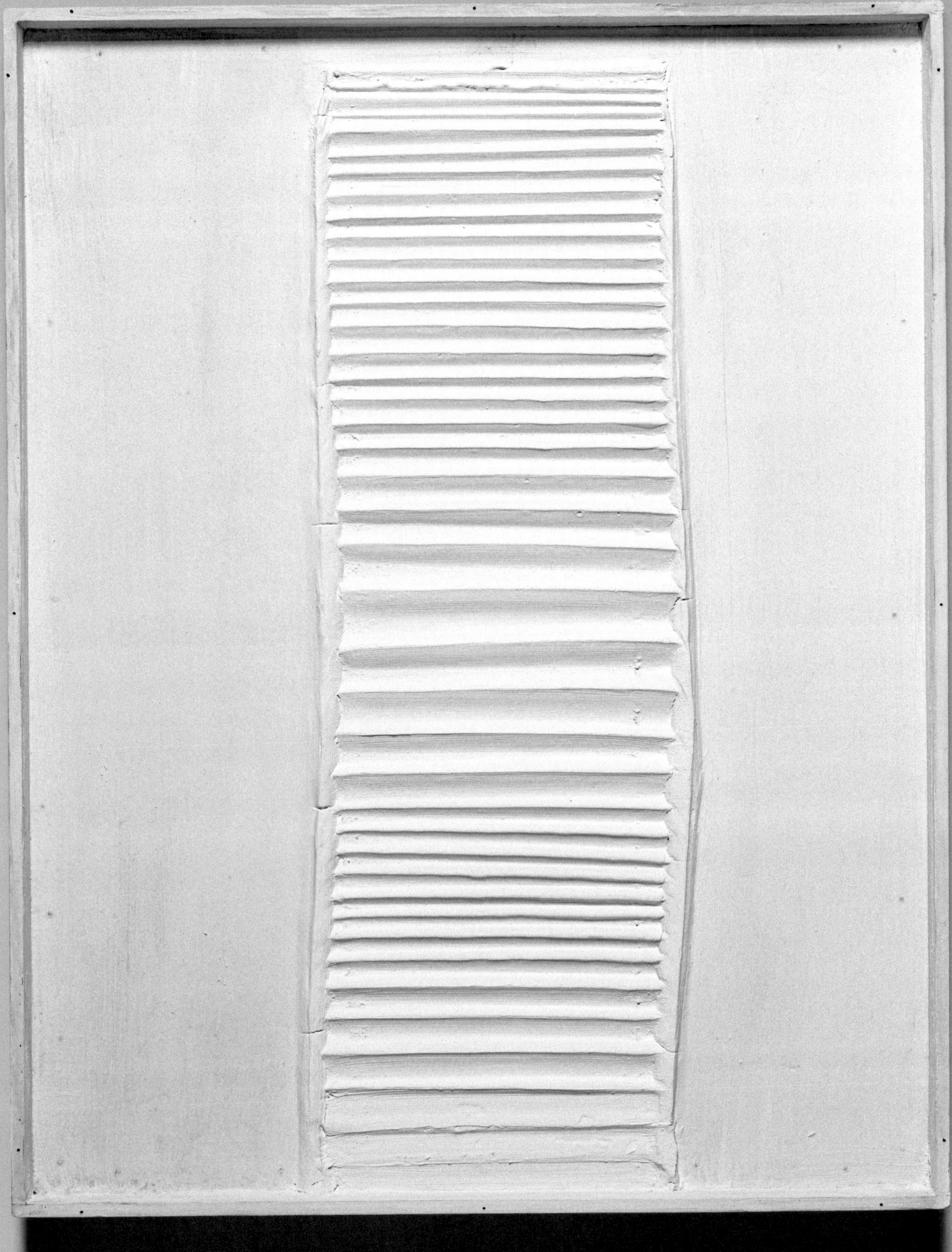

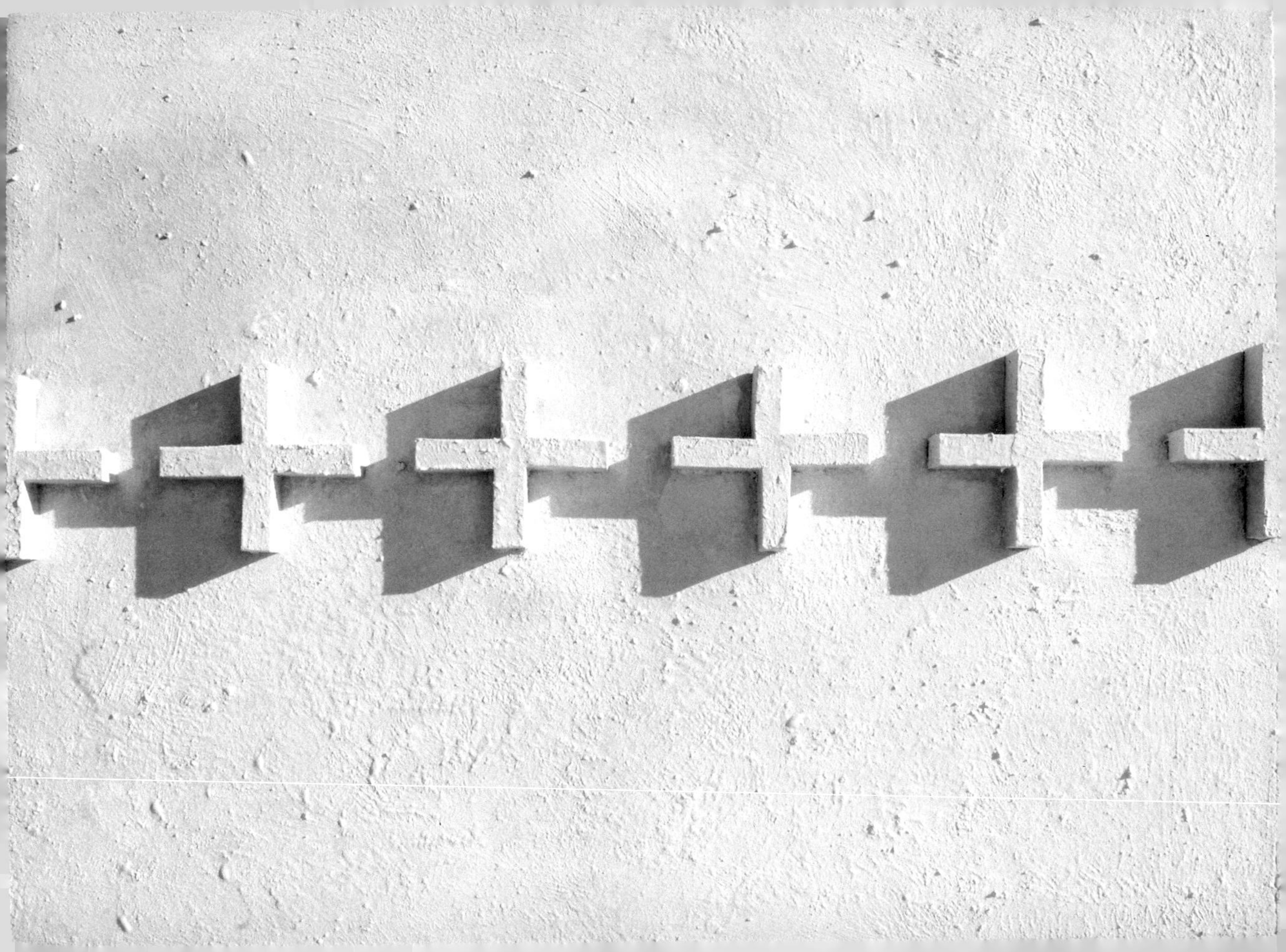

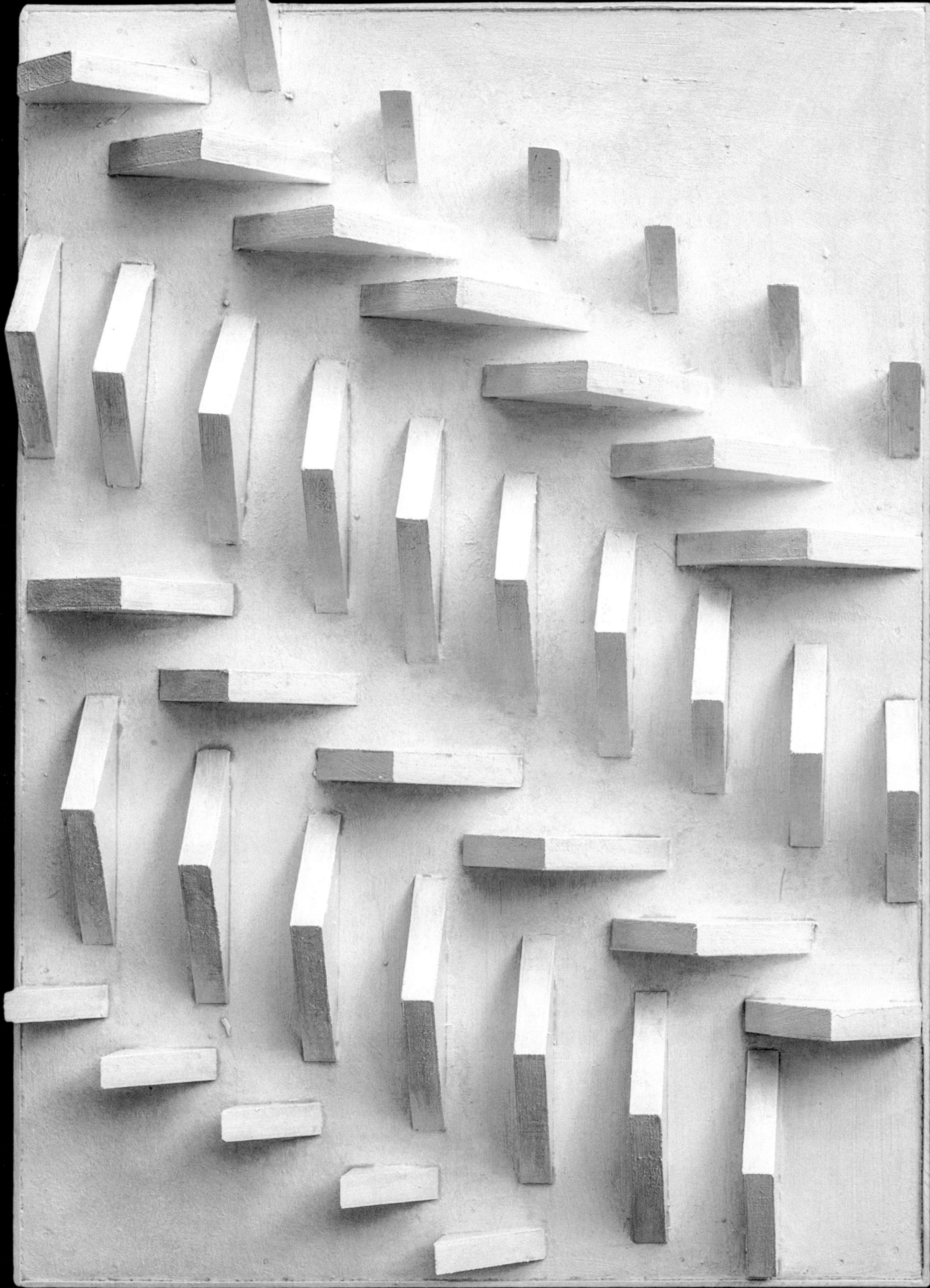

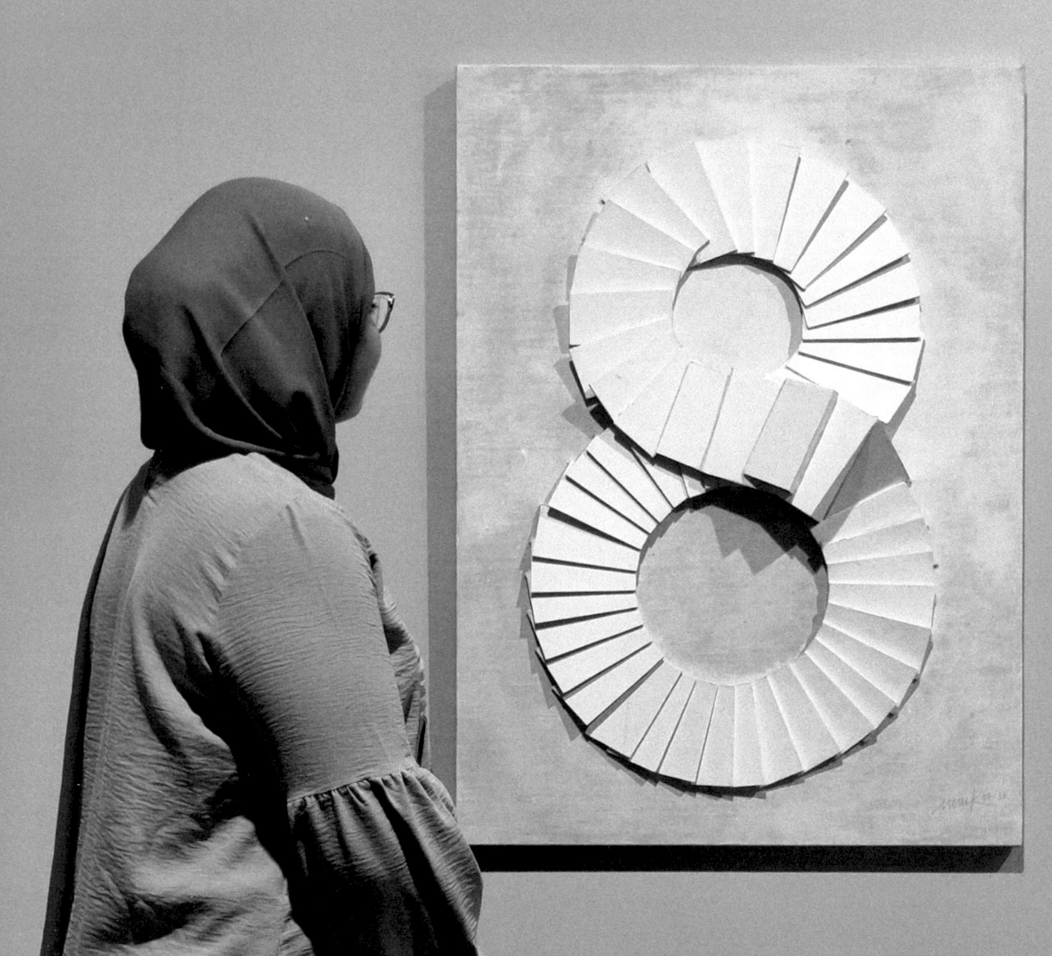

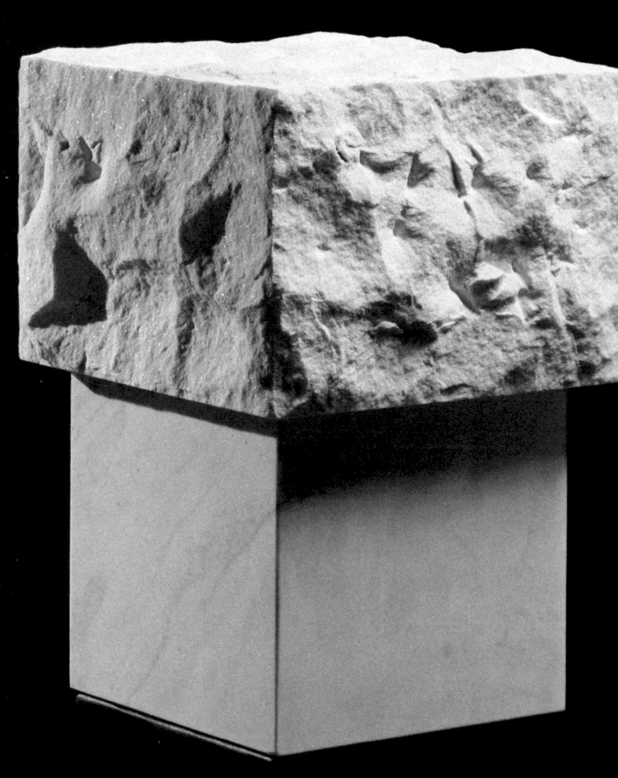

↑ *fig.* 225 Heinz Mack, *Wall Relief*, 1955–1957
← *fig.* 226 Heinz Mack, *Elementary Stone Block*, 2017
↗ *fig.* 227 Heinz Mack, *Rhythmic Progression of a Cube*, 1996 (idea: 1977)
→ *fig.* 228 *Mack at ZKM*, exhibition view, ZKM | Karlsruhe 2022

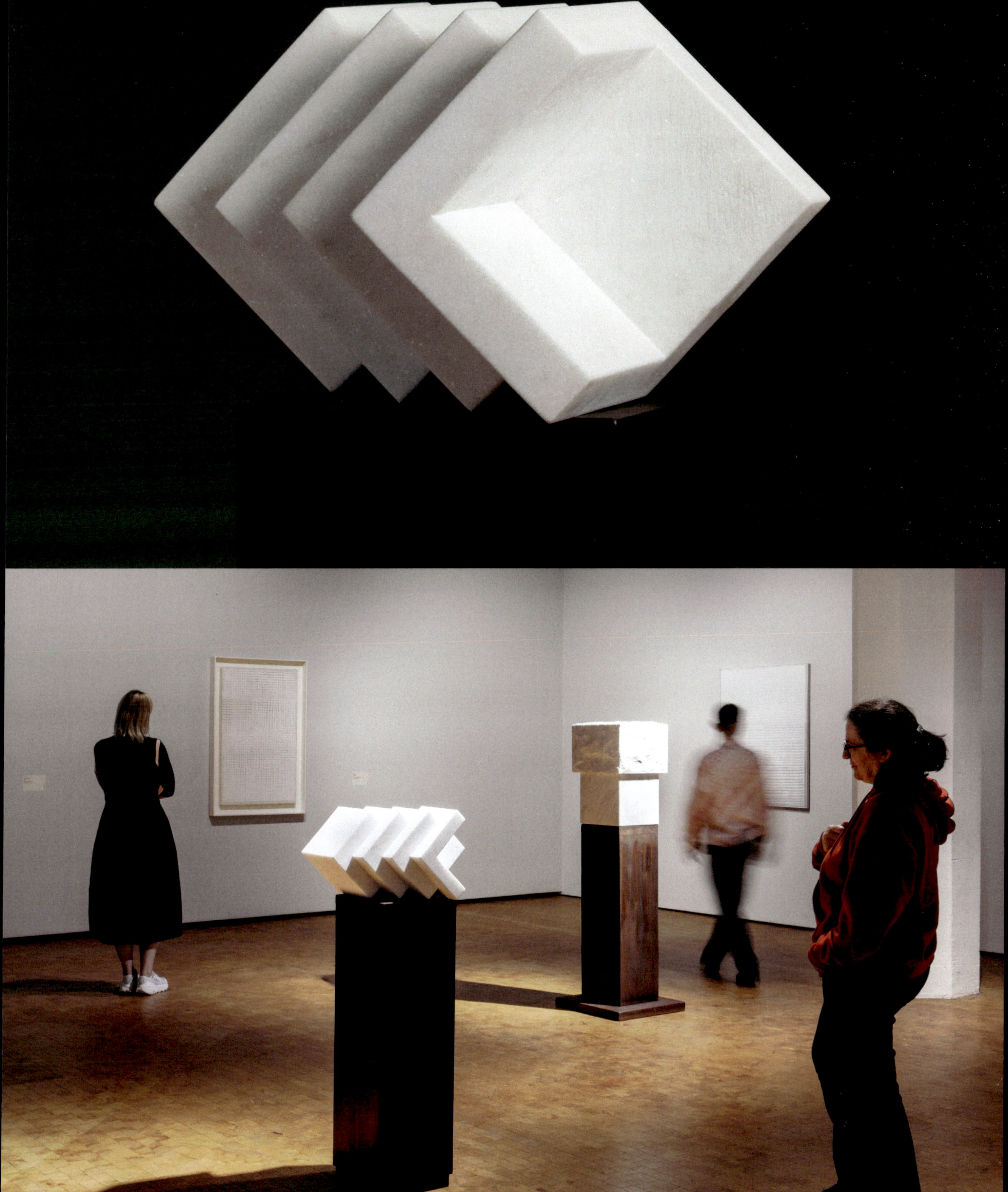

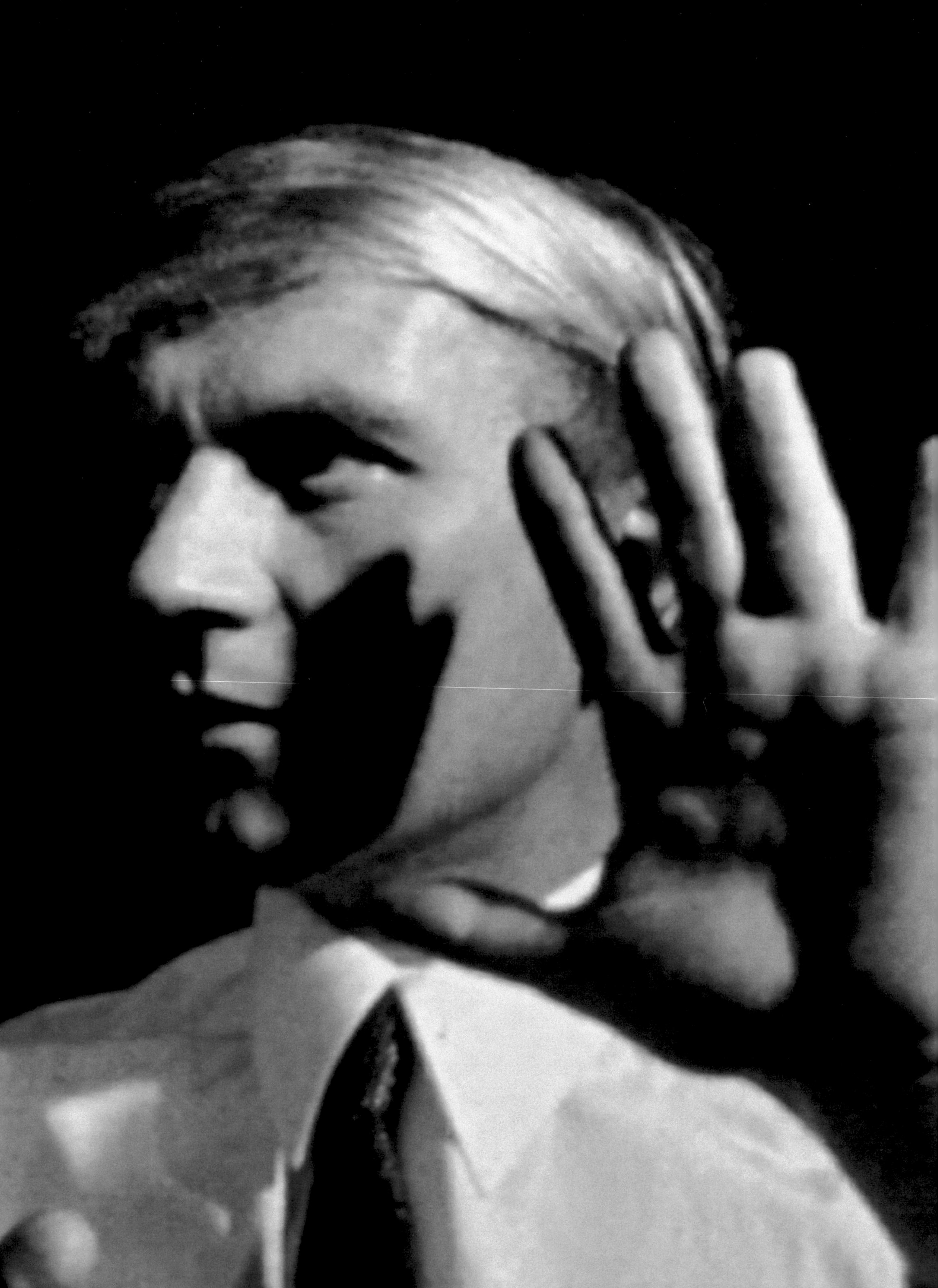

Small Cinema – Films by and about Heinz Mack

The media film, video, and photography play a unique role in the work of Heinz Mack. He assigns these technologies a subordinate function in relation to art, even though they fundamentally revolve around manipulation of light. In the photographic and cinematic processes, images are created by light. The TV set and the computer have monitors that are themselves a source of light. Since the advent of the modern era, light-based media technology has shaped art and enabled new forms of artistic expression. Mack, however, is reticent in engaging with them.

Yet photography and film do find their way into his work. His photographs not only have a documentary function, they also possess an experimental, highly aesthetically charged character. They condense complex ideas into a single image, similarly with the media of film and video. As early as 1962, the film *0 × 0 = Art* was made in collaboration with Gerd Winkler, which introduced the ZERO Group and its ideas. The film is an important document of its time. Various international artists, who were active in ZERO or were associated with the group, were filmed in their studios or while taking part in actions in public spaces.

A few years later, in 1968, Mack made the film *Tele-Mack* with Hans Emmerling, which was broadcast on public television in 1969 and won an award at the Venice Film Biennale in 1970. While shooting the film, Mack also realized parts of his extensive *Sahara Project* in the Tunisian desert. *Tele-Mack* documents the artist's work, but it is an artistic essay that has its own formal language, which reflects the spirit of its time.

In 1990, Mack made *Light Art* for television together with Ingrid LaPlante, a detailed portrait of the artist and his work. Several interviews and artistic actions featured in this film give it a personal touch, and the special lighting of the shots is enhanced by the medium of video.

The presentation of these three films by and about Mack is complemented by the documentary portrait *Mack. Light – Movement – Color* from 2011. For this film, Ralph Goertz and Werner Raeune accompanied the artist in daily life and in his studio.

← *fig. 229* *Tele-Mack*, 1968, film still, detail

*Film and photography should render dream visions visible, for words alone cannot describe ideas. Film and photography only prepare the ground for realizing the project; they are not its realization.**

Works in the exhibition:
All works courtesy of the artist
unless otherwise noted

0 × 0 = Kunst. Maler ohne Farbe und Pinsel
[0 × 0 = Art. Painter Without Paint and Brush]
1962
Film (digitized), b/w, sound, 33:08 min.
Direction: Gerd Winkler
Script: Gerd Winkler
Produced by Hessischer Rundfunk
→ *fig.* 232

Tele-Mack
1968
16 mm film (digitized), color, sound, 45:40 min.
Direction: Hans Emmerling, Heinz Mack
Camera: Edwin K. Braun
Editing: Gisela Kühn
Music: Heinrich Konietzny
Institut für Moderne Kunst Nürnberg, produced by Telefilm Saar GmbH on behalf of Saarländischer Rundfunk and WDR/ Westdeutsches Fernsehen
→ *figs.* 229, 231

***Lichtkunst* [Light Art]**
1990
Video, color, sound, 41:51 min.
A film by: Ingrid LaPlante
Camera: Kurt Chmel, Reinhold Vorschneider, Emmerich Pal
Sound: Wolfgang Brinschwitz
Cut: Hildegard Roser
Speaker: Christine Davis
A production of SWF Baden-Baden

Mack. Light – Movement – Color
2011
Video, color, sound, 42:00 min.
A film by: Ralph Goertz and Werner Raeune
Institut für Kunstdokumentation und Szenografie
→ *fig.* 230

* Heinz Mack in Henri Nannen, ed., *Mack. Expedition in künstliche Gärten*, photography by Thomas Höpker (Hamburg: Gruner + Jahr, 1977), n. p. Translated from the German.

→ *fig.* 230 *Mack. Light – Movement – Color*, 2011, exhibition view, ZKM | Karlsruhe 2023

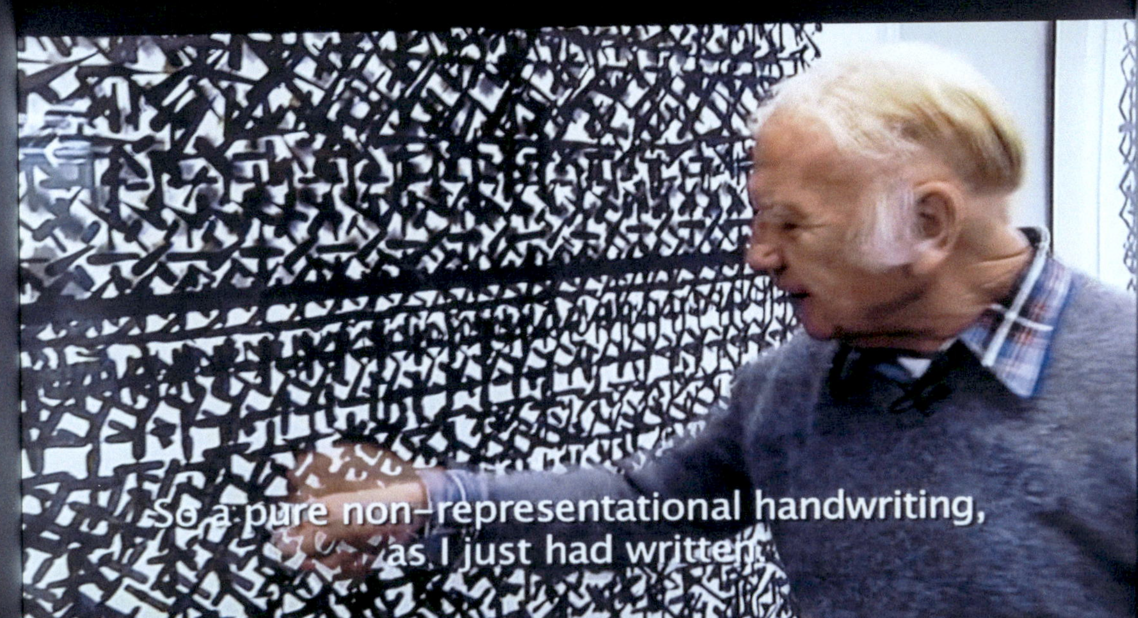
So a pure non-representational handwriting,
as I just had written.

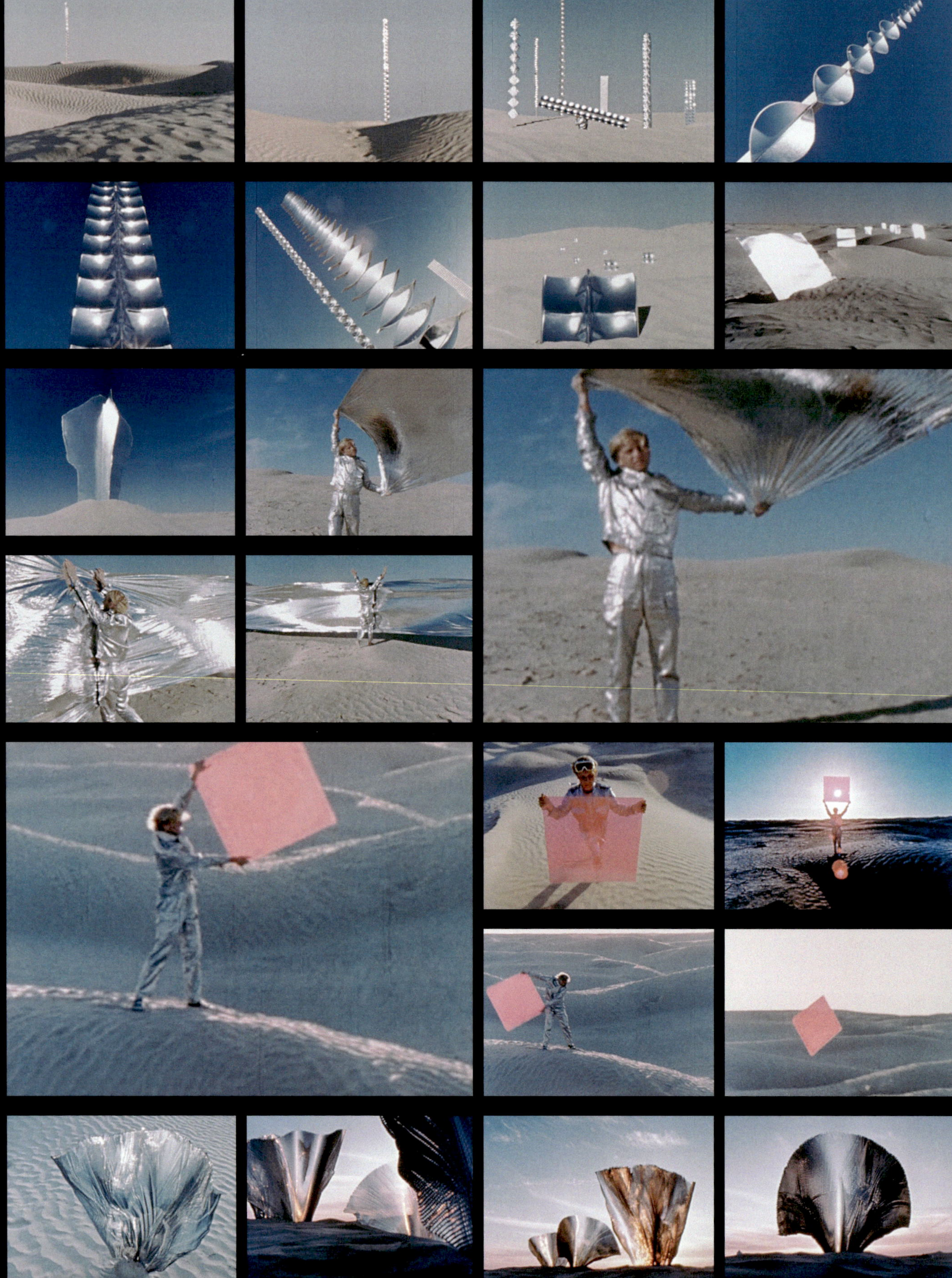

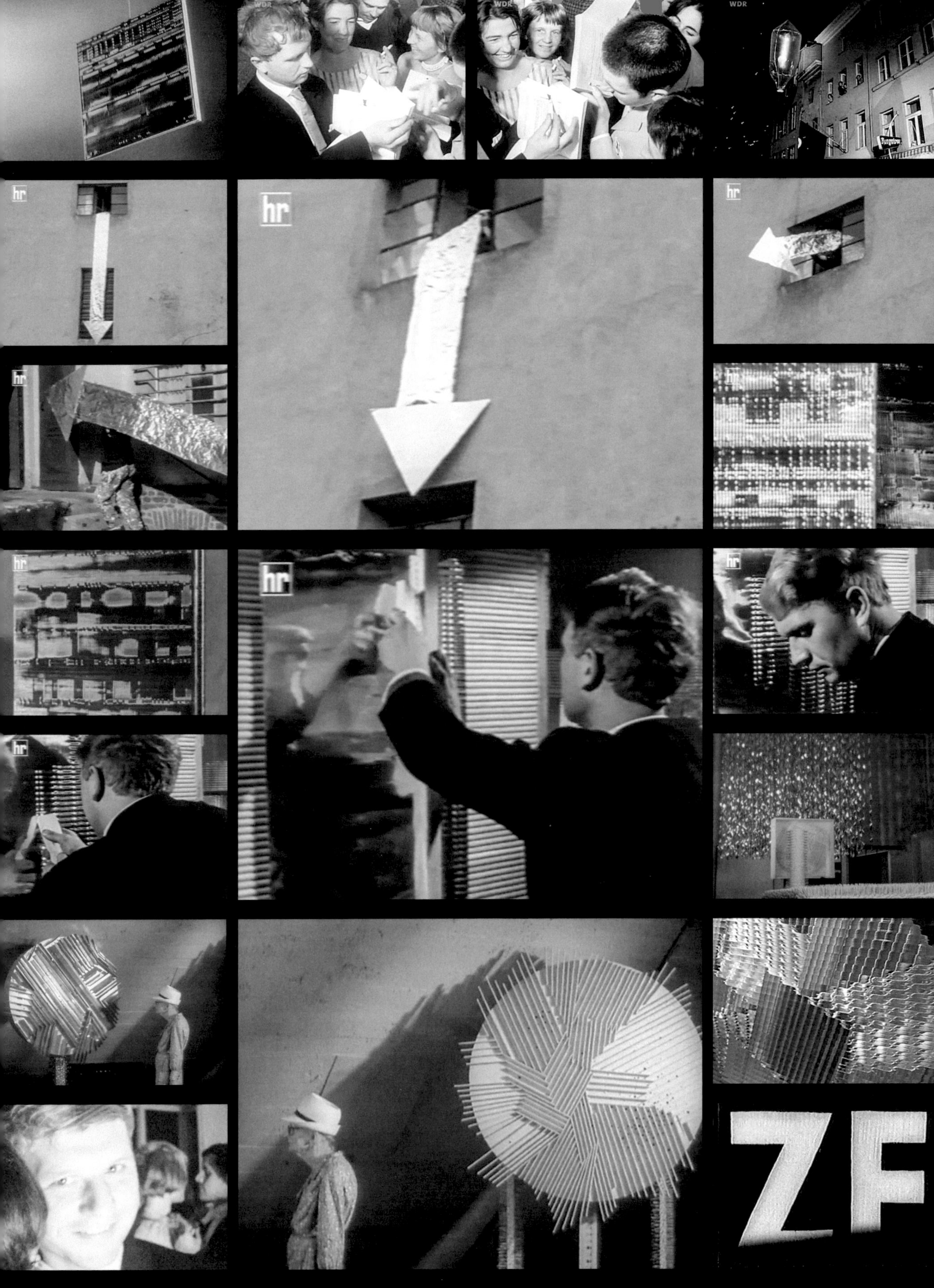

fig. 232 *0 × 0 = Kunst. Maler ohne Farbe und Pinsel* [0 × 0 = Art. Painter Without Paint and Brush], 1962, film stills

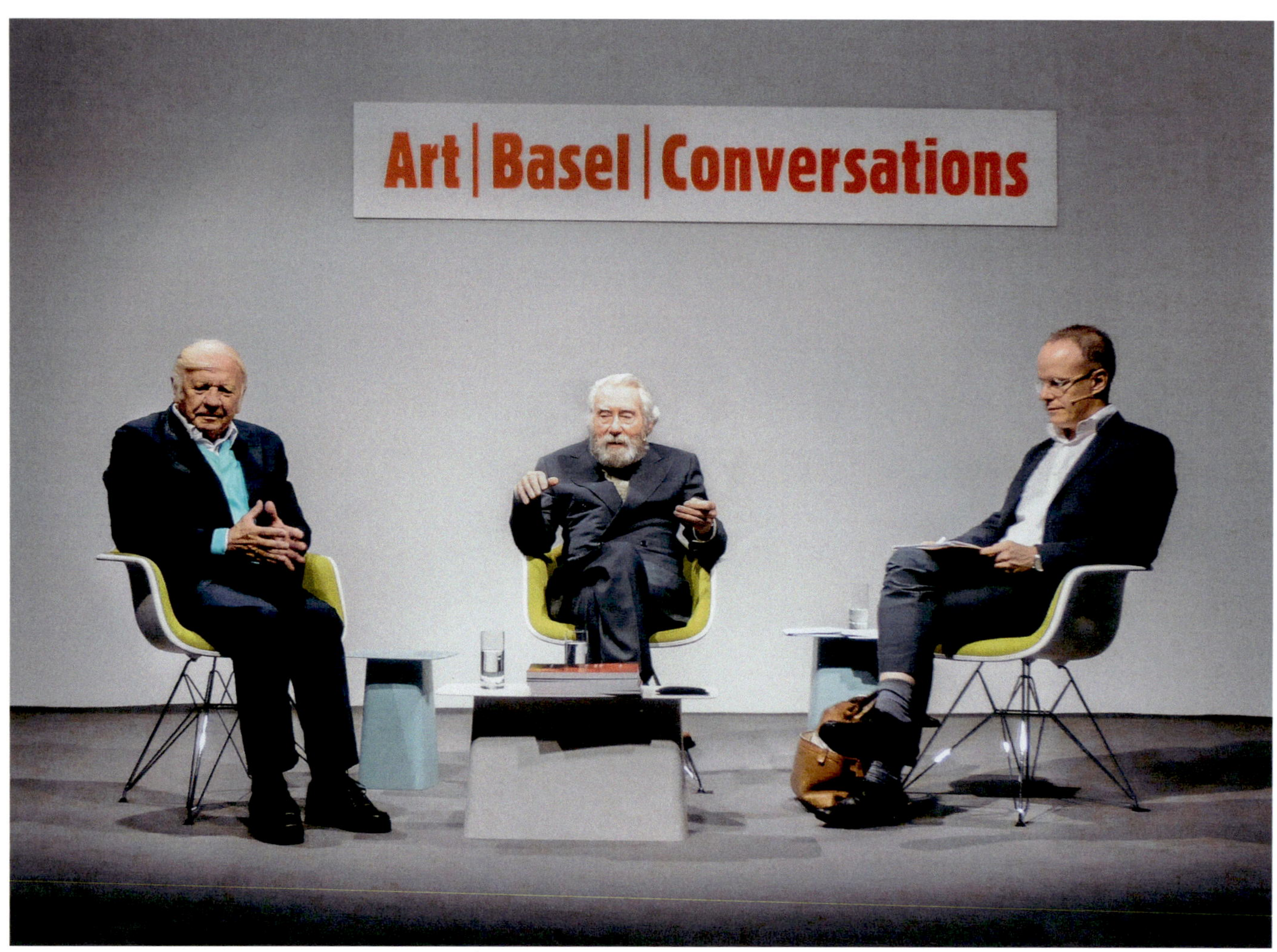

fig. 233 Heinz Mack, Otto Piene, and Hans Ulrich Obrist in conversation at Art Basel 2012

In conversation with Heinz Mack, Art Basel, 2012

HANS ULRICH OBRIST: To begin with the beginning, because we are focusing on the ZERO years today, I was thinking it could be very interesting to talk about the time before ZERO. As can be seen in your catalogue raisonné, you did work before ZERO and you were very interested in philosophy and science. So could you tell us about your beginnings, about your studies in philosophy and science and how you then came into art?

HEINZ MACK: Well, it's a little complicated. For instance, in a love affair, there's also the question of how did it begin? Sometimes, something starts without you having a consciousness about it. All in all [...] before ZERO started, we were involved in the so-called Tachism movement. And of course, with some expression, we did our best to get successful results. But I don't hesitate to mention that, in my personal case, this ended up in a catastrophe, because I started to doubt [...] and felt absolutely insecure in this situation. Somehow, I had a feeling that the evolution of art had come to an end, that everything what could be done had already been done. It then took some time to overcome this feeling and that's when the beginning of the beginning happened. We started to realize that art is – much like the title of the exhibition accompanying this art fair here in Basel[1] – unlimited, that ZERO is unlimited. [...]

HUO: One thing, which is interesting, is that artists of a younger generation have this interest in ZERO. For example, Ólafur Elíasson – very early on, about ten years ago – told me about his interest in ZERO. He said, he was so interested in the fact that you have this connection very early on to philosophy, to science [...]. When we did the interview[2] you told us that actually, philosophy was very important to you – light metaphysics, light mystics. [...] Can you maybe, before we talk about the beginnings of ZERO, talk about this philosophy background?

HM: Well, the general question came up – many years ago, around 1956-57 – how will art go on? That was the general question, discussed on a very high intellectual degree, perhaps influenced by our philosophical education at the university. But at the same time, there was never an attempt to develop any kind of theory. It was just the intention to discuss the substantial elements of what could be art [...]. These discussions not only happened between Otto Piene and me, Günther Uecker was involved, Yves Klein was involved, Piero Manzoni was involved, Lucio Fontana – who could have been our father, but acted like a friend of ours –, we all discussed more or less similar problems and our questions were directed towards the future. We were not so keen on learning about art history, we had done this when we were students. [...] In these discussions, there was also a very positive attitude towards modern

1 Since 2000, the *Unlimited* exhibition has taken place during Art Basel, an innovative platform for large-format art projects that go beyond the standards of a classic art fair exhibition stand.

2 "Simple is Complex: Daniel Birnbaum and Hans Ulrich Obrist in Conversation with Heinz Mack," in: Robert Fleck, ed., *Mack. Light – Space – Colour*, exh. cat. Kunst- und Ausstellungshalle der Bundesrepublik Deutschland Bonn (Cologne: Snoeck, 2011), 30-47.

developments, towards very high advanced technology. All these artists had no sentimental mood, but there was in a certain way a historical anticipation going back to the Renaissance, when it was clearly formulated: Art without science is no art, and science without art is no science. [...] ZERO was an era, it was a time between 1957 and 1967, with other words, just ten years I spent on ZERO – and Uecker and Piene just the same. In this time, we had been very keen on doing experiments, which did have a certain relation to science, too, and to technology. When you are ready to start from the very beginning, it's always helpful to start with experiments. Even a man like Picasso was very fond of experiments. [...]

Of course, philosophy, mediation and thinking about problems, belong to my world and to my work, too. But, as soon as possible, I decided to dismiss philosophy, because I wanted to avoid theories conquering me or getting power over my artistic work. I wanted to decide just by intuition what should be done in art. Intuition was the main factor and, this is still the case today, I go into my studio without theories. But if I discover something, which is completely new to me, then of course I start to think about it. I ask myself: What have you done here and what kind of relation does this have to the whole situation of art? For instance, you mentioned an artist who really got influenced by ZERO and perhaps especially by Heinz Mack. [...] So now I'm eighty years old and I have to realize that a younger generation is going on with ideas, with energy, sensitivity and sensibility, with hopes which we shared for ten years. And I hope the day will come, when I'm still alive, when we can compare what I did to what these younger artists are doing and what kind of relations there are. The more relations exist, the more I will get enthusiastic about the fact that I'm not totally alone. On the other hand, it belongs to the existential substance of an art existence to feel alone. It's a dialectic situation: On the hand, you are completely alone, when you go to your studio to work, and at the same time, you go to Basel to the art fair, where you are not alone anymore.

HUO: Now we come to ZERO. It was actually here at Art Basel, a couple of years ago, that we interviewed Albert Hoffmann, he was almost a hundred years old, the man who discovered LSD. It happens often that scientists locate very precisely an invention – Benoît Mandelbrot told me it was a rainy day, when suddenly on a blackboard he saw fractals, and Albert Hoffmann told us, it was a sunny day, when he discovered LSD. And in terms of this moment of ZERO, do you remember the day? I spoke to you [and Otto Piene] about it, when you found the name and you felt this necessity to become a group. When speaking to Uecker, who joined four years later, he told me he found it very interesting, because there was sort of a loneliness of the artist in the studio and the necessity of finding a dialogue with others. That's obviously something which is so interesting for our time, because now things are even more atomized, I think there's even more desire again for groups, and that's something we can learn from studying ZERO. So I was wondering, can you tell us about this epiphany, how the ZERO invention came about?

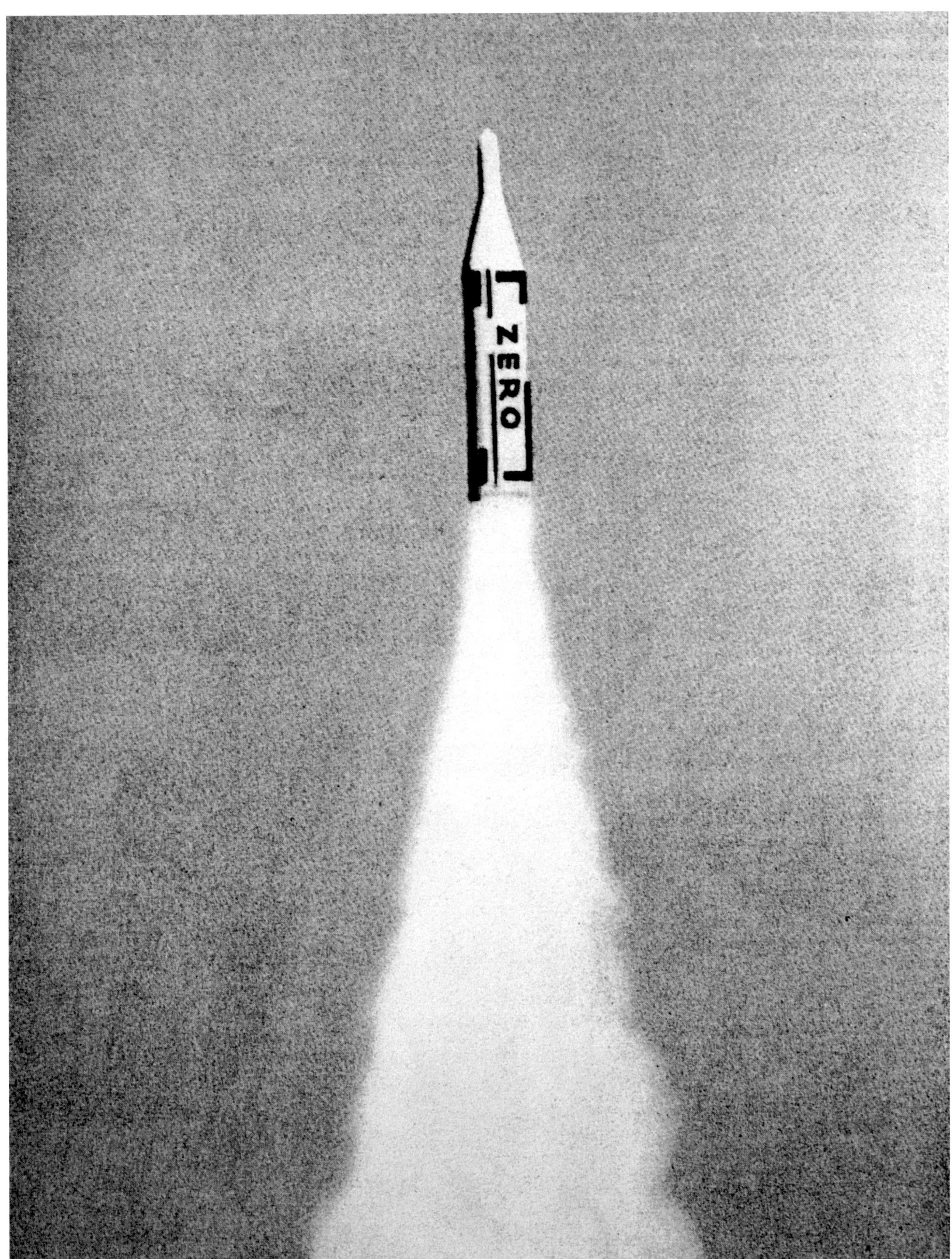

fig. 234 Heinz Mack, *ZERO Rocket*, 1961, photo collage for *ZERO*, no. 3 (1961)

HM: As soon as a certain – I even try to call it – friendship, a certain relationship between various artists came up, in this moment we felt a certain kind of community, a kind of identity in our feelings and in our ideas. And this duplicity of ideas, comparable between different artists, was a great matter. It was really something very striking, we felt very enthusiastic [...]. In the beginning I felt totally alone, but then I met artists like Fontana, Klein, Manzoni, Castellani, Tinguely, Schoonhoven and so on [...]. I was the one – I'm proud of that – who met Uecker on the road and I told him: Why don't you come to us? We are friends, we are a group, but not a kind of group like an institution. It was more like a feeling: There is somebody doing this work, which is not very far away from what I'm doing in my work. And this neighborhood, this *amitié*, this friendship was a big thing. And then of course the question came up: How should we call it? [...] And the idea of ZERO was really a very lucky one, because it was a word for an unlimited approach to an unlimited future. Of course, there was also this general common idea that whatever we are doing should be as simple and as striking as possible. In other words, we started with very, very strong elements: Just a point, just a line, just one color, just one cut in a canvas. All these gestures were very elementary, they excluded all other possibilities [...]. The word ZERO of course did have some relationship to the fact that, in those days, they started to reach the moon. Counting down from ten to ZERO and the rocket was going up – that was really a kind of parallel situation. I made a photo collage, in which you could see the rocket going up to the sky, and on the rocket I put the printed letters ZERO. So ZERO was starting towards the moon, this really was a big thing. [...]

fig. 234

HUO: I'm obviously interested to hear more about this tabula rasa moment, because I read this incredible book by Frank Kaplan [...], it's called *1959*.[3] It's about all these inventions that were made in the 1950s, the journey to outer space, to the moon, it's about all the revolutions of the 60s, as Kaplan says, they were actually invented in the 50s, so it would be great to hear more about this. [...]

HM: [...] What happened back then in science and technology, going up to the moon, it was a kind of expansion of the space. It belongs to the artistic point of view to expand the space, starting with the work of Yves Klein, with the work of Fontana and with our work, too. Instead of material like stones, stainless steel or color, we used light, the physical light, as a medium to expand the space. And this expansion meant a lot to me, too, because in 1959 I developed the so-called *Sahara Project*, which was published in 1961. In this project, I attempted to describe the possibility that art and even human life will totally change, if you go to a kind of reservation, to a landscape which is as untouched as the moon. [...] What I did [there] was to try, what will happen with my objects – in terms of light reflection, in terms of being a kind of instrument, like in music, but for light –, if these instruments are placed in the middle of the Sahara and [receive] sunlight in a very high intensity? I also went to the Arctic to find out: What does light mean in surroundings of extraordinary dimension? [...] An expansion of space always means an expansion of time. [...]

3 Fred Kaplan, *1959: The Year Everything Changed* (Chichester: John Wiley & Sons, 2009).

HUO: There was an early exhibition of ZERO at the Howard Wise Gallery in 57th street.[4] Very early on, this was an important presence of ZERO in New York. You emigrated to the United States, but you came back after a couple of years. So it's a very complex relationship you have with the United States and there have been many decades between the Howard Wise show and now that ZERO shows are happening again, while there was also a gap in between. Maybe it's interesting to talk a little more about that.

HM: The Howard Wise Gallery was very important and I really appreciate to remember that Howard was very kind to me. [...] He told me, you get one thousand dollars a year and afterwards we can see, if we can sell something. I like to mention this because at that time, all well-known and reputable galleries in New York and elsewhere were [only] devoted to German Expressionism. [...] Howard Wise was in this situation a kind of exception in New York compared to all the other gallerists. He was a very keen, very brave personality and he started to realize that movement, the kinetic work, means a lot and that the whole television era had become very important for art. [...]

In 1968, luckily a very good cinematographer and a very good director made a movie about my work and I gave it the title, naming it *Tele-Mack*. What was really exiting, this movie was not shown at midnight, when usually [on television] modern art is presented. It was shown just right after the evening news, so everyone in Germany was confronted with art. What I would like to mention, too: This kind of work like *Tele-Mack*, exists only as a film. Whatever you can see in this film, doesn't exist in reality any more. It was just a virtual exhibition. [...]

figs. 108, 123, 144, 231

Question from the audience: Now you talked about the beginning of ZERO. Could you tell us as well how it came to an end of ZERO? And, in your opinion, are the ideas of ZERO finished or are they still valid and of importance today?

HM: After ten years of cooperation and collaboration between different artists, mainly between Otto Piene, Günther Uecker and me, each personality developed his own power and this competition became a little bit dangerous. So we got jealous. And there is a general opinion too: after ten years there was the danger that the whole group idea became a kind of institution. And an institution does not belong to artists somehow. It will touch the freedom of the single artistic personality, the freedom of being responsible just for me alone and not being responsible for my colleagues. So, I was the one who said, let's stop the whole matter, and let's stop it in a very optimistic way. It was celebrated in Bonn with 1,000 people participating in this festival. But on the other hand, I am still Heinz Mack and I didn't stop to do my work in 1967. I went on with similar ideas. [...] So, ZERO is a part of my life but it is not my whole life.

4 *Group ZERO: Mack, Piene, Uecker*, Nov. 12 – Dec. 05, 1964, Howard Wise Gallery, New York.

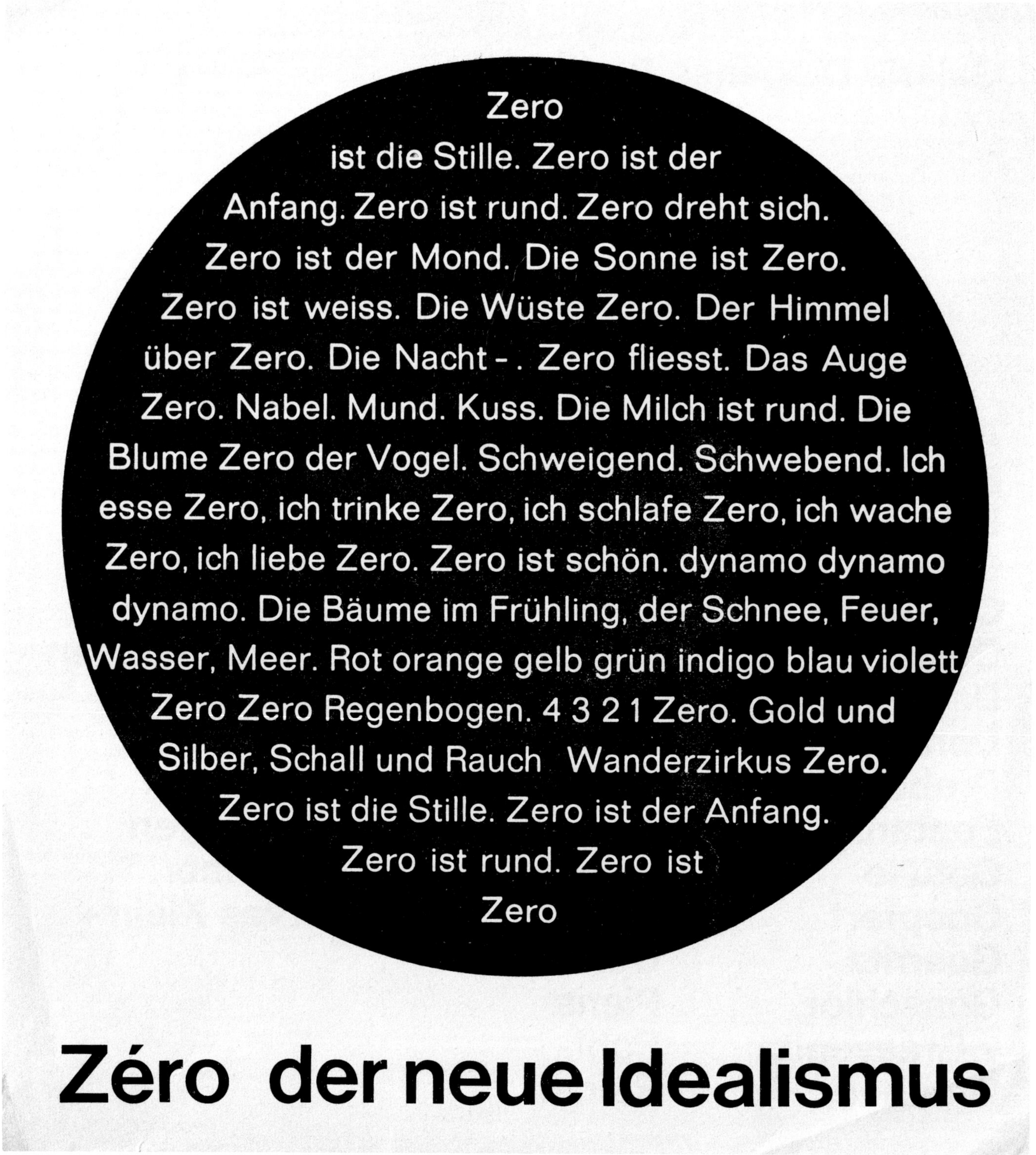

Zero
ist die Stille. Zero ist der
Anfang. Zero ist rund. Zero dreht sich.
Zero ist der Mond. Die Sonne ist Zero.
Zero ist weiss. Die Wüste Zero. Der Himmel
über Zero. Die Nacht - . Zero fliesst. Das Auge
Zero. Nabel. Mund. Kuss. Die Milch ist rund. Die
Blume Zero der Vogel. Schweigend. Schwebend. Ich
esse Zero, ich trinke Zero, ich schlafe Zero, ich wache
Zero, ich liebe Zero. Zero ist schön. dynamo dynamo
dynamo. Die Bäume im Frühling, der Schnee, Feuer,
Wasser, Meer. Rot orange gelb grün indigo blau violett
Zero Zero Regenbogen. 4 3 2 1 Zero. Gold und
Silber, Schall und Rauch Wanderzirkus Zero.
Zero ist die Stille. Zero ist der Anfang.
Zero ist rund. Zero ist
Zero

Zéro der neue Idealismus

fig. 235 *ZERO Manifesto*, from: *ZERO*, exh. cat. Galerie Diogenes, Berlin, 1963

fig. 235

HUO: My last question concerns the ZERO manifesto. One thing, which is obviously important in relation to every movement, is the manifesto. All the historic avantgardes in the twentieth century produced a whole catalogue of manifestos [...]. I think there's a great interest in looking at manifestos, because very often they are also a bridge between art and literature, because they are literary documents. So is the ZERO manifesto a literary document? [...]

HM: We hesitated to develop any kind of theory. So instead of using scientific language, we preferred the language of poetry. We were in a kind of Dada-mood, walking through the roads of the town, we developed this poem as a collaboration. And I still like the idea that behind all these words and symbols, it shows the world in which we placed our dreams. The poem was a manifestation of our dreams. The whole ZERO time was a time of dreams. [...] Perhaps a last word, if I may. Two thousand years ago the philosopher Seneca declared: Only the person who is awake, can realize what he has dreamed of.

This interview is an excerpt from: *Art Basel Conversations: Hans Ulrich Obrist in conversation with Heinz Mack and Otto Piene*, 13.6.2012, edited by Sophia Sotke and Ulrike Havemann.
The complete interview is available on YouTube, https://www.youtube.com/watch?v=96lynQzdi9I

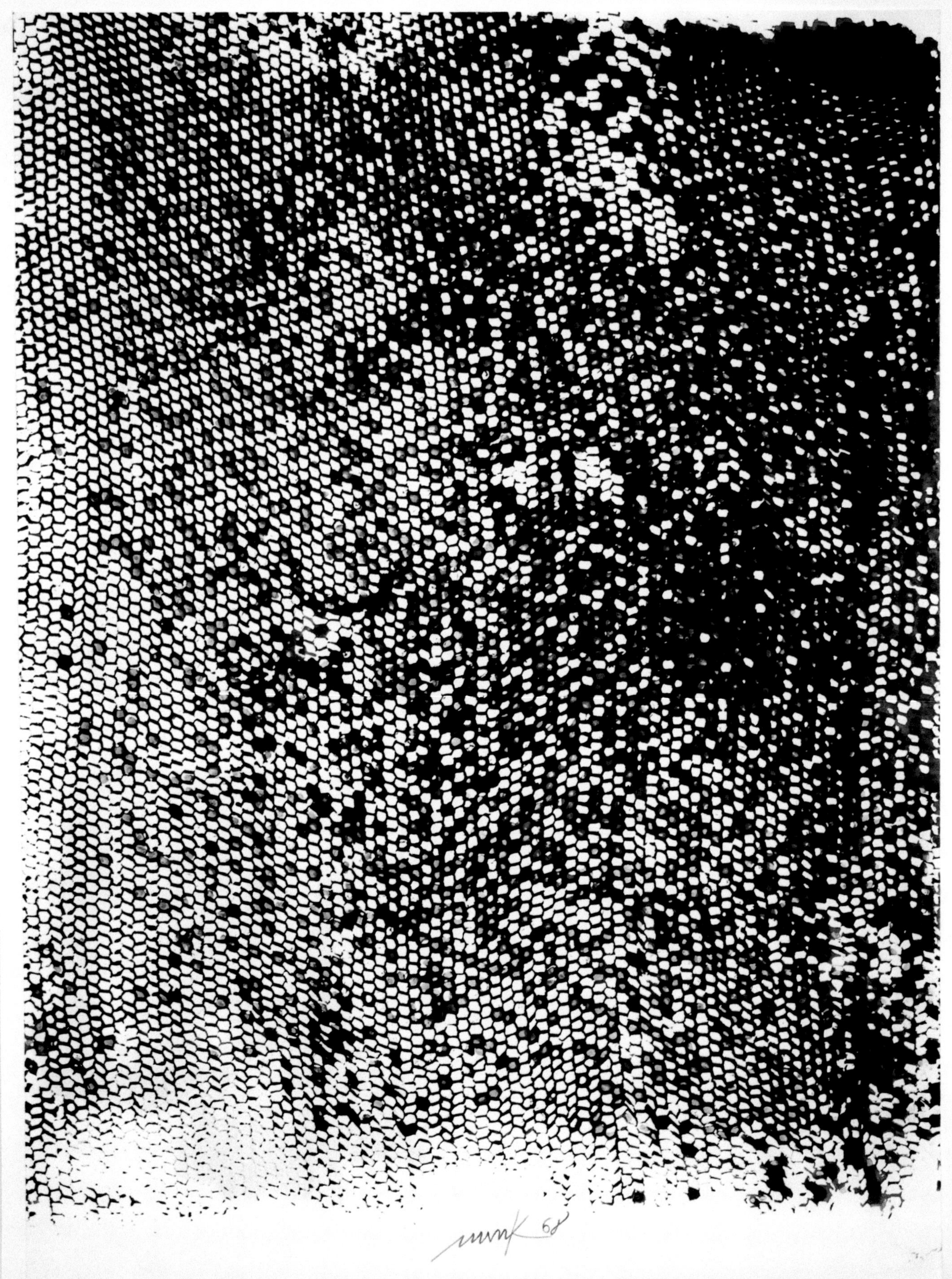

Affinities between Art and Science: Revisiting Mack's *Compendium*

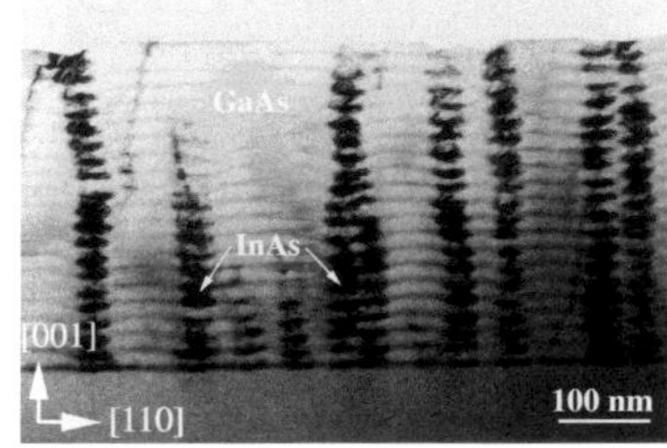

fig. 237 Self-organization of quantum dots in InAs/GaAs multilayers, transmission electron microscopy (TEM).

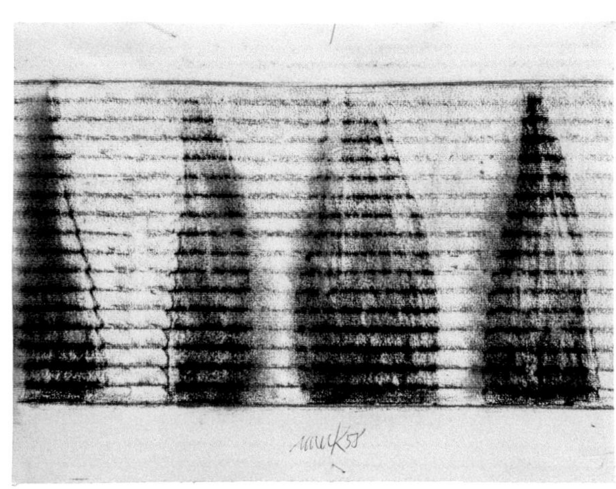

fig. 238 Heinz Mack, *Untitled*, 1958, charcoal on paper

"Our work is given form in order that it may function, in order that it may be a functioning organism. To achieve the same as nature, though only in parallel. Not to compete with nature but to produce something that says: it is as in nature." (Paul Klee)[1]

Compendium

Beginning in the ZERO era, Heinz Mack built a collection of images covering a broad range of subjects. This collection, which the artist calls his *Compendium*, contains images which serve as philosophically and aesthetically important points of reference in his œuvre, including a number of his own artworks. These images cover a wide range of subjects, including architecture, cosmos, technology, mirrors, light, transparency, natural elements, and many more. One series within this *Compendium* compares drawings by Heinz Mack to images from a collection of transmission electron microscopy (TEM) scans created at Forschungszentrum Jülich.[2] Mack's graphical sheets in this series are from the late 1950s. He saw parallels to his drawings in the scientific images, which is why they were included in his *Compendium* – also referred to by the artist as an extended "Musée Imaginaire" following a concept by André Malraux. Mack's scientific curiosity also led him to form a personal connection to Forschungszentrum Jülich, where the artist engaged in conversations with physicists studying atoms. For Mack's exhibition *Light – Space – Color* (Bundeskunsthalle Bonn, 2011), a moderated dialogue titled *Art meets Science* was held between Heinz Mack and Knut Urban, a physicist at Forschungszentrum Jülich's Ernst Ruska-Centre for Microscopy and Spectroscopy with Electrons. The topics of this dialogue included the visualization of structures and visual affinities between Mack's work and science. This discourse is revisited here, based on Mack's *Compendium* – the present contribution co-authored by an art historian and a nanoscientist is a dialectical examination of artistic and scientific images and techniques.

1 Eric Shanes, ed., *Paul Klee* (New York: Parkstone International, 2015), 274.

2 These images were published in: Martina Luysberg, Institute for Solid State Research Forschungszentrum Jülich, ed., *Transmissionselektronenmikroskopie (TEM): Atome zum Anfassen: Präsentation im Rahmen der Ausstellung "Der Stein der Weisen,"* exh. cat. Bundeshaus, Bonn (Jülich: Forschungszentrum, 2000). Founded as a nuclear research facility in 1956, Forschungszentrum Jülich is one of the largest research centers in Europe focusing on information, energy, and bioeconomy. Its mission is to contribute interdisciplinary work to solving major societal challenges regarding the future of information technology, the transformation of the energy system, and the development of a sustainable bioeconomy. See https://www.fz-juelich.de/en/about-us/what-we-stand-for/the-profile-of-forschungszentrum-julich.

fig. 237 / fig. 238

← *fig. 236* Heinz Mack, *The Diligence of Bees*, 1968, ink with brush on paper, 30 × 21 cm

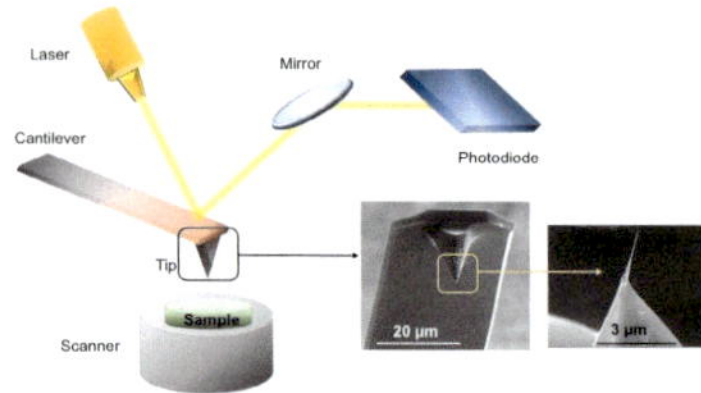

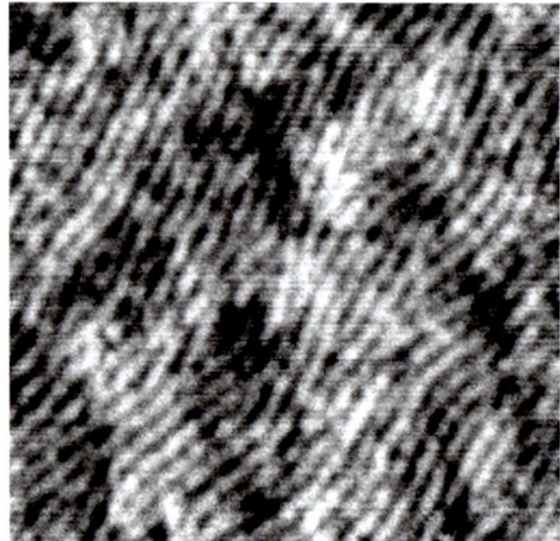

fig. 239 The principle of atomic force microscopy (AFM) (top) and AFM image of polymer chains (bottom)

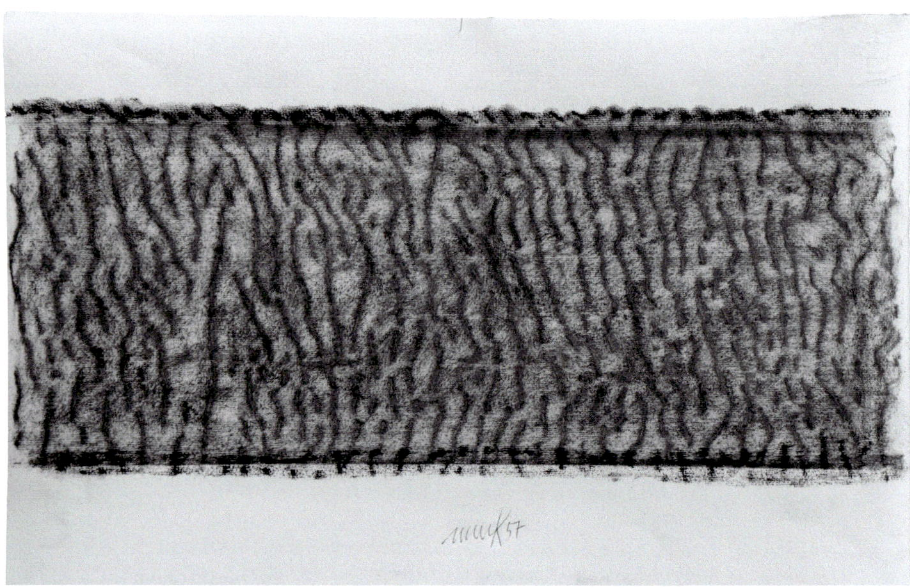

fig. 240 Heinz Mack, *Untitled*, 1957, charcoal on paper

What lies beneath the numerous and surprising formal similarities between these two visual realms? Is it a mere formal analogy, or is there a deeper level to the connection between Heinz Mack's artworks and the microcosms explored through the artificial eye of the transmission electron microscope? What is the relationship between Heinz Mack's artistic methodology and scientific concepts, and what ideas influenced his understanding of the interplay between technology, nature, and humanity? This investigation is particularly interested in those concepts which Heinz Mack defined as key characteristics of his artistic method: dynamic structure, randomness, dialectical concepts (tension created through interactions between opposites and its resolution), micro and macro, as well as beauty (of artificial and natural structures).[3]

figs. 247, 251

The similarities between Heinz Mack's artworks and the images produced by a scanning electron microscope begin at the technical level of image creation. Mack's drawings from the 1950s are frottages created with the use of grid-like reliefs placed beneath the paper, which were rotated or shifted multiple times throughout the rubbing process to generate repeating and overlapping patterns of lines. The artist's hand moved freely and spontaneously, determining the intensity of each component through variations in pressure: "The principle of my graphic art: The free movement of my hand, the emotional expression, is met with a sort of 'mechanical' resistance in the grid of a rigid relief underlay, meaning that the flying movement of the hand is rhythmically interrupted and set in vibration."[4]

fig. 239 / fig. 240

This description could easily be transferred to the principles of a specific microscopy technique known as atomic force microscopy (AFM). This method uses a cantilever probe which passes over surfaces like a feeling hand. As the probe follows the contours of the surface, its deflection is detected by a laser beam, and the resulting signal is transformed into images. AFM, which was developed almost 40 years ago, allows scientists to visualize polymer chains, DNA strands, and even events such as the opening and closing of channels within cell membranes.

3 As there are numerous examinations of light as a physical phenomenon in Mack's œuvre, it will not be addressed in detail here.

4 Heinz Mack, "Das Prinzip meiner Grafik," in *Mack. Objekte, Aktionen, Projekte*, exh. cat. Akademie der Künste Berlin (Berlin, 1972), 12. Translated from the German.

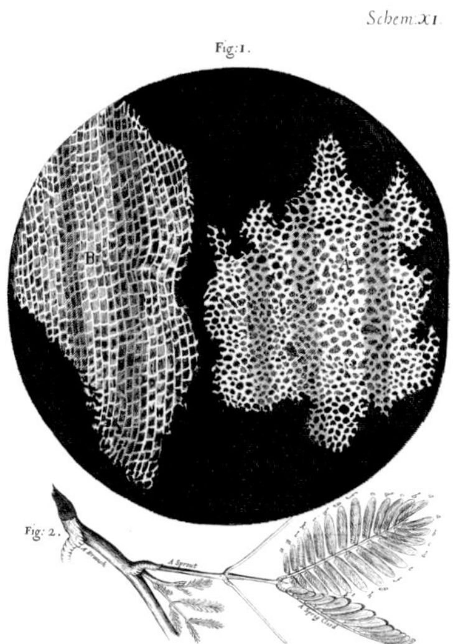

fig. 241 The cellular structure of cork seen through the Hooke microscope and a sprig of Sensitive Plant, 1665. Illustration from Robert Hooke, *Micrographia*, 1665.

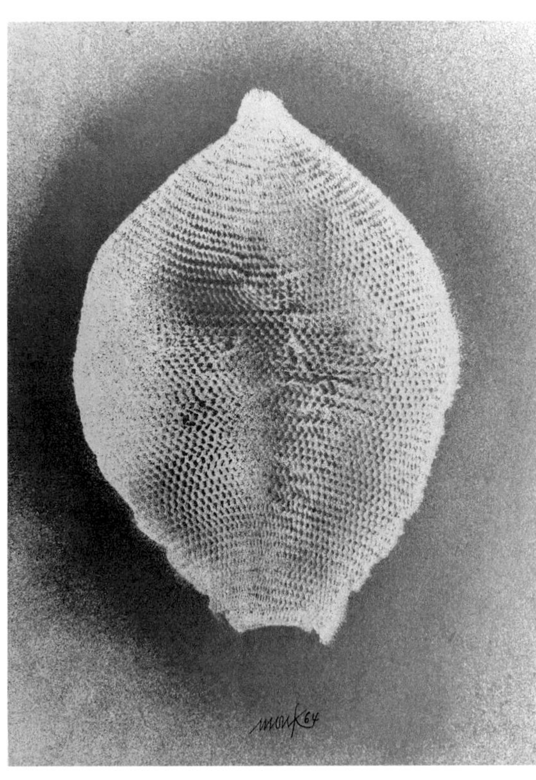

fig. 242 Heinz Mack, *Untitled*, 1964, silver spray through metal grid on paper, 30 × 21 cm

fig. 241 / fig. 242

Interestingly, the detailed images of material structures generated by this technology bear a striking resemblance to Mack's art. The same can be said of optical images obtained by Robert Hooke (1635–1703): Under an optical microscope, a plant leaf transforms into a lattice of hexagonal cells, which strongly resembles the artworks Mack created using honeycomb mesh. However, despite their resolution, even the most advanced optical microscopes cannot reach scales beyond a few hundred nanometers (0.000000001 m). The study of atoms and nanostructures at the innermost levels of natural structures, which are invisible to the human eye, requires more specialized tools.

This became possible in 1933, when Ernst Ruska constructed the first electron microscope utilizing electrons instead of light to visualize elements on a nanoscale. With the advent of electron microscopy (e.g., transmission electron microscopy, TEM), it became possible to investigate the deeper layers of matter: Atoms within semiconductors, crystalline boundaries in various metal oxides, or crystal lattices, and the positions of individual atoms within gold nanoparticles could now be visualized. But electron microscopes are not only capable of observing atoms; they can even be used to change the arrangement of atoms within crystals and thereby produce new hybrid materials. Research into quantum dots – nanoscale semiconductive crystalline particles with applications in bio- and medical imaging and the manufacturing of high-resolution displays and photovoltaic cells – which received a Nobel Prize in 2023, is a direct result of this ability to observe and manipulate matter.

While powerful, TEM has its own limitations. For one, the images obtained are snapshots of the larger structure that capture a moment in a highly dynamic system frozen in time, and secondly, TEM images are reconstructed from the behavior of transmitted electrons and can be influenced by the observer's interpretation.

fig. 244 / fig. 245

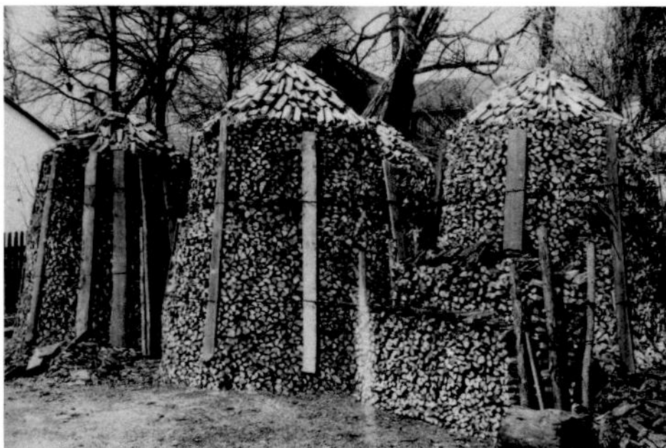
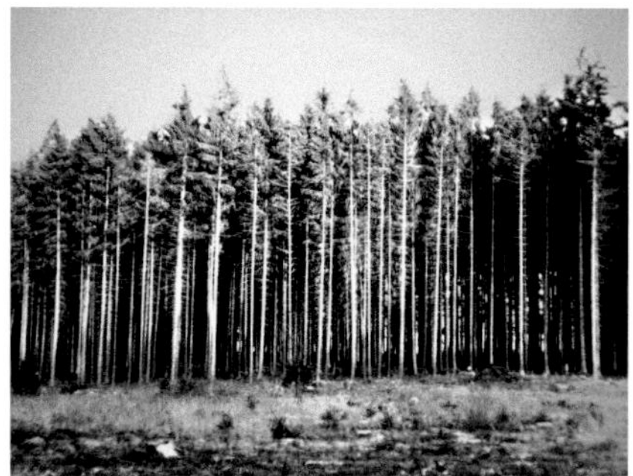
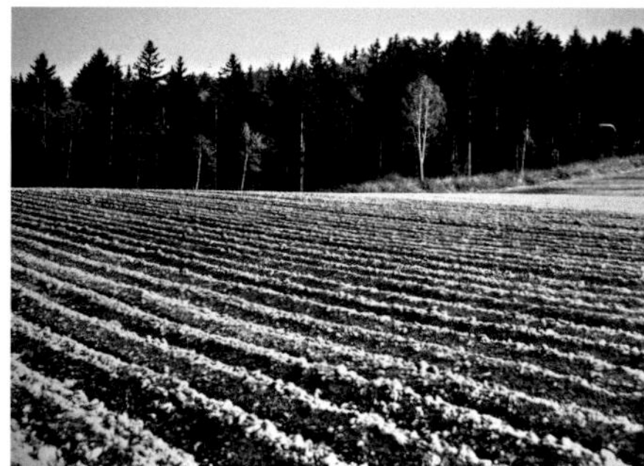

fig. 243 Heinz Mack, nature photographs from the surroundings of Lollar, mid-1940s

Dynamic Structure

Heinz Mack's theoretical elaborations on the concept of "dynamic structure" were consistently implemented in his artworks. For Mack, this concept was the amalgamation of all aspects in which he wanted to depart from the previous generation of artists. The combination of dynamic and structural elements is an essential characteristic of Heinz Mack's entire œuvre.

fig. 243

Heinz Mack's interest in structures became apparent early on. In his photographs taken during his youth on walks around Lollar, Hesse, and in his early works, sculptures and drawings created after his studies at the academy in Düsseldorf: Mack reduced natural forms to their structure, their "suggestive form."

His rejection of Tachism and its emphasis on the absence of form led Mack to create monochrome dynamic structures in his paintings and drawings from 1956 onwards. These structural artworks, based on grids and series of lines, are fundamentally different from other works that follow the principles of classical composition. The elements or units of structure as a system of order are homogenous and determine their inner order, whereas the heterogenous elements of composition are determined externally. Mack replaced composition with structure as an artistic device, which enabled him to leave the elements of narrative and illusionism behind. Much like structuralism in the humanities, which applies a rather ahistorical method of investigating invariable structures within societies instead of traditional developmental history, Mack broke free from the historical "isms" in art, as well as the history of style, developing a universal artistic language. This universal language was not an expression of some subjective artistic invention, but a reflection of principles of order based in reality.

The very first issue of the magazine *ZERO*, published in May of 1958, already contained his programmatic article *Die neue dynamische Struktur* [The New Dynamic Structure]. Around the same time, he created the drawings in his *Compendium*. The artist writes: "The pictorial device ... is an open mechanical sequence ... Every parallel zone is treated with essentially the same intensity of presence; in this regard, we can no longer speak of composition or variations on a formal theme. This would contradict the pictorial structure. The aspect of the pictorial structure is a dynamic one. The parallel zones not only have a static

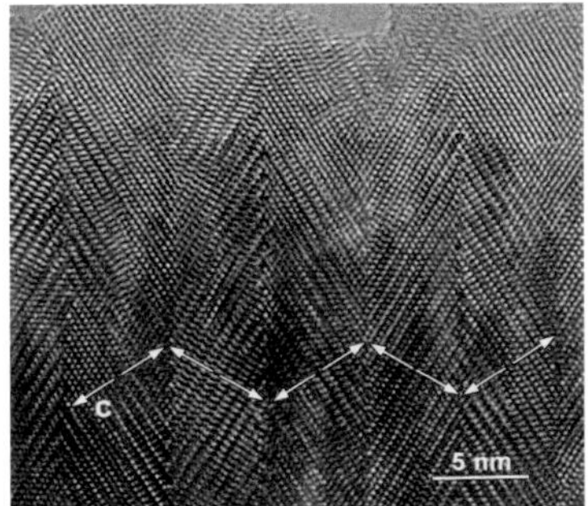

fig. 244 University of Bonn, twin boundaries in the crystal structure of zinc oxide, transmission electron microscopy.

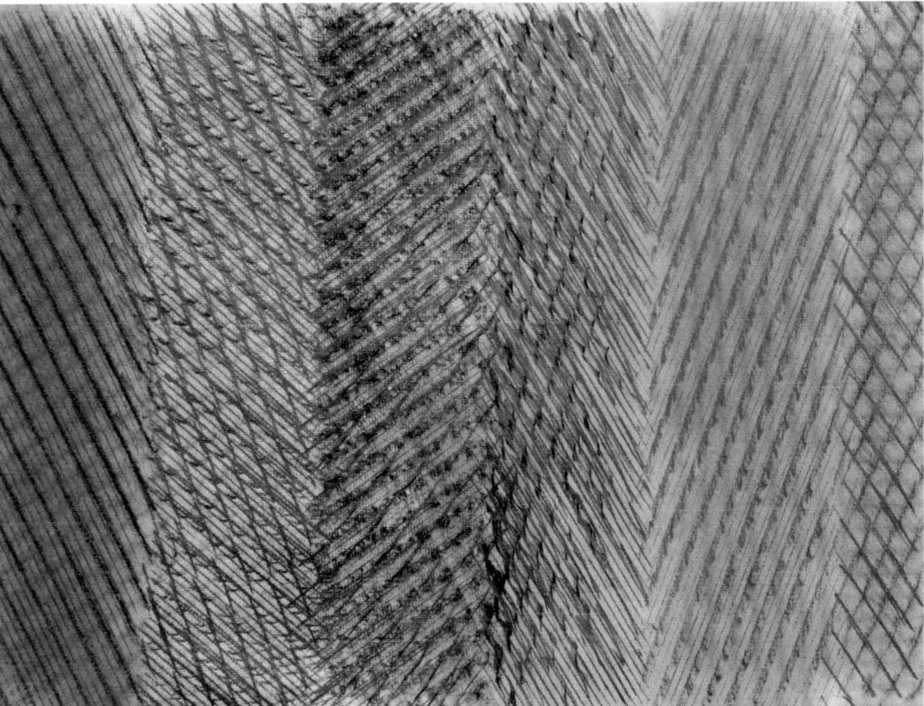

fig. 245 Heinz Mack, *Untitled*, ca. 1960

dimension, but also a dynamic one. The dialectical synopsis of static and dynamic elements gives rise to the virtual vibration, i.e., the pure and consistent pictorial movement, which cannot be found in nature; it is free of all suggestive illusionism ..."[5]

It is precisely this approach of viewing dynamic structure as the foundation of an artwork, which forms the bridge to scientific methods. The artist speaks of a "code that ... is unconsciously taken up by the artist, so that, during the process of creation all steps are decided intuitively, almost in the sense of a self-organisation in which all elements correspond with each other."[6] Heinz Mack's turn towards structures as an essential part of his methods stems from multiple sources: On the one hand, it derives from his exposure to structuralism; on the other hand, from his own observations of nature and his practice as a musician.[7]

fig. 247

However, the concept of structure first became relevant in the natural sciences and was only later transferred to structuralism as a fundamental concept. The technological development of optical scientific instruments and the refinement of investigative methods in mathematics, physics, chemistry, and biology enabled deeper insights into the nature of our world. The natural sciences strived to develop a structural description of the universe, in which they examined the elements and their interrelations. This exploration of structure and movement of matter in the nano-, micro-, and macrocosm has progressed by leaps and bounds in the twentieth and twenty-first centuries. In the natural sciences, from biology to crystallography,[8] the term "structure" refers to the spatial composition of a material or of matter as determined by its formation or production.

5 Heinz Mack, "Die neue dynamische Struktur," *ZERO*, no. 1 (1958): 15–16, here 16. Translated from the German.

6 Robert Fleck and Antonia Lehmann-Tolkmitt, *Heinz Mack. A Twenty-First-Century Artist: Monograph* (Munich: Hirmer, 2019), 81.

7 Music is the classic example of structural order within an aesthetic system.

8 See Brockhaus Enzyklopädie Online, "Struktur (Naturwissenschaften)," NE GmbH Brockhaus, https://brockhaus.de/ecs/enzy/article/struktur-naturwissenschaften

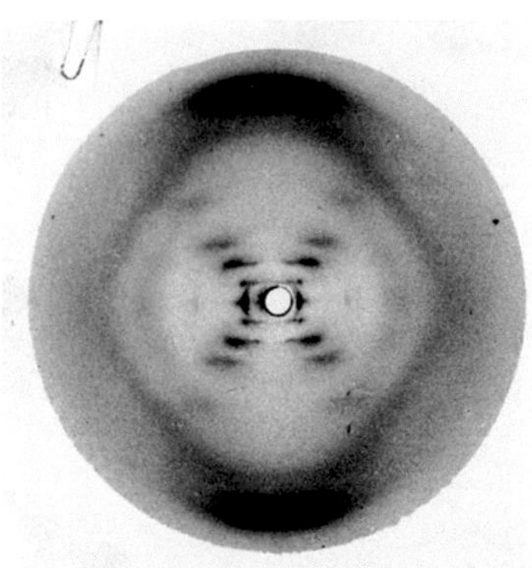

fig. 246 Rosalind Franklin, Raymond G. Gosling, *Photo 51*, 1953, crystallographic photo of sodium thymonucleate, type B.

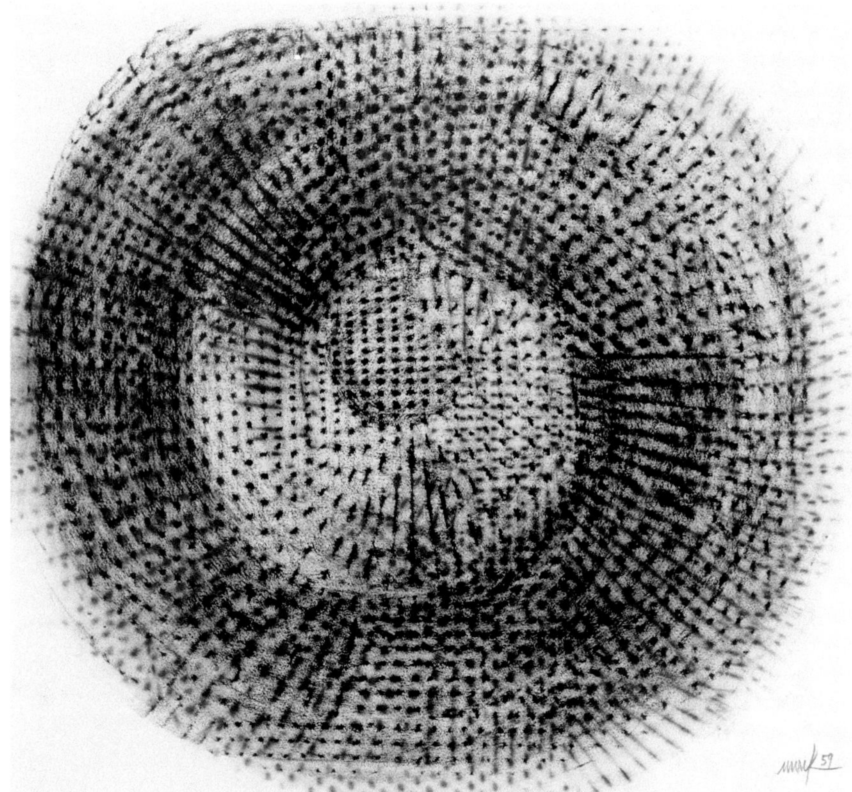

fig. 247 Heinz Mack, *Black Rotation*, 1959, frottage, wax crayon and charcoal on handmade paper, 54 × 56 cm

fig. 246

Indeed, X-ray crystallography played a pivotal role in unraveling the structures of numerous important biomolecules, ranging from DNA to proteins. The historic image known as *Photo 51*, captured by Rosalind Franklin, was instrumental in decoding the structure of DNA, catalyzing a revolution in molecular biology. This breakthrough has paved the way for contemporary processes such as genetic manipulation and early cancer diagnostics.

fig. 250 / fig. 251

Similar to Mack's art, where the arrangement of building blocks dictates the dynamics of their relationship with light or the observer, the positioning of atoms within the crystal lattice of a material determines its macroscopic properties and interaction with light. Assembling thousands of gold atoms within a volume of gold nanoparticles results in the formation of an electron cloud around the particles, known as a surface plasmon. Plasmonic gold nanoparticles interact with light differently than an ordinary gold surface, resulting in the distinctive red color of gold nanoparticles.

At the level of physical chemistry, all structures are dynamic. Even the seemingly most static structures are composed of vibrating molecules. In biology, we introduce the concept of dynamic self-assembly to elucidate the formation of complex biological structures. Self-assembled dynamic structures consist of building blocks that create functional structures capable of performing desired actions, adapting, changing, and healing. Every living tissue or organism is a dynamic structure characterized by the continous conversion of molecules and energy. Molecules vibrate, and in truth, nothing is ever truly static. Vibrations and movement are at the core of matter.

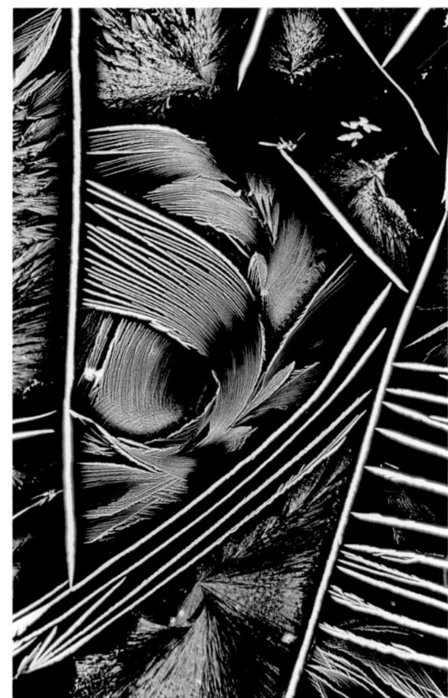

fig. 248 Manfred Kage, *Thiosemicarbazide*, 1956, light microscope, polarized light, 100 × magnification, 10 × lens, collection ZKM | Karlsruhe.

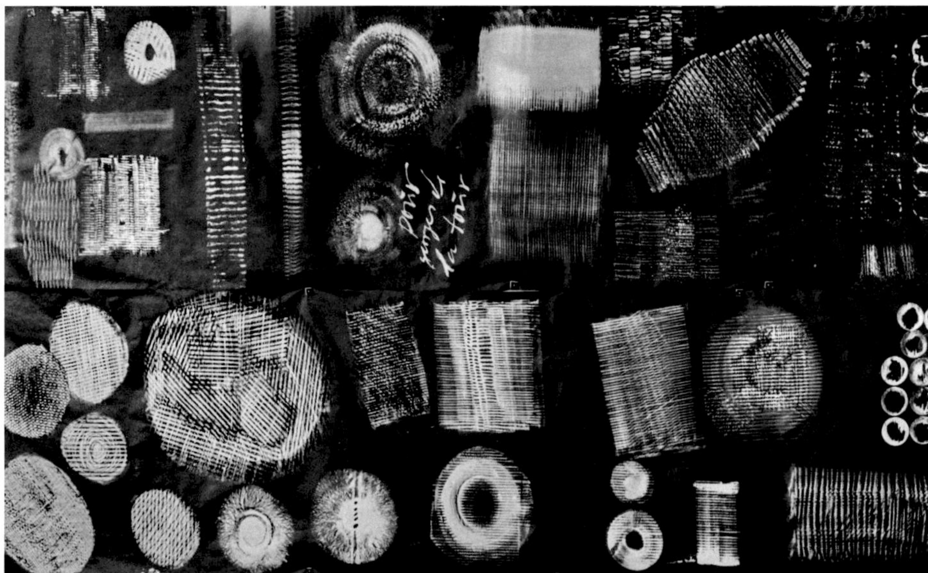

fig. 249 Heinz Mack, *Hommage à Georges de la Tour*, 1960, phosphorus wall painting, detail

Randomness

In addition to the stringency of structures, Mack also relies heavily on randomness and spontaneous invention as artistic means: "In my work I examine and strive for structural phenomena whose stringent logic I disturb or extend through aleatory interventions, in other words random actions. For if a creative process is completely determined, its results come across as undetermined, in fact positively chaotic in their arbitrariness, and thus they are the opposite of the intended stringency."[9]

Chance frequently serves as the catalyst for scientific discovery. Discoveries often happen unexpectedly, while researchers are searching for something entirely different: Nanoscale football-shaped structures made of carbon, known as fullerenes, were stumbled upon during the quest for complex carbon molecules in the aftermath of exploding supernovae.[10]

Recognizing that coincidence can lead to innovation requires a certain process. While the reconstruction of coincidences could hamper the creative process in art, and an artist might stop as soon as the aesthetic and poetic requirements of their work are met, a scientist must work to refine the process and establish a reproducible procedure which is more technical than it is creative. Regardless of whether the ultimate goal is achieved, coincidence requires a process to begin with a hypothesis. It demands an initial idea, which takes a creator on a journey, and a certain amount of intuition that enables the recognition of this unique, imperfect moment – a disruption in the known process that leads to something new.

The idea of a coincidence that produces the artistic structures in a dialectic process also has a counterpart in how quantum physicists approach the concept of coincidence. Determinism, which is fundamental to conventional Newtonian physics, is simply not applicable in quantum physics. Unlike conventional physics, quantum mechanics does not describe the state of an observable system in terms of actual values of a set of observable quantities, but in terms of the probabilities of the

9 Heinz Mack, "Structure," in: Heinz Mack, *Mack. Life and Work 1931–2011* (Cologne: Dumont, 2011), 481.

10 See Anothony J. Stace and Paul O'Brien, "Fullerenes; past, present and future, celebrating the 30th anniversary of Buckminster Fullerene," *Philosophical Transactions of the Royal Society A* 374 (2016), https://www.ncbi.nlm.nih.gov/pmc/articles/PMC4978749/pdf/rsta20160278.pdf.

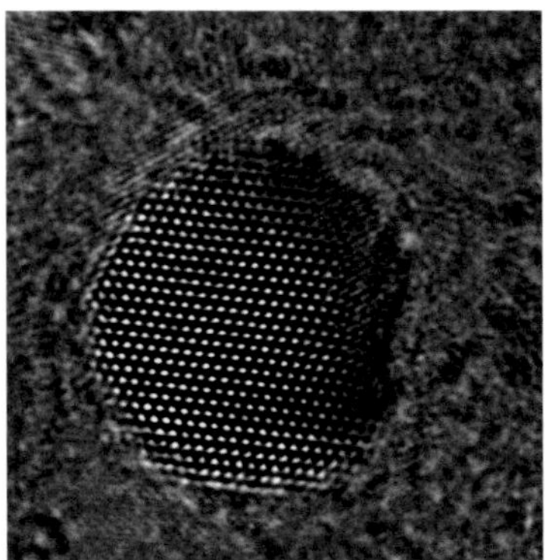

fig. 250 Lukas Stolzer and Ljiljana Fruk, TEM image of a gold nanoparticle

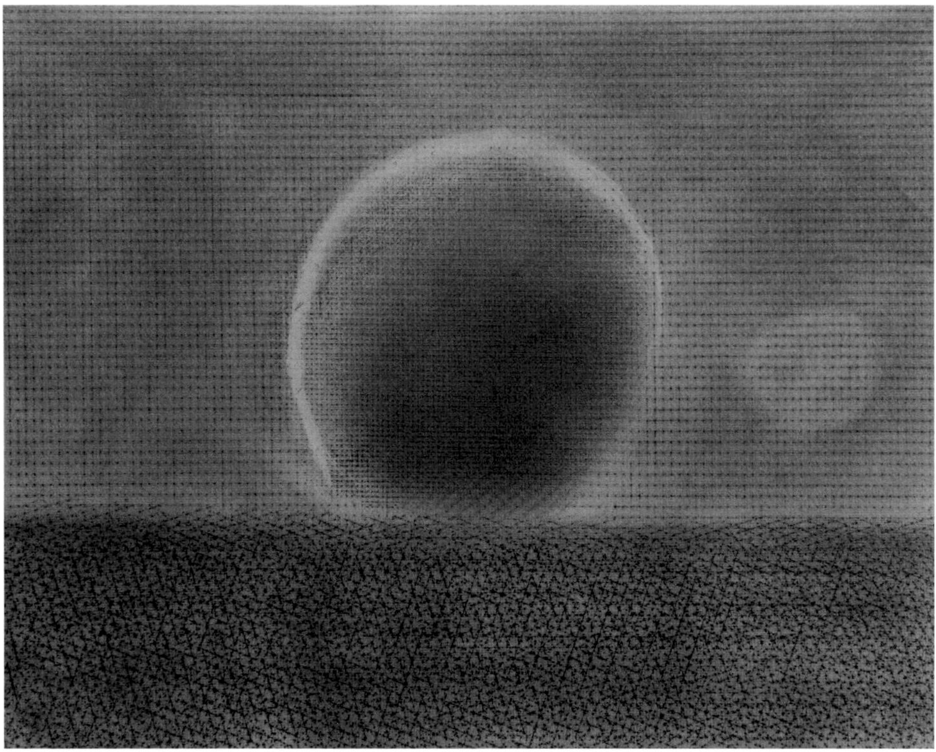

fig. 251 Heinz Mack, *Untitled*, 1958

possible values of those quantities. Quantum theory and its statistical laws are an expression of objective and actually occurring random fluctuations in the position and velocity of microscopic particles. Regularity and randomness are inseparably connected.

Imperfection and coincidence play a crucial role in the self-organization of matter. This is where unordered microscopic movements turn into ordered forms of movement. One example are the topological defects and other distortions of order within crystal lattices: The random placement of nitrogen atoms within the ordered framework of carbon nanodiamonds leads to the creation of a unique fluorescent structure capable of monitoring temperature within a single cell.[11] It is even assumed that "the objectively existing dialectic of necessity (regularity) and randomness is of great importance for the understanding of any complex development," as the mutual interaction of randomness and necessity is what makes the development of anything new possible in the first place.[12]

Guided by randomness, stochastic processes are prevalent in nature. In molecular biology, intrinsically random biochemical processes dictate how our cells function. While a human cell may appear homogeneous from the outside, resembling a well-mixed solution of biomolecules, it is, in fact, highly heterogeneous, densely packed with proteins and small molecules. Copies of the same protein might exhibit slight differences depending on their location, and these differences can vary over time. Determining gene activation and protein expression precisely remains challenging as long as the cell is alive. Dynamic structures are inherently stochastic, and the interplay of chance and necessity in biological structures and the evolution of species is one of the most intriguing questions in modern biology.

11 See Vadym N. Mochalin, Olga Shenderova, Dean Ho, and Yury Gogotski, "The properties and application of nanodiamonds, Nature Nanotechnology" (2011), 7, 11–23. DOI: **10.1038/nnano.2011.209**

12 See Christian Jooß, *Self-organization of Matter. A dialectical approach to evolution of matter in the microcosm and macrocosmos* (Berlin, Boston: De Gruyter, 2020), 5. https://doi.org/10.1515/9783110644203

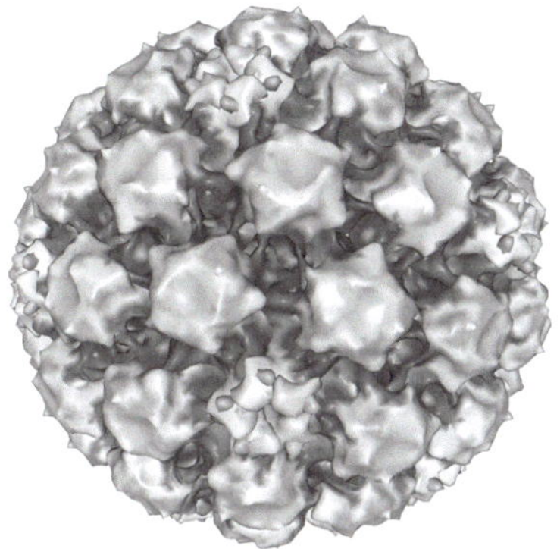

fig. 252 Ljiljana Fruk and A. Kerbs, bovine papillomavirus

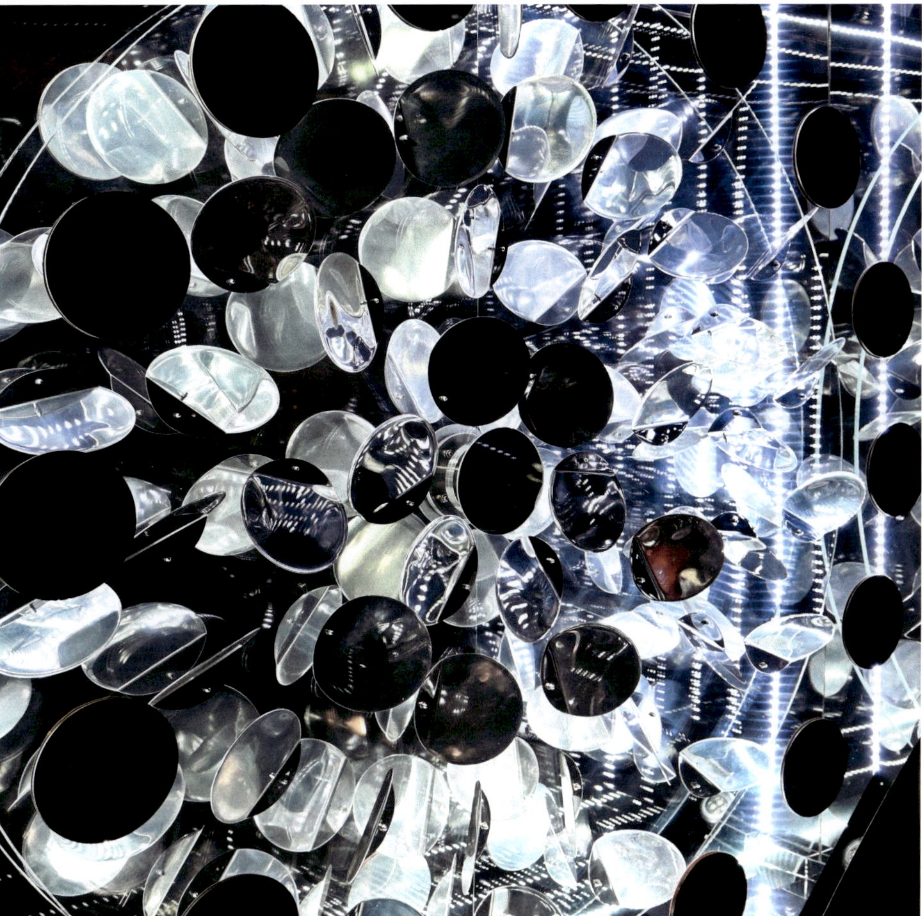

fig. 253 Heinz Mack, *Mirror Rotor*, 1960, detail

Dialectics

The dialectical principle of building and resolving tension plays a pivotal role in the emergence of Mack's artistic structures. It is especially crucial in his structural paintings and graphics. Necessity and randomness, surface and space, light and darkness, inside and outside, rhythm and meter unite to create one pictorial unit. This tension of opposites approaching each other and leading to a new unity or synthesis is mirrored in natural laws and scientific methodology.

There is an almost inconceivable amount of experimental scientific material showing that the different forms of matter in the universe form a system of mutually dependent and developmentally intertwined structures. These structures exist on scales ranging from less than femtometers to billions of light years. In physics, a dialectical-materialist approach offers a particularly systemic and relevant perspective on this phenomenon. It states that matter exists objectively and independently of our consciousness and is inherently subject to an infinite development that produces qualitatively new characteristics and types of motion on every level. This approach unifies humanity and nature in a harmonious way, which offers another parallel to Mack's œuvre. The dialectics of mutually conditional randomness and necessity is essentially expressed in the self-organization of matter and the formation of the infinite variety of structures in the universe.[13]

13 See Jooß, *Self-organization of Matter*, 1, 192, 193.

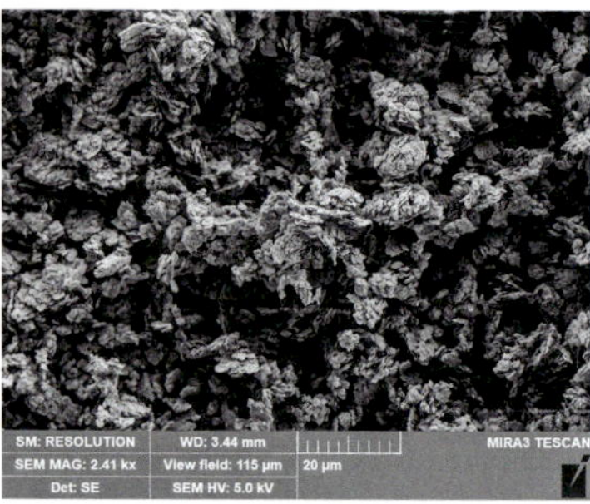

fig. 254 Fruk lab, SEM of laponite clay

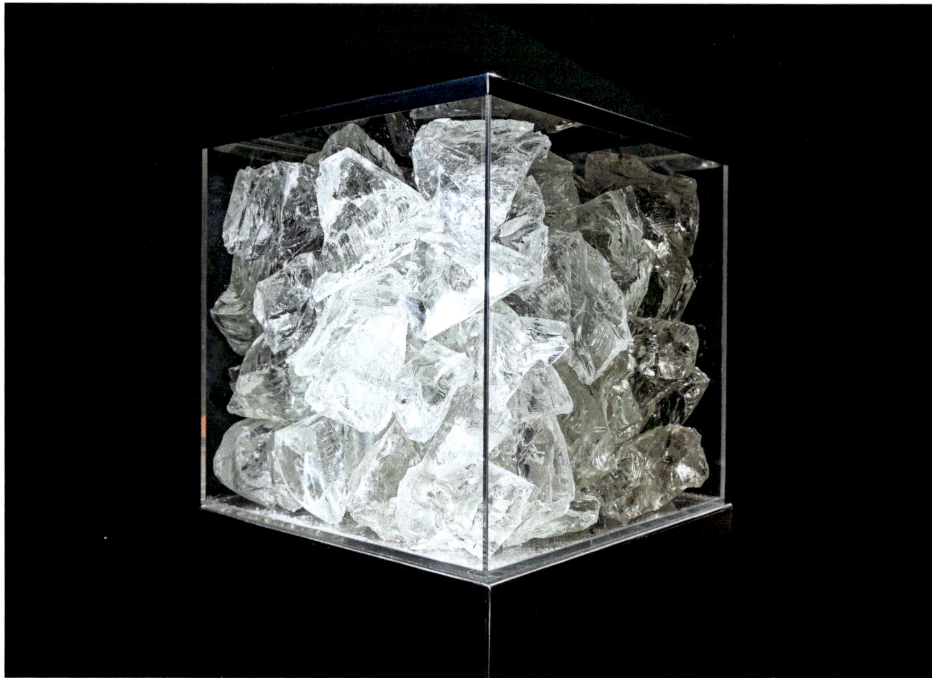

fig. 255 Heinz Mack, *Cube with Glass Chunks*, 2015 (idea: 1964)

Nano, micro, and macro

The universality of their languages enables Mack's structures to operate on the micro, nano, and macro levels: Any sense of dimension vanishes, much like in Charles and Ray Eames' *The Powers of 10*. Mack's orders resemble structures that might be seen in birds-eye views or if the eye could penetrate the microstructure of matter. From an artistic point of view, the distinction between scales and levels becomes blurred, and as Mack notes: "The immaterial world is not any less abundant than the material world."[14] Macro-level references to the real world in Mack's graphics pertain to cultural structures – for instance, when the structures he draws resemble cultivated farmland, vineyards, brickwork, or industrial plants – as well as natural structures, such as rock formations, sea shells, honeycombs, or sand dunes. In recent years, scientists have been discovering more examples of these types of formations also in the nanoworld, within the structure of graphene or organic nanopartilces such as viruses.

As science progresses, any structural level of matter previously considered "elementary" has turned out to consist of new, more basic structures. The development of novel instruments and methods of observation enables scientists to delve deeper not only into the microcosm, but also into the macrocosmos. Likewise, any structure that was once declared the largest has been surpassed by subsequent discoveries of even larger structures. The universe is characterized by hierarchical structures across a vast range of different scales.[15]

Mack's structures often resemble those found at the nanoscale, such as nanoscaled laponite clay, which can be utilized to stabilize sensitive biocatalysts that accelerate chemical reactions. Or, the movement and interaction of light with the art piece result in a projection that remarkably resembles the structure of inner networks within a living cell.

fig. 254 / *fig.* 255

14 Franz Joseph van der Grinten, *Mack: Zeichnungen Pastelle Tuschen* (Mönchengladbach: Kühlen, 2001), 82. Translated from the German.

15 See Jooß, *Self-organization of Matter*, 15.

fig. 256 / *fig.* 257

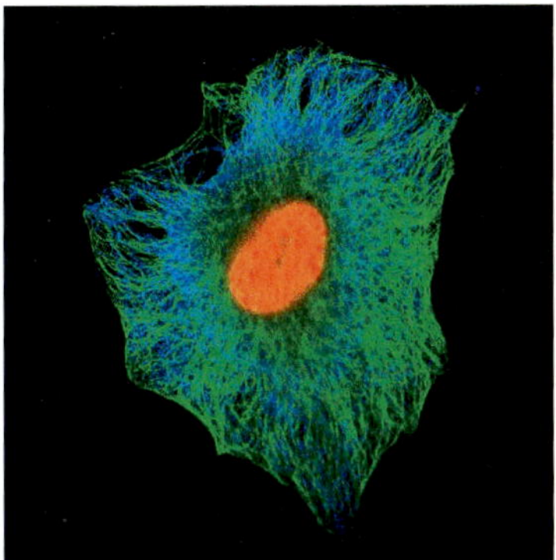

fig. 256 Matthew Daniels, human cell showing nucleus and tubulin

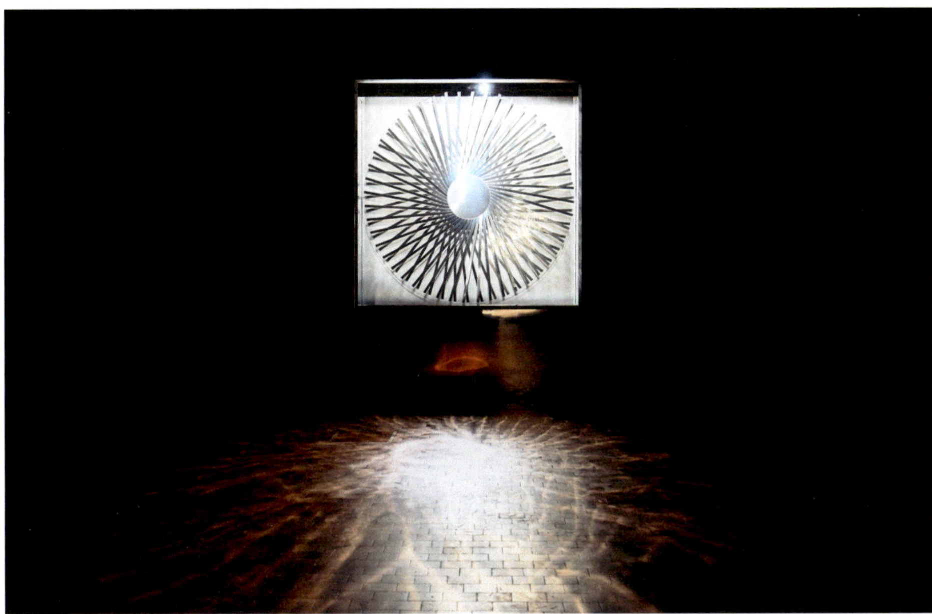

fig. 257 Heinz Mack, *Rotor for Light Grid II*, 1968

Beauty in artistic and natural structures

Heinz Mack's entire œuvre revolves around the question, What is beauty? For him, it is inextricably linked to the question, What is art?[16] Mack regards Friedrich Schiller, who was the first to recognize and stipulate the supremacy of form over content in art, as the starting point of a "new age of aesthetics."[17] In Mack's work, the immaterial prevails over matter. For Mack, beauty emerges from "immaterialization" through light and dynamization. This existential sense of connectedness with beauty (of nature) is the source of expressive power in Mack's work: "I find the beauty of nature deeply moving, it is the substantive essence and secret of nature. This also holds true for its microcosm."[18]

The perception of beauty is also at the focus of "molecular aesthetics," a discipline which is based on microscopic phenomena rather than the forms of human bodies or plants studied in traditional aesthetics.[19] Even in this realm of "immaterialized" matter, the laws of beauty, harmony, and symmetry still apply. Furthermore, deviations from the mathematical ideal in the form of surprise or novelty play a crucial role here as well: "What makes molecules beautiful? It may be their simplicity, a symmetrical structure. Or it may be their complexity, the richness of structural detail that is required for specific function. Sometimes the beauty of a molecule may be hidden, to be revealed only when its position in a sequence of transformations is made clear. Novelty, surprise, utility also play a role in molecular aesthetics. [...]"[20]

In the invisible world of quantum physics, beauty can also be found in the interactions between structures and the world surrounding them. At the nanoscale, the interactions of light and matter reveal hidden colors and result in new remarkable properties. Beauty is not static, but the result of dynamic processes and continuous change. The opalescent colors produced by the nanostructures in the wings of butterflies can vary depending on the viewing angle. Ultimately, beauty still lies in the eye of the beholder.

16 Heinz Mack, "Beauty is not dead, it only seems that way," in: Walter Smerling and Eva Müller-Remmert, eds., *Mack. Apollo in my Studio* (Cologne: Wienand, 2015), 94–103, here 95.

17 Ibid., 98.

18 Heinz Mack, "Mein Verhältnis zur Natur. Arbeitspapier von Heinz Mack," September 2022, unpublished typoscript (Archive Heinz Mack), 12. Translated from the German.

19 The concept of molecular aesthetics was established in a ZKM symposium (2011) and subsequent publication (2013): Peter Weibel and Ljiljana Fruk, eds., *Molecular Aesthetics* (Cambridge, MA: The MIT Press, 2013).

20 Roald Hoffmann, "Molecular Beauty", in: Weibel and Fruk, *Molecular Aesthetics*, 122–41, here 123.

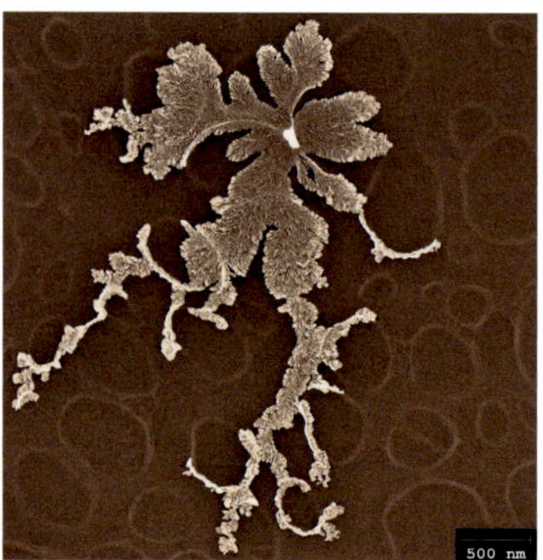

fig. 258 Yu-Chueh Hung and Ljiljana Fruk, University of Cambridge, 2015, gold nanoflower, consisting of gold nanoparticles grown on DNA.

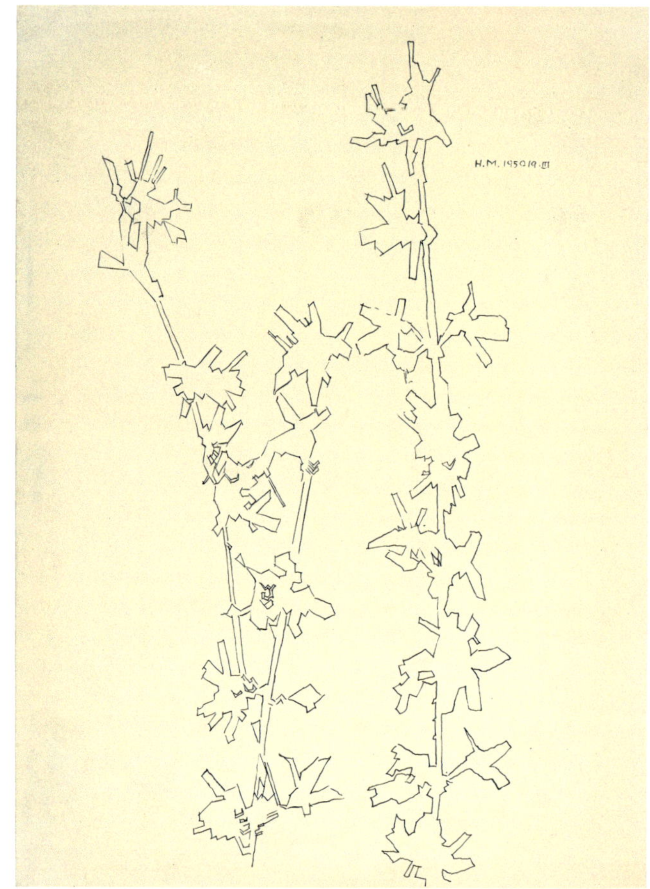

fig. 259 Heinz Mack, *Untitled*, 1950, ink on paper with steel pen, 29.5 × 21 cm

Reconciling "two cultures"

The extent of Heinz Mack's dedication to technology, nature, and science is extraordinary in the context of his time. His artistic position arose in a stark contrast to the climate of societal conservatism, which was perhaps best embodied in Konrad Adenauer's campaign for the 1957 federal elections and its slogan "Keine Experimente!" [No experiments!]. This period was characterized by a strict separation of the human sciences on the one hand and the technical and natural disciplines on the other hand, which the British physicist Charles Percy Snow criticized as a division of "two cultures" in his famous 1959 lecture *The Two Cultures*.[21] The German cultural scene was known for an increasingly pessimistic stance towards technology and its harsh criticism of any artistic innovations involving technology.[22]

So, which theoretical and philosophical positions were aligned with Mack and supportive of his artistic approach? In his school years, Mack studied the ideas of physicist and philosopher Carl Friedrich von Weizsäcker, including his twelve lectures published as *Die Geschichte der Natur* [The History of Nature].[23] Weizsäcker points out the mutual misunderstanding and the deep rift between natural and human sciences in his introduction, and his philosophical work aims to provide a solution for their reconciliation. He considers the human sciences a prerequisite of the natural sciences, as the history of humankind is ultimately embedded in the history of nature.[24]

21 For a summary of this debate, see Herbert W. Franke, *Kunst kontra Technik? Wechselwirkungen zwischen Kunst, Naturwissenschaft und Technik* (Frankfurt am Main: Fischer, 1978), 18–24.

22 See Susanne Kaufmann, "Heinz Mack: 'Ich wollte immer eine neue Kultur des Sehens,'" (radio feature, SWR Kultur, 11 October 2022), https://www.swr.de/swr2/leben-und-gesellschaft/heinz-mack-bildhauer-und-maler-swr2-zeitgenossen-2022-10-15-100.html.

23 C. F. von Weizsäcker, *Die Geschichte der Natur: Zwölf Vorlesungen von C. F. v. Weizsäcker* (Stuttgart: S. Hirzel Verlag, 1948), 8. In the 1970s, Weizsäcker also established an expanded concept of the structural sciences – a group of scientific disciplines between mathematics and empirical research founded on the unity of sciences (see Stefan Artmann, *Historische Epistemologie der Strukturwissenschaften* (Wilhelm Fink, 2010), 49–50).

24 Ibid., 8–9.

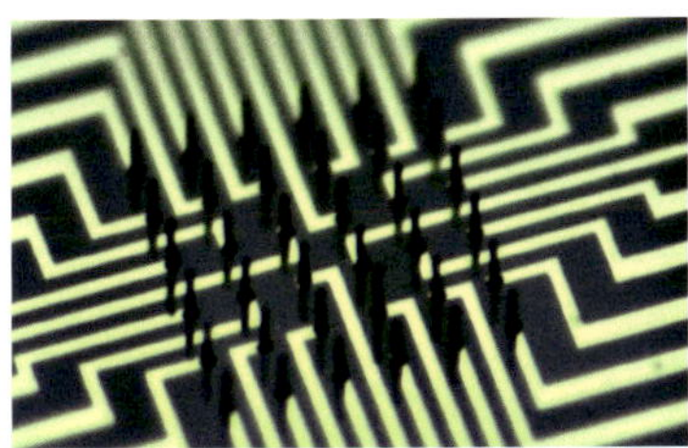

fig. 260 Jadranka Travas Sejdic, University of Auckland, polymer on electrodes

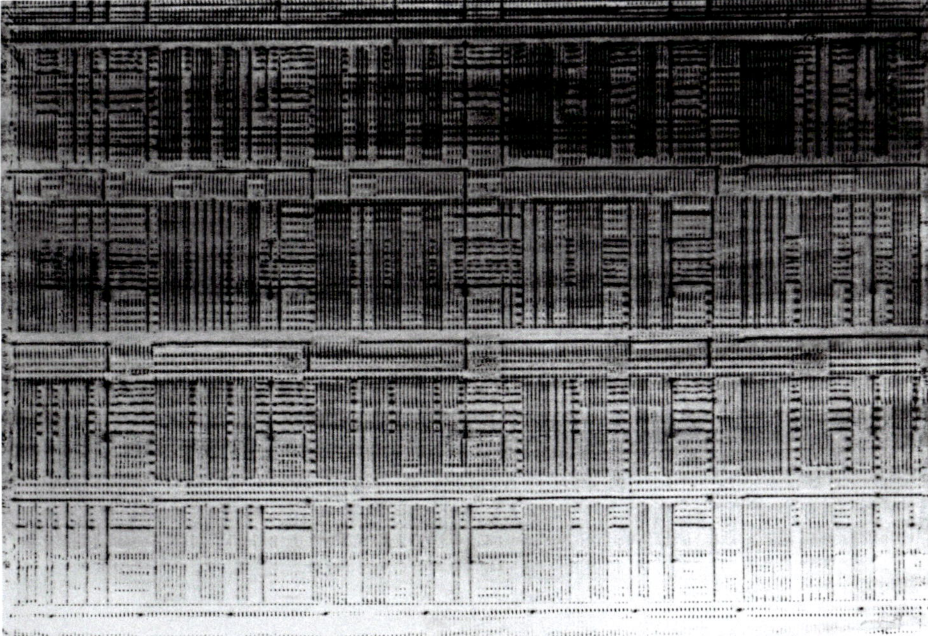

fig. 261 Heinz Mack, *IBM Grammar*, 1958, frottage of a light relief, black wax crayon on foiled paper, 50×70 cm

Another philosopher close to the ZERO group and Heinz Mack, also with a background in physics, was the disputatious thinker and Stuttgart professor of philosophy Max Bense. He viewed the rift between the cultures of natural and technological sciences and the arts and humanities as partly responsible for the rise of conservatism in Adenauer's republic.[25] In his writings, Bense pointed out the societal and political consequences of this rupture and strived to build the epistemological foundations for reconciling these two spheres philosophically. Following Descartes and Leibnitz, Bense viewed the mechanization of the world as an instrument of enlightenment and argued for a position of existential rationalism which would be in line with the conditions of our "technological existence" (Bense, 1949).[26]

As a pioneer of the "exact human sciences," Bense also wanted to create new foundations for aesthetics and establish it as an exact science by applying structural methods and analogies from the world of theoretical physics, such as the conceptualization of electrons not as objects, but as structures. Not unlike Mack, Bense assigned great significance to randomness in his aesthetical theory: Perfection can only arise from irritations by the non-perfect, lest perceptions become mere habits.[27]

Bense's theories were hotly debated in contemporary intellectual circles. In 1957, Mack and Otto Piene reached out to Bense and invited him to hold the opening speech for the sixth *Abendausstellung* [evening exhibition] at their studio in Düsseldorf. There were multiple points of overlap between the artists and Bense's philosophy, but also stark differences. His uninhibited openness towards technology and exact sciences, the visionary power of his claims, the unification of technology and art, and the search for structures – all this was in line with the young ZERO artists' objectives. The collaboration between Bense and Mack continued in the late 1960s, when Max Bense wrote an introductory chapter for the first book about Heinz Mack's *Sahara Project*.[28]

25 See Petra Boden, "Für 'eine stetige, wenn auch unendlich langsame Perfektion der Welt.' Max Bense zum Verhältnis von Natur- und Geisteswissenschaften," 45-59, here 46, in: Elke Uhl and Claus Zittel, eds., *Max Bense. Weltprogrammierung* (Stuttgart: J. B. Metzler Verlag, 2018).

26 See ibid. 45-59.

27 Max Bense, "Extrakt einer statistischen Ästhetik," *Das Kunstwerk* 12, no. 7 (1958): 39-42, here 42, in: Bense, *Programmierung des Schönen. Allgemeine Texttheorie und Textaesthetik* (Krefeld: Agis, 1960).

28 See Max Bense, "Das Sahara-Projekt Heinz Macks," 5-6, in: *Mack – Kunst in der Wüste*, ed. by Institut für moderne Kunst, Nürnberg (Starnberg: Josef Keller Verlag, 1969).

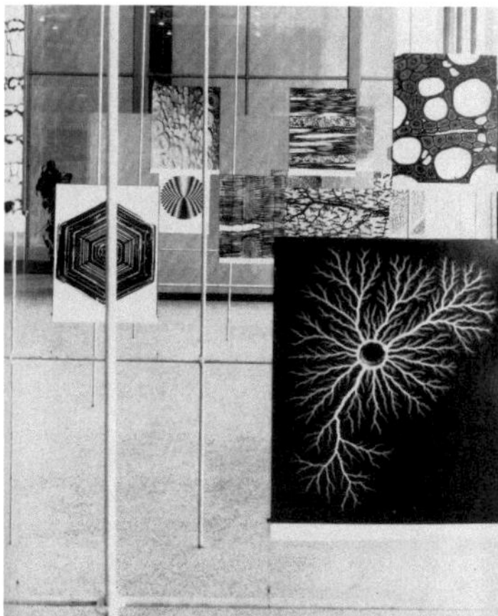

fig. 262 Exhibition view *The New Landscape, Massachusetts Institute of Technology*, 1951

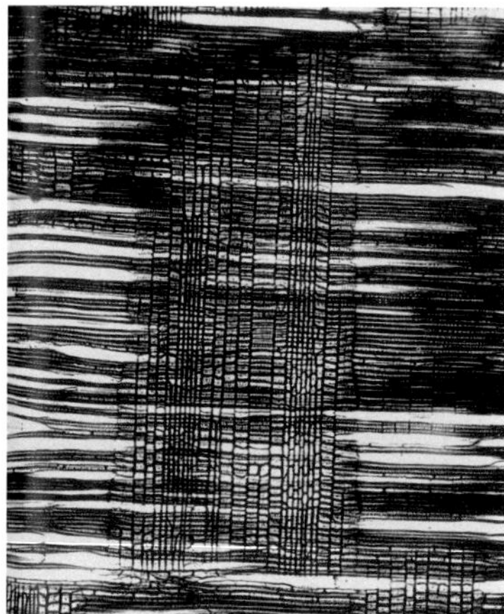

fig. 263 I.W. Bailey, Harvard University, Triplochiton, radial section

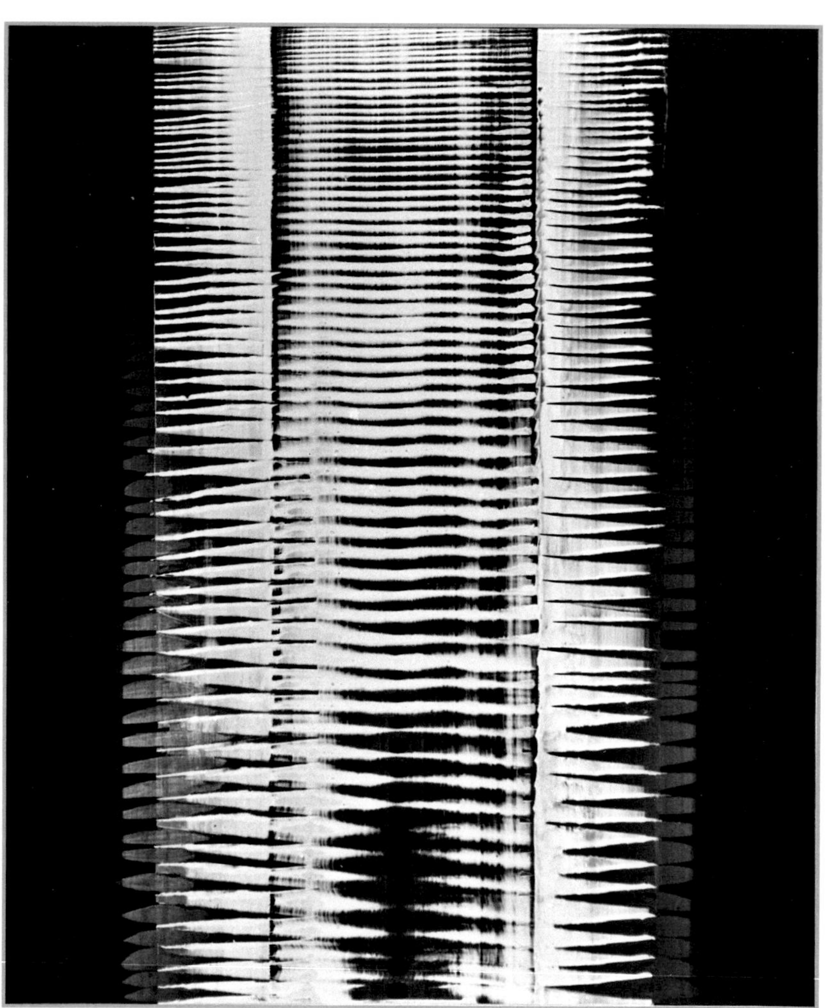

fig. 264 Heinz Mack, *Black Vibration*, 1957, synthetic resin on canvas, 130 × 105 cm, private collection

The holistic view of different spheres made possible by Mack's structural gaze enabled him to combine the seemingly contradictory fields of nature, technology, and humanity/culture without antagonism in his work. This structural principle can be applied to organic and inorganic matter, as well as artificial objects. But structure is not a rigid state: it creates itself and develops from a broad range of different forces. That is why Mack's works often seem like artistic sketches for new forms of interaction between modern technology and nature. Some drawings form the 1950s not only show structures resembling raster electron microscope images of atomic structures, but also bear a striking resemblance to complex technological artifacts such as integrated circuits. They are the visual anticipation of a technology that was only developed years later.

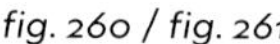

fig. 260 / fig. 261

In addition to these philosophical ties to Weizsäcker and Bense, Mack is closely linked to the visual culture of the 1950s and 1960s. Mack's practice of comparative vision can be linked to other investigations of co-visualities between artistic and natural structures.[29] Numerous popular scientific publications of the period showcased magnifications of natural structures,[30] and the comparative gaze was explored in artistic books and exhibitions: similarities between photographs of microscopic organic and inorganic structures, substances,

fig. 263 / fig. 268

29 See also: Lena Bader, Martin Gaier und Falk Wolf, eds., *Vergleichendes Sehen* (Munich: Wilhelm Fink, 2010); Matthias Bruhn und Gerhard Scholz, eds., *Morphologien*, in: *Bildwelten des Wissens. Kunsthistorisches Jahrbuch für Bildkritik*, vol. 9,2, ed. Horst Bredekamp, Matthias Bruhn und Gabriele Werner (Berlin: Akademie Verlag, 2013); Matthias Bruhn und Gerhard Scholtz, eds., *Der vergleichende Blick: Formanalyse in Natur- und Kulturwissenschaften* (Berlin: Reimer, 2017).

30 See Gustav Schenk, *Schöpfung aus dem Wassertropfen* (Berlin: Hartmann, 1954); Carl Strüwe, *Formen des Mikrokosmos* (Munich: Prestel, 1955); Juliane Roh, *Abstrakte Bilder der Natur* (Munich: Bruckmann, 1960).

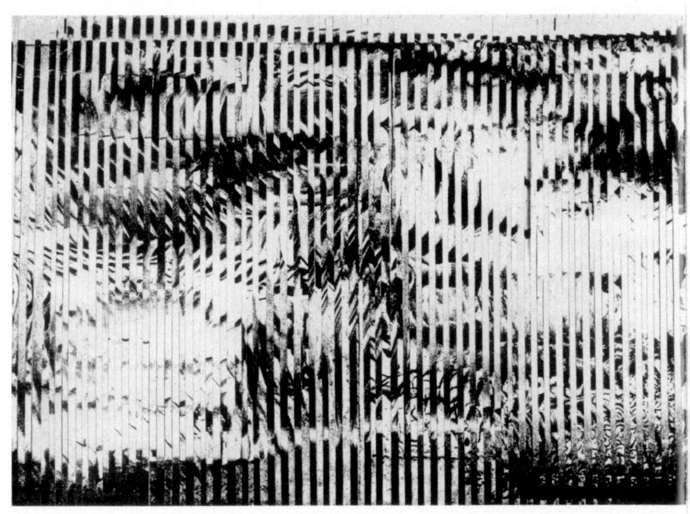

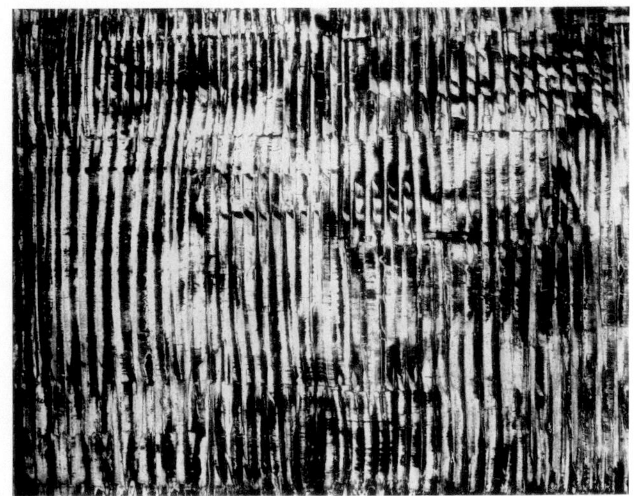

fig. 265 Double page from the publication *Das Kunstwerk* 4/XII (Oktober 1958), n. p., left page: stone structure (two prints of one photograph, cut up and spliced together); right page: Heinz Mack, *Untitled*, 1958, oil on canvas, 98 × 110 cm

fig. 262

fig. 269

or morphologies and abstract modern art. After an exhibition titled *The New Landscape* (1951), which presented affinities between the fine arts and the latest visualizations of scientific models, Georgy Kepes published *The New Landscape in Art and Science* in 1956, a "picture book,"[31] as he called it, which would serve as an important reference work for the relation between art and science for years to come: "Science has opened up resources for new sights and sounds, new tastes and textures. If we are to understand the new landscape, we need to touch it with our senses and build the images that will make it ours. For this we must remake our vision."[32] This documents the new perspective of imaging technologies such as x-rays, sonar, radar, high-powered telescopes, or electron microscopy, as well as the scientification of modern art. Kepes viewed the "domestication" of new discoveries in the natural sciences in integration "with the scientist's brain, the poet's heart, the painter's eye."[33] In 1965 and 1966, Kepes, who went on to found the Center for Advanced Visual Studies at MIT in 1967, published a series of six volumes titled "Vision + Value" – including the volume *Structure in Art and in Science* (1965), which is of particular interest for the present examination.[34]

fig. 265

Another example of comparative vision in this period can be found in a series of visual comparisons published in the magazine *Das Kunstwerk* alongside an article by Max Bense, which also included an artwork of Mack's.[35]

Such comparisons were also drawn in exhibitions of modern art throughout the German-speaking world at the time. *Kunst und Naturform* (1958, Kunsthalle Basel) was an organized exhibition that confronted photographs of microscopic organic and inorganic substances with non-figurative art.[36] While Kepes engaged in a rather critical examination of possible parallels between the two worlds of imagery, *Kunst und Naturform* paired the images in five chapters based on formal principles to point out the visual analogies.

fig. 269 / fig. 270

31 Georgy Kepes, ed., *The New Landscape in Art and Science* (Chicago: Paul Theobald and Co., 1956), 17.

32 Ibid., 20.

33 Ibid.

34 See Georgy Kepes, ed., *Structure in Art and in Science* (London: Studio Vista, 1965).

35 *Das Kunstwerk* 12, no. 4 (1959).

36 Georg Schmidt and Robert Schenk, eds., *Kunst und Naturform*, exh. cat. Kunsthalle Basel (Basel: Basilius,1960).

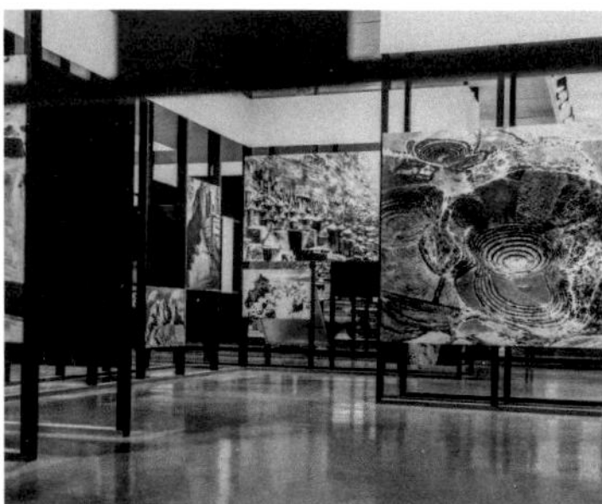

fig. 266 View into the exhibition *Architecture without Architects*, 1964, The Museum of Modern Art, New York

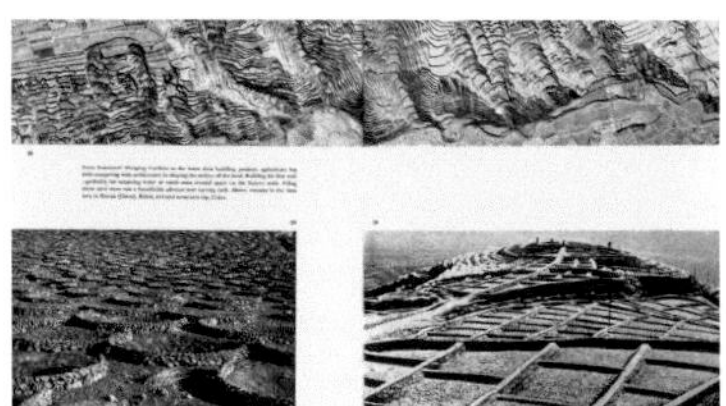

fig. 267 Double page from the exhibition catalog *Architecture without Architects*, 1964, The Museum of Modern Art, New York

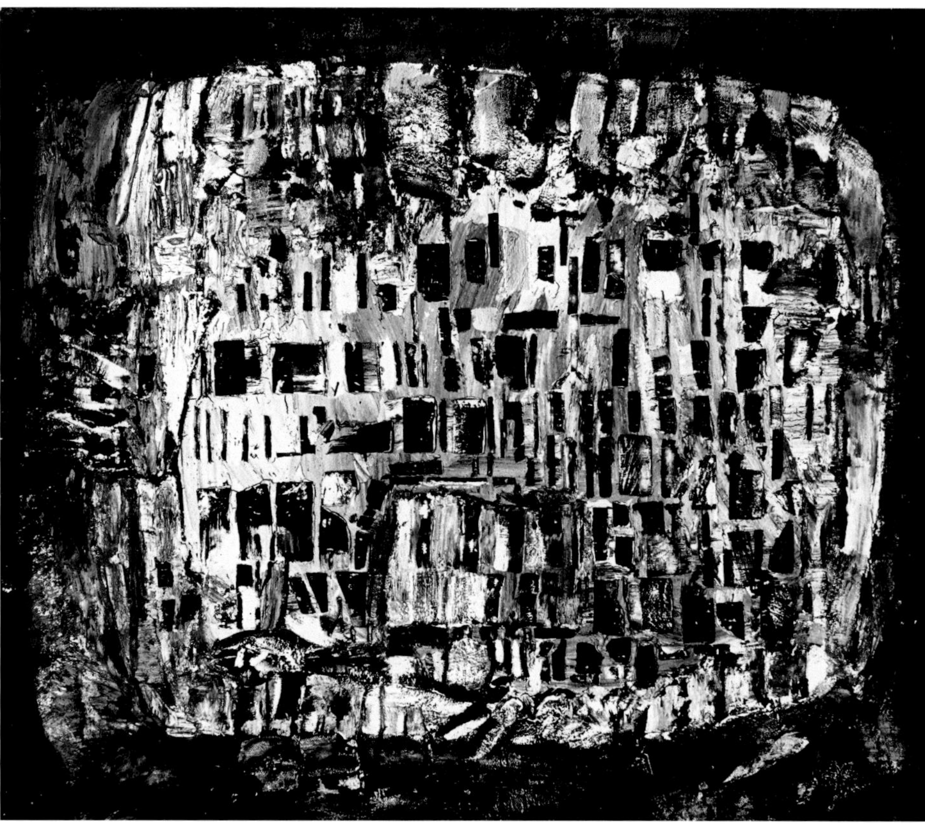

fig. 268 Heinz Mack, *Untitled*, ca. 1957, oil

fig. 266

On an international level, Bernard Rudofsky's exhibition *Architecture without Architects* (1964/1965), which Heinz Mack saw at MoMA during a visit to the United States, may have been influential.[37] More than 200 large-format black-and-white photographs showcased the cultural wealth of "anonymous architecture." Without any text or explanation, the exhibition only presented images of architectural traditions that were in stark contrast to the ideas of architectural modernism. While this was not a direct comparison of art and nature, many of the photographs were taken from a bird's-eye view or other perspectives that emphasized structural features and let the architecture seem almost like abstract patterns and ornaments.

The history of natural science in the twentieth century was shaped by a wealth of new theories, hypotheses, and discoveries, which changed our understanding of the composition and movements of material systems. Especially quantum mechanics, theories of relativity, molecular biology and genetics, nanochemistry, and material science were met with great interest from the art world. The relationship between Mack's art and the natural sciences is highly complex. Mack's work is characterized by its harmony with the physical laws of nature, the world of technology, and the natural sciences in the age of quantum physics. This not only gives rise to visual similarities, but also numerous parallels and analogies in the artistic creation of structures, the inclusion of dynamic and aleatory elements, and dialectical development, as well as the appreciation for phenomena of beauty.

37 See Heike van den Valentyn, "elementar," in: Heike van den Valentyn, ed., *MACK*, exh. cat. Kunstpalast Düsseldorf (Cologne: Verlag der Buchhandlung König, 2021), 14–37, here 17–18.

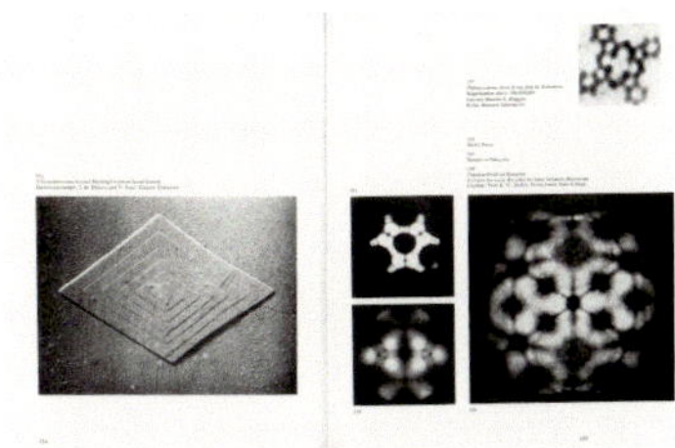

fig. 269 Double page from Gyorgy Kepes, *The New Landscape in Art and Science*, 1956

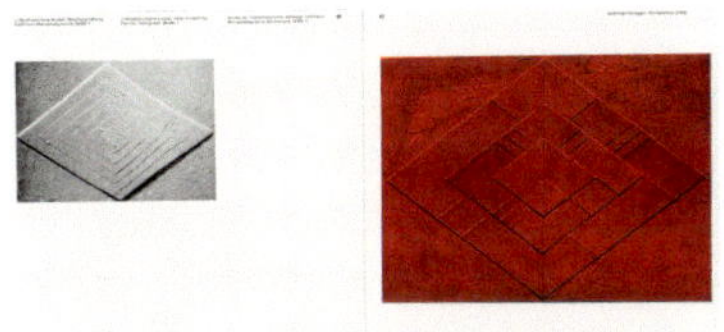

fig. 270 Double page from Georg Schmidt and Robert Schenk, *Form in Art and Nature*, 1960

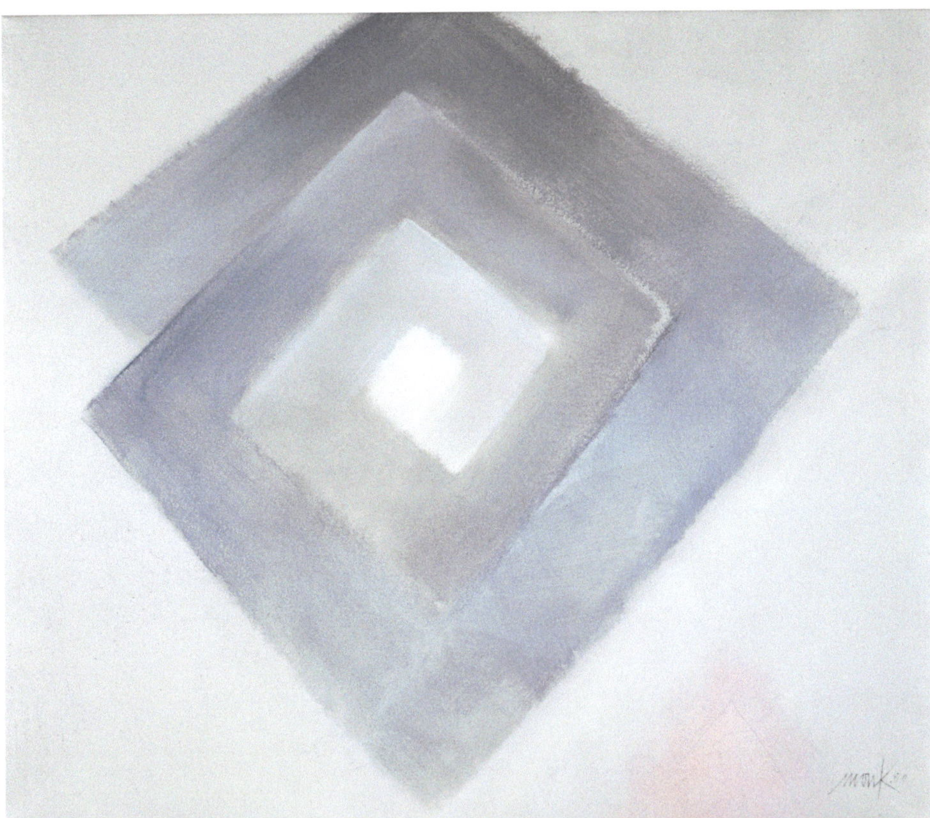

fig. 271 Heinz Mack, *Spiral with Edges (Chromatic Constellation)*, 2000, acrylic on canvas, 83×95 cm

The discovery of the universality of structures in the visual culture of the 1950s and the philosophies of C. F. von Weizsäcker and Max Bense form the cultural context for the transferral of scientific phenomena into the realm of visual art. The fundamental agreement between Mack's art and the sciences is also founded in the idea that everything can be constructed, which is a defining principle of human (technological) thought in the modern age. His art is thus firmly anchored in the paradigm of modern thought, which appreciates the value of artistic statements in the creation of new reality and emphasizes universalism instead of examining differences from a situated perspective.[38]

Translated from the German by Dan Lawler.

38 Special thanks to Henriette Pleiger and Sophia Sotke.

The *Compendium*

Art is magic delivered from the lie of being truth.[*]

When André Malraux published his book The Imaginary Museum (1947), *I felt reaffirmed in my inclination to compare everything to everything with regards to art, without always paying heed to the criteria of art history. [...] Influences lead to similarities, and ultimately, similarities resemble other similarities, which can be compared, which in turn is an essential prerequisite to critical art reception.*[**]

In the 1920s, the art and cultural scholar Aby Warburg developed his pictorial atlas *Mnemosyne*, which traces recurring visual themes, gestures, and patterns from antiquity through the Renaissance to contemporary culture. In 1947, André Malraux published the essay *Le Musée Imaginaire* (*The Imaginary Museum*), which imposed a new relationship with the work of art. This new relationship frees works of art from their function in what Malraux calls a "metamorphosis."

It was in this sense that Heinz Mack developed his *Compendium* over decades, finding analogies between his own visual world and images from science, technology, architecture, and art history. This collection of references contains images which serve as philosophically and aesthetically important points of orientation and inspiration in his œuvre.

Heinz Mack's *Compendium* is dedicated to a wide range of different topics from "flying objects" to the elements of air, water, fire, to the cosmos and to typography. On the following pages, the artist has made a representative selection to illustrate his way of working with this visual material.

* Theodor W. Adorno, *Minima Moralia: Reflections from Damaged Life: In nuce* (1951)
** Heinz Mack, *Mack. Malerei. Die Strukturen der chromatischen Konstellationen* (Munich: Hirmer, 2023), 195. Translated from the German.

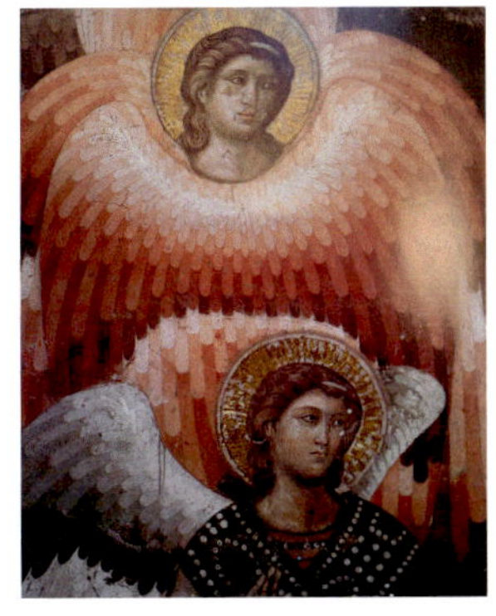

272

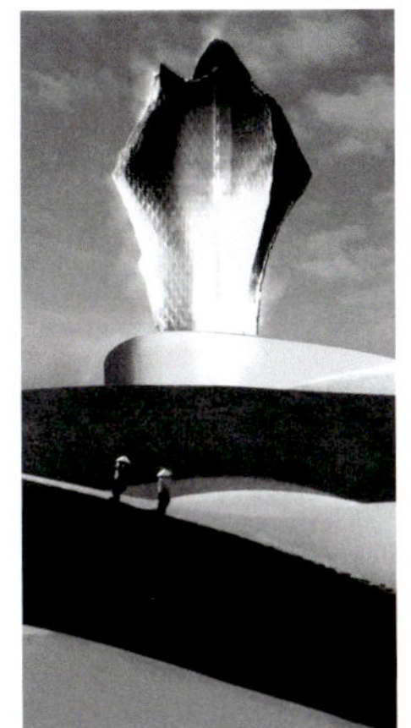

273

274

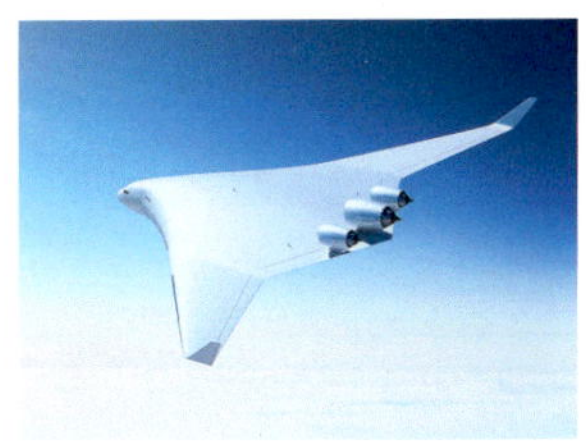

275

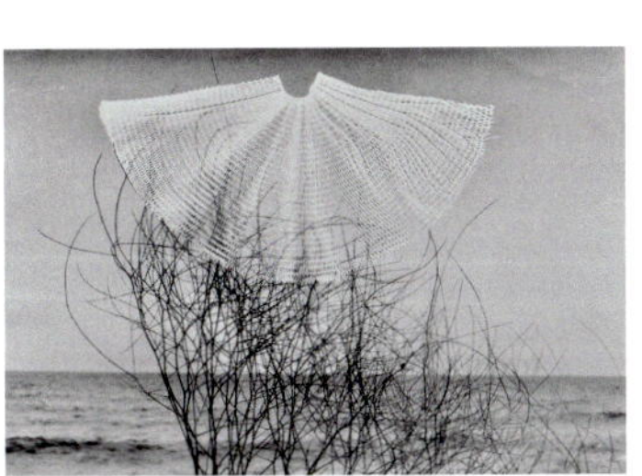

276

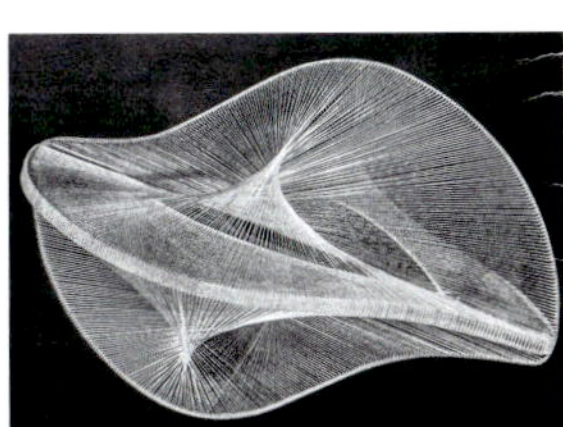

277

278

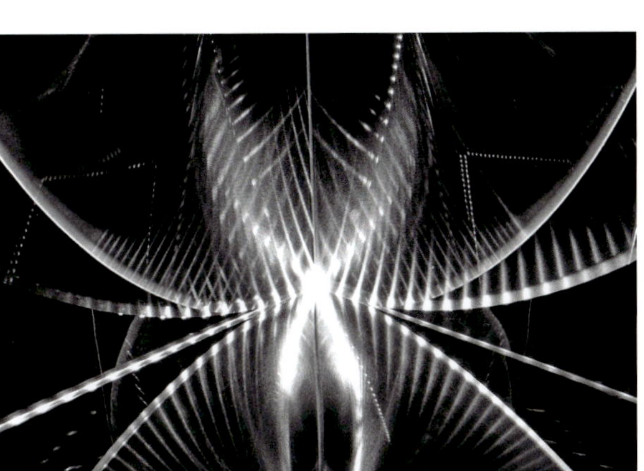
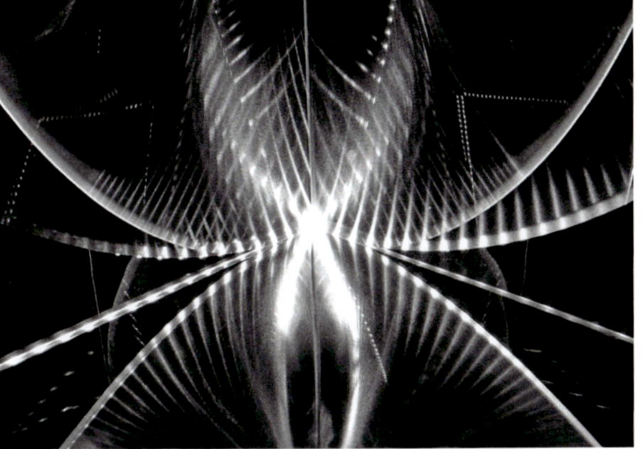

279

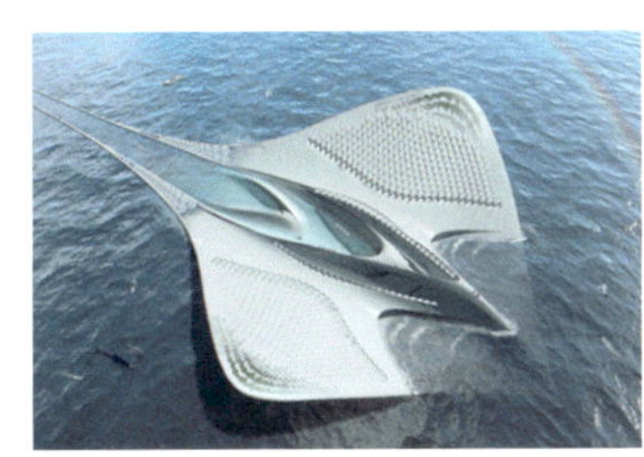

280

281

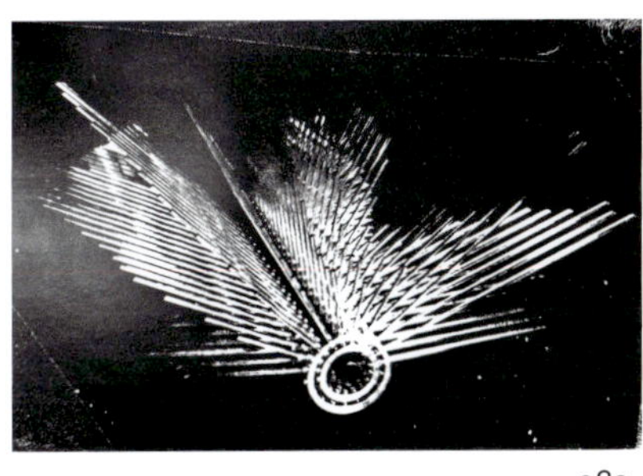

282

283

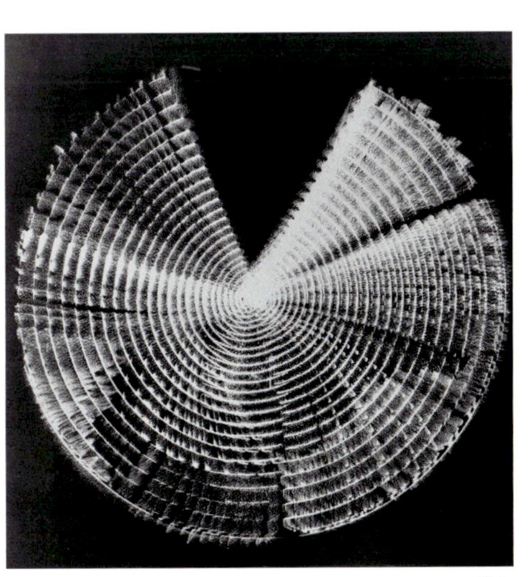

284

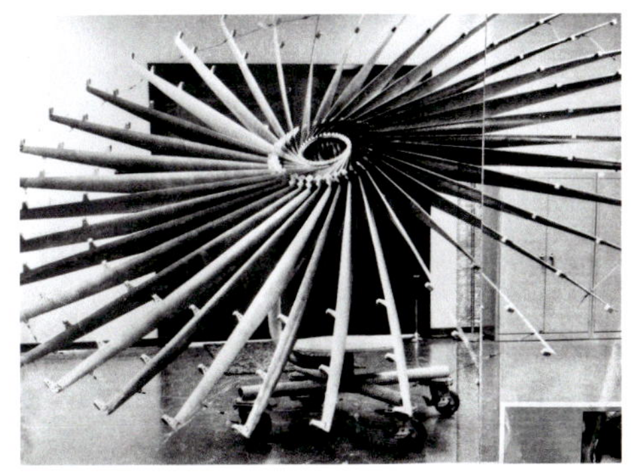

285

272 Pietro Cavallini, Jesus Christ with Angels, detail of the *Last Judgement*, ca. 1289–1293, Santa Cecilia in Trastevere, Rome

273 Heinz Mack, *Night Light Sculpture in the Desert*, ca. 1970

274 Cuckoo bird

275 Large futuristic passenger airplane in blended wing body shape

276 Heinz Mack, *Light Wing in the Sky*, ca. 1970

277 Naum Gabo, *Linear Construction No. 2*, 1970–71, Tate, London

278 Close-up of a Monarch Butterfly Wing

279 Heinz Mack, *Untitled*, 2016, photo experiment

280 Jacques Rougerie, model of the city of Merines

281 Seraphim fresco, 13th century, Sant Climent de Taüll, Catalonia

282 Heinz Mack, photo experiment with acrylic glass object

283 Windmill on Formentera, Baleares

284 Heinz Mack, *Wing Drawing*, ca. 1970

285 US Army, kinetic energy weapon for the Homing Overlay Experiment, 1980s

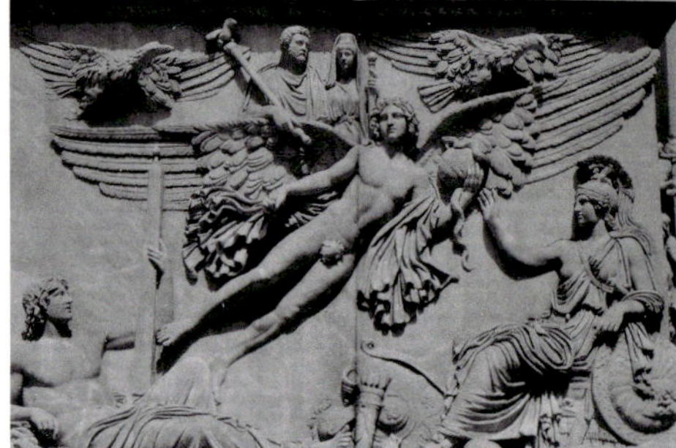
286

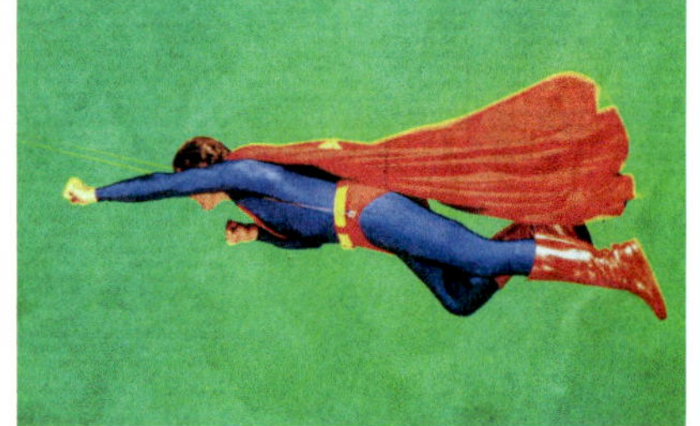
287

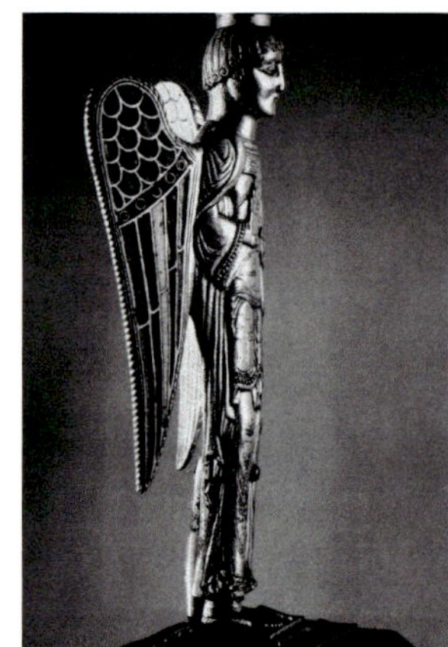
288

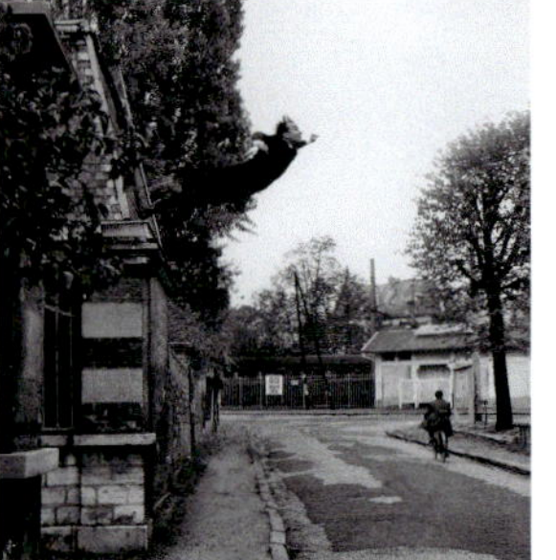
289

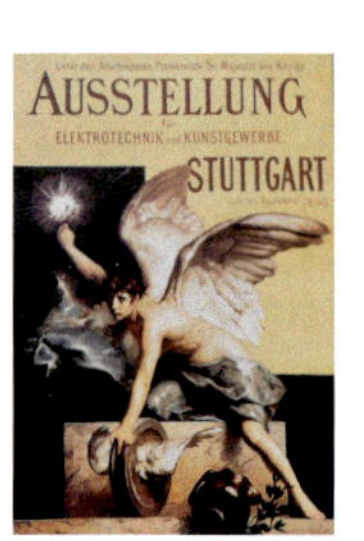

290

291

292

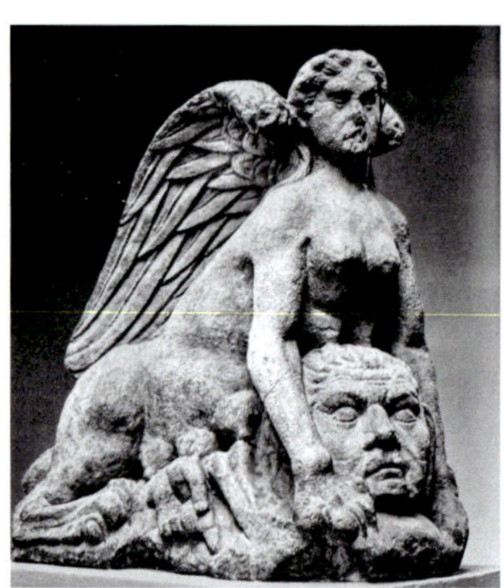
293

294

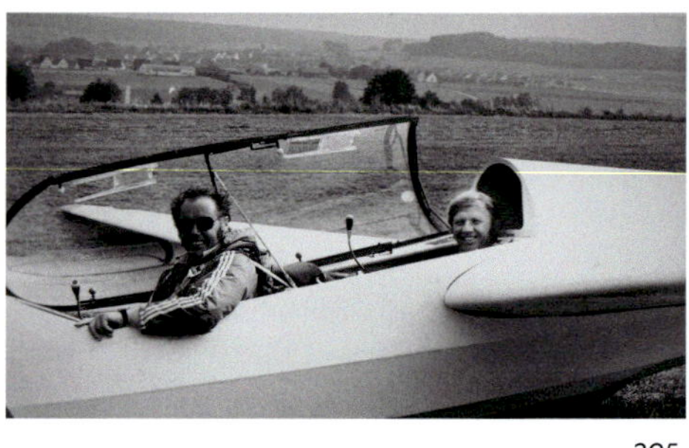
295

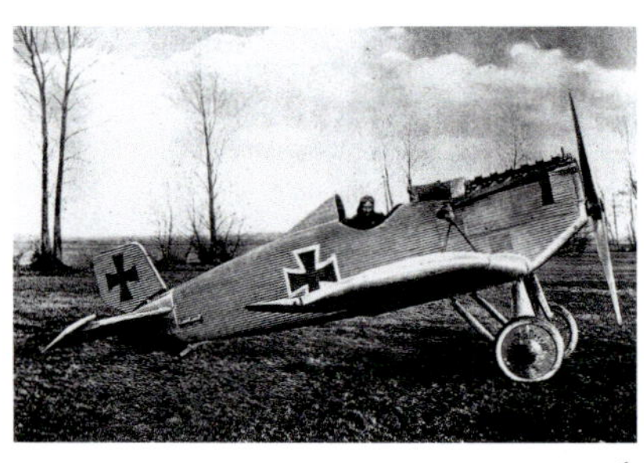
296

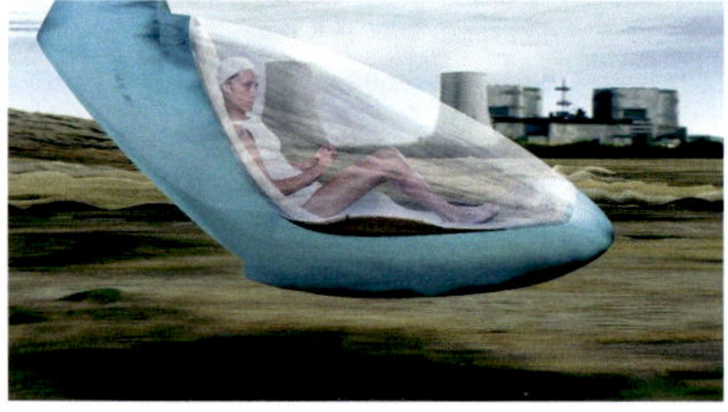
297

298

286 Column of Antonius Pius, Apotheosis of Antonius Pius and Faustina, 161 AD, Vatican Museums, Rome

287 *Lois & Clark: The New Adventures of Superman*, television series, 1993–1997, film still

288 Angel reliquary of Saint-Sulpice-les-Feuilles, mid 12th century, Museum of Fine Arts, Limoges

289 Yves Klein, *Leap into the Void*, 1960, Metropolitan Museum of Art, New York City

290 Electrical Engineering and Arts and Crafts, State Museum of Trade, Stuttgart, 1896, exhibition poster

291 Bill Suitor, wearing a rocket belt, drops into the stadium at the opening ceremony of the Olympic Summer Games, Los Angeles, 1984

292 Angel over the burning Babylon, Beatus Apocalypse, 10th century, Spain, book illumination

293 Colchester Sphinx, 43 AD, Roman sculpture found in Colchester, England

294 Heinz Mack, *Sky Art project*

295 Heinz Mack with Erich Reusch in an airplane

296 Junkers-J 9, all-metal airplane, 1917, postcard

297 Hussein Chalayan, *Place to Passage*, 2003, film still

298 Luigi Colani, Megalodon (shark), model of an ultra-high-capacity airliner, project for Boeing, 1977

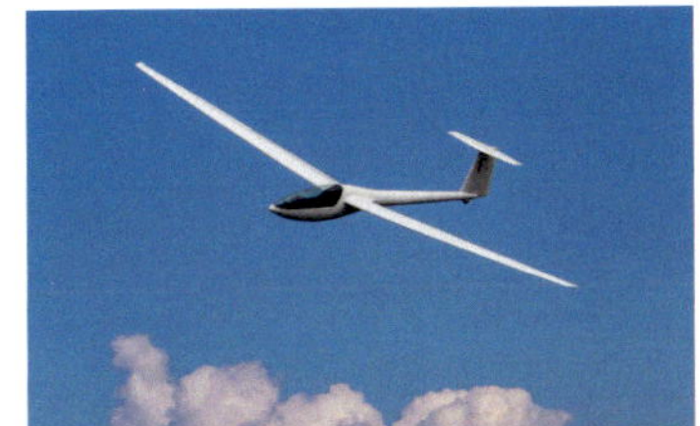

299

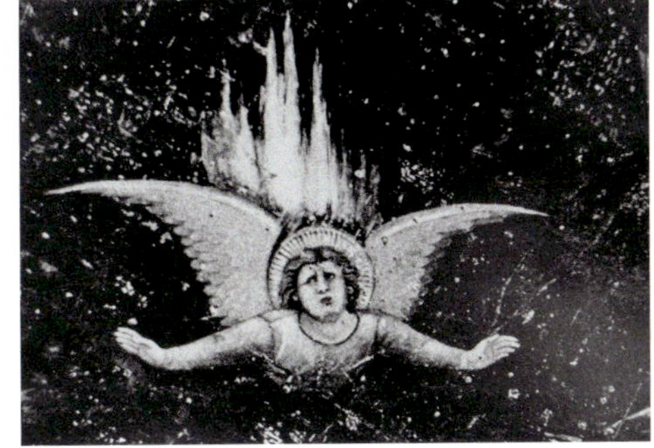

300

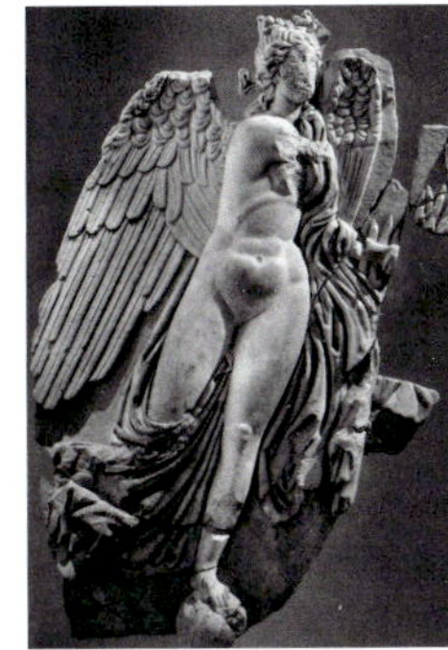

301

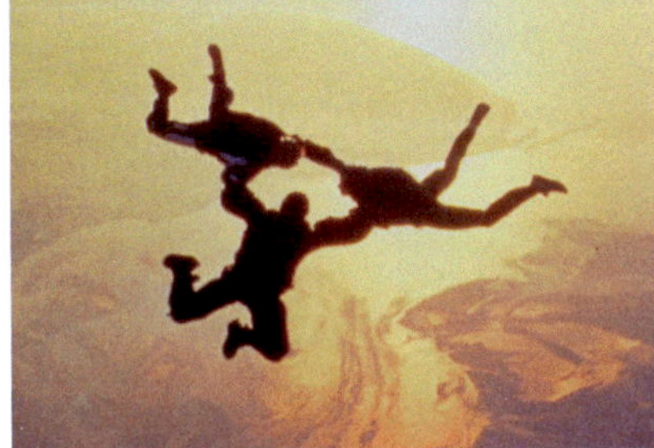

302

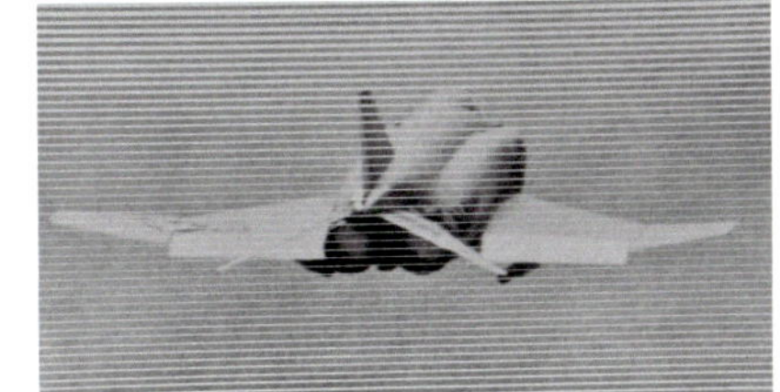

303

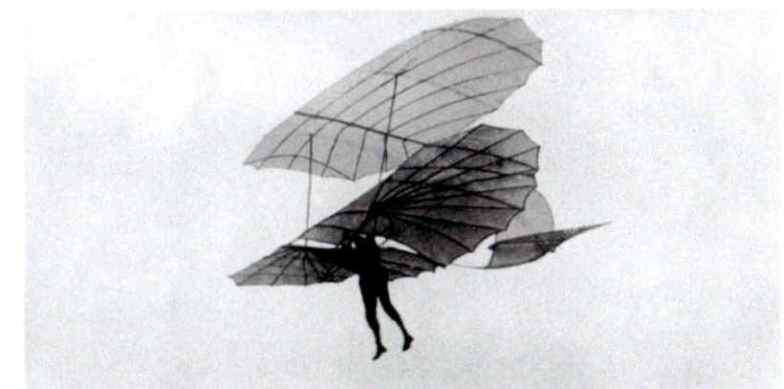

304

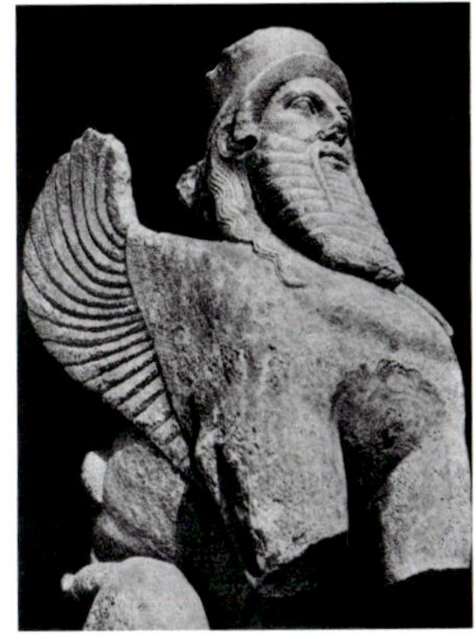

305

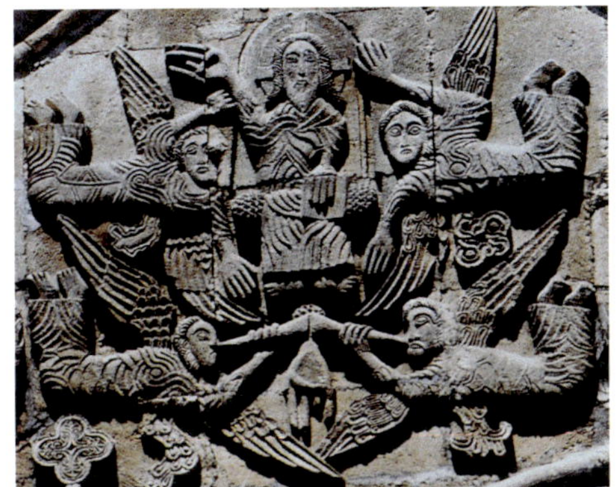

306

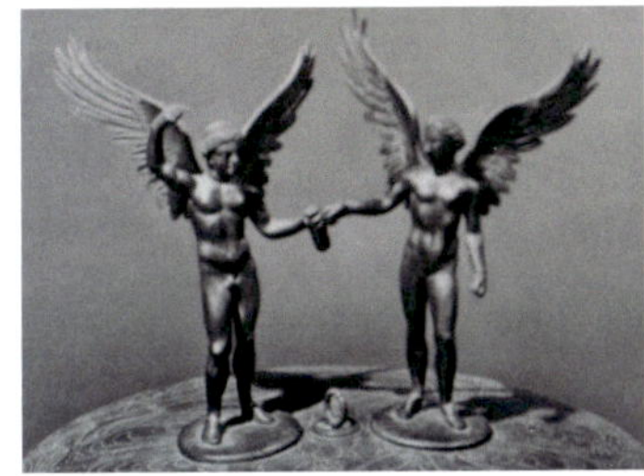

307

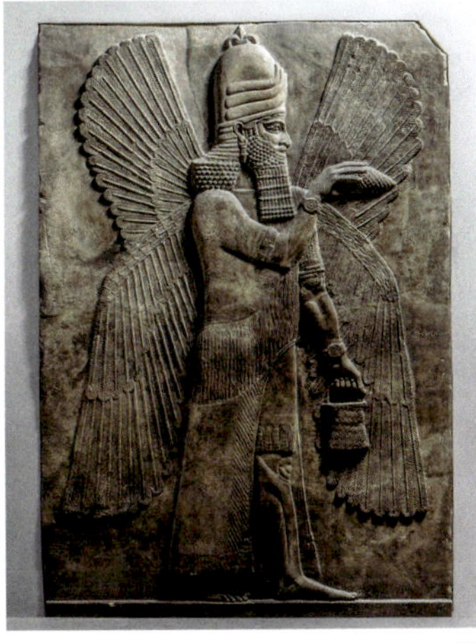

308

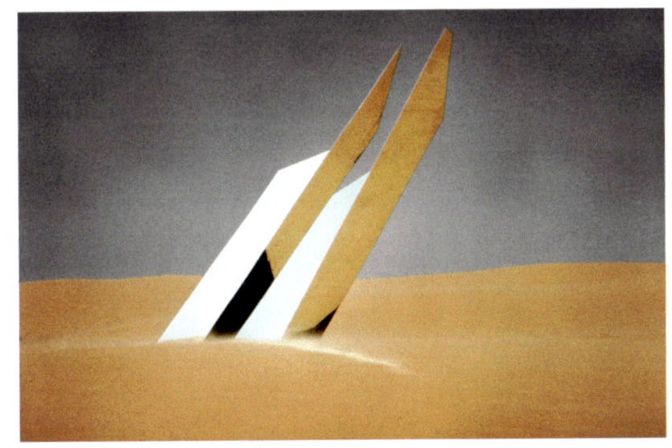

309

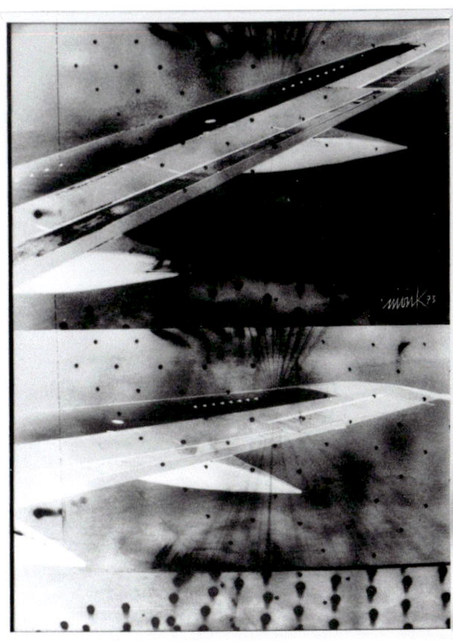

310

299 Glider plane

300 Ambrogio Lorenzetti, Angel, detail of the *Crucifixion*, 1336–1337, Basilica di San Francesco, Siena, fresco

301 *Victoria*, Arch of Septimius Severus, Lepcis Magna, ca. 200 AD, Saraya Museum, Tripoli, Libya

302 Skydiving

303 Heinz Mack, *Phantom-Jet – Thunderbird – Fire Bird*, 1966

304 Otto Lilienthal during one of his glider flights, 1896

305 Labranda Sphinx, 4th century BC, Iran

306 Relief on the southern façade, Nikortsminda Cathedral, Georgia, 1010–1014

307 Bronze cist with handle depicting the contest between Apollo and Marsyas, Palestrina, Columbella necropolis, Barberini Collection, Villa Poniatowski, 4th–3rd century BC

308 Neo-Assyrian, Orthostate, Sargon II, Khorsabad, 721–705 BC, Musée du Louvre, Paris

309 Heinz Mack, *The Saint-Exupéry Crash – Model of a Monument in the Algerian Desert*, 1976, photo: Thomas Höpker

310 Heinz Mack, *Untitled – Mirror Image in Great Height*, 1973

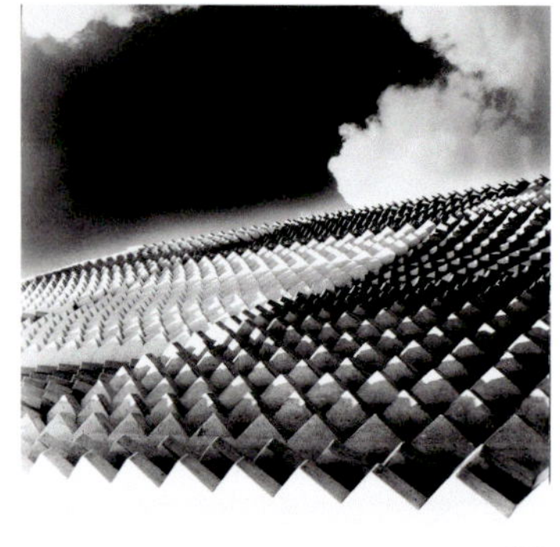
311

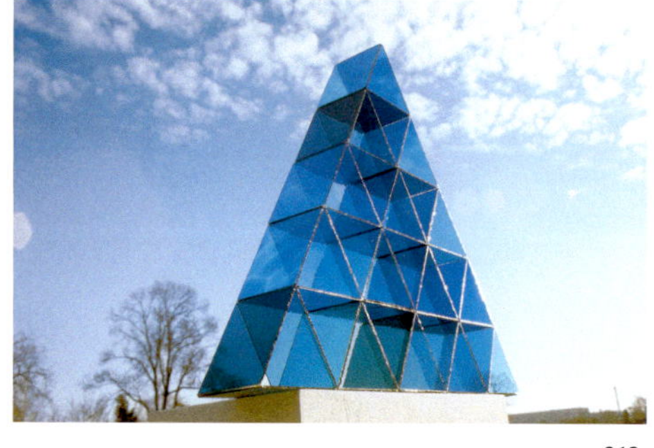
312

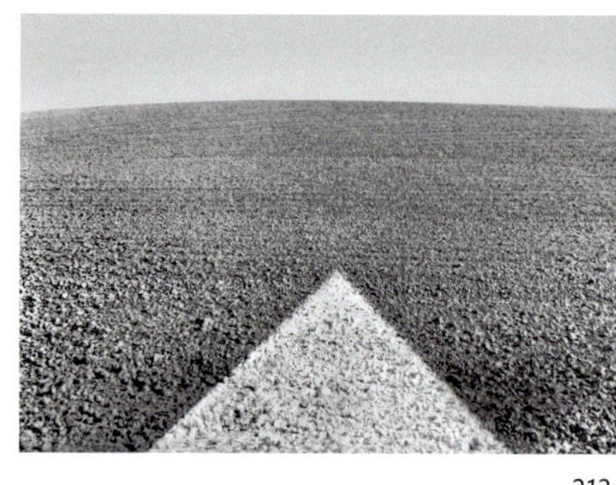
313

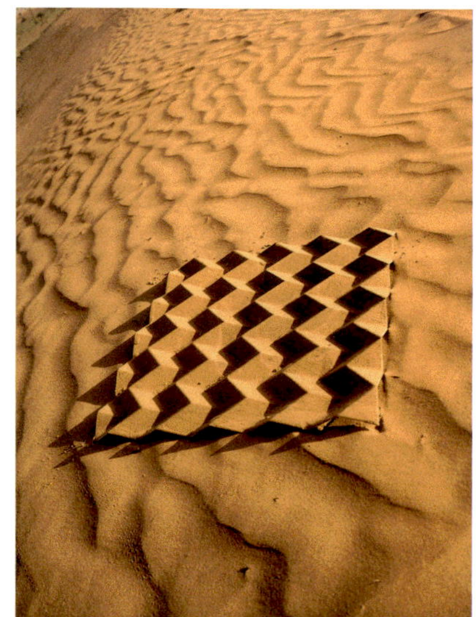
316

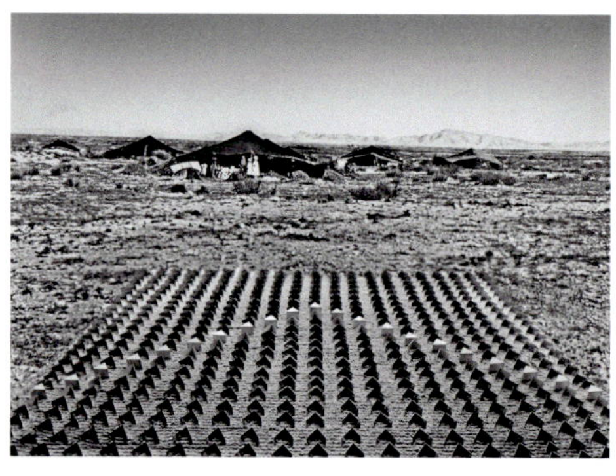
314

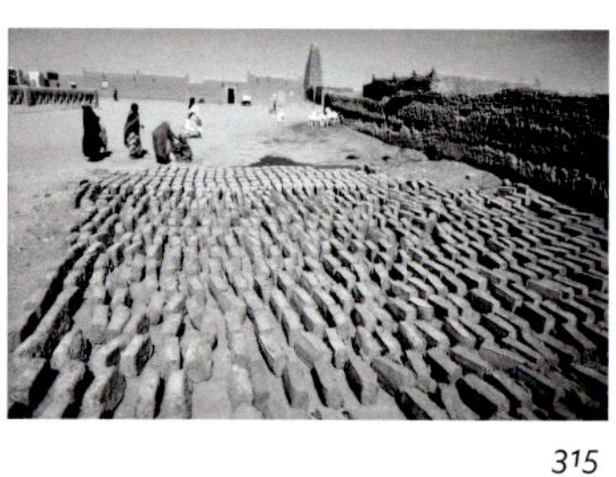
315

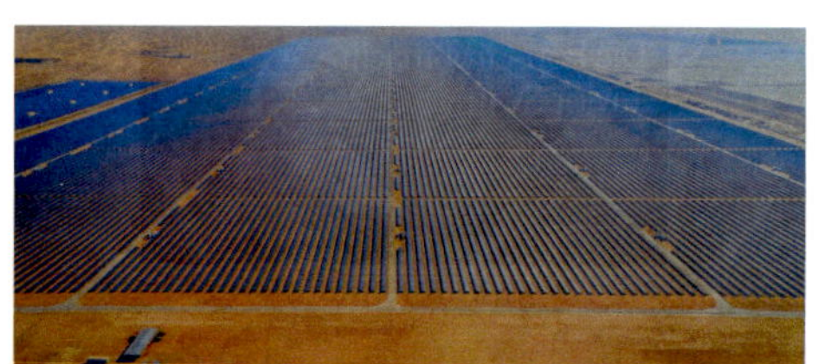
317

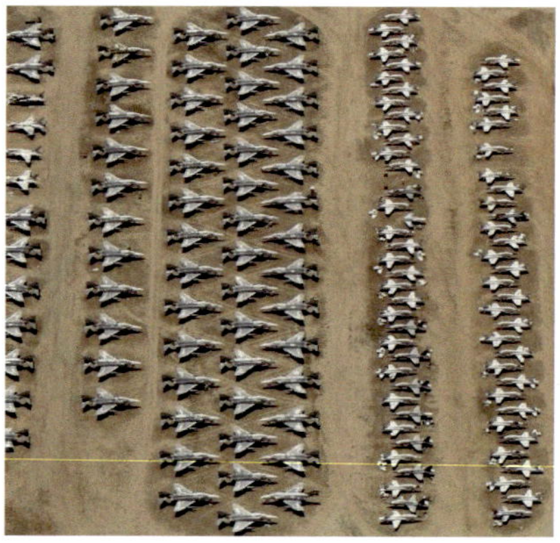

318

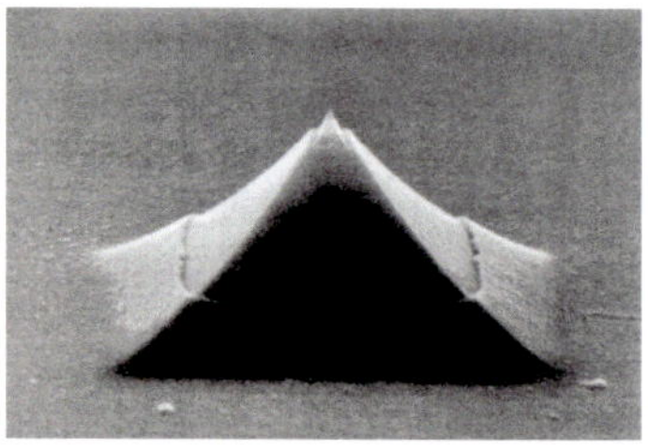

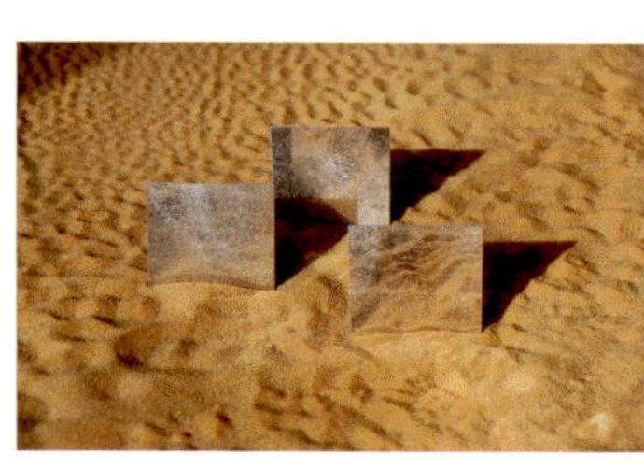
319

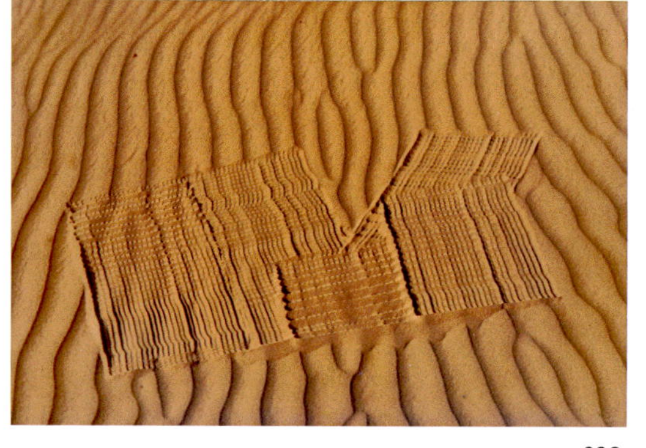
320

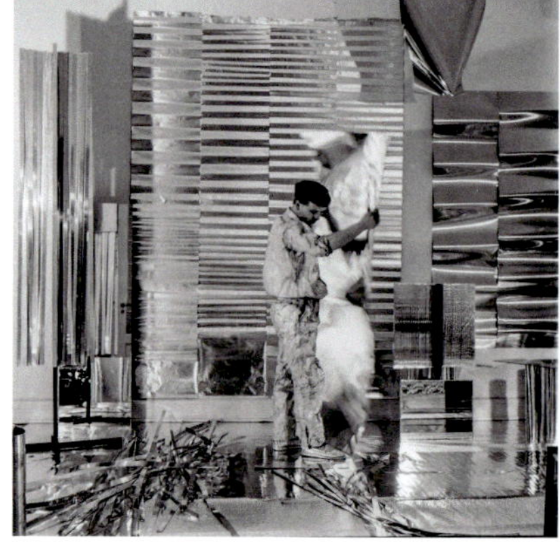
321

322

311 Heinz Mack, *Sahara Relief* 1960/61, Leverkusen, detail

312 Heinz Mack, *Architecture Pyramid*, 2004

313 Heinz Mack, *Marking of the Earth*, 1960, Hubbelrath near Düsseldorf

314 Heinz Mack, *Sand Relief from the Five Seasons of the Desert*, 1974/76

315 Clay bricks, laid out to dry, North Africa, mid 1950s, photo: Heinz Mack

316 Heinz Mack, *Counter Relief*, 1997, Wahiba sands, Oman

317 Al Maktoum Solar Park, Saih Al Salam Desert, Dubai, U.A.E.

318 Aircraft salvage yard, US Army Air Force base, Arizona desert

319 Pyramid-shaped photodiode made of silicon and aluminum

320 Heinz Mack, *Sand Relief*, 1976, Grand Erg Occidental, Algeria, photo: Thomas Höpker

321 Heinz Mack in his studio in Düsseldorf, ca. 1959

322 Heinz Mack, *Project for Mirrors in the Desert*, 1967

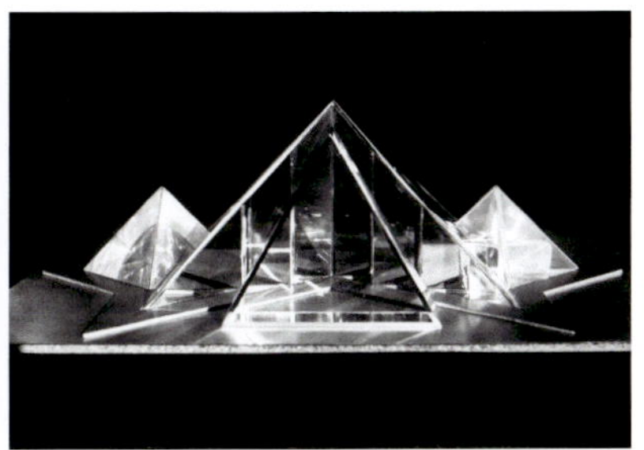
323

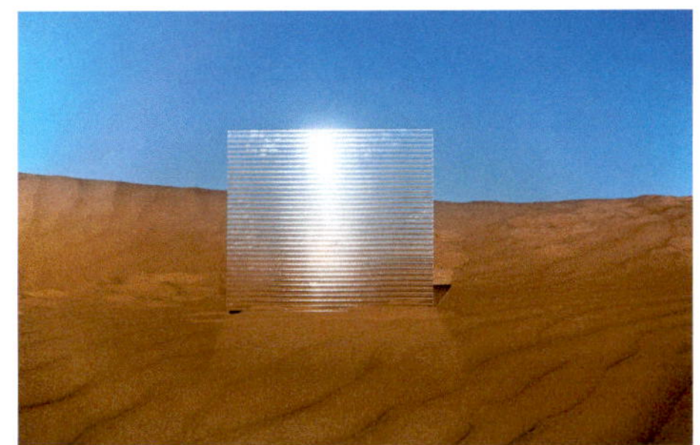
324

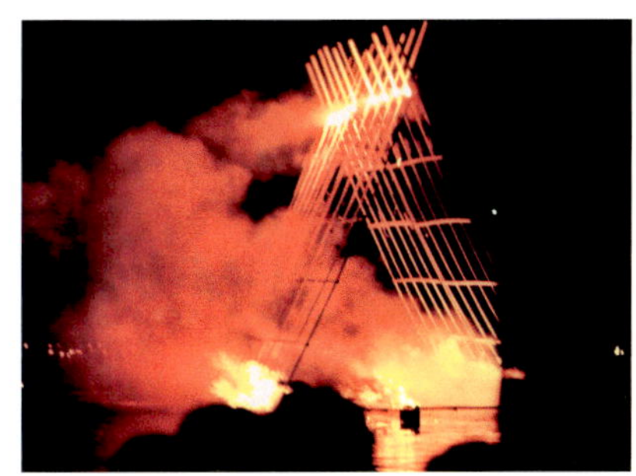
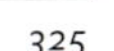
325

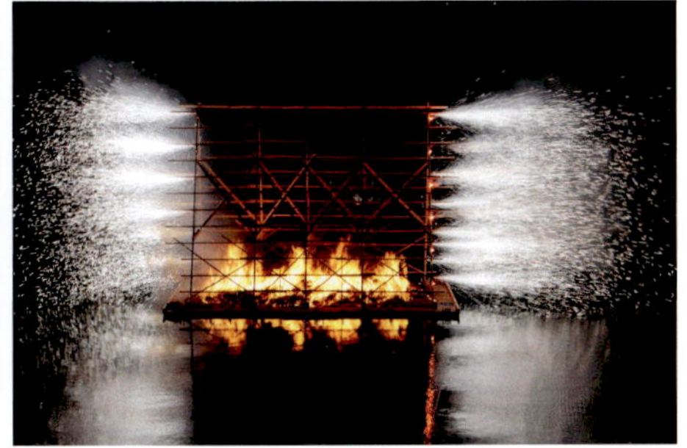
326

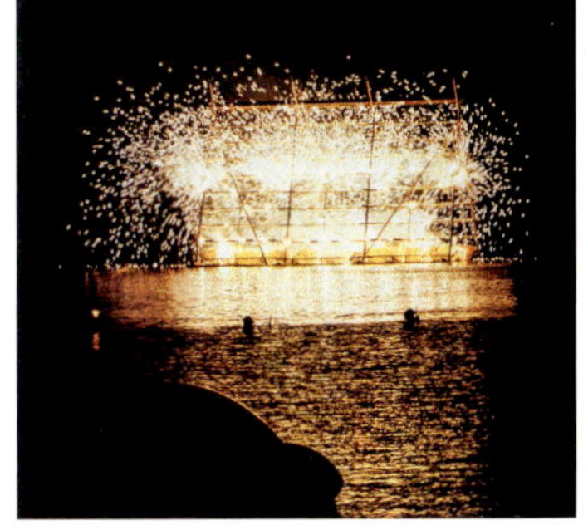
327

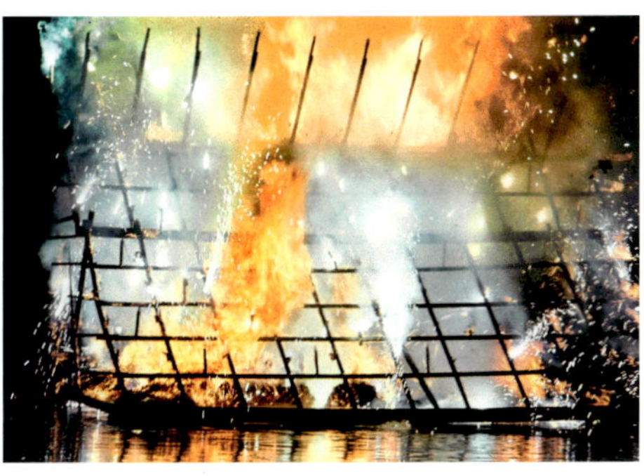
328

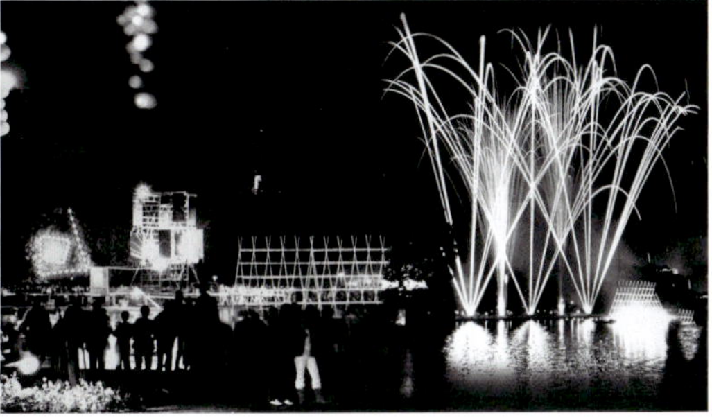
329

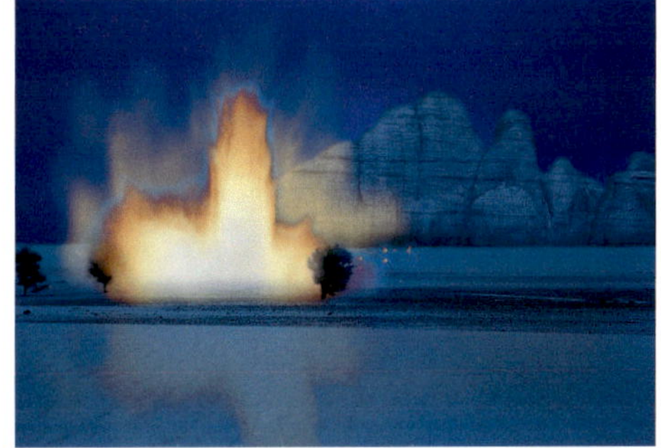
330

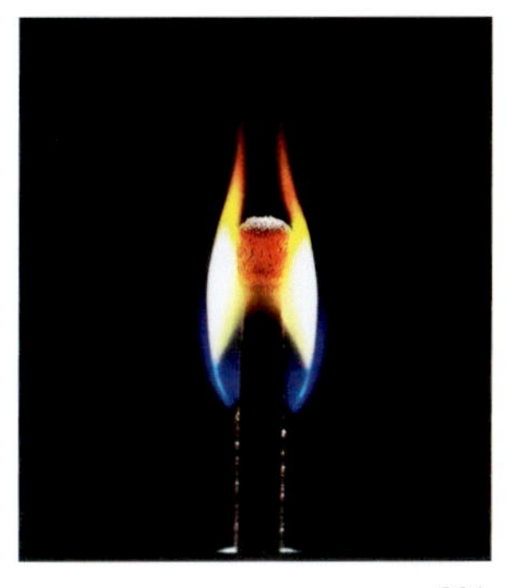
331

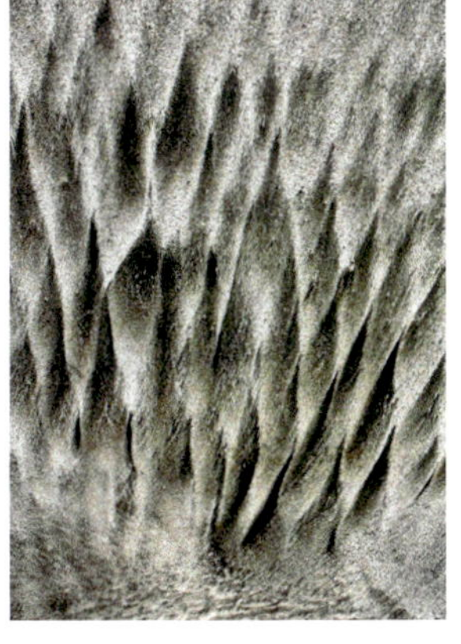
332

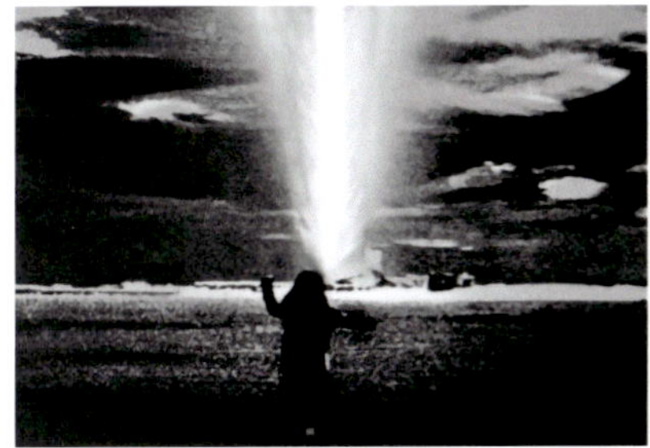
333

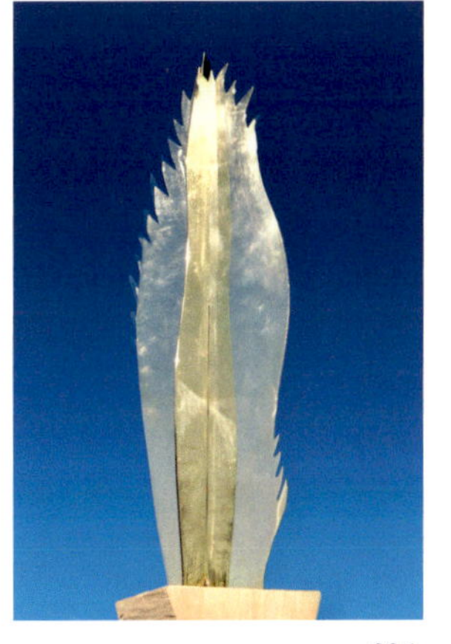
334

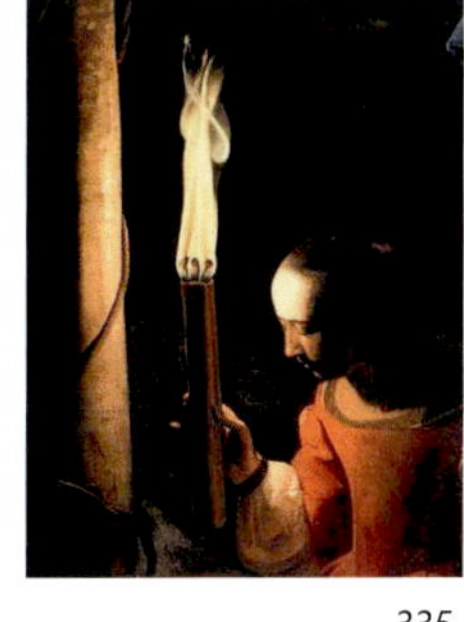
335

323 Heinz Mack, *Three Glass Pyramids*, 1983

324 Heinz Mack, *Light Filter for the Sky*, 1997, Wahiba sands, Oman

325 Heinz Mack, *Fire Ship*, still from the film *Tele-Mack*, 1968, photo: Edwin Braun

326 Heinz Mack, *Fire Ship*, 2010, Düsseldorf

327 Heinz Mack, *Fire Ship*, 2010, Düsseldorf

328 Heinz Mack, *Fire Ship* as part of the *Light Festival*, 1979, Stuttgart

329 Heinz Mack, *Light Festival*, 1979, Stuttgart

330 Heinz Mack, *Fire in the Desert – Experiment with Light*, 1968

331 Heinz Mack, *The Angel of Evil (Greeting to Aubertin)*, ca. 1968

332 Heinz Mack, *Nature Photography (Sand and Water)*

333 Heinz Mack, *Fire Fountain in the Tunisian desert*, 1968

334 Heinz Mack, *Flamma Eterna (3rd Hommage à Georges de la Tour)*, 1995

335 Georges de La Tour, *Saint Sebastian Tended by Saint Irene*, ca. 1649, Musée du Louvre, Paris

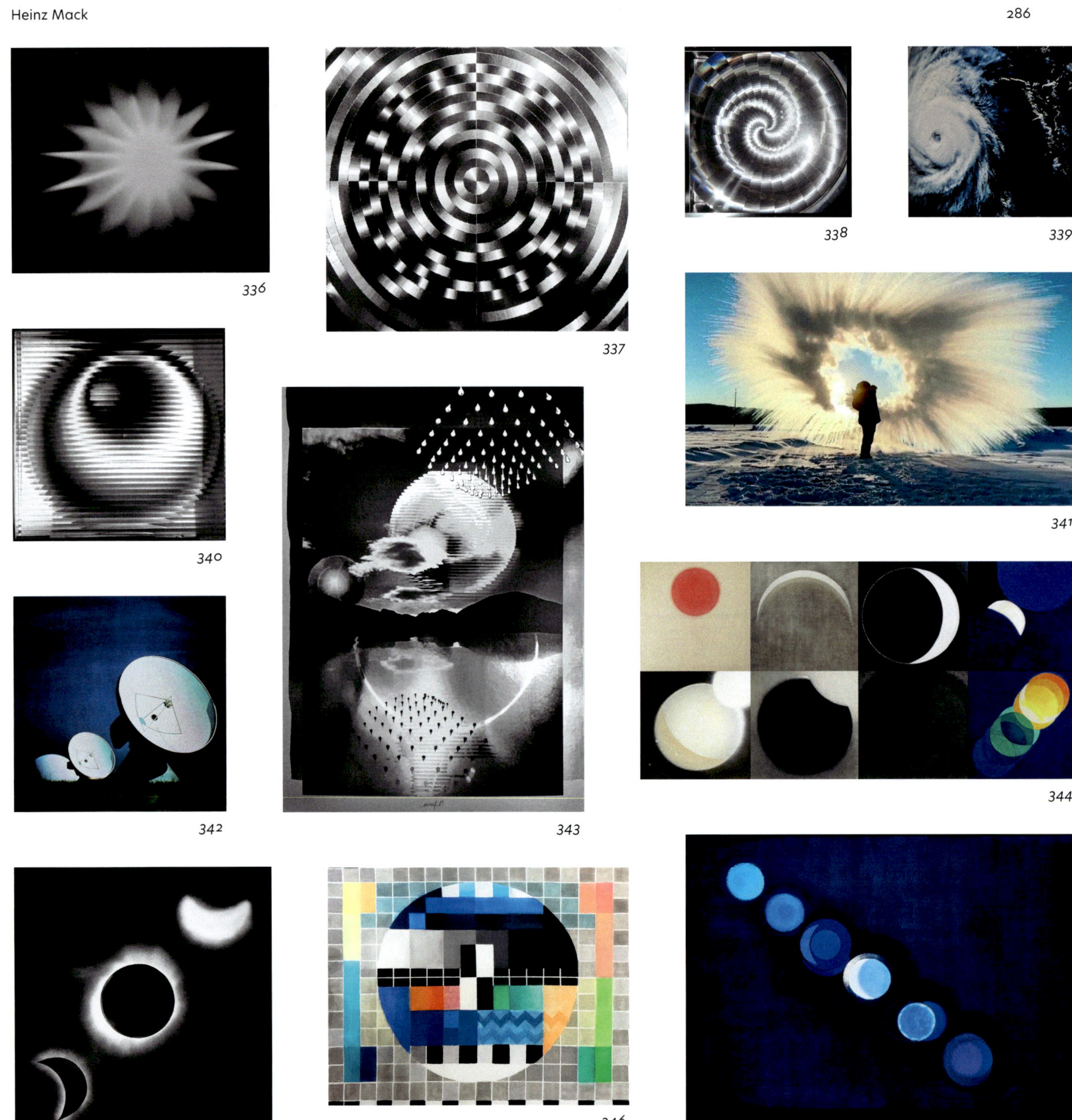

336 Heinz Mack, *Light Experiment*

337 Heinz Mack, *Untitled (from the Silver Light Suite)*, ca. 1968

338 Heinz Mack, *Untitled*, 2004, rotor

339 Hurricane, Miami

340 Heinz Mack, *Silver Moon Rotor*, 1971

341 Water experiment in frosty weather

342 Radio telescope

343 Heinz Mack, *Art in the Year 2000*, 1988

344 Heinz Mack, *Declination of the Moon*, 2005, chromatic constellation, 8-part ensemble

345 Heinz Mack, *Night View*, 2005, chromatic constellation

346 Heinz Mack, *Untitled*, 1997, chromatic constellation

347 Heinz Mack, *Caelum Stellatum*, 2000, chromatic constellation

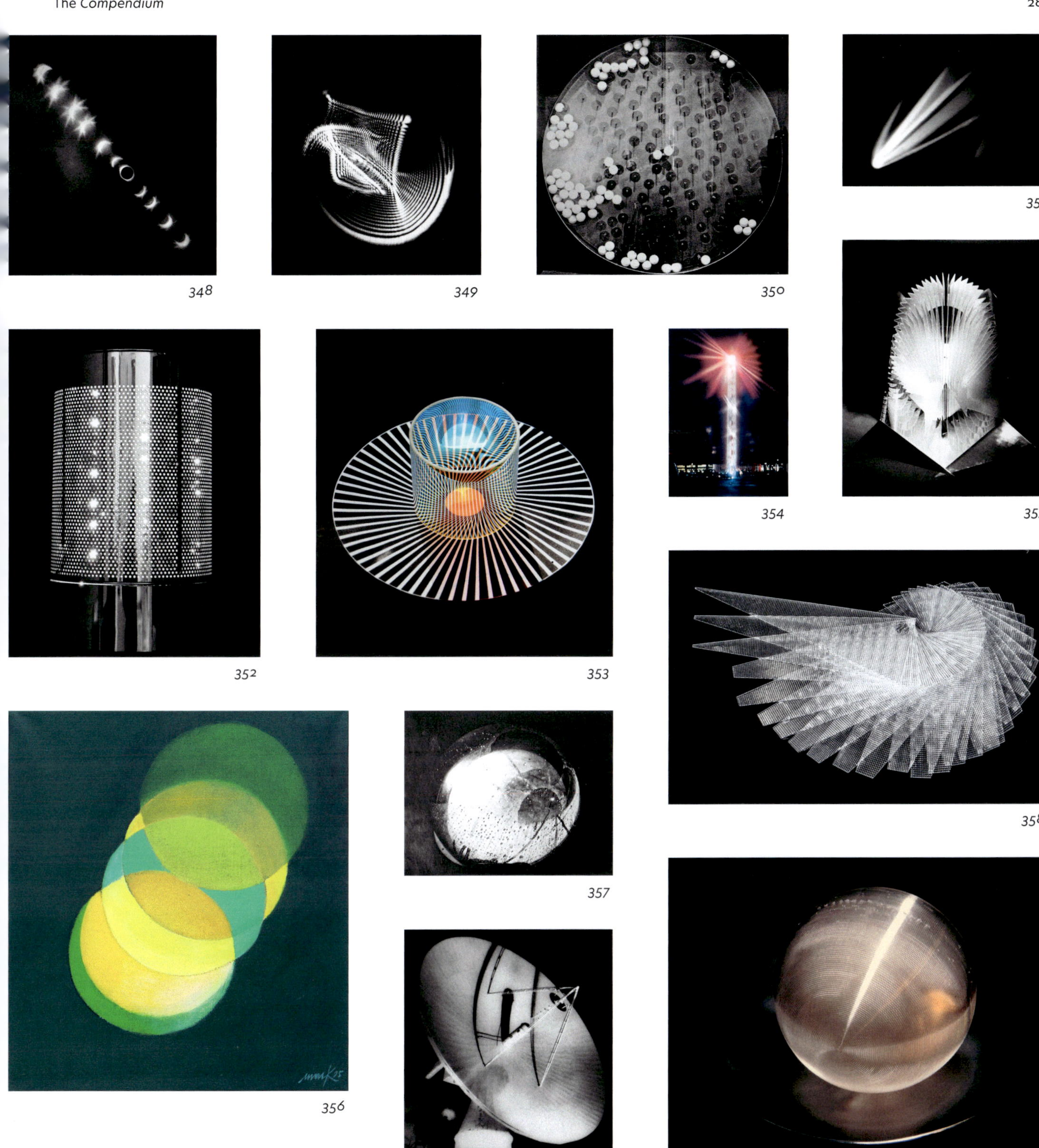

348 Heinz Mack, *Declination of the Sun in the Desert*, 1968

349 Heinz Mack, *Spherical Light Grid*, 1970

350 Heinz Mack, *Coincidence of Movement*, 1966/2009

351 Heinz Mack, *Light Trail of a Meteor*

352 Heinz Mack, *Untitled*, 1970/2010, light sculpture

353 Heinz Mack, *Untitled*, 2015, model for a glass pavilion with changing colors

354 Heinz Mack, *Project for a Light Pillar*

355 Heinz Mack, *Light Facets*, 1966

356 Heinz Mack, *Green Moon*, 1995, chromatic constellation

357 Heinz Mack, *Unisphere*, 1964

358 Heinz Mack, *Light Bird*, 1982

359 Radio telescope

360 Heinz Mack, *Project for a Dance Pavilion*, 1960

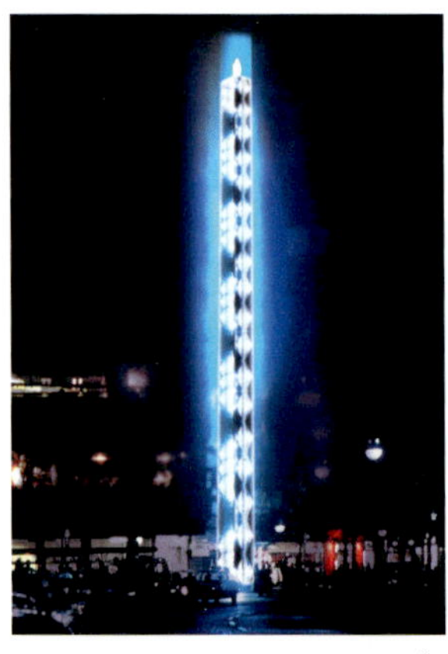
361

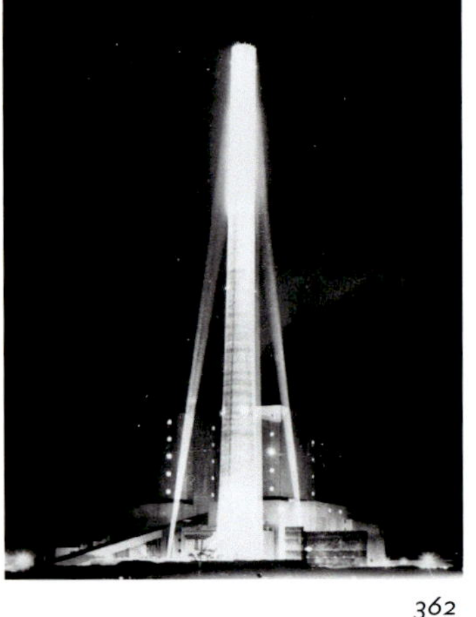
362

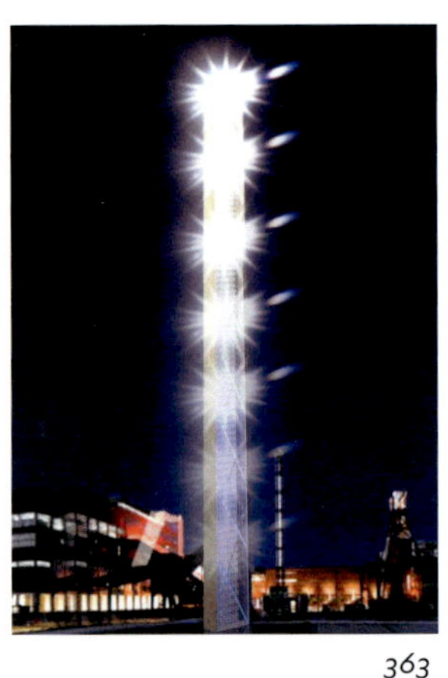
363

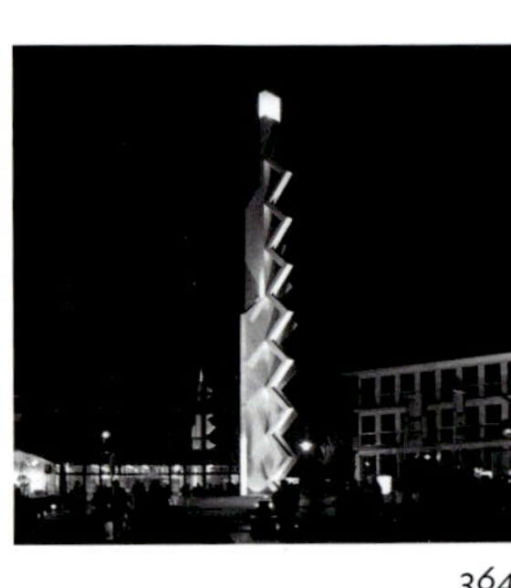
364

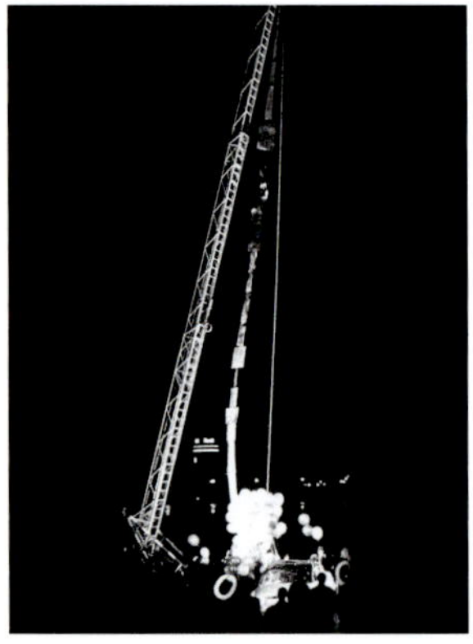
365

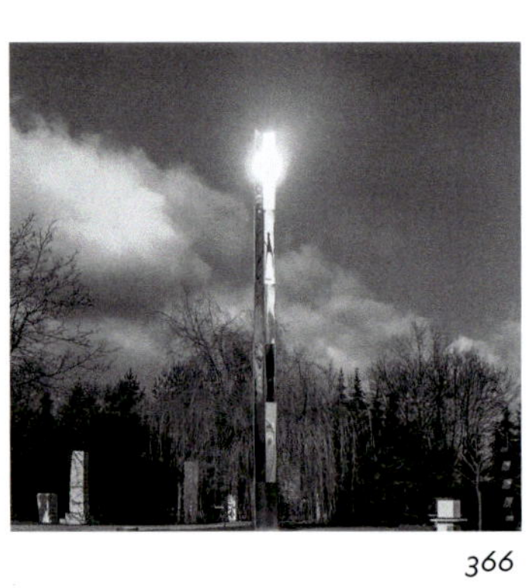
366

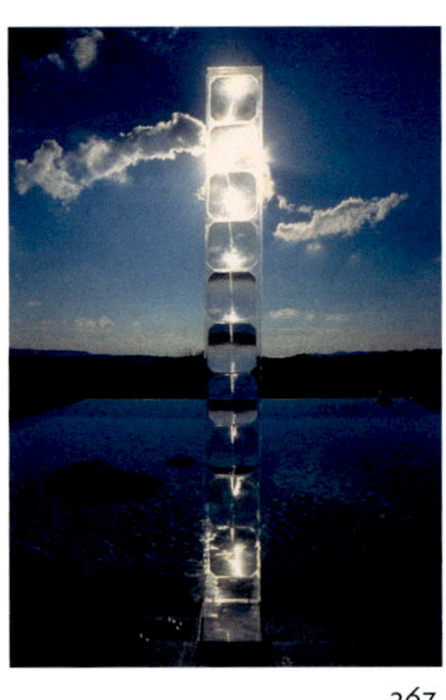
367

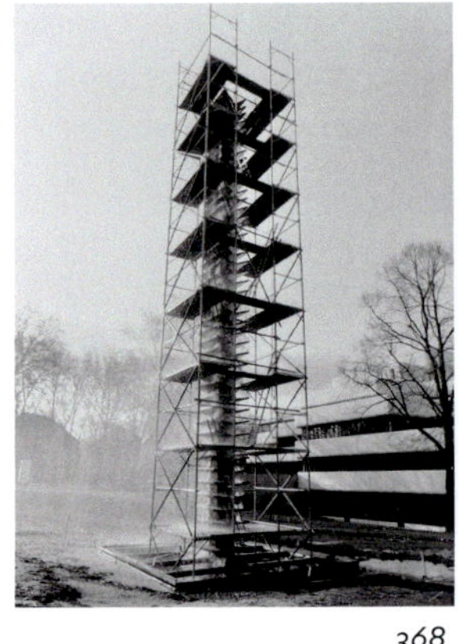
368

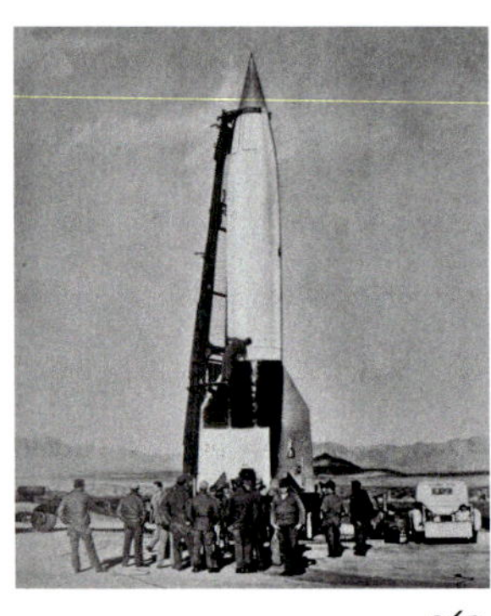
369

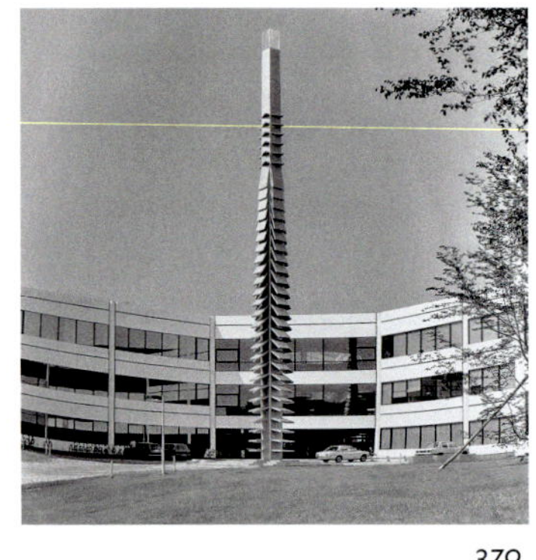
370

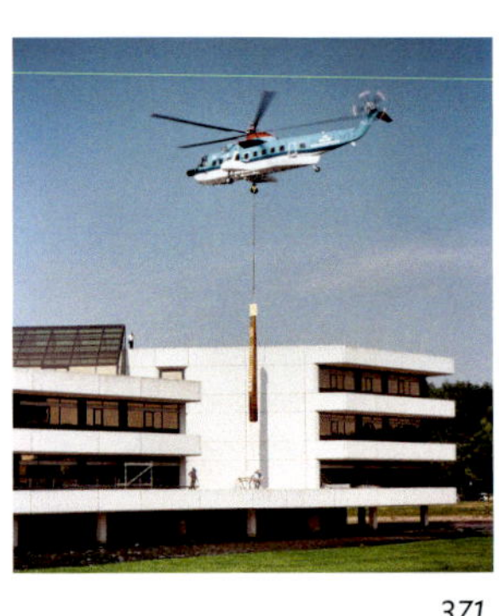
371

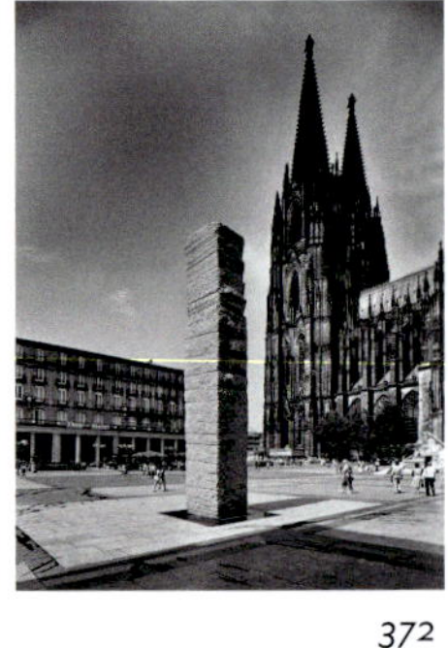
372

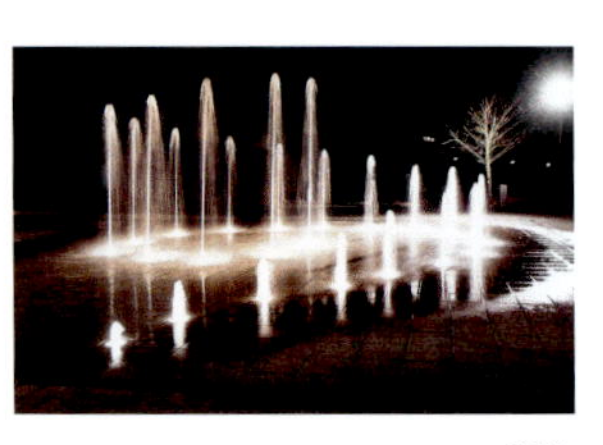
373

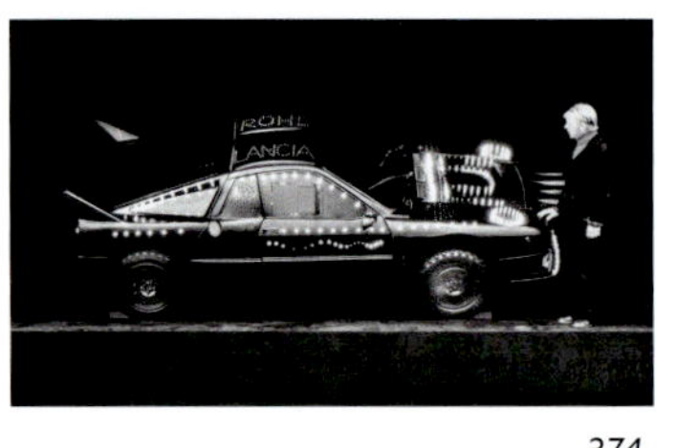
374

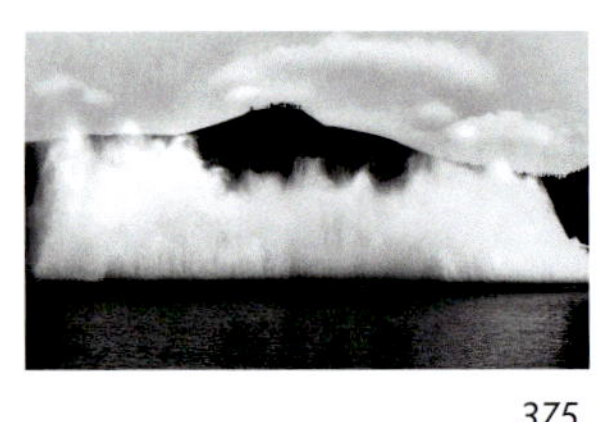
375

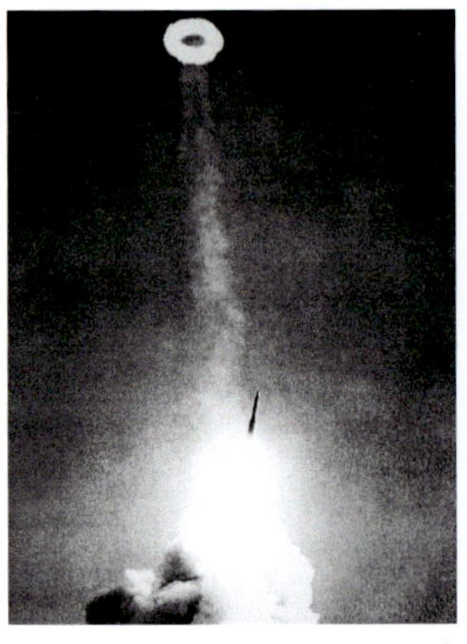
376

361 Heinz Mack, *Light Pillar*, 1987, Berlin

362 Heinz Mack, *Illumination of a Chimney*, ca. 1970

363 Heinz Mack, *Light Project for the Ruhr Festival*, 2002

364 Heinz Mack, *Large Vertical Rhythm*, 2008, Langenfeld

365 Heinz Mack, Relief Chain for the ZERO Demonstration on the Rhine meadows, 1962, photo: Reiner Ruthenbeck

366 Heinz Mack, *Model for the Great Stele*, 1989–90

367 Heinz Mack, *Stele with Ten Fresnel Lenses*, 1987

368 Heinz Mack, *Water Sculpture*, 1977, West German State Bank, Münster, under construction

369 V2 rocket, White Sands Missile Range Site of the US Air Force, New Mexico, late 1940s

370 Heinz Mack, *Sculpture for the Sky*, University of the Federal Armed Forces, 1976, Munich

371 Heinz Mack, *Construction of Falling and Rising Meteor*, 1984, Philips, Eindhoven

372 Heinz Mack, *Columne pro Caelo*, 1984, Cathedral plateau, Cologne

373 Heinz Mack, *Project for the Gustaf-Gründgens-Platz*, 2004, Düsseldorf

374 Heinz Mack, *Transformation of the Winning Car*, 1983, Lancia Rally

375 Heinz Mack, *Water Cloud on the Olympic Lake*, 1972, Munich

376 Heinz Mack, adaptation of a NASA photograph

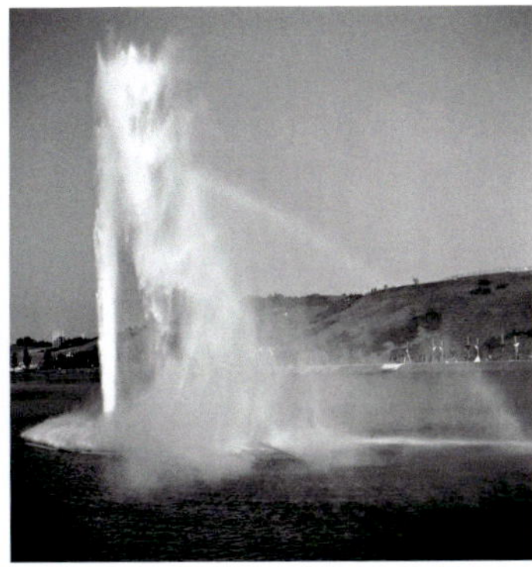

377

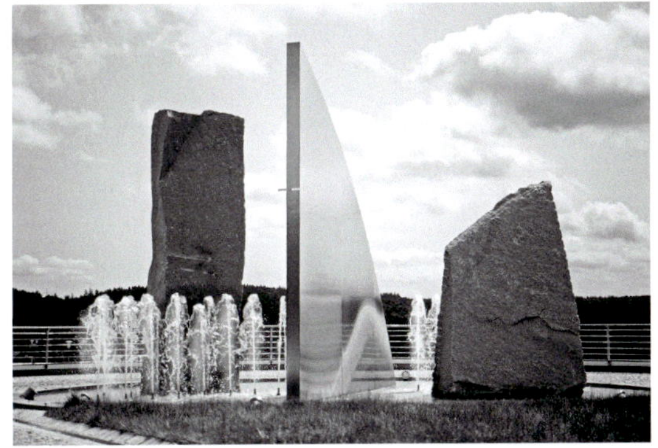

378

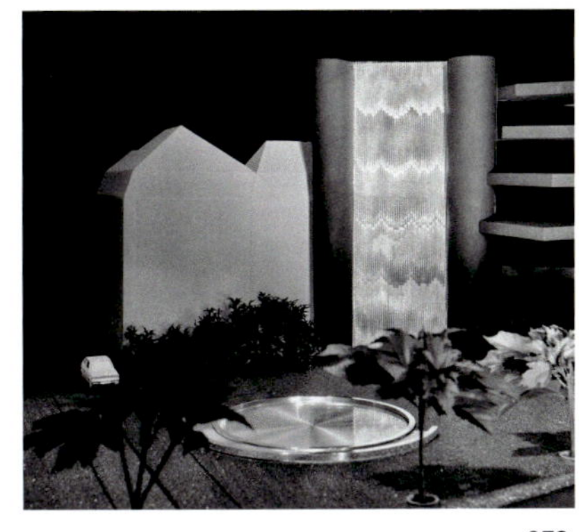

379

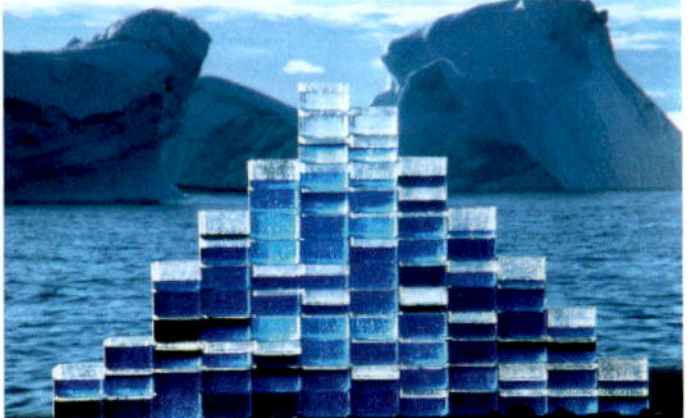

380

381

382

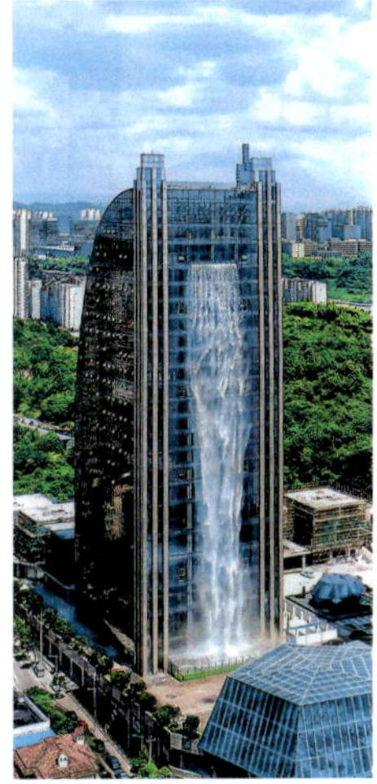

383

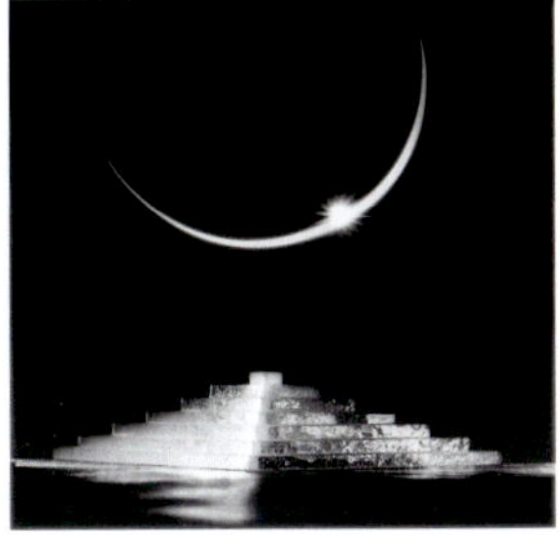

384

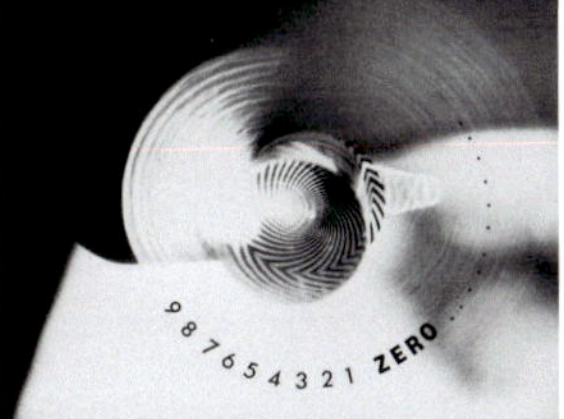

385

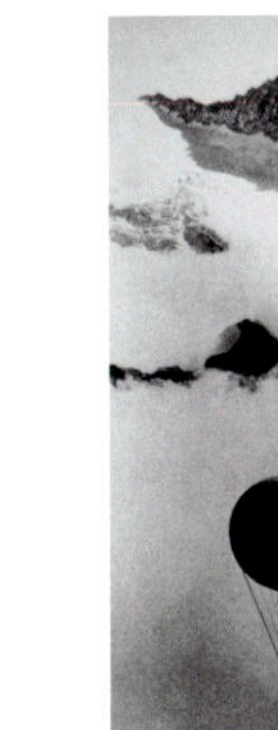

386

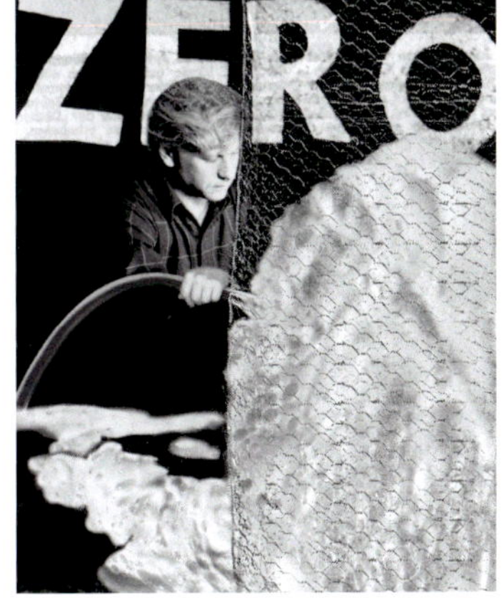

387

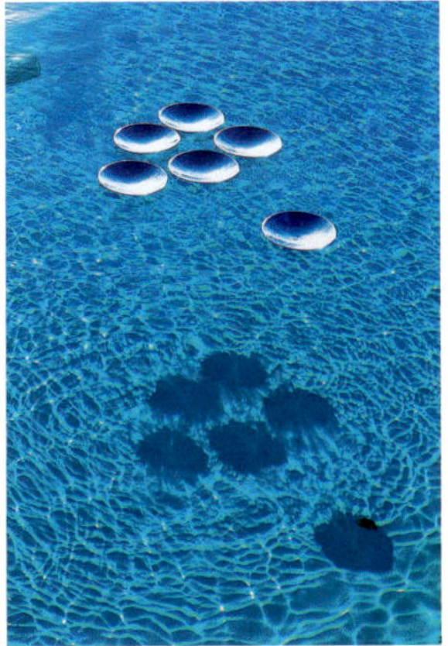

388

389

377 Heinz Mack, *Water Cloud on the Olympic Lake*, 1972, Munich

378 Heinz Mack, *Large Water Sculpture*, 1995, Media Center of Passau Publishing Group

379 Heinz Mack, *Design for a Monumental Water Wall*

380 Heinz Mack, *Model for a Floating Hotel in the Arctic*, 1976, Greenland, Arctic, photo: Thomas Höpker

381 Heinz Mack, *Water Light Sculpture*, 1991, Stadtsparkasse Mönchengladbach

382 Heinz Mack, *Water Cloud on the Olympic Lake*, 1972, Munich

383 Artificial waterfall on the façade of Liebian International Building, Guiyang, China

384 Heinz Mack, *Glass Pyramid*, 1968

385 Heinz Mack, *Design for a ZERO Exhibition Poster*, 1960s

386 Heinz Mack, *Balloon of the Arctic Expedition*, 1966/1976

387 Heinz Mack, *Foam Sculpture*, 1963

388 Heinz Mack, *Floating Islands on the Sea*, 1968

389 Heinz Mack, *ZERO project for Antarctica*

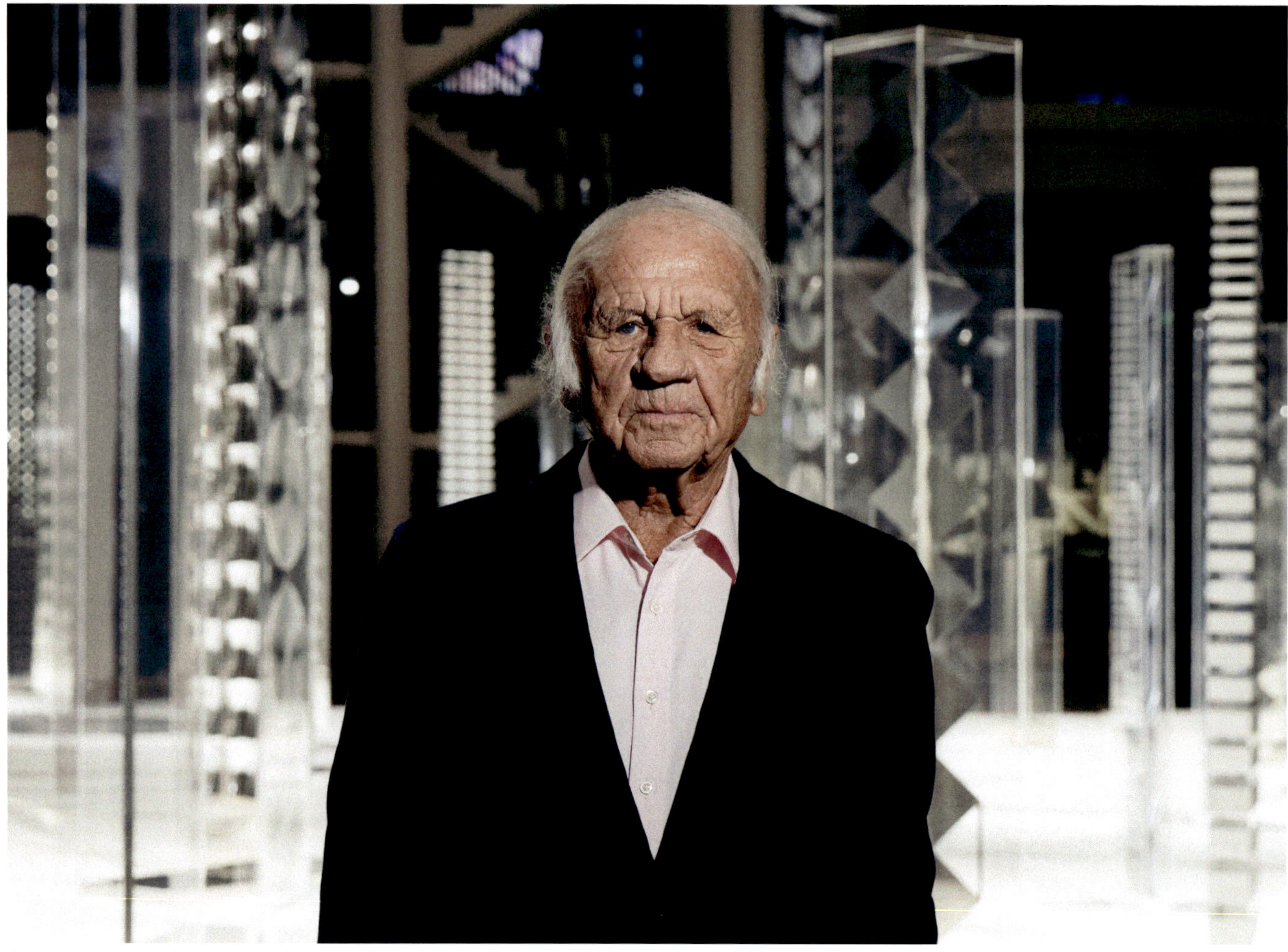

fig. 390 Heinz Mack, 92 years old, in the exhibition *MACK at ZKM*, 2023

Images on the following pages:
All works courtesy of the artist unless otherwise noted

Heinz Mack in his studio on Gladbacher Straße, Düsseldorf, around 1959, photo: Charles Wilp
→ *fig. 391*

Heinz Mack, *Sahara Relief*, 1960/1961, concrete, height: 13 m, formerly Mathildenhofschule, Leverkusen
→ *fig. 392*

ZERO – Edition, Exposition, Demonstration, Schmela Gallery, Düsseldorf, 1961, from WDR, *Hier und Heute*, TV feature, film (digitized), b/w, sound, 03:26 min.
→ *fig. 393*

ZERO room of documenta III, 1964, detail, from: *Wochenschau Deutschlandspiegel*, TV feature, film (digitized), b/w, sound, 00:14 min.
→ *fig. 394*

Heinz Mack, *Forest of Light*, 1966, exhibition view, Howard Wise Gallery, New York 1966
→ *fig. 395*

Shooting the film *Tele-Mack* in the Tunisian desert, 1968
→ *fig. 396*

Heinz Mack with his work *Water Cross in the Sand*, 1972, Kunsthalle Düsseldorf.
→ *fig. 397*

Fireworks at the *Light Festival*, Schlosspark Stuttgart, 1979
→ *fig. 398*

Heinz Mack, *Radial Light Relief*, emblem of the World Energy Conference, Munich, 1980, aluminum, Ø ca. 7 m
→ *fig. 399*

Heinz Mack, Overall design of the Jürgen-Ponto square, Frankfurt/Main, 1976–81
→ *fig. 400*

Heinz Mack, German Unity Square, Düsseldorf, 1986–88, stainless steel, granite, water, height: max. 11 m
→ *fig. 401*

Heinz Mack, *Great Stele*, 1989/90, stainless steel, height: 42 m, in front of the Mercedes-Benz Museum, DaimlerChrysler AG, Stuttgart
→ *fig. 402*

Heinz Mack, *Two Glass Prisms*, 2002, 2-part ensemble, mineral vapor-coated glass, stainless steel, lighting, height: 8 / 10 m, Vaduz, Liechtenstein
→ *fig. 403*

Heinz Mack, *The Sky Over Nine Colums*, 2014, 9 columns, 7.5 × 1.25 × 1.25 m each, mosaic stones 2 × 2 cm with 24-carat gold leaf
→ *fig. 404*

The artist's glass studio at Huppertzhof, Mönchengladbach, 2021
→ *fig. 405*

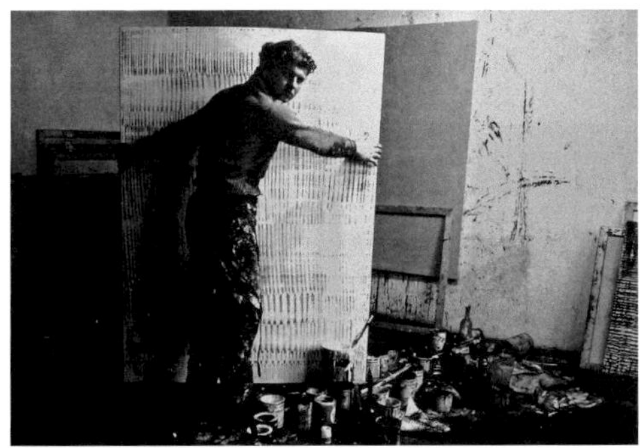

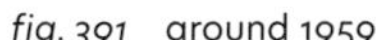

fig. 391 around 1959

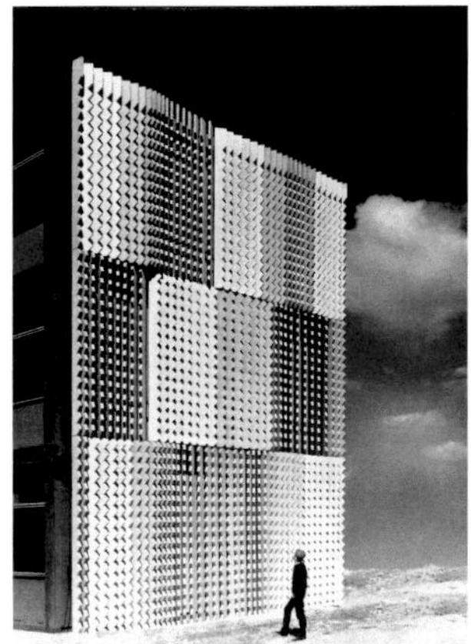

fig. 392 1960/1961

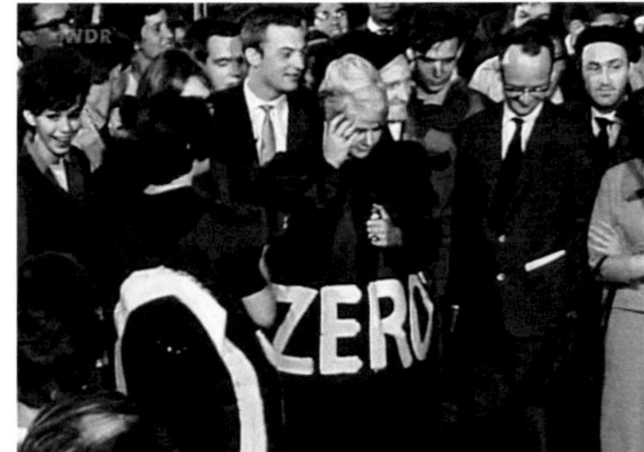

fig. 393 1961

Biography of Heinz Mack

1931 Born on March 8 in Lollar, Hesse, Germany

1950 Graduates high school in Krefeld, Germany

1950–1953 Studies at the Academy of Fine Arts of the State of North Rhine Westphalia, Düsseldorf, Germany

1953 State examination in art education

1953–1956 Studies in philosophy at the University of Cologne, Germany, state examination

1955 Studio at 69 Gladbacher Straße, Düsseldorf

First trip to the Sahara

1953–1958 Encounters with Georges Mathieu, Jean Tinguely, and Yves Klein

Visit to Constantin Brâncuși's Paris studio shortly after his death

Informal painting; development of *Dynamic Structures* in painting and drawing, as well as light reliefs in plaster and metal

1957 Heinz Mack and Otto Piene found artist group ZERO in Düsseldorf, which Günther Uecker joins in 1961. They organize the *Evening Exhibitions* that will later become legendary.

1958 On the occasion of the 7th and 8th *Evening Exhibition*, the catalogue magazines *ZERO*, no. 1 and no. 2 are published.

Art Prize of the City of Krefeld

Second trip to the Sahara

1958–1959 First light reliefs, light cubes, and light steles

From the idea of a vibrating light stele in the desert, a model of which is exhibited in Paris by Galerie Iris Clert in 1959, Mack develops the *Sahara Project*, a utopian concept that will accompany the artist from then on.

Encounters with Piero Manzoni, Enrico Castellani, and Lucio Fontana

1959 Kassel, Germany: Participation in the exhibition *Young German Painters* alongside documenta II

Antwerp, Belgium: Contribution to the exhibition *Vision in motion – Motion in vision* at Hessenhuis

1960 Berlin, Germany: First *Hommage à Georges de La Tour* at Diogenes Gallery with phosphor paintings and fire sculptures

1961 Leverkusen, Germany: Creation of two 13-meter-tall concrete reliefs for a school, the so-called *Sahara Reliefs*

Exhibition *Bewogen – Beweging* [Moved – Moving], Stedelijk Museum, Amsterdam, Netherlands, and Louisiana Museum, Humlebæk, Denmark

Düsseldorf: Event *ZERO – Edition, Exposition, Demonstration* at Schmela Gallery; publication ZERO, no. 3

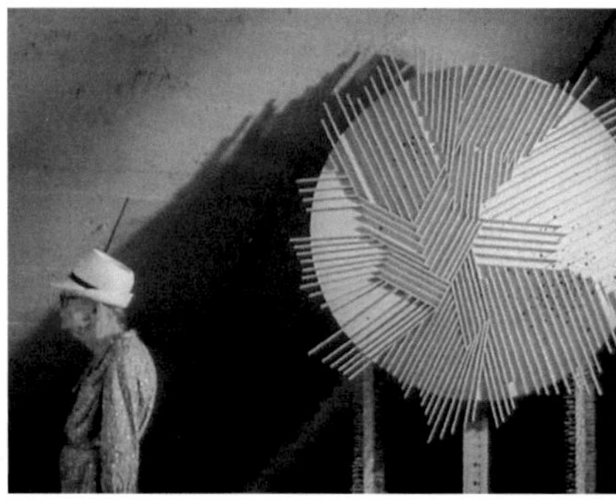
fig. 394 1964

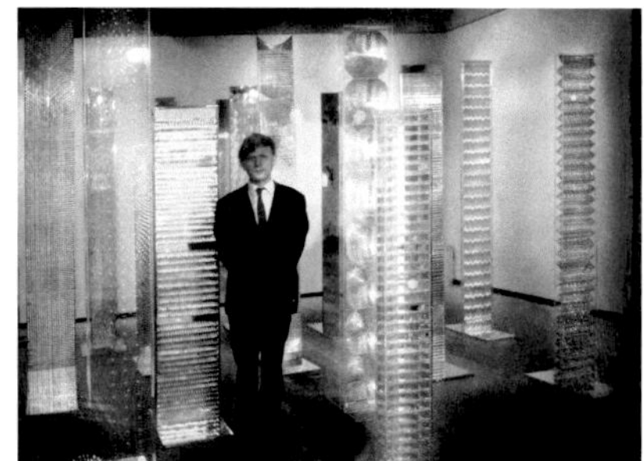
fig. 395 1966

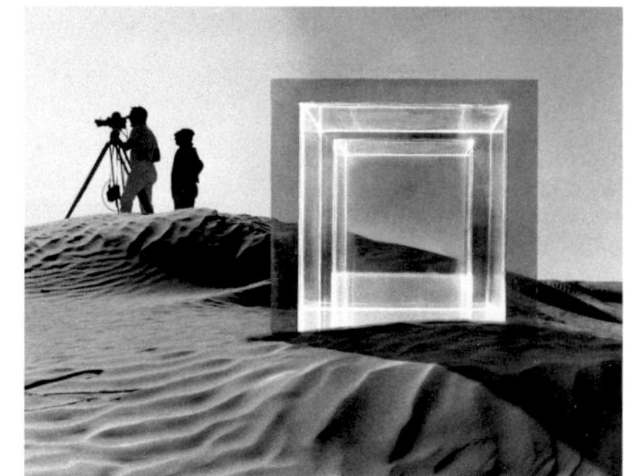
fig. 396 1968

1962 Düsseldorf: ZERO festival on the banks of the river Rhine and production of the ZERO film *0 × 0 = Art*

Brussels, Belgium: Exhibition *Dynamo – Mack, Piene, Uecker* at Palais des Beaux-Arts

1962–1963 Travels to Morocco and Tunisia, first light experiments in the desert

Studio at 104 Hüttenstraße in Düsseldorf together with Günther Uecker and Otto Piene – now home to the ZERO foundation.

1963 Premio Selezione Marzotto, Italy

1963–1966 Extended stay in New York; first studio at the Chelsea Hotel, second studio at 410 East 10th Street

1964 New York: Exhibition Group *ZERO – Mack, Piene, Uecker*, Howard Wise Gallery

Kassel: Participation in documenta III with the installation *Light Space – Homage to Fontana* by Mack, Piene, and Uecker

1965 1. Prix des arts plastiques, 4th Paris Biennale

Diourbel, Senegal: Design for a hospital entrance area

Trip to Mauritania

1966 Group ZERO splits up; last joint exhibition for the time being with Piene and Uecker in Bonn, Germany; the ZERO festival at Rolandseck train station with about 1,000 attendants marks the end of the ZERO time.

New York: first solo exhibition *Lights of Silver by Heinz Mack* at Howard Wise Gallery. Mack shows the *Forest of Light*, 20 steles mirroring Manhattan.

1967 Relocation of studio and residence to Huppertzhof in Mönchengladbach, Germany

Montreal, Canada: The sculpture *Light and Color* is shown in the German Pavilion at the World Fair.

Trip to Djerba, Tunisia

1968 Appointment as member of the Academy of Arts, Berlin

Trip to the Tunisian desert to shoot the film *Tele-Mack*, which receives the Adolf Grimme Recognition Award in 1970 and is honored at the Venice International Film Festival in 1971 in Italy

Mack paints his last canvas for the time being. Since then, he creates chromatic color images on paper, in which the spectrum of light is varied.

1970 Mack is appointed professor in Osaka, Japan, but resigns in the same year.

Participation in the design of the German Pavilion at the World Fair in Osaka with the objects *Mirror Plantation*, *Water Games*, and *Crown for the Color Spectrum* as well as a 12-meter-tall *Stele for the Sky* in front of the Expo Museum of Fine Arts, Osaka

Venice, Italy: Thomas Lenk, K.-G. Pfahler, Günther Uecker, and Heinz Mack represent Western Germany at the XXXV. Biennale di Venezia.

1970 Berlin: Design of *Light – Movement – Space*, a light environment for the German Industrial Exhibition, Berlin

1972 Munich, Germany: 36-meter-tall *Water Cloud* for the Olympic Stadium

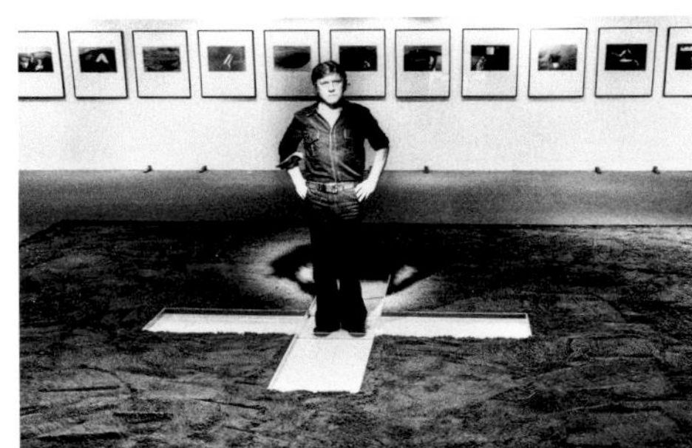
fig. 397 1972

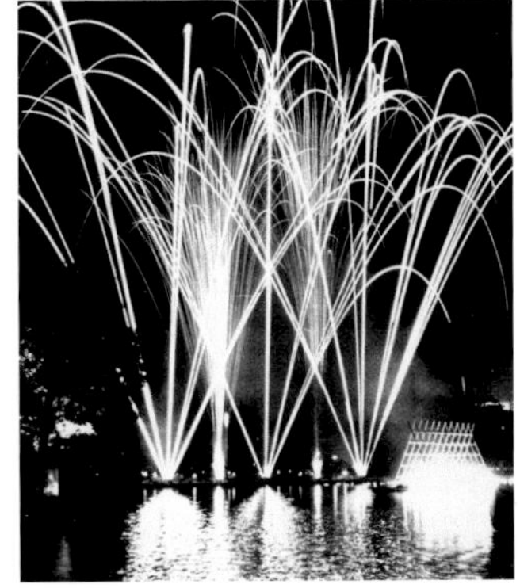
fig. 398 1979

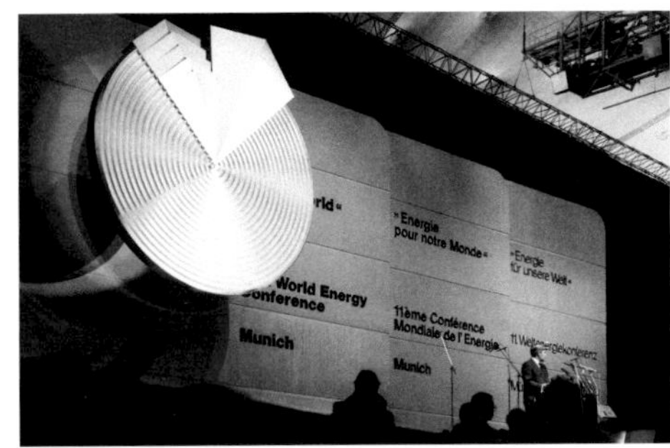

fig. 399 1980

1974 Commissioned by the UN in New York, Mack designs the 70-meter stele *Sign of Peace*, which is not realized due to the decision makers of the Federal Republic of Germany.

1975 Participation in the first northbound expedition through the Ténéré desert in Africa and trip to Djerba

1976 Bologna, Italy: Installation of *Ad Alta Potenza* at the Arte Fiera art fair

Working expeditions to the southern Algerian desert and the Arctic together with photographer Thomas Höpker. These trips are documented in the volume Henri Nannen, ed., *Mack. Expedition in künstliche Gärten* [Mack. Expedition into artificial gardens] (Hamburg: Gruner+Jahr, 1977).

1977 Kassel: Participation in documenta VI

1979 Stages a light festival in the castle gardens of Stuttgart, Germany, on behalf of the Deutscher Künstlerbund; builds a *Fire Ship* in Duisburg, Germany.

Eindhoven, Netherlands: 1st prize of the international competition *Light 79*; commission to create a light sculpture for Eindhoven's city park Stadswandelpark

1980 Munich: Artistic design of the World Energy Conference at the Olympic Hall

1981 Frankfurt/Main, Germany: Design of Jürgen-Ponto square outside the Silberturm sky scraper

1984 Eindhoven: Installation of the sculpture ensemble *Falling and Rising Meteor* for Philips (by helicopter)

1986 Moscow, USSR: Exhibition of *Great Light Spectrum* at the state exposition of North Rhine-Westphalia

1987 Berlin: Completion of a 30-meter light pillar in front of the Europa-Center building complex

Order of Merit of North Rhine-Westphalia

1988 Berlin: 18-meter *Bronze Obelisk* erected on Henriettenplatz

Duisburg: On the occasion of the 12th Duisburger Akzente with the topic *In Defiance of Danger*, the *Memorial for Anne Frank* is built.

Düsseldorf: Completion of the German Unity Square on Berliner Allee

1989 Neuss, Germany: Full design of a chapel for the archiepiscopal Collegium Marianum

Studio on the island of Ibiza, Spain

1990 Stuttgart: Mack creates the 42-meter-tall *Great Stele* made of stainless steel for the Daimler-Benz AG (today: Daimler AG) – the tallest sculpture in Europe.

1991 After a 23-year break from painting, Mack begins creating large canvases again, which he calls *Chromatic Constellations*.

The municipal Kunstmuseum Düsseldorf acquires the *ZERO space* created for documenta III in 1964 with works by Mack, Piene, and Uecker.

1992 Withdrawal from the Academy of Arts, Berlin

Grand Cultural Award of the Rhineland Savings Banks Association

1995 Cologne: Large mosaic for the headquarters of Kaufhof AG

Passau, Germany: *Large Water Sculpture* for the media center of Verlagsgruppe Passau

1997 Working trip to the desert of Oman

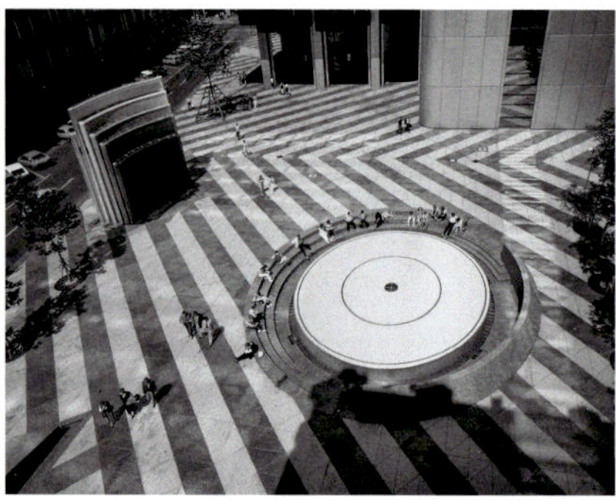

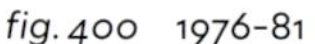

fig. 400 1976–81

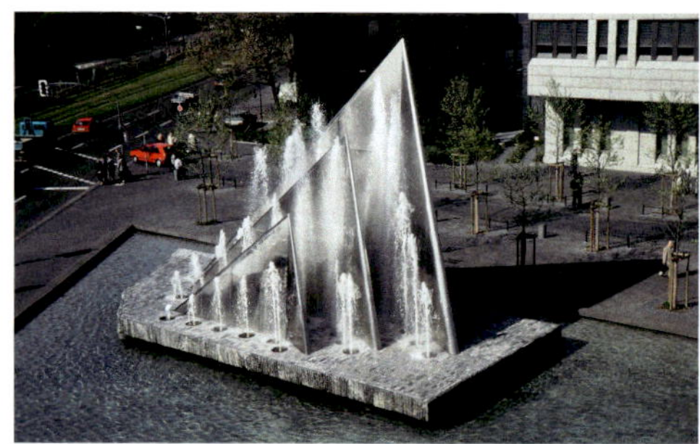

fig. 401 1986–88

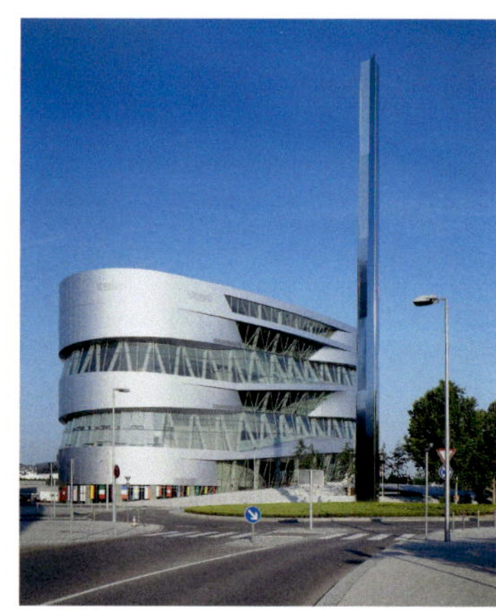

fig. 402 2000

1999 The artist volume *Mack. Ein Buch der Bilder zum West-östlichen Diwan von Johann Wolfgang v. Goethe* [Mack. A book of pictures to the West-Eastern Divan by Johann Wolfgang v. Goethe] is published in honor of Goethe's 250th birthday.

2000 Essen, Germany: Unveiling of seven 13-meter stainless steel steles outside the headquarters of Hypothekenbank Essen AG

2001 Numerous exhibitions and publications in honor of the artist's 70th birthday

Tehran, Iran: Exhibition *Heinz Mack – Elective Affinities*, Tehran Museum of Contemporary Art

Lectures in Tehran and Shiraz, Iran, on the occasion of the German Culture Days

2002 Vaduz, Lichtenstein: Completion of monumental glass sculpture *Two Glass Prisms* for the Zentrumsbank on Lindenplatz

2003 Graphic suite *On Bliss and Light* exploring the themes of happiness and light in the writings of Al-Ghazali

2004 Awarded the Great Cross of the Order of Merit of the Federal Republic of Germany in recognition of his work and activities as an ambassador of cultures

2006 Berlin: Exhibition *Heinz Mack – Transit between Occident and Orient*, Pergamon Museum

Düsseldorf: Exhibition *ZERO – International Avantgarde of the 1950s and 1960s*, Museum Kunstpalast

2007 Mönchengladbach: Monumental fountain sculpture for the headquarters of Santander Consumer Bank AG

2008 Langenfeld, Germany: Completion of the 17-meter tall sculpture *Large Vertical Rhythm*

Düsseldorf: Creation of the ZERO foundation; archives and numerous works by Mack, Piene, and Uecker are donated to the foundation. The focus is on research, promotion, and support of documentation and exhibitions of all international artists connected to the ZERO idea.

2009 Ring of Honor of the City of Mönchengladbach

Koblenz, Germany: Exhibition *Heinz Mack. Light of the ZERO Era*, Ludwig-Museum

2011 Numerous international exhibitions in honor of the artist's 80th birthday, including at Sperone Westwater Gallery in New York, Ben Brown Fine Arts in Hong Kong, the Art and Exhibition Hall of the Federal Republic of Germany in Bonn, Museum Abteiberg in Mönchengladbach, and Museum Kunstpalast in Düsseldorf.

Great Cross with Star of the Order of Merit of the Federal Republic of Germany

2012 Cultural Prize of the city of Dortmund from Kulturstiftung Dortmund, Germany, accompanied by a major solo exhibition at Museum Ostwall

2013 Brazil: ZERO exhibition tour in São Paulo, Curitiba, and Porto Alegre

Abu Dhabi, United Arab Emirates: Acquisition of a 6-part stele ensemble by Guggenheim Abu Dhabi

2014 Venice, Italy: *The Sky Over Nine Columns* is realized on the island of St. Giorgio Maggiore. The nine pillars each are seven meters

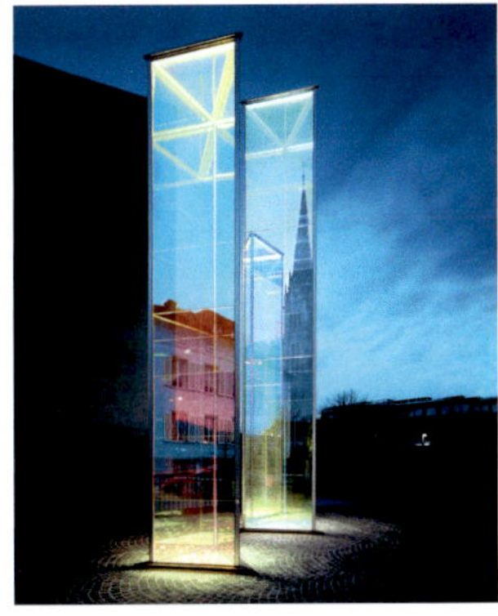
fig. 403 2002

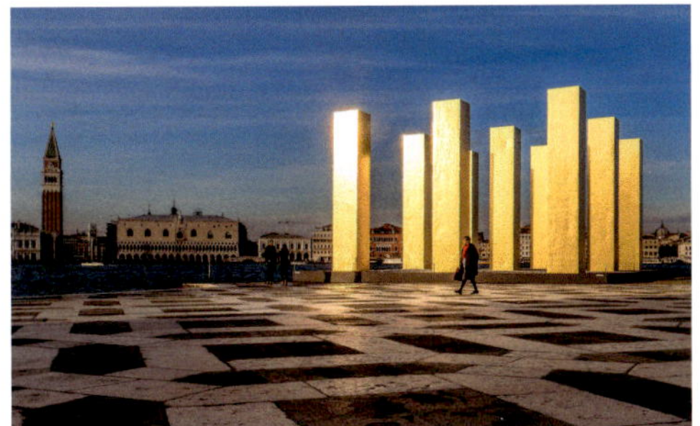
fig. 404 2014

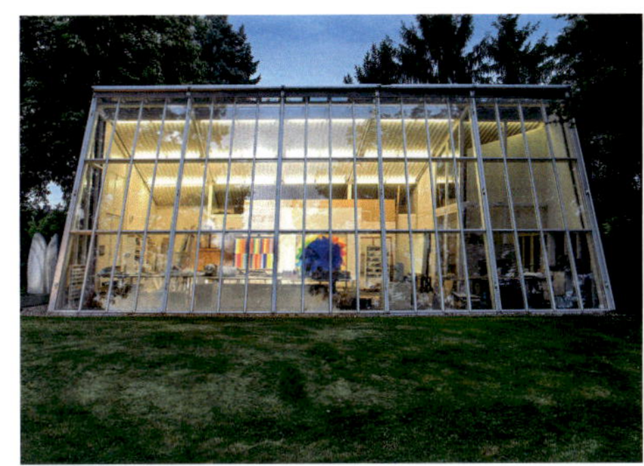
fig. 405 2021

tall and covered with more than 850,000 golden mosaic tiles. Further presentations follow in the sculpture garden of the Sakıp Sabancı Museum in Istanbul, Turkey, as well as in Valencia, Spain, and St. Moritz, Switzerland.

New York: Extensive ZERO exhibition at the Solomon R. Guggenheim Museum

2015 The ZERO exhibition from the Solomon R. Guggenheim Museum, New York, is shown at Martin-Gropius-Bau, Berlin, at Stedelijk Museum, Amsterdam, as well as at Sakıp Sabancı Museum, Istanbul. Over 700,000 visitors see the show.

The senate of the Düsseldorf Academy of Fine Arts unanimously elects Mack as an honorary member.

2016 Jan-Wellem-Ring for outstanding achievements for the city of Düsseldorf

2017 Herning, Denmark: Participation in the 7th Socle Du Monde Biennale at HEART Herning Museum of Modern Art

Berlin: For his artistic contributions to the remembrance of persecuted and murdered people and his commitment to tolerance and international understanding, Heinz Mack is honored with the Moses Mendelssohn Medal.

Düsseldorf: Mack is named Citizen of the Year

2018 Düsseldorf: Special exhibition *Taten des Lichts. Mack & Goethe* [Acts of Light. Mack and Goethe] at the Goethe-Museum

Hobart, Australia: First extensive presentation of ZERO in Australia at the Museum of Old and New Art in Hobart

Rotterdam, Netherlands: Conceived in 1966, The Mechanical Ballet is presented for the first time ever as part of the exhibition *Action ⟷ Reaction. 100 Years of Kinetic Art* at the Kunsthal.

2019 Dakar, Senegal: The first Mack exhibition on the African continent takes place at the Musée Théodore Monod d'art africain in Dakar, Senegal.

2021 The artist's 90th birthday is celebrated with numerous museum and gallery exhibitions, including at Museum Kunstpalast, Düsseldorf, and Museum Ritter, Waldenbuch, Germany.

Wuppertal, Germany: The Waldfrieden Sculpture Park shows monumental sculptures

2022 Venice, Italy: Participation in the 59th Biennale di Venezia with a solo exhibition at the Museo Correr

With *Mack – Sahara* by Sophia Sotke, the first in-depth academic examination of Heinz Mack's work within the context of ZERO and Land Art is published.

2023 Hagen, Germany: Solo exhibition *Heinz Mack. Das Licht in mir* [Heinz Mack. The Light Within Me] at Osthaus Museum

Karlsruhe, Germany: *Mack at ZKM*, extensive exhibition of kinetics, sculptures, and environments at ZKM | Center for Art and Media

To date, Heinz Mack has been represented in over 300 international solo exhibitions; around 150 publications accompany his work.

Mack at ZKM
ZKM | Center for Art and Media Karlsruhe
September 16, 2023 – April 14, 2024

Curated by: Daria Mille, Clara Runge
Curatorial assistance: Katharina Kern
Project assistance: Cornelia Eisendle, Marie Klauder, Vivien Ranger
Technical project management: Andrea Hartinger
Scenography: Matthias Gommel
Conservation: Marlies Peller, Leonie Rök
Registrar: Regina Linder
Technical team and construction: Martin Mangold, Volker Becker, Claudius Böhm, Götz Dipper, Mirco Fraß, Rainer Gabler, Gregor Gaissmaier, Jan Gerigk, Martin Häberle, Ronny Haas, Daniel Heiss, Christof Hierholzer, Werner Hutzenlaub, Gisbert Laaber, Bernd Lintermann, Nolan Ashvin Miranda, Christian Nainggolan, Marco Preitschopf, Martin Schläfke, Marc Schütze, Niklas Wallbaum, Manuel Weber
External companies: Artinate, COMYK, Essential-Art-Solutions, Pollux Edelstahlverarbeitung GmbH, Richfelder Kunstprojekte
Digital production: Andreas Brehmer
Video production: Christina Zartmann, Max Clausen, Andy Koch
Museum communication: Janine Burger, Lisa Bartling, Banu Beyer, Regine Frisch, Alexandra Hermann, Ulrich Steinberg
Marketing and PR: Helga Huskamp, Felix Brenner, Marlen Ernst, Emma Teuscher, Anne Thomé, Anouk Widmann
Copy editing: Gloria Custance, Ulrike Havemann
Graphic design: Demian Bern

ZKM | Center for Art and Media Karlsruhe
ZKM | Zentrum für Kunst und Medien Karlsruhe
ZKM | Centre d'Art et des Médias Karlsruhe
Lorenzstraße 19, 76135 Karlsruhe
Telephone: +49 (0)721/8100-1200
www.zkm.de
info@zkm.de

CEO and Chairman: Alistair Hudson
COO: Helga Huskamp
Head of administration: Boris Kirchner

In memory of Peter Weibel (1944–2023), on whose idea this exhibition is based.

With special thanks to the artist, Ute Mack, Sophia Sotke and the entire team of Studio Heinz Mack, the lenders, the ZERO foundation and the Friends of the ZERO foundation as well as the entire team of ZKM:
Lisa Bartling, Volker Becker, Paul Bethge, Banu Beyer, Benno Blome, Claudius Böhm, Andreas Brehmer, Felix Brenner, Marianne Bruder, Ludger Brümmer, Moritz Büchner, Klaus Burckhardt, Janine Burger, Max Clausen, Natascha Daher, Anne Däuper, Götz Dipper, Daniela Doermann, Nanna Doll, Sarah Donderer, Florian Draheim, Tatjana Draskovic, Ralf Eger, Marlen Ernst, Wolfgang Ernst, Uwe Faber, Corinna Fraß, Mirco Fraß, Regine Frisch, Rainer Gabler, Viola Gaiser, Gregor Gaissmaier, Hans Gass, Jan Gerigk, Sabine Grieb, Matthias Gommel, Julian Günther, Christian Haardt, Ronald Haas, Elke Hägele, Tobias Haller, Manfred Hahn, Fayza Harby-Bemmann, Idis Hartmann, Manfred Hauffen, Ulrike Havemann, Dirk Heesakker, Alexandra Hermann, Daniel Heiss, Christof Hierholzer, Anett Holzheid, Alistair Hudson, Helga Huskamp, Werner Hutzenlaub, Sabine Jäger, Yasha Jain, Johannes Jensen, Hartmut Jörg, Petra Julien, Hanna Jurisch, Samira Kaiser, Ines Karabuz, Dominik Kautz, Alexandra Kempf, Katharina Kern, Boris Kirchner, Tobias Klingenmayer, Paula Klotzki, Wolfgang Knapp, Felix Koberstein, Andy Koch, Andreas Kohlbecker, Sabine Krause, Ophelia Kühn, Peter Kuhn, Gisbert Laaber, Svenja Liebig, Nina Liechti, Regina Linder, Bernd Lintermann, Christian Lölkes, Elena Lorenz, Lucie Lorenz, Jens Lutz, Anna Maganuco, Henrike Mall, Martin Mangold, Tanja Mattes-Kunzmann, Marianne Meister, Svenia Messina, Daria Mille, Christiane Minter, Felix Mittelberger, Belinda Montúfar de Maschke, Henning Möller, Caroline Mössner, Dorcas Müller, Christian Nainggolan, Lívia Nolasco-Rózsás, Volker Nowicki, Cecilia Preiß, Marco Preitschopf, Malin Preuß, Tilo Reeb, Nicole Reiser, Elisabeth Sofia Rios Angles, Leonie Rök, Margit Rosen, Lilli Roser, Clara Runge, Marianne Schädler, Matthias Schleifer, Martin Schläfke, Friedrich Schroedter, Marc Schütze, Laura Schmidt, Michelle Schmidt, Heike Schneider, Sarah Donata Schneider, David Schulten, Jutta Schuhmann, Marina Siggelkow, Volker Sommerfeld, Ulrich Steinberg, Peter Steiner, Lucia Stockinger, Regina Strasser-Gnädig, Morgane Stricot, Miriam Stürner, Silke Sutter, Emma Teuscher, Dominique Theise, Marcus Thiel, Anne Thomé, Patrick Trappendreher, Nico Trautwein, Karl Valentin, Matthieu Vlaminck, Manuel Weber, Almut Werner, Christoph Wetzel, Anouk Widmann, Anika Wilcox, Dan Wilcox, Christina Zartmann, Philipp Ziegler, Petra Zimmermann.

Publication

Editor: Alistair Hudson
Project management: Ulrike Havemann
ZKM | Publications: Jens Lutz, Ulrike Havemann, Miriam Stürner
English editing: Dan Lawler
Translations from the German: Anna Galt, Gérard Goodrow, Dan Lawler
Chapter introductions: Katharina Kern, Clara Runge
Copy editing: Ulrike Havemann, Dan Lawler, Sophia Sotke
Graphic design: Demian Bern
Reprography: Repromayer Medienproduktion GmbH, Reutlingen
Project management, Hirmer Publishers: Jutta Allekotte, Katja Durchholz
Production: Katja Durchholz
Paper: Galaxi keramik 150 g, Peydur lissé 135 g
Typeface: New Hero by Miles Newlyn
Printing and binding: DZA Druckerei zu Altenburg GmbH

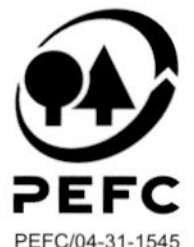

PEFC/04-31-1545

With special thanks to the artist, Ute Mack, Sophia Sotke and the entire team of Studio Heinz Mack, the authors and translators, and to EnBW for the generous support of the publication.

Printed in Germany

Published by: Hirmer Publishers, CEO: Kerstin Ludolph
Bayerstraße 57-59, 80335 Munich, Germany

ISBN: 978-3-7774-4434-5
www.hirmerpublishers.com
www.ukhirmerpuplishers.co

The Deutsche Nationalbibliothek lists this publication in the Deutsche Nationalbibliografie; detailed bibliographic data is available on the Internet at http://www.dnb.de.

In cooperation with:

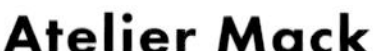

With the support of:

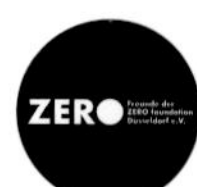

Founders of ZKM:

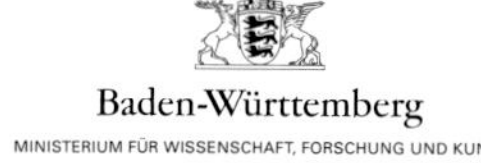

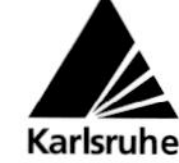

Premium partner of ZKM:

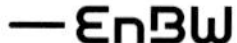

Image caption book cover:
fig. 1 Heinz Mack, *The Garden in the Garden*, 1979–1980, detail

Captions introductory image sequence:
fig. 2 Heinz Mack, *Cabinet of Light Treasures*, 1964, detail
fig. 3 Heinz Mack, *The Dance (Light-Relief)*, 1963, detail
fig. 4 Heinz Mack, *White Lamella Rotor*, 1963, detail
fig. 5 Heinz Mack, *Nemesis*, 2014, detail
fig. 6 Heinz Mack, *Helios*, 1973 (replica from 2019), detail
fig. 7 Heinz Mack, *The Garden in the Garden*, 1979–1980, detail

Image captions endpaper:
fig. 406 Heinz Mack, *Untitled*, 2006, detail
fig. 407 Heinz Mack, *Night-Light-Sculpture (Light Wing)*, 1970, detail

Image Credits:

Despite intensive research and best intentions, it was not possible in every case to establish the copyright holders. We ask the holders of such rights who feel they have not been properly acknowledged to contact us.

cover/fig. 1: photos © ZKM | Karlsruhe; photos: Demian Bern

fig. 2–8, 10–15, 17–19, 22, 24–26, 28–30, 32, 44, 55–59, 61, 64–74, 76, 79–85, 87, 91, 93, 94, 99–101, 103, 117, 118, 125, 128, 130, 131, 133, 136–139, 147–150, 152, 163, 188, 193, 211, 213–222, 226, 227: photos © ZKM | Karlsruhe; photos: Tobias Wootton

fig. 9, 23, 27, 31, 60, 75, 92, 129, 194, 195, 212, 228, 230, 390: photos © ZKM | Karlsruhe; photos: Felix Grünschloß

fig. 16, 34–41, 43, 45, 47–54, 62, 63, 77, 78, 86, 88–90, 95–98, 102, 109, 111, 113, 114, 119–122, 132, 135, 145, 146, *153, 154*, 156, 157, 159, 162, 168, 170, 175, 176, 192, 199, 209, 210, 223, 224, 229, 233–236, 238, 240, 242, 245, 247, 249, 251, 259, 261, 264, 268, 271, 275, 276, 279, 282, 284, 294, 295, 303, 310, 312–314, 316, 321–324, 326, 327, 330, 332–334, 336–338, 340, 343–358, 360–364, 366–368, 370–374, 378, 379, 381, 384–386, 388, 389, 395, 397–402, 405: photos © Archive Heinz Mack

fig. 20, 21, 33, 110, 253, 255, 257: photos © Archive Heinz Mack; photos: Tiziano Berra

fig. 42: © The Moholy-Nagy Foundation; photo © ZKM | Karlsruhe

fig. 46: photo © Archive Heinz Mack; photo: Walter Vogel

fig. 104–107, 112, 126, 127, 134, 155, 166, 169, 179, 182, 185, 189–191, 195–198, 200, 201, 203, 207, 208, 309, 320, 380: photos © Archive Heinz Mack; photos: Thomas Höpker

fig. 108, 116, 123, 140, 144, 231, 325, 396: photos © Archive Heinz Mack; photos: Edwin Braun

fig. 115: photo © Archive Heinz Mack; photo: Michael Richter

fig. 124: photo © Lothar Wolleh Estate, Berlin / Archive Heinz Mack; photo: Lothar Wolleh

fig. 141, 143, 151, 171, 177, 178, 243, 315: photos © Archive Heinz Mack; photos: Heinz Mack

fig. 142: photo © ACWA Power: NOOR III CSP IPP, Marocco

fig. 158: © Olafur Eliasson; photo © neugerriemschneider, Berlin / Tanya Bonakdar Gallery, New York / Los Angeles; photo: Olafur Eliasson

fig. 160: © Olafur Eliasson; photo © Galeria Elvira González, Madrid and neugerriemschneider, Berlin

fig. 161: © Olafur Eliasson; photo © ZKM | Karlsruhe; photo: Franz Wamhof

fig. 164, 165: photos © VG Bild-Kunst, Bonn 2024, photos: Jannes Linders

fig. 167: photo © Dan Graham Estate / Lisson Gallery

fig. 172: © Gisela Colón; photo © the artist and Desert X; photo: Lance Gerber Studio

fig. 173: © Alicia Kwade; photo © the artist and Desert X; photo: Lance Gerber Studio

fig. 174: photo © Gió Forma Architects; photo: Gió Forma

fig. 180, 181: © Abdullah Al Othman; photos © the artist and Desert X; photos: Lance Gerber Studio

fig. 183: © Philip K. Smith III; photo © the artist and Desert X; photo: Lance Gerber Studio

fig. 184: © Yu Honglei; photo © ZKM | Karlsruhe; photo: Felix Grünschloß

fig. 186, 187: © Soun-Gui Kim; photos © Soun-Gui Kim

fig. 202: photo © Dallas Museum of Art

fig. 204, 205: photos © VG Bild-Kunst, Bonn 2024

fig. 206: © Stein Henningsen; photo © Stein Henningsen

fig. 225: photo © ZKM | Karlsruhe; photo: Ulrike Havemann

fig. 232: photo © Hessischer Rundfunk

fig. 237, 244: reproductions from *Transmissionselektronenmikroskopie (TEM): Atome zum Anfassen*, exh. cat., Bundeshaus Bonn, 2000, n.p. / photos © Institut für Festkörperforschung und Institut für Schicht- und Ionentechnik, Forschungszentrum Jülich

fig. 239: photo © top: Ljiljana Fruk, University of Cambridge, bottom: Deepak Venkateshvaran, University of Cambridge

fig. 246 : source: https://scarc.library.oregonstate.edu/coll/pauling/dna/pictures/sci9.001.5.html

fig. 248: photo © KAGE MIKROFOTOGRAFIE

fig. 250: photo © Lukas Stolzer, Ljiljana Fruk, University of Cambridge, 2015

fig. 252: illustration from L. Fruk, A. Kerbs, *Bionanotechnology: Concepts and Applications* (Cambridge: Cambridge University Press 2021); photo © Ljiljana Fruk, A. Kerbs

fig. 254: photo © Fruk lab, Ljiljana Fruk, Anna Melekhova, University of Cambridge

fig. 256: photo © Matthew Daniels, Wellcome Collection. https://wellcomecollection.org/works/ap55rbmx

fig. 258: photo © Yu-Chueh Hung and Ljiljana Fruk, University of Cambridge, 2015

fig. 260: photo © Jadranka Travas Sejdic, University of Auckland / Wiley-VCH GmbH

fig. 262: reproduction from Gyorgy Kepes, *The New Landscape in Art and Science*, exh. cat. Massachusetts Institute of Technology, 1951 (Chicago: Theobald, 1956), 101.

fig. 263: reproduction from Gyorgy Kepes, *The New Landscape in Art and Science*, exh. cat. Massachusetts Institute of Technology, 1951 (Chicago: Theobald, 1956), 104.

fig. 265: reproduction from *das kunstwerk* 4/XII (Oktober 1958), n.p.

fig. 266: photo © Photographic Archive. The Museum of Modern Art Archives, New York. IN752.2.; photo: Rolf Petersen

fig. 267: reproduction from *Architecture without Architects*, exh. cat. (New York: The Museum of Modern Art, 1964).

fig. 269: reproduction from Gyorgy Kepes, *The New Landscape in Art and Science*, exh. cat. Massachusetts Institute of Technology, 1951 (Chicago: Theobald, 1956), 154/55.

fig. 270: reproduction from Georg Schmidt and Robert Schenk, *Form in Art and Nature* (Basilea: Basilius, 1960), 66/67.

fig. 274: photo © Mauritius

fig. 275: photo © Getty Images; photo: Michal Krakowiak

fig. 277: photo © Tate Gallery London, Inv. T01105

fig. 278: photo: © Tiger Stocks | Shutterstock

fig. 280: © Jacques Rougerie

fig. 289: © VG Bild-Kunst, Bonn 2024, photo © Metropolitan Museum of Art, New York; photo: Harry Shunk

fig. 297: © Hussein Chalayan; photo © neutral 2003

fig. 298: photo © Luigi Colani

fig. 299: photo © Nicola Colombo

fig. 304: photo © Henry Guttmann Collection / Hulton Archive / Getty Images

fig. 307: photo © Museo Nazionale Etrusco di Villa Giulia, Rome (Inv. 13135)

fig. 308: photo © Musée du Louvre, Paris (Inv. AO 19865)

fig. 311, 392: photos © Archive Heinz Mack; photos H. Erdman

fig. 317: photo © Amazing Aerial Agency

fig. 318: photo © COMPUTER BILD

fig. 319: photo © FAZ 2006

fig. 328, 329: photos © Archive Heinz Mack; photos: Ronkholz

fig. 331: photo © Archive Heinz Mack; photo: Penkert

fig. 335: photo © Musée du Louvre, Paris (Inv. RF 197953)

fig. 341: photo © VCG

fig. 365: photo © Archive Heinz Mack; photo: Reiner Ruthenbeck

fig. 369: photo © WSMR

fig. 383: photo © AFP / Getty Images

fig. 387: photo © Archive Heinz Mack; photo: dpa

fig. 391: photo © Archive Heinz Mack; photo: Charles Wilp

fig. 393: photo © WDR

fig. 394: photo © Bundesarchiv

fig. 403: photo © Archive Heinz Mack; photo: F. Kuyas

fig. 404: photo © Archive Heinz Mack; photo: Bruno Biancardi

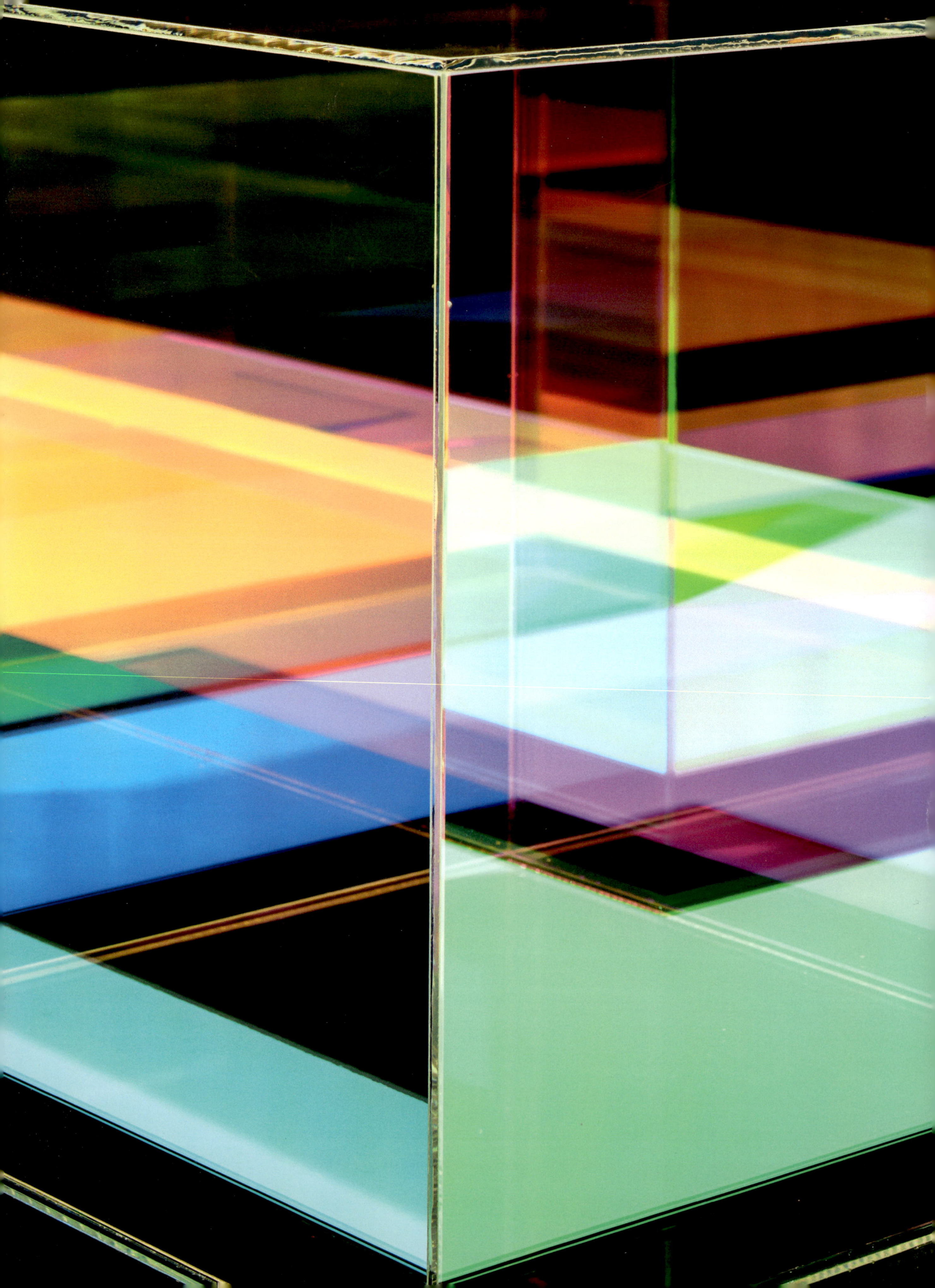